DIPLOMATARIUM ANGLICUM

ÆVI SAXONICI.

A COLLECTION

OF

ENGLISH CHARTERS,

FROM THE REIGN OF KING ÆTHELBERHT OF KENT, A.D. DC.V.
TO THAT OF WILLIAM THE CONQUEROR.

CONTAINING

I. MISCELLANEOUS CHARTERS. II. WILLS. III. GUILDS.
IV. MANUMISSIONS AND ACQUITTANCES.

WITH

A TRANSLATION OF THE ANGLO-SAXON.

BY

BENJAMIN THORPE,

MEMBER OF THE ROYAL ACADEMY OF SCIENCES AT MUNICH, AND OF THE SOCIETY OF
NETHERLANDISH LITERATURE AT LEYDEN.

THE LAWBOOK EXCHANGE, LTD.
Clark, New Jersey
2008

ISBN-13: 978-1-58477-924-7
ISBN-10: 1-58477-924-1

The quality of this reprint is equivalent to the quality of the original work.

The Lawbook Exchange, Ltd.
33 Terminal Avenue
Clark, New Jersey 07066-1321

Please see our website for a selection of our other publications and fine facsimile reprints of classic works of legal history:
www.lawbookexchange.com

Library of Congress Cataloging-in-Publication Data

Thorpe, Benjamin, 1782-1870.
Diplomatarium anglicum aevi saxonici : a collection of English charters, from the reign of King Aethelberht of Kent, A.D. DC. V. to that of William the Conqueror / by Benjamin Thorpe.
p. cm.
Latin and Anglo-Saxon with English translation.
"With a translation of the Anglo-Saxon."
Supplement to Kemble's "Codex diplomaticus aevi saxonici."
Originally published: London : Macmillian & Co., 1865.
Includes bibliographical references and index.
ISBN-13: 978-1-58477-924-7 (cloth : acid-free paper)
ISBN-10: 1-58477-924-1 (cloth : acid-free paper)
1. Great Britain--History--Anglo-Saxon period, 449-1066--Sources. 2. Great Britain--Charters, grants, privileges. 3. Wills--Great Britain. 4. Guilds--Great Britain. I. Title.
DA150.T518 2009
942.1'7--dc22 2008044524

Printed in the United States of America on acid-free paper

DIPLOMATARIUM ANGLICUM

ÆVI SAXONICI.

A COLLECTION

OF

ENGLISH CHARTERS,

FROM THE REIGN OF KING ÆTHELBERHT OF KENT, A.D. DC.V.
TO THAT OF WILLIAM THE CONQUEROR.

CONTAINING

I. MISCELLANEOUS CHARTERS. II. WILLS. III. GUILDS.
IV. MANUMISSIONS AND ACQUITTANCES.

WITH

A TRANSLATION OF THE ANGLO-SAXON.

BY

BENJAMIN THORPE,

MEMBER OF THE ROYAL ACADEMY OF SCIENCES AT MUNICH, AND OF THE SOCIETY OF
NETHERLANDISH LITERATURE AT LEYDEN.

LONDON:
MACMILLAN & CO., 16 BEDFORD STREET, COVENT GARDEN.
M.DCCC.LXV.

PRINTED BY TAYLOR AND FRANCIS,
RED LION COURT, FLEET STREET.

THIS VOLUME

IS

DEDICATED BY THE EDITOR

TO

JOSEPH MAYER, ESQ., F.R.A.S.,

TO WHOSE TASTE AND LIBERALITY EVERY LOVER OF

ARCHÆOLOGY, MONUMENTAL AND LITERARY,

OWES A LASTING DEBT OF GRATITUDE,

AND WITHOUT WHOSE AID, SPONTANEOUSLY OFFERED,

THIS COLLECTION OF OLD ENGLISH CHARTERS

WOULD HAVE LAIN

UNPUBLISHED AND UNKNOWN.

SUBSCRIBERS.

A. B. C., per Charles Roach Smith, Esq.
Edward Ackroyd, Esq., Bank Field, Halifax.
J. Adkins Barton, Esq., } Park Lodge, Bedford Place, Southampton.
Mrs. Barton, }
S. Amos, Esq., St. Ebb's, Hitchin, Herts.
William Armitage, Esq., Townfield House, Altringham, Cheshire.
Messrs. M. A. Asher & Co., Berlin. 4 copies.
Rev. J. Atkinson, Danby, Yorkshire.
Rev. C. Babington, St. John's Coll., Cambridge.
Francis Baigent, Esq., Winchester.
John Bailey, Esq., Welford Road, Leicester.
Rev. John Baron, Upton Scudamore, Warminster, Wilts.
W. Beaumont, Esq., Warrington.
Bedfordshire Archæological Society, per Rev. J. W. Haddick, 1 Windsor Terrace, Bedford, or care of A. T. Thomson, Esq., 49 Gloucester Terrace, Hyde Park.
W. H. Blaauw, Esq., F.S.A., Beechland, Uckfield, Sussex.
Mrs. Blackett, Hill Green, Stockbury, Sittingbourne.
Sir J. P. Boileau, Bart., F.R.A.S., 20 Upper Brook Street.
Beriah Botfield, Esq., M.P., F.R.A.S.[1]
Richard R. Brash, Esq., Sunday's Well, Cork.
W. H. Brockett, Esq., "The Observer" office, Gateshead.
Joseph Butterworth, Esq., F.S.A., 7 Fleet Street.
W. R. Callender, Esq., F.S.A., Victoria Park, Manchester.
Jos. Carlton, Esq., Booth Hall, Knutsford, Cheshire. 5 copies.
Edward Charlton, Esq., M.D., Newcastle-on-Tyne.
Ven. Archd. Churton, Crayke, near Easingwold, Yorkshire.
John Clayton, Esq., Town Clerk, Newcastle-on-Tyne.
John Cockle, Esq., M.D., 32 a, George Street, Hanover Square.
Rev. C. Collier, Training College, Winchester.
Rev. Dr. Corrie, Master of Jesus College, Cambridge.
Rev. H. O. Coxe, Keeper of Bodleian Library, Oxford.
The Earl of Darnley, Cobham Hall, Kent.
Robert Davies, Esq., F.S.A., The Mount, York.
Henry Dodd, Esq., City Wharf, Hoxton.
Rev. John Earle, Swanswick Rectory, near Bath.

---

[1] The names of deceased subscribers are printed in italics.

JAMES ESPINASSE, Esq., Recorder of Rochester, Boxley Lodge, near Maidstone.

JOHN EVANS, Esq., F.S.A., Nash Mills, King's Langley, Hemel Hempstead (care of Messrs. Dickinson & Co., Belle Sauvage Yard, Ludgate Hill).

WILLIAM EWING, Esq., Glasgow. 2 copies.

R. FERGUSON, Esq., Morton, Carlisle.

Mr. SEPTIMUS FLETCHER, Bookseller, Manchester.

General Fox, Addison Road, Kensington. 2 copies.

WILLIAM FRANCIS, Esq., Ph.D., F.G.S., &c., 1 Matson Villas, Richmond, S.W.

EDWARD A. FREEMAN, Esq., Somerleaze, Wells, Somersetshire.

THOMAS FREWEN, Esq., Northiam, Staplehurst, Kent.

J. F. GILBERT, Esq., Librarian to the Royal Irish Academy, 19 Dawson Street, Dublin.

NATHANIEL GOULD, Esq., F.S.A., 4 Tavistock Square.

Dr. J. Grimm, Berlin.

EDWIN GUEST, Esq., LL.D., Master of Caius Coll. Camb. 2 copies.

Rev. A. W. HADDON, Moreton in Marsh, Gloucestershire.

Dr. JUSTUS H. HALBERTSMA, Dr. LL.H.Philol., &c., Deventer.

H. R. HAMILTON, Esq., 32 A, George Street, Hanover Square.

Rev. CHARLES HENRY HARTSHORNE, Holdenby, Northamptonshire.

HENRY HEARN, Esq., St. Thomas's Street, Ryde, Isle of Wight.

J. HODGSON HINDE, Esq., Stetting Hall, Northumberland.

Rev. J. C. WILKES HOOK, Winchfield.

Rev. ABRAHAM HUME, LL.D., F.S.A., Everton, Liverpool.

The Earl of Ilchester.

CHARLES MOORE JESSOP, Esq., Surgeon, Inniskilling Dragoons, Mhow, Bengal.

JOHN JOLLIFFE, Esq., R.N., St. Angelo, Clarendon Road, Southsea, Hants.

Mr. DAVID KELLY, Bookseller, Manchester.

Rev. Professor KINGSLEY, Eversley, Hants.

Rev. LAMBERT B. LARKING, Ryarsh, near Maidstone.

LANCASHIRE INDEPENDENT COLLEGE, Manchester.

Dr. J. M. LAPPENBERG, For.F.S.A., Keeper of the Archives, Hamburg.

HENRY LATTER, Esq., Harbourne House, High Halden, Kent.

LIBRARY. St. Andrew's University.

——. Bank of England Literary Association, per C. J. RICHARDS, Esq.

——. Berlin, Royal.

——. Copenhagen, Great National.

——. —— University.

——. Leicester, Literary and Philos. Society.

——. Manchester, Owen's.

——. Windsor Castle, Royal.

W. H. D. Longstaff, Esq., F.S.A., Gateshead.
Rev. J. E. Major, St. John's College, Cambridge.
Thomas Martin, Esq., Reigate.
Hugh Mason, Esq., Ashton-under-Line. 2 copies.
Joseph Mayer, Esq., F.R.A.S., Liverpool. 30 copies.
Very Rev. Dr. Milman, Deanery, St. Paul's.
Rev. Dr. Moberly, Head Master of Winchester College.
Lord Monson, Burton Hall, Lincolnshire.
George Warde Norman, Esq., Bromley, Kent.
Frederic Ouvry, Esq., Treas. Soc. Antiq., 66 Lincoln's Inn Fields.
State-Councillor Dr. Pertz, Berlin.
George Plucknett, Esq., 1 Calthorpe Place, Gray's Inn Road.
Edward Pretty, Esq., F.S.A., Chillington House, Maidstone.
Dr. R. C. Alexander Prior, 48 York Terrace, Regent's Park.
Rev. F. Procter, Witton.
State-Councillor Regenburg, Copenhagen.
Samuel Rigby, Esq., Bruch Hall, Warrington, Lancashire.
E. William Robertson, Esq., Athenæum.
Evelyn P. Shirley, Esq., M.P., F.S.A., Eatington Park, Stratford-on-Avon.
Edm. Smirke, Esq.
Earl Somers, Priory, Reigate.
Lord Sondes, 32 Grosvenor Square.
Professor George Stephens, Copenhagen.
Lord Talbot de Malahide, F.R.A.S., Malahide Castle, near Dublin.
Miss Taylor, Alton Lodge, Richmond, Surrey.
Joseph Thompson, Esq., Sandy Nook and Pin Mills, Ardwick, Manchester.
Conferenceraad Chr. J. Thomsen, Copenhagen.
W. H. W. Tytheridge, Esq., General Register Office, Somerset House.
Weston S. Walford, Esq., F.S.A., 2 Plowden Buildings, Temple.
J. Green Waller, Esq., 68 Bolsover Street, Portland Place.
Charles Warne, Esq., F.S.A., Ewell, Surrey.
Edmund Waterton, Esq., F.S.A., Walton Hall, near Wakefield.
Sir James Watts, Abney Hall, near Manchester.
Conrad Wetter, Esq., Doct. Chem., 67 Myddelton Square.
Albert Way, Esq., M.A., F.S.A., Wonham Manor, Reigate.
J. C. Whiteman, Esq., Theydon Grove, near Epping.
Humphrey Wickham, Esq., Strood, Kent.
G. J. De Wilde, Esq., Northampton.
Thomas Willement, Esq., F.S.A., Davington Priory, Faversham.
Rev. Dr. Wilson, F.S.A., Pres. Trin. Coll., Oxford.
Professor J. J. A. Worsaae, For.F.S.A., Copenhagen.
William M. Wylie, Esq., F.S.A., Blackwater, Hants.

PREFACE.

WHILE the early history of a state, in the common acceptation of the term, supplies us with a narrative of the public acts and sufferings of its people and their rulers, it affords us little or no insight into its internal life. For an acquaintance with this, as far as it is attainable, recourse must be had to other sources of information: of these the most prolific is unquestionably those deeds or muniments comprised under the general denomination of CHARTERS. These documents of our ancient kings, prelates, and nobles impart to us information of the most valuable and interesting kind: they prove and rectify the chronology of the chronicles, and serve not unfrequently as a commentary on, and an exemplification of, the Laws, rendering intelligible many points which, without their aid, would be involved in obscurity[1]. The information derivable from the Charters of the pre-Normannic period has special reference, I. to the Constitutional Law of England anterior to the Conquest; II. to testamentary dispositions, heriots, marriage and other settlements, leases, mortgages, markets, tolls, customs, jurisdictions, rights, privileges, and immunities of both lay and ecclesiastical persons;

[1] Or, in the words of Mr. Kemble (Pref. to Cod. Dipl.): "In attempting to form an accurate conception of the Anglo-Saxon law, in its manifold bearings, we are compelled to resort to other evidence than is supplied by the written law itself. And the most important subsidiary evidence which we can now obtain, is furnished by the public and private instruments of the periods alluded to; those documents, in short, which pass under the general name of charters."

III. the royal authority, the law of real property, the Witenagemôt, or Great Council of the nation, and the inferior courts, viz. the Scîr-gemôt, or County Court, the Hundred-court, etc., with the forms of civil and criminal process. The Charters may in fact, as Mr. Kemble has observed, to a certain degree be considered, with respect to our early history, what letters, state papers, and pamphlets are to our later history, and may almost be regarded as the documentary annals of England, supplying us with information for which in History we seek in vain.

The remaining Charters, consisting almost exclusively of simple grants of land, will, it is to be hoped, ere long find an editor equally zealous with myself, and more competent. With a translation of, and commentary on, the Land-boundaries, they cannot fail of being of the highest interest and value to the topographical antiquary.

The First portion of this volume consists of Miscellaneous Charters, or of documents that are not simple grants of land, or are not comprised in the other portions. In common with the Wills, these documents occasionally afford a curious glimpse into the manners of the age, particularly some of the grants of immunity to monasteries from the burthen of entertaining the king's messengers, horses, hounds, hawks, etc., thus exhibiting a close counterpart to the tenures of the later Norman period. Of these charters many are unquestionably spurious, though some of them, hitherto regarded as forgeries, may perhaps be pronounced of a doubtful character. Such will be found distinguished by an asterisk[1].

[1] There are two documents in this volume, on which a few observations

I am, indeed, led to be diffident as to the authenticity of some documents by a comparison with others of the period, whereby their character appears at most questionable. But even those generally regarded as decided forgeries may not always be false with respect to their substance, being probably fabrications by the

may not here seem altogether out of place: The documents alluded to are those exhibiting the subscriptions of Ælfgifu and Æthelgifu as the wife and mother-in-law of king Eadwig. (See p. 191.) Two Roman Catholic writers (Milner, in his History of Winchester, and Lingard, in his History of England, and his Hist. and Antiq. of the A. S. Church) do not hesitate to pronounce Ælfgifu to have been the king's mistress; while others not of the Romish Church regard her as his lawful wife. I was among the latter; but doubts have, I regret to say, of late arisen in my mind as to the genuineness of these subscriptions. In the first place, among the numerous charters of Eadwig, there is not another in which either of these names appears. Secondly, it is only in the Abingdon Chronicle or Chartulary they are found, the original deed or deeds, if such ever existed, being no longer extant. Now we know that Eadwig was a most munificent benefactor to this abbey. I use the words of a much-lamented friend: "The donations to Abingdon in the time of Eadwig were splendid and numerous. His own immediate grants to our Lady of Abingdon, to St. Benet, the patron of monks, and to the abbot Æthelwold, amounted to fifty hides, and those made by his servants, with his consent and approbation, exceeded three hundred and forty. In the very last year of his reign he conferred on Abingdon a Charter (see p. 192) in the amplest form, confirming all its former privileges and possessions, and giving permission to the monks, on the death of their abbot Æthelwold, to elect his successor 'secundum regularia beati Benedicti instituta.'"—*Inquiry into the Life of King Eadwig, by* John Allen, p. 241[a]. Now supposing the good monks capable of perpetrating such a forgery, the deed, though reprehensible, admits of palliation, as springing from feelings of gratitude. According to one MS. of the Saxon Chronicle, we are told that, A.D. 958, archbishop Oda separated (totwæmde) Eadwig and Ælfgifu, because they were too near akin. Why does this statement not appear in the other MSS.? But be the relation of Eadwig to Ælfgifu whatever it may, nothing can excuse or palliate the atrocious barbarity of her persecutors, which calls forth feelings of the most intense horror and disgust.

---

[a] At the end of his Inquiry into the Rise and Growth of the Royal Prerogative in England. 8vo, 1849. Longman & Co.

monks, as vouchers for the possession of lands which justly belonged to them by prescription, or of which the original titles had been lost or destroyed, or of which the Norman conquerors had despoiled them. Such charters are usually distinguished by their magniloquence, their inordinate length, and the gaudy splendour of their illuminations, but with still greater certainty by their subscriptions and their occasional anachronisms. When, for instance, we find a charter of Æthelberht, a° 605[1], subscribed by such names as Angemundus, Pinca, Geddi, Graphio comes, etc., there seems no great risk of error in pronouncing it a forgery. On this subject it is well observed by Palgrave[2], "that there are many instruments in the shape and form of original charters, but which are probably copies, made long after the Conquest, for use and perusal; and to prevent the injury which might result to the ancient 'Land-bôc,' if touched by rude or careless hands. Occasionally the calligraphist attempted not merely to repeat the words, but to depicture the ancient characters; and as these imitations are easily detected by the skilful antiquary, he may be induced to condemn, as a forgery, a document which was merely intended to be an innocent facsimile." And again: "Interest may have tempted the monks to commit forgery; and they did not always resist this temptation so resolutely as might be wished for the honour of their order. Yet, in extenuation, if not in apology of this offence, it must be remembered that their falsifications were chiefly defensive. Lands which unquestionably belonged to the Church were frequently held merely by prescriptive possession, unaccompanied by deeds and charters. The right was lawful, but there

[1] Codex Diplom. i. p. 3. [2] Rise and Progress, ii. pp. ccix, ccx.

were no lawful means of proving the right. And when the monastery was troubled and impleaded by the Norman Justiciar, or the soke invaded by the Norman Baron, the abbot and his brethren would have recourse to the artifice of inventing a charter for the purpose of protecting property which, however lawfully acquired and honestly enjoyed, was like to be wrested from them by the captious niceties of Norman jurisprudence, or the greedy tyranny of the Norman sword"[1]. In documents, however, of the tenth and eleventh centuries, inflation is of itself no proof of forgery, but is a characteristic of the age, fully justifying the words of Malmesbury: "Angli pompatice dictare solent: id in omnibus antiquis chartis est animadvertere, quantum quibusdam verbis abstrusis et ex Græco petitis delectuntur." It should, however, be borne in mind that anachronisms may sometimes be placed to the account of an unskilful or careless copyist, particularly in the case of documents in the chartularies. It may further be observed, that Malmesbury, who lived at the time when such forgeries were most probably perpetrated, does not mention pomposity of diction as a proof of forgery. To the class of doubtful charters, or of forgeries in words rather than in matter, may perhaps be assigned some of those grants of lands, immunities, etc., to certain abbeys, as Peterborough, Glastonbury, and Crowland.

The WILLS and BEQUESTS, chiefly of royal and noble persons, archbishops, and bishops, and forming the SECOND PORTION of the volume, are, with few exceptions,

[1] A monk of St. Medard, being on his death-bed, confessed with great contrition and repentance, that he had forged numerous bulls of exemption in favour of various monasteries,—the abbey of St. Ouen in Normandy and of St. Augustine's Canterbury being among the number, to the prejudice of the rights of the ordinaries. *Anglia Sacra*, ii. Pref. p. v, and from the information of Mr. Petrie, cited by Palgrave, *ut sup.*

in our old vernacular tongue, and most of them hitherto untranslated either into Latin or modern English, and are consequently, to a great number of readers, a dead letter; though, in point of matter, as affording an insight into the private life of our ancestors, their dress, furniture, utensils, ornaments, etc., they are a mine of curious information. They are, moreover, the most ancient collection of similar documents existing in any old vernacular tongue of modern Europe. In the Wills we find the earliest mention of Heriots (the Relief of the Norman times), the introduction of which has been erroneously ascribed to Cnut, with whose enactments they bear a near resemblance; whence it would appear that he only stamped with legal authority what had previously, to a certain degree, been optional.

In the THIRD PORTION will be found the articles of Constitution of some of those corporations or fraternities known under the general denomination of GUILDS. These may, with great probability, be traced back to the sacrificial feasts of the heathens, and were, no doubt, the germ of the municipal system of the Germanic nations. Of these associations there were three kinds: 1st. Trade Guilds; 2nd. Frith, or Peace Guilds; 3rd. Guilds instituted for social or religious purposes.

In the Trade Guilds we may see the origin of our civic companies: but, besides these, there were some associations of foreign traders, chiefly from Flanders and the north of Germany, the foremost of which in rank, and perhaps in antiquity, was that of the Hanseatic merchants of the Steel-yard in Upper Thames Street, the origin of which may, with probability, be traced beyond the reign of Æthelred II.[1]

[1] See the title: De Institutis Lundoniæ in Anc. Laws and Inst. of England; Lappenberg, Urkundliche Geschichte des Hansischen Stahlhofes

Of Frith (Peace), or Social Guilds, there seems to be a trace as far back as the reign of Ine[1]. Of the former we still possess a precious monument in the Judicia Civitatis Lundoniæ, a deed of incorporation, by the prelates and reeves of the Londoners, for the repression of theft and maintenance of the public peace, which in its provisions is closely akin to the later institution of Frithborg[2] or, as it is mistranslated, *Frankpledge*.

The Third Class of Guilds, and that with which we are specially concerned, bears, with due allowance for difference of times and manners, a close resemblance to the Friendly or Benefit Societies or Clubs of our working classes, though composed of persons of a higher grade, and containing more of the religious element than these. Some of them, indeed, were exclusively ecclesiastical.

Under the title of MANUMISSIONS will be found a collection of attestations, from entries in the fly-leaves of MS. copies of the Gospels and Missals, many also from the Exeter MS. These are of considerable interest, not only as affording some insight into the state of a numerous class of the community, but as showing to what nationality they belonged. I allude to those of Cornwall and other western parts of the kingdom, in which Keltic, i. e. British, names chiefly prevail, thus informing us to what race those in a state of serfdom in

zu London, and Pauli's Pictures of Old England: *Engl. transl.* For the Guilds of the Continent, see the estimable work of Dr. W. E. Wilda, Das Gildenwesen im Mittelalter.

[1] Laws of Ine, 16.

[2] Under this denomination it first occurs in the Laws of the Confessor, where it is described as a known institution; but the law of "borh," or surety, existed from a very early period. It is mentioned, I believe, in the Laws of Ine, 41. Mr. Kemble has collected the several enactments relative to Frithborg in his Sax. in Eng. i. p. 249.

those shires for the most part belonged. Among these, some of our present surnames will be found, of which many were originally, no doubt, nicknames and personal, but afterwards became transmissible.

The form of manumission, as given in the Laws called Henry the First's, was as follows: Qui servum suum liberat, in ecclesia, vel mercato, vel comitatu, vel hundreto, coram testibus et palam faciat, et liberas ei vias et portas conscribat apertas, et lanceam et gladium, vel quæ liberorum arma sunt, in manibus ei ponat. Si quis de servitute redeat in liberum, in testem manumissionis, cum testibus redditionis, domino suo xxx. denarios reddat, scilicet, pretium corii sui, in signum quod eo dignus sit in æternum. From the History of Ramsey (apud Gale, cap. xxix.), we get another form of manumission: Per omnes terras suas, de xxx. hominibus numeratis XIII. manumisit, quemadmodum eum sors docuit, et in quadrivio positi pergerent quocunque voluissent. According to the Kentish law of king Wihtræd, in the 8th century, it appears that, if a serf be manumitted even at the altar, the property, "wêrgild" and "mund" of the serf belong to the manumittor; be the serf over the march wherever he may. From the Manumissions it will be seen that a serf could purchase the freedom of himself and family.

From the foregoing it will be seen that the instruments comprised in this volume, may not inaptly be regarded as the historic portion of the Charters. The remaining documents, consisting, as has been already said, almost wholly of simple grants of land, belong to the province of topography.

An Anglo-Saxon Charter, in its usual and restricted sense of a grant of land, privileges, immunities, and the like, consists in its completest form of the following parts, viz.[1]:

I. The Invocation. II. The Proem. III. The Grant. IV. The Sanction. V. The Date. VI. The Attestation.

I. The Invocation. This is a short, pious, ejaculatory sentence, with which the charter begins, such as, In nomine Domini nostri Jhesu Christi; or, In nomine sanctæ et individuæ Trinitatis, and the like.

II. The Proem, or Preamble. This is usually a pious effusion, sometimes, particularly in later documents, of inordinate length, and not seldom hardly intelligible, in praise of charity and beneficence, especially to the Church; on the vanity of the transitory goods of this life, in comparison with the everlasting heavenly treasures to be purchased by those virtues; on the necessity of committing all grants and contracts to writing, in order to prevent the violation or evasion to which they would be liable if intrusted only to memory.

III. The Grant itself. This is usually introduced by the word Quamobrem, or Quapropter, or one of similar import, having reference to the motive for making the grant, as Quamobrem ego Æthelberht, induced by these reasons, or exhortations, grant, etc. etc. If it be a grant of land, the boundaries immediately follow, usually in Anglo-Saxon, though the instrument itself be in Latin.

IV. The Sanction. This is a form, with few variations, of malediction on all who shall infringe, set aside, or diminish the grant or donation; and is followed by a benediction on those who shall augment or improve it.

V. Of the time-reckoning of the Anglo-Saxons prior

[1] See Cod. Dipl. i. Introd. page x.

to the introduction of Christianity in the year 597 we know nothing; but as all the documents with which we are here concerned are posterior to that event, the date, as may naturally be supposed, is computed from the year of the Incarnation, commencing on the 25th of December, or the 1st of January; for that, together with the Christian religion, Augustine introduced the Christian era, seems almost a matter of course; although there may not be found any undeniable instance of its use among us anterior to the year 676, under which date there is a charter of Osric, sub-king of the Hwiccas (Cod. Dip. No. XII.), the genuineness of which there appears no reason to question.

Besides the year of the Incarnation, the date of a charter is, in most cases, further determined by the number of the Indiction, consisting of a constantly recurring cycle of fifteen years. The Indiction, according to the best authorities, came into common use in 312, during the reign of Constantine, and, as the name implies, was the edict, or *indictio*, subscribed by the emperor, and fixed up in the principal city of each diocese during two months previous to the first day of September, and has reference to the fixing of the tributes. Of the origin of the Indictions nothing is known[1].

[1] The following are the words of Beda with reference to the Indictions (De Natura Rerum, cap. xlviii.). Secundus ordo circuli decennovalis complectitur Indictiones xv. annorum circuitu in sua semper vestigia reduces, quas antiqua Romanorum industria comperimus ad cavendum errorem qui de temporibus forte oboriri poterat institutas. Dum enim, verbi gratia, quilibet imperator, medio anni tempore, vita vel regno decederet, poterat evenire ut eundem annum unus historicus ejusdem regis adscriberet temporibus, eo quod ejus partem regnaret; alter vero historicus eundem successori illius potius attitulandum putaret, eo quod et hic partem æque ejus haberet in regno. Verum ne per hujuscemodi dissonantiam error temporibus inolesceret, statuerunt Indictiones, quibus uter-

There are two principal kinds of Indictions; the one known as the Cæsarean or Imperial Indiction, which, at least till the eighth century, was generally used in England and France, and began on the 24th of September; the other, the Pontifical, or Roman, which commenced on the 25th of December or 1st of January, according to which of those days was taken for the beginning of the year—thus obviating any confusion or difficulty that might arise from the year of the Indiction falling in two years of the Calendar: The Anglo-Saxon year commenced on the 25th of December.

In a few charters, besides the year of the Incarnation, we find that of the reign of the prince under whom they were issued, or, as it is usually termed, the regnal year [1]. When this commenced is matter of doubt; but a very reasonable hypothesis is that which dates it from the consecration of the king; though an objection to this hypothesis [2], less grave than it at first appears, has been raised, namely that Eadgar was not hallowed king until the

que scriptor, imo etiam vulgus omne, temporum cursum facillime servaret, quas pro facilitate quoque calculandi quindecim esse voluerunt, ut planissimo numero et ad multiplicandum promptissimo, compendiosius transacti temporis status in memoriam possit reduci. Quidam autem putant, quia quondam in republica post censum quinto anno peractum, urbs Roma lustrabatur, ad indicium ternæ lustrationis et census Indictiones esse conditas. Incipiunt autem Indictiones ab VIII. Calendas Octobris (Sept. 24), ibidemque terminantur. And in the next following chapter he gives the rule for finding the year of the Indiction: Hoc autem argumento quota sit anno quocumque computare volueris Indictio reperies: Sume annos ab incarnatione Domini quotquot fuerint in præsenti, verbi gratia, DCCXXV., adde semper tria, quia quarta Indictione, secundum Dionysium, natus est Dominus, fiunt DCCXXVIII.; hæc partire per XV.; quindecies quadrageni, sexcenti, quindecies octoni, centies et vicies, remanent octo: octava est Indictio. Si vero nihil remanserit, decimaquinta est.

[1] The earliest charter dated from the regnal year of the king is one of Cœnwulf of Mercia, a. 798. Cod. Dipl. i. p. 211.

[2] Nicolas, Chronology of History, p. 363, edit. 1838.

13th year of his reign; on which circumstance Lappenberg pertinently says: "Why this ceremony did not "take place earlier, or, if it had already been performed, "for what purpose it was at this time repeated, is matter "of uncertainty, though it has been brought into connexion with a tradition, according to which, Eadgar, as "a part of the penance imposed on him by Dunstan, for "the abduction of Wulfthryth, was forbidden to wear "the crown till the expiration of seven years[1]. This "story has been generally and perhaps justly regarded "as groundless; though it cannot be denied that a desire on the part of Eadgar to receive back his crown "from the hands of him who had forbidden him to wear "it, would be in perfect keeping with the spirit both of "that and of a much later age"[2]. At all events, this is a very anomalous circumstance, and hardly to be adduced as a proof against the hypothesis that the regnal years were reckoned from the consecration of the kings. Indeed it does not seem likely that a prince so pompous as Eadgar would have deferred such a solemnity till the thirteenth year of his reign, had not an earlier consecration taken place. It has also been suggested, and

[1] Osberni Vita S. Dunstani, in Acta Sanctorum, and an extract in Wharton, Anglia Sacra.

[2] England under the Anglo-Saxon Kings, ii. p. 142. On this passage Sir H. Nicolas (Chron. of Hist. p. 363) remarks: "Lappenberg's idea that the Saxon kings dated from their coronation and unction, appears untenable on grounds drawn from the old Teutonic law; and a remarkable fact in contradiction of that theory is furnished by Edgar, who was not crowned until a great many years after his accession, and who dated from his accession, and afterwards used the double date of his accession and coronation." Now I do not see that Lappenberg here expresses any idea or opinion on the subject; and the charters referred to are both marked by Kemble, and, I doubt not, very justly, as spurious (Cod. Dipl. Nos. 514, 584, and this vol. p. 211). Other instances are not wanting of a charter marked as forged being cited as an authority.

not without probability, that the regnal year of a king was reckoned from the day of his accession in one year to the same day in the next year. This calculation applies equally to the case of the regnal years being reckoned from the consecration or inauguration; for otherwise a small fragment of a year would be reckoned as the first of a reign; and only in the case of a king's accession or consecration falling on new-year's day could the regnal year and the dominical year coincide. For the sake of our chronology, it is to be regretted that the data whereon to found aught but conjecture are so few and insufficient.

VI. The Attestation, or Subscriptions. The list of subscriptions was always headed by the king, or by the person in whose name the document is promulgated. In the case of a charter issued by a sub-king (as of the Hwiccas or of Kent), or by a high dignitary, it is usually stated that the act is with the consent of the superior lord, who at the same time signs the instrument, expressing such consent, as, Ego Æthelred consensi et subscripsi. After the signature of the king, that of the queen usually occurs, then that of the ætheling, or heir to the throne; though these signatures are sometimes preceded by those of the chief ecclesiastical dignitaries. Next in succession come the names of the aldormen (duces), which are followed by those of the minor church-dignitaries, and these by the signatures of the thanes (ministri), &c. To this *ordo* exceptions are to be found, but it is that which is most generally followed. From the several charters promulgated in the name of the sovereign, it appears evident that they emanated from, and with the consent of, the great Council of the realm, or Witenagemôt, viz. "cum episcoporum ac principum meorum consensu"; while others of an inferior class probably issued from the Scîr-gemôt, or County court; though those of grants by archbishops and bishops are usually drawn up and signed by the members of the cathedral chapter.

From the original charters still extant, it appears that the names of the witnesses are in the same handwriting as the body of the charter; and even the crosses prefixed to the several signatures are most frequently in the same hand; thus apparently leaving to the attesting party (pro ignorantia litterarum) the sole office of touching the cross, and orally declaring the signature to be his own act and deed, as at the present day; though it appears probable that the cross was sometimes marked by the witness himself, as we find the expression (in a charter marked as spurious, it is true) "signum crucis aravi"[1], equivalent to the Old Norse, at rista runa, *to grave runes*. The *ignorantia litterarum* is, no doubt, chiefly applicable to the lay witnesses, as we cannot but suppose that most of the ecclesiastical dignitaries were at least capable of signing their names.

Seals, in the modern acceptation of the word, do not appear to have been used by the Anglo-Saxons in signing charters,—the term *sigillum*, which occurs in some instruments of a late date, being merely the diminutive of *signum*; so that *cum sigillo* sanctæ crucis is identical with *cum signo sanctæ crucis*. Other synonyms are tauma, agalma, indicium, trophæum, etc. etc.[2]

[1] Cod. Dipl. i. p. 218.

[2] That seals for other purposes were in use appears from the following:—A seal of Ethelwald (830–870) was dug up in a garden, about two hundred yards from the gate of the monastery at Eye in Suffolk, by a labourer, who gave it to the child of a workman employed on the farm. The child threw the seal into the fire, and it thus received some injury.

The following notice of the sources whence the materials of the present work are drawn, is copied nearly *verbatim* from Mr. Kemble's great work, the Codex Diplomaticus [1].

The repositories in which these documents are preserved, are the libraries of the British Museum, the Universities, and the various cathedrals, and, in very rare cases, those of private collections. Many are yet extant in their original form, viz. as single charters, on sheets of vellum of greater or less size; sometimes, too, we have even the duplicates and triplicates of the same charter, laid up in different repositories. A few are known to us from having been confirmed by the early English kings—the usual form in such a case being for the king to state that he had seen a certain charter, in manner and form following, and that he confirmed it. From the words used, this confirmation is, in England, called an *Inspeximus*, on the Continent, *Vidimus*; and the ancient charter is recited in the body of the new one. Many of these are found in the Exchequer, in the office of the King's Remembrancer; a few only in the Rolls of the Tower; a few are on single sheets of vellum, as they may have been drawn out for the Religious

It was afterwards purchased by Hudson Gurney, Esq., and presented by him to the British Museum. The seal is of yellow metal, mitre-shaped, composed of two rows of arches, supported by nine wolves' heads, the eyes of which are formed by small garnets. The legend exhibits a mixture of Greek and Latin characters: SIΓ̄ EÐILVVALDI EP̄. (Archæologia, vol. xx. p. 480). Of the seal of Edgitha, probably the daughter of Edgar, only an impression remains. She is represented nearly at full length, the effigy being surrounded by an inscription partly in Greek and partly in Latin: SIGILL' EAGDGYÐE REGAL' AÐELPHE (Hoare's Wilton Chartulary, Pref.). Note by Sir F. Palgrave, Rise and Progress, ii. ccxv.

[1] Vol. vi. Pref. p. vi.

House whose property it was desired to guard. The most numerous documents, however, are those which have been entered into Chartularies, or books belonging to the monasteries, and preserved by them as title-deeds, charters of privilege and immunity, and as evidences of property, or rank, precedence, and authority. From time to time these Registers or Chartularies were recopied, and, for the most part, translated in recopying into the form of speech current at the later period; thus they offer to the philologist a mass of data upon which inquiries into the progress and changes of language can be most securely founded. In many cases they have preserved to us copies of charters whose originals are no longer found; and as they have also preserved to us copies of many which we possess in their first and oldest form, they supply the means of comparison and induction as to the genuineness of others for which we have no authority but their own.

In undertaking this work my first idea was to produce an enlarged edition of the Codex Diplomaticus, on which this volume is based, and to which it owes its being, with a translation of every document in Anglo-Saxon, according to the plan submitted by the late Mr. Kemble and myself to Sir James Graham, then at the head of the Home Office; but to which we received no answer. Other occupations then for a time erased all thoughts on the subject from my memory. I afterwards offered the work to Sir John Romilly, as fitted to form one of the series in course of publication under his direction. My offer was rejected on the score of expense. To obviate this objection, and, at the same time, render the work more generally useful, I resolved on dividing the charters into two classes, one consisting of those directly or indirectly bearing on our early history, the other of those belonging to the province of topography, viz. the simple grants of land. A volume comprising the charters of the first-mentioned class I also offered to the Master of the Rolls, but this offer fared no better than the preceding one. This is the volume which I now submit to the public. Far from acting as an extinguisher over me and my work, this repulse had the effect of a spur. I instantly resolved on other means of bringing it forth, which have happily proved successful.

When engaged on the work, I applied to the Master of the Rolls for the loan of a collection of transcripts of Anglo-Saxon charters, which the late Mr. Petrie had caused to be made, and which had long been lying useless at the Rolls House. My request was obligingly met with immediate compliance, for which I here offer my very sincere thanks. When I made this request, Sir Francis Palgrave was Deputy Keeper of the Records. These transcripts, though known to, were never seen by Mr. Kemble. They consist of about 350 charters, of which many are from the Stowe collection, many from Westminster, and some from the collection of Sir Thomas Phillipps at Middlehill. Such as fell within my province, will be found in the Diplomatarium. Of all the documents not included in the Codex Diplomaticus I have copies; the others I collated with that work; and I now possess transcripts of 73 unprinted charters, which may one day serve as a supplement to Mr. Kemble's work.

This volume has been produced under adverse circumstances. More than a year ago I was attacked by illness which had nearly proved fatal, from which I still suffer, and by which the progress of the work was long retarded: its magnitude, which has exceeded my calculation, has put it beyond my power to adorn it with facsimiles with which it would have been enriched, had it been admitted into the series published "Under the Direction of the Master of the Rolls."

It was my intention to close this preface with a few strictures on some of the weightiest and most costly of the works published under the above-mentioned Direction; but I will reserve all such for the second part of a small pamphlet which I issued some time ago, entitled "Some Correspondence relative to the Materials of British History:" in this will be given the correspondence down to the final rejection of the Diplomatarium. I will here merely venture on the opinion, that good new editions of the best of our chronicles printed in the collections of Savile, Twysden, Gale, and others, would have been more welcome and infinitely more useful than, very few excepted, the entire mass of those printed under the said Direction. The rule for these publications is to admit no reprint: a worse, perhaps, it would be difficult to conceive; for if it be asked, Why has this or that work been suffered to lie for centuries in manuscript? what is the answer likely to be?

It was with deep regret that I found myself totally unable to avail myself of the kind permission granted me by the Earl of Ashburnham to collate the Anglo-Saxon charters at Ashburnham Place, formerly in the Duke of Buckingham's library at Stowe; but my obligation to his Lordship is not the less on that account, as well as my sincere thanks for his liberality. My chief object in desiring a visit to Ashburnham Place was to collate with the manuscript there the Will of king Ælfred; but I have since collated the text of Manning's edition with that of the Hyde Abbey copy, in the library of the Earl of Macclesfield at Shirburn Castle, as published by Mr. Edwards[1], and, with the exception of the later and apparently provincial orthography of the latter, have found them to accord without a variation worth noting.

To the Dean and authorities at Westminster I have also many thanks to offer, for their readiness in allowing the gentleman employed by me[2] to copy and collate whatever their rich manuscript stores contained connected with my object.

But to no one do I feel more grateful, for his sympathy and for his untiring zeal in furthering my undertaking, than to my friend Mr. Roach Smith: indeed I do not hesitate to declare that, but for his earnest co-operation, my attempt to edit the old charters of England must have proved abortive.

B. T.

Chiswick, July 12th, 1865.

[1] Chapters of the biographical History of the French Academy, with an Appendix relating to the unpublished Monastic Chronicle, entitled Liber de Hyda, by Edward Edwards. Trübner & Co. 1864.

I rejoice in being able to state that the entire Liber de Hyda is in the press, under the able editorship of Mr. Edwards, to whose kindness in supplying me with transcripts from that precious MS. I acknowledge myself greatly indebted.

[2] Mr. Henry R. Hamilton.

SYNOPSIS OF MS. AUTHORITIES.

Additional MSS. Brit. Museum. Nos. 4936, 5811, 5937, 9067 (Exeter MS. copy), 9381, 14847, 14907, 15350 (Winton MS.).
Arundel MS. 278. A modern copy of Ingulf's Hist. of Crowland.
Ashmole MS. Oxford.
Aula Trin. MS. at Trinity Hall, Cambridge.
Bodley MS. Wood I., Rawlinson, Tanner, Marshal.
C. C. C. Cant. MSS. at Corp. Chr. Coll. Cambridge. No. 59. C. xi. (Bath Chartulary).
Cotton. Cottonian Library in Brit. Mus. MSS. Augustus, A. ii. Claudius, A. iii. B. vi. C. ix. D. ii. x. Cleopatra, E. i. Domitian, A. vii. Faustina, A. iii. Julius, D. ii., Nero, D. i. E. i. Otho, B. xiv., Tiberius, A. xiii. (Worcester Chart.), B. iv. v. C. ix. E. iv. Titus, A. viii. Vespasian, A. v. B. xx. xxiv. D. xxii. E. xi. Vitellius, A. xiii. C. ix.
Harl. Harleian Library in Brit. Mus.
Lamb. Archiepiscopal Library at Lambeth.
Lansd. Lansdowne Library, in Brit. Mus.
B. P. Cant. Public Library, Cambridge. Ff. 2. 33, Ee. 3. 60, Ii. 2. 11.
Soc. Antiq. MS. No. 60 in Libr. Society of Antiquaries. Reg. of Peterborough Abbey.
Chart. in Arce Lond. Charters in the Tower of London.
Chart. Antiq. Cantuar. Single Charters in the Archives of Ch. Church, Canterbury—A. 207, B. i. 195, 207. C. 1282, E. 206, M. 14, 363, 369.
Chart. S. Nic. Pri. Exeter.
Chart. 8 Edward II. per Inspeximus.
Chart. Antiq. in Archivis S. Petri Westmonasterii. 1. In wooden box. Sec. x. No. viii. Liber Niger Quaternus.
Chart. Antiq. in Archiv. Eccl. Wigorn. Autograph of Windsor Charter, at Worcester.
Winton MS. See Additional MSS.
Ilchester MSS. in possession of the Earl of Ilchester.
Mag. Reg. Alb. penes D. & C. Eboraci.
Registrum B. penes D. & C. S. Pauli, Lond.
Registrum Malmesb., in Scaccario Regis Remem. Westm.
Registrum Chart. de Ramsey, in Scacc. Reg. Remem. Westm.
Registrum Scireburn., in the possession of Sir Thomas Phillips, Bart., at Middlehill, Worcestershire.

TABLE OF CONTENTS.

I. MISCELLANEOUS CHARTERS.

* This charter seems to be under a wrong date, it should probably be DCCIX. not DCXCIX.

* This charter should have been marked with an asterisk, fol. B. 136.

II. WILLS.

III. GUILDS.

IV. MANUMISSIONS.

*** Charters marked with an asterisk are considered spurious, or of doubtful authority.

DIPLOMATARIUM ANGLICUM ÆVI SAXONICI.

I. MISCELLANEOUS CHARTERS.

* KING ÆTHELBERHT OF KENT. JAN. 9TH DC.V.

✠ In nomine sancte et individue Trinitatis. Rex Anglorum Æthelbertus, misericordia Omnipotentis Dei catholicus, omnibus sue gentis fidelibus, et adventum glorie magni Dei et Salvatoris nostri Jesu Christi beata spe expectantibus, salutem viteque eterne beatitudinem. Largiente summi Regis clementia, ego Æthelbertus solio paterno confirmatus, paceque divinitus concessa, eo jam per decem quinquennia sceptrigera potestate potitus, et per venerabiles sacre fidei doctores, Spiritus Sancti gratia, irradiatus, ab errore falsorum deorum ad unius veri Dei cultum toto corde conversus; ne ingratus beneficiorum appaream illi a cujus sancta sede nobis in regione umbre mortis sedentibus lux veritatis emicuit, inter alias quas fabricavi ecclesias, monitu et hortatu beatissimi pape Gregorii et sancti patris nostri Augustini, ipsi beatissimo apostolorum principi Petro, et doctori gentium Paulo, ecclesiam a fundamentis construxi, eamque terris variisque possessionum donariis decorare studui, inibique monachos Deum timentes aggregari feci, et cum consilio ejusdem reverentissimi archipresulis Augustini, ex suo sancto sanctorum collegio venerabilem virum secum ab apostolica sede directum, Petrum monachum elegi, eisque, ut ecclesiasticus ordo exposcit, abbatem preposui. Hanc igitur ecclesiam ad provectum debiti culminis promovere desiderans, suarumque possessionum terminos dilatare gestiens, sana mente integroque consilio, cum Ædbaldi filii mei aliorumque nobilium obtimatum meorum consensu, ob redemptionem anime mee, et spem retributionis eterne, optuli ei etiam villam nomine Sturigao, alio nomine dictam Cistelet, cum omnibus redditibus ei jure competentibus, cum mancipiis, silvis, cultis vel incultis, pratis, pascuis, paludibus, fluminibus, et contiguis ei maritimis terminis eam ex una parte cingentibus, omnia mobilia vel immobilia in usus fratrum sub regulari tramite et monastica religione inibi Deo serviencium: missurium etiam argenteum, scapton aureum, iterum sellam cum freno, auro et gemmis ornatam, speculum argenteum, armilcaisia oloserica, camisiam ornatam, quod mihi xenium de domno papa Gregorio sedis apostolice directum fuerat, que omnia supradicte ecclesie gratanter obtuli. Quam etiam ecclesiam ipse servus Dei Augustinus sanctorum apostolorum ac martirum reliquiis variisque ecclesiasticis ornamentis ab apostolica sede sibi transmissis copiose ditavit, seseque in ea et cunctos successores suos ex auctoritate apostolica sepeliri precepit, scriptura dicente "Non esse civitatem mortuorum sed vivorum." Ibi etiam mihi et successoribus meis sepulturam providi, sperans me quandoque ab ipso apostolici ordinis principe cui Dominus potestatem ligandi atque solvendi dedit, et claves regni celorum tradidit, a peccatorum nexibus solvi, et eterne beatitudinis januam introduci.

Quod monasterium aut ecclesiam nullus episcoporum, nullus successorum meorum regum in aliquo ledere aut inquietare presumat, nullam omnino subjectionem in ea sibi usurpare audeat; sed abbas ipse qui ibi fuerit ordinatus, intus et foris, cum consilio fratrum, secundum timorem Dei, libere eam regat et ordinet, ita ut in die Domini dulcem illam piissimi Redemptoris nostri vocem mereatur audire, dicentis. "Euge serve bone et fidelis, quia super pauca fuisti fidelis, super multa te constituam: intra in gaudium Domini tui."

Hanc donationem meam in nomine Patris, et Filii, et Spiritus Sancti, largitate divina ut mihi tribuatur peccatorum remissio, per omnia cum consilio reverentissimi patris Augustini condidi, atque ad transcribendum Augemundum presbiterum ordinavi. De his ergo omnibus que hic scripta sunt, si quis aliquid inde minuere presumpserit, sciat se equissimo judici Deo et beatis apostolis Petro et Paulo rationem esse redditurum. Confirmata [est hec] donatio presentibus testibus reverentissimo patre Augustino Dorovernensis ecclesie archiepiscopo primo, Mellito quoque et Justo, Lundonie et Rofensis ecclesie presulibus, et religioso famulo Christi Laurencio presbitero, Ædbaldo filio meo, Hamigisilo [duce], Augemundo referendario, Hocca [et] Graphione [comitibus] Tangisilo et Pinca et Geddi et Aldhuno regis optimatibus, aliisque pluribus dignitatum diversarum personis.

Actum sane quadragesimo quinto anno regni nostri, sub die V. Idus Januarii.

---

* AUGUSTINUS.

✠ Augustinus episcopus Dorobernie sedis, famulus, quem, superna inspirante clementia, beatissimus papa Gregorius, Anglice genti Deo acquirende, legatarium misit ac ministrum, omnibus successoribus suis episcopis, cunctisque Anglie regibus, cum suis posteris, atque omnibus Dei fidelibus, et in fide et gratia, salutem et pacem. Patet omnibus quod Deo amabilis rex Athelbertus, primus Anglorum regum Christi regno sacratus, nostra instantia et sua prodiga benivolencia, inter ceteras ecclesias quas fecit et episcopia, monasterium extra metropolim suam Doroberniam, in honore principum apostolorum Petri et Pauli regaliter condidit, et regalibus opibus amplisque possessionibus ditavit, dilatavit, magnificavit, perpetuaque libertate et omni jure regio, cum omnibus rebus et judiciis intus et foris illo pertinentibus, munivit;

suoque regio privilegio et superni judicii imprecatione atque apostolica sancti pape Gregorii interminacione excommunicatoria contra omnem injuriam confirmavit. Ego quoque, ejusdem libertatis adjutor et patrocinator, omnes successores meos archiepiscopos, omnesque ecclesiasticas vel seculares potestates per Dominum Ihm Xpm et apostolorum ejus reverenciam obtestor, atque apostolica memorati patris nostri pape Gregorii interminacione interdico, ne quisquam unquam ullum potentatum aut dominatum aut imperium in hoc dominicum vel apostolicum monasterium, vel terras vel ecclesias ad illud pertinentes, usurpare præsumat, nec ulla prorsus subjugationis aut servitutis aut tributi condicione, vel in magno vel in minimo, Dei ministros inquietet aut opprimat. Abbatem a suis fratribus electum in eodem monasterio, non ad suum famulatum, sed ad dominicum ministerium, ordinet, nec sibi hunc obaudire sed Deo suadeat; nec vero sibi subjectum sed fratrem, set consortem, sed collegam et comministrum in opus dominicum eum reputet. Non ibi missas, quasi ad sue ditionis altare, nec ordinationes vel benedictiones usurpative, sine abbatis vel fratrum peticione excerceat. Nullum sibi jus consuetudinarium, vel in vilissima re exigat, quatinus pacis concordia unum sint in Domino utrimque. Nec quisquam, quod absit, dominandi dissidio in juditium incidat dyaboli, qui superbie tyrannide corruit de celo. Reges gencium, inquit Dominus, dominantur eorum, vos autem non sic. Cumque ab alienigenis, non a filiis, accipiantur tributa, sic ipse Dominus concludit: "Ergo liberi sunt filii." Qua ergo irreverencia patres ecclesiarum in filios regni Dei sibi vendicant dominationem, maxime autem in hanc ecclesiam sanctorum thesaurariam, in cujus materno utero tot pontificum Dorobernie, regumque ac principum, corpora speramus alma refovenda sepulture requie, ex auctoritate scilicet apostolica, et hinc ad eternam gloriam resuscitanda. Tales supremi Judicis amicos si quis offendere non metuens hujus privilegii statuta violaverit, vel violatorem imitando vim suam tenuerit, sciat se apostolico beati Petri gladio, per suum vicarium Gregorium puniendum, nisi emendaverit. Hec ergo omnia, ut hic sunt scripta, apostolica ipsius institutoris nostri Gregorii comprobacione et auctoritate servanda sancimus, suoque ore confirmamus, presente glorioso rege Athelberto, cum filio suo Athelbaldo[1], et collaudante cum ipso omnibus optimatibus regiis, atque ultro volentibus reverentissimis fratribus nostris, a sancta Romana ecclesia huc mecum vel ad me in evangelium Domini destinatis, scilicet Laurencio, quem nobis Deo favente successorem constituimus, et Mellito Londonie episcopo, et Justo Rofensi episcopo, et Petro venerabili ejusdem monasterii principum apostolorum abbate primo, cum ceteris in Domino adjutoribus meis, obnixe postulantibus, simulque in eos qui hec fideliter servaverint benedictionem; aut in impenitentes, quod nolumus, transgressores, dampnationem exercentibus.

---

* KING EADBALD OF KENT. DC.XVIII.

✠ In nomine Patris et Filii et Spiritus Sancti. Ego Ædbaldus rex, gloriosi regis Æthelberti filius, quem prothodoctor et apostolus Anglorum Augustinus cum suo regno ab eternis inferorum cruciatibus eripuit, et dealbatum fonte baptismatis sanctorum collegio copulavit, per venerabilem Laurencium, beati Augustini discipulum, quem ipse pater novelle adhuc Anglorum ecclesie sibi successorem in archiepiscopatum ordinaverat, tandem sermonibus assiduis et signis ac plagis in seipso pro me passis ac ostensis, a volutabro scelerum lotus, et ad agnitionem Creatoris omnium creaturarum promotus, Dominum Deum meum recognosco et adoro. Proinde ego Ædbaldus in solio paterno confirmatus, patris vestigia imitans, et ecclesias Dei quas viriliter instantia patris Augustini fundavit, et terris multisque honoribus ditavit, augens et confirmans, monasterio apostolorum Petri et Pauli in suburbio Dorovernie civitatis fundato, et prerogativo ecclesiastice libertatis privilegio munito, terris ac variis honoribus ditato, ad honorem Dei et sanctorum apostolorum Sanctique Augus-

[1] Eadbaldo.

tini, pro remedio animæ mei patris meeque parentumque meorum, gratanter concedo et amicabiliterque do quamdam partem terre regni mei, xxx. aratrorum, nomine Nortburne, in usum monachorum ibidem Deo famulancium, ubi ipse pater Augustinus et pater meus requiescunt, ubi etiam archiepiscopos et reges sibi succedentes requiescere decreverunt, ubi et corpus meum sepeliri precipio. Hanc autem præfatam terram, in omnibus ad se pertinentibus, pascuis, paludibus, pratis, silvis ac finibus maritimis, ita liberam et quietam dono ac dito sicut pater meus aut ego unquam liberius habuimus. Hujus donationis confirmationem tropheo agie crucis ✠ et carta mea regia consignavi, assidentibus et collaudantibus archiepiscopo, baptista scilicet meo, Laurencio, et subscribente cum regina mea Æmma filiisque meis Egfrido ac Ercumberto, cum duobus episcopis, Mellito Londoniæ et Justo Rofensis ecclesie, ceterisque multis comitibus et obtimatibus meis confaventibus et subscribentibus in hujus donationis fautores et auctores vitam eternam optantibus, in invidentes seu minuentes Dei omnipotentis et sanctorum apostolorum et patris nostri Augustini terribilem interminationem.

✠ Ego Laurentius, gratia Dei archiepiscopus, signo sancte crucis, sicut regem vidi facere, hoc donum confirmo. ✠ Ego Emma, Francorum regis filia, regis Æadbaldi copula, vexillo adorande crucis armavi. ✠ Ego Mellitus, Lundoniæ episcopus, signo sancte crucis que vidi astipulor. ✠ Ego Justus, Rofensis episcopus, laudo et subscribo. ✠ Ego Egbertus signo crucis libenter corroboro. ✠ Ego Ercumbertus, attestante venerande ✠ gratanter concedo, contestor, et subscribo. ✠ Ego Sueardus consensi. ✠ Ego Guthardus subscribo.

Actum est autem anno ab incarnatione Salvatoris nostri Jesu Christi sexcentesimo octavodecimo, Indictione sexta.

---

* KING CĒNWALH OF WESSEX. DC.LXXI.

☧ In nomine Domini nostri Jhesu Christi, ego Cenuualch regnante Deo rex hanc libertatem et potestatem sedi pontificali Sciréburnensis æcclesiæ, per privilegii cautionem, coram senioribus et testibus idoneis, communi consensu atque tractatu, firmiter atque inmarcessibiliter in æternum fore constituo, id est, ut omnium fiscalium ac secularium rerum, sive operum sive tributuum, et cunctorum negotiorum, seu in magnis seu in modicis, per omne modum universaliter sit libera, quia Dei singularis hæreditas est, et pontificalis officii sedis. De omnibus quoque curis et causis secularibus, fide catholica et recto baptismate perseverante, hoc decretum statuimus, ut ab universis gravitudinibus et secularium hominum turbinibus hæc eadem æcclesia, cum tota terra et possessione illius, semper immunis et secura permaneat, ut illic inhabitantes pura et sobria ac sincera mente laudem Domini celebrantes, et legem ejus diligenter tota plebe prædicantes, sine impedimento Deo servire valeant. Si enim aliquis successorum nostrorum, maligna fraude instructus, et spiritu cupiditatis illectus, hoc infringere ausus fuerit, sciat se in inferni suppliciis suspiraturum, et in faculis tartariis crematurum, et absque ullo remedio sine fine ejulaturum. Si quis vero hæc in bona parte augere misericorditer pro Dei nomine voluerit, augeat omnipotens Dominus bona ipsius, sive in hoc sæculo sive in futuro, centupliciter, et cum omnibus sanctis vitam mereatur æternam fæliciter. Scripta est autem hæc cartula hujus privilegii, consentiente et confirmante Laurentio archiepiscopo[1], simul rege Merciorum Wlfherio, cæteris patricia potestate præditis corroborantibus et subscribentibus anno Dominicæ incarnationis DC.LXXI.

---

* ARCHBISHOP THEODORE. DC.LXXX.

Regnante in perpetuum Deo et Domino nostro Jhesu Christo, qui cœlestia simul et terrestria imperio Patris cuncta quæ Sancti Spiritus gratia in æquitate disponit. Atque per ejusdem Dei prædestinationem hoc synodus congregatum fuerat in loco celeberrimo ubi nominatur Heðfeld, anno vero

[1] Laurentius ob. 621. Theodore was archbishop in 671.

Dominice incarnationis DC.LXXX. Indictio IX., præsidente autem Theodoro, gratia Dei episcopo, ceterisque episcopis et Dei sacerdotibus per universam Britanniam, pariter cum regibus Anglorum, Ægfrido regi Humbronentium et Atheldredo regi Marcentium, cum consensu Halduulfi regis Aesteranglorum atque Clotherio regi Cantuariorum, de multis necessitatibus tractantes, maxime de statu ecclesiarum Dei, quorum ab olitanis temporibus in primordia Christianitatis tocius Britannie constituta atque firmata noscuntur, quomodo vel qualiter, secundum normam rectitudinis his temporibus vel futuris ad servandum disposuimus, cum communi consilio omnium nostrorum regum, episcoporum, vel etiam tocius gentis Anglorum hanc discretionem statuimus atque decrevimus, nostrisque successoribus id ipsum in posterium præcipimus; huic duobus metropolitanis a primitibus locis, que sunt universe Britannie capita constituta prima, ut in Dorovernia civitate principali honor archiepiscopi et indumento paleg[1] habeatur, sicut archiepiscopo Augustino priscis jam temporibus at nunc usque detenta est a sui juris ditioni per singula loca XII. episcopi, seu omnis nationes Anglorum et Brittonum in australis partibus usque ad confinia Norðanhumbrorum; alia vero in Eboraica civitate fundata, similiterque sui juris ditioni XII. episcopi semper in futurum subjugati et partes aquilonales sicut disposuit prædecessoribus nostris pater noster Gregorius illis duobus sedibus ad servandum imperpetuum, ut ex illis præmemoratis civitatibus omnis ordo ecclesiastici officii cervatur atque inde ministratur, tam ordinatio episcoporum, vel etiam unctio regum, quamque canonicas instituciones que suis exhortacionibus et assiduis sollicitudinibus ad regimen Christianitatis pertineant. Et nunc ergo iterum ad memoriam retracti per dominum apostolicum Agathonem papam ita inrefragabilis et inviolabilis a nobis nostrisque successoribus utrorumque prænominatorum civitatum perpetuo stabilitate firmavi. Si quis vero, quod non optamus, obstinata contumacia his salubris statutis obpugnando contraire temptaverit, quisquis ille sit, sciat canonica subjacere sentencia, et a sinodali hujus

[1] pallii?

communione esse damnatum, vel a participatione corporis et sanguinis Domini nostri Jhesu Christi separatum.

Ego [Ægfridus] rex Humbrensium his synodalibus et canonicis constitutis consentiens subscribo. Ego [Æðelredus] rex Merciorum his sinodalibus et canonicis constitutis consentiens subscribo. Ego Alduulf rex Æstranglorum his sinodalibus et canonicis constitutis consentiens subscribo. Ego [Cloðerius] rex Cantuariorum his sinodalibus et canonicis constitutis consentiens subscribo. Ego Theodorius, gratia Dei archiepiscopus Britannie et civitatibus Dorovernie, consentiens subscribo.

---

* KING WIHTRÆD OF KENT. DC.XCIV.

✠ Anno ab incarnatione Domini DC.XCIIII. Whytredus gloriosus rex Kancie cum reverentissimo archiepiscopo Brihtwaldo precepit congregari concilium in loco qui nominatur Bachancild, presidente eodem concilio jam nominato clementissimo rege Cantuariorum Whytredo, et eodem venerando patre primate totius Britannie, simulque Tobia episcopo Roffensis ecclesie, cum abbatibus, abbatissis, presbyteris, diaconibus, ducibus, satrapis, pariter tractantes de statu ecclesiarum Dei in Anglia, et de hiis quæ a fidelibus regibus prædecessoribus ejus et propinquis, Æðelberto, videlicet, posterisque ejus, Deo omnipotenti in propriam hereditatem data fuerunt, qualiter secundum veram justiciam stare et permanere valeant; vel quomodo ea servare oporteat amodo et usque in finem seculi constituentes. Ego, inquit, Whytredus, rex terrenus, a Rege regum compunctus, zelo rectitudinis accensus, ex antiqua traditione sanctorum patrum didici, non esse licitum alicui homini in laico habitu constituto usurpare sibi, quasi propriam possessionem, quod fuerat ante Domino concessum et cruce Christi firmatum. Scimus enim, et veraciter constat, quia quod semel acceperit homo donatione alterius in propriam potestatem, nullatenus sine injuria illud iterum dimittet. Horrendum est itaque hominibus Deum vivum exspoliare, tunicamque ejus et hereditatem scindere. Cum ergo Deo oblatum aliquid fuerit de terrenis substantiis, ad hoc ut facilius promereri valeant offerentes eternam retributionem percipere in celis manifeste declaratur, quod quanto incautius homo secularis applicuit se in hereditatem regis eterni, tanto districtius a Deo punietur. Pro qua re firmiter decernimus, et in nomine omnipotentis Dei omniumque sanctorum præcipimus, omnibus successoribus nostris regibus, principibus, et omnibus in laico habitu constitutis, ut nulli unquam liceat alicujus ecclesie vel monasterii dominium habere quæ a me vel antecessoribus meis priscis temporibus tradita sunt Deo in perpetuam hereditatem et sanctis ejus: magis autem, sicut in canonibus precipitur, servandum est, ut quando aliquis de prelatis defungitur, episcopus, abbas, vel abbatissa, intimetur archiepiscopo proprie parochie, et cum ejus consilio et consensu, vita ac munditia ejus examinata, qui dignus invenitur eligatur, et nullo modo sine consensu et consultu archiepiscopi promoveatur. Neque enim de hac re aliquid pertinet ad decretum vel imperium regis. Illius autem est comites, duces, optimates, principes, prefectos, judices seculares, statuere; metropolitani vero est archiepiscopi ecclesias Dei replere, gubernare, episcopos, abbates, abbatissas, ceterosque prelatos, eligere, statuere, firmare, admonere, ne quis de ovibus Christi, scilicet eterni pastoris, aberret. Hec lex per evum in regno nostro in perpetuum permaneat omnibus ecclesiis Dei nostri, pro salute anime mee meorumque predecessorum, proque spe celestis regni. Igitur ex hac die et deinceps concedimus et donamus ecclesiis regni nostri liberas esse perpetua libertate ab omnibus difficultatibus secularis servitutis, ab omni debito vel pulsione regalium tributorum, ut possint pro nobis Deo omnipotenti hostias dignas offerre, nostraque peccata abluere immaculatis muneribus. Si quis autem rex post nos levatus in regnum, aut episcopus, aut abbas, seu aliqua alia persona contradixerit huic concilio, vel scripto judicio concilii facto, sciat se a corpore et sanguine Domini sequestratum, et sic excommunicatum sicut ille qui non habebit remissionem neque in hoc seculo neque in futuro, nisi ante mortem, secundum judicium archiepiscopi emendaverit. Hoc scriptum irrefragabile sua firmitate muniatur, servetur, et semper habeatur in ecclesia Salvatoris, que sita est in civitate Dorobernia, ubi primas habetur, ad exemplum omnium ecclesiarum, atque deffensionem que in Anglia habetur.

✠ Ego Wihtredus, auxilio Christi rex, hiis legibus constitutis pro me et Werberga[1] regina itemque filio nostro Ælrico subscripsi. ✠ Ego Brihtuualdus, gratia Dei archiepiscopus, hiis legibus constitutis subscripsi.

---

*KING INE OF WESSEX. DC.XCIX.

✠ In nomine Domini Dei nostri Jhesu Christi Salvatoris. Ea que secundum decreta canonum salubriter decernuntur, quamvis sermo tantum ad testimonium sufficeret, tamen pro incerta futuri temporis ambiguitate firmissima litterarum astipulatione roborentur. Quapropter ego Ini rex Saxonum terram juxta Abbendune, c.lxx.iii. cassatorum, Hean abbati libenter reddidi, quam Cissa rex sibi ac Cillan sorori sue atque abbatisse aliquando dederat: sed Ina rex eandem terram postea, dum regno potiretur diripiens ac reipublice restituit, nondum constructo monasterio in ea, nec ullo admodum oratorio erecto; rursus autem ad edificandum monasterium eidem Heano, patricio tunc temporis suo, eandem terram redonavit dicens: Ego Ina monarchus Saxonie regnante Domino, regalia gubernans sceptra, terram quam prædecessoris mei Cissa et ceteri Heano patricio sueque germane Cillan dedisse noscuntur, iterum cum consilio plurimorum reddo et relinco. Deinde predictus patricius Hean se cum omni facultate sua et præfata terra omnipotentis Dei servitio subdidit, meque ad construendum monasterium illud in loco supra nominato, id est juxta Abbendune, regulari-

[1] In a charter of 694, the queen of Wihtred is named Cynegyth, and in charters of 696 and 697, Æthelburh.—Cod. Dipl. i. 42, 48, 49.

terque regendum illud abbatem elegit, sponteque sua seipsum meo regimini commisit, votoque monachico constringens. At nunc nondum evoluto ad integrum quinquennio, ex quo hec vota vovit solvenda, immutare decreta cupiens, Inique regem in suffragium sibi repetite hereditatis assumpsit; quibus ego libenter cessi, præfatamque terram et monasteria que construximus, ut dixi, in toto retribuam. Insuper et de orientale parte fluminis Tamise xx. cassatos, quos mihi Cuthredus regulus et Merciorum rex Ethelredus, nec non et Ini rex Saxonum tradiderunt, adiciam x. quoque cassatos secus vadum Bestlesford, et c. in Bradenfeld, ubi monasterium erexi, quos Ini et Conred simul dederunt, pariter tribui, qui fiunt simul CC.LXXIII. cassatos. Votum autem monachi quod mihi spopondit relaxans clementer indulsi, presente venerando antistite Hedde, nec non Aldelmo abbate, et Wintra, et omni familia nostra in ecclesia. Si quis vero contra hoc decretum abbatatus venire temptaverit, vel has donationes regum religiosorum, tirannica fretus potestate, violenter demere vel auferre satagerit, sciat se coram Christo rationem in ultimo vivorum et mortuorum examine redditurum. Scripta est vero hæc cautionis singrapha anno ab incarnatione Christi DC.XCIX., Indictione XII.

✠ Ego Ine rex consensi. ✠ Ego Athelbald rex subscripsi. ✠ Ego Daniel episcopus subscripsi. ✠ Ego Befpha subscripsi. ✠ Ego Egfrid subscripsi. ✠ Ego Herrid subscripsi. ✠ Ego Aldbriht subscripsi. ✠ Ego Stranglic subscripsi. ✠ Ego Halda subscripsi. ✠ Ego Oba subscripsi. ✠ Ego Selred subscripsi. Ego Egbrith subscripsi.

---

* KING INE OF WESSEX. MAY 26TH DCC.IV.

In nomine Domini Dei nostri Salvatoris. Ego Yna regnante Domino rex, cum consilio et decreto præsulis nostri Aldelmi, simulque cunctorum Dei sacerdotum suggestione, et monachorum petitione qui in parochia [West][1] Saxonum

[1] The words between brackets are not in MS. Lansd.

conversantur, hanc libertatem ecclesiis impendo, et hanc privilegii dignitatem monasteriis confero; ut sine impedimento sæcularium rerum, et absque tributo fiscalium negociorum, liberis mentibus, Deo soli serviant, et monasticam cenobii disciplinam, Christo suffragium largiente regulariter exerceant; ac pro statu et prosperitate regni nostri, et indulgencia commissorum [criminum], ante conspectum divine Majestatis preces fundere dignentur: et orationum officia frequentantes in ecclesiis, pro nostra fragilitate interpellare nitantur. Si quis vero contra hujus decreti singrapham venire temptaverit, sciat se coram Christo novemque angelorum ordinibus in tremendo examine rationem redditurum. Hoc vero decretum, a nobis libenter consessum, taliter confirmari et servari decernimus, ut tam nobis vita comite propicia divinitate regni gubernacula regentibus [quam futuris successoribus hæreditatis jure regnandi monarchiam tenentibus], inextricabili lege firmiter roboretur. Nam pro ampliori firmitatis testamento, principes et senatores, judices et patricios subscribere fecimus, quorum nomina infra tenentur asscripta. Actum publice et confirmatum in loco qui appellatur Eburleagh. Septem Kalendarum Juniarum die. Indictione II[a]. Anno ab incarnatione Christi DCC.IIII. feliciter.

Signum manus Yni regis, qui hec omnia manu propria confirmavit.

Ego Aldelmus, servus servorum Dei, hoc decretum manu propria roboravi. Ego Hagona abbas consenciens subscripsi. Ego Adbertus abbas consenciens subscripsi. Ego Haeha abbas consenciens subscripsi. Ego Wintra abbas consenciens subscripsi. Ego Wedr abbas consenciens subscripsi. Ego Beornwald abbas consenciens subscripsi. Ego Wilgar abbas consenciens subscripsi. Ego Bealwlf abbas consenciens subscripsi. Ego Froda abbas consenciens subscripsi. Ego Witta abbas consenciens subscripsi. Signum manus Beoban. Signum manus Eanberht. Signum manus Ceonberht. Signum manus Coen. Signum manus Adilfridi. Signum manus Eascwaldi. Signum manus Duduc. Signum manus Ticcean. Signum manus Bealdhun.

* BISHOP ALDHELM. DCC.V.

✠ Nihil in hoc sæculo prolixa foelicitate perfruitur, nihil diuturna dominatione potitur, nihil quod non ad fatalem vitæ terminum veloci cursu tendere videatur. Et ideo sic nobis mundanarum rerum patrimonia sunt perfruenda, ut tamen æternæ patriæ emolumentis nunquam fraudemur. Hinc est quod ego Aldelmus, postquam me immeritum nullisque prædignis moribus comprobatum, in pontificatus officii sedem divina gratia subthronizasset, proposui arcano mentis meæ affectu, ut monasteriis meis, quibus jamdudum in abbatatus gradu constitutus, suffragante Domino, regulariter præfui, religiosum abbatem, quem sibi spontanea familiarum mearum optio consona voce elegisset, canonica creatione atque regulari sanctione constituerem.

His voluntariis propositionibus meis pia monachorum meorum restitit pertinacitas. Et cum hoc sedulo sæpiusque in conventu fratrum meorum fiducianter narrassem, nullus his votis meis placidissimum præbebat assensum, dicentes quod "Quamdiu vitali vegetaris spiritu nobiscumque præsentis vitæ deputaris stadio, tuæ semper dominationis jugo humillime colla subdere non dedignamur. Sed hoc supplici prece communique rogatu deprecamur, quod sub sacra scripturarum testificatione et favorabilium virorum claro consensu corrobores: ut nullus post obitum tuum, nec regalis audacitas, nec pontificalis auctoritas, vel aliquis æcclesiasticæ seu sæcularis dignitatis vir, sine nostro voluntatis arbitrio, in nobis sibi vendicet principatum." Huic debitæ monachorum meorum maximeque famulorum Dei petitioni libentissime consensi; et in monasterio quod juxta fluvium qui dicitur Uuinburna situm est, cui venerandi regis nostri germana Cuthburh præsidet, cum optabili famosissimi regis Ini consensu, et reverendissimi fratris et coepiscopi mei Danielis nutu, præsentatæ professionis devotionem decentissimam, et vernarum Domini postulationem, sacræ crucis signaculo confirmavi: itidem idem venerandus rex et prænominatus pontifex pari devotionis manu subscripserunt. Nec multo post, in sacrosancto concilio, quod juxta fluvium qui dicitur Woder congregatum esse dinoscitur, in idem omnium Saxonicæ gentis archimandritarum, cum regalis potentatus assensu et pontificalis prioratus nutu consensit auctoritas. Si quis vero contra hæc tam illustrium personarum decreta moliri machinetur, et sacra præsentis scedulæ scita prævaricari præsumpserit, sciat se ante terribilem divinæ Majestatis thronum cum prævaricatoribus præceptorum Domini lugubri damnationis judicio percellendum. Sunt autem hæc nomina monasteriorum, Maldubesberg, Froom, Bradanford. Scripta est hujus confirmationis cartula anno ab incarnatione Domini nostri Jhesu Christi DCCV. Indictione III.

KING ÆTHELBALD OF MERCIA. DCC.XVI.-DCC.XVII.

☧ In nomine Domini Jhesu. Ego Æðilbald, ex divina dispensatione Mercensium rex, rogatus a sancta familia Christi consistenti in loco cui nomen est Wigranceastre, aliquam agelli partem in qua sal confici solet, ad meridianam plagam fluminis quod dicunt Saluuerpe, in loco qui dicitur Lootwic et Coolbeorg, ad construendos tres casulos et sex caminos, pro redemptione anime mee, in voluntariam possidendi libertatem, concedens donabo; sex alios a supradicta Christi familia caminos, in duobus casulis, in quibus similiter sal conficitur, vicarios accipiens, ad aquilonalem videlicet partem fluminis memorati cui vocabulum est Saluuerpe. Hanc autem mutuam vicissitudinem idcirco fecisse nos constat, quia utrisque nobis magis aptum esse visum est.

Hanc autem libertatem ego Æðelbaldus, rex Merciorum, signo sancte crucis confirmabo. Ego Eguuinus episcopus. Ego Wilfridus dux. Ego Æþeluuard dux. Ego Stronglic dux. Ego Sigberhtus minister. Ego Eadberht minister. Ego Oba minister. Ego Eadwlf minister.

---

* KING ÆTHELBALD OF MERCIA. DCC.XVI.-DCC.XVII.

✠ In nomine Domini nostri Jhesu Christi. Ego Æðelbaldus, dum mihi Rex eternus, Omnipotens Deus, terrigeni regni absque merito portionem aliquam contulisset, cogitavi ut exinde aliquam partem, pro remedio anime mee, ad utilitatem ecclesiarum Dei perdonarem. Proinde unam portionem mansionis in wico emptorio salis quem nos Saltwich vocamus, cum conscientia principum ac ducum meorum, quorum nomina inferius perscripta sunt ac notata, pro spe superne remunerationis, ad ecclesiam beate Dei genitricis semperque virginis Marie, que fundata est in Cronuchomme, libenter concedens donabo; quatinus ab omni tributo fiscalis publici imperpetuum illa portio quam nostratim Sele nuncupamus libera sit. Si quis autem, quod absit, heredum meorum hanc donationem meam, quam pro redemptione anime mee trado, infringere ausus fuerit, sciat se ante tribunal Christi rationem redditurum, nisi satisfactione digna emendaverit. Si quis autem augere voluerit, augeat Deus partem illius in terra viventium.

Hanc vero donationem meam ego Æðelbaldus, dono Dei rex, pro majori stabilimento, signo sancte crucis munio. ✠ Ego Ecgwinus episcopus hanc donationem confirmans subscripsi. ✠ Ego Aðelwardus consensi et subscripsi. ✠ Ego Ædelrich consensi et subscripsi. ✠ Ego Eadberht consensi et subscripsi. Ego Wilfrid consensi et subscripsi. ✠ Ego Oua consensi et subscripsi. ✠ Ego Sigebald consensi et subscripsi. ✠ Ego Eoppa consensi et subscripsi.

---

* KING ÆTHELBALD OF MERCIA. DCC.XIX.

Cum plerumque contingere soleat, pro incerta temporum vicissitudine, ut ea quæ multarum et fidelium personarum testimonio consilioque roborata fuerunt, per contumaciam plurimorum, et machinamenta simulationis fraudulentæ, et sine ulla consideratione rationis, in animarum suarum periculo dissipentur, nisi autoritate literarum, et testimonio chirographorum in perpetuam memoriam fuerint consignata. Quapropter ego Ethelbaldus rex Merciorum, pro amore cœlestis patriæ, et pro redemptione animæ meæ, studendum esse providi, ut eam per bona opera liberam efficerem ab omni vinculo delictorum. Dum enim mihi Omnipotens, per misericordiam clementiæ suæ, absque ullo antecedente merito, sceptra regni largitus est, ideo libenter ex eo quod dedit retribuo. Hujus rei gratia, hanc donationem meam me vivente concedo, ut omnia monasteria et ecclesiæ regni mei a publicis vectigalibus, operibus, et oneribus absolvantur, nisi in instructione archium vel pontium quæ nunquam ulli possunt laxari. Præterea habeant famuli Dei propriam libertatem in proficuo silvarum, in fructu agrorum, in captura piscium; nec munuscula præbeant regi vel principibus, nisi voluntaria, sed liberi serviant Domino, in contemplatione pacifica, per totum regnum meum, usque in ævum.

---

* KING INE OF WESSEX. DCC.XXV.

CHARTER TO GLASTONBURY[1].

Adjuva nos Deus salutaris noster. Quecumque secundum decreta canonum atque ecclesiastica instituta salubri consilio diffiniuntur, quamquam sermo tantum absque textu sufficeret, tamen quoniam plerumque nostris temporibus tempestates et turbines secularium rerum, eciam portas ecclesie pulsant, iccirco opere precium censuimus, ob cautelam futurorum, ea quæ diffinita sunt paginis scripturarum annectere, ne in posterum oblivioni tradita ignorentur. Quapropter ego Ina, regali fretus dignitate a Domino, cum consilio Sexburge[2] regine, et licencia Beorthwaldi, Dorobernensis ecclesie pontificis, et omnium suffraganeorum suorum, necnon eciam hortatu Baldredi et Athelardi subregulorum, ecclesie vetuste que est in loco qui dicitur Glasteie, quam magnus sacerdos et

[1] A glaring monkish forgery.

[2] Æthelburh was the name of Ine's queen.

pontifex summus angelorum obsequio sibi ac perpetue virgini Marie, beato David, multis et inauditis miraculis, olim se sanctificasse innotuit, ex hiis quæ paterna hereditate possideo, et in dominium peculiare teneo, locis continuis et congruentibus concedo, ad supplementum vitæ regularis et ad usum monachorum: Brente decem hidas, Sowy duodecim hidas, Poulton viginti hidas, [Dulting viginti hidas,] Bledeneie unam hidam, cum omnibus hiis que antecessores mei eidem ecclesie contulerunt: Kenewalchius, qui, sancto Theodoro archiepiscopo interveniente, Ferlingmere, Beokery, Godenei, Martineseie, Edredeseie; Kentwinus rex, qui Glastingeie matrem sanctorum vocare solitus fuerat, et eam ab omni seculari et ecclesiastico obsequio immunem statuit, et hanc privilegii dignitatem concessit, ut habeant fratres ejusdem loci potestatem elegendi et constituendi sibi rectorem juxta regulam Sancti Benedicti: Hedde episcopus qui, Cedwalla annuente, et propria manu, licet paganus, confirmante, Lantocai; Baldred, qui Pennard, sex hidas; Athelard, qui Poholt, sexaginta hidas, me annuente et confirmante, dederunt. Quorum ego devocioni et benignæ peticioni assencio, et contra malignancium hominum et oblatrancium cœnum insidias, regalium munimine invigilo literarum, quatinus ecclesia Domini nostri Jhesu Christi, et perpetue virginis Marie, sicut in regno Britannie est prima, et fons et origo tocius religionis, ita et ipsa superenimentem privilegii obtineat dignitatem, nec ulli omnino homini ancillare obsequium faciat in terris, que super choros angelorum dominatur in celis. Igitur, summo pontifice Gregorio annuente, et ut matrem Domini sui in sinum et proteccionem sancte Romane ecclesie, me licet indignum cum ipsa suscipiente, consencientibus etiam omnibus Britannie regibus, archiepiscopis, episcopis, ducibus, atque abbatibus, statuo ego atque confirmo, quatinus omnes terre, et loca, et possessiones beate Marie Glasteie sint quieta, et ab omnibus regiis exaccionibus et operibus que indici solent, videlicet expedicione, pontis arcisve construccione, et ab omni[bus] archiepiscoporum et episcoporum promulgacionibus et perturbacionibus, sicut in antiquis ejusdem ecclesie cartis ratum esse invenitur, et a predecessoribus meis, Kenewalchio, Kentwino, Cedwalla, [et] Baldredo confirmatum esse dinoscitur, inconcussa et illabata permaneant. Et quecumque inmerserint cause, in homicidiis, sacrilegiis, veneficiis, furtis, rapinis, in disposicione ecclesiarum, [et] descripcione et ordinacione clericorum, in conventiculis sinodalibus, et in omnibus judiciariis examinacionibus, absque ullius hominis prejudicio, abbatis et conventus disposicione diffiniantur; sed et omnibus regni mei regibus, archiepiscopis, episcopis, ducibus, et principibus, super honorem suum et amorem meum precipio, et omnibus, tam meis quam eorum ministris, super salutem corporis sui precipio, ne ullus eorum in insulam Domini nostri Jhesu Christi, et perpetue virginis Marie Glasteie, nec ejusdem ecclesie possessiones, causa placitandi, perscrutandi, rapiendi, percipiendi, interdicendi, vel aliquid faciendi quod ibidem Deo famulantibus possit esse in scandalum, audeat intrare. Illud autem omnipotentis Dei et perpetue virginis Marie, et beatorum Petri et Pauli, et omnium intercessione sanctorum, interdiccione interdico, ne in ipsa Glastoniensi ecclesia, nec in ecclesiis sibi subditis, viz. Sowy, Brente, Merlinge, Schapewik, Strete, Buddecleighe, Piltun, nec in earum capellis, sed nec in insulis, aliqua interveniente occasione, episcopus cathedram sibi episcopalem statuere, nec missas solempnes celebrare, nec altaria consecrare, nec ecclesias dedicare, nec ordines facere, nec aliquid omnino disponere presumat, nisi ab abbate vel a fratribus invitatus fuerit. Quod si ad hec invitatus fuerit, nichil de rebus ecclesie, set nec de ipsis oblacionibus, ipse sibi aliquid usurpet. Duobus in locis ex ipsius ecclesie possessionibus, duas ei delegamus mansiones, unam in Pohelt, alteram in villa que Piltona dicitur, ut habeat ubi adveniens hospitetur, vel inde veniens sese recipiat. Neque enim eum ibi, nisi inportunitate temporis aut molestia corporis detentus fuerit, aut ab abbate vel a fratribus rogatus fuerit, nec amplius quam cum tribus aut cum quatuor clericis pernoctare licet. Hoc etiam provideat idem episcopus, ut singulis annis cum clericis suis qui Fontanetum sunt, ipsam matrem suam, Glastoniensem videlicet ecclesiam, feria secunda post Ascencionem Domini, cum letania recognoscat. Quod si, superbia inflatus, eam distulerit, et que superius dicta et confirmata sunt prevaricaverit, mansiones sibi superius delegatas amittat. Abbas vel monachi a quocunque voluerint episcopo qui Pascha canonicum celebret, ecclesiastica sacramenta in Glastoniensi ecclesia, aut in ecclesiis sibi subjectis, aut in earum capellis percipiant. Quisquis autem hujus mee munificencie et libertatis testamentum, quovis deinceps tempore, aliqua occasione, cujuslibet eciam dignitatis, vel professionis, vel gradus, pervertere vel in irritum deducere temptaverit, sciat se cum Juda proditore eterna confusione edacibus ineffabilium tormentorum periturum flammis. Scripta est autem hujus donacionis et privilegii pagina, anno Dominice incarnacionis septingentesimo vicesimo quinto, Indiccione quarta[1], sub presentia Ine regis et Beorthwaldi Dorobernensis pontificis, venerandorumque antistitum Danielis atque Fordredis, et aliorum quorum nomina inferius annotantur.

Ego Ina rex proprie manus subscripcione hanc donacionem et libertatem, sub sigillo sancte crucis, ratam fieri decerno. Ego Edelburga regina consensi. Ego Baldredus rex confirmavi. Ego Adelard frater reginæ consensi. Ego Beorthwaldus, Dorobernensis ecclesiæ archiepiscopus, Ine regis donacionem et libertatem, sub sigillo sancte crucis corroboravi. Ego Daniel, plebis Dei inspector, adquievi. Ego Fordredus episcopus signum crucis impressi. Waldehere prefectus. Bruta prefectus. Ethelheard. Umming prefectus. Winchelin comes: cum presencia populacionis, consenserunt et firmaverunt.

KING ÆTHELBERHT OF KENT. FEB. 20TH DCC.XXXII.[2]

✠ In nomine Domini Dei Salvatoris nostri Ihesu Christi. Est terrula quedam, id est quarta pars aratri unius juxta Liminee sali coquendo accommoda, quam ego Æthilberhtus

[1] The Indiction for 725 is 8.

[2] Æthelberht did not become sole king of Kent till 748, but appears to have reigned conjointly with his brother Eadberht from 725. See Malmesbury, p. 24, edit. E. H. S.

rex Cantuariorum dudum præstiteram antecessori tuo Hunberht, et tu, O Abba præsbyter Dun, jam per tempora plura, me annuente, eadem usus es præstatione. Hanc ipsam ego nunc terrulam juris mei, non pro pecunia aliqua sæculari, sed pro remedio tantum animæ meæ, tibi et ecclesiæ beatæ Mariæ, cui tua præ est sollicitudo, ita tribuo et dono ut a præsenti die et tempore vestræ sit potestatis eam semper habere ac possidere qualiter vobis placuerit. Et jus regium in ea deinceps nullum repperiatur omnino, excepto dumtaxat tale quale generale est in universis ecclesiasticis terris quæ in hac Cantia esse noscuntur, et ut jugiter firmitatem . . . . hæc ipsa mea donatio habeat, subter hic signum sanctæ crucis ex . . . . . testesque illius ut subscribant petam.

. . . . [d]ie vicesima Februarii mensis, anno regni nostri septimo; Indic. . . . [q]uinta decima. Doroverni.

Insuper ego Æthilberhtus rex addidi huic donationi, quam, pro remedio animæ meæ, dedi in omni anno, centum xx. plaustra onusta de lignis ad coquendum sal. Item dedi ei centum jugera ejusdem ruris, in loco qui dicitur Sandtun.

Termini vero terræ illius hec sunt. Ab oriente terra regis; ab austro fluvius qui dicitur Limenaee; ab occidente et in septentrione Hudan fleot.

✠ Signum scæ̃ crucis quod scripsit Æthilberhtus rex atque donator. ✠ Ego Tatuuinus episc̃. ad petitionem Æthilberhti regis subscripsi. ✠ Ego Albinus abbas, jubente piissimo rege Æthilberhto, subscripsi. ✠ Signum manus Balthhæardi. ✠ Signum manus Bynnan. ✠ Signum manus Æanberhti. ✠ Signum manus Æthiliæardi.

KING ÆTHELBALD OF MERCIA. DCC.XXXIV.

✠ In nomine Domini Dei Salvatoris nostri Jhesu Christi. Si ea quæ quisque pro recipienda a Deo mercede hominibus verbo suo largitur et donat stabilia jugiter potuissent durare, supervacaneum videretur ut litteris narrarentur ac firmarentur. Sed dum ad probanda donata, ad convincendumque volentem donata infringere nihil prorsus robustius esse videretur quam donationis manibus auctorum ac testium roborate non inmerito plurimi petunt, ut quæ eis conlata dinoscuntur paginaliter confirmentur: quorum postulationibus tanto libentius tantoque promptius consensus præbendus quanto et illis quæ præcatores sunt utilior res secundum hoc visibile sclm̃ nunc inpertitur. Et illis qui concessores existunt pro inpertito opere, pietatis uberior fructus secundum invisibile postmodum tribuetur. Quamobrem ego Ethilbaldus rex Merciorum, presentibus litteris, indico me dedisse, pro anima mea Alduulfo episcopo ecclesiæque beati Andreæ apostoli quam gubernat unius navis, sive illa proprie ipsius, sive cujuslibet alterius hominis sit, incessum, id est vectigal, mihi et antecessoribus meis jure regio in portu Lundonie usque hactenus conpetentem, quemammodum mansuetudinem nostram rogavit. Quæ donatio ut in perpetuum firma [et stabilis sit] ita ut nullus eam regum, vel optimatum, vel teloniariorum, vel etiam juniorum quilibet ipsorum, in parte aut in toto, [in irri]tum præsumat, aut possit adducere manu propria signum sanctæ crucis subter in hac pa[gina faciam, testesque] ut subscribant petam. Quisquis igitur id quod pro anima mea donavi, aut [donatu]m est inlibatum permanere permiserit, habeat communionem beatam cum præsente Christi ecclesia atque futura. Si quis autem non permiserit, separetur a societate [non solum sanc]torum hominum, sed etiam angelorum, manente hac donatione nostra nihilominus in sua firmitate.

Actum mense Septembrio dię Indic. II. anno regni nostri XVII.

✠ Ego Æthilbald rex subscripsi. ✠ Signum manus Oba.
✠ Ego Danihel episc̃. scripsi. ✠ Signum manus Sigibed.

Dorso.

✠ Hoc etiam iterum confirmatum est a Beorhtuulfo rege Merciorum, in vico regali Uuerburgeuuic.

✠ Ego Berhtuulf rex Merc̃ hanc meam donationem et prædecessoris mei Æthilbaldi regis cum signo sc̃e crucis Xp̃i confirmavi, his testibus consentientibus, et quorum nomina hic continentur, ad indulgentiam delictorum meorum atque prædecessoris mei Aeðelbaldi regis. Si quis autem successorum meorum regum aut principum, vel thelonariorum hanc donationem nostram infringere vel minuere voluerit, sciat se separatum a congregatione omnium sanctorum in tremendo die judicii, nisi prius digne emendaverit.

✠ Ego Berhtuulf rex Merc̃.	✠ Ego Tatnoth epis̃.
✠ Ego Ceolnoth arc̃.episc̃.	✠ Ego Hunberht dux.
✠ Ego Sæðryð regina.	✠ Ego Mucel dux.
✠ Ego Ceolred epis̃.	✠ Ego Hunstan dux.

ARCHBISHOP NOTHHELM[1]. DCC.XXXVI.-DCC.XXXVII.

✠ Gloriosissimus Mercensium rex Æthelred, cum comite suo, subregulo Huicciorum Oshero, rogatus ab eo, terram xx. cassatorum juxta fluvium, cui vocabulum est Tillath, duabus sanctimonialibus, Dunnan videlicet et ejus filiæ Bucgan, ad construendum in ea monasterium, in jus ecclesiasticum sub libera potestate, pro venia facinorum suorum, condonavit, propriæque manus subscriptione hanc eorum donationem firmavit. Præfata autem Dei famula Dunne, constructum in prædicto agello monasterium, cum agris suis necnon et cartulam descriptionis agri, cui tunc sola ipsa præerat, filiæ, nimirum filiæ suæ, in possessionem, ad Dominum migratura largita est. Sed quia hæc in parvula adhuc ætate erat posita, cartulam conscripti agri, necnon et omnem monasterii procurationem, quoad usque illa ad maturiorem pervenisset ætatem, matri illius maritate conservandam injunxit. Quæ cum cartulam reddi poposcisset, illa reddere nolens, furtu hanc sublatam respondit. Quo tandem omni negotio ad sanctam sacerdotalis concilii synodum perlato, decrevit omne venerabile concilium, cum reverentissimo archiepiscopo Nothelmo, hanc cartulam donationis, vel regum vel supradictæ Dei famulæ Dunnan, manifestissime describi, præfateque abbatissæ Hrotuuari reddi, ejusque possessionem monasterii firmissimam esse; damnato nimirum eo atque anathema-

[1] Of Canterbury.

tizato synodi sanctissimæ decreto, qui cartam illam subscriptionis agri primitivam, vel per furta vel quolibet modo fraudulenter auferendo subripere præsumpserit. Atque hoc decernit sacra synodus, ut post obitum ejus, sicut ante statutum fuit a senioribus ejus, ad episcopalem sedem castrum Uueogernensis liber hic, cum terra reddatur.

✠ Ego Nothelmus, gratia Dei archiepiscopus, canonice subscripsi. ✠ Ego Daniel episcopus subscripsi. ✠ Ego Incguuald episcopus subscripsi. ✠ Uuilfrith episcopus subscripsi. ✠ Ego Alduulf episcopus subscripsi. ✠ Ego Aluuine episcopus subscripsi. ✠ Ego Forthere episcopus subscripsi. ✠ Ego Cuthberht episcopus subscripsi. ✠ Ego Hereuuald episcopus subscripsi.

KING EADBERHT OF KENT. APRIL DCC.XXXVIII.

✠ In nomine Domini Dei nostri Jhesu Christi. Ego Eadberht, rex Cantuariorum, donavi aliquam partem terre, pro remedio anime mee atque indulgentia delictorum meorum, episcopatui beati Andreæ apostoli, ac venerabili viro Ealdulfo, ejus ecclesiæ antistiti, in regione que vocatur Hohg, in loco qui dicitur Andscohesham, id est decem aratrorum, juxta æstimationem provinciæ ejusdem. Hujus vero terræ possessionem ita prædicto episcopo largitus sum, cum omnibus ad eam pertinentibus, id est, campis, silvis, pratis, piscariis, salsilagene, atque omnibus utensilibus ejus, juxta notos terminos constitutos. Hoc quoque præcipimus, ut nullus præsumat propinquorum meorum vel successorum meorum hanc donationem meam minuere [vel] infringere quoquomodo. Si quis vero, quod non credimus, contra præceptum meum, huic donationi meæ malibolo animo contraire temptaverit, sciat se, in die judicii, rationem Deo redditurum, manentem tamen hanc cartulam nihilominus in sua firmitate. Si quis vero magis defendere [et] augere voluerit, addat Deus bona ejus in terra viventium.

✠ Hanc quoque donationem meam ego Eadberht, rex Cantuariorum, propria manu confirmavi, et signum sanctæ crucis infixi; testes quoque idoneos commites meos confirmare et subscribere feci. ✠ Ego Dimheahac commites meos confirmare et subscribere feci. ✠ Ego Hosberth commites meos confirmare et subscribere feci. ✠ Ego Nothbalth commites meos confirmare et subscribere feci. ✠ Ego Banta commites meos confirmare et subscribere feci. ✠ Ego Ruta commites meos confirmare et subscribere feci. ✠ Ego Tidbalth commites meos confirmare et subscribere feci.

✠ In nomine Domini Dei summi. Ego Alduulfus episcopus inprimis penitus ignoravi quod a Dorovernensis ecclesiæ præsule et rege hæc kartula confirmata esse debuisset, postea agnovi, et tam diligenter postulavi ab archiepiscopo Nothelmo et rege Æthilberto, præsidente meo largitore Eadberto, ut ipsi manu sua hanc donationem corroborassent; et sic in metropolitana urbe perfecte compleverunt. Actum mense April. Indic̃. VI., anno ab incarnatione Christi DCC.XXXVIII.

✠ Ego Nothelmus, gratia Dei archiepiscopus, testis consentiens subscripsi kanonice. ✠ Ego Æthilbertus rex præfatam donationem signo sancte crucis confirmavi. ✠ Ego Beornheard testis subscripsi. ✠ Signum manus Tunan. ✠ Signum manus Balthardi. ✠ Signum manus Eanberhti.

---

* KING ÆTHELBALD OF MERCIA. DCC.XXXVIII.

Ego Ethilbaldus rex Merciorum Deo omnipotenti gratiarum acciones in quantum possum persolvo, qui me ad tantum sublimitatis gradum eligere dignatus est, de tam humili et inquieta vita quam per tot annorum spacia transegi. Idcirco pro remedio anime mee, mihi in potestatem redacta, et pro munificentia sanctarum orationum servorum et ancillarum Dei, largifica munera summi Salvatoris Domini nostri Jesu Christi libenter ecclesiis Dei inpendo, et tibi Mildrithe abbatisse singulariter, et ecclesie tue, navis onuste transveccionis censum qui a thelonearíis nostris tributaria exactione impetitur, perdonans attribuo; ut ubique in regno nostro libera de omni regali fiscu et tributo maneat. Si quis hanc donationem a nobis perdonatam infringere vel in maximo vel in modico temptaverit, sciat se alienum a nostra communione, et maxime a cetu sanctorum, manere.

✠ Signum manus Æthilbaldi. ✠ Signum manus Cuthrædi. ✠ Signum manus Seleraedi. ✠ Signum manus Worres. ✠ Signum Cottan. ✠ Signum manus Cynrices. ✠ Signum manus Wlfridi. ✠ Signum manus Lullan. ✠ Signum manus Oban.

Actumque est die quarto Kalendarum Novembris, anno vicesimo secundo regni nostri, in loco qui dicitur Willanhalch.

KING ÆTHELBALD OF MERCIA. DCC.XLII.

✠ Anno Dominicæ incarnationis DCC.XLII. Indict. x., regni vero Æthilbaldi regis Merciorum XXVII. congregatum est magnum concilium apud Clovesho, præsidente eidem concilio Æthilbaldo rege Merciorum cum Cuthberto archiepiscopo Dorobernia cæterisque episcopis simul assidentibus, diligenter examinantes circa necessaria de statu[1] totius religionis et de symbolo ex antiquis sanctorum patrum institutionibus tradito, studioseque perquirentes qualiter[2] in primordio nascentis ecclesiæ hic in Anglia jubebatur haberi, aut ubi honor cœnobiorum secundum normam æquitatis servaretur. Hæc et hiis similia anxie inquirentes, antiquaque privilegia recitantes tandem pervenit ad manus libertas ecclesiarum et institutio vel præceptum Uuithrædi gloriosi regis de electione et auctoritate cœnobiorum in regno Cantiæ, quomodo et qualiter secundum imperium et electionem Cantuariensis metropolitani fieri [et][3] stare præcipitur; et præcepto itaque regis Æthelbaldi lectum est coram omnibus privilegium[4] præ-

[1] de statu. *Cott. Dom.* add.

[2] vel qualiter. *Cott. Dom.*

[3] Not in *Cott.*

[4] et hæc libertas. *Cott. Dom.* add.

fati Uithrædi gloriosi regis, et placuit cunctis hoc audientibus, pariterque dixerunt nullum aliud tam nobile tamque prudenter constitutum decretum inveniri potuisse secundum ecclesiasticam disciplinam[1], et ideo hoc ab omnibus firmari sanxerunt. Igitur ego Æthelbaldus rex Merciorum, pro salute animæ meæ, et stabilitate regni mei, proque venerantia[2] venerabilis archiepiscopi Cuthberti, propria manu munifica subscribens confirmo; ut per omnia libertas, honor, auctoritas, et securitas Christi ecclesiæ a nulla persona denegetur, sed sit libera ab omnibus sæcularibus servitiis, et omnes terræ ad illam pertinentes, exceptis expeditione, pontis et arcis constructione, et sicut sæpe præfatus rex Uuihtrædus pro se suisque constituit servandum ita per omnia irrefragabiliter et immutabiliter perdurare præcipimus. Si quis autem regum successorum nostrorum, seu episcoporum, seu principum, hoc salubre decretum infringere temptaverit, reddat rationem Deo omnipotenti in die tremendo. Si autem comes, presbyter, diaconus, clericus, vel monachus, huic constitutioni restiterit, sit suo gradu privatus, et a participatione corporis et sanguinis Domini separatus, et alienus a regno Dei, nisi ante placita satisfactione emendaverit quod malo superbiæ inique gessit: scriptum est enim "Quæcunque ligaveris super terram erunt ligata et in cœlo; et quæcunque solveris super terram erunt soluta et in cœlo."

✠ Ego Ethelbald rex, divino suffragio fultus, gentis Merciorum regens imperium, signum sanctæ crucis subscribo.

✠ Ego Cuthbertus archiepiscopus propria manu subscripsi.

✠ Ego Uuita episcopus consensi et subscripsi.

✠ Ego Torhthelm episcopus consensi et subscripsi.

✠ Ego Wilfredi episc. cons. et subs.

✠ Ego Cuthberht episc. cons. et subs.

✠ Ego Huetlac episc. cons. et subs.

✠ Ego Eanfrith episc. cons. et subs.

✠ Ego Egclaf episc. cons. et subs.

✠ Ego Aluuig episc. cons. et subs.

✠ Ego Hunvald episc. cons. et subs.

[1] et hoc annuentes stare ab omnibus firmare sanxerunt. *Cott. Dom.*
[2] reverentia. *Cott. Dom. Cantuar.*

✠ Ego Daniel episc. cons. et subs.
✠ Ego Aldwuulf episc. cons. et subs.
✠ Ego Æthelfrith episc. cons. et subs.
✠ Ego Herewald episc. cons. et subs.
✠ Ego Sigcga episc. cons. et subs.
✠ Ego Redwulf episc. cons. et subs.
✠ Ego Ofa patricius cons. et subs.
✠ Ego Aldwuulf dux cons. et subs.
✠ Ego Æthelmod indolis Merc. cons. et subs.
✠ Ego Heardberht dux cons. et subs.
✠ Ego Eadbald dux cons. et subs.
✠ Ego Bercul dux cons. et subs.
✠ Ego Cyneberht cons. et subs.
✠ Ego Freothoric cons. et subs.
✠ Ego Wermund abbas cons. et subs.
✠ Ego Cuthræd abbas cons. et subs.
✠ Ego Buna abbas cons. et subs.

KING ÆTHELBALD OF MERCIA. DCC.XLIII.-DCC.XLV.

✠ In usses Dryhtnes noman Hælendes Cristes· ic Æðelbald Myrcna cincg wæs beden from þæm arfullan bisceope Milrede þæt ic him alefde ⁊ his þæm halegan hirede alle nedbade tuegra sceopa þe þærto limpende beoð þet ic him forgefe þa þæm eadgan Petre apostola aldormen in þæm mynstre þeowiað· ꝥ is geseted in Huicca mægðe· in þære stowe þe mon hateð Weogernacester· þære bene swyðe arfulre geða-

✠ In the name of our Lord Jesus Christ. I Æthelbald king of the Mercians have been solicited by the venerable bishop Milred that I should allow to him and his holy convent all the dues of two ships which are thereto belonging—that I should grant them to those who serve the blessed Peter, the prince of apostles in the monastery which is seated in the province of the Hwiccas, in the place which is called Worcester.

funge ic wæs syllende for minre sawle læcedome. to ðon þæt for minum synnum hi heo geeaðmedden ꝥte heo wæren gelomlice þingeras wið Drihten. Swyðe lustfullice þa forgeofende. ic him alyfde alle nedbade tuegra sceopa. þa þe þær abædde beoð from þæm nedbaderum in Lundentunes hyðe. ond næfre ic ne mine lastweardas. ne ða nedbaderas geðristlæcen ꝥ heo hit onwenden oððe þon wiðgæn. Gif heo ꝥ nyllen. syn heo þonne amansumade from dælneomencge liceman ⁊ blodes usses Drihtnes Hælendes Cristes. ⁊ from alre neweste geleafulra syn heo asceadene and asyndrade. nymðe heo hit her mid þingonge bote gebete.

✠ Ic Æþelbald cincg mine agene sylene trymmende ic heo wrat. Milred bisceop þare halegan rode tacn he heron gefæstnode. Ingwuald ƀ geðafiende he hit wrat. Wilfrið ƀ; he hit wrat. Alda cinges gefera he hit wrat.

To that prayer I have given very honourable consent, for the healing of my soul; that for my sins they vouchsafe to be frequent mediators with the Lord. Very joyfully then giving, I have allowed them all the dues of the two ships which shall be there demanded by the collectors in the hithe of London town. And never I nor my successors, nor the collectors may ever presume this to frustrate or oppose. If they will not that, be they then excommunicated from participation of the body and blood of our Lord Jesus Christ; and from all proximity of the faithful be they severed and sundered, unless they here make amends with prayer.

✠ I Æthelbald king, confirming my own grant, have written it. Milred bishop has affixed hereon the sign of the holy rood. Ingwald bishop consenting has written it. Wilfrith bishop has written it. Alda the king's companion has written it.

---

* KING EADBERHT OF KENT. DCC.XLVII.

✠ Anno Dominicæ incarnationis DCC.XLVII., ego Eadbertus rex Cantie cum consensu optimatum meorum, Bregowini archiepiscopi et ceterorum principum meorum, concedo ecclesie que est apud Raculfe et tibi, Deneheah abba, tueque familie, pro salute anime mee, vectigal et tributum unius navis in portu ac villa que dicitur Forduuic, ad opus, ut prefatus sum, familie Sancte Marie, que in jam nominata ecclesia Deo serviunt. Simulque precipio, in nomine omnipotentis Dei, prefectis, prepositis, et actionariis, et omnibus fidelibus qui in illo portu habent vel habituri sunt aliquam potestatem, ut hec mea donatio sit stabilis et firma imperpetuum. Quod si aliquis, quod absit, hoc meum donum violare presumpserit, a Deo et sanctis ejus separatus, diabolo et angelis ejus sit conjunctus. Quod si una navis predicte familie perierit collisione, fractione, aut vetustate, iterum restituant aliam, et eadem conditione habeant, et sic in perpetuum.

KING ÆTHELBALD OF MERCIA. SEPT. 29TH DCC.XLVII.

In nomine Domini Dei Salvatoris nostri Jesu Christi. Si ea que quisque, pro recipienda a Deo mercede, hominibus verbo suo largitur et donat, stabilia jugiter potuissent durare, supervacaneum videretur ut litteris narrarentur ac fulcirentur; sed dum ad probanda donata ad convincendumque volentem donata infringere, nihil prorsus robustius esse videtur quam donationis [cartula] manibus auctorum ac testium roborate, non inmerito plurimi petunt, ut que eis prestita dinoscuntur paginaliter confirmentur; quorum postulationibus tanto libentius tantoque prompcius consensus prebendus est, quanto et illis qui precatores sunt utilior res secundum hoc visibile seculum nunc impertitur et illis qui concessores existunt, pro impertito opere pietatis, uberior fructus secundum invisibile postmodum tribuetur. Quamobrem ego Æthelbaldus rex Merciorum, presentibus apicibus, indico me concessisse atque donasse, pro anime mee salute, Mildrithe, religiose abbatisse, ejusque venerabili familie, que una cum ea conversatur in insula Thænet, totam exactionem navis earum, mihi et antecessoribus meis jure publico in Lundoniensi portu prius conpetentem, quemadmodum mansuetudinem nostram rogarent. Que concessio atque donatio, ut in perpetuum firma et stabilis sit, ita ut nullus eam regum, vel optimatum, vel theloneariorum, vel etiam juniorum quilibet ipsorum, in parte aut in toto, in irritum presumat ut possit adducere, manu propria signum sancte crucis subter in hac pagina faciam, testesque ut subscribant petam; proculdubio sperans quia sicut ego quod poposcerunt libenter concessi, sic ille quod promiserunt erga orationes pro me ibidem celebrandas, implebunt fideliter. Quisquis igitur id quod pio animo donavi, ita ut donatum est illibatum permanere permiserit, habeat communionem beatam cum presente Christi ecclesia atque futura. Quisquis autem non permiserit, separetur a societate non solum sanctorum hominum, sed etiam angelorum, manente hac donatione nostra in sua firmitate coram universis qui recta diligunt et custodiunt. Actum est die quarto kalendarum Novembris, anno xxxi° regni mei, Indictione xv[a] in loco qui dicitur Willanhalch.

✠ Ego Ædbaldus rex Merciorum hanc donationem meam firmavi et subscripsi manu mea. ✠ Signum manus Wori. ✠ Signum manus Cottan. ✠ Signum manus Cinrici. ✠ Signum manus Wilfridi. ✠ Signum manus Lullan. ✠ Signum Cuthredi. ✠ Signum manus Oban.

KING ÆTHELBALD OF MERCIA. MAY DCC.XLVIII.

In nomine Domini Salvatoris nostri. Omnem hominem qui secundum Deum vivit, et remunerari a Deo sperat et optat, oportet ut piis precibus assensum ex animo hilariter prebeat, quomodo certum est tanto facilius ea quæ ipse a Deo poposcerit consequi posse, quanto et ipse libencius hominibus recte postulata concesserit; quod tunc bonorum omnium largitori Deo acceptabile fit, cum pro ejus amore et utilitate famulancium ei peragitur. Quocirca ego Ethilbaldus Mercionum [rex], juxta petitionem vestram, tibi, Eadburge abbatisse tueque familie conversanti in monasterio beate Dei genitricis Marie, quod situm est in insula Thaneti, necnon et in monasterio apostolorum Petri et Pauli, quod tu ipsa non longe a predicto monasterio construxisti, unius navis, quod a Leubrico nuper emisti, dimidium vectigal atque tributum, quod meum erat, pro intuitu superne mercedis, et amore consanguinitatis religiosæ abbatisse Mildrede, cujus venerabile corpus a priori sepultura translatum in ipso monasterio apostolorum decenter posuisti, accipiendum possidendumque eterna donatione concedo; et, cuicunque volueritis heredum successorumque vestrorum, seu quolibet hominum, hoc ipsum de jure in re vestra perdonare liberam habeatis potestatem. Hinc igitur præcipio ac precor, in nomine Dei omnipotentis, patriciis, ducibus, comitibus, thelonеariis, accionariis, ac reliquis publicis dignitatibus, ut hec inoffense donatio per presentes ac posteros percurrat. Si autem contigerit, ut navis ista disrupta ac confracta sit, vel etiam vetustate detrita, aut omnino, quod absit, naufragio perdita, tunc quoque ad cumulum hujusce donationis hoc addo et concedo, ut alia in hujus donationis locum et conditionem construatur et habeatur. Et hoc non solum me vivente in hac vita, sed etiam post obitum meum, per succedentes semper generationes precipio, et per Jesum Christum judicem omnium, postulo fieri. Quisquis vero heredum successorumque meorum, vel aliorum quilibet hominum, sive secularium sive ecclesiasticorum, huic pie donationi nostre in aliqua re contraire quoquo tempore fuerit ausus, noverit se, quisque ille sit, audacis malicie sue rationem esse redditurum coram omnipotente Domino nostro, qui judicabit orbem terre in equitate, reddens unicuique secundum opera sua, Jesus Christus filius Dei, filiusque Sancte Marie semper virginis, cujus, scilicet, in prefato monasterio, sacris atque magnificis indesinenter die noctuque frequentatur et adoratur precibus, Judex seculi ipse Jesus Christus Dominus noster, Amen. Igitur manente hac cartula in sua semper firmitate, quam propria manu sacro signaculo roborare curavi, et testes nonnullos ut id ipsum consencientes agerent feci, quorum nomina infra tenentur. Actum mense Maio, in civitate Londonia. Indictione quarta decima[1]. Anno ab incarnatione Christi DCC.XLVIII°.

✠ Ego Æthilbaldus rex Merciorum suprascriptam donationem meam signo sancte crucis, in hac cartula expresso, diligenter confirmavi. ✠ Ego Ædbeortus rex Cancie testis, consenciens subscripsi. ✠ Signum manus Cuthberti archiepiscopi. ✠ Signum Milredi episcopi. ✠ Signum Egcuulfi episcopi. ✠ Signum manus Obani ducis. ✠ Signum manus Kyneberti. ✠ Signum Eoppani. ✠ Signum Friðurici. ✠ Signum Ealhmundi. ✠ Signum Panti thelonearii.

KING ÆTHELBALD OF MERCIA. DCC.XLIX.

Plerunque contingere solet pro incerta futurorum temporum vicissitudine, ut ea que prius multarum fidelium personarum testimonio consilioque roborata fuerunt, ut fraudulenter per contumaciam plurimorum, et machinamenta simulationis, sine ulla consideratione rationis periculose dissipentur, nisi auctoritate litterarum, et testamento cyrographorum eterne memorie inserta sint. Quapropter ego Æthelbaldus rex Merciorum, pro amore celestis patrie, et pro remedio anime mee, hoc maxime agendum esse previdi, ut eam bonis operibus liberam efficerem ab omnibus vinculis piaculorum. Dum enim mihi omnipotens Deus, per misericordiam clementie, absque ullo antecedente merito, sceptra regiminis honorifice largitus est, ideo ei libenter et voluntarie ex eo quod accepi iterum retribuo. Hujus rei gratia hanc donationem, Deo teste, me vivente concedo, ut monasteria et ecclesie a publicis vectigalibus, et ab omnibus operibus oneribusque, auctore Deo, servientes absoluti maneant, nisi sola que communiter fruenda sint, omnique populo, edicto regis, facienda jubentur, id est instructionibus pontium, vel necessariis defensionibus arcium contra hostes, non sunt renuenda.

[1] The Indiction for 748 is I.

Sed nec hoc pretermittendum est, cum necessarium constat ecclesiis Dei, quia Æthelbaldus rex, pro expiatione delictorum suorum, et retributione mercedis eterne, famulis Dei propriam libertatem in fructibus silvarum agrorumque, sive in cæteris utilitatibus fluminum, vel raptura piscium, habere donavit; et ut munuscula ab ecclesiis in seculare convivium regis vel principum a subditis minime exigantur, nisi amore et voluntate prebentur; sed cunctas tribulationes que nocere vel impedire possunt in domo Dei, omnibus principibus sub ejus potestate degentibus demittere et auferre precipit; quatenus sublimitas regni ejus prosperis successibus polleat in terris, et meritorum manipuli multipliciter maturescunt in celis. Qui vero hec benigna mentis intentione atque inlesa cogitatione custodierit, eterna claritate coronetur, ornetur, glorificetur. Si quis hoc, quod absit, cujuslibet persone, tyrannica cupiditate instinctus, contra hanc donationis cartulam, seculari potentia fretus, venire nititur, sit sub anathemato Jude, proditoris Domini nostri Jhesu Christi. Ad confirmandum vero hoc nostre beneficentie munus, hii testes adfuerunt, et nostri magistratus optimates et duces fidelissimique amici consenserunt et scripserunt.

✠ Ego Ædelbald, divinis fultus suffragiis, hiis statutis consentiens confirmandoque, signum crucis aravi. ✠ Ego Huita Mercensis ecclesie humilis episcopus subscripsi. ✠ Ego Torhthelm gracia Dei episcopus signum crucis infixi. ✠ Ego Headberht primatum tenens subscripsi. ✠ Ego Eada his statutis consentiens subscripsi. ✠ Ego Cyneberht his gestis consentiens subscripsi. ✠ Ego Bercul patricius his donis consentiens subscripsi. ✠ Ego Friothuric consentiens subscripsi. ✠ Ego Eopa his statutis consentiens subscripsi. ✠ Ego Eadbald subscripsi. ✠ Ego Byrnhelm subscripsi. ✠ Ego Mocca subscripsi. ✠ Ego Aldceorl subscripsi. ✠ Ego Alhmund subscripsi.

Hujus scedulæ scriptio Dominicæ incarnationis anno DCC.XLVIIII. Indictione secunda, in loco celebre, cujus vocabulum est Godmundeslæch XXXIII. anno Ædelbaldi regis, peracta est.

* KING EADBERHT OF KENT. DCC.LXI.

Regnante in perpetuum Domino nostro Jesu Christo. Unicuique mortalium vite sue terminus omnipotentis Dei dispensatione incertus esse dinoscitur; venit enim Dominus ad visitandum servum suum in die qua non sperat, et hora qua non putat. Qua de re ego Eadbertus rex Canciæ[1], anno xxxvi° regni nostri, una cum consensu et consilio archiepiscopi Bregwini et principum meorum, pro eterna redemptione anime mee, aliquid ex his que mihi idem ipse Dominus et Salvator noster, cunctorum bonorum largitor, tribuerit, statuens donare decreveram; id est, duarum navium transvectionis censum, qui etiam juris nostri [erat] in loco cujus vocabulum est ad Serræ, juxta petitionem venerabilis abbatisse Sigeburge, ejusque sacre conversationis familie in monasterio Sancti Petri, quod situm est in insula Tenæt; sicut a regibus Merciorum, Æthilbaldo videlicet clementissimo et rege Offan[2], longe ante concessum est tributum in loco cujus vocabulum est Lundenwic; alterius vero quod nuper edificatum est in monasterio ejusdem religiose Dei famule omne tributum atque vectigal concedimus, quod etiam a theloneariis nostris juste impetitur publicis in locis que appellantur Fordwik et Seorre. Hinc igitur precipio et precor, in nomine omnipotentis Dei, patriciis, ducibus, comitibus, theloneariis, actionariis, publicis dignitatibus, ut hec nostra concessio in Dei donatione eternaliter sit confirmata; ita ut nec mihi nec alicui successorum meorum, regum sive principum, seu cujuslibet conditionis dignitatibus, nefario temeritatis ausu, de supradicta donatione nostra aliquid fraudare vel minuere liceat. Si autem contigerit, ut navis ista rupta et confracta sit, vel nimia vetustate consumpta, sive etiam, quod absit, naufragio perdita, ut alia in loco illius ad utilitatem ibidem Deo serviencium famulorum Christi et famularum construatur; ad hanc videlicet conditionem, ut quicquid in suis mercimoniis in diversis speciebus adquirere pos-

[1] According to Beda (H. E. v. 23), the Sax. Chron., and Florence, Eadberht succeeded his father Wihtræd in 725, and died in 748.

[2] Offa reigned from 757 to 796.

sint, nobis fideliter inoffense offerre debeant, simul cum ipsa navi, ad locum qui appellatur Fordewik. Et quicunque de hac donatione nostra, quod etiam specialiter omnipotenti Deo firmiter concessum est, aliquid, nefario caliditatis ausu, abstrahere vel minuere temptaverit, sciat se a consortio sanctorum omnium separatum, et cum diabolo et angelis ejus in perpetuum esse dampnandum; quoniam sanctum locum istum dehonestare conatus est, in quo primi apostolorum principis Petri intercessio orationibus assiduis et elemosinis floret pro omni populo Christiano. Iccirco vivens benedictione Dei carebit, et moriens maledictioni debite subjacebit, nisi digna satisfactione emendaverit quod nuper studuit depravare. Quicunque vero hec augenda custodierit, sit benedictus in perpetuum, et beatissimam vocem audire mereatur cum sanctis: "Venite benedicti Patris mei."

✠ Ego Edbertus rex hanc donationem a me factam propria manu signo sancte crucis roboravi. ✠ Ego Bregowinus archiepiscopus ad petitionem Edberti regis signum sancte crucis expressi. ✠ Signum manus Jamberti abbatis. ✠ Signum manus Dæne abbatis. ✠ Signum Bruni abbatis. ✠ Signum manus Baltheardi comitis. ✠ Signum Eathelhun principis. ✠ Signum manus Redfridi. ✠ Signum manus Budda. ✠ Signum manus Eathelberti. ✠ Signum manus Eadda. ✠ Signum manus Egesasi. ✠ Signum manus Aldred.

DÛNWALD, A THANE. DCC.LXII.

✠ In nomine Domini nostri Jesu Christi. Ego Dunwaldus minister, dum adjuveret, inclite memorie regis Ethelberti, nunc vero pecuniam illius pro anime ejus salute ad limina apostolorum Rome cum aliis perferre desiderans, villam unam, post obitum meum, ni forsitan hoc prius me vivente placeat peragendum, que jam ad Quenegatum urbis Dorovernis in foro posita est, quam nunc Hringwine tenet; quam idem mihi prefatus rex cum aliis terrulis jure proprio cum tributo illius possidendam, et cuicunque voluerim tradendam, condonavit; hanc videlicet ad ecclesiam prope positam beati Petri et Pauli, ubi scilicet corpus ejusdem domini mei regis Æthelberti requiescit, pro anime illius et salute mea, eterna donatione cum tributo illius possidenda attribuo; et ut nulla esset inposterum de hac contentio, hoc ipsum in libello prime donationis mee faciendum descripsi. Et ideo nunc, cum consensu venerabilis archiepiscopi nostri Bregwini, hunc libellum hujusce donationis mee describi feci et manu propria roboravi, et illum atque alios religiosos testes ut id ipsum faciant adhibeo. Actum anno incarnationis Christi DCC.LXII°.

✠ Ego Bregwinus, gratia Dei archiepiscopus, signum sanctæ crucis subscripsi. ✠ Ego Dunwald præfatam donationem meam signo sancte crucis roboravi. ✠ Ego Baltheardus dux subscripsi. ✠ Ego Kyneardus presbiter consensi et subscripsi. ✠ Ego Jambertus abbas testis subscripsi.

Hec terra circumcincta est hiis terminibus: a Quenegatum in meridiem extensas habens tres perticas, et inde in occidentem rectissima linea dividit terram regis et istum XXXIII. perticis usque in maceriam que in aquilonali parte civitatis muro adjacet, virgas habens XXXIII.

---

* KING OFFA OF MERCIA. DCC.LIX.-DCC.LXIV.

✠ In nomine Regnantis in perpetuum. Ego Offa rex Merciorum illam donationem quam rex gloriosus Ethilbaldus Deo omnipotenti, gratiarum persolvens actiones, Mildrithe abbatisse, de navis onuste transvectionis censu, qui a thelonearlis exigebatur, conferre voluit, pro remedio anime mee, et pro munificentia orationum sanctarum, tibi Sigeburge, ejusdem monasterii abbatisse, condonans attribuo. Ad hanc conditionem signum Salvatoris nostri propria manu firmavi, et testes ut subscriberent rogavi.

✠ Ego Bregwinus archiepiscopus consensi et subscripsi. ✠ Signum Tottan episcopi. ✠ Signum Milredi episcopi. ✠ Signum Egwlfi episcopi. ✠ Signum Eardulfi episcopi.

HEATHORED AND WULFHEARD. DCC.LXXXIX.

✠ Seculi namque labentis tempora velocius vento aërem[1] tranant; ideo omnes firmas statutiones serie litterarum adnotamus, ne forte in posterum aliquis ignorantiæ avaritiæve ea decreta infringere præsumat quæ venerabilium virorum fiunt verbis confirmata. Anno Dominicæ incarnationis DCC°LXXX°VIIII° Indictione vero XII^{a}, qui est annus XXXI. regni Offan, strenuissimi Merciorum regis, factum est pontificale conciliabulum in loco famoso qui dicitur Celchyð, praesidentibus duobus archiepiscopis, Jamberhto scilicet et Hygeberhto, mediante quoque Offan rege cum universis principibus suis; ibi inter alia plura aliqua contentio facta est inter Heaðoredum episcopum et Wulfheardum filium Cussan, de hereditate Hemeles et Dudæ, quod post obitum suorum nominarent ad Weogernacestræ, hoc est Intanbeorgas et Bradanlæg; voluisset[2] ergo Uulfheardus illum agellulum avertere ab ecclesia præfata in Weogornaceast̃. cum ignorantia et insipientia si potuisset. Tunc ille episcopus illum refutabat cum his testibus qui eorum nomina infra scripta liquescunt coram synodali testimonio. Et aiebat quod ei rectum non fieret ulli alio post se tradere præter et [antedi]ctam civitatem, hoc est Weogorinaceast̃. Et præter eorum præce et amore qui illam terram [adqui]sierunt et ad æcclesiam præfatam dedissent, illi senatores familiæ consentientes fuerunt ut illud custodiret et haberet diem suum. Tunc archiepiscopus simul cum universis provincialibus episcopis ita finem composuerunt et reconciliaverunt, ut Uulfheardus terram possideret tamdiu viveret, et postquam viam patrum incederet, sine aliqua contradictione [illuc ad] Weogornense aec[clesiae] terras atque libellus cum semetipso redderet [ubi corpora requiescunt Hemeles et Dudæ.]

[1] MSS. Tib. and Nero read "ad finem tranant."

[2] MS. Nero reads: Wlfheardus ergo voluit illas a Weogorna civitate avertere, cum insipientia, si potuisset; sed episcopus illum vicit cum testibus quorum nomina infra notantur, coram universa sinodo; et aiebat quod rectum non esset ulli alii post se tradere nisi ad Weogernam civitatem, et preter eorum prece et amore qui illam terram adquisierunt et ad præfatam æcclesiam dederunt. Tunc archiepiscopus, etc.

✠ Ego Offa rex Merc̃. consentiendo imposui.
✠ Ego Jamberht gratia Dei arc̃.ep̃s sigillo sanctæ crucis roboravi.
✠ Ego Hygeberht simłt. arc̃.ep̃. consen. et subs.
✠ Ego Ceolwulf ep̃. cons̃. et sub.
✠ Ego Heardred ep̃. cons̃.
✠ Ego Unuuona ep̃. cons̃. et subscripsi.
✠ Ego Heaðored ep̃. cons̃.
✠ Ego Alheard episcopus consensi et subscripsi.
✠ Ego Ceolmund ep̃. consensi.
✠ Ego Æðelmod ep̃.
✠ Ego Cyneberht ep̃.
✠ Ego Wermund ep̃.
✠ Ego Bodwine ab.
✠ Ego Utel ab.
✠ Ego Fordred.
✠ Ego Wulfheard simul subs et confirmavi.
✠ . . . . berht pr̃.
✠ . . . . mundi p̃.
✠ Sig. Alhmundi pr̃.
✠ Sig̃. Ceolmundi p̃.
✠ Sig̃. Æðelhardi p̃.
✠ Sig̃. Bynnan[1].

KING OFFA OF MERCIA. DCC.XCI.-DCC.XCVI.

✠ In nomine Domini nostri Ihesu Christi [qui cuncta regit secula[2].] Ego Offa trado illam terram æt Westbyrig cum omnibus ad se rite pertinentibus, id est sexaginta manentium, et in alio loco æt Heanbyrig xx. manentium to Weogerna cestre, pro remedio animæ meae ac parentum meorum, post obitum meum et filii mei Egcfriði, et eadem libertatis dicione in omnibus rebus jure permanendam qua eam ante Æþelbaldus rex, avo meo Eanulfo conscripserat; id est, ut sit libera tam in terrarum donatione seu in omnibus causis parvis vel magnis inconcuṣsa permaneat usque in sæculum, tamdiu fides Christiana apud Anglos in Brittannia maneat. [Soluta sit ab omni vi regum et principum

[1] The variations in the subscriptions are numerous.
[2] Wanting in MS. Nero.

et subditorum ipsorum, in summo Dei nomine præcipimus, præter his vectigalibus, hoc est,

þæs gafoles æt Westbyrig twa tunnan fulle hlutres aloð· ⁊ cumb fulne liðes aloð· ⁊ cumb fulne Welisces aloð· ⁊ VII. hriðru· ⁊ six weðeras· ⁊ XL. cysa· ⁊ VI. lang þero· ⁊ þritig ombra rues cornes· feower ambru meolwes,

for the rent at Westbury two tuns full of clear ale, and a coomb full of mild ale, and a coomb full of Welsh ale, and VII. oxen, and six wethers, and XL. cheeses, and VI. 'lang þero', and thirty ambers of rye corn, four ambers of meal,

ad regalem vicum[1].] Hoc itaque cum consensu et consilio pontificum et senatorum meorum firmo fœdere dejudicaverunt. Nulla regalis vel principalis aut aliqua sæcularis dignitas de nostra hereditate plus his in modico vel in magno appetendo, per vim aut petitionem aliquid exigerit, [absque hoc tantum quod haec præsens cartula continet[2].] Hi sunt testes:

✠ Ego Offa gratia Dei rex hoc regi singulis annis statum ..... censum manus meae propriæ signo confirmo. ✠ Ego Ecgferð ejusdem regis filius consensi et subscripsi. ✠ Ego Æþelheard archiepiscopus consensi et subscripsi. ✠ Ego Heaðored episcopus consensi et subscripsi. ✠ Ego Unuuona episcopus consensi et subscripsi. ✠ Signum Brordani patricii. ✠ Signum Beonnan abbatis. ✠ Signum Alhmundi abbatis. ✠ Signum Wigmundi abbatis. ✠ Signum Forðredi abbatis. ✠ Signum Bynna principis. ✠ Signum Esne ducis. ✠ Signum Æþelmund ducis. ✠ Signum Alhmund ducis. ✠ Signum Wigberht ducis. ✠ Signum Wigcgan ducis. ✠ Signum Eadgar ducis. ✠ Signum Alhmund ducis.

ARCHBISHOP ÆTHELHEARD. DCC.XCVIII.

✠ Regnante imperpetuum Deo et Domino nostro Jhesu Christo. Ego Æðelhardus, larga omnipotentis Dei gratia annuente, Dorobernensis ecclesie metropolitanus; cum prestantissimo rege nostro Cenulfo, convocans universos provin-

[1] Wanting in MS. Nero.

[2] Supplied from Nero.

ciales episcopos nostros, duces, et abbates, et cujuscunque dignitatis viros, ad sinodale concilium, in locum qui nominatur Clouesho, ibi sollicito ab eis scrutinio quesivimus, qualiter apud eos fides catholica haberetur, et quomodo Christiana religio exerceretur. Hiis ita exquisitis, una omnium voce ita responsum est: "Notum sit paternitati tue, quia sicut primitus a sancta Romana et apostolica sede, beatissimo papa Gregorio dirigente, exarata est, ita credimus; et quod credimus absque ambiguitate, quantum possumus exercere satagimus." Postquam autem super hiis uberius tractatum est, ita exorsi sumus: "Necessarium est, fratres charissimi, ecclesias Dei et venerabiles viros, qui jam multo tempore terrarum dispendio et absumptione cirographorum miserabiliter laboraverant, corrigere." Hiis dictis, prolatæ sunt inscriptiones monasterii quod vocatur Coccham in medium, terrarumque sibi adjacentium; quod videlicet monasterium, cum omnibus ad illud pertinentibus terris, rex inclytus Merciorum Æðelbaldus ecclesie Salvatoris, que sita est in civitate Dorobernie, dedit; utque illius donatio perseverantior fieret, ex eadem terra cespitem et cunctos libellos prememorati cenobii, per venerabilem virum Cuðbertum archiepiscopum misit, et super altare Salvatoris, pro perpetua sua salute, poni precepit. Sed post mortem prefati pontificis, easdem inscriptiones Dæiheah et Osbertus, quos idem pontifex alumnos nutrivit, maligno acti spiritu furati sunt, et Cenulfo regi Occidentalium Saxonum detulerunt; at ille, accipiens statim testimonia litterarum, predictum cenobium cum omnibus ad illud rite pertinentibus suis usibus coaptavit, neglectis prenominati archiepiscopi Cuðberti dictis et factis. Item, Bregwinus et Ianbertus archiepiscopi, per singulas sinodus suas, questi sunt de injuria ecclesie Salvatoris illata; et apud Cenulfum regem Occidentalium Saxonum, et apud Offam regem Merciorum, qui videlicet sepe memoratum cenobium Coccham et alias urbes quamplurimas Cenulfo rege abstulit, et imperio Merciorum subegit. Tandem Cenulfus rex, sera ductus penitentia, telligraphia, id est, libellos quos a supradictis hominibus, Dæiheh et Osberto, injuste perceperat, cum magna pecunia, ecclesie Christi in

Doroberniam remisit, humillime rogans ne sub tante authoritatis anathemate periclitaretur. Verum rex Offa prememoratum cenobium Coccham, sicut sine litteris accepit, ita quanto tempore vixit detinuit, et absque litterarum testimonio suis post se heredibus reliquit. Secundo autem anno regni Cenulfi facta est sinodus, sicut supra est prelibatum, apud Cloueshо; at ego Æðelhardus, gratia Dei Dorobernensis archiepiscopus, et Cuba primicherius mecum, et multi alii ex illa ecclesia Christi sapientes, libellos prefati cenobii Coccham in concilium detulimus; cumque coram sinodo relecti fuissent, omnium voce decretum est justum esse ut metropolis ecclesia sepe prefatum cenobium Coccham, cujus inscriptiones in suo gremio habebat, perciperet, quo sub tanto tempore tam injuste spoliata fuerat. Tunc autem placuit mihi Æðelhardo, Dei gratia archisacerdoti, et Cyneðryðe abbatisse, que eodem tempore sepedicto cenobio prefuit, ac senioribus ex utralibet parte, Cantia scilicet et Bedeforde, ad hoc ibidem congregatis, quatenus ipsa Cyneðriða in regione Cantia daret mihi, pro commutatione sepe prefati cenobii, terram centum et decem manentium, sexaginta cassatorum, videlicet, in loco qui dicitur Fleote, et triginta in loco qui dicitur Teneham; in tertio quoque loco, ubi dicitur Creges æwylma, viginti. Quas scilicet terras olim rex Offa sibi viventi conscribere fecit, suisque heredibus post eum; et, post eorum cursum vite, ecclesie que sita est apud Beodeford consignari precepit. Hoc etiam coram omni sinodo elegimus; ut ipsa abbatissa a me percipiet sepe nominatum cenobium cum suis inscriptionibus; et ego terras et libellos terrarum illarum quas mihi in Cantia reddit, ab ea acciperem, quatenus nulla imposterum inter nos heredesque nostros et Offe regis surgat controversia, sed quod sub tam nobilis sinodi testimonio inter nos confirmatum est indirupto federe servetur imperpetuum. Ego quoque Æðelhardus archiepiscopus concedo Cyniðriðe abbatisse monasterium quod situm est in loco qui dicitur Pectanege ad habendum, quod mihi rex pius Egfridus hereditario jure possidendum donavit atque conscripsit.

---

* ARCHBISHOP ÆTHELHEARD. DCC.XCVIII.

✠ Anno Dominicæ incarnationis DCC.XCVIII. congregatum est magnum concilium in loco ubi dicitur Bachanchilde, presidente eidem concilio Ceneuulfo rege necnon reverentissimo archiepiscopo Æðelardo, cum episcopis, abbatibus, et multis aliis idoneis personis. Tunc idem venerabilis pater et primas totius Britannie, Æðelardus sic exorsus est: "Ego Æðelardus, gratia Dei humilis sanctæ Dorobernensis æcclesiæ archiepiscopus, unanimo concilio totius sancte sinodi, in nomine Dei omnipotentis, et per ejus tremendum judicium, precipio, sicut ego mandatum a domino apostolico Leone papa percepi, ut ex hoc tempore nunquam temerario ausu super hereditatem Domini, id est, ecclesias, laici presumant dominium suscipere. Sed sicut in privilegiis ab apostolica sede datis habetur, seu etiam ab apostolicis viris, in initio nascentis ecclesie traditum est per sanctos canones, vel etiam a propriis possessoribus monasteriorum constitutum est, ea regula et observantia discipline sua [monastica] jura studeant observare. Si ergo, quod absit, ipsi hoc nostrum mandatum, et domini apostolici preceptum spreverint et pro nichilo ducunt, sciant se a presenti ecclesia justorum segregatos, et in die judicii ante tribunal Christi, nisi emendaverint, rationem reddituros." Hec sunt nomina sanctorum episcoporum et abbatum, qui cum totius sinodi consensu, pro confirmatione predicte rei, signum sancte crucis subscripserunt.

✠ Ego Æðelardus archiepiscopus Dorobernensis civitatis signum sancte crucis subscripsi. ✠ Ego Hedde episcopus subscripsi. ✠ Ego Worr episcopus subscripsi. ✠ Ego Eguuinus episcopus subscripsi. ✠ Ego Forðerus episcopus subscripsi. ✠ Ego Daniel episcopus subscripsi. ✠ Ego Eadbriht episcopus subscripsi. ✠ Ego Acca episcopus subscripsi. ✠ Ego Inguualdus episcopus subscripsi. ✠ Ego Heardrid episcopus subscripsi. ✠ Ego Noðbertus episcopus subscripsi. ✠ Ego Wulfredus archidiaconus subscripsi. ✠ Signum Aldulfi episcopi Licifeldensis. ✠ Ego Eaduulf Siddensis episcopus subscripsi. ✠ Ego Osmundus Lundoniensis episcopus subscripsi. ✠ Ego Tiidfridus Dammoce episcopus subscripsi. ✠ Ego Fortredus abbas subscripsi. ✠ Ego Wernbrihtus Legorensis subscripsi. ✠ Ego Ealhmundus episcopus Uuintoniensis subscripsi. ✠ Ego Wermundus Hrofensis episcopus subscripsi. ✠ Ego Felogyldus abbas subscripsi. ✠ Ego Wlfredus archidiaconus subscripsi.

KING CÊNWULF OF MERCIA. DCC.XCIX.

✠ In nomine Domini Dei Salvatoris nostri Jhesu Christi Ego Cenulf rex una cum conjuge mea Cenegiðа regina, referentes gratias Largitori bonorum, Domino Jhesu Christo, qui dilatavit terminos nostros juxta paternam antiquitatem, in commune pertractavimus aliquam partem terre nobis conlate ad vicem rependere, ne ingrati Dei beneficiis videremur Largitori nostro. Qua de re, a presenti die et tempore, tibi pastori et familie ecclesie Christi Deoque dicate, terram juris nostri que sita est in provincia Cantie que quondam apellata est Geddingc et Wudutun, aratrorum IIII., contulimus in perpetuum posidendam, et cum omnibus ad eandem pertinentibus pratis, campis, silvis, pascuis, et quicquit ad supradictam terram pertinet, a quattuor partibus, horientis, occidentis, aquilonis, et meridie, tuo husui et familie tue, et remisionem delictis nostris ditionique subiciatis, teneatis, posideatis, donetis, commutetis, venundetis, vel quicquit exinde facere volueritis, liberam abeatis potestatem, successoresque vestri defendant, in perpetuum; numquam me eredesque mei contra hanc cartulam descriptionis nostræ aliquando esse venturos. Ad cujus cumulum etiam confirmationis, cespitem uius supradicte terre super sanctum altare Salvatoris posui, et, propria manu, pro ignorantia litterarum, signum sancte crucis in ac cartula expressi; set et Cenegiðа idem fecit, principesque mei, ut pari modo propriis manibus facerent, rogavi, quorum nomina subter adnexa sunt. Si quis, quod apsit, contra anc cartulam a me factam, [1]ego credes mei', contraire presumserint noverint se a par-

[1] ' Sic MS.

ticipatione corporis et sanguinis Domini Jhesu Christi esse alienos, et a ceto fidelium segregandos hic et in eternum. Quam sepedictam cartulam scribendam dictavi, et tibi, pastor, cui supra tradidi conservandam.

His vero notissimis terminibus circumgyrata est. In aquilone publica stratus; in oriente ita est; in meridie terra Sancte Eanswiðe; in occidente Denetun.

Actum est XVI. Kalendas Agusti, Indictione VII., anno regni nostri III.

Signum manus Cenulfi regis. Signum manus Đeodori episcopi. Signum manus Adriani abbatis. Ego Redun episcopus. Piot dux consensi. Tiolf dux consensi. Cynelm filius regis. Biornhard minister. Egheard diaconus.

KING CÊNWULF OF MERCIA. DCCC.I.

✠ Anno Dominicæ incarnationis DCCC.I., regni vero Cœnulphi regis Merciorum anno quinto, orta est aliqua dissensio inter Cœnulphum et Weðunum episcopum Australium Saxonum, de terra illius predicti episcopi, id est, in Denton XXV. Dicebat rex ut rectius attingere deberet ad monasterium in Beadyngham; dicebat episcopus quod ejus antecessoribus dudum datum fuerat ad ecclesiam que est in Selesegh. Cogitabat rex eum in aliqua parte sue hereditatis dispoliare, nisi episcopus predicte provincie Weðun, cum testimonio ac verbis canonicis regem resipisceret, ac perniciosam meditationem regalis potentie mitigaret, et humili supplicatione poposcit ut eum insontem innocentemque non condemnasset, neque deprivasset hereditati ecclesie. Tunc rex verbis legalibus episcopo promendo consentiens, concessitque episcopo ut ad propria cum cedula remeasset, ibidemque sine ullo conflictu sempieternaliter cum suis successoribus mansisset. Et hoc coram omni sinodo æt Celchiðe ascribere demandavit, ut nullus successorum ejus eum in aliquo molestet, vel ecclesiam agitaret, sub hoc testimonio quorum nomina caraxatur esse videntur.

Ego Cœnulf rex Merciorum hoc consensi et subscripsi ✠. Signum manus Hugberti episcopi ✠. Signum manus Æðilhardi archiepiscopi. Signum manus Ealdwlfi [episcopi] ✠. Signum manus Cunberti episcopi ✠. Signum manus Uiberti episcopi ✠. Signum manus Deneberti episcopi ✠. Signum manus Wlfhardi episcopi ✠. Signum manus Eadwlfi episcopi.

BISHOP DENEBERHT. DCCC.III.

✠ In nomine Domini nostri Jhesu Xp̃i. Ea quæ secundum aecclesiasticam disciplinam ac synodalia decreta salubriter definiuntur, quamvis solus sermo sufficeret, tamen, pro evitando futuri temporis ambiguitate, fidelissimis scripturis et documentis sunt commendata. Quapropter ego Deneberhtus episcopus fui memor pristinæ locutionis antecessoris mei Hioþoredi episcopi et Wulfheardi circa terram illam æt Intanbeorgan, simul etiam æt Bradanleage, tunc Wulfheardus iterum coram synodali testimonio confirmavit cum signo crucis Xp̃i Deneberhto episcopo et ejus familiæ in Weogornæ civitate, ut illud noluisset umquam avertere ab aecclesia ante nominata, præter ut ante veraciter ac firmiter definitum haberet, ut hoc per omnia firmum et fixum perpetuo inter eos permaneret. Haec commemoratio facta est in loco qui dicitur Clofesho, an̄. Dominicæ incarnat̃. DCCC^{o}III° Indic̃. XI., die II. Non̄. Octob̃.

✠ Ego Æðelheard arc̃.ep̃.
✠ Ego Alduulf ep̃s.
✠ Ego Werenberht ep̃s.
✠ Ego Eadwlf ep̃.
✠ Ego Denebriht ep̃.
✠ Ego Wulfheard ep̃.
✠ Ego Uuigberht ep̃.
✠ Ego Alhmund ep̃.
✠ Ego Alhheard ep̃.
✠ Ego Tidferð ep̃.
✠ Ego Osmund ep̃.
✠ Ego Wermund ep̃.
✠ Ego Wihtun ep̃.
✠ Ego Cenwulf rex Merc̃. consensi et subscripsi.
✠ Ego Heaberht princ̃s.
✠ Ego Beornoð princ̃s.

✠ Ego Ceolward princ̃s.
✠ Ego Cynehelm princ̃s.
✠ Ego Wicga princ̃s.
✠ Ego Wigheard princ̃s.
✠ Ego Byrnwald princ̃s.
✠ Ego Aldred princ̃s.

ENDORSED ON THE FOREGOING CHARTER.
DCCC.XIX.–DCCC.XXI.

✠ Ceolulf rex wilnade ðæs landes æt Bremesgræfan to Heaberhte bisceope ⁊ to his higun. ⁊ ða sende he his ærendwreocan to Wulfhearde to Intanbeorgum. ⁊ heht ꝥ he cuome to him ⁊ to ðæm higum. ða dyde he swa. Ða heo him to spræcon se bisceop ⁊ his weotan ymbe ꝥ land ꝥ he his him geuðe ꝥ heo mehtan ðone freodom begeotan. ⁊ ða wæs he eadmodlice ondeta ꝥ he swa walde. ⁊ to him wilniende wæs ðætte heo him funden swylce londare swylce he mid arum on beon mehte ⁊ his wic ðær on byrig beon mihte on his life. Ða sende he monn to ðæm arcebisceope ⁊ to Eadberhte ⁊ to Dynne. ⁊ him heht sæcgan ꝥ he wilnade ðæs londes æt Intanbeorgan. Ða se ærcebisceop ⁊ Eadberht hit wærun ærndiende to cyninge. Ða cuom Dynne to gelærde ðone cyning ꝥ he his no geþæf wæs. Ða wæs higen ⁊ hlaforde

✠ King Ceolulf desired the land at Bromsgrove for bishop Heaberht and for his monastery; and he then sent his messenger to Wulfheard at Inkberrow, and commanded him to come to him and to the convent; and he did so. Then they, the bishop and his 'witan,' spoke to him about the land, that he should grant it to them, that they might obtain the freedom. And then he humbly agreed that he so would, and was desirous that they should find him such a landed property as he with dignity might reside on, and might have his dwelling there in the town for his life. He then sent a man to the archbishop, and to Eadberht, and to Dynne, and commanded him to say that he desired the land at Inkberrow. Then the archbishop and Eadberht sent to inform the king. Then Dynne came and informed the lond unbefliten eghwæs ⁊ seoððan ā oð his daga ende.

king that he was no consenting party. Then was the land given to the convent and the lord, uncontested of every one, and ever afterwards until his days' end.

ARCHBISHOP ÆTHELHEARD. DCCC.III.

Gloria in excelsis Deo, et in terra pax hominibus bonæ voluntatis.

✠ Scimus autem quod multis in Deum fideliter confidentibus notum et manifestum est; et nihil tamen illis placabile in eo visum est, qui in gentibus Anglorum commorantur, quod Offa rex Merciorum in diebus Iaenberhti archiepiscopus, cum maxima fraude honorem et unitatem sedis Sc̃i Agustini, patris nostri, in Dorovernensi civitate dividere et discindere præsumsit; et quomodo post obitum prædicti pontificis, Æðelheardus ar̃cep̃is. Dei gratia donanti illius successor post curricula annorum erga plurima Dei ecclesiarum jura limina apostolorum et apostolicæ sedis beatissimum papam Leonem visitare contigit. Inter alias necessarias legationes etiam discissionem injuste factam archiepiscopalis sedis narravit; et ipse apostolicus papa ut audivit et intellexit quod injuste fuisset factum, statim sui privilegii auctoritatis præceptum posuit, et in Brittanniam misit, et præcipit ut honor Sc̃i Agustini sedis cum omnibus suis parrohhiis integerrime redintegraretur, juxta quod Sc̃s Gregorius, nostræ gentis apostolus et magister, conposuit, et honorabili ar̃cepiscopo Æðelheardo in patriam pervenienti per omnia redderetur, et Coenuulfus rex pius Merciorum ita complevit cum senatoribus suis. Anno vero Dominicæ incarnationis DCCC^{o}III°, Indictione XI^{a}, die IIII^{a} idus Octobris, Ego Æðelheardus ar̃cep̃isc. cum omnibus XII. ep̃isco sancto sede beati Agustini subjectis, per apostolica præcepta domni papæ Leonis, in synodo qui factus est in loco celebri qui vocatur Clofeshoas, unianimo consilio totius sancti synodi, in nomine Dei omnipotentis præcipientes, et omnium sanctorum illius, et per ejus tremendum judicium, ut numquam reges, neque episcopi, neque principes, neque ullius tyrannicæ potestatis homines honorem Sc̄i Agustini et suæ sc̄æ sedis diminuere, vel in aliquantula particula dividere præsumerint; sed in eo per omnia dignitatis honore plenissime semper permaneat, quo utique in constitutione beati Gregorii, et in privilegiis apostolicorum suorum successorum habeatur, nec non etiam et in sanctorum canonum rectum haberi sanctionibus videatur. Nunc etiam Deo cooperanti, et domno apostolico papæ Leoni, ego Æðelheardus ar̄cep̄is., et alii coepiscopi nostri, et nobiscum omnes dignitates nostri synodi, cum vexillis crucis Xp̄i unanimiter primatum sc̄æ sedis firmantes, hoc quoque præcipientes, et signo sc̄æ crucis scribentes, ut ar̄cepiscopalis sedes in Liccidfeldensi monasterio numquam habeatur, ex hoc tempore, neque in alio loco aliquo, nisi tantummodo in Dorobernensi civitate, ubi Xp̄i ecclesia est, et ubi primus in hac insula catholica fides renituit, et a Sc̄o Agustino sacrum baptismum celebretur. Insuper etiam cartam a Romana sede missam per Hadrianum papam de palleo et de archiepiscopatus sede in Liccedfeldensi monasterio, cum consensu et licentia domni apostolici Leonis papæ præscribimus aliquid valere, quia per subreptitionem et male blandam suggestionem adipiscebatur: et idcirco manifestissimis signis cælestis regis, primatum monarchiæ archiprincipatus permanere canonicis et apostolicis munitionibus statuimus ubi sc̄m evangelium Xp̄i per beatum patrem Agustinum in provincia Anglorum primum prædicatur, et deinde per gratiam Sc̄i Spiritus late diffusum est. Si quis vero, contra apostolicis præceptis et nostrorum omnium, ausus sit tunicam Xp̄i scindere, et unitatem sc̄e Dei ecclesiæ dividere, sciat se, nisi digne emendaverit quod inique contra sacras canones fecit, æternaliter esse damnatum.

Hic sunt nomina sanctorum episcoporum et abbatum qui præscriptam cyrographi cartulam, in synodo qui factus est æt

Cloveshoum, anno adventus Domini DCCC.III., cum signo s͠cæ crucis Xp͠i firmaverunt:

✠ Æðelheardus arc͠ep͠is.
✠ Alduulfus ep͠is.
✠ Uuerenberhtus ep͠is.
✠ Alcheardus ep͠is.
✠ Uuigberhtus ep͠is.
✠ Alhmundus ep͠is.
✠ Osmundus ep͠is.
✠ Eaduulfus ep͠is.
✠ Deneberhtus ep͠is.
✠ Uuihthunus ep͠is.
✠ Tidfriðus ep͠is.
✠ Uulfheardus ep͠is.
✠ Alhmundus pr͠s ab͞.
✠ Beonna pr͠s ab͞.
✠ Foðred͠ pr͠s ab͞.
✠ Uuigmundus pr͠s ab͞.

ARCHBISHOP ÆTHELHEARD. DCCC.III.

✠ Ego Æðelheardus, gratia Dei humilis sancte Dorobernensis ecclesie arc͠episc͠. unanimo concilio totius s͠ce sinodi congregationibus omnium monasteriorum que olim a fidelibus Xp͠o Dn͠o perpetuam in libertatem dedita fuerunt. In nomine Dei Omnipotentis, et per ejus tremendum judicium precipio, sicut et ego mandatum a domno apostolico Leone papa percepi, ut ex hoc tempore nunquam temerario ausu super hereditatem Domini laicos et sæculares sibi præsumant dominos eligere; sed sicut in privilegiis ab apostolica sede datis habetur, seu etiam ab apostolicis viris, in initio nascentis ecclesie traditum est per sanctos canones, vel etiam a propriis possessoribus monasteriorum constitutum, ea regula et observantia discipline sua monastica jura studeant observare. Si ergo, quod absit, ipsi hoc nostrum mandatum, et domini apostolici papæ spreverint et pro nihilo ducunt, sciant se ante tribunal Xp͠i, nisi ante emendari voluerint, rationem reddituros.

Hæc sunt nomina sanctorum episcoporum et venerabilium abbatum et presbiterorum, et diaconorum qui, cum totius s͠ce sinodi consensu, pro confirmatione predicte rei, signum s͠ce crucis subscripserunt.

✠ Ego Æðelheardus, gratia Dei arc͠epis͠ Dorobernensis civitatis, signum s͠cæ crucis subscripsi.

✠ Æðelheah ab̄. ✠ Wernoð p̄r.
✠ Feologeld p̄r. ab̄. ✠ Beornmod p̄r.
✠ Uulfheard p̄r. ✠ Uulfred arc̄. diac.

✠ Ego Aldulfus, Liccedfeldensis ecclesie epis̄., siḡ. crucis subscripsi.

✠ Hygberht ab̄. ✠ Monn p̄r. ✠ Eadhere p̄r.
✠ Lulla p̄r. ✠ Wigferð p̄r. ✠ Cuðberht p̄r.

✠ Ego Werenberht, Legorensis civitatis epis̄., siḡ. crucis subscripsi.

✠ Alhmund p̄r. ab̄. ✠ Berhthæð p̄r.
✠ Beonna p̄r. ab̄. ✠ Eadred p̄r.
✠ Forðred p̄r. ab̄. ✠ Æðelhæh p̄r.
✠ Uuigmund p̄r. ab̄. ✠ Eanred p̄r.
✠ Eadberht p̄r. ✠ Mon p̄r.

✠ Ego Eadwulf, Syddensis civitatis episc̄., siḡ. crucis subscripsi.

✠ Eadred p̄r. ab̄. ✠ Eaduulf p̄r.
✠ Dæghelm p̄r. ab̄. ✠ Hereberht p̄r.
✠ Plegberht p̄r. ✠ Heaðored p̄r.

✠ Ego Deneberht, Wegoranensis civitatis epis̄., siḡ. crucis subscripsi.

✠ Hyseberht ab̄. ✠ Freoðomund ab̄.
✠ Þingeferð ab̄. ✠ Cœnferð p̄r.
✠ Pæga ab̄. ✠ Seleræd p̄r.

✠ Ego Wulfheard, Herefordensis ecclesie epis̄., siḡ. crucis subscripsi.

✠ Cuðred ab̄. ✠ Monn p̄r.
✠ Strygel p̄r. ✠ Heaðobald diac̄.
✠ Dycga p̄r. ✠ Werferð.

✠ Ego Wigberht, Sciraburnensis ecclesie epis̄., siḡ. crucis subscripsi.

✠ Muca ab̄. ✠ Berhtmund ab̄.
✠ Eadberht ab̄.

✠ Ego Ealhmund, Wintanæ civitatis episc̄., siḡ. crucis subscripsi.

✠ Cuðberht ab̄. ✠ Lulla ab̄.
✠ Cufa ab̄. ✠ Notheard p̄r.
✠ Marcus ab̄. ✠ Wigðegn p̄r.

✠ Ego Alhheard, Elmhamis ecclesie episc̃., sig̃. crucis subscripsi.

✠ Folcberht p̃r.
✠ Freoðuberht p̃r.
✠ Eadberht p̃r.
✠ Wulflaf p̃r.
✠ Hunfrið diac̃.
✠ Beornhelm diac̃.

✠ Ego Tidfrið, Dummucæ civitatis episc̃., sig̃. crucis subscripsi.

✠ Wulfheard ab̃.
✠ Lull ab̃.
✠ Ceolhelm p̃r.
✠ Cynulf p̃r.
✠ Tilberht p̃r.
✠ Eadberht p̃r.

✠ Ego Osmund, Lundonensis civitatis episc̃., sig̃. crucis subscripsi.

✠ Heahstan p̃r. ab̃.
✠ Wigheard p̃r.
✠ Tidhun p̃r.
✠ Freoðored p̃r.
✠ Æðelhelm.

✠ Ego Wermund, Hrofensis civitatis epis̃., sig̃. crucis subscripsi.

✠ Lullinge p̃r.
✠ Tuda p̃r.
✠ Beagnoð p̃r.
✠ Heahberht p̃r.
✠ Wigheard p̃r.
✠ Heared diac̃.

✠ Ego Uuihthun, Selesegi ecclesie episc̃., sig̃. crucis subscripsi.

✠ Ceolmund ab̃.
✠ Dudd p̃r.
✠ Eadberht p̃r.
✠ Beorcol p̃r.
✠ Heahferð.
✠ Cynebald.

Actum est in celebri loco qui vocatur Clofeshoas. Anno ab incarnatione Domini DCCC.III., Indictione XI., die quarta Idus Octobres.

BISHOPS DENEBERHT AND WULFHEARD. DCCC.III.

✠ Anno Dominice incarnationis DCCC°III° Indict. XI[a] vero qui est annus VII. regni Cenwulfi pii regis Merciorum, factum est sinodale conciliabulum æt Clofeshoum, presidente Æþelheardo archiepiscopo; ubi cum universi provinciales episcopi, cum abbatibus et presbiteris de necessariis et pluribus universe aecclesie statutis congregarentur; ibi etiam inter alia plura facta est contentio inter Deneberhtum, Uueogernensis aecclesie antistitem, Uulfheardumque, Herefordensem presulem. Sunt autem monasteria in parochia Deneberhti Celtanhom, Beccanford, quae olim in antiquis diebus ad Herefordensem æcclesiam præstita fuerunt, in quibus postulabat suam pastum qui ei episcopali jure pertinebat, ipse Deneberht sibi reddi. Uulfheard autem e contra narrabat, ut ei nullam dare debuisset, neque umquam antecessores illius aliquam ibi haberent. Et si erat umquam, jam xxx. annis et eo amplius nemo illum, neque antecessores ejus, hujuscemodi pastu pulsaret neque tangeret. Deneberht autem cum testimonio narrabat, ut Uuermund episcopus pastum acciperet æt Beccanforda, Haðoredus similiter æt Celtanhomme, insuper et ipse Wulfheard ei pecuniam daret pro pastu, hæcque cum testimonio conprobavit. Cum vero hujuscemodi hinc et inde multa contenderunt, ventum est ad sermonem, ut archiepiscopus Deneberhtum rogabat dimidia sibi hujus pastus præstare et altero anno semper æt Beccanforda suam refectionem acciperet, altero æt Celtanhomme. Ille autem respondebat, se et velle et debere in omnibus ejus parere præceptis; hoc modo tamen in testimonio totius sinodi in diem ejus prestare et non amplius; idque litteris confirmare, ut sciant omnes qui ejus sunt successores, quod ipse numquam intermittit quod Uueogernensi aecclesie ad utilitatem recte pertinet. Haec autem pacis conciliatio facta est sub die IIII. Iduum Octobrium. Eodem die, in simili contentione placiti sunt Werenberhtus, Mediterraneorum Anglorum episcopus, et Aldulfus Licetfeldensis præsul; Uuigberhtus similiter Sciraburnensis antistes et Alhmundus Wentani pastor aecclesiæ, tale aliquid inter se habentes, omnes ad vere fraternitatis pacem adunati, perrexerunt unusquisque ad suam. Erat autem dies v. feria, et hii sunt testes hujus pacis.

✠ Ego Æðilheard archiepiscopus consensi. ✠ Ego Aldulf episcopus. ✠ Ego Werenberht episcopus. ✠ Ego Eadulf episcopus. ✠ Ego Deneberht episcopus. ✠ Ego Alheard episcopus. ✠ Ego Tidferð episcopus. ✠ Ego Wigberht episcopus.

ÆTHELRIC. DCCC.IV.

☧ In nomine Domini Dei summi, Regis regum, qui in altis habitat et prospicit omnia celestia et terrestria. Anno ab incarnatione Christi DCCC.IIII. Indictione XII. ego Æthelric, filius Æthelmundi, cum conscientia sinodali invitatus ad Sinodum, et in judicio stare, in loco qui dicitur Clofeshoh, cum libris et ruris, id est, æt Westmynster, quod prius propinqui mei tradiderunt michi et donaverunt, ibi Æthelhardus archiepiscopus michi regebat atque judicaverat, cum testimonio Cœnwulfi regis et optimatibus ejus, coram omni sinodo, quando scripturas meas perscrutarent, ut liber essem terram meam atque libellos dare quocunque volui. Postea commendavi amicis meis ad servandum, quando quesivi Sanctum Petrum et Sanctum Paulum, pro remedio anime mee, et, iterum me revertente ad patriam, accepi terram meam, et pretium reddidi, quasi ante pacti sumus, et pacifici fuerimus ad invicem. Facta est autem post paucos annos alia sinodus æt Aclea. Tunc in illo sinodo coram episcopis, rege, et principibus ejus, rememoravi pristine libertatis mee, que mihi ante judicatum est, et cum licentia eorum testificavi, in presenti testimonio, quemadmodum meam hereditatem dare voluissem, et sic dixi: Hec sunt nomina illarum terrarum, que dabo ad locum, qui dicitur Deorhyrst, pro me et Æthelmundo patre meo, si mihi contingat ut illic corpus meum requiescat, Todanhom, et æt Sture, Screfleh, et Cohhanleh, ea conditione, ut illa congregatio vota eorum faciat firma, sicut mihi promiserunt. Iterum dabo Werferðæ XI. manentium Bremesgræfan et Feccanhom, ut habeat suum diem, et postea reddat ad Wegornaceastre. Verum etiam do XXX. manentium Under Ofre ad Gleawcestre; et quando michi contingat exitus diei mei, tunc dabo Ciolburge matri mee, si diutius vivit quam ego, terram XLIII. manentium æt Westmynstre, et æt Stoce, ut habeat sua die, et postea reddat ad Weogornensem ecclesiam. Pro qua re ea vivente ut ibi habeat protectionem et defensionem contra Berclinga contentione: et si aliquis homo in aliqua contentione juramentum ei decreverit contra Berclingas, liberrima erit ad reddendum, cum recto consilio propinquorum meorum, qui michi hereditatem donabant, et meo, quo ei dabo. Et si non habeat patrocinium in civitate Weogornensi, postea primum querat ad archiepiscopum in Cantia. Et si ibi non habeat, sit libera cum ruris et libris ad eligendum patrocinium ubi placitum sibi fuerit. Si aliter fiat, ut non opto, aliquis homo contendat contra libros meos, vel hereditatem, indigne, tunc habeat Aldulfus episcopus in Liccetfelda istius cartule comparem, et amici et necessarii mei et fidelissimi alias, id est, Eadberht Eadgaring, et Æthelheah Esning, ad confirmationem hujus rei. Rogo etiam Æðelric, pro amore omnipotentis Dei, et precipio, et obsecro per omnes virtutes celorum, ut nullus homo hanc positionem crucis Christi, que tantorum virorum testimonio confirmata est, non presumat minuere. Si ausus est aliquis confirmationem istam infringere, deleatur nomen ejus de laude Dei, si non satisfactione emendaverit.

✠ Ego Coenwulf, rex Merciorum hanc munificentiam signo sancte crucis subscripsi. ✠ Ego Æðelheardus archiepiscopus Dorovernensis civitatis signum sancte crucis subscripsi. ✠ Ego Alduulfus Licetfeldensis episcopus consensi. ✠ Ego Werenberht episcopus consensi. ✠ Ego Denebyrht episcopus consensi. ✠ Ego Wulfheard episcopus consensi. ✠ Ego Eadwulfus episcopus consensi. ✠ Ego Heaberht dux subscripsi. ✠ Ego Beornoð dux subscripsi. ✠ Ego Ciolward dux subscripsi. ✠ Ego Cynehelm dux subscripsi. ✠ Ego Wicga dux subscripsi. ✠ Ego Wigheard dux subscripsi. ✠ Ego Byrnwald dux subscripsi. ✠ Ego Aldred dux consensi et subscripsi.

KING CÈNWULF OF MERCIA. DCCC.VI.

✠ Kenulfus, Dei misericordia rex Merciorum, omnibus Mediterraneis Anglis per universam Merciam fidem confitentibus Christianam, pacem perfectam, sempiternamque salutem. Omnes et singuli scitote, quia Dominus sanctum suum mirificavit, signis celeberrimis et preclaris prodigiis, beatissimum Christi confessorem Guthlacum, in monasterio Croylandensi corporaliter quiescentem, et novis ac innumeris miraculis, prout ego et regina mea in nostra peregrinatione nuper oculis nostris vidimus, quotidie clarius ad totius mundi notitiam coruscantem. Unde ad supplicationem religiosissimi viri et spiritualis patris æc confessarii nostri, dñi Siwardi, abbatis dicti monasterii, consulente idem ac commonente venerabili patre domino Wlfredo archiepiscopo Dorobernensi, tunc nostre peregrinationis comite, dictum monasterium Croylandie, cum tota insula adjacente, sicut in carta quondam regis Ethelbaldi, fundatoris sui, per limites est distincta: monachos etiam ejusdem monasterii, et conversos, ac servos universos, in custodiam capio mee protectionis. Insuper peregrinos omnes illuc causa devotionis accedentes, et cum signo Sancti Guthlaci in suis capuciis vel capellis recedentes, liberos et solutos ab omni passagio et thelonio, ubicunque venerint per totum regnum Mercie perenniter esse volo. Sed et eleemosynam quam Thoroldus vicecomes Lincolnie dedit dictis monachis in Bokenhale; item eleemosynam quam Geulphus filius Malti dedit illis in Halingtoñ; item eleemosinam quam Fregistus, miles validissimus, quondam magister meus, dedit illis in Langtoft; et eleemosynam quam Algarus miles etiam dudum meus, dedit illis in Baston et in Repingale, Deo, ac Sancto Guthlaco, dictoque monasterio ac monachis in eo Deo servientibus, in perpetuam possessionem concedo, confero, et confirmo.

✠ Anno incarnationis Christi octingentesimo sexto istud cyrographum ego Kenulphus Merciorum rex signo sanctæ crucis consignavi. ✠ Ego Wlfredus archiepiscopus Dorobernensis fieri consului. ✠ Ego Kinebertus episcopus Winchester subnotavi. ✠ Ego Wonwona episcopus Legecestrensis consensi. ✠ Ego Celredes abbas de Medeshamsted, germanus frater domini Siwardi abbatis, multum procuravi. ✠ Ego Cuthredus rex Cantuariorum, ad imperium domini mei regis Kenulphi, assensum dedi. ✠ Celwulf frater domini regis Kenulphi approbavi. ✠ Ego Algarus minister affui. ✠ Ego Sigga presbiter, precipiente domino meo rege Kenulpho, hoc chirographum, manu mea scriptum, in præsentia dictorum venerabilium patrum et dominorum meorum, prefato venerabili domino Siwardo abbati Croylandie commendavi.

KING CÈNWULF OF MERCIA. AUG. 1st DCCC.XI.

✠ In nomine Dei summi Regis æterni. Anno autem incarnationis ejusdem Domini Salvatoris mundi Jħu Xp̃i DCCC°XI°, Indictione vero IIII.; porro quoque imperii piissimi regis Merciorum Cœnuulfi anno XV°, præsulatus etiam Uulfredi archipontificis anno VI°, prima Kalendarum die Augustarum, in loco preclaro oppidoque regali Lundaniæ vicu concilium pergrande collectum habebatur, in quo videlicet ipse rex Cœnuulf atque Uulfred arc̃.episc̃. cum coepiscopis illius duobus, verbi gratia, Deneberht Huuicciorum episc̃., Ætheluulf episcop̃. Australium Saxonum, cum principibus ducibusque et majores natu, quorum nomina infra caraxantur: inter alias quoque diversarum rerum causas in illo habentes concilio interpretatas, placuit pio regi Cœnuulfo, cum consilio et consensu totius concilii illius, id est episcoporum, principum, ducum, judicumve majorumque natu, pro honore Dei Omnipotentis, ac pro expiatione piaculorum ejus, atque pro reverentissima dilectione Uulfredi arc̃episc̃i, seu etiam pro ejus larga pecuniarum remuneratione, hoc est centum et viginti VI. mancosas, pro his rebus in Occidentale Cantiæ, in regione suburbanaque regis oppido, ibi ab incolis Rogingaham nuncupato, terram duorum aratruum, quod Appincglond illic nominatur, et rursum in alio loco et in regione suburbana ad oppidum regis, quod ab incolis ibi Fefresham appellatur, terram quoque duorum aratruum in locis nominatis illic ðæt Suiðhunincglond æt Grafenea, atque iterum in civitate Dorovernia, in australe parte ecclesiæ Salvatoris, duas possessiunculas et tertiam dimediam, id est, in nostra loquella, ðriddan healf haga, et prata duo ad eas prius et modo pertinentia in orientale parte Sture fluminis sita; Cœnuulf rex has terrulas sui propriæ puplicæ juris, cum prædicto concilii consensu, ac pro cunctis antedictis causis, Uulfredo suo archipontifici donare ac conscribere in propriam atque in perennem hereditatem habendum fruendumque; et ad tractandum, cum campis, pascuis, pratibus, silvis, saltibus, piscuosis ac maritimis fretis, paludibus, vallibusque, dulcis salsuginesque salisque, stationibus coctionesque, et cum cunctis fructibus internis externisque, vel aliunde usquam ad eas rite vel unquam pertinentia, in talem sibi usum qualem semetipsi utillimum optimumve fore videretur, firmiter pleniterque dejudicavit. Integram quoque libertatem his terrulis atque ruriculis rex Cœnuulf cum auctoritate supra dicti concilii decreverat, ut perpetue sint liberæ ab omnibus puplicis tributis et a cunctis regalium rerum vel operum debitis, sive principum seu ducum vel procuratorum, aut etiam ab omni sæcularium causarum rerumve gravedine, exceptis his debitis, id est pontis instructione, et contra paganos expeditione, atque arcis munitione distructioneve. Cum tamen hoc universo populo opportunitas summa poposcerit, et necessitas eximia hoc agendum cunctos undecumque coherceret, tunc et illi rite sua reddent.

✠ Ego Cœnuulf, Dñi misericordia rex Merciorum, hujus nostræ dationis ac libertatis remunerationem mente consona propriisque manibus crucis Xp̃i signo confirmare roborareque subscripsi.

✠ Ælfþryð regina consentiens subscripsit.
✠ Sigred rex subscripsit.
✠ Uulfred archiepis̃, Xp̃i gratia, subscripsit.
✠ Deneberht epis̃ subscripsit.
✠ Beornmod epis̃ subscripsit.
✠ Æðeluulf epis̃ subscripsit.
✠ Heardberht princ̃. subscrip̃.
✠ Beornnoð princ̃. subscrip̃.
✠ Cynehelm princ̃. subscrip̃.
✠ Eadberht dux cons̃. subscrip̃.
✠ Ecguulf dux cons̃. subscrip̃.
✠ Eanberht dux cons̃. subscrip̃.
✠ Heahferð dux cons̃. subscrip̃.
✠ Cyneberht propiñ. ejus sub̃.
✠ Cœnwald propiñ. ejus sub̃.
✠ Æðelheah pedes sessor sub̃.

✠ Cuœnburg abba sub.
✠ Seleburg abb. subscripsit.
✠ Cuðred pr. subscripsit.

KING CÊNWULF OF MERCIA. NOV. 9TH DCCC.XI.

✠ Regnante Domino nostro in ævum per secula cuncta. Anno vero incarnationis ejusdem Salvatoris mundi, Domini nostri Jhesu Christi DCCC.XI. Indictione autem IIII., imperii vero nostri a Deo dati anno XVI., die vero V. idus Novembris. Tunc ego Coenulfus rex Merciorum hoc opusculum, Deo auxiliante atque favente in plenitudine, provincia Wictionum inchoavi, famoso in loco quem solicoli antiquo nomine Wincelcumbam appellare suescunt. Ecclesiam quæ modo pulcherrima clarescit, scemate jam nempe preparata enituit, ibi Wulfredus quoque presul Cantuariæ, in honore Jhesu Christi Domini nostri beatæque Mariæ genitricis Dei, quæ suo contulit gremio regem quem cæli capere terraque nequiverant, dedicavit; ibi quoque meum in Domino corpus pausare decrevi. Complacuit autem mihi Kenulfo, ut ad consecrationem ante nominatæ æcclesiæ universos accercissem Merciorum optimates, episcopos, principes, comites, procuratores, meosque propinquos, necnon et Cuthredum regem Cantuariorum, atque Sigredum regem Orientalium Saxonum, cum omnibus qui testes nostris sinodalibus concilialibus aderant. Quam vero basilicam ad laudem et ad honorem Domini nostri Jhesu Christi, et pro amore reginæ cælestis, atque expiatione piaculorum meorum, ædificavi, non modo ad roborationem hereditatis mee, atque ad solidationem apostolici privilegii quod mihi apostolici pontifices cum auctoritate beati Petri principis apostolorum, direxerunt. Ego etenim Kenulfus, Dei arridenti gratia rex Merciorum, ad gratiarum actionem pro devotione illorum qui mihi et mee hereditati benivola mente cum auctoritate apostolorum affirmatione, atque cunctorum sinodalium nostrorum reconciliationem firmiter roboraverunt: jam autem pro confirmatione meæ hereditatis, quam dominus Leo papa primus affirmabat cum suo privilegio; et postea

Paschalis summus pontifex, cum preceptis suæ auctoritatis, et universis Merciorum optimatibus, in tribus sinodis, unanimo concilio, in perpetuam hereditatem mihi meisque heredibus dona mea omnibus archontis Merciorum, necnon et aliarum provinciarum, in auro argentoque, et in omnibus utensilibus meis, letus erogavi, necnon in equis electissimis, unicuique secundum dignitatem gradus sui; et universis qui agros non habebant, libram in argento purissimo tribui, atque in auro mundissimo, unoquoque presbitero, manc̃. tradidi unum, et omni servo Dei solidum unum; et ea dona innumerabilia sunt, sicut nostram regalem dignitatem decebat, quæ nullus enumerare valet; neque numeranda sunt quæ tunc meæ erogavi genti, ea conditione, ut mihi meisque heredibus plena libertate hereditas mea eo firmior atque stabilior æternaliter perduraret. Ego Kenulphus etiam rex Merciorum vexillum sanctæ crucis, in quo passus est Jhesus Christus Dominus noster, ad hoc conquisivi, ut animæ meæ, et omnium bonorum secularium, seu heredum immobiliter patrocinando, contra tumultum pravorum tutatrix atque defensatrix perpetuis temporibus permansisset. Et si quis aliquid ab hoc vexillo per vim studeat auferre, majoris sive minoris personæ, sciat se anathematis vinculo innodatum, et a sancte crucis tutela coram Deo in die judicii separatum, nisi ante hic cum satisfactione emendaverit: et ab illo patrocinio predicto sanctam istam æcclesiam, sub almæ Trinitatis nutu, atque angelorum, et archangelorum, patriarcharum, prophetarum, apostolorum, martirum, confessorum, virginum, atque omnium sanctorum protectione corroboratam sciatis permanere. Hoc quoque ego Kenulfus rex, et omnes qui in nostris sinodalibus conciliis testes atque conscii hujus rei presentati fuissent, dijudicavimus atque unanimo consensu constituimus, ut si homo aliquis culpabilis vitæ suæ, aut in aliquo delicto, oculte publiceve delinquens, pervenisset ad apicem hereditatis meæ, et nostram æcclesiam, atque vexillum salutiferæ crucis requireret, firmissimam ibi pacem atque indulgentiam inveniret; et nullus fuisset homo aliqua audacitate fretus, quoquo modo torvave cogitatione, aliquid per vim exinde rapere, nec diminuere, neque agros meæ hereditatis foras transdonare, vel accommodare, nisi ad tempus et ad conditionis statutum unius hominis; sed immobiliter permansissent, quasi in nostris tribus sinodis firmiter decrevimus æternaliter perdurare. Hii omnes hujus rei veritatis testes extiterunt, et sacratissimo crucis Christi signaculo roborando confirmaverunt.

Ego Kenulfus rex Merciorum hujus definitionis reconciliationem signo sanctæ crucis confirmavi. Ego Cuthredus rex Cantuariæ consentiens signum salutifere crucis impono. Ego Siredus rex Orientalium Saxonum signum crucis salutiferæ corroborans impono. Ego Wlfredus Cantuariæ archiepiscopus consensi et subscripsi. Ego Aldulfus [Licetfeldensis[1]] episcopus consensi et subscripsi. Ego Denebertus [Uuigorniensis] episcopus consensi et subscripsi. Ego Werenbrihtus [Leogerensis] episcopus consensi et subscripsi. Ego Wlfhardus [Hecana, quæ nunc Hereford dicitur] episcopus consensi et subscripsi. Ego Tilferthus [Agustaldensis] episcopus subscripsi. Ego Ætheluulfus [Eastanglorum] episcopus consensi et subscripsi. Ego Eadulfus [Cridiatunensis] episcopus consensi et subscripsi. Ego Alchbertus [Suhtsaxonia] episcopus consensi et subscripsi. Ego Æthelnothus [Lundoniensis] episcopus consensi et subscripsi. Ego Wibertus [Sciireburniensis] episcopus consensi et subscripsi. Ego Beormonus[2] [Rovecestrensis] episcopus consensi et subscripsi. Ego Wignothus [Exoniensis] episcopus consensi et subscripsi. Ego Eambeorthus dux consensi et subscripsi. Ego Heardbearhtus dux consensi et subscripsi. Ego Beornothus dux consensi et subscripsi. Ego Cynhelmus dux consensi et subscripsi. Ego Ceolbertus dux consensi et subscripsi. Ego Aldredus dux consensi et subscripsi. Ego Wlfredus dux consensi et subscripsi. Ego Heahferthus dux consensi et subscripsi. Ego Ciolverthus dux consensi et subscripsi. Ego Heatferthus dux consensi et subscripsi. Ego Plesa dux consensi et subscripsi.

[1] The names of the sees within brackets are written over the names of the witnesses in a coeval hand.

[2] So MS. for Beornmodus.

ARCHBISHOP WULFRED. DCCC.XIII.

✠ In nomine sancti Salvatoris Dei et Domini nostri Jhesu Christi. Anno ab incarnatione ejusdem Dei et redemptionis mundi DCCC.XIII. Indict. VI. presidente Christi gratia archipontifice Uulfredo metropolitano sedem ecclesie Christi, que sita est in Dorovernia civitate, anno VII.[1] episcopatus ejusdem archiepiscopi, divina ac fraterna pietate ductus amore Deo auxiliante renovando et restaurando pro honore et amore Dei sanctum monasterium Dorovernensis ecclesie reedificando refici auxiliantibus ejusdem ecclesie presbiteris et diaconibus cunctoque clero Domino Deo servientium simul. Ego Uulfredus, misericordia Dei archisacerdos, pro intimo cordis affectu, dabo et concedo familia Christi habere et perfruere domos quas sivi pro labore construxerunt, jure perpetuo hereditatis, munificentia illis viventibus seu decedentibus cuicumque relinquere vel donare voluerint unusquisque liberam habeant facultatem in eodem monasterio donandi, sed nec alicui foras extra congregationi. Ita etiam in Christi caritate obsecrans precipio omnibus successoribus meis hanc predictam donationem inconcussa et inviolatam salva ratione servandam, sed sine semper in evum; hac tamen conditione, ut Deo humiliores et gratiores omnium beneficiorum Dei semper existant, seduloque frequentatione canonicis horis ecclesiam Christi visitent, orantes ac deprecantes pro seipsis propriis piaculis, et pro aliorum remissione peccatorum, misericordiam Domini implorent: necnon domum refectionis et dormitorium communiter frequentent, juxta regulam monasterialis discipline vite observant, ut in omnibus honorificetur Deus, et vita nostra et bona conversatio nobis nostrisque proficiat in bonum. Si quis illorum per audaciam sue male voluntatis hanc predictam constitutionem inritam habere, et in oblivionem deducere, et congregare convivias ad vescendum et bibendum, seu etiam dormiendum in propriis cellulis, sciat se, quisquis ille sit, reatum se esse proprie domi, et in potestate archiepiscopi ad habendum, et cuicunque ei placuerit donandum k̃ manentem itaque hanc cartulam in sua nihilominus firmitate.

[1] Wulfred succeeded to Canterbury in 803.

✠ Ego Uulfred gratia Dei archiepisc̄. signo sancte crucis Christi firmans subscripsi.

✠ Ego Uuernoth pr̄ ab̄. coñ. ⁊ subscripsi.

✠ Ego Wulfheard pr̄ coñ. ⁊ sub̄.

✠ Ego Heamund pr̄ coñ. ⁊ sub̄.

✠ Ego Osuulf pr̄ coñ. ⁊ sub̄.

✠ Ego Ceolstan pr̄ coñ. ⁊ sub̄.

✠ Ego Tudda pr̄ coñ. ⁊ sub̄.

✠ Ego Diornoth pr̄ coñ. ⁊ sub̄.

✠ Ego Guthmund pr̄ coñ. ⁊ sub̄.

✠ Ego Cuthberht pr̄ coñ. ⁊ sub̄.

✠ Ego Cœnhere coñ. ⁊ sub̄.

✠ Ego Brunheard coñ. ⁊ sub̄.

✠ Ego Hæhferth coñ. ⁊ sub̄.

KING CÊNWULF OF MERCIA. DCCC.XXI.

✠ In nomine Dei et Domini nostri Jhesu Christi, veri Redemptoris mundi. Anno vero Dominice incarnationis DCCC.XXI., Indiccione XIIII., ego Coenulfus rex Merciorum, ab eodem Deo et Domino nostro, populis et tribubus præordinatus in regem, anno imperii nostri XXV., fui rogatus ab apostolica sede, per privilegium domni apostolici gloriosissimi Leonis papæ, et per Rethunum venerabilem episcopum, ut sibimet vel suis propinquis seu ipsa familia que habitat in monasterio quod situm est in Abbandune ecclesie quod ibidem dedicatum est in honore sancte Marie semper virginis et Dei genitricis, domine nostre, ut illud monasterium vel omnia loca que ad ipsum pertinere dinoscuntur, cum rebus mobilibus et immobilibus, in notis causis et ignotis, in modicis et in magnis, in [nomine] Domini Dei omnipotentis et beatissimi Petri principis apostolorum, donans donabo perpetuis temporibus eternam libertatem, in sancte Trinitatis patrocinio, omnia loca ad præfatum monasterium pertinentia, quorum infra nominantur nomina: Culanhom, Chenigtun, Hengesteseig, Cumanora, Earmundelæh, Eatun, Sunniggawille, Sondford, Wdtun, Gaging, Deniceswurþ, Ceornei, Gooseig, Færhom, Wæthenesfeld, Scrivenanhom, Burgtuun, Læhhamstede, Boxora, Wælingford, mid heora geburatunum [1] [id est cum appendiciis suis], Wicham cum suis campis, sicut Ceadwalla rex perdonavit, cum illa silva integra que dicitur Spene Wohanlæh et Trindlæh, Eastun cum omnibus agellulis ad præfata loca pertinentibus, concedens perdonabo, sicut prædiximus, perpetuam libertatem. Et mandatum mandamus, in nomine Patris et Filii et Spiritus Sancti, ut nullus superveniat hominum superbia inflatus, nec rex suum pastum requirat, vel habentes homines quos nos dicimus fæstingmen, nec eos qui accipitres portant, vel falcones, vel caballos ducunt, sive canes, nec penam mittere super eos quoquomodo audeat. Nec princeps nec graffio hanc lenitatem præfatam in alicujus oneris molestia mutare audeat, aut in diebus nostris vel successorum nostrorum. Si pro alico delicto accusatur homo Dei, ecclesie ille custos solus cum suo juramento, si audeat, illum castiget. Sin autem, ut recipiat aliam justiciam hujus vicissitudinis conditionem, præfatum delictum cum simplo præcio componat. Expeditionem cum XII. vassallis et cum tantis scutis exerceant; antiquos pontes et arces renovent; ceterum plena et integra libertate glorientur. Maxime cum ipsi diebus Dominicis VII. missas pro nobis saluberrimas offerant, et armis spiritualibus, centum psalteriis, contra invisibiles hostes dimicare non cessent. Si quis autem præscriptis statutis noluerit obedire, sciat se alienum esse a consortio sancte Dei ecclesie et a participatione corporis et sanguinis Domini nostri Jhesu Christi, per auctoritatem beati Petri apostoli, nisi digne emendaverit quod contra Dei ecclesiam fecisset. Dederunt enim, pro hujusmodi rei gratia, in auro et argento, cxx. libras, et centum manentes ad villam regalem que dicitur Suðtun.——Que postquam vir ille prudentissimus patravit, in summa pacis securitate coad vixit cenobium illud gubernavit.

[1] Culeham, Chenitun, Hengestesie, Cumenoran, Earmundesle, Eatun, Sunningawelle, Sandford x. manentium, Wdetun, Geinge, Denicheswurde, Ceornei, Goseig, Fernham, Wacenesfeld, Scriuenham, Burgtun, Lechamstede, Boxora, Weliford. *Cott. Claud. C.* ix.

KING CEOLWULF OF MERCIA. SEPT. 17TH DCCC.XXII.

✠ In nomine Jħu Xp̄i Salvatoris mundi, qui est, et qui erat, et qui venturus est, per quem reges regunt et dividunt regna terrarum, sicut dispensatur universæ terre distribuit secundum mensuram sui propriæ voluntatis. Ita iedem Dei gratia concedente, Ego Ceolwulf, rex Merciorum, vel etiam Contwariorum, dabo et concedo Uulfredo venerabile arc̄epis̄ aliquam partem terre juris mei, id est, v. aratro, in provincio Cantiæ ubi nominatur Mylentun, in propriam potestatem, ad abendum, possidendum, commutandumque, vel etiam post se relinquendum cuicumque ei karorum placuerit, cum omnibus usis ad eam rite pertinentibus, cum campis, silbis, pratis, pascuis, aquis, molinis, piscationibus, aucupationibus, venationibus, et quicquit in se abentibus, insuper etiam hanc p̄dictam terram liberabo ab omni servitute secularium rerum, a pastu regis, episcopis, principum, seu prefectum, exactorum, ducorum canorum vel æquorum seu accipitrum, ab refectione et habitu illorum omnium qui dicuntur fæstingmen, ab omnibus laboribus, operibus, et oneribus sive difficultatibus, quit plus minusve numerabo vel dico, ab omni gravitatibus magioribus minoriis, notis ignotis, undique liberata permaneat in æfum, nisi is quattuor causis que nunc nominabo; expeditione contra paganos ostes, et pontes constructione, seu arcis munitione vel destructione in eodem gente et singulare pretium foras reddat, secundum ritum gentes illius. Et tamen nullam penam foras alicui persolvat, set semper sine aliqua vi ullius causæ in integritate liber et secura perseveret, Uulfredo episcopi et eredibus ejus in posterum cum certissimis terminis suis: Ab oriente Cymesinc; in australe se Hole welle; ab occidente Diorente; ab aquilone Scorham silba, similiter qui dicitur Cert; ab occidente et aquilone Greotan Edesces lond; in oriente Cymesinges Cert; et in austra Ondred. Item in Ondrede pastum et pascua porcorum et armentum seu caprorum, suis locis: in Hyrst Sciofingden, Snad hyrst: et si quis scire desiderat quare hanc donam tam devotissime dedissem vel liberassim, sciat illi recitatur quod inprimis, pro amore Dei omnipotentis, et pro venerabili gradui preticti pontificis, seu etiam consecrationis meæ, quan ab eo eodem die, per Dei gratiam accepi, nec non pro eju placabili pecunia, id est anulus aureus abens LXXV. mancusas ut ab eo accepi.

Actum est anno Dominice incãti DCCC.XXII., Indict. XV., di vero XV. kl. Octob., in loco regale qui dicitur Bydictun, i testis consentientibus et scribentibus quorum nomina infr abentur.

✠ Ego Ceolwulf rex Merciorum hanc meam donationen proprio manu subscribo.

✠ Ego Wulfred arhc̃.ep̃is consensiens subscribo.
✠ Ego Æðelwald ep̃is consensi ⁊ subscribo.
✠ Ego Reðhun ep̃is consensi ⁊ subscribo.
✠ Ego Wulfheard ep̃is consensi ⁊ subscribo.
✠ Ego Heaberht ep̃is consensi ⁊ subscribo.
✠ Ego Sigered dux consensi ⁊ subscribo.
✠ Ego Eadberht dux consensi ⁊ subscribo.
✠ Ego Wulfred dux consensi ⁊ s̃ub.
✠ Ego Muca dux consensi ⁊ s̃ub.
✠ Ego Eaṭferð dux consensi ⁊ s̃ub.
✠ Ego Bofa dux consensi ⁊ s̃ub.
✠ Ego Piot p̃rs consensi ⁊ s̃ub.
✠ Ego Eadbald.
✠ Ego Cyneberht.
✠ Ego Wighelm.
✠ Ego Beadheard.
✠ Tunred.

KING ECGBERHT. DCCC.XXIII.

✠ In nomine Domini nostri Jhesu Christi. Ego Ecgberhtus gratia Dei rex Anglorum, cum consensu episcoporum ac principum meorum, hanc libertatem donavi ecclesie que sita est in civitate Hrobi, et omnibus agellis qui ad ecclesiam Sancti Andree apostoli pertinent, pro remedio anime mee et filii nostri Ætheluulfi, quem regem constituimus in Cantia ut omnes agri sint liberi ab omni regali servitio, a pastu regum et principum, ducum et prefectuum, exactorumque, ab equorum et falconum accepitrumque, et canum acceptione, et illorum hominum refectione quos nos festingmenn nominamus, a parafrithis, et ab omnibus difficultatibus regalis vel secularis servitutis, notis et ignotis, cum furis comprehensione intus et foris, majoris minorisve, preter pontis constructionem et expeditionem eternaliter liberata permaneat.

✠ Ego Ecgbertus, rex Anglorum, hanc donationem meam hujus libertatis signo sancti crucis Christi confirmavi et subscripsi. ✠ Ego Ætheluulf rex consensi et subscripsi. ✠ Ego Uulfred archiepiscopus consensi et subscripsi. ✠ Ego Wigðegn episcopus consensi et subscripsi. ✠ Ego Ealhstan episcopus consensi et subscripsi. ✠ Ego Beornmod episcopus consensi et subscripsi. ✠ Ego Wulfhard dux consensi et subscripsi. ✠ Ego Monuedi dux consensi et subscripsi. ✠ Ego Osmod dux consensi et subscripsi. ✠ Ego Dudda dux. Aldred. Oshere. Æðeluulf. Duduc. Boba. Ealhhere. Sigesteb. Æðelhard.

KING BEORNUULF OF MERCIA. OCT. 30TH DCCC.XXIV.

✠ Regnante inperpetuum Domino nostro Jhesu Christo, qui mundi monarchiam sua semper virtute gubernat in æternum: anno vero ab incarnatione Domini nostri Jhesu Christi DCCC.XXIIII., Indictione autem II., regnante Beornulfo, rege Merciorum, factum est pontificale et sinodale conciliabulum, in loco qui dicitur Clofeshoas, præsidente ibi rege præfato, ac venerando viro Wulfredo archiepiscopo, illo conventu regente ac moderante. Illic omnes episcopi nostri, et abbates, et universi Mercensium principes, et multi sapientissimi viri congregati adessent; ubi inter alia plura colloquia, aliqua contentio allata est inter Heaberhtum episcopum et illam familiam æt Berclea, de hereditate Æthelrici filii Æthelmundi, hoc est monasterium quod nominatur Westburhg. Habuit autem episcopus ante nominatus terram illam cum libris, sicut Æthelricus ante præcepit, ut ad Weogernensem ecclesiam redderetur. Statuta est autem atque decreta ab archiepiscopo, et ab omni sancta sinodo illa consentiente, ut episcopus qui monasterium et agellum cum libris haberet, cum juramento Dei servorum, presbiterorum, diaconorum, et plurimorum monachorum, sibi in propriam possessionem terram illam cum adjuratione adjurasset. Et ita finita est præscripta illa contentio coram episcopo: post xxx. noctes illud juramentum to Westmynstre deductum est. Quapropter, si quis hunc agrum ab illa ecclesia in Ceastre nititur evellere, contra decreta sacrorum canonum sciat se facere, quia sancti canones decernunt, quicquid sancta synodus universalis, cum catholico archiepiscopo suo adjudicaverit, nullo modo fractum vel irritum esse faciendum. Hæc autem gesta sunt. Hii sunt testes et confirmatores hujus rei, quorum nomina hic infra notantur, die III. kal. Novembris.

✠ Ego Beornulf, rex Merciorum, hanc cartulam synodalis decreti signo sanctæ crucis Christi confirmavi.

✠ Ego Wulfred archiepiscopus hanc synodalem sententiam cum signo gloriosæ crucis corroboravi. ✠ Ego Oethelwald episcopus consensi. ✠ Hræthhun episcopus consensi. ✠ Eadwulf episcopus consensi. ✠ Heaberht episcopus consensi. ✠ Beonna episcopus consensi. ✠ Ego Wigthegn episcopus consensi. ✠ Ego Cioberht episcopus consensi. ✠ Ego Wermund episcopus consensi. ✠ Ego Cynred episcopus consensi. ✠ Ego Hunberht episcopus consensi. ✠ Ego Eanmund abbas consensi. ✠ Ego Cuðwulf abbas consensi. ✠ Ego Wihtred abbas consensi. ✠ Ego Wilferth abbas consensi. ✠ Ego Beornoth dux. ✠ Sigered dux. ✠ Eadwulf dux. ✠ Mucel dux. ✠ Ludeca dux. ✠ Eadberht dux. ✠ Ecgberht dux. ✠ Alhheard dux. ✠ Uhtred dux. ✠ Bynna, frater regis. ✠ Piot presbiter. ✠ Cyneberht. ✠ Noðhelm præco a domno Eugenio papa. ✠ Bola. ✠ Aldred theloniarius consensi. ✠ Wighelm. ✠ Beadheard. ✠ Eadbald consensi.

✠ Æt þam aðe wæs æt Westmynstre efen fiftig mæssepreosta· ⁊ x. diaconas· ⁊ ealra oðra preosta sixtig ⁊ hundteontig. [Hoc est. Eidem juramento apud Westmonasterium prestito aderant quinquaginta sacrifici et x. diaconi, et ex omnibus aliis presbyteris, centum et sexaginta.]

✠ Her sindon þara mæssepreosta naman þe on þam aðe stodon ⁊ on wæron.

[Id est. Hæc sunt sacrificorum nomina qui juramento illi astiterunt, et idem præstiterunt.]

✠ Friomund abbas.
✠ Eadberht abbas.
✠ Ecgberht abbas.
✠ Badheard presbiter.
✠ Monn presbiter.
✠ Plegberht presbiter.
✠ Cuðbald presbiter.
✠ Hehstæf presbiter.
✠ Brada presbiter.
✠ Ecgmund presbiter.
✠ Brada presbiter.
✠ Wigberht presbiter.
✠ Berhthun presbiter.
✠ Regngar presbiter.
✠ Cuðberht presbiter.
✠ Snyda presbiter.
✠ Berhtred presbiter.
✠ Monn presbiter.
✠ Cuthbald presbiter.
✠ Alhmund presbiter.
✠ Luhhede presbiter.
✠ Ecgberht presbiter.
✠ Tidbald presbiter.
✠ Sucga presbiter.
✠ Eadgar presbiter.
✠ Alhhere presbiter.
✠ Eastmund presbiter.
✠ Mecga presbiter.
✠ Wigberht presbiter.
✠ Beorred presbiter.
✠ Hehferð diaconus.
✠ Tidberht presbiter.
✠ Berhtwulf presbiter.
✠ Cuðberht presbiter.
✠ Ciolheard presbiter.
✠ Ecgheard presbiter.
✠ Tidberht presbiter.
✠ Alhmund presbiter.
✠ Wigberht presbiter.
✠ Hwita presbiter.
✠ Beorhred presbiter.
✠ Hunlaf presbiter.
✠ Cynemund presbiter.
✠ Byrnhelm presbiter.
✠ Heaðoberht presbiter.
✠ Esne presbiter.
✠ Preost presbiter.
✠ Dudeman presbiter.
✠ Eadberht presbiter.
✠ Monnel presbiter.
✠ Beornwald presbiter.
✠ Berhthelm diaconus.
✠ Wighelm diaconus.
✠ Cynemund diaconus.
✠ Ceofa diaconus.
✠ Dynne diaconus.

KING BEORNWULF OF MERCIA. DCCC.XXV.

✠ In nomine Trino divino, qui est Deus benedictus in sæcula. Amen. Ðȳ gere ðe wes from Cristes gebyrde agān eahtahund wintra ⁊ xxv. ⁊ sio æfterre indictio[1] wæs in rīme· ⁊ wæs Biornwulfes rice Mercna cyninges· ða wæs sionoðlic gemōt on ðære mæran stowe ðe mon hateð Clofeshoas· ⁊ ðær se siolfa cyning Biornwulf ond his biscopas ond his aldormenn ond alle ða wioton ðisse ðiode ðær gesomnade wæron. Ðа wæs tiolo micel sprec ymb wudu leswe to Suðtune ongægum west on Scyrhylte. Waldon ða swangerefan ða læswe forður gedrifan· ond ðone wudu geþicgan ðonne hit aldgeryhto weron. Ðonne cuæð se biscop ⁊ ðara hina wiotan þet hio him neren maran ondeta þonne hit aræded wæs on Æðelbaldes dæge þrim hund swīna mæst· ond se biscop þa tugen ahten twæde þæs wuda ond þæs mæstes. Ða geræhte Wulfred arcebiscop ond alle þa wiotan þet se biscop ond þa higen mosten mid aðe gecyðan þet hit sua wære aræden on Æðel-

✠ In nomine Trino divino, qui est Deus benedictus in sæcula. Amen. In the year that was agone from Christ's birth eight hundred and xxv. winters, and the Indiction was the [1]second in number, and it was the reign of Beornwulf king of the Mercians, then there was a synodal meeting in the famed place which is called Clovesho. And there the same king Beornwulf and his bishops, and his aldormen, and all the 'witan' of this nation were assembled. Then there was very great speech about the wood-pasture at Sutton towards the west in Shireholt. The swain-reeves would drive the pasture further, and feed off the wood further than the old rights extended. Then said the bishop and the [2]witnesses of the convent, that they were liable to him for no more than had been decided in Æthelbald's time, viz. mast for three hundred swine; and the bishop and the convent held two parts of the wood and the mast. Then archbishop Wulfred and all the 'witan'

[1] The Indiction for 825 is 3.

[2] Or wise men.

baldes dæge· ond him mare to ne sohte. Ond he þa sona se biscop beweddade Eadwulfe þæm aldormen þæs aðæs biforan allum þæm wiotum· ond hine mon þonne gelædde ymb xxx. næhta to þæm biscopstole et Wiogærnaceastre. In þa tiid wæs Hama swangerefa to Suðtune· ond he rād þæt he wæs et ceastre· ⁊ þone aað gesæh· ond gesceawade sua hine his aldormon het Eadwulf· ond he hine hweðre ne grette.

directed, that the bishop and the convent must declare on oath, that it was so decided in Æthelbald's day, and that they did not seek for more. And he the bishop then forthwith engaged to Eadwulf the aldorman to make oath before all the 'witan'; and they then led him, about xxx. nights after, to the episcopal see at Worcester. At that time Hama was swain-reeve at Sutton; and he rode so that he was at Worcester and saw and beheld the oath, as his aldorman Eadwulf commanded him; and yet he did not greet him.

Hii sunt nomina et vocabula qui in synodali concilio fuerunt congregati.

✠ Signum manus Biornwulfi regis Merciorum. ✠ Wulfred archiepiscopus consensi hanc conditionem. ✠ Œðelwald episcopus consensi. ✠ Hræðhun episcopus consensi. ✠ Heaberht episcopus consensi. ✠ Bionna episcopus consensi. ✠ Eadwulf episcopus consensi. ✠ Wilred episcopus consensi. ✠ Wigðegn episcopus consensi. ✠ Alhstan episcopus consensi. ✠ Humberht episcopus. ✠ Ceolberht episcopus. ✠ Cynred episcopus. ✠ Torhthelm prior. ✠ Eanmund abbas. ✠ Wihtred abbas. ✠ Cuðwulf abbas. ✠ Eanmund abbas. ✠ Eadberht dux. ✠ Biornnoð dux. ✠ Sigered dux. ✠ Cuðred dux. ✠ Eadwulf dux. ✠ Mucel dux. ✠ Uhtred dux. ✠ Alhheard dux. ✠ Bolam. ✠ Aldran. ✠ Bynna. ✠ Wighelm. ✠ Heabert. ✠ Eadgar presbiter. ✠ Wigberht presbiter. ✠ Heahstæf presbiter. ✠ Brada presbiter. ✠ Cuðbald presbiter. ✠ Regengar presbiter. ✠ Cuðbert presbiter. ✠ Ecgmund presbiter. ✠ Heahferhð diaconus. ✠ Wighelm diaconus. ✠ Cyneberht diaconus.

mid allra oðerra priosta butan ðissum mæssepriostum· efen LX.	With all the other priests, except these mass-priests, just LX.

ARCHBISHOP WULFRED. DCCC.XXV.

✠ In nomine Domini. Anno ab incarnatione Christi DCCC.XXV., Indictione tertia, anno secundo regni Beornulfi regis Merciorum, synodus fuit ad Clobe[s]ham, præsidente archiepiscopo Wulfredo; post mortem vero Cœnulfi regis Merciorum multe discordie et innumerabiles dissonanciæ extollebantur contra uniuscujusque principalium personarum, regum, et episcoporum, et pastorum ecclesiarum Dei, erga plurima secularia negotia; ita ut multum dispoliate fuerant per loca diversa ecclesie Christi, in rebus, in terris, in tributo, in omnibus causis . . . . ea episcopus Australium Saxonum Cœnredus fuerat spoliatus de aliqua parte terre illius XXV. ecclesie que vocitatur Deanton, quod Plegheard abbas dudum tradidit ad sedem episcopalem que est in Selesegh, cum corpore suo, quod ei rex Offa ante condonaverat et conscripserat de hereditate ecclesie Bedingehommes, quam ipse sibi adquisierat in hereditatem propriam. Tunc in præfata synodo. judicatum est, ut ille episcopus, cum consensu et unanimi consilio episcoporum et abbatum seu principum, in jus proprium ecclesie, hereditatem sine ullo obstaculo accipiat; sicut et ante prius at Cælchyðe judicatum est inter Cœnulfum regem et Weðunum de ejusdem terre assumptione, coram archiepiscopo Æðilheardo, tertio anno Cœnulfi regis. Et hec acta sunt coram omni concilio at Clobeshom, cum consensu et licentia regis et principum et archiepiscoporum, quorum nomina infra annotantur, et cum signo sancte crucis Christi impresserunt et confirmaverunt.

Ego Wulfredus archiepiscopus signum Salvatoris pro ampliore firmitate conscribo et confirmo has testimoniæ causas ✠.

Aðelwal[d] episcopus ✠. Ceobberht episcopus ✠. Redunin episcopus ✠. Eaðberht episcopus ✠. Eadulf episcopus ✠. Wihtred abbas ✠. Syred dux ✠. Eadwlf dux ✠. Eadberht dux ✠. Ealhstan ✠. Ealdred ✠. Eadbald ✠. Si quis vero, quod absit, hanc munificentiam frangere temptaverit, sciat se anathematizatum [et] ab omni sinodali societate separatum, nisi ante satisfactione Deo et hominibus emendaverit.

ARCHBISHOP WULFRED. DCCC.XXV.

✠ Anno vero Dominicae incarnationis DCCC.XXV., Indict. IIIª, de diversis Saxoniae partibus congregatum est synodale concilium in loco preclaro quæ nominatur æt Clofeshoum, præsidente autem huic venerabili concilio Uulfredo arcepiscopo, anno XX° episcopatus sui; seu etiam Beornuulfo regi Merciorum, anno III° regni ejus, cæterisque episcopis et abbatibus, necnon et ducibus, omniumque dignitatum optimatibus, ecclesiasticarum vel sæcularium personum, ecclesiarum Dei utilitatem et necessitatem tractantes atque scrutantes, monasterialisque vitæ regulam et observantiam, seu etiam generositatem stabilitatemque regni terrestris consiliantes ac quærentes. Inter ea etiam ab omnibus illic in eadem synodo residentibus trutinatum ac quæsitum fuerat: Quis cum justitia et æquitate conservatus fuisset; quis autem cum injustitia et violentia fraudatus dispoliatusque in sua persona fieret. Tandundem vero inter aliarum allocutionum verba patefactum est, quod præfatus archiepiscopus Uulfredus, per inimicitiam et violentiam avaritiamque Coenwulfi regis, sive quae hic in nostra propria gente peracta sunt, seu etiam ultra mare ad illam apostolicam sedem, per ejus jussionem et inmissionem adlata sunt. Hoc est vero quod in testimonio totius populi omni dominatione propria privatus est, vel in his liberis monasteriis aet Suðmynstre ⁊ æt Ræculfo omnibus rebus ac possessionibus quæ ad illos pertinebant cum violentia ac rapacitate ejusdem præfatæ regis despoliatus est.

Nec ille solus episcopus his aliisque rebus perplurimis inhonoratus fuisset, sed per eadem supradictas accussationes et discordias tota gens Ancglorum VI. ferme annorum curricula sua primordiali auctoritate sacræque baptismatis ministerio privata est; postea etiam ille prædictus rex Coenwulf cum suis sapientibus ad regalem villam Lundoniæ perveniens ad hoc eodemque concilio illum archiepiscopum cum suo foedu foenoreque principum suorum invitabat. Tuncque in eodem concilio cum maxima districtione illo episcopo mandavit quod omnibus rebus quæ illius dominationis sunt disspoliatus debuisset fieri, omnique de patria ista esse profugus, et numquam nec verbis domne papæ nec cæsaris, seu alterius alicujus gradu huc in patriam iterum recipisse, nisi hoc consentire voluisset, hoc est quod illam terram æt Iogneshomme ccc. manent. reddidisset, istamque pecuniam tradidisset c.xx. librarum. Sed et ille episcopus hanc reconciliationem diu recussans, spontaneaque voluntate omnino insons nolens consentire, sed tamen tantundem præ ista supradicta increpatione rapacitatis et fuge coactus, hac condicione hanc reconciliationem sic invitus consensit, ut omni potestate obedientiaque, quæ ad illius episcopalem sedem pertinebant juxta auctoritatem gradus ejus dignus fuisset, sicut prædecessores ejus juxta justam ordinem in pristinis temporibus ante per omnia habuerant. Sed et hocque ille rex Coenwulf illo episcopo reconciliavit, ut omnium supradictarum sucggillationum discordiarumque insontem et securum contra domne papan fecisset; aut si hoc facere non potuisset, illam pecuniam quam ei dedisset iterum episcopo omnia reddidisset. Sed nihil hujus condicte condicionis impletum est. Sed hæc continua omnia fallata sunt, quia post eadem reconciliationem tribus annis integris æt Suðmynstre, tam in pastu et pecunia vestimentisque, ac omni oboedientia quae ad illam archiepiscopalem sedem pertinebat, sine omni honore fraudatus est; aliisque in locis perplurimis illius parochiae inhonoratus est. Postea vero contigit ut in temporibus prædicti Beornwulfi regis ad illamque praenominatam synodum aet Clofeshoum, ille archiepiscopus Uulfred Cwoenðryðam abbt. heredem Coenwulfi cum eadem hereditate illius invitabat, emendationemque sibi omnium supradictarum molestiarum injuriarumque postulavit, quas ille idem rex Coenwulf sibi et ecclesiae Xp̃i ac porochiae ejus iniqua pravitate perpetrasset. Tunc vero omnis ille synodus ad æquitatem invenerunt, huncque judicium unanimo consensu constituerunt, quod illi episcopo reddere omnia debuisset quod violentia abstulerat, in omnibus rebus quibus cum aliqua injuria in omni spatio illa spoliata fuerat, et alteram similem partem ad hoc ipsum adjecisse, et omnem usum emendasse qui in ipsa spatio confracta fuerat. Postea autem placuit Beornwulfo regi, pro amicitia hereditatis Coenwulfi regis heredesque illius, cum suis sapientibus, illo prænominato archiepiscopo istarum supradictarum rerum reconciliationem et emendationem diligentissime facere decrevisset, humilique præce deposcebat ut huic reconciliatione, pro amore Dei et amicitia illius adnueret, quia hereditas et heres ejus ad intercessorem et ad patronem eum expetivit. Hoc est ut terram c. manent. in quattuor locis suscipere deprecabat: id est æt Hearge, Herefreðing lond, ⁊ æt Wembalea, ⁊ æt Geddincggum. In postremo autem ille prænominatus episcopus illius regis allegationibus accommodans, non tamen spontanea voluntate, sed pro amore Dei et amicabili amicitia illius regis, hanc prædictam reconciliationem consentiendo suscepisset, ut illa abbatissa Cwoenðryð, filia Coenwulfi, heresque illius hanc prædictam terram conputati c. manent. illo archiepiscopo cum propriis et antiquis telligraphis, et cum eadem libertate quam ante habuerat, in perpetuam hereditatem ad habendam et possidendam, postque dies ejus cuicumque ei placuerit dereliquendum tradiderat. Insuper etiam ille Beornwulf rex, cum testimonio consilioque ejusdem synodi, illam terram, que ante non fuerat liberata, hujus prædictae donationis eadem libertate liberabat sicut et altera terra æt Hearge jamdudum liberata fuerat, et in altera kartula conscripta habetur. Sed statim ista prædicta reconciliatio confracta est, quia XII. mensibus istius praenominati terræ III. manentes abstracte sunt, librosque XLVII. manent. in tribus locis reddita non fuerunt: hoc est æt Boclonde, ⁊ æt Wembalea, ⁊ æt Herefreðing londe. Iterumque, secundo anno postquam hæc omnia ita peracta sunt, hæc eadem abbt.

illius episcopi colloquium flagitabat, eumque in provincia Hwicciorum expetivit, illo in loco quæ nominatur Oslafeshlau, eique suam insipientiam confessa est retardate reconciliationis; hoc est illius terræ quam ante negaberat; tuncque in eodem loco episcopus, illa abbt̃. præsente, exponebat quod ille omnium antiquorum causarum quas ante reconciliaverunt liberatus fuisset, cum illa perfecta non fuerunt quæ ante spondata habuisset. Tum autem illa abbt. cum omni humilitate promiserat, ut omne quod ei reddita non fuerat cum omni devotione diligentissimæ emendare voluisset: quosdamque libros, quos ante non habebat, in eodem concilio illi reddebat; agellum quoque IIII. manent̃., pro ejus amabili amicitia, ad illam prænominatam terram æt Hearge donabit. Similiter etiam et in provincia Cantiæ XXX. manent̃. terram, ubi dicitur æt Cumbe, cum ejusdem libellis, ad emendationem illi in sempiternam hereditatem donasset, ut ista prædicta reconciliatio stabilis firmaque permaneret; ut omnis hereditas Coenwulfi heredesque illius firmaliter sint liberati. Tuncque episcopus hoc idem consensit, hac condicione, ut illorum prædictorum agellorum nomina de antiquis privilegiis quæ sunt æt Wincelcumbe eradati fuerint, iterumque in posterum non sunt prolati. Si autem iterum aliqua altercatio ab alicui herede Coenwulfi inposterum elata fuerit, absque omni dubitatione sciat me liberum esse measque heredes ⁊ ecclesiam Xp̃i justitiam et emendationem ad heredem illam requirere, omniaque suprascripta injuria inreconciliata permanere. Hæc sunt autem nomina illorum hominum quae ex alia parte conscribuntur, qui cum totius synodalis auctoritate hujus reconciliationis testes adfuerunt, et signo sc̃æ crucis Xp̃i propriis manibus conscripserunt.

✠ Ego Cwoenðryð abb. hanc reconciliationem propriis manibus, cum signo sc̃æ crucis Xp̃i, robor̃. ⁊ sub.

✠ Ego Beornwulf rex Merc̃. cum signo sc̃æ crucis Xp̃i confirmabo ⁊ sub.

✠ Ego Uulfredus gratia Dei arc̃episc̃. hanc eadem reconciliationem cum signo sc̃æ crucis Xp̃i rob. ⁊ sub.

✠ Ego Aeðelwald episc̃. cons̃. ⁊ sub.

✠ Ego Reðhun episc̃. cons̃. ⁊ sub.

✠ Ego Eadwulf episc̃. cons̃. ⁊ suƀ.
✠ Ego Haeberht episc̃. cons̃. ⁊ suƀ.
✠ Ego Beornmod episc̃. cons̃. ⁊ suƀ.
✠ Ego Beonna episc̃. cons̃. ⁊ suƀ.
✠ Ego Wigðægn episc̃. cons̃. ⁊ suƀ.
✠ Ego Alhstan episc̃. cons̃. ⁊ suƀ.
✠ Ego Humberht episc̃. cons̃. ⁊ suƀ.
✠ Ego Willred electus cons̃. ⁊ suƀ.
✠ Ego Ceolberht episc̃. cons̃. ⁊ suƀ.
✠ Ego Cynred episc̃. cons̃. ⁊ suƀ.
✠ Ego Cuðwulf pr̃ aƀƀ. cons̃. ⁊ suƀ.
✠ Ego Willferð pr̃ aƀƀ. cons̃. ⁊ suƀ.
✠ Ego Eanmund aƀƀ. cons̃. ⁊ suƀ.
✠ Ego Eanmund pr̃ aƀƀ. cons̃. ⁊ suƀ.
✠ Ego Torhthelm prior cons̃. ⁊ suƀ.
✠ Ego Wiohtred aƀƀ. cons̃. ⁊ suƀ.
✠ Ego Piott pr̃ cons̃. ⁊ suƀ.
✠ Ego Beornnoð dux cons̃. ⁊ suƀ.
✠ Ego Eadberht dux cons̃. ⁊ suƀ.
✠ Ego Eadwulf dux cons̃. ⁊ suƀ.
✠ Ego Ecgberht dux cons̃. ⁊ suƀ.
✠ Ego Alchhard dux cons̃. ⁊ suƀ.
✠ Ego Cyneberht dux cons̃. ⁊ suƀ.
✠ Ego Sigered dux cons̃. ⁊ suƀ.
✠ Ego Mucel dux cons̃. ⁊ suƀ.
✠ Ego Cuðred dux cons̃. ⁊ suƀ.
✠ Ego Eadwulf dux cons̃. ⁊ suƀ.
✠ Ego Wulfred dux cons̃. ⁊ suƀ.
✠ Ego Bynna fr̃ regis cons̃. ⁊ suƀ.
✠ Ego Aldred cons̃. ⁊ suƀ.
✠ Ego Wighelm cons̃. ⁊ suƀ.
✠ Ego Aldred cons̃. ⁊ suƀ.
✠ Ego Bola pedisecus cons̃. ⁊ suƀ.
✠ Ego Alhstan cons̃. ⁊ suƀ.
✠ Ego Eadbald cons̃. ⁊ suƀ.
✠ Ego Feologeld pr̃ aƀƀ. cons̃. ⁊ suƀ.
✠ Ego Oswulf pr̃ cons̃. ⁊ suƀ.
✠ Ego Hunferð pr̃ cons̃. ⁊ suƀ.

✠ Ego Coena pr̃ cons̃. ⁊ sub̃.
✠ Ego Osmund pr̃ cons̃. ⁊ sub̃.
✠ Ego Tudda pr̃ cons̃. ⁊ sub̃.
✠ Ego Brunhard pr̃ cons̃. ⁊ sub̃.
✠ Ego Deornoð pr̃ cons̃. ⁊ sub̃.
✠ Ego Bægmund pr̃ cons̃. ⁊ sub̃.
✠ Ego Hunred pr̃ cons̃. ⁊ sub̃.
✠ Ego Cynehard diac̃. cons̃. ⁊ sub̃.
✠ Ego Wigmund diac̃. cons̃. ⁊ sub̃.
✠ Ego Dægmund diac̃. cons̃. ⁊ sub̃.
✠ Ego Wihtred pr̃ cons̃. ⁊ sub̃.
✠ Ego Wærhard cons̃. ⁊ sub̃.
✠ Ego Eadwulf pr̃ cons̃. ⁊ sub̃.
✠ Ego Duda cons̃. ⁊ sub̃.
✠ Ego Coenhard cons̃. ⁊ sub̃.
✠ Ego Alhhere cons̃. ⁊ sub̃.
✠ Ego Aelfgyð cons̃. ⁊ sub̃.
✠ Ego Beonne cons̃. ⁊ sub̃.
✠ Ego Bægswið cons̃. ⁊ sub̃.
✠ Ego Aloburg cons̃. ⁊ sub̃.
✠ Ego Exgburg cons̃. ⁊ sub̃.

KING ÆTHELWULF OF KENT. DCCC.XXVII.

Regnante eternaliter Rege omnium seculorum Domino et Salvatore nostro Jhesu Christo. Orbita labentis seculi cotidiano deficit occasu. Hoc quoque indicio fideles quique opido commonentur quo bonorum operum exempla sectantes patrum in benivolencie proficiendo successu, temporalium vicissitudine bonorum, perpetua et incommutabilia regni celorum mereantur adipisci gaudia sine termino permansura. Quapropter ego Æthelwlfus rex, favente Dei Omnipotentis clemencia, omnes terras, villas, possessiones, prata, pascua, ad quoddam monasterium, quod sub nomine sancte Trinitatis et apostolorum principis Petri constat honore dedicatum, quod famoso apud Anglos nuncupatur Certeseg onomate, omniaque ad idem monasterium rite pertinencia, ejusque familie venerande sub custodia primorum regulariter cum metu Christi degencium, videlicet ad sustentacionem illius cenobii, pro amore Christi, libenti animo concedo et confirmo, quo illic unanimiter Domino servientes pro meis non desistant intervenire peccaminibus atque offensionibus innumeris. Hoc etiam in ista donacionis et confirmacionis cartula, ut si aliquando aliquis, quod absit, suasione diabolica vel avaricie fascibus accensus, regum successorum, in magno vel in modico, vi vel voluntate, minuere temptaverit, sciat se a Christi consorcio et omnium sanctorum separatum, et cum Iuda traditore in inferno inferiori dampnatum, nisi ante satisfactione digna plenerrime emendaverit. Acta est hec præfata donacio et confirmacio anno ab incarnatione Domini DCCC.XXVII. hiis consencientibus:

Ego Ætheluulfus rex hanc libertatis donacionem et confirmacionem vexillo sancte crucis subscribo et confirmo ✠. Ego Swithunus episcopus Wintonie subscribo ✠. Ego Æthelstanus episcopus Syreburnie subscribo ✠. Ego Hunfridus abbas subscribo ✠. Ego Osmundus presbiter subscribo ✠.

KING ECGBERHT. DCCC.XXVIII.

✠ In nomine Domini nostri Jhesu Christi, Ego Ecgbertus gratia Dei rex Anglorum, cum consensu episcoporum ac principum meorum, hanc libertatem donabi ecclesiæ quæ sita est in civitate Hrobi, et omnibus agellis quæ ad ecclesiam Sancti Andreæ apostoli pertinent, pro remedio animæ meæ et filii nostri Ætheluulfi, quem regem constituimus in Cantia, ut omnes agros sint libera ab omni regali servitio, a pastu regum et principum, ducum et præfectum, exactorumque, ab equorum et falconum accipitrumque et canum acceptione, et illorum hominum refectione, quod nos festingmenn nominamus, a parafrithis, et ab omnibus difficultatibus regalis vel sæcularis servitutis, notis et ignotis, cum furis comprehensione, intus et foris, majoris minorisve, præter pontis constructione, et expeditione, eternaliter liberata permaneat. Hanc libertatem prædictæ ecclesiæ donabi pro humili obedientia venerabilis episcopi Beornmodi, et pro amore apostoli Sancti Andreæ, et beati Paulini archiepiscopi, cujus corpus in prædicta ecclesia requiescit; sic etiam omnibus successoribus vel heredibus meis; necnon cuicunque gradu regibus seu principibus, in nomine sanctæ Trinitatis, et per tremendum Dei judicium, præcipio, ut hæc donatio mea firma et inlabata inconcussaque permaneat. Si quis vero hoc benivola mente observare voluerit, servetur ei benedictio sempiterna hic in eternum; si autem, quod absit, aliquis insurrexerit, tyrannica potestate fretus, seu diabolica temeritate instigatus, qui hanc libertatem infringere aut minuere, vel in aliut convertere temptaverit quam a nobis constitutum est, sciat se separatum a communione sanctæ Dei ecclesiæ, et a participatione omnium sanctorum Dei, et eternis ignibus esse nodatum, nisi prius digne et perfecte hic in sæculo emendare voluerit. Scripta est hæc cartula anno dominicæ incarnationis DCCC.XXVIII., Indictione VI., his testibus consentientibus et signo sanctæ crucis Christi confirmantibus, quorum nomina infra tenentur ascripta:

✠ Ego Ecgbertus rex Anglorum hanc donationem meam hujus libertatis signo sanctæ crucis Christi confirmavi et subscripsi. ✠ Ego Atheluulf rex consensi et subscripsi. ✠ Ego Wulfred archiepiscopus consensi et subscripsi. ✠ Ego Wigðegn episcopus consensi et subscripsi. ✠ Ego Ealhstan episcopus subscripsi et consensi. ✠ Ego Beornmod episcopus consensi et subscripsi. ✠ Ego Wulfhard dux consensi et subscripsi. ✠ Ego Monnede dux consensi et subscripsi. ✠ Ego Osmod dux consensi et subscripsi. ✠ Ego Dudda dux consensi et subscripsi. ✠ Ego Aldred consensi et subscripsi. ✠ Ego Oshere consensi et subscripsi. ✠ Ego Æthelwulf consensi et subscripsi. ✠ Ego Duduc consensi et subscripsi. ✠ Ego Boba consensi et subscripsi. ✠ Ego Ealhhere consensi et subscripsi. ✠ Ego Sigesteb consensi et subscripsi. ✠ Ego Aðelhard consensi et subscripsi.

* KING WIGLÂF OF MERCIA. MAY 26TH DCCC.XXXIII.

Witlafius dispositione divina rex Merciorum, omnibus Christicolis universam Merciam inhabitantibus salutem sempiternam. Magnalia Dei prædicare et publicare minime mihi verecundum, sed vere videtur honorificum et gloriosum; unde aperte confiteor Domino qui in altis habitat, humilia respiciens in cælo et in terra, quoniam ad tempus iratus est mihi, conversus est furor suus, et consolatus est me, humilians in ira sua peccatorem usque ad terram, detrahens usque ad pulverem, et iterum in misericordia sua suscitans de pulvere egenum, et de stercore erigens pauperem, ut sedeam cum principibus, et solium gloriæ teneam. In die igitur bonorum ne immemor sim malorum, memor ero Rahab et Babilonis; scientium me non Rahab meretricis, sed Etheldrithæ sanctissimæ virginis, cognatæ meæ, pro sponsi sui agni immaculati amore Croylandiæ reclusæ, et in tempore tribulationis meæ me in cella sua quatuor mensium spatio diligentissime abscondentis a facie inimici et persequentis; memor etiam ero Babilonis, non turris confusionis, sed sanctissimæ ecclesiæ Croylandensis, quæ terra turris ad cælum ascendens, vigiliis et orationibus, psalmis et lectionibus, disciplinis et afflictionibus, lachrimis et singultibus, eleemosinis et innumeris aliis devotionibus pietatisque officiis, pro sæculo peccatore fortissimam violentiam regno cælorum ingerit die ac nocte. Itaque quoniam venerabilis pater dominus Siwardus abbas Croylandiæ protexit me in tabernaculo suo in die malorum, celans et salvans a facie tribulantis, ultra privilegia meorum antecessorum regum Merciorum, qui prædictum monasterium variis libertatibus et donariis nobiliter illustrarunt, offero et ego magno altari prædicti monasterii, de paupertate mea, calicem aureum, crucem auream, et tabulam capellæ propriæ laminis aureis deauratam, me profitens dictæ ecclesiæ perpetuum pro viribus defensorem. Insuper præcipio omnibus ministris meis per universam Merciam constitutis, quod abbati Croylandiæ, monachis, et omnibus fratribus illius sanctissimi monasterii, cum ad civitates et castella regia pro quocunque negotio accesserint, tanquam Wimundo filio meo, vel mihi, obediant in omnibus et ministrent, nihil pro expensis, quas ipsi vel sui fecerint ibidem, ab eis accipientes, sed cum litera vel signo dictorum monachorum, archarius meus expensas omnes hujusmodi, cum dicti ministri mei annumeraverint, pro fisco integre acceptabit.

Volo etiam et præcipio, quod quicunque in regno meo, pro quocunque delicto, reus inventus et legibus obnoxius fuerit, si fugerit ad dictum monasterium, et coram abbate dicti monasterii qui pro tempore fuerit, gratiam sanctissimi confessoris Guthlaci ibidem corporaliter quiescentis invocans, fidelitatem ei et servitium juraverit sempiternum, salvus et securus sub protectione abbatis et monachorum suorum, in quocunque servitio, per totam insulam Croylandiæ ipsum posuerint, sicut in asylo, vel in camera mea propria, pace mea et impunitate gaudeat, nullusque ministrorum meorum ultra ipsum insequi audeat, nec in aliquo molestare, sub pæna perditionis dextri sui pedis, quicunque de meo regno istud meum privilegium tentaverit in aliquo violare. Licebitque dicto fugitivo, in quibusque aquis quæ dictam insulam ambiunt, navigare et piscari, ac aliter, quomodocumque a dominis suis assignatus fuerit laborare, absque ministrorum meorum vel alicujus alterius calumnia vel gravamine. Quod si extra dictas aquas vel metas dicti monasterii captus aliquando fuerit, pænam quam quondam meruit, sive mortem, sive membrorum suorum mutilationem, si ministri mei, vel quicumque sui adversarii, per juramentum sex hominum fide dignorum, probare poterunt, quod extra metas suas inventus fuerit, absque ulla gratia sustinebit. Dictas vero metas monasterii Croyland, in quinque ejus aquas prædictas tam ministris meis, quam abbati et monachis suis, pro suis dictis fugitivis, describi feci et notari. Dictæ namque aquæ vocantur istis nominibus, videlicet Shepshee ad orientem, in cujus ripa occidentali crux lignea stat vetusta, et distat ab ipsa aqua per decem pedes, æqualiter posita in medio inter duos angulos ejusdem insulæ, scilicet Aswictoft, qui est angulus et meta dictæ insulæ contra vulturnum, et Tedwarker, qui est angulus et meta dictæ insulæ contra subsolanum. Secunda aqua, quæ claudit dictam insulam ad austrum, vocatur Southee, in cujus ripa posita est crux lapidea, distans a Namanlandhirne per quinque perticatas, et a Southee per sex perticatas, ubi Southee intrat in aquam de Nene quæ currit ad pontem de Croyland: sed metæ fugitivorum in illa parte diriguntur in mariscum occidentale per Einfet contra affricum, et sic usque ad Folwardstaking contra chorum, et sic divertendo ad boream, ubi Southlake intrat in aquam de Weland ex opposito lapideæ crucis, quæ stat in boreali ripa dictæ aquæ de Weland, distans ab ipsa aqua per quinque pedes, quæ currit inde ad prædictum pontem de Croyland: sed metæ fugitivorum ab illa cruce diriguntur in mariscum boreale directe usque ad Oggot, qui est angulus metarum contra favonium, et sic redeundo versus orientem per Wodelade usque ad Apinholt, et ibi ascendendo per aquam de Weland, quæ est quarta aqua claudens insulam in illa parte, sicut tertia aqua de Nene claudit eam ex altera parte pontis de Croyland, usque ad Seweram de Asendick, cadentis in Weland, ubi stans fracta crux lapidea distat ab ipsa aqua de Asendick [per tres perticatas in ejus ripa australi; et ipsa aqua de Asendyk] [1] est quinta aqua claudens ab illo loco insulam prædictam contra aquilonem usque ad Aswictoft. Si extra istas quinque aquas et metas prænominatas fugitivus inventus fuerit, tanquam Semei extra Jerusalem, publicis legibus subjiciendus, pænam quam meruit patietur. Quod si intra prædictas aquas et metas, et prædictarum aquarum ripas exteriores, homicidium, furtum, vel aliam forisfacturam fecerit, per balivos dicti monasterii capiendus juxta [demerita] [1] in ipsa insula, cujus immunitatem perdidit, patietur, et ibidem judicandus in carcere abbatis condemnabitur. Et ut istud meum privilegium firmius et fortius ad posteros perseveret, per dominum meum Egbertum regem West Saxoniæ, et Athelwlfum filium ejus illud obtinui confirmari.

Offero etiam secretario dicti monasterii, in ministerium sanctissimi altaris, clamidem coccineam, qua indutus eram in coronatione mea, ad capam inde sive casulam faciendam, et in ecclesiæ sanctissimæ ornamentum, velum meum aureum quo inciditur excidium Troiæ, in meo anniversario, si placuerit, in

[1] Wanting in MS.

parietibus suspendendum. Offero etiam refectorario dicti monasterii, ad usum præsidentis quotidie in refectorio, cyphum meum deauratum, et per totam partem exteriorem barbaris victoribus[1] ad dracones pugnantibus celatum, quem crucibolum meum solitus sum vocare, quia signum crucis per transversum ciphi imprimitur interius, cum quatuor angulis simili impressione protuberantibus; et cornu meæ mensæ, ut senes monasterii bibant inde in festis sanctorum, et in suis benedictionibus meminerint aliquando animæ Witlafii donatoris.

Confirmo etiam dicto monasterio omnes terras et tenementa, possessiones, et earum peculia, et omnia alia donaria, quæ prædecessores mei, reges Merciorum, et eorum proceres, vel alii fideles Christiani, sive Judei, dictis monachis dederunt, vendiderunt, vel invadiaverunt, aut aliquo alio modo in perpetuam possessionem tradiderunt; et specialiter donum Thoroldi quondam vicecomitis Lincolniæ in Bokenhale, videlicet, duas carucatas terræ et dimidiam, et viginti sex acras prati, et quinquaginta acras sylvæ, [et LXX. acras][2] de Brushæ. Item donum Geolphi filii Malte in Halington, videlicet, quatuor bovatas terræ de innland[3], et decem bovatas in servitio, et triginta quatuor acras prati in Gernthorp. Item donum Fregisti militis, videlicet, totam villam de Langtoft, et in campis ejusdem villæ sex carucatas terræ arabilis, habentes in longitudine XV. quarentenas, et IX. quarentenas in latitudine; et centum acras prati, et silvam et mariscum duarum leucarum in longitudine, et duarum leucarum in latitudine. Et ecclesiam ejusdem villæ, et XL. acras de eodem feodo in campo de Depyng. Item donum Algari militis, scilicet Northlang in Baston, videlicet, quatuor carucatas terræ arabilis, continentes in longitudine octo quarentenas, et VIII. quarentenas in latitudine, et XLV. acras prati, et mariscum continens in longitudine sexdecem quarentenas, et VIII. quarentenas in latitudine, et ecclesiam ejusdem villæ, et unum molendinum, et dimidium alterius molendini, et totam piscariam in aqua a molendino versus occidens usque ad finem marisci ejusdem

[1] vinitoribus. *Ingulf.*

[2] Wanting in MS.

[3] MS. Luland, *Ingulf*, Iuland.

villæ versus orientem. Item donum ejusdem Algari militis in Repingale, videlicet, tres carucatas terræ arabilis, et XL. acras prati. Item donum Normanni quondam vicecomitis in Sutton juxta Bosworth, duas carucatas terræ, et unum molendinum ventricium. Item donum ejusdem Normanni in Stapelton, videlicet, manerium et duas carucatas terræ. Item donum ejusdem in Badby, videlicet, quatuor hidas terræ cum appendiciis. Item donum domini Algari comitis in Holbeche, et in Cappelade, videlicet, quatuor carucatas, et sex bovatas, et XVIII. acras prati, et mariscum. Item donum ejusdem in villa sua de Spaldeling, videlicet, tres carucatas prati. [Item donum ejusdem in villa sua de Pyncebek, videlicet, unam carucatam terræ. Item donum ejusdem in Algarkirke villa sua, videlicet, undecim bovatas terræ; et in parochia de Sutterton tres carucatas terræ, et unam bovatam, et XXVI. acras prati,][1] et IIII. salinas, cum ecclesia ejusdem villæ. Item donum Oswii militis in Draitona, videlicet, octo hidas terræ, et IIII. virgatas, et ecclesiam ejusdem villæ. Item donum Asketelli coqui mei in Glapthorn[2], videlicet, tres virgatas terræ. Item donum Wulgeti pincernæ mei, in Peiekirk, tres virgatas terræ. Item donum [Edulphi][1] nuncii mei, in Laithorp, unam bovatam terræ. Item donum Siwardi vicecomitis, in Kirkby, tres bovatas terræ, unam mansionem, et tria cotagia. Et in Standona donum Sigburgæ comitissæ, v. hidas terræ. Et donum Wulnoti dapifieri mei, in Adingtona, videlicet, duas hidas terræ, et piscariam, cum advocatione ecclesiæ ejusdem villæ; et in alia Adingtona, ex dono ejusdem, unam virgatam terræ. Istas terras et tenementa prædicto monasterio Croylandiæ, et monachis ibidem Deo servientibus, in pacificam et perpetuam possessionem concedo, trado, et confirmo, habenda de me et hæredibus meis quibuscunque regibus Merciorum post me successuris, in puram et perpetuam eleemosinam libere, quiete, et solute ab omnibus oneribus sæcularibus, exactionibus, et vectigalibus universis, quocumque nomine censeantur. Quod si quis adversarius, instigante diabolo, in quibuscunque prædictis terris aut tenementis, tot regum spatio pacifice possessis, et eorum

[1] Wanting in MS. [2] MS. Glaphton.

auctoritate confirmatis, calumniam ponere voluerit in futurum, me et successores meos, reges Merciorum, profiteor præsenti chirographo, et polliceor, dicti monasterii futuros in perpetuum defensores.

✠ Istud chirographum domino Siwardo abbati meo patri, et Etheldrithæ sanctissimæ virgini, pro Christi amore ibidem reclusæ, carne quidem cognatæ meæ, sed, quod majus est, in Christo charissimæ sorori, quondam promissum, in præsentia dominorum meorum Egberti regis West Saxoniæ et Athelwulphi filii ejus, coram pontificibus et proceribus majoribus totius Angliæ, in civitate Lundonia ubi omnes congregati sumus pro consilio capiendo contra Danicos piratas Angliæ littora assidue infestantes, signo sanctæ crucis confirmavi. ✠ Ego Celnothus archiepiscopus Dorobornensis consului. ✠ Ego Enbaldus Eboracensis archiepiscopus consignavi. ✠ Ego Osmundus Londoniensis episcopus collaudavi. ✠ Ego Helmstanus episcopus Wintoniensis assensum præbui. ✠ Ego Herewinus Lichfeldensis episcopus consensi. ✠ Ego Cedda Herfordensis episcopus aspiravi. ✠ Ego Adelstanus Shireburnensis episcopus procuravi. ✠ Ego Humbrithus Helmamensis episcopus approbavi. ✠ Ego Wilredus Dommocensis episcopus annui. ✠ Ego Herferdus Wigornensis episcopus gratum habui. ✠ Ego Godwinus Roffensis episcopus favi. ✠ Ego Hedda abbas de Medeshamsted ratificavi. ✠ Ego Ambertus abbas Ripadii interfui. ✠ Ego Kinewinus abbas de Bardinei astiti. ✠ Ego Egbertus rex West Saxoniæ concessi. ✠ Ego Adelwlphus filius regis Uuest Saxoniæ consensum dedi. ✠ Ego Wlhardus dux affui. ✠ Ego Athelmus dux audivi. ✠ Ego Herebrithus dux acceptavi. ✠ Ego Swithinus presbiter regis Egberti præsens fui. ✠ Ego Bosa scriba regis Withlafii manu mea chirographum istud scripsi. ✠ Ego Withlafius Domini nostri Jhesu Christi gratia rex Merciorum, ad sanctæ matris ecclesiæ honorem, et divini cultus exaltationem, anno incarnationis ejusdem nostri Salvatoris D.CCC.XXXIII°, in festo Sancti Augustini confessoris, doctoris, et apostoli nostræ gentis, hæc paucula offero, pluraque offerrem, quin corpus meum in morte mea tam sancto monasterio promitterem, nisi antea sepulturam meam Ripadio devovissem. Veruntamen spiritus meus permanebit vobiscum in æternum.

KING ECGBERHT OF WESSEX. DCCC.XXXV.

✠ In nomine Dei et Domini nostri Jhesu Christi, Redemptoris mundi. Anno Dominice incarnationis D°ccc°xxx°v°, Indiccione XIII., Ego Ecberht rex Occidentalium Saxonum dedi monasterium illud Mercham, quinquaginta manentium, ad Abbendune, cum licentia et consensu tocius nostre gentis et unanimitate omnium optimatum. Hec donatio fuit facta in Pascha in Dorkecestre; et postera vice eandem donationem liberaliter in Natali confirmavimus, anno imperii nostri XXXIIII. Et sic mandamus, in nomine Patris et Filii et Spiritus Sancti, ut nullus superveniat hominum ibi superbia inflatus, nec rex suum pastum requirat, vel habentes homines quos festigmen, nec eos qui accipitres portant vel falcones, vel caballos ducunt sive canes. Nec penam mittere super eos quomodo audeat, nec princeps nec graphio hanc lenitatem prefatam in alicujus oneris molestiam mutare audeat, aut in diebus nostris vel successorum nostrorum. Si pro aliquo delicto accusatur homo Dei, ecclesie ille custos solus cum suo juramento, si audeat, illum castiget. Sin autem, ut recipiat alienam justiciam, hujus vicissitudinis conditionem, præfatum delictum cum simplo precio componat. Quid plura? Ne cui hominum per vim aliquid ibi tribuatur, neque in palefridis, neque in refectiones, sed ab his omnibus liber permaneat. De illa autem tribulatione que witereden nominatur sit libera, nisi tamen singuli precium solverit ut talia accipiant. Fures quoque quos appellant weregeld ðeofas, si foris rapiantur, precium ejus dimidium illi ecclesie, et dimidium regi detur. Et si intus rapitur, totum reddatur ad ecclesiam. Similiter de hereditate peregrinorum, id est Gallorum et Brittonum et horum similium, ecclesie reddatur. Precium quoque sanguinis peregrinorum, id est weregeld, dimidiam partem rex teneat, dimidiam ecclesie antedicte reddant. Silva quoque omnis que illi ecclesie et suburbanis ejus suppetit, in omnibus causis sit libera, et non secetur ibi ad regis vel principis edificia aliqua pars materiæ grossi vel gracilis, sed ab omnibus defensa et libera maneat. Si quis autem præscriptis statutis noluerit obedire, sciat se alienum esse a consortio sancte Dei ecclesie, et a participatione corporis et sanguinis Domini nostri Jhesu Christi, per auctoritatem beati Petri apostoli, nisi digne emendaverit quod contra Dei ecclesiam fecisset.

✠ Ego Ecgbert rex concessi et subscripsi.
✠ Ego Æthelwlf filius regis concessi et subscripsi.
✠ Ego Ælfstan episcopus concessi et subscripsi.
✠ Ego Rethun episcopus concessi et subscripsi.
✠ Ego Kinred episcopus concessi et subscripsi.
✠ Ego Wlflaf abbas concessi et subscripsi.
✠ Ego Eadwald abbas concessi et subscripsi.
✠ Ego Wlfar dux concessi et subscripsi.
✠ Ego Osmod dux concessi et subscripsi.
✠ Ego Wigfred dux consensi et subscripsi.

✠ Et multi alii hanc libertatem præscriptam, cum his testibus infra nominatis, firmiter in Jhesu Christo cum signaculo sancte crucis confirmantes roboravimus.

KING WIGLÂF OF MERCIA. DCCC.XXXVI.

Regnum Dei querendum est super universa lucra terrena, Paulo testante apostolo; quae enim videntur temporalia sunt, sed quæ non videntur aeterna sunt. Quid prodest homini totum mundum lucrare, si anima ejus detrimentum patietur? Quapropter ego Uuiglaf, rex Merciorum, cum meis episcopis et ducibus et magistratibus, illut monasterium in Heanbyrg in circuitu cum silva ad eam pertinentem, et cum campis et pratis et cum omnibus utensilibus et cum putheis salis et fornacibus plumbis, et villis et omnia illuc pertinentia in cœlestem culmen generaliter per totum gentem Merciorum, et pro absolutione criminum nostrorum liberaliter liberamus a modicis et a magnis causis, a notis et ignotis, praeter vallis et pontes constructionem.

Factum est hæc donatio in Craeft, anno Dominicæ incarnationis DCCC°XXX°VI°, Indic̃. vero XIIII°, regni autem nostri a Deo concessi VII°[1], pro redemtione animae meae placabile atque dilectabile mente praedicta loca liberabo, cum universis casallis que ipsis locis universis sunt subditi, hoc modo per aevum liberabo a pastu regis et principum, et ab omni constructione regalis villæ, et a difficultate illa quam nos Saxonice Faestingmenn dicimus, haec omnia mente concedo spontaneo. Scitote ergo vos qui hanc labens regnum post me obtineatis, quare hoc munus et hanc libertatem scripsi et scribere præcepi, quod in Deum meum desidero, et in ejus ineffabilem misericordiam confido, ut Dominus noster Jhesus Christus meas iniquitates quas per ignorantiam feci, Deus delere faciat. Credo per hoc bonum a cunctis me emundare dignetur, quod scriptum est, "Peccatum ibi emenda ubi nascitur," modo posteros meos per gloriosum et præmirabile nomen Domini nostri Jhesu Xp̃i, humiliter supplico ut elemosinam quam in altitudinem caeli culminis in manus Domini datam, habeo communiter pro me et pro totum gentem Merciorum tam benigniter stare demittetis et multiplicare dignemini.

✠ Ego Wiglaf rex Merciorum. ✠ Cyneðryþ regina. ✠ Ceolnoð archiep̃i. ✠ Cyneferð ep̃i. ✠ Raeþhun ep̃i. ✠ Eaduulf ep̃i. ✠ Heaberht ep̃i. ✠ Eaduulf ep̃i. ✠ Alhstan ep̃i. ✠ Beormod ep̃i. ✠ Husa ep̃i. ✠ Cunda ep̃i. ✠ Ceolberht ep̃i. ✠ Cynred ep̃i. ✠ Eanmund ab̃. ✠ Weohtred ab̃. ✠ Beornhelm ab̃. ✠ Ego Sigred dux hanc donationem signo crucis Xp̃i confirmavi. ✠ Mucoel dux. ✠ Tiduulf dux. ✠ Aeþelhard dux. ✠ Cyneberht dux. ✠ Aeþeluulf dux. ✠ Alhhelm dux. ✠ Humberht dux. ✠ Aelfstan dux. ✠ Mucoel dux. ✠ Wicga. ✠ Aldred. ✠ Aldberht. ✠ Aelfred. ✠ Hwithyse. ✠ Werenberht. ✠ Wulfred. ✠ Wiglaf. ✠ Eanuulf. ✠ Alhmund. ✠ Berhtuulf. ✠ Ecghard.

[1] Wiglâf became king in 825, was expelled by the Danes, but restored in 828, which year he seems here to regard as that of his accession.

✠ Ðes friodom waes bigeten aet Wiglafe cyninge mid ðaem tuentigum hida aet Iddeshale· end ðaes londes friodom aet Habecaham mid þy ten hida londe aet Felda bi Waeduman· end Mucele Esninge ðaet ten hida lond aet Crogleage hæbben heora dæg· ⁊ æfter heora dæge agefe mon þæt land into þære halgan stowe into Weogurnacestre.

In dorso. Þis is Heanbirige friodum· se waes bigeten mid þy londe aet Iddeshale· ⁊ aet Heanbyrig ten hida þaes londes· ⁊ aet Felda ten hida on Beansetun· ⁊ biscop gesalde Sigrede aldormenn six hund scillinga on golde· ⁊ Mucele aldormenn ten hida lond æt Crogleage.

✠ This freedom was obtained from king Wiglaf for the twenty hides at Iddeshall; and the freedom of the land at Hawkham for the ten hides of land at Field by Wæduman; and to Mukel Esning the ten hides of land at Crowle; to hold for their day; and after their day, let the land be given up to the holy place in Worcester.

Indorsed. This is the freedom of Hanbury, which was obtained for the land at Iddeshall and ten hides of land at Hanbury, and ten hides at Felda in Beansetan. And the bishop gave to Sigred aldorman six hundred shillings in gold, and to Mukel aldorman ten hides of land at Crowle.

KING BERHTUULF OF MERCIA. MAR. 28TH DCCC.XL.

✠ Alto et agio et omnipotentissimo Deo nostro, ac sanctæ et gloriose Trinitati, virtus honor et potestas sit in perpetuum. Amen. Anno autem ab incarnatione ejusdem Dei et Domini nostri Jhesu Christi DCCC°XL°. Indictione III. contigit autem quod Berhtwlf rex Merciorum tollerat a nobis et tradidit terram nostram quod recte ac jure sub propria potestate ac libera possessione cum firma donatione tradita est et concessa et firmata ad sedem episcopalem, id est, ad Uueogernensem ecclesiam, rex prefatus suobus propriis hominibus condonavit, sicut se inimici homines docuerunt, hoc est, Stoltun, Uuassanburna, Cyneburgingctun, Tateringctun,

Codeswelle. Tunc perrexit ille episcopus Heahberht, cum suis secum senioribus, in Pascha, ad Tomeworðie, et suas libertates et cartulas ante nominatorum terrarum secum habentes, et ibi ante regem ejusque proceres fuerunt allecta, et ibi Merciorum optimates dejudicaverunt illi, ut male ac injuste despoliati essent in suo proprio. Tunc illis terra sua reddita est cum pace, et simul etiam ille episcopus hanc donativum regem perdonavit iterum in Welesburnan: hoc est IIII. caballos bene electos, et unum anulum in XXX. mancusis, et discum fabrefactum in tribus pundis, et duas albas cornas in IIII. libris: et ille regina dedit duos equos bonos, et duas steapas in twæm pundum, et unam cuppam deauratam in duobus pundis. Et tunc rex cum testimonio has terras firmiter liberavit sibi in evum, coram suis archontis, unius cujusque necessitatis et sustulionis, et illud etiam cum signaculo sancte crucis Christi suo manu firmiter roborando scripsit et munivit.

Si quis vero rex, aut princeps, vel alicujus gradus homo, hanc nostram elemosinam et libertatem per diabolicam avaritiam deceptus sit, ut frangere vel minuere temptaverit, sciat se separatum a consortio omnium sanctorum Dei in die magni judicii, ante tribunal Christi, nisi hic Deo et hominibus cum bona satisfactione emendaverit. Et hii testes adfuerant, qui hoc consenserunt et scripserunt, quorum hic nomina in altera plaga cartule flavescunt.

✠ Ego Berhtwulf rex Merciorum hanc meam libertatem et donationem cum vexillo sancte crucis munio, ut fixa permaneat in evum.

✠ Ego Sæðryð regina consensi. ✠ Ego Cyneferð episcopus consensi. ✠ Ego Heaberht episcopus consensi. ✠ Ego Berehtred episcopus consensi. ✠ Ego Cuðwulf episcopus consensi. ✠ Ego Eammund abbud. ✠ Ego Hunberht dux. ✠ Ego Æðelheard dux. ✠ Ego Mucel dux. ✠ Ego Dudda dux. ✠ Ego Cyneberht dux. ✠ Ego Sigered dux. ✠ Ego Æðelwulf dux. ✠ Ego Mucel dux. ✠ Ego Eadwulf. ✠ Ego Wicga. ✠ Ego Eaduulf. ✠ Ego Ælfred. ✠ Hwithyse. ✠ Ego Aldberht.

KING BERHTUULF OF MERCIA. DEC. 25TH DCCC.XLI.[1]

✠ Aio et alto Domino Deo Zabaoth regnanti in ævum: Siquidem humani generis prosapio de primo patre et matre oriundus in hanc sæculum venit, et sic per longa vaga temporum spatium diversis nationibus derimuntur, ut janitor caelestis bibliothece et vas electionis, predicator egregius, apostolus Paulus, dixit, preteriit enim figura hujus mundi, quomodo in velocitate dies et anni deficiunt: et iterum sagax sophista, qui quondam Solymis dives regnavit in arvis, katolectico versu cecinit dicens, "Non semper licet gaudere: fugit hora qua jacemur." Et ideo sunt omnes nostræ seriæ litterarum apicibus confirmandas, ne posteris ex memoria labere possit quicquid facta præcedentium patrum ac regum firmiter statuerunt. Qua de rê, ego Berhtuulf, Domino disponente, rex Merciorum, mihi et omnibus Mercis in æternam elemosinam, donans donabo Eanmundo venerabili abbate et ejus familie on Breodune, cum licentia et testimonia obtimatum gentis Merciorum, hanc libertatis gratiam, id est, ut sit liberatum et obsolutum illud monasterium in æternitatem ab illis incommodiis quam nos Saxonica lingua fæstingmen dicimus, Christo Domino teste et omnibus sanctis in celis, tam diu fides catholica et baptismum Christi in Brittannia servetur. Ob hujus rei gratia, ipse vero supradictus Eanmund abbas et illius sancta congregatio Breodunensis monasterii dederunt mihi et omnibus Mercis regaliter perfruendum et possedendum, in famoso vico in Tomeworðie, magnum discum argenteum valde bene operatum ac faleratum in magno pretio, et c.xc. mancusas in auro puro; similiter etiam decantaverunt duodecim vicibus c. psalterios, et c.xx. missas, pro Berhtwlfum regem, et pro illius caros amicos, et pro omnem gentem Merciorum, ut eorum libertas firmior ac stabilior permaneat in evum[2], et ut illius regis memoria et amicorum ejus, qui hanc pietatem in elemosinam sempiternam omnibus Mercis ille congregatione on Breodune donaverat, in eorum sacris orationibus jugiter permaneat usque in

[1] A choice specimen of monastic Latin in the 9th century.

[2] MS. eorum.

evum. Insuper, in Dei omnipotentis nomine, et novem ordinibus angelorum, et omnium electorum Christi, præceptum ponimus, ut nullus unquam regum vel principum, aut alicujus personis homo, magnis sive modicis, in aliquo tempore hanc præscriptam libertatis gratiam infringere ausus sit, sed semper stabilis et indisscussa firmiterque firmata ille congregatione on Breodune, coram Deo et hominibus jugiter permaneat in evum. Haec autem cartula caraxata est anno Dominice incarnationis DCCC°XLI. Indictione IIII., in die natalis Domini, in celebre vico on Tomeworðie, his testibus consentientibus et signum crucis Christi scribentibus, quorum subter nomina notata sunt.

✠ Ego Berhtuulf, largiflua Dei munificentia rex Merciorum, hanc meam libertatis gratiam ac omnium Merciorum cum signo sancte crucis firmiter consignabo. ✠ Ego Sæðryð regina consensi et subscripsi. ✠ Ego Cyneferð episcopus consensi. ✠ Ego Aldred episcopus consensi. ✠ Ego Berehtred episcopus consensi. ✠ Ego Heaberht episcopus consensi. ✠ Ego Cuðuulf episcopus consensi. ✠ Ego Eanmund abbas consensi. ✠ Ego Wihtred abbas consensi. ✠ Ego Ceolred abbas consensi.

KING BERHTWULF OF MERCIA. DCCC.XLIV.

Regnante in perpetuum Domino nostro Jhesu Christo. Ceolred antistes, cum consciencia et licentia venerabilium familiarum mearum, dabo Berhtwlfo, regi Merciorum, illud territorium at Peginga burnan, XIIII. manentium juxta amnem que dicitur Temes, pro libertate horum monasteriorum, ut habeat eandem terram, perfruat et possideat in diem illius, et post se cuicunque voluerit relinquat in perpetuam hereditatem. Ego Berhtwlfus, rex Merciorum, donabo Ædelwlfe duci libertatem et territorium et Pægeinga burnan in perpetuam hereditatem. Hoc est, verbi gratia, ut sint liberati a pastu principum et a difficultate illa quot nos Saxonice dicimus Festigmen; nec homines illuc mittant qui osceptros vel falcones portant, aut canes aut caballos ducunt; set sint liberati perpetualiter in evum. Si quis autem hoc servaret vel augere voluerit, benedictionem a Domino Deo celi percipiat hic et in futuro. Si quis autem, quod non optamus, in aliqua parte frangere vel minuere voluerit, sciat se rationem redditurum ante tribunal nostri judicis, nisi ante ea Deo et hominibus emendaverit. Hoc autem factum est anno Dominice incarnationis DCCC°XL°IIII°, Indictione vero VI., regni autem regis Bertulfi IIII° anno. His testibus contestantibus et scribentibus; et cum signo sancte crucis corroboraverunt, quorum nomina infra notantur.

✠ Ego Bertulf rex concessi et subscripsi. ✠ Ego Sæþryð regina consensi et subscripsi. ✠ Ego Ceolred episcopus consensi et subscripsi. ✠ Ego Hunbrht episcopus consensi et subscripsi. ✠ Ego Heabrht episcopus consensi et subscripsi. ✠ Ego Eanmund abbas consensi et subscripsi. ✠ Ego Mucel dux consensi et subscripsi. ✠ Ego Humbrht dux consensi et subscripsi. ✠ Ego Ælfstan dux consensi et subscripsi. ✠ Ego Cynebrht dux consensi et subscripsi. ✠ Ego Æðel dux consensi et subscripsi. ✠ Ego Beornoð subscripsi. ✠ Ego Ælfred subscripsi. ✠ Ego Wlfred subscripsi.

KING ÆTHELWULF OF WESSEX. NOV. 5TH DCCC.XLIV.

✠ Regnante Domino nostro in perpetuum. Dum in nostris temporibus bellorum incendiis et direptione opum nostrarum, necnon et vastantium crudelissima depredatione hostium barbarorum, paganorumque gentium multiplici affligencium usque ad internecionem, tempora cernimus incumbere periculosa. Quamobrem ego Æðelwlfus rex Occidentalium Saxonum, cum consilio episcoporum ac principum meorum, consilium salubre atque uniforme remedium affirmavi, ut aliquam portionem terrarum hæreditariam antea possidentibus gradibus omnibus, sive famulis et famulabus Dei Deo servientibus, sive laicis, semper decimam mansionem ubi minimum sit tum decimam partem [omnium bonorum] in libertatem perpetuam perdonare dijudicavi, ut sit tuta atque munita ab omnibus secularibus servitutibus, fiscis regalibus, tributis majoribus et minoribus, sive taxationibus quæ nos dicimus[1] Uuintereden; sitque libera omnium rerum; pro remissione animarum et peccatorum nostrorum, Deo soli ad serviendum, sine expeditione, et pontis instructione, et arcis munitione, ut eo diligentius pro nobis ad Deum preces sine cessatione fundant, quo eorum servitutem secularem in aliqua parte levigemus. Placuit autem tunc postea episcopis Alhstano Scireburnensis ecclesiæ, et Helmstano Wintanceastrensis æcclesiæ, cum suis abbatibus et servis Dei, consilium inire, ut omnes fratres et sorores nostri in unaquaque ecclesia, omni ebdomada Mercoris die, hoc est Wodnesdæg, omnis congregatio cantet quinquaginta psalmos, et unusquisque presbiter duas missas, unam pro rege Aðelwlfo, et aliam pro ducibus ejus huic dono consentientibus, pro mercede et refrigerio delictorum suorum: pro rege vivente, "Deus qui justificas"; pro ducibus viventibus, "Prætende Domini." Postquam autem defuncti fuerint, pro rege defuncto, singulariter; pro principibus defunctis, communiter. Et hoc sit tam firmiter constitutum omnibus diebus Christianitatis, [quasi libertas constituta est] quamdiu fides crescit in gente Anglorum. Et hoc sub testimonio satrapum nostrorum plurimorum, ad confirmationem quorum nomina subter annexa notantur. Scripta est autem hæc donationis cartula anno Dominicæ incarnationis DCCC.XLIIII., Indictione VII., die quoque nonarum Novembris, in civitate Wentana, in ecclesia Sancti Petri, ante altare capitale; et hoc fecerunt pro honore Sancti Michaelis archangeli, et Sanctæ Mariæ reginæ gloriosæ Dei genitricis, simulque et beati Petri apostolorum principis, necnon et sancti patris nostri Gregorii papæ, atque omnium sanctorum. Et tunc, pro ampliori firmitate, rex Æðelwlfus posuit cartulam supra altare Sancti Petri, et episcopi pro fide Dei acceperunt; et postea per omnes ecclesias transmiserunt in suis parochiis, secundum quod prædictum est. Terra autem ista quam in libertatem ponamus ad Meldunesburgensem ecclesiam pertinet. Ðæt is at Ellendune þrity hyde, ⁊ æt Elmhamstede fyftene hyde, æt Wttune tien hyde, et Cherltune tuentig

[1] Witerǣden.

hyde, et Minty uif hyde, at Rodburne tien hyde. Et qui hoc auger voluerit, augeat Deus bona illius in regione viventium. Si quis autem, diabolica fraude deceptus, in magnis aut in modicis, hoc infringere vel minuere temptaverit, sit anathematizatus ab omnibus fidelibus hic et in futuro seculo, nisi antea per satisfactionem emendaverit.

✠ Ego Æðelwlf rex consensi et subscripsi. ✠ Ego Elmstan episcopus subscripsi. ✠ Ego Ælstan episcopus subscripsi. ✠ Ego Æðelwlf dux subscripsi. ✠ Ego Osric dux subscripsi. ✠ Ego Eanwlf dux subscripsi. ✠ Ego Æðelric dux subscripsi. ✠ Ego Ceanwlf dux subscripsi. ✠ Ego Cearl dux subscripsi. ✠ Ego Æðelmund abbas subscripsi. ✠ Ego Wlflaf abbas subscripsi. ✠ Ego Beorhtelm abbas subscripsi. ✠ Ego Ægheard minister. ✠ Ego Milred minister. ✠ Ego Osmund minister. ✠ Ego Ælla minister. ✠ Ego Wlfhere minister. ✠ Ego Ælfstan minister. ✠ Ego Ceolmund minister. ✠ Ego Kyneheah minister. ✠ Ego Kyneheah minister. ✠ Ego Dudda minister. ✠ Ego Æðelred minister. ✠ Ego Wihtgar minister. ✠ Ego Eadred minister. ✠ Ego Æðelbald minister. ✠ Ego Lulling minister. ✠ Ego Cealmund minister.

KING ÆTHELUULF OF WESSEX. DCCC.XLIV.

✠ In nomine Dei summi Regis æterni. Plerumque etenim contingere solet ut res possessæ hæreditatis acquisitæ in contentionem plerisque et altercationis conflictum deveniunt, nisi cum idoneis testibus, et subscriptionibus sapientium, et fidelium personarum testimoniis tractata et confirmata fuerint. Quapropter sapientes salubrem consilium prudentium quærunt, et cyrographorum cautionibus, et heroicorum virorum testimoniis confirmantur, ne imposterum aliquibus altercationibus, vel scrupulo falsi suspicionis corrumpuntur, aut nebulo ignorantiæ in aliquo fuscetur. Idcirco etenim Osuulf, Dei gratia dux atque princeps provinciæ Orientalis Cantiæ, circa suæ propriæ hæreditatis jura tractare studuit; et hoc coram beatæ memoriæ Uulfredo archiepiscopo, coramque abbatis Uernotho atque Feolgeldo cæterisque fidelissimis et religiosissimis, Ceolstano, viz. Athelhuno atque Heremodo, presbyteris æcclesiæ Christi, necnon sæpe coram sociis suis et amicis fidissimis, qualiter post discessionem suam circa hæreditatem suam imposterum agere voluisse; id est, ut post dies uxoris suæ et filii ejus Earduulfi filiæ quoque suæ Ealfthrythæ, ad æcclesiis Dei omnia dare Deo et sanctis ejus sibi in sempiternam hæreditatem sub eorum testimonia dare præcepit, sicut in altera kartula manifeste et lucide comprobatur. Sed tamen post obitum Osuulfi ducis surrexit excitata a quibusdam quæstio et contentio magno circa hæreditatem Osuulfi contra uxorem ejus Beornthrythæ; cujus altercationis conflictum neque a domino archiepiscopo nec ab aliquibus personis inferioribus ullo modo sedare potuit, sed utrique partes ad synodale concilium advocari et invitari jubebantur: et cum ad synodum devenissent, et diligenti investigatione veritatis sententia utrarumque partium a sancto synodo, quæ facta est in loco præclaro æt Æclea, quærendo examineretur, inventum est nihil justius nec rectius esse posse constare quam sic perseverare hæreditatem Osuulfi sicut ipse Osuulf prius proprio arbitrio per omnia donare coram prædictis testibus decreverat; atque ita hoc etiam ab illo sancti synodo perpetuæ perdurare dejudicatum est. Insuper etiam sancta illa synodus decrevere statuit, ut illa altercatio nunquam amplius per aliquam inquietudinis discordiam, post illum diem et deinceps excitando moveretur, et hoc cum signo sanctæ crucis Christi perenniter perdurare conscripserunt. Et si quis post hæc alicujus personis homo, diabolica instigatus temeritate, insurrexerit, qui hoc kanonica et synodalia decreta infringere temptaverit, a societate sanctorum omnium et a cœtu congregationis et communionis ipsorum sciret se esse alienatum, synodali judicio statuerunt. Sed heu pro dolor, ille antiquus venenatissimus serpens, qui protuplaustu piacula indidit, et humanum genus sibi per hæc subdidit, ceu cælydra infesta et pestifera, in quorundam pectore adhuc turgescit, et ad excitandas seditiones discordiasque committendas post curricula quantorum annorum, id est, XXXIIII., iterum æcclesiam Christi et hæreditatem sanctorum ejus adgravere et depravere impia nisu ac prava voluntate conatus est; atque illam prædictum altercationis conflictum renovare et excitare, post synodalia decreta ac probabilium patrum sanctiones, studuit. Quamobrem congregata multitudine spiritalium sæculariumque personum in Dorovernia civitate, anno Dominicæ incarnationis DCCC.XLIIII. Indict. [VII.] Ætheluulfo regi præsente atque Æthelstano filio ejus, Ceolnotho quoque archimetropolitano archiepiscopo, necnon Tatnoth presbitero electo ad episcopalem sedem Dorobrevi, id est, civitatis Hrofi, cum principibus, ducibus, abbatibus, et cunctis generalis dignitatis optimatibus, inter quas etiam ille venenatissimus anguis cognomento Ætheluulf, ad turbandum et inquietandum æcclesiam Dei deveniens, sicut sæpe progenies et parentes ejus fecerunt, prolatis falsis machinamentis e latebris cordis suæ, dicens hæreditatem Osuulfi ducis cum auro et argento patris sui, Æthelheah, esse comparatum, et per hoc spoliare æcclesiam Dei et sanctos cœnubias ad quas hæreditas illa pertinebat, cum pravis sequacibus nisus est. Tunc ille archiepiscopus Ceolnoth et familia ejus, id est, æcclesiæ Christi illa, per ordinem replicavit qualiter in illo sancto synodo de illo reconciliatum et dejudicatum est. At ille nolens adquiescere, neque judicio synodis et probabilium patrum sanctionibus, neque adsertione et veredica voce episcopi vel alicujus personis; tunc etenim a sapientibus et prudentibus trutinatum ac dijudicatum est, familiam æcclesiæ Christi, et familiam æt Folcanstane, familiam quoque at Dobrum, necnon familiam æt Liminge, ad quos hæreditas illa pertinebat, justo juramenta hæreditatem illam sibi ipsis contra hæreditatem Æthelheahes castigare; nam et ita fecerunt. Juraverunt XXX. homines de familiis prædictis, XII. presbiteri, cæteri communi gradus; et sic etiam illa altercatio utrarumque partium perenniter sedari decretum est; et illa altercatio nunquam amplius, per aliquam inquietudinis discordiam, post diem illum excitando moveatur; et firmiter decreverunt, ut sub anathematis vinculo esset nodatus, qui hanc reconciliationem in aliquo irritum faceret, sicut et ille excommunicatus constat a consortio sanctorum omnium, et a communione synodalis concilii, et familiis nostris æcclesiæque Dei alienus existat, qui hoc kanonica statuta et synodalia præcepta infringere studuit, nisi digne Deo et hominibus præsumptionis suæ conamen emendare voluerit. Et hoc signo sanctæ crucis Christi roborando omnes pariter conscripserunt.

✠ Ego Ætheluulf, Deo dispensante, rex Occidentalium Anglorum, hanc prædictam reconciliationem familiæ Christi et hæreditatis Æthelheahes, et omnem altercationis conflictum, qui inter se concitatum habuerunt, sedatum esse demonstrans; et hoc cum sapientibus meis signo sanctæ crucis Christi perenni titulo roborabo et subscribo, quorum subter in scedula liquescunt vocabula.

✠ Ego Ætheluulf dux coñ. et sub̄. ✠ Ego Cyneuulf coñ. et sub̄. ✠ Ego Lulling coñ. et sub̄. ✠ Ego Æthelheah coñ. et sub̄. ✠ Ego Æthelheah coñ. et sub̄. ✠ Ego Gishard coñ. et sub̄.

✠ Ego Ceolnoth, gratia Dei metropolitanus archiepisc̃., cum presbyteris et familia sua, hoc, id est signo sanctæ crucis Christi roborando subscripsi.

✠ Ego Alchhere dux coñ. et sub̄. ✠ Ego Ætheluulf dux coñ. et sub̄. ✠ Ego Freothoric ab̄b̄. coñ. et sub̄. ✠ Ego Æthelmund coñ. et sub̄. ✠ Ego Æthelred coñ. et sub̄. ✠ Ego Freothoric coñ. et sub̄. ✠ Ego Denemod coñ. et sub̄. ✠ Ego Beornfreth coñ. et sub̄. ✠ Ego Osfere coñ.

Hæc sunt etiam nomina familiæ Christi, et illius familiæ æt Folcanstane, necnon æt Dobrum, atque æt Liminge qui hanc jurationem juraverunt, quorum nomina subter adnotantur.

✠ Ego Abba pr̃ coñ. et sub̄. ✠ Ego Brunheard pr̃ coñ. et sub̄. ✠ Ego Hunred pr̃ coñ. et sub̄. ✠ Ego Hysenoð pr̃ coñ. et sub̄. ✠ Ego Uuigmund pr̃ coñ. et sub̄. ✠ Ego Eof pr̃ coñ. et sub̄. ✠ Ego Degmund pr̃ coñ. et sub̄. ✠ Ego Uuealdhere pr̃ coñ. et sub̄. ✠ Ego Æthelred pr̃ coñ. et sub̄. ✠ Ego Cichus coñ. et sub̄. ✠ Ego Sigemund coñ. et sub̄. ✠ Ego Bornfred coñ. et sub̄. ✠ Ego Uuynna coñ. et sub̄. ✠ Ego Sygeanoth coñ. et sub̄. ✠ Ego Uuihtred coñ. et sub̄. ✠ Ego Uuillmund coñ. et sub̄. ✠ Ego Beornmod coñ. et sub̄. ✠ Ego Cynuulf. ✠ Ego Uuillhere. ✠ Ego Berht-noth. ✠ Ego . . . . . ✠ Ego Ceolbald coñ. ✠ Ego Alchhere. ✠ Ego Duddel. ✠ Ego Æthelhere. ✠ Ego Northhere.

KING BERHTUULF OF MERCIA. DEC. 25TH DCCC.XLV.

✠ In nomine Domini. Certe fugitiva et caduca itaque est status istius mundi, et omnia quæ videntur hic vento velocius ad finem trahunt, et quæ non videntur fixa ac mansura in æternum permaneant. Ideo cum istis temporalibus ac transitoriis hujus sæculi divitiis æterna præmia, ac semper gaudia manentia, studeamus in cælestibus comparare, vocante nos ad se Domino nostro Jhesu Christo, qui ait, "Venite ad me omnes qui laboratis, et honorati estis, et ego reficiam vos." Qua de re ego Berhtuulf, gratia divina largiente, rex Merciorum, de remedio anime meæ præcogitans, diemque tremendum distincti examinis ante oculis cordis mei componens, cogitavique, quod aliquit de istius mundani regni perceptione pro memetipsum in perpetuam elemosinam ac libertatem æcclesiasticam, Deo vivo, in æternum erogarem; ideo, cum consensu et licentia episcoporum et principum meorum, et omnium seniorum gentis nostræ, donabo Heaberhto, meo venerabili episcopo, hujus libertatis privilegium, et ejus familie in Uuegerna cæstre, illius monasterii bi Eafene, quod appellatur Ufera Stretford, cujus quantitas est xx. manentium, eo quod placabile pecunio acceptus fui, id est, x. libris argenti, ea conditione, ut libera permaneat in sempiternum. Soluta et liberata sit ab omni jugo humane servitutis, ab omnibus sæcularibus tributis et vectigalibus; cum cunctis utilitatibus ad illam ecclesiam recte pertinentibus, campis vel silviunculis, pascuis vel pratis, fluminibus vel piscationibus; ab opere regali et pastu regis et principis, vel juniorum eorum; ab hospitorum refectione vel venatorum, etiam equorum regis, falconum et ancipitruum, et puerorum qui ducunt canes. Quid plura? ab omni tribulatione noti et ignoti, magni et modici, libera consistit in ævum, quamdiu fides Christiane religionis apud Anglos in Brittannia insula permaneat. Si quis vero regum aut principum vel præfectorum, aut alicujus gradus homo hanc nostram conscriptam libertatem, per diabolicam gastrimoniam deceptus, frangere vel minuere temptaverit, sciat se separatum a consortio sanctorum in die magni judicii, et in æterna dampnatione dampnandum cum diabulo et angelis ejus, nisi ante hic Theo pontocratore[1] et hominibus, cum bona satisfactione emendaverit. Hii testes adfuerunt, quorum nomina hic infra flavescunt. Gesta est autem hæc donatio anno Domini incarnationis DCCC°XLV°, Indictione VIII[a], in loco regali qui dicitur Tomeuuorðig, in Nativitate Domini.

✠ Ego Berhtuulf rex Merciorum hanc meam largifluam libertatem cum vexillo sanctæ crucis Christi roboravi, ut fixa permaneat in æternum. ✠ Ego Sæðryð regina consensi et subscripsi. ✠ Ego Hunberht[2] episcopus consensi et subscripsi. ✠ Ego Heaberht episcopus consensi et subscripsi. ✠ Ego Ciorred episcopus consensi et subscripsi. ✠ Ego Berhtred episcopus consensi et subscripsi. ✠ Ego Cuthuulf episcopus consensi et subscripsi. ✠ Ego Uuihtred episcopus[3] consensi et subscripsi. ✠ Ego Eanmund abbas consensi et subscripsi. ✠ Ego Ætheluulf presbiter consensi et subscripsi. ✠ Ego Berhtric filius regis consensi. ✠ Ego Mucel dux consensi et subscripsi. ✠ Ego Humberht dux consensi. ✠ Ego Ælfstan dux consensi. ✠ Ego Cyneberht dux consensi. ✠ Ego Ætheluulf dux consensi. ✠ Ego Mucel dux consensi. ✠ Ego Sigered dux consensi. ✠ Ego Dudda dux consensi. ✠ Ego Aldberht dux consensi. ✠ Ego Ælfred. ✠ Ego Uuicga. ✠ Ego Æthelheah. ✠ Ego Eadgar. ✠ Ego Uuiglaf. ✠ Ego Eaduulf. ✠ Ego Uulfred.

KING BERHTUULF OF MERCIA. DCCC.XLVIII.

✠ In nomine alme et agye Sophiæ, qui monarchiam mundi tocius ac celsitudinem cœlorum abditamque profunditatem turgentis oceani, in altis et in imis, omnia cum suo

[1] Θεῷ παντοκράτορι. [2] Tunberht? [3] abbas?

majestatis imperio, qui in primordio mundi creavit, et nunc in ævum gubernat et regit, summus Pater, omnipotens Deus. Status hujus mundi in velocitate deficiet, et rotunda sæculorum volubilitas facesset, sic alternando creaturarum qualitas decrescit, sic mutando mortalis vitæ fragilitas fatescit. De qua miserrima humani status vicissitudine Æcclesiastes, cœlesti afflatus spiritu, competentem protulit sententiam: "Generatio, inquid, venit et generatio vadit: alii nascuntur et alii moriuntur." Ita universa divitiarum facultas et temporalis gazæ possessio, quam præcessorum anxia sollicitudo per indefessa laborum emolumenta lucratur, proh dolor, incertis heredibus, interdum optatis interdum exosis, relinquitur. Quemadmodum psalmista inprovidam humani generis socordiam conquerens increpitet: "Thesaurizat et ignorat cui congregat ea." Ideo sunt omnes nostras serie et sermocinationis litterarum apicibus confirmandos, ne unquam ulla oblivione tradantur, sed perpetua memoria serventur, quicquid reges ac præcedentes patres firmiter constituerunt. Qua de re ego Berhtwulfus, divino fultus suffragio rex Merciorum, cum consensu et consilio principum ac magistratuum Mærcianorum gentis, donans donabo venerabili abbati Æanmundo et ejus familiæ sanctæ congregationis Breodunensis monasterii istam libertatis gratiam illius monasterii æt Breodune, mihi et omnibus Mærcis, tam pro Deo quam pro sæculo, in elemosinam sempiternam. Id est, ut sit liberatum et absolutum illud monasterium ab illis causis quas cumfeorme et eafor vocitemus; tam a pastu ancipitrorum meorum omnium, quam etiam venatorum omnium, vel a pastu equorum meorum omnium, sive ministrorum eorum. Quid plura? ab omni illa incommoditate æfres et cumfeorme, nisi istis causis quas hic nominamus: præcones si trans mare venirent ad regem venturi, vel nuntii de gente Occidentalium Saxonum, vel de gente Norþanhymbrorum, si venirent ad horam tertiam diei, vel ad medium diem, dabitur illis prandium; si venirent supra nonam horam, tunc dabitur eis noctis pastum; et iterum de mane pergent in viam suam. Ob hujus ergo rei gratiam, ipse vero supradictus Eanmund abbas ac illius supranominata familia æt Breodune, ad commercium hujus libertatis, cum testimonio obtimatum gentis Merciorum, dederunt Berhtuulfo regi Merciorum c.lxxx. mancusas in auro puro, et terram xv. manentium in duobus locis, æt Stanlege et æt Bellanforde, ut ista libertatis gratia cum Dei testimonio, et omnium sanctorum in cœlo, et eorum hominum in terra qui Dei præcepta custodiunt, et tremendum diem judicii metuunt, et honorem sancte crucis Christi colunt, ac illorum baptismatis donum firmiter perenniterque firmatum, nullo homine interdicente, sed Deo favente ac angelis ejus, stabilis permaneat, tamdiu fides Christiana ac baptismum Christi apud Anglorum gentem in Brittannia maneat. Insuper etiam ego Humberht princeps optinebam a domino meo Berhtuulfo regi Merciorum, cum consensu optimatum, illo abbati Eanmundo et familiæ illius supradictæ on Breodune, hanc libertatis gratiam pro eorum venerabili pecunia, quod mihi impendebant in uno vaso prætioso potatorio, quod fuit de nobile genere pulchraliter factum, et ex parte cum auro ornatum. Hoc est ut sit illud monasterium on Breodune liberatum et absolutum ab omnibus causis, magnis vel modicis, notis ac ignotis, quæ mihi aut principibus Tonsetorum unquam ante ea pertinebant ex illo monasterio, tamdiu voluerit Deus ut baptismi gratia et recta fides cum regibus ac principibus Christianis in populo fideli firmiter fideliterque permaneat in ævum. Et ut memoria regis Beorhtuulfi, ac Humberhti principis, et omnium optimatum gentis Merciorum, in eorum sacris orationibus, diebus ac noctibus, memoretur, et nullus homo alicujus personis, rex aut princeps, magnis sive modicis, in aliquo tempore, diabolica potestate fretus, per tirannicam phylargiriam vel gastrimargiam, hanc nostram statutionem fringere præsumat; sed semper stabilis et indiscussa hæc donatio conservetur inperpetuum; et ut merita ac elemosinæ nostræ ante Deum florescant, ac nomina nostra coram throno Domini scribantur in libro viventium. Amen. Hæc scedula scripta est anno Dominice incarnationis dccc.xlviii., Indictione vero xi., in venerabili monasterio primum æt Hrypadune, et iterum karaxata atque confirmata fuit cum ista testimonia quorum subter nomina notata sunt.

Ego Berhtuulf, Domino disponente rex Merciorum, hanc

nostram diui ....[1] et meam donationem, mihi et omnibus Mercis in elemosinam sempiternam, firmiter donabo, atque cum signo sanctæ crucis consignabo. Ego Seþryþ regina consensi et subscripsi. Ego Tunberht episcopus consensi et subscripsi. Ego Ciolred episcopus consensi et subscripsi. Ego Berhtred episcopus consensi et subscripsi. Ego Alchan episcopus consensi et subscripsi. Ego Cuþuulf episcopus consensi et subscripsi. Ego Eanmund abbas consensi et subscripsi. Ego Withred abbas consensi et subscripsi. Signum Muceli principis. Signum Humberhti principis. Signum Æthelhardi principis. Signum Aldberti principis. Signum Dudan principis. Signum Sigredi principis. Signum Wiglafi principis. Signum Muceli principis. Signum Ælfstanis principis. Signum Hunstanis principis.

[1] Sic MS.

ABBOT CEOLRED. DCCC.LII.

✠ In nomine Patris et Filii et Spiritus Sancti. Ceolred abƀ ⁊ ðа higan on Medeshamstede sellað Wulfrede ðet land æt Sempingaham· in ðas gerednisse· ðet he hit hæbbe ⁊ bruce sua lange sua he life· ⁊ anum ærfeuuarde æfter him· ⁊ elce gere sextig foðra wuda to ðæm ham on Hornan ðæm wuda· ⁊ tuelf foðer græfan· ⁊ sex foður gerda. End forðon we him ðis land sellað ðet he ðes landes fulne friodom bigete in ǽce ærfeweardnisse æt Sempingaham ⁊ æt Slioforda· ⁊ bruce þere cirican lafard on Medeshamstede ðes landes æt Slioforda· ⁊ Wulfred

✠ In nomine Patris et Filii et Spiritus Sancti. Ceolred abbot and the convent at Medeshamstede give to Wulfred the land at Sempringham, on this condition: that he have and enjoy it as long as he lives, and one heir after him, and every year [give] sixty fothers of wood to the 'hām' in the wood of Horn, and twelve fothers of pit coal, and six fothers of faggots. And we give him this land that he may obtain the land's full freedom in perpetual inheritance, at Sempringham and at Sleaford. And let the lord of the church at Medesðes on Sempingaham· ⁊ he geselle eghwelce gere to Medeshamstede tua tunnan fulle luhtres aloð· ⁊ tua slegneat· ⁊ sex hund lafes· ⁊ ten mittan Wælsces aloð· ⁊ þere cirican laforde geselle eghwelce gere hors ⁊ ðrittig scillinga· ⁊ hine ane niht gefeormige fiftene mitta luhtres aloð. v. mitta Welsces aloð· fiftene sestras liðes· ⁊ hi sion symle in allum here life eadmode ⁊ hearsume ⁊ underþeodde. ⁊ ofer here tuega dæg þonne agefe hio þet land into þere cirican to Medeshamstede mid freodome· ⁊ we him þis sellað mid felda ⁊ mid wuda ⁊ mid fenne sua þerto belimpeð. Sið heora tuuege dæg agan sie· þonne agefe mon tuuenti hida higuum to biodland· ⁊ þere cirican lafarde xii. hida land æt Forde ⁊ æt Cegle· ⁊ he þes feormied tuuege hida landes æt Læhcotum his erfeweorda sweolcum swelce him ðonne gesibbast wære· ⁊ þat were Fulfredes cynne gefre swa sua þet oðer into þere cirican. Anno vero Dominicæ incarnationis DCCC.LII., Indictione xv. hoc factum est.

hamstede enjoy the land at Sleaford, and Wulfred that at Sempringham: and let him give every year to Medeshamstede two tuns full of bright ale, and two neats for slaughter, and six hundred loaves, and ten measures of Welsh ale. And let him give every year to the lord of the church, a horse and thirty shillings, and one night's entertainment, fifteen measures of bright ale, five measures of Welsh ale, fifteen sesters of mild [ale]: and be they always, in all their life, humble and obedient and under subjection. And after the day of the two, let them restore the land to the church at Medeshamstede with freedom. And we give him this with field and with wood and with fen as thereto belong. When the day of those two is agone, then let be given twenty hides to the convent for table-land, and to the lord of the church xii. hides of land at Ford and at Keal; and he for this shall cultivate two hides of land at Læhcotum to such of his heirs as may then be nearest of kin to him. And be that to Wulfred's kin freed so as the other is to the church. Anno vero Dominicæ incarnationis DCCC.LII. Indictione xv.

Her sindan ðа naman ðere monna þe þis wreotan ⁊ festnedan.	Here are the names of the men who wrote and ratified this.

Burgred rex. Cælnoth archiepiscopus. Tunberht episcopus. Ceored episcopus. Alchun episcopus. Berhtred episcopus. Wihtred abbas. Werheard abbas. Æthelhard dux. Hunberht dux. Aldbert dux. Beornhard dux. Mucel dux. Osmund dux. Ælfstan dux. Aldred dux. Wenberht dux. Eadulf.

Ic Ceolred abƀ þas ure selene mid Cristes rode tacne trymme ⁊ festnie.	I Ceolred abbot confirm and ratify this our gift with the sign of Christ's rood.

Aldberht præpositus. Alcheard presbiter. Eanred presbiter. Wilheard presbiter. Cenferð presbiter. Cyneweald presbiter. Eaduuald presbiter. Egberht diaconus. Humberht diaconus. Aldhelm. Byrnuuald. Tunwulf.

KING ÆTHELWULF OF WESSEX. APRIL 22ND DCCC.LIV.[1]

✠ Regnante imperpetuum Domino nostro Jhesu Christo, summo et ineffabili rerum Creatore omnium, tempora qui sua multimoda disponens temporibus potencia ut voluerit finem inponet, et hac vita degentibus cunctis certum ut proposuerat dierum terminum constituet; iccirco cunctis agendum ut hic bonis actibus future beatitudinis felicitatem perpetualiter adipisci mereantur. Quapropter ego Aðelwlf, gracia Dei Occidentalium Saxonum rex, in sancta et celeberrima paschali solempnitate, pro mee remedio anime, et regni prosperitate et populi, ab omnipotente Deo michi collati salute, consilium salubre cum episcopis, comitibus, cunctisque optimatibus meis, ego humiliter pro amore Dei perfeci, ut decimam partem terrarum per regnum nostrum non solum sanctis ecclesiis dare, verum eciam et ministris in eisdem constitutis in perpetuam libertatem habere concessimus, ita ut talis donacio fixa incommutabilisque permaneat, ab omni regali servicio, et

[1] This and the three following charters are all that are known to be extant of Æthelwulf's cession of a tenth of his lands.

omnium secularium absoluta servitute. Placuit autem Athelstano Sciraboruensis ecclesie episcopo, et Suuithino episcopo Wyntonceastrensis ecclesie, cum omnibus Deo servientibus, ut in unaquaque ebdomada, die Sabbati, unanimis congregacio famulorum famularumque Dei L. psalmos cantet, et unusquisque frater duas missas, unam pro Aðelwulpho rege, et aliam pro episcopis et ducibus: oracio pro rege vivente: "Deus, qui justificas impium"; pro episcopis et ducibus viventibus: "Pretende Domine"; postquam ii defuncti fuerint, pro rege defuncto specialiter, pro episcopis et ducibus defunctis communiter hanc conferentibus donacionem, ut tam roborata perseveret quamdiu fides Christianaque religio in Anglorum gente inconcussa pervigeat. Hoc in honorem Domini nostri Jhesu Christi fecimus, et beate ac semper virginis Marie, ac omnium sanctorum, et paschalis festi reverencia, ut Deus omnipotens nobisque et nostris posteris misericordiam afferat: et hoc sub testimonio satrapum nostrorum plurimorum ad confirmacionem, quorum nomina subter annexa vocentur. Scripta est hec cartula anno Dominice incarnacionis DCCC.LIIII., indictione prima, die vero paschali, in palacio nostro quod dicitur Wiltone. Terra ista quam in libertatem ponimus ad ecclesiam pertinet ad Glastingaburi:

Ðæt is þanne erest on Boklond toun fif hide; in be Pennard sex hidas, on Cotenesfelde ān hywysce· ⁊ on Cerawicombe· and þoðer del of Branok hyalf hiwisce· and al þat oðer del.

That then is first: In Buckland town five hides; in by Pennard six hides; in Cotensfield one hide; and in Cerawicomb, and the other part of Branok half a hide and all the other part.

Qui hanc augere voluerit nostre donacionem satisfactionis, augeat Deus omnipotens dies ejus prosperos. Si vero quis minuere vel immutare presumpserit, noscat se ante tribunal Christi redditurum rationem, nisi prius satisfactione emendaverit.

✠ Ego Aðelwolf rex subscripsi. ✠ Swiðon episcopus. ✠ Aðelstanus episcopus. ✠ Eanwlf dux. ✠ Wlfer dux. ✠ Wulfluf abbas. ✠ Wyeffard abbas. ✠ Aðelred frater regis. ✠ Alfreð filius regis. ✠ Erue minister regis et multi alii.

KING ÆTHELUULF. APRIL 22ND DCCC.LIV.

✠ Regnnante inperpetuum Domino nostro Jhū Xp̄o, summo et ineffabili rerum Creatori ac Moderatori omnium, tempora, qui sua multimoda disponens temporibus potenciam ut voluerit, finem inponet et in ac vita degentibus cunctis certum ut proposuerat dierum terminum constituet; idcirco cunctis agendum est ut a bonis actibus future beatitudinis felicitatem perpetualiter adipisci mereatur. Quapropter ego Æðelulf, gracia Dei Occiduntalium Saxonum rex, in sancta ac celeberima paxchali solemnitate, pro mee remedio anime et regni prosperitate et populi ab omnipotenti Deo conlato, consilium salubre cum episcopis committibus et cunctis optimatibus, me perfecci ut decimam partem terrarum per regnum non solum sanctis ecclesiis darem, verum eciam et ministris nostris in eodem constitutis in perpetuam libertatem concessiris ita ut alis donacio fixa incommutabilisque permaneat ab omni regali servicio, et omnium secularium opsoluto servitute. Placuit Alhstano episcopo Sciraburnanscis eclesie æt Suiðhun Uuentane eclesie episc̄. cum omnibus Deo serventibus, in unaquaque efdomada die Sabato unianimis congregacio famulorum famularum Dei L. salmos cantent, et unusquisque pr̃ duos missas, unam pro Aðeluluo rege, alteram pro episc̄. et ducibus: pro rege vivente "Deus qui justificos impium"; pro episc̄. et ducibus "Pretende Domine." Pro rege defuncto specialiter, pro episc̄. ⁊ ducibus communiter ãnc consentientibus donacionem, ut tam roborato perseveret quamdiu fides ⁊ xp̄iana relegio in Agelorum gente inconcusso pungeat. Oc fecimus in onorem Domini nostri Jhū Xp̄i, ⁊ beate ac semper virginis Marie, ⁊ omnium sanctorum t . . . um, ⁊ pasxalis festi reverencia, ut Deus omnipotens et nostris posterris propiciare dignet. Scripta est hec cartula anno ap incarnacione Domino nostri Jhū Xp̄i DCCC.LIIII. Indiccione II., die vero Paxali, in palacio nostro quod dicitur Wiltun. Qui augere voluerit nostram donacionem satisfaccionis augeað omnipotens Deus dies prosperos. Si quis minuere vel mutare presumserið, noscat se ante tribunal Xp̄i reddituram racionem, nisi prius satisfacione emendaverit. Ista est libertas quam Æðelulf rex suo ministro Wiferðe in perpetuum ereditatem abere concessit: I. cassati in loco qui dicitur Heregeardingc hiwisce, istis terminis circumdatis:

Ærest on ða norðigge eastewearde· ðone on ða miclan med· ðone on Tydginc mæd· ðonne on ðam ylendic· ðone up to Mealmehtan leahe· ðone to Scelces stede· ðone on Æschyrste æstewerde· ðone to Hunig yrste· ðone to Đunresfelda· ðonne on Fontanhlewe· ðonne on Wernan broc· ðonne on Wrennan wylle· ðonne on þ wætersłæd· ðæt forð on hagan· eft to ðære norðigge eastewearde.	First to the North island eastward; then to the great mead, then to Tydging mead; then to the island dike; then up to Mealmehte lea; then to Scalc's place; then to Ashhurst eastward; then to Honeyhurst; then to Thundersfield; then to Fontanlow; then to Wernan brook; then to Wrenwell; then to the water-slade; then on to the "haga"; again to the North island eastward.

et istis testibus consentientibus, quorum nomina inufra scribuntur.

✠ Æðelulf rex.	✠ Cyneuulf mī.
✠ Alhstan episc̄.	✠ Cuðuulf mī.
✠ Suiðhun episc̄.	✠ Cyneeah mī.
✠ Æðelbal episc̄.	✠ Niðmud mī.
✠ Eanulf dux.	✠ Ecgheard m̃.
✠ Osric dux.	✠ Osmud m̃.
✠ Æðelbreht dux.	✠ Milred m̃.
✠ Eannulf dux.	✠ Lullig m̃.
✠ Lullede dux.	✠ Ecuulf m̃.
✠ Hunlaf abƀ.	✠ Uulfred m̃.
✠ Hunerferð abƀ.	✠ Alhstan m̃.
✠ Esne mī.	✠ Aldred m̃.
✠ Æðred fili reg.	✠ Eanmund m̃.
✠ Ælfred fili reg.	✠ Cyma m̃.

Dorso. ✠ ðis seondan ðes landes bec ðe Æðelulf cyning Wiferðe his ðegne salde.	*Indorsed.* ✠ These are the land's books that king Æthelwulf gave to Wiferð his thane.

KING ÆTHELUULF. APRIL 22ND DCCC.LIV.

✠ Regnante imperpetuum Domino nostro Jhesu Christo, summo et ineffabili rerum Creatori [ac Moderatori] omnium, tempora qui sua multimoda disponens temporibus potencia, ut voluerit finem imponet, et in hac vita degentibus cunctis certum ut proposuerat dierum terminum constituet. Idcirco cunctis agendum, ut hic bonis actibus future beatitudinis felicitatem perpetualiter adipisci mereantur. Quapropter ego Athelwulf, gratia Dei Occidentalium Saxonum rex, in sancta ac celeberima paschali solempnitate, pro mee remedio anime, et regni prosperitate, et populi ab omnipotenti Deo michi collata salute, consilium salubre cum episcopis, comitibus, cunctisque optimatibus meis, ego humiliter pro amore Dei perfeci, ut decimam partem terrarum per regnum nostrum non solum sanctis ecclesiis dare, verum etiam et ministris nostris in eodem constitutis imperpetuam libertatem habere concessimus, ita ut talis donatio fixa incommutabilisque permaneat, ab omni regali servitio et omnium secularium absoluta servitute. Placuit autem Alstano Sciraburnensis ecclesie episcopo, et Swithuno episcopo Wyntancestrensi ecclesie, cum omnibus Deo servientibus, ut in unaquaque ebdomada, die Sabbati, unanimis congregacio famulorum famularumque Dei quinquaginta psalmos cantet, et unusquisque presbyter duas missas, unam pro Athelwulfo rege et aliam pro episcopo et ducibus ejus. Pro rege vivente, "Deus qui justificas impium"; pro episcopis et ducibus viventibus, "Pretende Domine." Postquam autem defuncti fuerint, pro rege defuncto specialiter; pro episcopis et principibus defunctis communiter, hanc consencientibus donationem, ut tam roborata perseveret, quamdiu fides et Christiana religio in Anglorum gente inconcussa pervigeat. Hoc autem in honorem Domini nostri Jhesu Christi fecimus, et beate ac semper virginis Marie, et omnium sanctorum, et paschalis festi reverencia, ut Deus omnipotens et nobis et nostris posteris misericordiam ejus adferret; et hoc sub testimonio satrapum nostrorum populorum ad confirmationem, quorum nomina subter annexa notantur. Scripta est autem hec cartula anno Dominice incarnationis DCCC.LIIII.

Indictione 1[a], die vero Paschali, in palatio nostro qui dicitur Wylton.

Terra autem ista quam in libertate ponamus ad ecclesiam pertinentem at Malmesburg.

Þer is þat erest at Pirigtune· fif ⁊ þrittig hyde· at Cwacot fiftiene hyde· at Suð-tune fif· at Corsaburnan fif hyda· at Criddanwylle tien hyda· at Cemele tien hyde· at Domeccesige þridde half hiwisc.

There is the first at Purton five and thirty hides; at Quacket fifteen hides; at Sutton five; at Corsbourne five hides; at Cridwell ten hides; at Kemble ten hides; at Dauntsey two hides and a half.

Qui autem augere voluerit nostre donationem satisfactionis, augeat omnipotens Deus dies ejus prosperos. Si vero quis minuere vel immutare præsumpserit, noverit se ante tribunal Christi redditurum rationem, nisi prius satisfactione emendaverit.

Aeþelwlf rex. Aelstan episcopus. Swithun episcopus. Osrich dux. Eanwlf dux. Athelbold dux. Lulling minister. Uuerfd abbas. Ulfhere dux. Cyma minister. Aeþelred minister. Lullede dux. Eanwlf dux. Ecgheard minister. Cyne minister. Aethelbert dux. Aelstan minister. Cuþwlf minister. Ulflaf abbas. Eanmund minister. Osmund minister. Cynewlf minister. Niþmund minister. Milred minister. Milred minister. Ulfred minister. Aldred minister.

KING ÆTHELWULF. NOV. 5TH DCCC.LV.

✠ Regnante Domino nostro in perpetuum. Dum in nostris temporibus bellorum incendia et direptiones opum nostrarum, necnon et vastantium crudelissimas hostium deprædationes barbarorum, paganarumque nationum multiplices tribulationes, ad affligendum nos pro peccatis nostris usque ad internecionem, tempora cernimus incumbere periculosa. Quamobrem ego Ethelwulphus rex Westsaxonum, cum consilio episcoporum ac principum meorum, consilium salubre atque uniforme remedium affirmantes consensimus, ut aliquam portionem terrarum hæreditariam antea possidentibus omnibus gradibus, sive famulis et famulabus Dei Deo servientibus, sive laicis miseris, semper decimam mansionem ubi minimam sit, tum decimam partem omnium bonorum, in libertatem perpetuam donari sanctæ ecclesiæ dijudicavi, ut sit tuta et munita ab omnibus secularibus servitutibus, imo regalibus tributis, majoribus et minoribus, sive taxationibus quæ nos dicimus [1]Winterden; sitque libera omnium rerum, pro remissione animarum et peccatorum nostrorum, ad serviendum Deo soli, sine expeditione, et pontis extructione, et arcis munitione; ut eo diligentius pro nobis ad Deum sine cessatione preces fundant, quo eorum servitutem in aliqua parte levigamus. Acta sunt hæc apud Wintoniam, in ecclesia Sancti Petri, anno Dominicæ incarnationis DCCC.LV. Indictione III. nonas Novembris, ante majus altare, pro' honore gloriosæ virginis et Dei genetricis Mariæ, Sanctique Michaelis archangeli, et beati Petri apostolorum principis, necnon et beati patris nostri Gregorii papæ. Præsentibus et subscribentibus archiepiscopis et episcopis Angliæ universis, necnon Beorredo rege Merciæ, et Edmundo Eastanglorum rege; abbatum et abbatissarum, ducum, comitum, procerumque totius terræ, aliorumque fidelium infinita multitudine, qui omnes regium chirographum laudaverunt; dignitates vero sua nomina subscripserunt.

Rex vero Ethelwulphus, pro firmitate ampliore, obtulit hanc chartulam scriptam super altare Sancti Petri apostoli; et episcopi, pro fide Dei illam acceperunt et per omnes ecclesias postea transmiserunt in suis parochiis publicandam.

In a donation of land, etc. by Æthelwulf in DCCC.LV. reference is made to this grant of a tenth, viz., ✠ "In nomine Trino divino. Ego Etheluulf rex Occidentalium Saxonum, necnon et Cantuariorum, pro decimatione agrorum, quam Deo donante ceteris ministris meis facere decrevi, tibi Dunne ministro meo dabo unam villam," etc. etc.—*Cod. Diplom.* ii. p. 57.

[1] Witereden?

KING BURHRED OF MERCIA. DCCC.LV.

✠ In nomine omnipotentis Dei et Domini nostri Jhesu Christi, qui vivit in sæcula. Amen. Ego Burgredus, Deo auxiliante omnium regnorum Regnatore concedente, rex Mercensium, mihi in elemosinam perpetuam largiendo hujus libertatis compositione et privilegium, meo praeclaro pontifice et fidele amico Alhuuino et ejus familiae in Weogerna civitate, cum consilio et licentia pontorum procerum meorum, in hiis territoriis et locis anc libertatem illis firmiter perdonabo et scribo: hoc est bi Cunelgan decem manentium; æt Eadbaldingtune ⁊ æt Pultune VIIII. cassatorum; æt Beorondes lea similiter VI. cassatorum; and æt Esege V. manentium; ita ab omnibus servitutibus et tributalibus rebus, magnis vel modicis, reis vel principis, aut juniorum illorum, in perpetuum sint liberati has terras omni rei, nisi tantum quattuor causis, pontis et arcis et expeditione contra hostes, et singulare praetium contra alium, et ad poenam nihil foras resolvat. Et illam terram trium manentium in Beonetlege, in occidentale plaga Sebrine, etiam liberabo a pascua porcorum re[g]is, quod nominamus fearnleswe. Propter hujus libertatis traditione, ille praenominatus epis mihi perdonabat duas bradiolas aureas fabrefactas, quas pensarent XLV. mancusas. Si quis autem benivola mente hujus libertatis donant, et nostrae elemosinæ largitionem augere, vel adjuvare, vel servare voluerit, ordinetur, coronetur, et benedicetur, hic in praesenti et in futuro, cum justis; et qui in aliquo fraude vel disceptione, per diabolicam gastrimoniam, istam libertatem frangere aut minuere temptaverit, sciat se cum rapacibus et peccatoribus esse conjunctum, et sine ullo honore in aeterna dampnatione cum diabulo dampnatum et sociis ejus, nisi hic cum satisfactione emendaverit Deo et hominibus.

Gesta est autem hujus libertatis donatum anno Dominice incarnationis DCCC.LV°, Indictione III^a, in loco qui vocatur Oswaldesdun, quando fuerunt pagani in Wreocensetum.

✠ Ego Burgred, rex Merciorum, hanc libertatem praescriptam mea manu consensi et subscripsi. ✠ Ego Æðelsuuið regina libertatem istam consensi. ✠ Ego Ciored episcopus consensi et subscripsi. ✠ Ego Alhhun episcopus consensi et subscripsi. ✠ Ego Berhtred episcopus consensi et subscripsi. ✠ Ego Cuðwulf episcopus consensi et subscripsi. ✠ Ego Hunberht dux. ✠ Ego Æþelheard dux. ✠ Ego Beornnoð dux. ✠ Ego Beornoð dux. ✠ Ego Aldberht dux. ✠ Ego Werberht dux. ✠ Ego Mucel dux. ✠ Ego Æþelwulf dux. ✠ Ego Omund dux. ✠ Ego Bernhard dux. ✠ Ego Eadgar. ✠ Ego Eadwulf. ✠ Ego Werberht. ✠ Ego Aldberht. ✠ Ego Ciolmund. ✠ Ego Baldred. ✠ Ego Mucel. ✠ Ego Æþelwulf. ✠ Ego Baldred. ✠ Ego Æþelheard.

KING BURHRED OF MERCIA. DCCC.LV.

✠ Regnante in perpetuum agio et alto Prosatori nostro, universitatis Creatore in sæculorum sæcula. Amen. Ego quidem Burhredus, omnipotentissimo Domino largiente rex Merciorum, donabo ac trado, pro redemptione animæ meæ, et pro absolutione peccaminum meorum, et pro spe superne remunerationis, meo fidele et percaro præsule et amico Alhwino hujus libertatis munificentiam et donatio: id est, monasterium quod nominatur Bloccanleeh, liberabo illud a pastu et ab refectione omnium ancipitrum et falconum in terra Mercensium, et omnium venatorum regis vel principis, nisi ipsorum tantum qui in provincia Hwicciorum sunt; similiter et a pastu et refectione illorum hominum quos Saxonice nominamus Wahlfæreld· ⁊ heora fæsting· ⁊ ealra Angelcynnes monna ⁊ ælþeodigra rædefæstinge, tam nobilium quam ignobilium: istorum omnium sint liberati prænominatorum in perpetuum, quamdiu Christiana fides in Brittannia insula aput Anglos perseverat. Propter hujus præfati libertatis donatione, ille episcopus Alhuuine mihi donabat placabilem pretium, hoc est ccc.torum solidorum in argento, ut eo liberior perfruantur hujus meæ elimosine in eternum. Si quis autem hanc donationem vel libertatem meam cum bona voluntate augere vel servare, aut in omnibus custodire conaverit, sciat se in celestibus habere consortium cum justis, et in æternum requies illius cum Deo et angelis ejus: et si aliquis, quod non optamus, sit, qui convertere hoc voluerit, et ad malum servitutem vel ergastulum mutare maluerit, sciat se separatum et anathematum a consortio omnium sanctorum Dei in celis, et cum diabolo et angelis ejus sine fine in perpetuum dampnatum, nisi ante hic Deo et hominibus cum satisfactione emendaverit. Gesta est hujus liber[tatis] cartula anno Dominicæ incarnationis DCCC.LV. Indictione III., in vico celebre qui a multis vocitatur Tomanworðigne; et hii testes adfuerunt quorum hic nomina infra notantur.

✠ Ego Burhred rex Merc̃. hanc meam donationem et elemosinam signo crucis Xp̃i muniat.

✠ Ego Æðelswyð regina consensi.

✠ Ego Tumberht ep̃s c̃s.

✠ Ego Ceorred ep̃s consensi.

✠ Ego Berehtred ep̃s consensi.

✠ Ego Alhiwine ep̃s c̃s.

✠ Ego Cuðuulf ep̃s c̃s.

✠ Ego Humbriht dux. ✠ Æðelheard dux. ✠ Beornnoð dux. ✠ Ego Aldberhti dux. ✠ Ego Weremberhti dux. ✠ Mucel dux.

---

* KING ÆTHELWULF OF WESSEX. AFTER DCCC.LVI.

On þæs naman þe on eces lifes bec on heofonan þa awrit þe her on life wel gecwemaþ· ic Aðulf kyningc on ðysum gewrite geswutelie be Ciltacumbes freulse ðone þe Kynegyls kyningc þe ærest kininga cristen gewearþ on West Sexan his fulluht fæder Sc̃e Birine biscope geuþe· ⁊ siþþan ælc þæra kyninga þe æfter oðran on West Sexan wæron gefriðodon ⁊ gefyrðredon þeah

In the name of Him, who in the book of everlasting life in heaven, has written down those with whom here in life he is well pleased, I Athulf king, by this writing make known concerning the freedom of Chilcombe, which king Kynegils, who first of the kings of West Saxony became a Christian, granted to his baptismal father St Birinus bishop; and after-þe he ær on gewrite ne stode oð hit to me com þe nu se nygoþa kyningc eom. Eac ic her geswutelie þæt ic þisne freols ætforan Sc̃e Petre on Rome ⁊ þam halgan papan Leone swa gefæstnode swa swa me ⁊ eallan ðeodscype gewearþ on Englaland ær ic to Rome fore. ꝥ wæs þæt mon ælles ðises freolses are æfre for ane hide werian scolde· forþam þe Godes ar æfre freogre beon sceal þonne ænig woruld ar· ⁊ min sune eac Ælfred þe mid me for· ⁊ þær to kyninge gehalgod wæs· þan papan on hand gesealde þæt he ðisne freols æfre gefyrþrian wolde· ⁊ his bearn· gif him God ænigra geuþe· to þam ylcan sprittan wolde. Ic eac· beforan þam ylcan papan· ealle þa land are þe ic on Angla þeode hæfde· Gode into halgan stowon· for me ⁊ for ealle þeode geteoðode· ⁊ on Rome· be þes papan fyrþrunge ⁊ leaue· mynster geworhte· Gode to loue· ⁊ Sc̃a Marian his halgan meder to wyrþmynte· ⁊ þær Englisce scole gesette· þe æfre nihtes ⁊ dæges for ure þeode Gode þywian scolde· ⁊ þaþa ic on

wards each of the kings, who were successively in West Saxony has protected and promoted, although it before stood not in writing, until it came to me who am now the ninth king. I also here declare that I, before St Peter at Rome and the holy pope Leo, so confirmed this freedom as was agreed on by me and all the nation in England, before I journeyed to Rome. That was, that for all the land enjoying this freedom, there should ever be defence for one hide[1]; because God's property should ever be more privileged than any secular property. And my son Ælfred also, who journeyed with me, and was there consecrated king, gave pledge to the pope, that he would ever promote this privilege, and his children, if God should grant him any, would rear up to the same. I also, before the same pope, conceded all the landed property which I had in the nation of the Angles, to God for holy places, for myself and for all the nation; and at Rome, by the pope's furtherance and leave, wrought

[1] That is for the 'Fyrd,' or military levy. Had the land been lay-property, it would no doubt have been rated according to the real number of hides.

eard com ic oncyðde ealle folce hwæt ic on Rome gedon hæfde. Þa þancodon hy þyses Gode ⁊ me swyþe georne. ⁊ heom eall þis swyþe wel licode. ⁊ cwædon þæt heora þances þis on ecnesse stande. Nu halsie ic. þurh þa halgan þrimnisse ⁊ Sc̄s Petrus. ⁊ ealne þane haligdom þe ic on Rome. for me ⁊ for ealne þeodscype gesohte. þet næfre ne kyningc. ne æþelingc. ne biscop. ne ealdorman. ne þegen. ne gerefa. hine silfne swa earme forwyrce þæt he þisne freols gelyttlie þe be swylcre gewittnesse gefestnod is. buton tweonan se þe hit deð he abilhð Gode ⁊ Sc̄e Petre ⁊ eallan þam halgan þe on Romes cyrcean restaþ. ⁊ him seluan ece hellewite ungesæliglice getilaþ. Eac se halga forsæda papa Leo Godes curs. ⁊ Sc̄e Petres. ⁊ ealra halgena. ⁊ his on þæne gesette þe þis æfre undo. ⁊ eac eall þes þeodscype. ge on gehadodan ge on læwedan ꝥ ylce dyde þa ic ongean com. ⁊ him þis cyþde.

monasteries to the glory of God and the honour of St Mary, his holy mother; and there founded an English school, which ever, by night and by day, should serve God for our nation. And when I came home I declared to all the people what I had done at Rome. Then they for this thanked God and me very earnestly, and all this they well liked, and said, that with their good will it should for ever stand. I now beseech by the holy Trinity, and St Peter, and all the sacred things, which I sought for myself and for all the nation at Rome, that never any king or ætheling, or bishop, or aldorman, or thane, or reeve, so miserably fordo himself, that he diminish this privilege, which is confirmed by such witness. Without doubt, he who shall do it will incense God and St Peter, and all the saints who rest in the churches of Rome, and for himself will unhappily prepare hell torment everlasting. Also the holy pope aforesaid Leo will set the curse of God, and St Peter, and all saints, and his own, on him who shall ever undo this. And also all this nation, both ecclesiastic and lay, did the same when I came back and announced this to them.

KING BURHRED OF MERCIA. APRIL 18TH DCCC.LVII.

✠ In nomine Domini Dei excelsi, qui est spes omnium finium terre, et in mare longe. Ego autem Burhredus [Omnipot]entissimo Deo concedente, rex Me[rciorum, donabo ac] trado Alhuno, episcopo meo, pro remedio anime mee, aliquam parvam portionem libertatis, cum consensu consiliatorum meorum, gaziferi agelluli in vico Lundonie; hoc est, ubi nominatur Ceolmundingchaga, qui est non longe from Westgetum positus, sibi episcopis in propriam libertatem ad habendum, vel ad Uueogerna civitate pertinentem, cum omnibus rebus que ad se recte pertinent, modicis et magnis; hoc est, quod habeat intus liberaliter modium et pondera et mensura, sicut in porto mos est ad fruendam. Hec libertas hujus agri comparata est a rege cum sexaginta solidorum argenti, et ante empta cum tanto pecunia uno libra et Ceolmunde præfecto. Pax et securitas sit omnibus servantibus hanc libertatem; contradicentibus vero et rennuentibus eterni regis ultio sibi incumbat, si non digne emendaverint Deo et hominibus.

Gesta sunt hec anno Dominicæ incarnationis DCCC.LVII. Indictione vero V., in loco famosa qui dicitur Tomanworðig, in sancta pascha Domini. Ad censum vero regi reddatur in anno de agriunculo illo XII. denarios.

Hii fuerunt testes quorum nomina hic sunt:

✠ Ego Burgred rex Merciorum hanc libertatem, quam episcopis donavi, signo crucis Christi munio et confirmo. ✠ Ego Æthelswyð [re]gina hanc donationem regis consensi et subscripsi. ✠ Ego Tumberht episcopus. ✠ Ego Ceorred episcopus. Ego Alhun episcopus. Ego Byrhtred episcopus. Ego Cuðuulf episcopus. Ego Hunberht dux. [Ego Beor]htnoð dux. Ego Ealdberht dux. Ego Mucel dux. [Ego Aðulf dux.] Ego Beornhard dux. Ego Eadred dux.

KING ÆTHELBERHT OF KENT. DCCC.LVIII.

✠ Regnante in perpetuum Domino Deo nostro omnipotenti Sabaot. Ego Eðelbearht rex, cum consensu ac licentia meorum secularium optimatum divinorumque personarum, liventi animo dabo et concedo meo fideli ministro Wullafe aliquam partem terre juris mei, hoc est v. aratra in illa loco ubi Wasngwelle nominatur, in bicissitudinem alterius terre, hoc est et Mersaham. Hanc terram supranominatam et Wassingwellan ego Eðelbearht ab omni servitute regali operis eternaliter liverabo, sicut ante fuerat illa prenominata terra et Mersaham. Hec sunt etenim marisci q: ad eandem terram rite ac recte pertinent ꝗ hega ante abuerat; id est, an Wiwarawic, ꝗ ante subjecta erat

to Wii ⁊ to Leanaham· ⁊ et Febresham, I. sealtern ⁊ II. wenagang mid cyninges wenum to Blean ðem wiada· ⁊ IIII. oxnum gers mid cyninges oxnum an Wiwarawic· xxx. statera kasei et item x. statera in alia Wiwarawic· et xx. lamba ⁊ xx. fehta.

at Wye and at Lenham, and at Faversham I. salt-house, and II. wainloads with the king's wains at Blean wood; and grass for IV. oxen, with the king's oxen in Wiwarawic; xxx. stateræ of cheese, and likewise x. stateræ in the other Wiwarawic; and xx. lambs, and xx. 'fehta.'

Hec autem terra suprascripta et Wassingwellan his notissimis terminibus antiquitus circumjacentibus ab occidente cyninges folcland quæ abet Wighelm et Wulflaf, ab aquilone Cuðrices dun Heregeðeland; ab oriente Wighelmes land; a meritie biscepes land to Cert II. q: molina ad illam eandem terram pertinentia; una an Wassingwellan, alia an Hwiteceldan. Hec sunt pascua porcorum, quot nostra lingua denbera nominamus: hoc est Lamburnanden, Orricesden, Teligden, Stanehtandenn, et illa silva Sandhyrst nominata, q: pertinet to Wassingwellan. Hancq: livertatem huic eodem agellulo illo q: Wullafe similiter et Wassingwellan, cum consensu ac licentia meorum optimatum liventer largitus sum, ut omnium regalium tributum et vi exactorum operum et penalium rerum principali dominatione, furisq: comprehensione, et cuncta seculari gravidine, absque expeditione sola, et pontium structura, et arcium munitionibus, secura et inmunis permaneat. Si autem aliquis, q̄ absit, diabolika fraude deceptus, et mundana cupiditatæ inlectus, hoc infringere vel irritum facere conaverit, sciat se a consortione katholicorum segregatum, et in die magni æxaminis, quando celum et terra moventur coram Xp̄o et exercitu celesti, nisi ante emendaverit, rationem reddituram esse. Hactum est autem anno Dominice incarnationis DCCC.LVIII., Indictione VI., his testibus consentientibus ac conscribentibus, quorum hic nomina infra karaxant̃.

Hec sunt prata:

to Wassingwellan Stocmed healf be norðan Hegforde be Sturemeda· sue ðerto limpað.	at Washingwell Stockmead-side, to the north of Hedgeford, as thereto belong.

✠ Ego Eðelbearht rex hanc meam donationem cum signo sc̃e crucis Xp̄i rovoravo et subscribo.

✠ Ego Eðelmod dux cons̃. ⁊ sb̃scr.
✠ Ego Eastmund pedesecus cons̃. ⁊ sb̃scr.
✠ Ego Wullaf cons̃. ⁊ sb̃scr.
✠ Ego Eðered cons̃. ⁊ sb̃scr.
✠ Ego Sigenoð cons̃. ⁊ sb̃scr.
✠ Ego Beagmund cons̃. ⁊ sb̃scr.
✠ Ego Ese cons̃. ⁊ sb̃scr.
✠ Ego Dun cons̃. ⁊ sb̃scr.
✠ Ego Oslac cons̃. ⁊ sb̃scr.
✠ Ego Dudda cons̃. ⁊ sb̃scr.
✠ Ego Mucel cons̃. ⁊ sb̃scr.
✠ Ego Burgnoð cons̃.
✠ Ego Eðelweald cons̃.
✠ Ego Eadweald cons̃.
✠ Ego Lulla cons̃.
✠ Ego Acka cons̃.
✠ Ego Cynelaf cons̃.
✠ Ego Eðelhere cons̃.
✠ Ego Wighelm cons̃.
✠ Ego Noðmund cons̃.
✠ Ego Sigemund cons̃.
✠ Ego Hunfreð cons̃.

Dorso. ✠ Ðis siondan ðes landes boec et Wassingwellan ðet Eðelbearht cyning Wullafe sealde his ðegne wið oðrum sue miclum lande et Mersaham. Se cyning sealde ⁊ gebocade Wullafe fif sulung landes et Wassing-	*Indorsed.* This is the charter of the land at Washingwell, which king Æthelberht gave to Wullaf his thane for so much other land at Mersham. The king gave and chartered to Wullaf five sulungs of land at Washingwell

wellan wið ðem fif sulungum et Mersaham. ⁊ se cyning dyde ðet land et Mersaham him to folclande. ða hie ðem landum iehwerfed hefdan. butan ðem merscum. ⁊ butan ðem sealtern et Fefresham. ⁊ butan ðem wioda ðe to ðem sealtern limpð.

for the five sulungs at Mersham; and the king made the land at Mersham into folkland, when he had exchanged the lands, except the marshes, and except the salt-house at Faversham, and except the wood which belongs to the salt-house.

KING ÆTHELBERHT OF WESSEX. DCCC.LXIII.

✠ In nomine Trino divino, Regi regnanti in perpetuum, Domino Deo Hsabaoth, cui patent cuncta penetralia cordis et corporis terrestria simul et cœlestia, necnon super æthera regnans in sedibus altis, ima et alta omnia sua dicione gubernans, cujus amore et eternis premiis ✠ ego Eðelbearht, rex Occidentalium Saxonum, necnon et Cantuariorum, dabo et concedo meo fideli ministro et principi meo Eðelredo aliquam partem terre juris mei, hoc est VIII. aratra in illa loco hubi nominatur Mersaham, in sempiternum hereditatem sibi abendum et possidendum, feliciterque in dies ejus perfruendum, post dies ejus cuicumque hei heredi placuerit derelinquendum, liberam per omnia habeat potestatem, cum campis, silvis, pratis, pascuis, aquis, venationibus, pascuis porcorum, simulque mariscis, et cum omnibus utilitatibus rite ac recte ad eandem terram pertinentibus. Hoc feci pro ejus humili hobœdientia, simulque pro ejus placavili atque conpetenti pecunia, quam ab eo accepi, hoc est CCCCtos mancusas auri purissimi. Hanc autem terram supranominatam et Mersaham ✠ ego Eðelbearht rex ab omni servitute regali operis, intus et foris, magnis ac modicis, notis et ignotis, perenniter liveravo, nisi his tantum tribus causis, hoc est, expeditione, et arcis munitione, pontisque constructione, et illud foras reddat quot sivi intus faciendi appetat. Hæc autem terra prenominata his notissimis terminibus circumcingitur: A meritie et ab occidente Stur usque Blancanryðe; ab aquilone et ab oriente Eadwaldes bocland to Bradeburnan; estque una semis aratra ab oriente Sture, que jacet at confinium usque Garulfi regis ministri to Mersaham et medan be eastan ee, sue þer mid rihte to þem lande limpað (as there rightfully belong to the land), unamque salis coquinariam, hoc est, I. sealternsteall. ⁊ þer cota to (and two cots there), in illa loco ubi nominatur Herewic; et IIII. carris transductionem in silba regis sex ebdomades a die Pentecosten, hubi alteri homines silbam cedunt, hoc est, in regis communione, hec sunt pascua porcorum, que nostra lingua Saxhonica denbera nominamus; hoc est, Husneah, Efreðingdenn, Herbedingdenn, Wafingdenn, Widefingdenn, Bleccingdenn; necnon xx. statera casei of Mersce (from the Marsh) ad Mersaham reddatur, et XL. agnos, et XL. vellera ovium, et duorum dierum refectio, vel xxx. argenteis, hoc est, semicum libra redimatur. Hsi quis vero heredum successorumque meorum, regum, principum, ducum, optimatum, sive exactorum, hanc meam donationem servare voluerit, servetur ei desuper benedictio sempiterna; hsi autem, absit, quod non optamus, alicujus personis homo, diabolica temeritate instigatus, surrexerit qui hanc meam donationem vel livertatem infringere, vel minuere, aut in aliut conbertere quam a nobis constitutum est temptaverit, sciat se ante tribunal summi et eterni Judicis rationem esse redditurum, nisi ante digna hsatisque placabili factione Deo et hominibus emendare studuerit.

Hacta est autem hec eadem donatio vel livertas in illa loco que vocitatur Biernefeld, anno Dominice incarnationis DCCC.LXIII., Indictione XI., testibus consentientibus, et signo sc̃e crucis Xp̃i confirmantibus, quorum hic nomina infra ac in scedula patefacta liquescunt.

✠ Ego Eðelbearht rex hanc meam donationem vel livertatem cum vexillo sc̃e crucis Xp̃i rob. ⁊ sb. ✠ Ego Eðered dux cons. ⁊ sb. ✠ Ego Eðered fil. reg. cons. ⁊ sb. ✠ Ego Dryhtweald dux cons. ⁊ sb. ✠ Ego Mucel m̃. cons. ⁊ sb. ✠ Ego Heahmund pr̃. cons. ⁊ sb. ✠ Ego Heremod pr̃. cons. ⁊ sb. ✠ Ego Garulf m̃. cons. ⁊ sb. ✠ Ego Eastmund m̃. cons. ⁊ sb. ✠ Ego Uulfred m̃. cons. ⁊ sb. ✠ Ego Wigstan m̃.

cons̄. ⁊ sb̄. ✠ Ego Ecgferð m̄. cons̄. ⁊ sb̄. ✠ Ego Ealdred m̄. cons̄. ⁊ sb̄. ✠ Ego Sigenoð m̄. ✠ Ego Elfstan m̄. ✠ Ego Wighelm m̄. ✠ Ego Piahtred m̄. ✠ Item at stabilitatem hujus suprascripte donationis vel livertatis, ✠ Ego Ciolnoð, gratia Dei arc̄iepisc̄., mea propria manu signum sc̄e crucis Xp̄i impressi. ✠ Ego Deimund pr̄. ab̄. cons̄. ⁊ sb̄. ✠ Ego Biarnulf pr̄. ab̄. cons̄. ⁊ sb̄. ✠ Ego Eðelweald pr̄. cons̄. ⁊ sb̄. ✠ Ego Noðheard pr̄. cons̄. ⁊ sb̄. ✠ Ego Osmund pr. cons̄. ⁊ sb̄. ✠ Ego Iab pr̄. cons̄. ⁊ sb̄. ✠ Ego Wighelm pr̄. cons̄. ⁊ sb̄. ✠ Ego Tida pr̄. cons̄. ⁊ sb̄. ✠ Ego Biarnheah arc̄d. cons̄. ⁊ sb̄. ✠ Ego Osulf arc̄hd. cons̄. ⁊ sb̄. ✠ Ego Ealhstan cons̄. ⁊ sb̄. ✠ Ego Sigefreð arc̄hd. cons̄. ⁊ sb̄. ✠ Ego Diarweald sb̄d. cons̄. ⁊ sb̄. ✠ Ego Sefreð sb̄. cons̄. ⁊ sb̄. ✠ Ego Osmund cons̄. ⁊ sb̄. ✠ Ego Dudda cons̄. ⁊ sb̄. ✠ Ego Beagmund cons̄. ⁊ sb̄. ✠ Ego Osweald cons̄. ⁊ sb̄. ✠ Ego Lulla cons̄. ⁊ sb̄. ✠ Ego Hunfreð cons̄. ⁊ sb̄. ✠ Ego Lulla cons̄. ⁊ sb̄. ✠ Ego Eadulf cons̄. ⁊ sb̄. ✠ Ego Osbearht cons̄. ⁊ sb̄. ✠ Ego Wealdhelm cons̄. ⁊ sb̄. ✠ Ego Ealdhere cons̄. ⁊ sb̄. ✠ Ego Diara cons̄. ⁊ sb̄. ✠ Ego Garulf cons̄. ⁊ sb̄. ✠ Ego Elric cons̄. ⁊ sb̄. ✠ Ego Dudda cons̄. ⁊ sb̄. ✠ Ego Eðelwulf cons̄. ⁊ sb̄.

Ic Eadwald sello ⁊ forgeofu þis lond et Wifelesbeorge Agustines higum into hiora beode· minre sawle to are ⁊ to lecdome· ⁊ eow for Godes lufe bidde þet ge hit minre sawle nyt gedeo· ⁊ me hit for Gode leanie eow to elmessum. Amen.

I Eadwald give and concede this land at Wivlesborough, to the brotherhood of St Augustine's, for their table; for the honour and medicament of my soul; and I pray you, for the love of God, that ye render it useful to my soul, and before God requite me for it as alms to you. Amen.

KING ÆTHELBERHT OF WESSEX. DCCC.LXIV.

LIBERTAS QUAM ATHELBERTUS REX CONCESSIT SCIREBURNENSI ECCLESIÆ.

✠ Regnante in perpetuum Domino nostro Ihesu Christo. Ricsiendum urum Dryhtne Hælendum Criste in ecnisse· þæm hiehstan ⁊ þæm untosprecendlican ealra þinga ⁊ ealra tīda Scippende· se ðe on manegum þingum his mihtum setteð· eac swylce þam ure hefenlican ⁊ þæm unasecgendlican rīce· ꝥte he þisses līfes eadinysse ⁊ gesælinysse on ænigum þingum ne forlæte. Forþon ic Æðelbreht mid Godes gife Westsaxna kyning witodlice ic þence· ⁊ me on gemynde is mid þissum eorðlicum þingum ða ecelican gestreon to begitanne· sicut Salomon dixit. "Redemptio animæ propriæ divitiæ"· swa swa Salomon cwæð· þæt we sceoldon mid urum spedum urum saulum þa ecan gesælinesse begitan. Forþon ic cuðlice· mid geþeahte· ⁊ mid geþafonge ⁊ leafe minra biscepa ⁊ aldormanna· ⁊ nohte þon læs mīnra broðera Æðelredes ⁊ Ælfredes· ⁊ ealra þara selestena witona þæs rīces· ic forgyfe for me selfne ⁊ for mīne ða

✠ Regnante in perpetuum Domino nostro Ihesu Christo. Our Lord Jesus Christ ruling in eternity, the highest and the most ineffable Creator of all things, and of all times, who holds many things in subjection by his powers, so also our heavenly and ineffable kingdom, so that he the happiness and prosperity of this life in no things abandons. Therefore I Æthelberht, by God's grace king of the West Saxons, certainly think and have in mind with these earthly things to beget everlasting reward; sicut Salomon dixit: "Redemptio animæ propriæ divitiæ"; as Solomon said: that we should, with our riches, beget for our souls eternal happiness. Therefore I, to wit, with the counsel and leave of my bishops and aldormen, and not less of my brothers Æthelred and Ælfred, and of all the most excellent 'witan' of the kingdom, I give for myself and for my dearest friends living, and also for veneration of the soul of my father liofestan līfiende frynd· ⁊ eac swylce for arwurðnesse Æðelwulfes saule mīnes fæder· ⁊ Æðelbaldes mīnes broðor· soðlice þisne freols to þære halgan stowe æt Scireburnan· þære Æðelbaldes cyninges lichama hine resteð· ꝥ hit sy fæstlice ⁊ unawended ⁊ ecelice gefreod alra cynelicra ⁊ alra dōmlicra þeowdōma· ge þeoffenges ge æghwelcre unieðnesse[1] ealles worldlices broces· nymðe fyrde ⁊ bryce weorces. Gif hwa þonne sye ꝥ he hine for Godes lufan to ðan geeaðmedan wille ꝥ he þas ure gyfe geieacnian wille oððe gemonifældan wille· geiece him ælmihti God eal gōd her on worlde· ⁊ his dagas gesundfulle. Gyf þanne hwilc man to ðan geþristlæce· oððe mid deofles searwum to ðam beswicen sye ꝥ he þis on ænigum þingum lytlum oððe myclum þence to gebrecanne oððe to onwendanne· wite he þonne ꝥ he þæs agieldende sie beforan Cristes þrymsetle· þonne ealle heofonware ⁊ eorðware on his andweardnesse beoð onstyrede ⁊ onhrerede· nymðe he hit ǣr her on worlde mid ryhte gebete.

Ðis wæs gewriten þæs gære ðe wæs agān fram Cristes

[1] MS. ieðnesse.

Æthelwulf, and of my brother Æthelbald, verily this immunity to the holy place at Sherborne, where the body of king Æthelbald rests, that it be firmly and immutably and eternally freed from all royal and all judicial services, both of 'þeoffeng' and from every annoyance of all worldly cares, except the 'fyrd' and bridge-work. If then there be any one who, for love of God, will so vouchsafe, that he will augment or multiply this our gift, may God Almighty augment all good to him here in the world, and cause his days to prosper. But if any man be so audacious, or by the devil's wiles so deceived, that he in any things, little or great, think to break or to avert this, be it then known to him that he may have to make retribution for it before the throne of Christ, when all the inhabitants of heaven and of earth shall be stirred and excited in his presence, unless he previously, here in the world, make just atonement.

This was written in the year that was agone from the birth of Christ eight hundred acennednesse eahta hund wintra ⁊ feower ⁊ sixtig. ⁊ in þam tacencircole ꝥ twelfte gear. þe deg wæs septimo kał. Ianuarii.

Ðis wæs gedon in þam cynelican setle on þære stowe þe is genæmned Dornwaraceaster beforan þissum witum geþafigendum. þe hære namon her benioðan gewritene ⁊ gesewene sindon. ✠ Ic Æðelbreht cyning mid þære halgan rode tacne þis het swiðe geornlice getrymman ⁊ gefæstnian.

Ða æfter þyssum hit gelamp. þan ilcan geare þæsne þis on midnewinter wæs gedon. ꝥ Æðelbreht se cining. on frigedæg. twam nihtum ǣr Estron. ðisne freols mid his ágenre hande unnende mode ufan þone heah altare alegde æt ham æt Sciréburnan. in andweardnesse ealre þære broðorlican gesamnunga. ealdra ⁊ geongra. ⁊ eac swylce his mægan Æðelredes ⁊ Ælfredes. ⁊ his oðræ witona. þe ðær ða mid him wæron for hine selfne lifigende ⁊ for his twegen broðre þe þær ða andwearde stodon. ⁊ for hyra ealra fæder saule Æðelwulfes cyninges. ⁊ Æðelbaldes cyninges hyra broðor. ðe his lichama in þære stowe resteð.

and sixty-four winters, and in the twelfth year of the Indiction. The day was the seventh of the Kalends of January (Dec. 26th).

This was done in the royal residence, in the place which is named Dorchester, before these consenting witnesses, whose names are here beneath written and seen. ✠ I Æthelberht king, with the sign of the holy rood, very earnestly command this to be confirmed and ratified[1].

Then after this it happened, in the same year, after this had been done at Midwinter, that king Æthelberht, on Friday, two nights before Easter, with his own hand and with munificent spirit, laid this immunity upon the high altar in the monastery at Sherborne, in the presence of all the brotherly congregation, old and young, and also of his brothers, Æthelred and Ælfred, and his other 'witan' who were then there with him, for himself living, and for his two brothers who there stood present, and for the soul of the father of them all, king Æthelwulf, and of their brother, king Æthelbald, whose body rests in that place.

[1] The other signatures are wanting.

He þisne freodō̄m· on ælmihtiges Godes namon ⁊ on ealra his halgra· fæstlice bebead þæt hine nā̄n his æfterfylgendra eft ne onwende· ne on anegum dælum· læssan ne on maran· hine ne oncyrde· ac he swa ecelice forð þurwunede swa lange swa God wolde ꝥ cristengeleafamidEngolcynne untosceacen weoxa· ealra þara worldcundra hefinesse ðe her beforan nemde syondon· ⁊ se hæbbe Godes miltse ⁊ his halgra· se ðe þis mid gō̄de trymman wille ⁊ healdon. Gyf þonne hwa sie ꝥ he his on ænegum dæle wanian þence oððe brecan· þanne næbbe he naðer ne Godes miltse ne his haligra· nymðe he hit ǣr mid ryhte gebete.

Ðis wæs gedon beforan þære gewitnesse þe hyro naman her bynyoðan gemearcode standað.

This immunity he, in the name of Almighty God, has strongly commanded that none of his successors either divert, or in any of its parts, great or small, change; but that it should continue on eternally, as long as God shall will that Christian belief wax unimpaired among the English race, by all the worldly ills which are here before named. And let him have the mercy of God and his saints, who will confirm and observe this with good. But if any one be who in any part think to impair or violate it, then may he never have God's mercy nor his saints', unless he make just reparation.

This was done before the witnesses whose names stand marked here beneath[1].

[1] The names are wanting.

EALHERE. DCCC.LX.–DCCC.LXVI.

✠ In nomine Domini, ego Ealhere dabo et concedo Oswige et Weahtræde aliquam partem terre . . . . virgas in latitudine contra ejus pecunia que accepi ab eo, hoc est cc. et LXX. denarios et . . . . hereditatem illis habendum et possidendum feliciterque in diebus eorum perfruendum . . . . derelinquendum liberam per omnia habeant potestates, et si quis hanc meam donationem . . . . benedictio: si autem absit, quod non optamus, ut alicujus personis homo, cum diabolica . . . . infringere aut minuere temptaverit, sciat se ante tribunal Xp̄i racionem . . . . et hominibus emendare vo . . . . it his testibus consencientibus a conscribentibus . . . .

Ego Æðelbearht rex hanc me . . . . . ne cum vexillo sc̄e crucis Xp̄i roborabo et subscribo. Ego . . . . . Ego Cialnoð arh̄i epı̄c conseñ . . . . [B]ryhtwald dux. Ego Mucel m̄. Ego Eastmund m̄. Ego Ealhere m̄. . . . . Ego Ælfred filius reḡ. hos omnes consenserunt et signo sc̄e crucis conscripš. Ego Eðelwine. . . . . Ego Æðelstan et ingan burgware. Ego Æðelhelm et cniahta gealdan. Ego Herewine et herred . . . .

KING CEOLWULF OF MERCIA. DCCC.LXXV.

✠ In nomine sancte et individue Trinitatis, anno ejusdem incarnationis humane DCCC.LXXV., Indict. VIII., Ego Ceolwulf, gratia Dei gratuita largiente rex Merciorum, aliquid mihi in elemosinam donare precogitavi, ut sempiterne mercedis portionem acceptarem; ideo rogatus a Werfriðo antiste Huicciorum, et familia in Uueogernacestre, istam libertatem, cum meorum omnium unanimo consensu episcoporum et principum, ac etiam cunctorum optimatum nostre gentis, perpetualiter donavi, ut tota parochia Hwicciorum a pastu æquorum regis, et eorum qui eos ducunt, absoluta et secura permansisset; et ille episcopus dedit regi Ceolwulfo sex manentes, ubi appellatur Dæglesford, et hoc divinum servitium pro expiatione peccaminum Ceolwulfi regis diffiniunt, ut in illis monasteriis in quibus prenominata servitus persolvi deberet, memoria et Oratio Dominica cotidie ad celum mitteretur, quamdiu Christiana fides in ista gente servaretur. Tunc etiam supradictus rex ante nominato episcopo dedit LX. mancusos auri, ea conditione, ut ipse istam terram habuisset, et tribus heredibus, quibus voluisset, post se relinquisset, et post dies istorum heredum antedicta terra ad Uueogernensem civitatem rediret, pro anima Ceolwulfi regis et posterorum illius; et tamen libertas supradicta perpetualiter permaneret. Omnipotens Deus illos custodiat, qui hoc donum custodire dignentur; et qui violare temptaverint, sciant se rationem reddituros in tremendo examinis die. Hii sunt testes et confirmatores hujus donationis, quorum nomina infra signo sancte crucis notantur. ✠ Ego Ceolwulf, rex Merciorum, hanc conditionem propria manu confirmo. ✠ Ego Eadberht episcopus consensi. ✠ Ego Uuærferð· episcopus consensi. ✠ Ego Deorlaf episcopus. ✠ Ego Beorhtnoð dux. ✠ Ego Æðelhun dux.

ÆTHELRED ALDORMAN OF MERCIA. DCCC.LXXXIII.

✠ Sæculi namque labentis tempora, sicut umbræ fugientes, sic velociter tranant, varieque eventuum status in cogitationes hominum conscendunt. Ideo omnes firmas statutiones nostras litterarum serie confirmamus, ne posteris cadant ex memoria precedentium decreta patrum; Grecorum talibus exemplis statuta sunt, qui quod scire volunt litteris tradunt, ne ex memoria labetur. Estque nobis necesse premeditandum in fugabundis temporibus sæculi quomodo ad æternam felicitatem pervenire valeamus; quia cuncta que videntur fugitiva sunt et caduca, que autem non videntur perhenniter sunt manentia;

for þære wisan ic Æðelræd eldorman· inbryrdendre Godes gefe gewelegod ⁊ gewlenced mid sume dæle Mercna rices for Godes lufan ⁊ for alesnessa minra gylta ⁊ synna· ⁊ for benum abbodes ⁊ þære heorædene æt Berclea· ⁊ eac for ealre Merce· ic heo gefreoge ecelice þæs gafoles þe hio nu get to cyninges handa ageofan sceolan of þam dæle þe	for which cause I Æthelred aldorman, through the inspiring grace of God, enriched and exalted with a part of the Mercians' realm, for love of God, and for the remission of my guilts and sins, and for the prayers of the abbot and the society at Berkeley, and also for all Mercia, I free them for ever from the tax which they still have to pay

þær ungefreod to lafe wæs ðære cyningefeorme· ge on hlutrum alað· ge on beore· ge on hunige· ge [on] hryþrum· ge on swynum· ge on sceapum. And þæt ic dyde for hiora godcundre gebedredenne· ⁊ for þan eac þe hio me hiora landes sumne dæl in ece ærfewerdnesse to forleortan· þæt is æt Stoce twelf hida· ⁊ ðritig mancusa goldes hio sealdan eāc me· ⁊ ꝥ ic ꝥ mynster fram æghwelcum gafolum gefreoge þe to þiode hlafarde belimpeð· litles oððe micles· cuðes ge uncuðes· butan angilde wið oþrum· and fæstengewerce· ⁊ fyrdsocne· ⁊ brycggeweorce· ⁊ ꝥ ic do mid Ælfredes cyninges leafe ⁊ gewitnesse· ⁊ mid ealra Myrcna witena· godcundra hada ⁊ woroldcundra. And nu æft ꝥ ilce land æt Stoce· ꝥ is twelf hida· ic selle Cynulfe Ceoluhtes suna in þreora manna dæg· for syxtigum mancesa clænes goldes· æghwelces þinges to freon· ge wið cyning· ge wið

into the king's hand, viz. from the part which was left unfreed of the royal farm, in clear ale, in beer, in honey, in cattle, in swine, and in sheep. And that I have done for their divine prayers, and also because they have relinquished to me a part of their land in perpetuity. That is, at Stoke twelve hides; and they have also given me thirty mancuses of gold, and that I free the monastery from all the taxes which belong to the lord of the people, little or great, known or unknown, except the 'angild'[1] to others, and fortress-work, and 'fyrdsocn,' and bridge-work. And that I do with the leave and witness of king Ælfred and of all the 'witan' of the Mercians, of divine and secular conditions. And now again that same land at Stoke, that is the twelve hides, I give to Cynulf Ceoluht's son, for sixty mancuses of pure gold, free of everything towards the king, the aldorman, or the

[1] Angild is a simple payment or compensation, opp. to twygild, a double payment; but here and a few lines lower, where, in connection with the *trinoda necessitas*, it appears as an exception to the several exemptions from imposts, I understand the passage to mean that the enfranchisement does not include the dues to individuals, as the aldorman, reeve, &c., but the royal dues only. The words ⁊ noht út to wite, on the next page, I cannot explain. The 'angild' is the payment to the individual; the 'wite,' the penalty due to the state for the infraction of the law.

ealdorman· ge wið gerefan· æghwelces þeodomes· lytles and micles· butan fyrdsocne· and fæstengeworce· ⁊ brycggeworce· ⁊ angylde wið oðrum· ⁊ noht ut to wite. Ond we beodað ꝥ nænig mon on Ceoluhte[1]· ge sib oððe fremde· hit gereafige in ænigum þingum þa hwyle þe he lyfie· forðon þe he hit geearnode æt Mercna hlafordum mid rihtre eadmodnysse. Ond nu we beodað in Godes almihtiges naman· ꝥ ðes bufancwedena freodom þæs mynstres æt Berclea· ⁊ eac sio geofu þæs landes þe we Cynulfe syllað in ðreora manna [dæg]· unbereafod ðorhwunige on ēcnesse· on þas gerad· ꝥ æfter Cynewulfes ⁊ his erfewerda twega· þæt twelf hida land æt Stoce· butan ælcum wiðercwide· sio agefen to Wigornacestre þam bisceopstole· for Æðelred ealdormon ⁊ for ealle Merce· him to ecre ælmessan. Eac we biddað ⁊ alsiað· in naman ðære halgan þrinesse· þæt gif hwelc mon sio þæt he mid yfle wyllan oht ðæs abrecan wylle ðe on ðisse cartan awriten is· wite he þonne ꝥ hē hit dē ofer Godes est· ⁊ ofer ealra his haligra· ⁊ eāc

reeve, of every service, little and great, except fyrdsocn and fortress-work, and bridge-work, and 'angyld' to others, and naught out for 'wite'. And we command that no man, either relative or stranger, in any way, bereave Ceoluht[1] of it, as long as he lives; because he has merited it of the lords of the Mercians through right obedience. And we now, in the name of Almighty God, command, that this abovesaid immunity to the monastery at Berkeley, and also the gift of the land, which we give to Cynulf for three men's day, continue unimpaired for ever, on this condition, that after the death of Cynewulf and his two heirs, the twelve hides of land at Stoke be, without any contention, given to the episcopal see at Worcester, for Æthelred aldorman and for all Mercians, in perpetual alms. We also pray and beseech, in the name of the holy Trinity, that if any man there be, who with evil will shall in aught violate this which is written in this charter, be it known to him that he does it against the pleasure of God and of all his

[1] Cynulfe?

ofer monna godcundra hada ⁊ woroldcundra· elces ðæra þe ænig riht geþencean cunne oððe wylle· ⁊ he hit gebete beforan þam heahsetle ðæs ecean Deman· butan he hit ær mid rihtre bote gebetan wille Gode ⁊ monnum.

saints, and also of men of divine and secular conditions, of all those who can think or will any right: and let him make reparation before the throne of the eternal Judge, unless he will previously, with just compensation, make amends to God and men.

Acta est autem hujus donationis munificentia anno Dominicæ incarnationis DCCC.LXXXIII., Indict. autem I., his testibus consentientibus et subscribentibus, quorum hic nomina notescunt.

✠ Ego Ælfred rex hujus traditionis munificentiam signo sanctæ crucis adfirmo. ✠ Ego Æðelred dux hanc meam donationem signo sanctæ crucis inpono. ✠ Ego Wulfred episcopus consensi. ✠ Ego Werferð episcopus consensi. ✠ Ego Deorlaf episcopus consensi. ✠ Ego Æðelferð dux consensi. ✠ Ego Earduulf consensi et subscripsi. ✠ Ego Æðelwold dux consensi. ✠ Ego Eadnoð consensi et subscripsi. ✠ Ego Ælfred consensi et subscripsi. ✠ Ego Æðelhun abbas consensi et subscripsi. ✠ Wigheard presbiter. ✠ Wighelm. ✠ Luda. ✠ Wilferð. ✠ Ecghun. ✠ Acha.

Terra autem ista hiis circumcingitur terminibus, etc.

Ærest of Hæslwellan in Hæsldene· þonne on Waldeswellan· of Waldeswellan on Sweordes stane in Eowcumb· of Eowcumbe in Afene stream· of Afene streame eft up·. þæt in Hrycgleage· þonne of Hrycgleage· þæt on Penpau· of Penpau þæt in Sæferne stream· of Hæslwellan eft· þæt in Leadgedelf· of Leadgedelfe on Mylepul· of Mylenpulle eft in Afene stream.

First from Hazlewell in Hazledean; then to Woldswell; from Woldswell to Sweordes stone in Ewcombe; from Ewcombe to the Avon's stream; from the Avon's stream again up; then to Ridgeley; from Ridgeley, then to Penpau; from Penpau then to the Severn's stream; from Hazlewell again; then to Leadgedelf; from Leadgedelf to Millpool; from Millpool again to the Avon's stream.

ÆTHELRED ALDORMAN OF MERCIA. DCCC.LXXXVII.

✠ Regnante imperpetuum Domino nostro Jhesu Christo, cujus imperio hujus seculi labentis prosperitas in adversis successibus sedulo permixta et conturbata cernitur, omniaque visibilia atque desiderabilia pomparum mundi ornamenta ab ipsis amatoribus suis cotidie fugiendo transeunt. Quapropter quique sapientes ac beati cum his fugitivis seculi eterna gaudia jugiter mansura celestis patrie magnopere mercanda sunt. Quapropter ego Æðelred, gratia Domini largiflua concedente, dux et patricius gentis Merciorum, cum licentia et impositione manus Ælfredi regis, una cum testimonio et consensu seniorum ejusdem gentis, episcoporum vel principum, pro redemptione animarum nostrarum, et pro sospitate, nec non et stabilitate regni Merciorum, nobis in eternam elemosinam, quandam ruris portionem Domino Deo et Sancto Petro, liberatam ab omni tributo regali, magno vel modico, noto vel ignoto, hoc est, æt Berhtanwellan VI. mansiones, et æt Wætlingtune VIII., cum omnibus pertinentibus ad rura eadem, in silvis et in campis, sicut exterius finibus certis dinota consistunt, ad ecclesiam illam que vocatur æt Readanoran pertinentes, utrasque terras in unam possessionis hereditatem, id est, ad episcopalem sedem, scilicet Uueogernensis civitatis, plena videlicet mentis devotione concedendo humiliter donavimus. Insuper etiam, huic donationi in augmentum, sex homines, qui prius pertinebant ad villam regiam in Beonsincgtune, cum omni prole et stirpe eorum, ad eandem conscripsimus ecclesiam, cum consensu prefati regis et eorundem optimatum meorum, ut, sine contradictione alicujus, nobilis vel ignobilis, semper ad terram ecclesie supradicte pertineant, in sempiternam hereditatem hec possidenda donavimus. Si qui autem, quod absit, ausu philargirie, hoc nostrum traditionis donum in aliqua corrumpenda fedare pertemptent, sciant se rationem reddituros in die judicii, cum Anna et Saphira, nisi prius digna satisfactione emendare maluerint. Acta sunt hec anno Dominice incarnationis DCCC.LXXXVII., Indict. vero V.

Ðis earon þara manna	These are the names of the

noman þe gewritene earon from Bynsingtune to Readanoran in ꝥ bisceoprice to Uueogernacestre· mid heora teame ⁊ mid þy tudre þe from him cume· ā on ece yrfewardnesse. Alhmund· Tidulf· Tidheh· Lull· Eadwulf. Hoc autem rus his finibus ambitur. Æt Byrhtanwellan from Ceolulfes treowe· ondlong Longanhylles on Fildena weg· þonan on Holandene up on Cadandune to Æðelheges gemære· þonan to Ecgfriðes gemære· þonne ā big Ecgfriðes gemære to Cuceshæma gemære· ꝥ to Incghæma gemære suð þurh Eastleh· ꝥ to Gisles bæce· ꝥ ondlong Gisles bæces· ꝥ eft to Ceolwulfes treowe· ⁊ ꝥ mæðlond betweonum Egsanfordam ⁊ Strætforda· be Norðan broce· ⁊ þone wudu þærto þe Scylfhrycg is haten.

men that are written from Bynsington to Radnor in the bishopric of Worcester, with their families and with the offspring which shall from them come, ever in perpetuity: Alhmund, Tidulf, Tidheh, Lull, Eadwulf. Hoc autem rus his finibus ambitur: At Brightwell from Ceolulf's tree, along Longanhills to Fieldenway; thence to Hollowdean up to Chadlington to Æthelhere's boundary; thence to Ecgfrith's boundary; then keeping along Ecgfrith's boundary to Cuxham boundary; then to Ingham boundary south through Eastlea; then to Gilsbeck; then along Gilsbeck; then again to Ceolwulf's tree; and the meadowland between Exford and Stratford, by Northbrook and the wood thereto, which is named Shelfridge.

Hec nomina sunt qui hanc libertatis donationem consentientes, signo crucis subscripserunt.

✠ Ego Ælfred rex consensi et subscripsi. ✠ Ego Æðered dux hoc nostrum donum signo crucis confirmavi. ✠ Ego Æðelflæd conjunx subscribens confirmavi. ✠ Ego Uulfred episcopus. ✠ Ego Uuerfrið episcopus. ✠ Ego Deorlaf episcopus.

* KING ÆLFRED. DCCC.LXXXIX.

✠ Sedule namque nonnullis, et maxime per instantis vitæ turbidam discordiæ rabiem, in hac decrepita finis mundialis canitiæ contingere solet, quod simplicem memorialis præcordii oculum turbines obliviose obscenitatis quatientes reverberant, seu nebulæ neglegentiarum nubiferis deprivationum fuscationibus a recte possessionis jure radiantem justitiæ Phoebum obnubilant; quapropter necesse cuilibet homini est, ut litteratoriis apicibus omnia atquisita seu possessa, ob præsentium sive succedentium cautelam, quæ a catholicis vel heroicis viris cujuslibet persone majoris minorisve potestatis, Deo ejusque sanctis per celorum celsitudinem tradita sunt, etiam testimonio et roboratione ipsorum firme rationis serie firmentur, rectoque caraxantis stilo in scedulis notentur. Anno igitur postquam almifica cælestini luminis gemma per agrum virginalis pudicitiæ humano generi desiderabilis mistici spiraminis specimine enituit, octingentesimo octuagesimo nono, Indictione VII., cujus denique splendoris et gratiæ nobis jubare radiante, ego Ælfred rex Anglorum et Saxonum, et Æðelred subregulus et patricius Merciorum, cum testimonio et licentia seu consensu senatorum, episcoporum seu ducum utriusque gentis, pro revelatione facinorum nostrorum, et pro adquirenda deifice remunerationis requiæ, Uuærfriðo, eximio Huicciorum antistiti, ad æcclesiam Uueogernensem, in Lundonia unam curtem, que verbotenus ad antiquum petrosum ædificium, id est, æt Hwætmundes stane a civibus apellatur, a strata publica usque in murum ejusdem civitatis, cujus longitudo est perticarum XXVI., et latitudo in superiori parte perticarum XIII. et pedum VII., et in inferiori loco perticarum XI. et VI. pedum, ad plenam libertatem infra totius rei sempiternaliter possidendum, in ecclesiasticum jus conscribimus, et concedentes donamus; et intro urnam et trutinam, ad mensurandum in emendo sive vendendo ad usum, sive ad necessitatem propriam et liberam omnimodis habeat; et totius debiti vel pene fiscalis, vel publice rei, nisi ad dominium episcopi ecclesie Uueogernensis quæ intus contingat, absoluta persistat. Si autem foris vel in strata publica seu in ripa emtorali quislibet suorum mercaverit, juxta quod rectum sit, thelon ad manum regis subeat; quod si intus in curte predicto quislibet emerit vel vendiderit, thelon debitum ad manum episcopi supra memorati reddatur; et semper quamdiu unda sacri baptismatis populi Anglorum sive Saxonum per fidem Christiane religionis aspergentur, seu ipsorum auctoritatis dominio urbs Lundonia habilis subjaceat ad Uueogernensem civitatem subdita persistat. Contestamur et obsecramus unius cujusque personas hominum, presentium sive subsequentium, ut hoc nostrum donum inviolatum et integrum, sicut presens pagina testatur, permaneat. Si qui vero, ut non optamus, serpentino suggestionis demonicæ toxico inflati, hujus tramitis seriem in aliquo temptaverint foedare, noverint se cum Anna et Zaphira herebica aeterne anathematis machera perforandos, nisi prius digna satisfactione emendare maluerint.

Haec autem sunt nomina illorum qui huic nostræ donationi testes et consentientes fuerunt, et trophico sancte crucis vexillo roborantes, propriis manibus subscripserunt.

✠ Ego Ælfred, rex Anglorum et Saxonum, hanc donationem confirmans, signo crucis subscribo. ✠ Ego Æðelred, subregulus et patricius Merciorum, hanc donationem signo crucis subscripsi. ✠ Ego Æþelflæd consensi. ✠ Ego Uulfred episcopus consensi. ✠ Ego Alhard episcopus consensi. ✠ Ego Uuærfred episcopus consensi. ✠ Ego Deneuulf episcopus consensi. ✠ Ego Uulfsige episcopus consensi.

ÆTHELRED ALDORMAN OF MERCIA AND ÆTHELFLÆD. DCCC.LXXXVI.-DCCC.XCIX.

✠ Ðæm ælmihtigan Gode þære soðan ānnesse ⁊ þære halgan þrynnesse on heofonum sie lof ⁊ wuldor ⁊ dæda þoncung[1] ealra þæra gōda þe he us forgifen hafað· for þæs	✠ To almighty God the true Unity and the holy Trinity in heaven, be praise and glory, and thanksgiving, for all the good which he has given us; for whose love, in

[1] Perhaps meant for a translation of *gratiarum actio*.

lufan æt ærestan Æþelred ealdorman ⁊ Æðelflæd· ⁊ for Sc̃e Petres ⁊ þære cyricean æt Weogernaceastre· ⁊ eac for Wærferðes bisceopes bene· heora freondes· hehtan bewyrcean þa burh æt Weogernaceastre eallum þæm folce to gebeorge· ⁊ eac þæron Godes lof to arǽrenne· ⁊ heo nu cyðað on Godes gewitnesse on þisse be͂c· ꝥ heo wyllað on ælcum þæra gerihta þe to heora hlaforddóme gebyrað· oððe on ceapstowe· oððe on stræte· ge binnan byrg ge butan· geunnan healfes Gode ⁊ Sc̃e Petre ⁊ þære cyrcean hlaforde ꝥ þy ārlicor on þære stowe beon mæge· ⁊ eac ðy eað be sumum dǽle þæs heoredes helpan· ⁊ ꝥ heora gemynd on ecnesse þy fæstlicor on þære stowe seo· þa hwile ðe Godes hearsumnes on þam mynstre beo. Ond Wærferð bisceop ⁊ se heored habbað geseted þas godcundnysse beforan þære ðe him mon dæghwamlice deð· ge be heora life ge æfter heora life· ꝥ þonne æt eolcum uhtsonge· ⁊ æt eolcum æfensonge· ⁊ æt eolcum undernsonge· De profundis þone sealm þa hwile þe heo lifgeon· ⁊ æfter heora life· Laudate Dominum· ⁊

the first place, Æthelred aldorman and Æthelflæd, and for St Peter's and the church at Worcester, and also for the prayer of their friend bishop Werferth, have commanded the 'burh' at Worcester to be constructed as a protection to all the people, and also to raise the praise of God therein. And they now declare, with God's witness, by this charter, that of all those rights which belong to their lordship, either in market-place or in street, both within burgh and without, they will give the half to God and St Peter and the lord of the church, that it may be the more honourable in that place, and also the more easily, in some part, help the convent, and that their remembrance may to eternity be the firmer in that place, while obedience to God shall be in that monastery. And bishop Werferth and the convent have established this divine office before that which is daily offered him, both during [1]their life and after their life; that namely at every uht-song, and at every even-song, and at every undern-song the psalm 'De

[1] Æthelred and Æthelflæd.

ælce Sæternesdæge· on Sc̃e Petres circean þrittig sealma ⁊ heora mæssan· ægðer ge for heo lifgende ge eac forð-geleorde. Ond þonne cyþeð Æþelræd ⁊ Æþelflæd ꝥ heo willað mid estfullan mode þisses unnan Gode ⁊ Sc̃e Petre on Ælfredes cyninges gewitnesse ⁊ ealra þæra witena ðe on Myrcna lande syndon· butan ꝥ se wagnscilling ⁊ se seampending gonge to þæs cyninges handa· swa he ealning dyde æt Saltwic· ah elles ge landfeoh· ge fihtewite· ge stale· ge woh ceapung· ge burhwealles sceatinge· ge ælc þæra wonessa þe to ænigre bote gebyrie ꝥ hit āge healf þære cyrcean hlaford· Godes þances ⁊ Sc̃e Petres· swa swa hit mon to ceapstowe gesette ⁊ on strætum· ond wiðutan ða ceapstowe seo se bisceop his landes ⁊ ealra his gerihta wyrðe· swa hit ǣr ure fore-gengan gesetton ⁊ gefreodan. And Æþelræd ⁊ Æþelflæd þis dydon on Ælfredes cyninges gewitnesse· ⁊ on Myrcna witena· þara naman her beæftan awritene standað· ⁊ on Godes ealmihtiges naman halsiað ealle heora æfter-fylgendan ꝥ nænig mon þæs ælmessan ne wanige ðe heo for Godes lufan ⁊ Sc̃e Petres

profundis', while they live, and after their life, 'Laudate Dominum'; and every Saturday, in St Peter's church, thirty psalms, and their mass, both for them living, and also hence departed. And then Æthelred and Æthelflæd declare that, with devout mind, they desire to give this to God and St Peter, with the witness of King Ælfred and of all the 'witan' who are in the land of the Mercians; except that the wain-shilling and the load-penny go into the king's hand, as it always did at Saltwich; but else, of land-money, fight-wite, theft, 'woh-ceapung', burh-wealles 'sceating', and every one of those wrongs which are incident to any bôt, let the lord of the church have half, for the sake of God and St Peter; as it was settled for the market-place, and in the streets; and without the market-place be the bishop worthy of all his land and of all his rights; as it our predecessors before established and privileged it. And Æthelred and Æthelflæd have done this with the witness of king Ælfred and of the 'witan' of the Mercians, whose names stand written hereafter. And in to ðære cyricean geseald habbað.

the name of God Almighty, they beseech all their successors, that no man may impair this alms, which they, for love of God and St Peter, have given to the church.

ÆTHELRED ALDORMAN OF MERCIA. DCCC.XCVI.

✠ Rixiendum ussum Dryhtene þæm Hælendan Crist. Æfter þon þe agan wæs ehta hund wintra ⁊ syx ⁊ hund nigontig efter his acennednesse· ⁊ þy feowerteoðan gebonn gere· þa þy gere gebeon Æþelred ealderman alle Mercna weotan tosomne to Gleaweceastre· biscopas· ⁊ aldermen· ⁊ alle his duguðe· ⁊ ꝥ dyde be Ælfredes cyninges gewitnesse ⁊ leafe· ⁊ heo þa ðær smeadan hu heo rihtlicost heora þeodscipe ægðer ge for Gode ge for weorlde gehealdan mehton· ⁊ ec monige men ryhtan· ge godcundra hada· ge weorldcundra· ge on londum· ge on mā þara þinga þe heo onforhaldne weran. Ða cydde Werferð biscop þam weotum ꝥ him wære forneh eall ꝥ wudulond ongereafad· þe to Wuduceastre belomp· ꝥ Æþelbald cyning gesealde to Weogernaceastre him to ecre

✠ Under the rule of our Lord Jesus Christ. After that eight hundred and ninety-six winters were passed after his birth, and in the fourteenth year of the Indiction, then in that year Æthelred aldorman summoned all the 'witan' of the Mercians together at Gloucester, bishops, and aldormen, and all his chief men; and did that with the knowledge and leave of king Ælfred. And they there deliberated how they might most righteously govern their people, both before God and before the world; and also do right to many men, both of divine conditions and worldly; both in lands and in more of the things which had been withheld from them. Then bishop Werferth made known to the 'witan' that almost all the woodland had been reft from him that belonged to Wood-ælmessan. Wilferðe ƀ to mæstlonde ⁊ to wudulonde. ⁊ ꝥ sæde ꝥ hit wære sum genumen to Bislege. sum to Æfeningum. sum to Scorranstane. sum to Þornbyrig. þæs þe he wende. Ða cwædon ealle þa weotan ꝥ mon uðe þære cyrcan rihtes swa wel swa oðerre. ⁊ þa sona wæs Eþelwald þæs wordes. ꝥ he no þes rihtes wiðsacan wolde. ⁊ sæde ꝥ Aldberht ⁊ Alhhun ƀ wæron ær ymb ꝥ ylce. ⁊ cwæð ꝥ he ælcre circan āā his dæla rihtes uðe. ⁊ hit swa swiðe mildlice ageaf þan ƀ. ⁊ heht his geneat Ecglaf hatte ridan mid ceastersetna preoste Wulfhun hatte. ⁊ he hine þa gelædde ealle þa gemæru swa he him of þam aldan bocum rædde. hu hit ær Æþelbald cyning gemærude ⁊ gesealde. Ða wilnede Æþelwald swa þeh to þam ƀ ⁊ to þam higen ꝥ heo him mildemode alefdan ꝥ he his moste brucan ða hwile þe he wære. ⁊ heo Alhmund his sunu. ⁊ heo hit woldon habban on his læne ⁊ hina. ⁊ he næfre ne heora nowþer hine bereafian wolde þære mæstreddene þe he him alefed hæfde on Longan hrycge. þam tidum þe hine God him salde. Ond he þa Æþelwald

chester, which king Æthelbald gave to Worcester in perpetual alms, as mast-land and woodland, to bishop Wilferth; and said that, as he believed, some was taken from Bisley, some from Avening, some from Sherston, some from Thornbury. Then said all the 'witan', that right should be done to that church as well as to another. And then Æthelwald forthwith declared that he would not oppose the right, and said that Aldberht and bishop Alhhun had before been stirring in the same matter; and added, that to every church he would always give his share of right. And so very mildly gave it up to the bishop, and ordered his 'geneat', named Ecglaf, to ride with the townsmen's priest, named Wulfhun; and he then led him along all the boundaries, as he read them to him from the old books, how king Æthelbald had before increased and given it. Then, however, Æthelwald desired of the bishop and the convent that they would kindly allow him to enjoy it while he lived, and Alhmund his son; and they would hold it in fee of him and the convent; and ꝥ word gecwæð· ꝥ hit āā hæfde ofer Godes est þe hit hæfde butan þære cyrcan hlaforde þe he hit to ageaf· butan Alhmunde· ⁊ ꝥ þonne on þa geran[1] þe he heolde þa ylcan freondreddene þe he heold wið þone ƀ. Gif hit þonne gebirie ꝥ Alhmund swa þa freondreddene healdan nolde· oððe hine mon oferricte ꝥ he ne moste londes wyrðe beon· oððe þridda wend· gif him ær his ende geselde ꝥ þonne þære cyrcan hlaford fenge to his londe. Swa hit Mercna weotan on þam gemote gerahton· ⁊ him þa bec wisedon þæs londes· ⁊ þis wæs gedōn on Æþelredes gewitnesse aldermonnes· and on Æþælflæde· ⁊ Æþulfes aldormonnes· ⁊ Æþelferðes aldormonnes· ⁊ Alhelmes aldrm̄es· ⁊ Eadnoðes· ⁊ Ælfrædes· ⁊ Werferðes· ⁊ Æþelwaldes mæssepreostes· ⁊ his agenra maga Æþelstanes ⁊ Æþelhunes· ⁊ eac Alhmundes his agenes sunu.

he never, nor either of them, would bereave him of the pannage right, which he had allowed him in Longridge, for the time in which God gave it[2] to him. And then he Æthelwald said the words, that he would ever have it against God's pleasure who had it, except the church's lord to whom he restored it, except Alhmund; and that then on the condition that he should hold the same friendly relation which he held towards the bishop. But if it happen that Alhmund should not hold that friendly relation, or be proved not to be landworthy; or thirdly, if his end should previously happen, that then the lord of the church should take to his land. So did the 'witan' of the Mercians declare it in the 'gemôt'; and showed him the charters of the land. And this was done with the witness of Æthelred aldorman, and of Æthelflæd, and of Æthulf aldorman, and of Æthelferth aldorman, and of Athelm aldorman, and of Eadnoth, and Ælfred, and Werferth, and Æthelwald masspriest, and of his own kinsmen, Æthelstân and Æthelhûn, and also of Alhmund his own son.

[1] gerad?

[2] Longridge.

And þus se ceastersetna preost hit gerad. ⁊ se Æþelwaldes geneat mid hine. ærost on Gemyðlege. ⁊ þanon on Roddanbeorg sylfne. þanon on Smececumb. þanon on Sengetlege. þanon on Heardanlege. þære is oðer noma Dryganleg. ꝥ swa on þa læssan Nægleslege. ⁊ swa to Æþelferðes londe. Þus him gewisede se Æþelwaldes mo[n] þa gemæru swa him þa ealdan bec ryhtan ⁊ wisedon.	And thus the townsmen's priest rode it, and Æthelwald's 'geneat' with him. First to Gemythley, and thence to Rodborough itself; thence to Smechcombe; thence to Sugley; thence to Hardley, of which there is another name, Dryganley; then so to the less Nailsworth; and so to Æthelferth's land. Thus did Æthelwald's man point out to him the boundaries, as the old charters directed and indicated.

ÆTHELWULF ALDORMAN. DCCC.XCVII.

✠ Anno Dominice incarnationis DCCC.XCVII. Indictione vero XV., eo anno contigit, quod Ætheluulf venerabilis dux recitavit et investigavit hereditarios libros Cenwulfi regis, et in privilegiis illius scriptum inveniebat, quod nullus hæres post eum licentiam haberet hereditatem Cenuulfi, que pertinet ad Wincelcumbe, alicui hominum longius donandam vel conscribendam quam dies unius hominis; sed si quis hoc observare noluisset, vel contraire, longius spatium addendo conatus fuisset, sciret se anathematizandum esse, nisi digna satisfactione emendaret. Accidit autem tunc, inter alias locutiones, quod Æðeluulf loquebatur de illa terra quæ appellatur in Uptune v. manentium ad Uullafum, qui tunc eam possidebat, quoniam de hereditate ipsius Cenuulfi erat. Tunc ille dicebat, quod Cyneþryð patri suo illam terram dies trium hominum donasset, et Ælfled sibi postea trium addidisset; sed Æðelred et illi omnes adjudicabant quod illa donatio aliter stare non posset, nisi sicuti in diebus Cenuulfi constitutum erat. Tunc ille predictus Wullaf reddidit Æðeluulfo pristinos libellos a Cyneþrida et Ælfleda conscriptos, et Æðeluulfus ei istum postea scribere precipiebat. Ea namque dictione, ut habeat et perfruatur per tempora vite sue, et postea sine contradictione reddatur ad sedem episcopalem que est in Uueogernensi civitate, antistiti, qualiscumque rector et gubernator illius tunc exstiterit, pro redemptione anime Cenuulfi regis et omnium heredum ipsius, necnon quoque et pro renovatione et reconciliatione pacis inter illam familiam que est in Uueogernensi civitate et illam que est in Uuincelcumbe, et sedatione discordie et conviti-arum quas ante inter se habuerunt. Et ut illa pax, quam Uuærfriðus episcopus et Æðeluulfus dux, cum testimonio Ælfredi regis, et Æðelredi ducis Merciorum, atque omnium senatorum ipsorum, invenerunt, firmior ac stabilior inter illas perpetualiter permaneret. Et hec diffinitio cum Uullafo facta est cum testimonio supradictarum familiarum et eorum hominum quorum nomina infra caraxata patebunt.

✠ Ego Uuerfrið episcopus consensi. ✠ Ego Berhthun presbiter. ✠ Ego Berhtmund presbiter. ✠ Ego Tidbald presbiter. ✠ Ego Cynelm diaconus. ✠ Ego Ecgferð diaconus. ✠ Ego Wigheard. ✠ Ego Æðeluulf dux. ✠ Ego Wigred. ✠ Cenbriht. ✠ Wynhelm. ✠ Alhelm. ✠ Ego Deorbriht. ✠ Æðelswyð. ✠ Wigswyð. ✠ Lulle.

KING EADWARD THE ELDER. DCCCC.

Regnante imperpetuum Domino nostro Ihesu Christo, et omnia de summo cæli apice visibilia et invisibilia ordinabiliter gubernante, presentisque vitæ semper curriculo cotidie decrescente. Quapropter ego Eadward, gratia Dei Angul Saxonum rex, litterarum memoriæ commendare procuraverim, quod in diebus avi mei Æðelwlfi regis et Ælfredi regis patris mei factum fuerat; hoc est quod ille Aðulf rex moriens commendavit Ælfredo regi, filio suo, illam terram æt Ceolseldene et æt Sweores holte, ea conditione, quod ille Ælfred rex, post obitum suum, dimitteret eandem terram illi familie venerabili in Wintonia civitate, specialiter ad refectorium suum, habendam et possidendam perfruendamque perpetualiter, cum silvis, campis, pratis, et pascuis, atque omnibus ad se pertinentibus, in sempiternam hereditatem. Attamen ego Eadward rex utramque præfatam terram ab illa venerabili præfata familia in Wintonia civitate comparavi, dedique pro utraque præfata terra x. manentes in illo loco qui dicitur æt Stoce be Hysseburnan, cum omnibus hominibus qui in illa terra erant quando Ælfred rex obiit, et etiam cum illis omnibus hominibus qui tunc fuerunt æt Hisseburna quando Ælfred rex viam universe carnis adiit. Sunt autem utræque terræ ab omni censu mundiali et regali libere et expedite, excepta expeditione, et arcis et pontis constructione.

Anno autem Dominicæ incarnationis DCCCC^{mo}, Indictione III°, quando Ælfred rex obiit, et Eadward rex, filius suus, regnum suscepit, hæc cartula scripta est in Wintonia civitate, coram illis idoneis testibus quorum nomina subterscripta sunt.

✠ Ego Eadward rex signaculo sanctæ crucis corroboravi. ✠ Ego Denewulf episcopus. ✠ Ego Asser episcopus. ✠ Ego Æþelweard filius regis. ✠ Ego Ordlaf dux. ✠ Ego Ordgar dux. ✠ Ego Ælfred dux. ✠ Ego Tata presbiter. ✠ Ego Werulf presbiter. ✠ Ego Beornstan presbiter. ✠ Ego Æþelstan presbiter. ✠ Ego Waldo presbiter. ✠ Ego Osferð minister. ✠ Ego Witbrord minister. ✠ Ego Deormod minister. ✠ Ego Beorhthelm minister. ✠ Ego Wulfhelm minister. ✠ Ego Beornstan minister. ✠ Ego Ælfred minister.

Her synd gewrĩten þa gerihta þæ ða ceorlas sculan don to Hysseburnan. Ærest æt hilcan hiwisce feowerti penega tõ herfestes emnihte. ⁊ VI. ciricmittan eãlað. ⁊ III. sesðlar hlafhwetes. ⁊ III. æceras geẽrian on heora agenre hwile ⁊ mid heora agenan sæda gesawan. ⁊ on hyra agenre hwile on bærene	Here are written the services which the churls have to render at Hussebourn. First, for every family forty pence at the autumnal equinox, and V. church-mittas of ale, and III. sesters of loaf-wheat; and to plough three acres, in their own time, and sow them with their own seed; and in their own time

gebringan· ⁊ þreo pund gauolbæres· ⁊ healfne æcer gauolmæde on hiora agienre hwile· ⁊ þæt on hreace gebringan· ⁊ IIII. foðera aclofenas gauolwyda to scidhræce· on hiora agenre hwile· ⁊ XVI. gyrda gauoltininga[2] eác on hiora agenre hwile· ⁊ to Eastran two ewe mid twam lamban· ⁊ we [talað] two geong sceap tó eald sceapan· ⁊ hi sculan waxan sceáp ⁊ sciran on hiora agenre hwile· ⁊ ælce wucan wircen ðæt hi man háte· butan ðrim· an to middanwintra· oðeru to Eastran· þridde tó gangdagan.

Ðis synd þa landgemero.

Ærest of Twyfyrde andlang weges to Fearnhlince· þanan andlang weges to Æsesbeorge· þanan on gerihte to þære pirigan· þonne ⁊lang weges on Ceardices beorg· þonne on Wiðiggrafe· þonne on ðone weg þe scyt ofer ða díc· þonne andlang weges on þa coppedan ác· þanan andlang weges of[3] he to wuda lið· þonne on gerihte on Stod-

to bring [the produce] into the barns; and three pounds[1] of gafol-barley, and half an acre of gafol meadow, in their own time; and to bring it in a reek; and IIII. fothers of cloven gafol-wood for a shingle-reek, in their own time; and XVI. rods of gafol-palings, also in their own time. And at Easter two ewes with two lambs. And we reckon two young sheep as an old sheep. And they shall wax and shear the sheep, in their own time; and they shall do every week what they are ordered, excepting three: one at Midwinter, a second at Easter, a third in the Rogation days.

These are the land-boundaries.

First from Twyford along the way to Farnlinch; thence along the way to Æsesbeorg; thence right on to the pear-tree; then along the way to Cerdic's hill; then to Withy grove; then to the way that leads over the ditch; then along the way to the copped oak; thence along the way which leads to the wood; then right on southward to Stud-

[1] Compare with "Rectitudines Singularum Personarum," in 'Ancient Laws and Institutes of England.'

[2] From týnan?

[3] Apparently a clerical error for oð.

leage suþewearde· þonne andlang Mearcweges ūtt wið Feldbeorga· þonne andlang Mearcweges to þan hagan be suþan Feārnleāge· andlang hagan ūtt to Ubbanleāge stigele· þonne ⁊lang hagan to Wocces geate· þanan andlang hagan ōn Tyrwenes sledes heafad· þonne andlang hagan ūtt to Bitan cnolle on ðone līthagan· andlang þære þorngræfan þwyres ofer Hysseburnan on Gosdæne· þonne andlang þæs weges þe lið andlang Gosdæne þwyres ofer in Waldes weg· þonne andlang weges on þone beorg æt Wæcces treōwe· þanan onbutan Higdune þornes tō Bruneshamme· þonne andlang hagan to þam grundeliesan pytte· þanan on gerihte andlang hagan to Hremmes dene· ꝥ andlang hagan on ðære ealdan mapolder be suþan Tutan mære· þonne andlang hagan on Sotceorles æcer· þanan ofer ða dæne ūpp be wyrtwalan· þonne onbutan ðone garan on þone piwinðlan· þonne onbutan þone garan on þone biwindlan· þonne andlang Mearcweges to Wifan stocce· þanan andlang þæs ealdan weges to

ley; then along the boundary way out towards Felborough; then along the boundary way to the 'haga' south of Farleigh; along the 'haga' out to Ubley stile; then along the 'haga' to Wockes gate; thence along the 'haga' to the head of Tyrwen's 'slade'; then along the 'haga' out to Bita's knoll to the 'lithaga', along the thorn-grove across over Hussebourn to Gosden; then along the way that leads by Gosden across over to Walde's way; then along the way to the hill at Wecke's tree; thence round Higdon thorns to Brun's ham; then along the 'haga' to the bottomless pit; thence right on along the 'haga' to Raven's dean; then along the 'haga' to the old maple south of Tuta's mere; then along the 'haga' to Sotchurl's field; thence over the dean up by the 'wyrtwal'; then round the 'gore' to the windle-tree[1]; then round the 'gore' to the windle-tree; then along the boundary to 'Wifan stock'; thence along the old way to Bradley; thence to Geapa gore; thence to the hoar apple-tree; then along the dike out to the Terstan

[1] Translation conjectural, on the supposition that biwindla may be synonymous with windeltreow, *withy*, *windle*.

Bradan lea· þonne an westeweard Geapan garan· þanan to þære haran apoldre· þonne ⁊lang dīc ūtt on Terstan on þone syþeran steð· þonne ⁊lang steþes· ꝥ beneoðan Beamwǣr on þone norþere steþ· andlang staðes æft on Twyfyrde.

to the south bank; then along the bank; then below Beamweir to the north bank; along the bank again to Twyford.

Anno autem Dominicæ incarnationis DCCCC^{mo} Indictione III., quando Ælfred rex obiit, et Eadward rex, filius suus, regnum suscepit, hæc cartula scripta est in Wintonia civitate, coram illis idoneis testibus, quorum nomina subterscripta sunt.

Ego Eadward rex signaculo sanctæ crucis corroboravi. Ego Denewulf episcopus. Ego Asser episcopus. Ego Aðelweard filius regis. Ego Ordlaf dux. Ego Ordgar dux. Ego Tata presbiter. Ego Werulf presbiter. Ego Beornstan presbiter. Ego Æðelstan presbiter. Ego Waldo presbiter. Ego Osferð minister. Ego Witbrord minister. Ego Deormod minister. Ego Beorhtelm minister. Ego Ælfred minister. Ego Wulfred minister. Ego Wulfhelm minister. Ego Beornstan minister.

BISHOP DENEWULF. DCCC.LXXIX.-DCCCC.IX.

✠ Denewulf bisceop ⁊ ða hȳwan on Wintanceāstre ænlænað Ælfrede his deg XL. hida landes æt Alresforda· æfter þære læna þe Tunbryht bisceop ær alende his yldran· ⁊ agan wēs on ðæt gerad þet he gesylle ælce geāre to hærfestes emnihte ðreo pund to gafole ⁊ cyresceattas ⁊ cyresceatweorc· ⁊ þenne þæs

✠ Bishop Denewulf and the convent at Winchester have leased to Ælfred, for his day, XL. hides of land at Alresford, according to the lease which bishop Tunberht formerly leased to his parents, and was settled on the condition that he give every year, at the autumnal equinox, three pounds as rent, and neod bið his men beon gearuwe ge tō ripe ge to huntoðe. ⁊ efter his dege gānge seo ar unbeflītan into Sc̄e Petre.

church-shots and church-shot work, and when there be need, that his men be ready both to reap and hunt; and after his day, that the property pass uncontested to St Peter.

Þis synt þara wītena handsetena ⁊ ðere hina ðe on þære geðafunge wēron.

These are signatures of the witnesses and the inmates who were at this agreement.

Ðæt is Denewulf bisceop· and Tata bisceop· and Byrnstan bisceop· and Wighelm diaconus· and Æþelstan clericus· and Eadwulf clericus· and Ælfstan clericus· and Wulfstan clericus· and Wulfric clericus· and Winsige clericus· and Wulfred clericus· and Beorhtsige clericus· and Ælfsige clericus· and Wulfhelm clericus· and Wulfsige clericus· and Wiglaf clericus· and Æðelm clericus· and Cynestan clericus· and Aðeric clericus· and Ðruðgar clericus· and Wulfred minister· and Beornulf minister· and Winstan minister· and Aðulf minister.

KING EADWARD THE ELDER. DCCCC.I.

Ðis is þæra [x. hida] land bōc to bi Wilig þæ Eadweard cing gebocade Aðelwulf bisceope on æce yrfe.

This is the charter of the [x. hides] at Wiley, which king Eadward chartered to bishop Æthelwulf in perpetual inheritance.

In nomine altitonantis mundi Satoris. Provida namque jamdudum ac prævalens æcclesiarum censuit institutio, observandumque succedentibus diffinitione cautissima decrevit, ut dationes piissimorum regum pro mutabili temporum varietate cartarum monumentis tradere, subque testimonio cyrographi concludere, quominus ingruente caligosa oblivione origo veritatis cassaretur. Idcirco, præsentibus, absentibus, posteris cunctis, hujus descriptionis tenore declaratur, quia Eadweard, Angul-Saxonum, Dei gratia annuente, rex, aliquam agelli partem proprii juris donans in perpetuam possessionem, jure hereditario, Aðelwlfo concedo, proque ejus amabili subjectione eo firmius ei corroboro prefate telluris magnitudinem, id est, x. cassatorum in loco qui dicitur bi Wilig, cum omnibus ad se rite pertinentibus, id est pratis, pascuis, silvis, aquis, aquarumque decursibus, ut habeat et possideat feliciterque condonet cuicumque voluerit in omnibus cum libero mentis arbitrio; ei equidem liberam in omnibus præfatam conscribimus terram, preter arcis munitionem, et pontis constructionem, et expeditionem. Ista vero prænominata tellus primitus fuit præpeditus a quodam duce, nomine Wulhere, et ejus uxore, quando ille utrumque et suum dominum, regem Ælfredum, et patriam, ultra jusjurandum quam regi et suis omnibus optimatibus juraverat, sine licentia dereliquit. Tunc etiam, cum omnium juditio sapientium Gevisorum et Mercensium, potestatem et hereditatem dereliquit agrorum; nunc vero in calce hujus singraphæ legentibus et audientibus omnibus patet, quia omnibus illis antiquis libris, si quis habeat, sit proscriptum, et nil ultra prævaleant, in modico vel in magno.

Hæc vero præfata terra his terminibus circumcincta esse videtur.

Ærest on Codanford· þonne andune andlang Wilig on Hyssa pol· þæt on þære gebyge· þæt be eastan Cynelmingham ofer þa mæde on Hafocwylle· þonne andlang mærfyr on greatan þorn· þonne andlang weges on Landscorehlinc· þone andlang Scorehlinces on Alercum· þonne ofer Radune sweoran ofer Nacum on Trindlea· þæt swa on Wilafes treow· þæt ofer þone Heðfeld on dicgeat· ðet west andlang dic on Wylle weg· ðæ andlang Wylle weges on Widancum· ðonne ⁊lang

First to Codford; then down along Wiley to Hyssa pool; then to the bending; then to the east of Kynelmingham, over the mead to Hawkwell; then along the boundary furrow to the great thorn; then along the way to Landscore link; then along Score link to Alercombe; then over Rawdon neck over Nacombe to Trindley; then so to Wilaf's tree, then over the heath field to the dike gate; then along the dike to the well-way; then along the well-way to Witcombe; then again along the weges æft on Odenford· of Odanforda on Codanford.

way to Odford; from Odford to Codford.

Si quis autem hujus nostræ donationis cartulam augere vel amplificare voluerit, augeat Deus bona sua in regione vivorum. Si autem evenerit, quod non optamus, ut alicujus personæ supervenerit qui hoc infringere vel mutare voluerit, sciat se esse epicarmai a consortio Dei et sanctorum ejus, nisi prius digna satisfactione Deo et omnibus emendaverit.

Ðis gewrit cyð Deormodes foresprece ⁊ Aðulfes ymb þæt land æt Wilig· þæt is þæt Aþulf hit gesealde Deorswiðe on agene æht to ateonne swa hire leofost wære· ægðer ge on hire lyfe ge æfter hire lyfe· ⁊ ageaf hire þa bǣc ðy ilcan deg ðe hi man him geāf on ðissa manna gewitnesse.

This writing makes known the agreement of Deormod and, Athulf concerning the land at Wiley. That is, that Athulf gave it to Deorswith in full possession, to dispose of as to her might be most desirable, both in her life and after her life; and gave over to her the titles on the same day on which they were given to him in these men's witness.

Scripta est autem hæc cartula anno Dominicæ incarnationis DCCCCI., Indictione vero IIII. His testibus consentientibus sanctæque crucis vexillum adponentibus, quorum nomina infra caraxata esse videntur.

✠ Ego Eadweard rex. ✠ Ego Æðelweard filius regis. ✠ Ego Ordgar dux. ✠ Ego Ordlaf dux. ✠ Ego Sigulf dux. ✠ Ego Heahferd dux. ✠ Ego Ordgar dux. ✠ Ego Deormod dux. ✠ Ego Ælfstan dux. ✠ Ego Beorstan dux. ✠ Ego Æðelferd dux. ✠ Ego Ælfheah dux. ✠ Ego Ælfred dux. ✠ Ego Beorhtsige minister. ✠ Ego Occa minister. ✠ Ego Wulfhere minister. ✠ Ego Ælfhere minister. ✠ Ego Ælfred minister. ✠ Ego Ælfred minister. ✠ Ego Buga minister. ✠ Ego Cufa minister. ✠ Ego Æðelstan minister. ✠ Ego Wulfhun minister. ✠ Ego Witulf minister. ✠ Ego Ælfheah minister. ✠ Ego Uffa minister. ✠ Ego Wulfhere minister. ✠ Ego Burhtric minister. ✠ Ego Dudig minister. ✠ Ego Beorsige minister. ✠ Ego Wulfsige minister. ✠ Ego Witbroð minister. ✠ Ego Odda minister. ✠ Ego Eardulf minister. ✠ Ego Ælfstan minister.

BISHOP DENEWULF. DCCCC.II.

In nomine Domini. Denewulf bisceop ⁊ þa hiwan in Wintanceastre leton tō Beornulfa hiora landes xv. hida æt Eblesburnam· wið þam gafole ðe he wið bisceop ⁊ wið hiwan ared· ðæt is xlv. scill to hærfestes emnihte· sīe simle agyfeð on ða gerad ðæt hine nage nan man ōf to aceapienne· ne his bearn æfter his dege þa wile þe hi ða gerihta forðbringan a magen· ⁊ eac ælce geare fultumien to þære cyrican bōte þe ðet land to hyrð· be ðem dæle þe ðet oðer folc do ælc be his landes meðe· ⁊ þa cyricsceattes mid rihte agyfe· ⁊ fyrðe ⁊ brycge ⁊ festergeweorc hewe swa mon ofer eall folc do· ⁊ ðis wes gedōn on þara witena gewitnesse ⁊ ða furðe[3] ðe hiora naman her benioðan standaþ awritene· ðe geare ðe wes agān fram Cristes acennesse twa winter ⁊ nigan hund· ⁊ ðet

In nomine Domini. Bishop Denewulf and the convent at Winchester have let to Beornulf xv. hides of their land at Ebbesborne, in consideration of the rent which he has settled with the bishop and the convent, that is that xlv. shillings, at the autumnal equinox, be always paid, on the condition that no man may buy him off[1], nor his children after his day, as long as they may perform the services, and also, every year contribute to the repair of the church which belongs to the land, in the proportion which other folk do, each according to the condition of his land; and rightly pay the church-shots, and the 'fyrd,' and bridge- and fastness-work hew[2], as is done by all the folk. And this was done with the witness of the 'witan,' and also of those whose names stand here beneath written;

[1] That is, off the land, by offering a higher rent.

[2] That is, hew the timber, if the reading is correct.

[3] ða furðe—apparently an error of the copyist.

wes gedōn on þære mæran stowe on Wintanceastre.

in the year that was agone from Christ's birth nine hundred and two winters. And that was done in the famous place of Winchester.

[Denewulf] bisceop lyfde Beornulfe his mege þæt he moste þa inberðan menn hamettan to Eblesburnan. nū hebbe ic hi hamet. Lufe ⁊ hire ðreo bearn. ⁊ Luhan ⁊ his seax bearn.

Bishop Denewulf has allowed Beornulf his kinsman to house the inborn people at Ebbesborne. I have now housed Lufe and her three children, and Luha and his six children.

Þonne geærendodon me ða hīwan on Wintanceastre ðet þa men mostan on þan londe wunien. hæfde swa īc swa minra freonda swelce hit hæfde. þonne weron þær ðreo wīteþeowe men burbærde. ⁊ ðreo ðeowberde ða me salde bisceop ⁊ þa hiwan to ryhtre æhta. ⁊ hire team.

Then the convent at Winchester sent me word, that the men must dwell on the land, whether I or any of my friends had it. There were then three penal serfs there boor-born, and three serf-born: these the bishop and the convent gave me in lawful possession, with their families.

Ðis wes gedon ða man þa cyricean halgode æt Hysseburnan. on ðara manna gewitnesse þe hira naman her neoðan standat.

This was done when the church was hallowed at Hussebourne, in witness of the men whose names stand here beneath.

Ærest Denewulf bisceop. and Tata presbiter. and Beornstan presbiter. and Wigea diaconus. and Æþelstan presbiter. and Eadwulf presbiter. and Dyrewine presbiter. and Wulfhere Cidding. and Wulfstan presbiter. and Eadulf cempa. and Beorhtsige presbiter. and Windsige presbiter. and Ælfsige presbiter. and Denewulf bisceop. and Tata presbiter. and Byrnstan presbiter. and Eadstan diaconus. and Æþelstan presbiter. and Eadulf presbiter. and Ædelstan presbiter. and Ælfstan presbiter. and Wulfstan presbiter. and Wigea presbiter. and Wulfric presbiter. and Eahtan presbiter. and

Winsige minister. and Wulfred minister. and Beorsige minister. and Ælfsige minister. and Eadulf minister. and Wulfhelm minister. and Wulsige minister.

KING EADWARD, ÆTHELRED, AND ÆTHELFLÆD. DCCCC.III.

✠ Regnante in perpetuum et mundi monarchiam gubernante, altithrone Patris Sobole, qui cœlestia simul et terrena moderatur: illius etenim anno incarnationis an. DCCCC.III., Indictione vero sexta, contigit quod Æðelfriðo duci omnes hereditarii libri ignis vastatione combusti perierant. Tali igitur necessitate cogente, prædictus dux rogavit Eadweardum regem, Æðelredum quoque, et Æðelflædam, qui tunc principatum et potestatem gentis Merciæ sub prædicto rege tenuerunt, omnes etiam senatores Merciorum, ut ei consentirent et licentiam darent alios libros rescribendi. Tunc illi unanimiter omnes devota mente consenserunt ut alii ei libri rescriberentur, eodem modo quo et priores scripti erant, in quantum eos memoriter recordari potuisset. Si vero quoslibet recordari minime potuisset, tunc ei ista kartula in auxilio et adfirmatione fieret, ut nullus eum contentiose cum aliis libris affligere valuisset, nec propinquus nec alienus, quamvis aliquis homo aliquem de vetustis libris protulerit, quem prius fraudulenter, in hora ipsius incendii, vel alio quolibet tempore, per furtum abstraxisset. Novimus namque quod omnia quæ in hoc mundo contingere solent, aliquando citius aliquando vero tardius, ex memoria mortalium elapsa deveniunt, nisi in scedulis litterarum caracteribus adnotantur. Quapropter in hac kartula innotescere ratum atque gratum satisque commodum duximus, de illa videlicet terra[1] æt ðæn easteran Hrisanbyrge, cujus quantitas est xxx. cassatorum, quod eam

[1] The text is from MS. Stowe, which accords with MS. Bodley, as far as the words 'videlicet terra,' after which the latter reads thus: [terra] at Wringtone, cujus quantitas est viginti cassatorum. Et hanc præfatam largitionem ego Edred (sic MS.) et totus senatus Anglorum devoto animo

Aðulf Æðelgyðe filiæ suæ cum hereditaria libertate in propriam et[1] perpetuam donavit hereditatem.

KING EADWARD THE ELDER. DCCCC.IV.

EADWARDES CININGES FREOLS TO TANTUNÆ.
KING EADWARD'S FREEDOM TO TAUNTON.

Regnante imperpetuum Domino nostro Jhesu Christo, cujus potestas nec crescit nec minuit, omnibusque presentis vitæ curriculis cotidie semper subterlabentibus suæque condicioni omnibus visibilibus et invisibilibus inevitabiliter velint nolint cotidiæ subdentibus. Quapropter ego Eadward, divina indulgente clementia, Angul Saxonum rex, omnia quæcunque dicta aut facta vel etiam pacta sunt in nostris temporibus relatui digna pro necessitate animæ meæ, et pro communi nostra necessitate, necnon etiam subsequentis posteritatis nostræ, litterarum memoriæ commendare procuravi, ne aut fusca oblivionis caligine oblitterata, vel incuria scriptorum et testium id agente ignorata, regnantibus post nos et suis optimatibus ad lites et contentiones de cætero devenirent. Qua de re in hac cartula demonstrare conor quod ego cum consilio et consensu optimatum meorum, quorum nomina infra scripta sunt, libertatem illius monasterii quod Saxonicæ Tantun dicitur, cum omnibus ad se pertinentibus villis, campis, silvis, pascuis, pratis, et piscium capturis, in sempiterno graphio in cruce Christi Denewulfo episcopo et illi venerabili familiæ in Wentana civitate commoranti, ab omnibus regalibus, fiscalibus, et commitialibus, necnon et ab omnibus mundialibus taxationibus expeditam, excepta expe-

---

Æðelfriðo duci in perpetuam hereditatem persolvimus, ut nemo post nos percipientes sine indignatione Dei omnipotentis illam irritam faciat. ✠ Ego Æðelred consensi et confirmavi. ✠ Ego Eadward rex consensi et subscripsi.

Hanc præfatam hereditatem Æðelstan dux filius Æðelredi, consensus et factus monachus, optulit secum ad monasterium Glastingense, illamque sibi largitus est Æðelstan rex.

[1] MS. ad.

ditione et arcis et pontis constructione, toto mentis affectu dedi; ea conditione quo semper prefatum monasterium pertineat atque deserviat episcopali sedi in Wintonia civitate, sine ulla controversia et sine disceptatione, nec in nostro tempore, nec etiam ab ullo nostro successore, hæc donatio commutetur aut violetur in sempiternum. Sed et hoc alacri animo Christo concessi ut episcopi homines, tam nobiles quam ignobiles, in præfato rure degentes hoc idem jus in omni haberent dignitate quo regis homines perfruuntur, regalibus fiscis commorantes, et omnia secularium rerum judicia ad usus præsulum exerceantur eodem modo quo regalium negotiorum discutiuntur judicia. Prædicte etiam villæ mercimonium, quod Anglicæ þæs tunes cyping appellatur, censusque omnis civilis, sancte Dei æcclesiæ in Wintonia civitate, sine retractionis obstaculo, cum omnibus commodis æternaliter deserviat; erat namque antea in illo supradicto monasterio pastus unius noctis regi, et VIII. canum, et unius caniculari pastus, et pastus novem noctium accipitrariis regis, et quicquid rex vellet inde ducere usque ad Curig vel Willettun, cum plaustris et equis; et si advene de aliis regionibus advenirent, debebant ducatum habere ad aliam regalem villam quæ proxima fuisset in illorum via. Ille quoque episcopus et illa venerabilis familia michi LX. manentes in illis illustribus locis quæ Saxonicæ ita nominantur: id est x. manentes æt Crauuancumbe, æt x. æt Cumbtune, æt xx. æt Bananwylle, xx. quoque æt Stoce juxta Scealdeburnan, perpetualiter in sempiterno graphio in cruce Christi, pro prefati monasterii libertate, ab omni regali censu et comitiali, omnique mundana exactione equaliter expeditas, excepta expeditione, et arcis et pontis constructione, libenti animo condonaverunt. Hoc etiam sub divino testamento precipimus et imperamus, ne umquam aliqua commutatio vel vicissitudo illius nostræ donationis et confirmationis in utraque parte fiat, quamdiu illa Christianitas in ista insula consistat. Si quis hanc nostram donationem et commutationem custodire et augere voluerit, custodiat illum Deus et augeat illi omnia bona præsentis et futuræ vitæ; sin vero, aliqua mala machinatione, minuere vel infringere voluerit, sciat se ante celsissimi Judicis horribile tribunal rationem redditurum in die judicii, si non prius hic digna emendaverit pœnitentia. Hæc autem cartula scripta est anno Dominicæ incarnationis DCCCC.IIII., Indictione VII., in villa venatoria quæ Saxonicæ dicitur Bicanleag, coram idoneis testibus, quorum nomina subsequenter scripta sunt.

Ego Eadward rex. Ego Pleigmund archiepiscopus. Ego Denewulf episcopus. Ego Wulfsige episcopus. Ego Æþelweard filius regis. Ego Ordlaf dux. Ego Osulf dux. Ego Ordgar dux. Ego Heahferd dux. Ego Ælfwald dux. Ego Johan presbyter. Ego Werulf presbyter. Ego Tata presbyter. Ego Æþelstan presbyter. Ego Byrnstan presbyter. Ego Searu presbyter. Ego Wealda presbyter. Ego Friðestan minister. Ego Wighelm minister. Ego Witbord minister. Ego Deormod minister. Ego Beorthelm minister. Ego Odda minister. Ego Wlfred minister. Ego Buga minister. Ego Ealhmund minister. Ego Wlfstan minister. Ego Æþelferð minister. Ego Wlfhelm minister. Ego Wlfhun minister. Ego Wlfhere minister. Ego Wlfric minister.

KING EADWARD THE ELDER. DCCCC.I.-DCCCC.IX.

✠ In nomine Domini. Ic Eadwerd kinig begeat æt Denulfe biscepe ⁊ æt ðæn hiwun on Winteceastre þa Windcirican ⁊ ðæt stæinene slapern. ⁊ ðærto ðæs landes be suðan ðære cirican. ⁊ ðæn slepern XXIIII. gerda on lange. ⁊ on brǽde ðar hit bradest is fif geurda. ⁊ ðær hit unbradost is anne geurde. to ðæn ðæt ic ðær mynster on gestaðolode for mī ne saule hælo. ⁊ mī nes ðæs arwyrdan fader Ælfredes cyninges. ⁊ ic let. be ealra West Sexna

✠ In nomine Domini. I king Eadward have obtained from bishop Denewulf and from the convent at Winchester, the 'Wind-church' and the stone dormitory, and thereto of the land south of the church and the dormitory XXIV. rods in length, and in breadth, where it is broadest, five rods, and where it is least broad, one rod; in order that I might thereon found a monastery, for the health of my soul and of my venerable father king Ælfred.

witena geðeahte ⁊ leafe· to biscepe ⁊ to þan hiwun Sc̃e Andreas ciricau ⁊ ðone worðig ðe ðærto gaunnan wes into ðære stowe· on ece erfe· ðæt hit nage nan man fram ðære stowe to dælanne. Ðonne is ðisse eaca ðe eallra Westseaxna witan ðærto eacan me gebocodon on ece erfe. Ærest suðrichte from ðan beoðærn to Sc̃e Gregories cirican· ðonne from ðære suðwest hyrnan Sc̃e Gregories cirican XII. geurda westrichte to ðære strete· ðonne richte norð XIII. geurde to þære norðstræte· ðonne eastrichte XLIII. geurde· ⁊ VI. fet to ðære eaststrete· ðonne suðrichte XX. geurde ⁊ VI. fet to ðære suðstrete· þonne westrichte be ðære suðstrete to ðæn lictune VII. geurde ⁊ VI. fet· ðonne richt norð V. geurde· ðonne is ðæs imbganges ealles ðrio furlanges ⁊ ðreo metgeurda.

And I have let, with the counsel and leave of all the 'witan' of the West Saxons, to the bishop and the convent, the church of St Andrew and the 'worðig' which was thereto granted to the place, in perpetual inheritance, so that no man may separate it from the place. Now this is the augmentation which the 'witan' of all the West Saxons have in addition chartered to me in perpetual inheritance. First direct south from the refectory to St Gregory's church; then from the south-west corner of St Gregory's church, XII. rods due west to the street; then direct north, XIII. rods to the north street; then due east XLIII. rods and VI. feet to the east street; then due south XX. rods and VI. feet to the south street; then due west, by the south street, to the cemetery, VII. rods and VI. feet; then direct north, V. rods. Then is the circuit of the whole, three furlongs and three rods.

✠ Eadwearð rex. ✠ Ealdereð frater regis[1]. ✠ Plemunð archiepiscopus. ✠ Denewulf episcopus. ✠ Wilfærd episcopus. ✠ Wulfrige episcopus. ✠ Asser episcopus. ✠ Wighen episcopus. ✠ Eodmund episcopus. ✠ Eadgar episcopus. ✠ Wimund episcopus. ✠ Brinhelm abbod. ✠ Witbrorð minister. ✠ Deormoð minister. ✠ Beorthsige minister. ✠ Ocea minister. ✠ Adelstan minister.

[1] Eadward's brother was named Æþelweard; ob. 922.

✠ Wulfhelm minister. ✠ Alla minister. ✠ Heorstan minister. ✠ Wulfhelm minister. ✠ Beorstan presbiter. ✠ Tata presbiter. ✠ Brichtulf presbiter.

KING EADWARD THE ELDER. DCCCC.I.-DCCCC.IX.

In nomine Domini. Eadward̄ cyning ⁊ þa hiwan in Wintanceastre lætað to Dænewulfe bisceōpe twentig hida landes be Ticceburnan· swa geirfað swa hit nu stent· þreōra manna deg· æfter his dege swilcum frand to tolætenne swilce hīm leofost beoð[1]· on þa gerad þe man [his] gemynd æfter his dege to þære halgan stowe do in Wintanceastre· swa swa hē þænne finde þæt hit mæðlic sie ⁊ aberendlīc· be þæs landes meðe· ælce geāre ·to þære edmeltide[2]· þæt mon geselle twelf seoxtres beōras· ⁊ twelf geswettes Wilisc ealoð· ⁊ twentig ambra hluttor ealoð· ⁊ tu hund greates hlafes· ⁊ þridde smales· ⁊ tu hrieðeru· oþer sealt oþer fersc· ⁊ six weðeras· ⁊ feower swin· ⁊ feor fliccu· ⁊ twentig cysa· gyf hīt on lencten gebyrige ꝥ þæ þonne þære flæscun

In nomine Domini. King Eadward and the convent at Winchester let to bishop Denewulf twenty hides of land at Tichbourne, so stocked as it now stands, for three men's day; after his day to let it to such friend as to him shall be most desirable: on the condition that after his [Eadward's] day his commemoration be solemnized in the holy place at Winchester, as he [Denewulf] may then find it fitting and bearable, according to the condition of the land: viz. That every year at the return of the day, there be given twelve sesters of beer, and twelve of sweet Welsh ale, and twenty ambers of clear ale, and two hundred great loaves, and a third of small, and two oxen, one salt, the other fresh, and six wethers, and four swine, and four flitches, and twenty

[1] MS. boð.

[2] Edmel, *dies naturalis*; Fris. etmal; Dutch etmaal. See *Outzen*, Gloss.

geweorð on fisce gestriene buton ꝥ þis forgenge sie. Gif hit þænne sie se ðe þæt land hæbbe ꝥ he þis his geagenes þances tuwa forgymeleasie. buton hit hæres[2] unæmetta sie. þonne bid hic hiwan for Godæs lufan to tidsongum min gemund dōn. þonne bebeodað hie on Godes ælmihtiges naman. ⁊ on Sanctes Petres. ⁊ on Sanctes Paules. þæt hi fon to þan lande ⁊ min gemund þær on þam gerihtum þæ þærto belimpað arerad. be þam ilcan þe hit her bufan gecweden is. buton þæt hi for Godes lufan to tidsangum min gemund dōn. þonne bebeodad hie on Godes ælmihtiges naman. ⁊ on Sanctes Petres. ⁊ on Sanctes Paules. þæ hit hiera yrfe is. ꝥ hit swa umbesæccen gange into þære cyrican swa hit þa on dæg wes þa hit man him to læt. ⁊ þis gewrit. was awriten on Wintanceastre. on þara witena gewitnesse þe hiera naman hær bæniþan awriten standad. þæt is genemned Eadward cyning. and

cheeses. If it happen in Lent, then let the worth of the flesh be obtained in fish, unless it be extremely abundant[1]. But if it be that he who has the land spontaneously twice neglect this, unless there be a failure[3] of the harvest, then I pray the convent, for love of God, to solemnize my commemoration at their daily offices. Then [we] command them, in the name of Almighty God, and of St Peter and St Paul, that they take to the land, and there establish my commemoration with the rites which thereto belong, in the same manner, as it is here above said, except that they, for love of God, solemnize my commemoration in their daily offices. Then [we] command them, in the name of Almighty God, and of St Peter and St Paul, whose property it is, that it pass to the church as uncontested as it was on the day when it was let to him. And this writ was written at Winchester

[1] And, consequently, so cheap as not to require the expenditure of the whole value. My translation of forgenge by *abundant* is conjectural, as, indeed, is that of the entire passage. The dictionaries render genge by *valens*.

[2] An error for hærfestes?

[3] Or strictly *an obstruction*, caused, we may easily suppose, by warfare.

Plegmund arcebisceop· and Friðestan bisceop·

on the witness of the 'witan' whose names stand here beneath written. That is, the said Eadward king, and Plegmund arcebisceop· and Friðestan bisceop·

and Osulf dux· and Deormod minister· and Tata presbiter· and Beornstan presbiter· and Æþelstan presbiter· and Ælfstan presbiter· and Ealhstan presbiter· and Wulfric presbiter· and Æþelbyrth presbiter· and Yðelbeard presbiter· and Wigelm diaconus· and Beornulf minister· and Æþelstan clericus· and Eadulf clericus· and Ælfstan clericus· and Æþelweard clericus· and Wulfhelm clericus· and Wulfstan clericus· and Wulfric clericus· and Winsige clericus· and Beorhtsige clericus· and Ælfsige clericus· and Eadulf clericus· and Wulfsige clericus· and Winsige clericus· and Wulfsige clericus· and Wilaf clericus· and Wulfstan clericus· and Æðelhelm clericus· and Cynestan clericus· and Heremod clericus· and Đrudgar clericus· and Æðric clericus· and Ælfred clericus· and Uffa clericus.

Đis synt ða gemæro to Ticceburnan.

Ærest on Ellenforð· þanon on þone miclan hlinc· ðonne on Æpphangran eastewеardne· ðanon on Hormæres wudu middeweardne· þanon on gerihte to Scealdæmeres hamme· þonon on Mælanbeorh middeweardne· þonne þær to wuda on þone heal· andlang weges utt to Higleáge· þanon norh ⁊ west inn an þone heal· þanon ⁊lang leage· þonne ⁊lang weges to Torscagan· þanon ⁊lang weges upp on Gandran dune· andlang weges to readan anstigan· þanon ⁊lang weges

These are the boundaries at Tichbourne.

First to Ellenford; thence to the great link; then to Epphanger eastward; thence to Hormer's wood southward; thence right on to Shaldmersham; thence to Melbury southward; then there at the wood to the hall; along the way out to Highley; thence north and west in at the hall; thence along the lea; then along the way to Torshaw; thence along the way up to Gander down; along the way to the red 'anstig'; thence along the on Ceaforleāge· þanon on þone miclan hlinc· þanon on Cuþænes ford norðeweardne· þanon on Tornageāt· þanon ūtt þurþ Beaddes scagan to Aclea· andlang weges ūtt tō felda· þanon be wyrtwalan on langan leāge norðwearde· þanon to Hindsceata· þanon on Ostercumb norþeweardne· þanon to Mænan leāge· þanon on Ostercumb suðewearðne· þanon ⁊lang weges on Wines heafod· þonne ⁊lang weges ūtt on Ellenford.

way to Chaverley; thence to the great link; thence to Cuthen's ford northward; thence to Torngate, thence out through Bead's shaw to Oakley; along the way out to the field; thence by the 'wyrtwal' to the long lea northward; thence to Hind-sceat; thence to Ostercomb northward; thence to Mæne lea; thence to Ostercombe southward; thence along the way to Wines head; thence along the way to Ellenford.

BISHOP DENEWULF. DCCCC.I.-DCCCC.IX.

In nomine Domini. Ego Denewulfus episcopus indico Edwardo regi domino meo de terra illa Beaddinctun, de qua egisti apud me, ut ego eam tibi commodarem. Unde, mī care, nunc ā conventu Wintonie optinui, et apud seniores et apud juniores, quod ipsi bono favore concedunt michi ut eam tibi per cartam tradam quamdiu vixerïs, sive ad possidendum sive ad commodandum alteri, cuicunque tibi magis placuerit. Hujus terræ sunt LXX. hidæ, et est modo tota bene procurata, quæ quando dominus meus michi eam tradidit omni peccunia caruit et pauperibus hominibus erat destitutum. Tunc ego ipse peccuniam meam in ea reparare studui, unde interim pauperes vixerunt, et nunc nos eam tibi libenter concedimus. Sed nunc familia ipsa expetit te ut post dies tuos loco suo iterum restituatur. Modo habetur ibi pecunia quantum pro hyemæ residuum fuit: IX. veteres boves, et IIII. et C.XI. veteres porci, et L. arietes, preter jus porcorum quos porcarii debent habere, et XX. bacones. Non fuit ibi frumenti quid, nisi quantulum fuit præparatum ad firmam episcopi. Sunt autem ibi xc. acræ seminatæ. Nunc vero rogamus, et ego ipse episcopus et tota familia Wincestriæ, et hoc tibi ad elemosinam, quo pro amore Dei et ipsius sanctæ æcclesiæ terram ejusdem loci amplius non expetas; quia videtur eis rex tua necessaria præceptio, quatinus nec tibi nec nobis Deus debeat imputare hanc imminutionem diebus nostris actam, quia ibi affuit magna ex parte Dei obtestatio eorum qui eandem terram eidem loco concesserunt.

IDEM ANGLICE.

Ic Denewulf bisceop kyðæ Eadwarde kyninge minum hlafurdæ ymb þæt land on Beaddinctune þæ ðu mæ firmdig to wæræ ðæt ic þæ lendæ. Þonnæ min leof hæbbe ic nū æt ðam hiwum fundæn on Wintæceastræ· gæ æt gieldran gæ æt giengran· þæt hīe mæ mid ealræ æstæ unnun his mæ ðæt to bociannæ þinnæ deg· swuðæ to brucannæ swuðum to lænannæ ðæ þæ leofust bið. Þonnæ his þæs londæs hundseofontig hida· and is nu eall gewæred· and ða hit æst min laford mæ to læt· þa wæs hit ierfælæas and mið æðnum folce aburod. And ic ða sælf þæt ierfæ togestrindæ þæt ðær mon siððan bi wæs· and wæ his þæ nū swyðæ eadmodlicæ unnon. Þonnæ min leōf siōndon hiwun nu firmdige þæt hit æfter þīnun degæ to þæræ stowæ æft agyfæn sīe. Ðonnæ īs þær nū irfæs

I bishop Denewulf announce to king Eadward my lord concerning the land at Bedhampton, which thou wast desirous that I should lease to thee. Now, then, my beloved, I have settled with the convent at Winchester, both with old and with young, that they, with all good will, have granted me to charter it to thee, for thy day, whether to enjoy it or to lease it as to thee shall be most desirable. Now of this land there are seventy hides, and it is now all stocked; and when my lord first let it to me, it was unprovided with cattle, and laid waste by heathen folk: and I myself then provided the cattle, and there people were afterwards. And we now very humbly grant it to thee. Now, my beloved, the convent are desirous that after thy day it be again given up to the place.

þæs þæs stranga wintær læfæd hæfð nigon ealð hriðru· and feower and hundændlæftig ealdra swina· and fiftig wæþæra· butan þam scipæ and swinun þæ ða hirdas habban sculon· ðara ís twæntig ealdra· and þær is hundendlæftig ealdra sceapa ⁊ seofæn þeowæ mæn· and twæntig flicca· and næs þær cornæs mare þonnæ þær wæs bisceopæs færm gægearwodu· and þær hundniogontig gæsawænra æcæra. Þonnæ biddæð þæ bisceop ⁊ þa hiwan on Wintanceastræ ðæt to ælmæssan· for Godæs lufan ⁊ for ðæræ haligan ciricean· þæt ðu þære stowæ londæs maræn ne willnie· forðam þe him ðyncð ymbæ ðine[1] hæs· þæt naðær ne þæ ne us God ne þurfa oncunnan for þæræ waniungæ on urum dæge· forþam þe ðæræ wæs swiðæ micel Godes bæbodd þa mæn þa lond to þære stowæ gesealdæ.

Now of cattle which the severe winter has left, there are nine old oxen, and a hundred and fourteen old swine, and fifty wethers, besides the sheep and swine which the herds are to have, of which there are twenty old; and there are a hundred and ten old sheep, and seven serf men, and twenty flitches: and there was no more corn there than was provided for the bishop's sustenance. And there are ninety sown acres. Now the bishop and the convent at Winchester pray thee in charity, for love of God, and for the holy church, that thou wilt not desire more land of that place, because it seems to them, with reference to thy behest, that God should have no need to accuse either thee or us for its diminution in our day; because of that the command of God was very strong when those lands were given to the place.

KING EADWARD THE ELDER. DCCCC.IX.

DONUM ET RESTITUTIO SIVE CONFIRMATIO REGIS EADWARDI DE ALRESFORDA AD VETUS CENOBIUM.

Summo atque æterno rege æternaliter regnante, atque

[1] MS. ðync ðynbæ dune.

omnia visibilia et invisibilia ordinabiliter atque incommutabiliter dispensante et gubernante. Intelligens omnia penæ preterita dicta vel facta quæ in antecessorum nostrorum diebus evenerunt fuscæ oblivioni tradita, nisi ea quæ discrete et sapienter litterarum apicibus commendata sunt, coniciensque presentia et futura eodem modo labi, nisi prefato ordine litterarum caracteribus diligenter et studiose a presentium et futurorum temporum regibus et presulibus insignita fuerint. Quapropter ego Eaduuard, divina indulgente clementia, Angul-saxonum rex, rogatus fui ã meo dilecto episcopo Friðestano territoria æcclesiæ Dei cui deserviebat pertinentia novis litterarum apicibus renovare, et veterum librorum monimenta, recenti recuperata auctoritate, restaurare; idcirco votis ejus libenter obtemperans, renovare studui territorium illius telluris quæ Alresford usitato dicitur vocabulo, prefato episcopo cathedram beati Petri, apostolorum principis, Paulique, ejusque co-apostoli præsidenti, uti Cenwald atque Ine Egcbyrthque, mei antecessores Domino nostro Ihesu Christo, omnium rerum Conditori, æterna concesserant libertate. Prefatum equidem rus, pro stupro cujusdam militis, cui accommodatum fuerat ut censum singulis annis persolveret indictum, a prefata æcclesia injuste abstractum nuper fuerat; sed Denewlf Uuentanæ æcclesiæ cathedram illo in tempore regens, pateram, centum auri siglis appendentem, regi qui tunc temporis Angul-saxoniam regebat, licet non juste, tribuit, et possessionem ad usus succedentium presulum æcclesiæ Dei restituit. Precavendo igitur ne tale periculum posteris futuro tempore miserabiliter eveniat; Ego Eaduuardus, divina largiente gratia, Angul-saxonum rex, et Plegmund, Dorubernensis æcclesiæ archiepiscopus, cæterique suffraganei, quorum inferius vocabula notantur. In nomine almæ Trinitatis atque individuæ Unitatis præcipimus, tam Friðestano, ejusdem Wentane sedis episcopo, quam cunctis ejus successoribus, ut nulli secularium militum, nec ipsum rus, nec aliud aliquot ad æcclesiam Dei pertinens, pro munere quolibet, ne talis perturbatio æcclesiæ Dei contingat ut per stuprum prefati militis contigit, dare vel accommodare præsumat. Qui autem temerarius nefas interdictum præsumpserit, anathema sit, et auctoritate beati Petri, cujus possessio est, dampnatus intereat, nisi cum ejulato magno quod contra nostrum decretum abstulit penitendo ante obitum suum restituerit.

Hæc cartula scripta est anno ab incarnatione Domini DCCCC.VIIII., Indictione XII. Maneat igitur gratis terminibus veterum librorum manifestatione harum XL^rum mansionum quantitas indissoluta, his testibus infra notatis unanimi consentientibus judicio.

Ego Eaduuard rex hanc restaurationem a me renovatam signum sanctæ crucis propria manu scribendo firmavi, quando episcopium Uuentane civitatis in duas parrochias divisi. Ego Plegmund archiepiscopus mellifluam donationem præfati regis subscripsi cum signaculo sanctæ crucis. Ego Friðestan episcopus, cum consilio ejusdem regis, hoc roboravi atque conexi cum triumpho æterni regis. Ego Wulfsige episcopus conexi et subscripsi. Ego Wighelm episcopus conexi et subscripsi. Ego Celmund episcopus conexi et subscripsi. Ego Æðelweard frater regis. Ego Æðelstan filius regis. Ego Ælfweard filius regis. Ego Osferð dux consensi. Ego Orlaf dux consensi. Ego Beorhtulf dux consensi. Ego Ordgar dux consensi. Ego Heahferð dux consensi. Ego Werulf presbiter. Ego Æþelstan presbiter. Ego Beornstan presbiter. Ego Ealhstan presbiter. Ego Deormod minister. Ego Withbrord minister. Ego Odda minister. Ego Ælfwold minister. Ego Ælfred minister. Ego Aðulf minister. Ego Æþelferð minister. Ego Wulfheard minister. Ego Ælfric minister. Ego Wulfhelm minister. Ego Uffa minister. Ego Ælfstan minister. Ego Ælfreð minister. Ego Ælfstan minister. Ego Ælfstan minister. Ego Wulfhere minister. Ego Adulf minister. Ego Wulfhun minister. Ego Wullaf minister. Ego Buga minister. Ego Ælfred minister. Ego Æðelnoð minister. Ego Wulfric minister.

BISHOP WERFERTH[1]. DCCC.LXXII.-DCCCC.XV.

✠ In usses Dryhtnes naman Hælendes Cristes. Ic Werferð bisceop cyðe swa me Alchun bisceop sægde· ⁊ eac mine gewrytu wisodon· þæt Mired bisceop gesealde Eanbalde ꝥ land æt Soppanbyrg mid þis bebode· ⁊ seoððan Eanbald hit sealde Eastmunde· ⁊ him bebead Mired bisceop bebod on Godes ealmihtiges noman· ⁊ on þære halgæn þrinesse· ꝥ ða hwile þe ænig man wære on hira mægðe þe godcundes hades beon walde· ⁊ þæs wyrðe wære· ꝥ he þonne fenge to þam lande æt Soppanbyrg· gif hit þonne hwæt elles geselde· ꝥ hit næfre on lædu hand ne wende· ac hit seoððan eode to þam bisceop-stole to Weogornaceastre· for heora ealra saule. Ond he þa Eastmund ǽr his ende bebead· on þæs lifgendan Godes noman· þam mēn þe to þam lande fenge· ꝥ he þonne on þa ilcan wisan to fenge þe Mired bisceop bebead· gif he þonne to þan gedyrstig wære ꝥ he þæt abrǽce· ꝥ he wiste hine scyldigne beforan Godes heahsetle æt þam miclan dome. Ða æfter Eastmundes forð-

✠ In the name of our Lord Jesus Christ, I bishop Werferth declare, as bishop Alchun said to me, and as my writings have also shown, that bishop Milred gave to Eanbald the land at Sodbury, with this injunction, (and Eanbald afterwards gave it to Eastmund, and to him enjoined the injunction of bishop Milred, in the name of God Almighty and of the holy Trinity,) viz. that as long as there should be any man in their family who would be of divine order, and were worthy thereof, that he should succeed to the land at Sodbury; but if it happened aught otherwise, that it should never pass to a lay hand, but it should afterwards go to the episcopal see of Worcester, for the souls of them all. And he, Eastmund, then, before his end, enjoined, in the name of the living God, the man who should succeed to the land, that he should succeed thereto on the same condition as bishop Milred had enjoined; but if he were so presumptuous as to break it, that he should know himself

[1] Of Worcester.

siðe. bereafode seo mægð þæs ilcan londes ge þa gastas þara forðgewitenra manna ge þone bisceop ⁊ þa cirecean æt Weogornaceastre. ⁊ Heahberht bisceop oft þæs myngode oððe þæs landes bæd. ⁊ seoððan Alchun bisceop for oft. þa hwile þe he wæs. ⁊ eac ic Werferð bisceop oft his bæd. ⁊ we ne mihton to nanum rihte becuman ær Æþelred wæs Myrcna hlaford. Ða gesamnode he Mercna weotan to Saltwīc ymbe mænigfealde þearfe. ge Godes dæles ge worolde dæles. Þa spræc ic on þa magas mid þe erfegewrite. ⁊ wilnade me rihtes. Ða beweddode me Eadnoð ⁊ Ælfred ⁊ Ælfstan. þæt hio oðer þara dydon. oððe hit me ageafon. oððe on hira mægðe þone man funden þe to þam hade fenge ⁊ to lande. ⁊ me wære gehearsum for Gode ⁊ for worolde. Þa Eadnoð þe þæt land hæfde gebead hit ealre þære mægðe hwæðer hit ænig swa gegan wolde. Ða wæs ælc þæs wordes. ꝥ him leofre wære ꝥ he land foreode þonne he þæne had underfenge. Ða gesohte he Æþelred ⁊ Æþelflæde ⁊ eac Æþelnoð urne ealra freond. ⁊ heo ealle to me wilnodon ꝥ ic hine læte æt

guilty before God's throne, at the great doom. Then, after Eastmund's decease, the family bereaved of the same land both the ghosts of the men departed and the bishop and the church of Worcester. And bishop Heahberht often called this to remembrance, or demanded the land; and bishop Alchun afterwards very often, while he existed; and I also, bishop Werferth, have often demanded it; but we could obtain no right before Æthelred was lord of the Mercians. He then assembled the 'witan' of the Mercians at Saltwich, on account of manifold things needful, both on the part of God, and on the part of the world. I then pleaded against the kinsmen, producing the deed of inheritance, and desired right. Then Eadnoth, and Ælfred, and Ælfstan pledged me, that they would one or the other, either they would give it up to me, or would find a man in their family who would take to orders and to the land, and would be obedient to me before God and before the world. Then Eadnoth, who had the land, offered it to all the family, whether any one would so obtain it. Then me ꝥ land begeotan him to agenre æhte· swelcum erfewæardum to syllenne swelce he wolde. ⁊ ic þa swa dyde ealles swyðost for hiora bene· ⁊ he eac me gesealde feowertig mancesa· ⁊ ic þa mid mira higna leafe æt Weogornaceastre him sealde ꝥ lond on ece erfe· ⁊ þa bēc. ⁊ ꝥ Eastmundes erfegewrit· ⁊ eac ure agen rædengewrit· ꝥ wære him to þam gerade ꝥ land tolæten þe mon ælce gere gesylle fiftene scillingas clænes feos to Tettanbyrg þam bisceope· ⁊ him eac þone ne[1] scrift healde. Ond ic Eadnoð eac beode minum erfeweardum· on Godes ælmihtiges naman· ꝥ heo næfre þis feoh gelitliæn· ah sien ā þæm bisceope mid rihte holde· ⁊ þære heorædene æt Weogornaceastre. God ælmihtig þa gehealde for bæm lifum þe unne ꝥ þeos gerædnis stondon mote in ēcnesse· ⁊ þis syndon þara manna naman þe æt þæ[2] rednisse wæron· ⁊ æt gewitnysse· þe her beneoðan awritene syndon.

[1] No doubt a repetition of the preceding syllable.

[2] þære?

every one declared that he would rather forgo the land, than he would take holy orders. He then sought Æthelred and Æthelflæd, and also Æthelnoth, the friend of us all; and they all desired of me that I would let him get the land of me in absolute possession, to give to such heirs as he would. And I then did so, above all for their prayer: and he also gave me forty mancuses. And I then, with the leave of my convent at Worcester, gave him the land in perpetual heritage, and the charters, and Eastmund's deed of inheritance, and also our own agreement, that the land should be relinquished to him, on the condition that every year there should be fifteen shillings of pure money given at Tetbury to the bishop, and the written contract with him be also observed. And I Eadnoth also enjoin my heirs, in the name of God Almighty, that they never diminish this money, but be ever rightly faithful to the bishop and the convent at Worcester. May God Almighty preserve them in both lives, who grant that this agreement may stand to eternity. And these are the names of the men who were at the agreement, and at the witnessing, which are here beneath written.

✠ Ic Wærferð bisceop· mid minre agenre handa· þas sylene getrimme ⁊ gefæstnie.

✠ I Werferth bishop, with my own hand, this donation confirm and ratify.

✠ Beornferð pr̃.
✠ Werfrið pr̃.
✠ Berhthun pr̃.
✠ Tidbald pr̃.
✠ Oslac pr̃.
✠ Berhthelm.

✠ Wigheard.
✠ Wulfred.
✠ Cynehelm.
✠ Wulfhun.
✠ Eardwulf.
✠ Beornferð.

ANONYMOUS. DCCCC.I.–DCCCC.XXIV.

✠ Leof[1] ic þe cyðe hu hit wæs ymb þæt lond æt Funtial· þa fif hida þe Æðelm Higa ymb spycð· ða Helmstan þa undæde gedyde þæt he Æðeredes belt forstæl· þa ongon Higa him specan sona on mid oðran onspecendan· ⁊ wolde him oðflitan ðæt lond. Ða sohte he me· ⁊ bæd me ðæt ic him wære forespeca· forðon ic his hæfde ær onfongen æt biscopes handa ær he ða undæde gedyde. Ða spæc ic him fore· ⁊ þingade him to Ælfrede

✠ Beloved! I will declare to thee how it was concerning the land at Fonthill, the five hides about which Æthelm Higa sues. When Helmstân did the misdeed of stealing Æthered's belt. Then Higa began forthwith, with other accusers, to implead him, and would litigate the land from him. Then sought he me, and prayed me that I would be his advocate, because I had formerly received him at the bishop's hand, before he did that misdeed. I then pleaded

[1] The person addressed is King Eadward the Elder, son of Ælfred. There is much in this document that I do not pretend to understand. See 'Saxons in England,' i. pp. 310, 313, ii. p. 51.

cinge. Ða God forgelde his saule· ða lyfde he ðæt he moste beon ryhtes wyrðe for mire forspæce· ⁊ ryht race wið Æðelm ymb ðæt lond. Ða het he hie seman. Ða wæs ic ðara monna sum þe ðærto genemned wæran· ⁊ Wihtbord· ⁊ Ælfric wæs ða hrælðen· ⁊ Byrhthelm· ⁊ Wulfhun þes blaca æt Sumortune· ⁊ Strica· ⁊ Ubba· ⁊ ma monna þonne ic nu genemnan mæge. Ða reahte heora ægðer his spell. Ða þuhte us eallan þæt Helmstan moste gan forð mid ðon bocon· ⁊ geagnigean him ðæt lond ðæt he hit hæfde swa Æðeldryð hit Osulfe on æht gesealde wið gemedan feo· ⁊ heo cwæð to Osulfe ðæt heo hit ahte him wel to syllanne· forðon hit wæs hire morgengifu ða heo æst to Aðulfe com· ⁊ Helmstan þis eal on þon aðe befeng· ⁊ Ælfred cing ða Osulfe his hondsetene sealde· ða he ðæt lond æt Æðeldryðe bohte· ðæt hit swa stondan moste· ⁊ Eadweard his· ⁊ Æðelnað his· ⁊ Deormod his· ⁊ ælces þara monna ðe mon ða habban wolde. Ða we hie æt Weardoran nu semdan· þa bær mon ða boc forð· ⁊ rædde hie· þa stod seo hondseten eal ðæron. Ða þuhte

for him, and interceded for him to king Ælfred. Then, may God reward his soul! then he allowed that he might be right-worthy, on account of my advocacy, and plead his right against Æthelm about the land. He then commanded them to come to an agreement. Then was I one of the men who were named thereto, and Wihtbord, and Ælfric, who was then keeper of the wardrobe, and Byrhthelm, and Wulfhûn the Black at Somerton, and Strica, and Ubba, and more men than I can now name. Then each of them said his say. Then it seemed to us all that Helmstân must come forth with the titles, and prove his right to the land, that he had it as Æthelthryth had sold it to Osulf, in possession, for a fair pecuniary consideration. And she said to Osulf, that she well possessed it to sell, because it was her morning-gift, when she first came to Athulf. And Helmstân included all this in the oath. And king Ælfred gave his sign manual to Osulf, when he bought the land of Æthelthryth, that it must so stand; and Eadward his, and Æthelnath his, and Deormôd his, and every one us eallan ðe æt þære some wæran. þæt Helmstan wære aðe þæs ðe near. Đa næs Æðelm na fullice geðafa ær we eodan in to cinge. ⁊ sædan eall hu we hit reahtan. ⁊ be hwy we hit reahtan. ⁊ Æðelm stod self þærinne mid. ⁊ cing stod þwoh his honda æt Weardoran innan þon bure. Đa he ðæt gedon hæfde. ða ascade he Æðelm hwy hit him ryht ne ðuhte ðæt we him gereaht hæfdan. cwæð ðæt he nan ryhtre geðencan ne meahte þonne he þone að agifan moste gif he meahte. Đa cwæð ic þæt he wolde cunnigan. ⁊ bæd ðone cing ðæt he hit andagade. ⁊ he swa dyde. ⁊ he gelædde ða to ðon andagan ðone að be fullan. ⁊ bæd me ðæt ic him fultemade. ⁊ cwæð ðæt him wære leofre ðæt he .... alde ðonne se að forburste. oððe hit æf .... æde. Đa cwæð ic ðæt ic him wolde fylstan to ryhte. ⁊ næfre to nanan wo. on ða gerade þet he his [bóc[1]] me uðe. ⁊ he me ðæt in wedde gesealde. ⁊ we ridan ða to ðon andagan. ic ⁊ Wihtbord rad mid me. ⁊ Byrhthelm rad ðider mid Æðelme. ⁊ we gehyrdan ealle ðæt he ðone að be fulan

of the men that it was wished to have. When we had now brought them to an agreement at Wardour, the titles were brought forth and read, when the sign manual stood all thereon. It then seemed to us all who were at the agreement, that Helmstân was so much nearer to the oath. Then did Æthelm not fully assent, before we went in to the king, and said all how we had arranged it, and why we had so arranged it. And Æthelm himself stood therein with us; and the king stood washing his hands at Wardour, within the chamber. When he had done that, he asked Æthelm, why that did not seem right to him, which we had arranged; and said that he could not conceive anything more right, than that he [Helmstân] should give the oath if he could. Then said I that he would make the trial, and prayed the king that he would adjourn it; and he did so; and then, on the day fixed, he would take the oath fully; and prayed me that I would support him, and said that he would rather .... than that the oath should fail, or

[1] Not in MS.

ageaf. Ða we cwædan ealle ðæt hit wære geendodu spæc· ða se dom wæs gefylled· ⁊ leof hwonne bið angu spæc geendedu· gif mon ne mæg· nowðer ne mid wed ne mid aða geendigan· oððe gif mon ælcne dom wile onwendan· ðe Ælfred cing gesette· hwonne habbe we þonne gemotad. And he me ða boc ða ageaf swa he me on ðon wedde ær geseald hæfde· sona swa se að agifen wæs· ⁊ ic him gehet ðæt he moste ðes londes brucan ða hwile ðe he lifde· ⁊ gif he hine wolde butan bysmore gehealdan. Ða on ufan ðæt· ymb an oðer healf gear· nat ic hweðer ðe ymb tua· ða forstæl he ða unlædan oxan æt Funtial· ðe he mid ealle fore forwearð· ⁊ draf to cytlid· ⁊ hine mon þæræt aparade· ⁊ his speremon ahredde ða spor wreclas [1]. Ða he fleah ða torypte hine an brember [2] ofer ðæt nebb. Ða he ætsacan wolde þa sæde him mon þæt to tacne. Ða swaf Eanulf Penearding on· wæs gerefa· ða genom eal ðæt yrfe him on þæt he ahte to Tyssebyrig. Ða ascade ic hine hwy he swa dyde· ða cwæð he ðæt he wære ðeof·

. . . . I then said that I would aid him to right, and never to any wrong, on the condition that he should give me his [title], and he gave it me in pledge; and we rode then on the appointed day, I, and Wihtbord rode with me; and Byrhthelm rode thither with Æthelm; and we all heard that he gave the oath fully. Then we all said that the suit was ended, when the judgment was completed. And, Beloved! when shall any cause be ended, if it cannot be ended either with pledge or with oath? or if every decision may be set aside which king Ælfred laid down, when then shall we have finished? And he then gave up to me his book, as he had before given it in pledge, as soon as the oath was given; and I promised him that he might enjoy the land while he lived, and provided he would hold himself without reproach. Then after that about a year and a half, or, I know not whether, about two [years], he stole the unguarded oxen at Fonthill, for which he totally ruined himself, and drove them to a 'cytlid' [3]; and there

[1] his . . . . . wreclas. This I do not understand.

[2] MS. breber.

[3] Perhaps another name for cotlif, *a cottage, or small holding.*

⁊ mon gerehte ðæt yrfe cinge· forðon he wæs cinges mon· ⁊ Ordlaf feng to his londe· for ðon hit wæs his læn ðæt he on sæte· he ne meahte na his forwyrcan· ⁊ tu hine hete ða flyman. Ða gesahte he ðines fæder lic· ⁊ brohte insigle to me· ⁊ ic wæs æt Cippanhomme mit te. Ða ageaf ic ðæt insigle ðe· ⁊ ðu him forgeafe his eard ⁊ ða are ðe he get on gebogen hæfð· ⁊ ic feng to minan londe· ⁊ sealde hit ðon biscope ða on ðine gewitnesse ⁊ ðinra weotena· ða fif hida wið ðon londe æt Lidgeard [1]wið fif hidan[1]· ⁊ biscop ⁊ eal hiwan forgeafan me ða feower· ⁊ an wæs teoðing lond. Ðonne leof is me micel neodðearf ðæt hit mote stondan swa hit nu gedon is ⁊ gefyrn wæs. Gif hit elleshwæt bið· ðonne sceal ic ⁊ wylle beon gehealden on ðon ðe ðe to ælmessan ryht ðincð.

he was discovered, and his tracer . . . . As he fled a bramble tore him on the face. When he would deny, they told him that as a token. Then Eanulf Penearding turned upon him, who was the reeve; then took all the property from him that he owned in Tisbury. I then asked him why he did so, when he said that he (Helmstân) was a thief, and the property was confiscated to the king, because he was the king's man. And Ordlaf took to his land, because being his fee on which he resided, he could not forfeit it. And thou then didst declare him a fugitive. Then sought he thy father's body, and brought a signet to me; and I was at Chippenham with thee. Then delivered I the signet to thee, and thou didst grant him his country, and the property on which he has yet dwelt. And I took to my land, and then gave it to the bishop, in witness of thee and thy 'witan', viz. the five hides for the land at Liddiard. And the bishop and all the convent then gave me four, and one was tithing land. Now, Beloved! it is to me much needful that it

[1]' delendum?

	might stand as it now is done and formerly was. If it shall be otherwise, then I shall and will be held to that which shall appear to thee right eleemosinarily.
In dorso. ✠ ⁊ Æðelm Higa eode of ðam geflite ða cing wæs æt Worgemynster· on Ordlafes gewitnesse· ⁊ on Osferðes· ⁊ on Oddan· ⁊ on Wihtbordes· ⁊ on Ælfstanes ðys blerian· ⁊ on Æðelnoðes.	*Indorsed.* ✠ And Æthelm Higa gave up the suit when the king was at Warminster, in witness of Ordlaf, and Osferth, and Odda, and Wihtbord, and Ælfstân the Bald, and Æthelnôth.

ÆTHELFLÆD OF MERCIA. DCCCC.XV.-DCCCC.XXII.

Regnante Christo Mediatore nostro, Filio Dei et Salvatione mundi, qui sceptra regit, et alta tociusque telluris orbem, post opere et umbratione conceptioneque Sancti Spiritus, ex sacratissimo prosiliens virginis alvo, cujus imperio cuncta optemperant celestia, tremuntque terrestria, et formidant infernalia. Hujus gloriosissime incarnationis anno DCCC°LXX°VIII° [1] ego Æþelfled, juvante superna pietate, et largiente clementia Christi, gubernacula regens Merciorum, cum consilio episcoporum optimatumque meorum, dedi licentiam Eadrice meo ministro comparandi terram x. manentium æt Fernbeorngen, sibi suisque hæredibus perpetualiter possidendam. Terram quidem hanc ego Eadric placabili pecunia comparavi æt Wullafe, liberam ab omnibus tributis notis vel ignotis, nisi expeditione et arcis construccione, et singulare precium contra aliud [2]. Terram vero hanc Offa rex Merciorum tradidit Bynnan, abavo Wullafi, et litteris consignavit. Casu quidem

[1] This date is erroneous: the genuineness of the document is more than doubtful; Æthelhun succeeded to the see of Worcester in 915, and died in 922.

[2] alium? The equivalent in Saxon is, butan angilde wið oðrum. See p. 130.

contigit, anno eclypsi solis, perdicio prioris libri; nunc autem nostra licentia et confirmatione anticus præscribitur liber; si causa alicujus rei inveniatur, igne cremetur. Karaxata est autem cartula hujus donationis et confirmationis anno divine incarnationis sicut supra invenitur, et die v. Idus Septembris, in loco qui dicitur Weardburg. Hoc autem servantibus prosperitas, vita, salus; minuentibus vero et frangentibus mors, pena et perdicio. Nomina vero hujus confirmationis et testimonii hic infra nitescunt.

✠ Ego Æþelfled hanc meam licentiam confirmo signaculo sancte crucis. ✠ Ego Ælfwyn[1] episcopus consensi et subscripsi. ✠ Ego Ælfwine episcopus consensi et subscripsi. ✠ Ego Æþelhun episcopus consensi et subscripsi. ✠ Ego Eadgar episcopus consensi et subscripsi. ✠ Ego Ælfred episcopus consensi et subscripsi. ✠ Ego Æþelferd dux consensi et subscripsi. ✠ Ego Ælfred dux consensi et subscripsi. ✠ Ego Æþelhun abbas consensi et subscripsi. ✠ Ego Ecgberht abbas consensi et subscripsi. ✠ Ego Cynað abbas consensi et subscripsi. ✠ Ego Wihtred consensi et subscripsi. ✠ Ego Berhsige consensi et subscripsi. ✠ Ego Æþelnaþ consensi et subscripsi. ✠ Ego Æþelward consensi et subscripsi. ✠ Ego Ælfstan consensi et subscripsi.

---

* KING ÆTHELSTÂN.

"THE ORIGINAL CHARTER TO THE BURGESSES OF MALMESBURY."

Athelstanus rex Anglorum do, pro me et meis successoribus, burgensibus meis et eorum omnibus successoribus Meldulfuensis burgi quod habeant et teneant semper omnes functiones et liberas consuetudines suas, sicut tenuerunt tempore regis Eadwardi patris mei, illibate et honorifice. Et præcipio omnibus subter imperio meo, quod non faciant eis injuriam, et sint quieti absque calumpnia et scot. Et do et concedo eis illam brueram regiam quinque hydarum terre

[1] This is a female name: perhaps for "episcopus" we should read *filia Æþelflede*.

juxta villunculam meam de Nortona, propter auxilium eorum in conflictu meo contra Danos. Confecta est hujus donacionis cartula cum signo meo, per testimonium Eadmundi fratris mei, et per consilium magistri Wolsini cancellarii mei, et Odonis thesaurarii mei, et Godwyny.

Godwynus qui fert vexillum regis perquisivit hoc pro burgensibus.

KING ÆTHELSTÂN.

✠ On þam halgan naman ures Hælendes Cristes· se ðe us gescop þa ða we sylfe næron, ⁊ us eft alysde mid his agenum life· ða ða [we] fordone wæron þurh ðæs deofles lare· ⁊ mid ealle forscylgode into þam ecan susle· ac his myccle arfæstnesse us alysde of þam. Nu ic Æðelstan cyning ofer Ængla þeode cyðe minum witum· ⁊ on þisum gewrite mid wordum afæstnige· ꝥ ic wille friggen ealle þa lande are into Sanctes Paules mynstre· ⁊ þæreto gesetan þysne priuelege· þæt is synderlic freols· S. Paul to lofe ðan halgan apostle ðe þeos stow is halig· minre saule to alysednesse ⁊ mine synnan to forgifenesse· be þam ðe Sybba cyng hit ærest gefreode· ⁊ se halga Erkenwold· ⁊ hig begen þærto· gebugen· mid ealle Gode geðeowode· ⁊ ða stowe gegodeden· ⁊ se

✠ In the holy name of our Saviour Christ, who created us when we ourselves were not, and afterwards redeemed us with his own life, when we were fordone through the devil's lore, and totally condemned into eternal sulphur; but his great mercy liberated us therefrom. Now I Æthelstân, king over the Angles' nation, make known to my 'witan', and in this writing by words confirm, that I will free all the landed property [belonging] to St Paul's monastery, and thereto add this privilege, that is an extraordinary immunity, to the praise of St Paul, the holy apostle, to whom this place is holy, for the redemption of my soul and forgiveness of my sins, according to that which king Sebbi first privileged it, and the holy Erkenwold; and they both re-mære biscop S. Erkenwold þæne freols gefette on Rome birig ðe on þisse cartan is awriten. ⁊ manega oðre freolsas heron gewriten synd ðe mine forgengan gesetten heora saule to alysednesse. Se ðe ðysne freols geeacnige God his lief[1] her on life. ⁊ him heofonarices myrhðe sylle þonne he heonon faran sceole. Se ðe þænne ða are þænce to þeofigenne oððe on oððre wis on to awendenne[2] on oðre hit her beforen awriten is. sy his lif her gelittled. ⁊ ðenne he heonon faran sceole. sy ā his wunung on helle grund. buton he hit her ær his ænde ðe stiðelicor gebete wið þæne æcan God ðe ah ealra þinga geweald. Forþi we swa fæstlice ðysne freols bebeodað þat we swa moten eft ealle ætgædere heofonan rices myrhðe habban mid ðam ecan Gode þe ah ealra þinge geweald. Amen.

tired thereto, and wholly served God, and endowed the place; and the great bishop St Erkenwold obtained this privilege in Rome, which is written in this charter; and many other privileges are herein written, which my predecessors established, for the redemption of their souls. Whoever shall augment this privilege, may God preserve him here in life, and give him the joy of heaven's kingdom when he shall go hence. But whoever shall think to rob this property, or in other wise to avert it to other than is here before written, be his life shortened, and when he shall go hence, be his habitation in the ground of hell; unless before his end he the more rigidly compensate towards the everlasting God, who has power of all things. Therefore do we so firmly command this privilege [to be observed], that we may so hereafter all altogether have the joy of heaven's kingdom, with the everlasting God, who has power of all things. Amen.

THE SAME IN LATIN.

✠ In sancto nomine nostri Servatoris Christi, qui nos creavit quando nosmet ipsi non eramus, et nos redemit cum sua propria vita, quando perditi fuimus ex diaboli doctrina, et

[1] his lief. Not understanding this, I have translated the Latin.
[2] MS. awadenne.

penitus damnati in æternum sulphur; sed ejus magna clementia nos liberavit ab eo. Nunc ego Aðelstanus, rex super Anglicam gentem, notum facio meis sapientibus, et in hoc scripto verbis confirmo, quod liberabo omnem terram ad Sancti Pauli monasterium [spectantem]; et insuper constituam istud privilegium, hoc est singularem immunitatem in laudem Sancti Pauli illius sancti apostoli, cui hic locus est sacratus, in animæ meæ redemptionem et peccatorum meorum remissionem, secundum quod Sebba rex eundem [locum] primo liberavit, et Sanctus Erkenwaldus; quorum ambo eo se contulerunt, omnino Deo inservierunt, et illum locum locupletarunt; magnusque ille episcopus Sanctus Erkenwaldus illud privilegium impetravit Romæ quod in hac carta scribitur; et plura alia privilegia hic inscribuntur, quæ mei prædecessores irrogarunt in animarum suarum redemptionem. Qui hoc privilegium adauxerit, Deus ejus vitam in hoc mundo [conservet], et ei cœlorum regni gaudia concedat quando hinc decesserit. Qui vero quid illinc abstulerit sive in alium usum converterit, aliter [scilicet] quam hic suprascriptum est, sit ejus vita hic decurtata, et quando hinc decesserit semper sit ejus habitatio in inferni fundo, nisi id hic ante finem suum diligentius compenset apud æternum Deum qui omnium rerum habet potestatem. Idcirco tam firmiter hoc privilegium [observari] præcipimus, ut ita nos omnes denuo possimus simul coelorum regni gaudia assequi cum æterno Deo, qui omnium rerum habet potestatem. Amen.

KING ÆTHELSTÂN.

✠ In nomine Domini nostri Jhesu Christi. Ego Æðelstanus rex do Sancto Cuðberto hunc textum evangeliorum, duo casulas, et unam albam, et unam stolam cum manipulo, et unum cingulum, et tres altaris cooperimenta, et unum calicem argenteum, et duas pateras, alteram auro paratam alteram Græco opere fabrefactam, et unum thuribulum argenteum, et unam crucem auro et ebore artificiose paratam, et unum regium pallium auro textum, et duas tabulas auro et argento fabrefactas, et duo candelabra argentea auro parata, et unum missalem, et duos evangeliorum textus auro et argento ornatos, et unam Sancti Cuðberti vitam metrice et prosaice scriptam, et septem pallia, et tres cortinas, et tria tapentia, et duas coppas argenteas cum cooperculis, et quatuor magnas campanas, et tria cornua auro et argento fabrefacta, et duo vexilla, et unam lanceam, et duas armillas aureas, et meam villam dilectam Wyremuðe australem cum suis appendiciis, id est, Wertun, Uffentun, Sylceswyrðe, duas Weothehoppas, Byrdene, Seham, Setun, Daltun, Daldene, Heseldene. Hæc omnia do sub Dei et Sancti Cuðberti testimonio; ut si quis inde aliquid abstulerit, damnetur in die judicii cum Juda traditore, et trudatur in ignem æternum qui paratus est diabolo et angelis ejus.

---

* KING ÆTHELSTÂN.

✠ In nomine sanctæ et individuæ Trinitatis. Adelstanus rex, Dei gratia, regni Angliæ, omnibus hominibus suis Eboraci, et per totam Angliam salutem. Sciatis quod ego confirmo ecclesiæ et capitulo Ripon pacem suam, et omnes libertates et consuetudines suas; et concedo eis curiam suam de omnibus quærelis et in omnibus curiis de hominibus S. Wilfridi, pro ipsis et hominibus suis, vel contra ipsos, vel inter se ad invicem, vel quæ fieri p . . . . . . et judicium suum pro Frodmortell; et quod homines sint credendi per suum ya, et per suum na; et omnes suas terras, habitas et habendas, et homines suos ita liberos, quod nec rex Angliæ, nec ministri ejus, nec archiepiscopus Eboraci, nec ministri ejus, aliquid faciant vel habeant quod est ad terras suas vel ad socam capituli. Testibus G. archiepiscopo Eboracensi, et P. præposito Beverlaci.

---

* CARTA ADELSTANI REGIS SANCTO JOHANNI BEVERLACI; ANNO DOMINI DCCCC.XXV. DE PRIVILEGIIS.

þat witen alle þat ever been,
þat þis charter heren and seen,
þat I þe king Adelstan
has yaten and given to seint John
of Beverlike, þat sai I yow,
tol and theam, þat wit ye now,
soke and sake over al þat land,
þat es given into his hand,
on ever ilke kinges dai,
be it all free þan and ay;
be it almousend be all free
wit ilke man and eeke wit mee
þat wil i be him þat me scop,
bot til an ercebiscop,
and til þe seven minstre prestes
þat serves God þer saint John restes.
þat give i God and seint John
her befor you ever ilkan.
All my herst corn ineldeel,
to uphald his minstre weel:
þa fourþreve be heven kinge
of ilka plough of estriding.
If it swa betid, or swa gaas,
þat ani man her again taas,
be he baron, be he erle,
clark, prest, parson, or cherel;
na be he na þat ilk Gome,
I will forsaye þat he come
(þat wit ye weel or and or)
till saint John mynstre dor.
And þar i will (swo Crist me red)
þat he bet his misded,
or he be cursed son on on
wit al þat servis saint John.

Yif hit swa betid and swa es,
þat þe man in mansing es :
i sai yow over fourti daghes,
(swilk þan be sain John laghes)
þat þe chapitel of Beverlike
til þe scirif of Everwike
send þair writ son onan,
þat þis mansed man betan.
Þe scirref þan say i ye,
witouten any writ one me,
sal nimen him (swo Crist me red),
and into my prison lede,
and hald him (þat is my wilt)
til he bet his misgilt.
If men reises newe laghes,
in any oþer kinges daghes,
be þay fromed, be þay yemed
wit yham of the mynstre demed,
þe mercy of ye misdeed,
gif i saint John, swo Crist me red,
yif man be cald of limes or lif,
or men chalenges land in strif
wit my bodlaik, wit writ of right,
y wil saint John have ye might,
þat man þar for noght fight in feeld,
nowþer wit staf no wit sheeld;
bot twelve men wil i þat it telle,
swo sal it be swo heer ibelle.
And he þat him swo werne may,
overcomen be he ever and ay,
als he in feld war overcomen,
þe cravantise of him be nomen.
Þat yat i God and saint John
her befor iow ever ilkon.
If man be founden slan idrunkend,
sterved on saint John rike, his aghen men,
wiþouten swike his aghen bailiffs make ye sight,
nan oþer coroner have ye might.

Swa mikel fredom give i ye
swa hert may think or eghe see,
þat have i þought and forbiseen,
i will þat þer ever been,
samening and mynstre lif
last follike witouten strif.
God help alle þas ilk men
þat helpes to þe þeowen. Amen.

CARTA ADELSTANI REGIS SANCTO WILFRIDO DE RIPPON CONCESSA.

Wyt all that es and es gan
þat ik king Adelstan
as gyven as frelich as I may,
and to þe capitel of seint Wilfrai,
of my free devotion,
þair pees at Rippon.
On ilke side þe kyrke a mile,
for all ill deedes and ylke agyle,
and wiþin þair kirke yate,
at þe stan þe Griþstole hate;
wiþin þe kirke dore and þe quare,
þair have pees for les and mare.
Ilkan of þis stedes sal have pees
of frodmortell and il deedes
þat þair don is, tol, tem,
with iren and with water deme;
and þat þe land of seint Wilfrai
of alkyn geld fre sal be ay.
At na man at langes me to
in þair Herpsac sal have at do;
and for ik will at þai be save,
I will at þai alkyn freedom have;
and in al þinges be als free
as hert may thynke or eygh may se,
at te power of a kinge
masts make free any þynge.

And my seale have I sett þerto,
for I will at na man it undo.

---

* KING ÆTHELSTÂN. DEC. 21ST DCCCC.XXXV.

Fortuna fallentis sæculi procax, non lacteo inmarcessibilium liliorum candore amabilis, sed fellita ejulande corrupcionis amaritudine odibilis, fœtentis filios in valle lacrimarum carnis rictibus debachando venenose mordaciter dilacerat; quæ quamvis arridendo sit infelicibus attrectabilis, Acherontici tamen ad yma Cociti, ni satus alti subveniat boantis, impudenter est decursibus. Et ideo quia ipsa ruinosa deficiendo taliter dilabitur, summopere festinandum est ad amena indicibilis leticie arva, ubi angelica ymnidice jubilationis organa mellifluaque vernancium rosarum odoramina a bonis beatisque naribus inestimabiliter dulcia capiuntur, sineque calce auribus cliviparum suavia audiuntur. Cujus amore felicitatis illectus, fastidiunt jam infima dulcescunt superna; ejusque pro percipiendi semperque specie concupiscibili fruendi, Ego Athelstanus, rex Anglorum, per Omnipotentis dexteram tocius Britannie regni solio sublimatus, quandam telluris particulam venerabili familie Maldubiensi, pro animabus patruelium meorum, filiorum Athelwardi clitonis, videlicet Alwynis et Athelwinis, sub estimatione x. cassatorum, in loco qui dicitur Wdetun, servienti familie Deo et Sancto Petro imperpetuum jus largitus sum [1]. Hoc præcipiens, in nomine Dei, ut nos-

[1] The copy in Malmesbury (Gale, Scriptt. xv. i. p. 364) has the following reading and interpolation :—sub æstimatione VI. cassatorum in loco qui dicitur Breoni, et sub æstimatione V. cassatorum in loco qui dicitur Summerford ; item V. in loco qui dicitur Nortun, item V. in loco qui dicitur Ewulm : hoc præcipiens ut nemo nostrorum successorum hoc nostrum donum, quamdiu Christianitas vigeat, vel ex minimo interrumpere tentet ; quod si quis tentaverit, a Deo se damnandum in perpetuum sciat. Sciant autem sapientes nostræ regionis nos has præfatas terras non injuste rapuisse, rapinamque Deo dedisse, sed sic eas accepi quemadmodum judicaverunt omnes optimates regni Anglorum, insuper et apostolicus papa Romanæ ecclesiæ Johannes, Elfredo defuncto, qui nostræ felicitatis et vitæ æmulus

trorum nemo successorum hoc nostrum donum, quamdiu Christianitas vigeat, vel ex minimo irrumpere temptet; quod si quisque temptaverit, a Deo imperpetuum dampnandum. Hujus namque a Deo Dominoque Jhesu Christo, innuente atque inspirante voluntatis scedula, anno Dominice incarnationis DCCCC.XXXVIII.[1], regni vero gratis michi commissi XI°, Indictione VIII., Epacta XIIII., Concurrente III., XII. Kal. Jan., luna vertentis mensis X., in civitate celeberrima que Dorneacester appellatur, tota optimatum generalitate sub alis regie dapsilitatis ovanti, perscripta est. Cujus etiam inconcusse firmitatis auctoritas hiis testibus roborata constat, quorum nomina subtus grammulis depicta annotantur.

Ego Athelstanus, ierarchia florentis Albionis prædictus rex, cum signo sancte semperque venerande crucis corroboravi hunc indiculum, et subscripsi. Ego Wlfhelmus, Dorobernensis ecclesie archiepiscopus, consensi. Ego Wlfstanus Eboracensis ecclesie archiepiscopus consensi et subscripsi. Ego Eugenius subregulus consensi et signavi. Ego Morcant subregulus. Ego Howel subregulus consensi et signavi. Ego Cunan episcopus signavi. Ego Jutual subregulus[2] consensi et subscripsi. Ego Wlfhelm episcopus consensi. Ego Afwyne episcopus consensi et subscripsi. Ego Aelfwold dux consensi. Ego Uhtred dux consensi et subscripsi. Ego Urm dux consensi. Ego Osulf dux consensi et subscripsi.

---

exstitit, nequitiæ inimicorum meorum consentiens, quando me voluerunt, patre meo defuncto, cæcare in Wintonia civitate, si non me Dominus sua pietate eripuisset. Sed denudatis eorum machinamentis, remissus est ad Romanam ecclesiam, ut ibi se coram Johanne apostolico jurejurando defenderet; et hoc fecit coram altari Sancti Petri. Sed facto juramento cecidit coram altari, et in manibus famulorum suorum portatus est ad scholam Anglorum, et in III. nocte vitam finivit. Et nunc apostolicus ad nos remisit, et quid de eo ageretur consuluit. Nos autem, optimatum nostrorum rogatu, concessimus, ut portaretur ad cæteros Christianos, quamvis indignus. Et sic indicta est mihi possessio illius omnis in magnis et modicis, etc. Hujus namque, &c.

[1] This date is erroneous.

[2] MS. Jutwal episcopus.

KING ÆTHELSTÂN. DCCCC.XXXVIII.

☧ Regnante in æternum Christo Filio Dei, qui sicut tempora temporibus, ita etiam dat regna quibus vult regibus, Ego Æðelstanus, humilis et devotus rex Anglorum, venerabili ep̃o Frithestano Uuentanæ æcclesiæ, quæ in honore sanctorum apostolorum Petri et Pauli consecrata est, hanc cartulam fieri jussi; atque in ea, pro indulgentia peccatorum meorum, libertatem renovavi quam Æðelheard rex dudum constituit; quia volo ut pro pace regni et gentis salute æcclesia Uuentana, quæ caput est ecclesiarum quæ in Occidentalium Saxonum provinciis construuntur, æternam libertatem et reverentiam et dominationem principalem sine fine possideat. Prefatus autem rex Æðelheard, sicut rogatus fuit a Fryðegyþa regina, dedit ad villam Tantun, quæ nunc est possessio et hereditas episcopalis Uuentanæ ecclesiæ, IIII[or] mansas in loco qui dicitur Wiðiglea, ad pascua pecorum, et IIIes in loco qui Cearn nuncupatur, ad coquendam salis copiam. Istarum autem VII. mansarum quantitas, justo valde judicio totius populi et seniorum et primatum, ablata fuit ab eis qui eorum possessores fuerunt, quia aperto crimine furti, usque ad mortem obnoxii inventi sunt. Ideoque decretum est ab omni populo ut libri illorum, quos ad has terras abebant, æternaliter dampnarentur; et quicumque eos in adjutorium sui umquam proferre presumeret, anathematizatus et maledictus ab omnibus Xp̃ianis haberetur. Nos quoque nostris temporibus dampnamus et maledicimus omnem hominem qui libertatem sc̃æ et Deo dilectæ Uuentanæ ecclesiæ in magnis vel in modicis corrumpere seu diminuere presumpserit; nec habeat hereditatem in regno Xp̃i et Dei quicumque huic sanctissimæ ecclesiæ inimicus vel adversarius, sive exterminator extiterit; nisi ante finem suum, cum manifesta pœnitentia, malitiam suam purgaverit. Et quicumque huic ecclesiæ adjutor et amicus esse studuerit, benedictionem et salutem longam, et felicitatem temporum, et indulgentiam peccatorum, atque societatem regni cælorum consequatur in secula seculorum.

Limites terrarum predictarum diffunduntur sicut sermo Anglicus monstrat subsequens.

✠ Ærest on Ucingcford· of ðæs cumbes heafde on þone smalan weg þurh ðone mor to Wiðigslæde· þæt to Brocenan beorge· swa to Wuduforda· ꝥ to Lulles beorge· swa forð ⁊lang . . . . . arpaðes to Mægenstanes dene· swa to Wiðlea gate· ꝥ to Nædran beorge· ꝥ ðurh þone mor be riht gemære on Wiðigmor· ðæt eft on Ucingcford.

✠ Ærest of sæ up on Hengestesrigc· ðonan norð on Gyrd weg· swa norð ⁊lang hricges on middeweardne Sealtera cumb· ꝥ be cumbe ing on Holan broc· ꝥ ⁊lang streames ing on Hlosmoc· adune on stream on seofan æceras· þær of streame eft onbutan seofan æceras· eft suð on Hlosmoc· ðæt adune on stream· oððа suran apeldran· ꝥ suð on ða norð ræwe· ðanan eft ofer Cern on Gata ford· ðæt suð bufan litlan graf· swa suð on Earnes hlingc· of Earnes hlince eft ut on sæ.

✠ First to Uckford; from the combe's head to the narrow way through the moor to Withislade; then to Brokenborough; so to Woodford, then to Lulsborough, so on along the high road to Mainstone dean; so to Widley gate; then to Nadderborough; then through the moor, by the right boundary to Widmore; then again to Uckford.

✠ First from the sea to Henstridge; thence north to Yardway; so north along the ridge to the south of Saltercombe; then by the combe meadow to Holbrook; then along the stream meadow to Losmock; down to the stream to the seven acres; thence from the stream again round the seven acres; again south to Losmock; then down to the stream as far as the sour appletree; then south to the north row; then again over Cerne to Gatford; then south above the little grove; so south to Erneslink; from Ernslink again to the sea.

Acta est hæc præfata donatio anno ab incarnatione Dñi nostri Jhesu Xp̃i DCCCC.XXXVIII., in quo anno bellum factum est in loco qui Bruninga feld dicitur, ubi Anglis victoria data est de cælo.

✠ Ego Æðelstanus rex hoc donum meum regiæ potestatis libertate confirmavi.

✠ Ego Wulfhelm archieps̃ hanc donationem sc̃æ crucis titulo consecravi.

✠ Ego Frithestan, Wintaniensis eps̃, consignavi.

✠ Ego Þeodred, Lundoniensis eps̃, consolidavi.

✠ Ego Cenwald eps̃ prædictum donum conlaudavi.

✠ Ego Oda eps̃ hanc cartulam corroboravi.

✠ Ego Æþelgar eps̃ sancta cruce signavi et conclusi.

✠ Ego Alfwold dux.	✠ Ego Ælfhere mı̄.
✠ Ego Uhtred dux.	✠ Ego Wihtgar mı̄.
✠ Ego Odda mı̄.	✠ Ego Aþelwold mı̄.
✠ Ego Wulfgar mı̄.	✠ Ego Ælfheah mı̄.
✠ Ego Sigered mı̄.	✠ Ego Ælfred mı̄.
✠ Ego Ælfric mı̄.	✠ Ego Wulfmær mı̄.
✠ Ego Eadmund mı̄.	✠ Ego Ordeh mı̄.
✠ Ego Wulfsige mı̄.	

Dorso. Þis is seo boc þe Æþelstan cing gebocode Friþestane bisceope to Wiþiglea ⁊ to Cearn. Þis syndon Tantunes land.	This is the charter which king Æthelstan chartered to bishop Frithestan for Widley and Cerne: these are Taunton's lands.

KING EADMUND. DCCCC.XLIV.

CHARTER TO GLASTONBURY.

In nomine Domini nostri Ihesu Christi. Ego Edmundus rex Anglorum cæterarumque in circuitu gencium persistencium gubernator et rector, cum concilio et consensu optimatum meorum, pro eterne retributionis spe, et relaxatione peccaminum meorum, concedo ecclesie sancte Dei genitricis Marie Glastonie, et venerabili viro Dunstano, quem ibidem abbatem constitui, libertatem et potestatem, jura et consuetudines, et omnes forisfacturas omnium terrarum suarum, id est, burgbrice, hundred socna athas, ordelas, infangenetheofas, hamsocna, et frithbrice, et foresteall, et tol et team, in omni regno meo; et sint terre sue sibi libere et solute ab omni calumpnia, sicut mee michi habentur. Sed præcipue ipsa villa Glastonia, in qua celeberima vetusta æcclesia sancte [Dei] genitricis sita est, pre ceteris sit liberior cum terminis suis; abbati tantum ejusdem loci tantummodo potestas sit, tam in notis causis quam in ignotis, in modicis et in magnis, et in hiis etiam que sunt super et subtus terram, in aridis et in rivis, in silvis et in planis. Et eandem auctoritatem puniendi aut dimittendi delinquentium in ea commissa habeat quam mea curia, quemadmodum mei antecessores concesserunt, et statuendo firmaverunt, videlicet pater meus Edwardus, et Elfredus pater ejus, et Kentwynes, Ines, Cuthredus, et alii quamplures qui locum illum honorantes gloriosum habuerunt, et apostolica auctoritate roboraverunt. Et ne quisquam mortalium, seu episcopus, aut dux, aut princeps, aut quislibet ministrorum eorum, audeat eam omnino intrare, causa placitandi, vel rapiendi, vel quippiam faciendi, quod contrarium possit esse inibi Deo servientibus, Dei interdictione prohibeo. Quisquis igitur benevola mente meam donacionem vel devocionem ampliare, et privilegii dignitatem servare satagerit, in hoc præsenti seculo vita illius prospera sit, et longiturne vite gaudia teneat. Si quis autem propria temeritate violenter invadere temptaverit, sciat se procul dubio ante tribunal districti judicis titubantem tremebundumque racionem redditurum, nisi prius digna satisfactione emendare maluerit. Acta est autem hujus privilegii pagina anno Dominice incarnationis nongentesimo quadragesimo quarto, Indictione secunda.

Ego Edmundus rex Anglorum prefatam donacionem, cum sigillo sancte crucis, confirmavi. Ego Eadred, ejusdem regis frater consensi. Ego Eadgiua, ejusdem regis mater, prædictum donum consignavi. Ego Oda, Dorobernensis ecclesie archiepiscopus, ejusdem regis donacionem, cum tropheo agie crucis, subarravi. Ego Wlfstanus archiepiscopus præfatam donacionem confirmavi. Ego Elfheah, Wintoniensis ecclesie episcopus, triumphalem tropheum agie crucis impressi. Ego Wlfhelm, Fontanensis episcopus, corroboravi.

Scriptaque est litteris aureis in libro evangeliorum quem

eidem ecclesie obtulit, opere satis eleganti composito, qui textus Sancti Dunstani dicitur.

KING EADRED. DCCCC.XLVII.

Þis is þæs landes boc æt Tantune ðe Eadred cing edniwon gæbocode sanctæ Trinitatæ ⁊ Sanctæ Petræ ⁊ Paulæ into Ealdan mynstre.

This is the Book of the land at Taunton, which king Eadred booked anew to the Holy Trinity and St Peter, and St Paul, at the Old monastery.

✠ In nomine Dei summi et altissimi Jhesu Christi. Subtilissimo mentis certamine Deum quem diligimus et credimus, intima mentis affectione timeamus et amemus; quia Psalmista, qui quondam Sullimis regnabat dives in arvis, conquerelando ac lamentabili voce ita protulit, dicens, "Thesaurizat, et ignorat cui congregat ea," eo quod interdum [non] optatis et sepius exosis relinquitur quod prius homo per ambitionem seculi concupivit; tamen, miserationis Omnipotentis Dei largitate, caducis opibus æternæ celestis vitæ premia mercari queamus. Quapropter ego Eadredus, rex Anglorum cæterarumque gentium in circuitu persistentium gubernator et rector, sanctæ Dei æcclesiæ Wentana civitate locatæ, ac beato Petro apostolorum principi, ejusque coapostolo Paulo dicate, Ælfheago ejusdem sedis pontifice impetrante, uti Fryðegyð regina, penæ in exordio Christianæ religionis, reverende Trinitatis ejusque prænominatis apostolis devota mente concesserat, ac Aðelwlf rex augmentando amplificaverat, itidemque Eadward rex, novis litterarum apicibus, iterum restauraverat, cum isdem territoriis quas Aðelwlf rex hereditaria carta conscribi jusserat, c. scilicet ac xxx. quantitatem manentium continentem loco celebri qui Tantun nominatur, æterna restituendo largitus sum hereditate. Prefato siquidem regi Eadwardo lx. telluris manse, quattuor locorum partibus disperse sicut ipsius territorii cartula, quam præfatus rex edere jussit, liquido testatur, a quodam episcopo Denewlfo videlicet, pro ejusdem telluris libertate concesse sunt. Maneat igitur meum hoc inmobile donum æterna libertate jocundum cum omnibus quæ rite ad prædicta loca pertinere dinoscuntur, campis, pascuis, pratis, excepto communi labore, expeditione, pontis arcisve constructione. Si qui denique, michi non optanti, hanc libertatis cartam, livore depressi, violare satagerint, agminibus tetre caliginis lapsi, vocem audiant examinationis die arbitris sibi dicentis, "Discedite a me maledicti in ignem æternum," ubi cum demonibus ferreis sartaginibus crudeli torqueantur in pœna, si non ante mortem digna hoc emendaverint pœnitentia. Acta est hæc prefata donatio anno Dominicæ incarnationis DCCCC.XLVII., Indictione V.

Ego Eadredus rex Anglorum prefatam donationem sub sigillo sanctæ crucis indeclinabiliter consensi atque roboravi. Ego Eadgyfu, ejusdem regis mater, cum sigillo sanctæ crucis confirmavi. Ego Oda, Dorobernensis æcclesiæ archiepiscopus, ejusdem regis principatum et benivolentiam cum sigillo sanctæ crucis conclusi. Ego Wulfstanus archons, divinæ servitutis officio mancipatus, Eboracæ civitatis archiepiscopus, sigillum sanctæ crucis impressi. Ego Þeodred, Lundoniensis æcclesiæ episcopus, conclusi. Ego Ælfheah, Wintoniensis æcclesiæ episcopus, testudinem sanctæ crucis subscripsi et confirmavi. Ego Cenuuald episcopus prædictum donum consensi. Ego Ælfric episcopus consignavi. Ego Æðelgar episcopus roboravi. Ego Ælfred episcopus conclusi. Ego Æðelstan dux. Ego Eadric dux. Ego Æðelstan dux. Ego Wulfgar dux. Ego Æþelmund dux. Ego Ealhhelm dux. Ego Ælfstan minister. Ego Eadmund minister. Ego Wlfric minister. Ego Ælfric minister. Ego Wulfric minister. Ego Ælfsige minister. Ego Æðelnoð minister. Ego Ælfred minister. Ego Ælfheah minister. Ego Æðereð minister.

BISHOP BYRHTHELM AND ABBOT ÆTHELWOLD. DCCCC.LVI.

✠ Ðis is seo gerædnes þe Byrhtelm biscop and Aþeluuold abƀ hæfdon ymbe hira landgehwerf. Ðæt is þonne þe se biscop gesealde þa hida æt Cenintune into þære cyricean æt Abbendune to ecan yrfe· ⁊ se abbud gesealde ꝥ seofontyne hyda æt Crydanbrigce þan biscope to ecenesse· ge on life ge efter life· ⁊ hi eac ealra þinga gehwyrfdon· ge on cucan ceape ge on oðrum[1]· swa swa hi betwehs him geraeddon· ⁊ þis wæs Eadwiges leaf cyninges· ⁊ þis syndon ða gewitnessa· Ælfgifu ðæs cininges wif· ⁊ Æðelgifu þæs cyninges wifes modur· Ælfsige biscop· Osulf biscop· Coenwald biscop· Byrhtnoð ealdorman· Ælfheah cyninges discþen· Eadric his brodur.

✠ This is the agreement that bishop Byrhthelm and abbot Æthelwold had concerning the exchange of their land. That then is, that the bishop gave the hides at Kennington to the church at Abingdon in perpetuity, and the abbot gave the seventeen hides at Crydanbridge to the bishop for ever, both during life and after life. And they also exchanged all things both in live stock and in other, as they settled between themselves. And this was with the leave of king Eadwig. And these are the witnesses: Ælgifu the king's wife, and Æthelgifu the king's wife's mother, Ælfsige bp., Osulf bp., Cœnwald bp., Byrhtnoth aldorman, Ælfheah the king's sewer, Eadric his brother.

✠ Dominus autem abbas Athelwoldus commutationem ejusdem terre, id est Cenintun, concedente eodem rege, egit aput Brihtelmum episcopum. In cujus vicissitudine ipse episcopus accepit illam villam que appellatur Crydanbrigce. Testes autem fuerunt hujus commutationis: Ælfgifa regis uxor, et Athelgifa mater ejus, Ælfsige episcopus, Osulfus episcopus, Kenwald episcopus, et multi alii.

[1] MS. oðeorn, or a word resembling it.

KING EADWIG. MAY 17TH DCCCC.LIX.

PRIVILEGIUM EDWII REGIS DE VILLA ABBEND. ET DE ABBATE ELIGENDO DE PROPRIA CONGREGATIONE.

✠ Ortodoxorum vigoris ecclesiastici monitu creberrime instruimur, ut illi oppido subjecti suppeditantes famulemur, qui totius mundi fabricam miro ineffabilique serie disponens, micocrosmum, Adam videlicet, tandem quadriformi plasmatum materia almo ad sui similitudinem instinctum spiramine, universis que in infimis formaverat, uno probandi causa excepto vetitoque, præficiens Paradisiace amenitatis jocunditate conlaterana, Eva scilicet comite decentissime collocavit. Larvarica, pro dolor! seductus cavillatione, versipellis suasibilisque tergiversatione viraginis pellectus anathematis alogia ambro pomum momordit vetitum, et sibi ac posteris, in hoc erumnoso dejectus seculo, letum promeruit perpetuum. Vaticinantibus siquidem prophetis, et celitus superni Regis diuturna clandestino præsagia dogmate promentibus nitide ortodoxis, eulogium ex supernis deferens: non ut Judeorum seditiosa elingue fatetur loquacitas; sed priscorum atque modernorum lepidissimam ambiens facundiam, Arrianas, Sabellianasque proterendo nenias anagogico infrustrans famine, nosque ab obtunsi cecitate umbraminis ad supernorum alacrimoniam patrimoniorum advocans, angelus supernis elapsus liminibus in aurem intemerate virginis, ut evangelica promulgant famina, stupenda cecinisse videtur carmina; cui ecclesia tota, videlicet catholica, consona voce altiboando proclamat, "Beata es, virgo Maria, que credidisti, perficientur in te que dicta sunt tibi a Domino." Mirum dictu! incarnatur verbum et incorporatur scilicet illud de quo evangelista supereminens universorum altitudine sensuum inquit, "In principio erat verbum, et verbum erat apud Deum, et Deus erat verbum," et reliqua. Qua videlicet sumpta de virgine incarnatione, antique virginis facinus demitur, et cunctis mulieribus nitidis precluens taumatibus decus irrogatur. Intacta igitur redolente Christi divinitate, passaque ipsius humanitate, libertas addictis clementer contigit servulis. Hinc ego Eadwig, Altitrono amminiculante, Anglorum ceterarumque gentium in circuitu triviatim persistentium basileus, ut hujus libertatis Altitroni Moderatoris clementia merear optinere consortium, cenobio loco celebri, qui ab hujus prosapie solicolis Æbbandun nobili nuncupatur vocabulo situm, genitricique Domini nostri semper virgini Marie, necnon beato Petro apostolorum principi, ejusque coapostolo Paulo dedicatum habetur, monachis regulariter degentibus monastici eternam privilegii concedo libertatem, quatenus post decessum Æðeluuoldi abbatis egregii, cujus temporibus hec libertatis restauratio, Christo suffragante, concessa est, quem sibi universa præfati cenobii congregatio apto elegerit consilio, secundum regularia beati Benedicti instituta, abbatem juste ex eodem fratrum cuneo eligens constituat. Hujus privilegii libertas deinceps usu perpetuo a cunctis teneatur catholicis, nec extraneorum quispiam, tirannica fretus contumatia, in prædicto monasterio jus arripiens exerceat potestatis; sed ejusdem cenobii collegium perpetue, ut prædixi, libertatis glorietur privilegio. Sit autem præfatum monasterium omni terrene servitutis eodem tenore liberum, quo a prædecessoribus nostris catholicis, a sancto Leone, videlicet, papa, et Coenulfo rege catholico, vetusto continetur privilegio, Rethuno abbate optinente, solutum: agri equidem ad usus monachorum Domino nostro Jhesu Christo ejusque genitrici Marie priscis modernisque temporibus a regibus et religiosis utriusque sexus hominibus, et a meipso meoque patruo Eadredo, rege fidelissimo restituendo jure concessi sunt, ejusdem perpetualiter sint libertatis. Nam rex præfatus rus quod Abbendun nuncupatur, quod rex Ceadwala Domino nostro ejusque genitrici Marie priscis temporibus devoto concesserat animo, in quo prædecessores nostri, diabolica decepti avaricia edificium regale sibi injuste construxerant æcclesie Dei restituens, interdixit ut regum nemo inibi pastum requireret, nec edificium in sempiternum construeret; quod ego Eadwig Anglorum basileus, optimatum meorum usus consilio, tam meis quam meorum successorum temporibus fixum in nomine Patris et Filii et Spiritus Sancti fieri in eternum præcipio. Si quis vero tam epilempticus, philargyrie seductus amentia, quod non optamus, hanc nostre munificientie dapsilitatem ausu temerario infringere temptaverit, sit ipse alienatus a consortio sancte Dei ecclesie, necnon et a participatione sacrosancti corporis et sanguinis Jhesu Christi filii Dei, per quem totus terrarum orbis ab antico humani generis inimico liberatus est; et cum Juda Christi proditore sinistra in parte deputatus, nisi prius hic digna satisfactione humilis penituerit quod contra sanctam Dei ecclesiam rebellis agere præsumpsit, nec in vita hac practica veniam, nec in theorica requiem apostata obtineat ullam, sed eternis baratri incendiis trusus, cum Anania et Saphira jugiter miserrimus crucietur. Anno Dominice incarnationis DCCCC.LIX., indictione II[a], regni autem mei IIII[o], XVI. Kalendas Junii scripta est hujus munificentie singrafa, his testibus consentientibus, quorum inferius nomina, secundum uniuscujusque dignitatem caraxantur.

✠ Ego Eadwig, Britanniæ Anglorum monarcus, præformatas propinquorum sed et regum donationes hoc taumate agie crucis roboravi. ✠ Ego Odo, Dorobornensis ecclesie archiepiscopus, ejusdem benivolentiam subscripsi. ✠ Ego Eadgiuu, ejusdem regis ava, hanc donationem cum sigillo sancte crucis confirmavi. ✠ Ego Osulf plebi Dei famulus, canonica subscriptione manu propria firmavi. ✠ Ego Brihtelm episcopus, jubente rege, signum sancte crucis impressi. ✠ Ego Alfwold presul tropheum agie crucis imposui. ✠ Ego Brihtelm antistes testudinem sancte crucis subscripsi et confirmavi. ✠ Ego Daniel pontifex consensum prebui figens crucem. ✠ Ego Ælfheah dux donum ejusdem regis confirmavi. ✠ Ego Aðelwold abbas hoc eulogium manu propria apicibus depinxi. ✠ Ego Alfric abbas crucis vexillo corroboravi. ✠ Ego Alfwold abbas crucis modum manu propria infixi. ✠ Ego Eadmund dux consensi et subscripsi. ✠ Ego Wulfgar custos. ✠ Ego Æscwig custos. ✠ Ego Alfnoð custos. ✠ Ego Alfgar minister. ✠ Ego Brihtferþ minister. ✠ Ego Eadric minister. ✠ Ego Wulfgar discifer. ✠ Ego Æðelsige pincerna. ✠ Ego Ælfsige minister. ✠ Ego Ælfred minister. ✠ Ego Ealdred minister. ✠ Ego Lefincg minister. ✠ Ego Ælfsige minister. ✠ Ego Ælfwig minister. ✠ Ego Ælfwine minister. ✠ Ego Æþelweard minister.

✠ Ego Wulfric minister. ✠ Ego Cyneric minister. ✠ Ego Wihtsige minister. ✠ Ego Leofa minister. ✠ Ego Ælfric minister. ✠ Ego Leofstan minister. ✠ Ego Wulfric minister. ✠ Ego Eadric minister. ✠ Ego Æðelstan minister. ✠ Ego Alfwold minister. ✠ Ego Æþelweard minister. ✠ Ego Ælfric minister. ✠ Ego Æþelferð minister. ✠ Ego Osweard minister. ✠ Ego Osulf minister. ✠ Ego Osuuig minister. ✠ Ego Ordgar minister. ✠ Ego Brihtric minister. ✠ Ego Æþelferð minister. ✠ Ego Ælfsige minister. ✠ Ego Æþelsige minister. ✠ Ego Wulfhere minister. ✠ Ego Leofric minister. ✠ Ego Alfwold minister. ✠ Ego Ælfmær minister. ✠ Ego Ordwold minister. ✠ Ego Ordnoð minister. ✠ Ego Ælfheah minister. ✠ Ego Eadred minister. ✠ Ego Cyneric minister. ✠ Ego Alfwold minister. ✠ Ego Ealdred minister. ✠ Ego Eanulf minister. ✠ Ego Ælfnoð minister. ✠ Ego Ælfric minister. ✠ Ego Wulfric minister. ✠ Ego Wulfgar minister. ✠ Ego Ceoleah minister. ✠ Ego Brihtric minister. ✠ Ego Aþelwold minister. ✠ Ego Leofincg minister. ✠ Ego Ælfsige minister. ✠ Ego Æþeric minister. ✠ Ego Brihtelm minister. ✠ Ego Ælfweard minister. ✠ Ego Eadric minister. ✠ Ego Brihtwald minister. ✠ Ego Æþelferð minister. ✠ Ego Ælfric minister. ✠ Ego Ælfmer minister. ✠ Ego Eadulf minister. ✠ Ego Sigelm minister. ✠ Ego Eadric minister. ✠ Ego Æðelm minister.

---

* BISHOP DŪNSTĀN. APRIL 1ST DCCCC.LIX.

Dunstanus, Dei misericordia Londoniensis episcopus, omnibus episcopis abbatibus, et cunctis æcclesiæ filiis, præsentibus et futuris, inperpetuum. Quum, fratres karissimi, inimicus humani generis semper laborat superseminare zizannia in agro Dominice sationis, et quos non potest incitare ad graviora delicta plerunque de minimis occasionibus incendit ad lites et discordias, cavendum est, eis maxime qui in æcclesiasticis ordinibus eminere videntur, ut publice ac privatim, quanta virtute possunt, amputent omnes occasiones per quas inter servos Dei scandala possunt oriri, ut quietam et tranquillam vitam agamus in caritate Domini. Quapropter noverit omnium catholice æcclesie cultorum generalis universitas, quod domnus gloriosissimus Eadgarus Anglorum rex, divino irradiatus lumine, religiosa petitione humilitatis nostræ extremitatem poposcit, propter frequentes monachorum et clericorum simultationes, ut et nos et canonicorum nostrorum communis fraternitas securitatis et incommutabilitatis privilegium ederemus, pro reverencia summi apostolorum principis Petri, ad basilicam ipsius quæ dicitur Westmonasterium, ubi reliquiæ ipsius virtutum miraculis coruscant, quamquam multo ante nos tempore, beatus papa Gregorius de eadem re sentenciam tulerit, dicens inter alia, "Interdicimus in nomine Domini Jhesu Christi, ex autoritate beati Petri apostolorum principis, cujus vice huic æcclesiæ presidemus, ut nullus episcoporum vel secularium ulterius presumat de redditibus, rebus, vel kartis monasteriorum, vel privilegiis que ad ea pertinent, quocumque modo seu qualibet occasione, vel dolos vel inmissiones facere; sed si qua forte occasio inter ea evenerit, et pacifice non potuerit ordinari, apud electos abbates et alios patres timentes Deum, sine voluntaria dilatione, mediis sacrosanctis evangeliis, finiatur." Item post pauca, "Missas quoque publicas ab episcopis in cœnobiis fieri omnino prohibemus, ne in servorum Dei recessibus et eorum receptaculis ulla prebeatur occasio conventus vel mulierum fiat novus introitus, quod omnino non expedit animabus eorum. Nec audeant ibi cathedram collocare, vel quamlibet potestatem habere imperandi, nec aliquam ordinationem, quamvis levissimam, faciendi, nisi ab abbate fuerint rogati, quatinus monachi semper maneant in abbatum suorum potestate." Idem alio loco: "Grave nimis et contra sacerdotale constat esse propositum, cujusque monasterii privilegia olim indulta confundere, et ad irritum quæ sunt pro quiete disposita niti deducere." Item Leo papa Marciano Augusto: "Privilegia monasteriorum sanctorum patrum auctoritate instituta nulla possunt improbitate convelli, nulla novitate mutari." Item ex decretis Anacleti papæ: "Privilegia monasteriorum intemerata et inviolata perpetuis decernimus manere temporibus." Item beatus Augustinus, in libris de ecclesiasticis ordinibus, docet: "Sub quiete monachos regulariter viventes sua singulari lege debere quiescere, et ab omni infestatione clericorum intrepidos permanere, ne secularis strepitus eos lædat quos districta regula servitutis Domini moderatur." Item ex Concilio Hispalensi secundo: "Statuimus pari sententia, ut cenobia que antiquitus instituta sunt, immobili et inconcussa stabilitate permaneant solidata. Si quis autem, quod absit, nostrum vel succedentium sacerdotum quodlibet monasterium, aut vi cupiditatis expoliandum, aut simulatione aliqua fraudis convellendum, vel dissolvendum temptaverit, anathema effectus, maneat a regno Dei extraneus, nec proficiat illi bonum fidei vel operis ad salutem, qui tantæ et tam salutaris vitæ destruxerit tramitem." Hanc ergo scriptorum istorum sententiam considerantes, vel ideo quia supradicti domni Eadgari regis petitio nobis quasi jussio est, cui difficillimum est resisti, seu pro reverentia tanti apostoli, cujus patrocinio se ipse commisit, seu ut ipsis monachis secundum sanctum ordinem vivere liceat, et ut tam pro nobis quam pro omnibus æcclesiæ nostræ fratribus Deum orent, hoc privilegium plena voluntate una cum consensu fratrum meorum ipsis concessi, per quod decerno atque obtestificatione divini nominis interdico, ut nec ego deinceps nec ullus successorum meorum episcoporum Londoniensium hoc audeat infringere, vel temerario ausu aliquatenus violare, videlicet, ut omnis presbiter vel clericus ex iis qui in ipso procinctu beatissimi Petri, et omnes illi qui in circumscripto spatio, sicut designant cruces, vel fossata, vel alia signa, illi æcclesiæ serviunt, sint liberi et absoluti ab omni debito et redditione circadarum et synodorum. Tamen volumus et, pro amore vel reverentia Sancti Petri, concedimus, ut ex nostro vel successorum nostrorum episcopatu sine pretio crisma et oleum accipiant. Concedimus etiam illi loco cymiterium liberum, sicut et a regibus ab antiquis temporibus concessum fuerat, ita ut quicunque, de quocunque loco vel cujuscunque conditionis, petierit se ibi sepeliri, non impediatur vel prohibeatur, vel ab episcopo, vel ab archidiacono, vel a parrochiano suo presbitero. Et si quis eorum, presbiter vel clericus, forte aut occisus, quod absit, aut vulneratus fuerit, aut ex eis omnibus alicujus injuriæ acclamatio surrexerit, quicquid ex his omnibus ad nos attinere videtur, hoc totum abbati qui in ipso sancto loco præfuerit, cæterisque fratribus, habendum et disponendum concedimus. Si autem, quod absit, etiam de rebus eorum furtum fuerit factum, et abbati vel fratribus visum fuerit ut examinatio ex hoc debeat agitari, habebunt licentiam accipiendi a nostro episcopatu benedictum ferrum, vel si qua alia sunt instrumenta aut benedictiones ad hujusmodi rem exercendam, absque exactione pretii a calumpniatore vel calumpniato intra procinctum monasterii tantum, sed extra efferendi ad villas suas vel causas aliorum agendas non habebunt potestatem. Relaxamus etiam eos qui intra villam ipsius procinctus commorantur a collecta denariorum quam Romeschot appellant, sicut relaxatum est a regibus Offa, et Kenulfo, et Eadgaro, et omnia quæ ad libertatem et exaltationem illius loci per nostram auctoritatem accedere possunt, hilari et prompta voluntate concedimus: nimirum cum ego illi sancto loco, quasi multorum regum temporibus neglecto prefuerim, quem postea additis ei aliquantis terris venerabili Wulsino ejusdem loci monacho commendavimus servandum, quâs scilicet terras hic denotare non omittimus. In primis circa illud monasterium v. mansas a venerabili rege Eadgaro c.xx. mancusis auri, una cum loco emi, et cum redditibus et cum terris, quas antiqui reges, scilicet, Offa, Kenulfus, et Alfredus, illi sancto loco benigne dederant. Item v. mansas in Blecenham, et sex in Loþereslêge a prefato rege emi x. mancusis auri, et addidi monasterio prefato. Item mercatus sum a venerabili Ethelwoldo Wintoniensi episcopo x. mansas, et x. a quodam Wulnoþo milite regis octoginta libris probati argenti, easque sub uno territorio addidi præfato monasterio, in loco scilicet qui Hendun dicitur. Item tres cassatos emi a quodam Eadnoþo regis ministro XII. libris, in loco qui Codenhleâw nuncupatur, et addidi prædicto loco. Quidam autem minister regis in Middelsexan mansitando, Elfwine vocitamine, qui adiens limina sanctorum apostolorum Petri et Pauli, Rome scilicet, et gratia inopie petiit a me quoddam amminiculum, qui commodans ei xxx. libras argenti, suscepi ab eo VIII. mansas cujusdam telluris in Hanewelle, et addidi loco sepe nominato. Item x. cassatos emi ab Ælfego duce ducentis mancusis auri in loco qui Sunnabyri dicitur, et dedi præfato cenobio. Et illam possessionem in Scepertune emi ab Ealfleda vidua LX. Bizanteis nummis, et dedi loco præscripto. Item Ælfhelm Wolga, pro anime sue remedio, V. mansas largitus est cenobitis in Westmunster conversantibus, in loco qui Brikandun vulgari vocitamine dicitur. Item Ælfwine præfectus regis de Kent III. cassatos cenobio præfato, pro animula sua conjugisque, largitus est in loco qui Sillinctune dicitur. Et illa possessio in Perham, post dies Wulnoþi, redeat ad præfatum cenobium, quam ab eodem mercatus sum xxx. mancusis auri. Et illud prædiolum in Padintune æcclesiæ prædicte addidi. Item prædium illud in Cofenlea præfate æcclesiæ adjeci. Item prædium in Æwelle illi sancto loco in perpetuam perstrinxi possessionem.

Ego Eadgarus rex Anglorum hujus libertatis donationem, culminis totius regimen gubernans, episcopo Dunstano desiderante, libenter concessi, et signo sancto regiaque potestate roboravi ✠ in Christi nomine, sub horum testimonio quorum nomina flavescunt infra. ✠ Ego Dunstanus, ac si peccator et nomine tantum episcopus, hanc libertatis scedulam inpressione sigilli nostri et anuli, insuper et agalmate sancte crucis, diligenter consignavi; ac deinde manibus ad cœlum extensis dixi: Si quis hanc munificentiæ libertatem sanctum prædictumque locum, in terris, vel decimis, vel aliis redditibus, seu in aliquo, nostris et futuris temporibus, melioraverit vel adauxerit, augeat illi Deus perpetuitatis beatitudinem, atque in nostris orationibus et benedictione ab omnibus peccatis suis absolutus fœliciter permaneat. Qui vero hanc nostram auctoritatem vel immunitatem infringere voluerint, vel alios ad hoc conduxerint, et tam ea que præteritis vel nostris temporibus sunt data quam ea que in futuro a fidelibus danda sunt, stolido conamine absumere cogitaverint, vel aliquod amminiculum, aut calices, aut cruces, seu indumenta altaris, vel sacros codices, aurum, argentum, vel qualemcunque speciem ibidem collatam eripere temptaverint, vel alias de rebus illius æcclesiæ hæreditaverint, fratribusque ejusdem loci vim inferre præsumpserint, vel eos injuste contristaverint, necnon et hanc scedulam cartulasque regum vel aliorum fidelium, ad defensionem et tuitionem loci ibidem data auferre seu evertere studuerint, ignibus æternis, cruciatibus perpetuis illos damus, maledicimus atque excommunicamus, portas cœli eis claudimus, et deleantur nomina eorum de libro vitæ, sitque pars eorum cum Juda Domini traditore, nisi resipiscant et tribus annis a communione fratrum sequestrati pœnitentiam agant. ✠ Ego Oswoldus, Eborum æcclesiæ archiepiscopus, hujus munificientiæ conservatores benedixi; contradictores vero perpetuo dampnavi, dicens: Effundat Dominus super eos iram suam, et furor iræ suæ comprehendat eos. ✠ Ego Ælfstanus, Roffensis æcclesiæ episcopus, hanc libertatem augmentantes Regi regum commendavi; destructores autem sic dicendo maledixi: Veniat mors super illos, et descendant in inferum viventes. ✠ Ego Ælfeagus, Wintoniensis æcclesiæ episcopus, illius loci adauctores Jhesu Christo consignavi; invasores nempe æternis cruciatibus tradidi, dicens: Non sit illis pax, non misericordia, non pietas, sed terror infernorum, crudelitas pœnarum, impietas cruciatuum. ✠ Ego Escwius, episcopus Dorecensis æcclesiæ, hoc adjeci: Erubescant destructores præsentis loci, et conturbentur in sæculum sæculi, et confundantur et pereant; benefactores autem in æternum vivant. ✠ Ego Aðulfus, præsul Herefordensis æcclesiæ, hoc idem hoc dicens affirmavi: Maledicti sint raptores illius sanctæ æcclesiæ in omnibus operibus suis, et in omnibus viis suis, et in cunctis adinventionibus suis pravis; benefactores vero adeo benedicantur. ✠ Ego Æþelsinus, episcopus Schiresburnensis æcclesiæ, supradicta sic conclusi: Quicunque inferior vel sublimior contra hunc libellum quicquam sinistrum audere præsumpserit, vivus ad inferos raptus, inter omnia perpetua mala inperpetuum dampnetur.

Anno ab incarnatione Domini DCCCC^{mo}L^{mo}IX^{no}, imperii autem gloriosi regis Eadgari IIII., ego Aldredus abbas hanc scedulam scripsi, kalendas Aprilis, episcopo Dunstano rogante, quam idem episcopus Londoniæ et Wigorniæ, necnon et totius Angliæ decanus, super altare beati Petri in eadem æcclesia, quæ manibus angelicis consecrata dinoscitur, optulit atque ibidem in ævum, propter iniquitates simulationesque futurorum, atque inopinata mala quæ sæpe prædicebat futura eam servari ad defensionem loci præcepit: Indictione vera II[a].

QUEEN EADGIFU[1]. DCCCC.LXI.

✠ Eadgifu cyþ þam arc̃.-bisc̃. ⁊ Cristes cyrcean hyrede· hu hire land com æt Culing-on· ꝥ is þæt hire læfde hire fæder land ⁊ bóc· swa he mid rihte beget· ⁊ him his yldran lefdon. Hit gelamp ꝥ hire fæder aborgude xxx. punda æt Godan· ⁊ betæht him þæt land þæs feos to anwedde· ⁊ he hit hæfde VII. winter. Đa gelamp emb þa tíd þæt man beonn ealle Cantware to wigge· to Holme. Þa nolde Sigelm hire fæder to wigge faran mid nanes mannes scette unagifnum· ⁊ agef þa Godan xxx. punda· ⁊ becwæð Ead-gife his dehter land· ⁊ bóc sealde. Đa he on wigge afeallen wæs· þa ætsóc Goda þæs feos ægiftes· ⁊ þæs landes wyrnde· oð þæs on syxtan geare. Đa spræc hit fæstlice Byrhsige Dyrincg swa lange oð þa witan þe þa wæron ge-rehton Eadgife þæt heo sceolde

✠ Eadgifu makes known to the archbishop and the convent at Christchurch how her land came [to her] at Cooling. That is, that her father left her land and charter, as he lawfully acquired them, and parents had left to him. It happened that her father borrowed xxx. pounds of Goda, and delivered that land to him, in pledge for the money, and he had it VII. winters. Then about that time it happened that all the Kentish men were summoned to war at Holme. Then Sigelm would not go to war with any man's money unpaid, and then paid Goda the xxx. pounds, and bequeathed the land and gave the charter to his daughter Eadgifu. When he had fallen in the war, Goda denied the payment of the money, and refused the land, until the sixth year after.

[1] Wife of Eadward the Elder.

hire fæder hand geclænsian be swa miclan feo. ⁊ heo þæs að lædde on ealre ðeode gewitnesse to Æglesforda. ⁊ ðær geclænsude hire fæder þæs ægiftes be xxx. punda aðe. Ða gyt heo ne moste landes brucan ær hire frynd fundon æt Eadwearde cyncge þæt he him þet land forbead swa he æniges brucan wolde. ⁊ he hit swa alet. Ða gelamp on fyrste ꝥ se cynincg Godan oncuðe swa swyðe swa him man ætrehte béc ⁊ land ealle þa þe he ahte. ⁊ se cynincg hine þa ⁊ ealle his are mid bocum ⁊ landum forgeaf Eadgife to ateonne swa swa heo wolde. Ða cwæð heo ꝥ heo ne dorste for Gode him swa leanian swa he hire to geearnud hæfde. ⁊ agef him ealle his land. butan twam sulungum æt Osterlande. ⁊ nolde þa béc agifan ær heo wyste hu getriwlice he hi æt landum healdan wolde. Ða gewat Eadweard cyncg. ⁊ fencg Æðelstán to ríce. Ða Godan sæl þuhte. þa gesohte he þone kynincg Æðelstán. ⁊ bæd ꝥ he him geþingude wiþ Eadgife his bóca edgift. ⁊ se cyncg þa swa dyde. ⁊ heo him ealle agef butan Osterlandes béc. ⁊ he þa bóc unnendre handa hire to let. ⁊ þara oþerra mid eaðmettum geþan-

Then Byrsige Dyring urgently sued for it so long until the 'witan' who then were, decreed to Eadgifu, that she should clear her father's hand according to so much money. And she took an oath of it in witness of all the people at Aylesford, and cleared her father of the payment by an oath of xxx. pounds. Still she might not enjoy the land before her friends had obtained from king Eadward, that he forbade him that land, as he would enjoy any, and so he relinquished it. Then it happened after a time that the king accused Goda so strongly, that his charters and all the lands that he owned were decreed forfeited. And the king gave him and all his property, with charters and lands, to Eadgifu, to dispose of as she would. Then said she that she durst not before God so requite him as he had merited from her, and gave him up all his lands, except two sulungs at Osterland; but would not give up the charters before she knew how faithfully he would conduct himself with regard to the lands. Then king Eadward departed, and Æthelstân succeeded to the kingdom. Then it seemed cude· ⁊ ufenan þæt twelfa sum hire āð sealde for geborenne ⁊ ungeborenne· ꝥ þis æfre gesett spræc wære· ⁊ þis wæs gedon on Æðelstānes kynincges gewitnesse· ⁊ his wytena æt Hamme wiþ Læwe· ⁊ Eadgifu hæfde land mid bōcum þara twegra cyninga dagas hire suna. Ða Eadred geendude· ⁊ man Eadgife berypte ælcere are. Þa namon Godan twegen suna. Leofstān ⁊ Leofric· on Eadgife þas twa foresprecenan land æt Culingon ⁊ æt Osterland· ⁊ sædon þam cilde Eadwige· þe þa gecoren wæs· ꝥ hy rihtur hiora wæren þonne hire· ꝥ þa swa wæs oð Eadgar astiðude· ⁊ he ⁊ his wytan gerehton ꝥ hy mānfull reaflac gedon hæfden· ⁊ hi hire are gerehton ⁊ agefon. Ða nam Eadgifu be þæs cynincges leafe ⁊ gewitnesse· ⁊ ealra his bisceopa· þa bēc· ⁊ land betæhte in to Cristes cyrcean· mid hire agenum handum up on þone altare lede· þan hyrede on ecnesse to āre· ⁊ hire sawle to reste· ⁊ cwæþ ꝥ Crist sylf mid eallum heofonlicum mægne þane awyrgde on ecnesse þe þas gife æfre awende oþþe gewanude. Ðus com þeos ār in to Cristes cyrcean hyrede.

to Goda a favourable moment, and he sought king Æthelstân, and prayed him that he would intercede with Eadgifu for the restoration of his charters; and the king then so did; and she gave him up all except the charters of Osterland, and he that charter gratefully relinquished to her, and for the others humbly thanked her, and besides that, with eleven others took an oath to her, for born and unborn, that this should for ever be a settled suit. And this was done in witness of king Æthelstân and his 'witan' at Ham by Lewes. And Eadgifu had the land with the charters during the days of the two kings her sons. Then Eadred died, and Eadgifu was bereft of all her property. Then the two sons of Goda, Leofstân and Leofric, took from Eadgifu the two aforesaid lands at Cooling and Osterland, and said to the child Eadwig, who was then chosen [king], that they were theirs more rightly than hers. That then was so until Eadgar resolved, and he and his 'witan' decreed that they had done a wicked robbery; and they decreed to her and restored her property. Eadgifu then, with the leave and witness of the king and all his bishops, took the charters and delivered the lands to Christchurch, and with her own hands laid them on the altar, in perpetual property to the convent, and for her soul's rest; and said that Christ himself, with all the heavenly might, would curse to eternity him who should ever avert or invalidate this gift. Thus came this property to the convent at Christchurch.

IDEM LATINE.

✠ Anno Dominicæ Incarnationis DCCCC.LXI. Ego Eadgiua regina, et mater Eadmundi et Eadredi regum, pro salute animæ meæ, concedo æcclesiæ Christi in Dorobernia, monachis ibidem Deo servientibus, has terras, Meapeham, Culinges, Leanham, Peccham, Fernlege, Munccetun, Ealdintun, liberas ab omni sæculari gravitate, exceptis tribus, pontis et arcis constrùctione, expeditione. Qualiter autem istæ terræ michi venerunt, operæ pretium duxi intimare omnibus: scilicet Odoni archisacerdoti tociusque Britanniæ primati, et familiæ Christi, id est, monachis in Dorobernia civitate. Contigit aliquando patrem meum Sigelmum habere necessitatem xxx. librarum, quas a quodam principe nomine Goda mutuo accepit, et pro vadimonio eidem dedit terram quæ nominatur Culinges, qui tenuit eam septem annis. Septimo itaque anno expeditio præparabatur per omnem Cantiam, cum qua Sigelmum patrem ire oportuit. Cum vero se pararet, venerunt illi in mente xxx. libræ quas Godæ debebat, quas statim ei reddere fecit. Et quia nec filium nec filiam nisi me habuit, heredem me fecit illius terræ et omnium terrarum suarum, et libros michi dedit. Forte tunc evenit patrem meum in bello cecidisse: postquam autem idem Goda audivit defunctum in bello esse, negavit sibi triginta libras persolutas fuisse, terramque quam pro vadimonio a patre meo accepit detinuit fere per sex annos. Sexto vero anno quidam propinquus meus nomine Byrsige Dyring cepit instanter aperte conqueri apud optimates et principes et sapientes regni de injuria propinquæ suæ a Godone facta. Optimates autem et sapientes pro justicia invenerunt, et justo judicio decreverunt, quod ego, quæ filia et heres ejus sum, patrem meum purgare deberem, videlicet sacramento xxx. librarum, easdem triginta libras patrem meum persolvisse; quod, teste toto regno, apud Agelesford peregi. Sed non tunc quidem potui terram meam habere quoad usque amici mei regem Eaduuardum adierunt, et illum pro eadem terra requisierunt. Qui videlicet rex eidem Godoni, super omnem honorem quem de rege tenuit, prædictam terram interdixit, sicque terram dimisit. Non multo autem post tempore contigit eundem Godonem coram rege ita inculpari, quod per judicium judicatus sit perdere omnia quæ de rege tenuit, vitamque ejus esse in judicio regis. Rex autem dedit eundem michi et omnia sua cum libris omnium terrarum suarum, ut de eo facerem secundum quod promeruit; sed reddidi ei omnes terras suas excepta terra duorum aratrorum apud Osterland: libros autem terrarum non reddidi ei, probare enim volui quam fidem de beneficio contra tot injurias michi ab illo illatas tenere vellet. Defuncto autem domino meo rege Eaduuardo, Æðelstanus filius suscepit regnum; quem videlicet regem requisivit idem Godo, ut pro eo me rogaret quatinus ei redderem libros terrarum suarum. Ego autem libenter, devicta amore videlicet regis Æðelstani, ei omnes libros terrarum suarum reddidi, excepto libro de Osterlande, quem scilicet humiliter bona voluntate dimisit. Insuper pro se et omnibus parentibus suis, natis et nondum natis, nuncquam querimoniam facturos de prædicta terra, secum acceptis undecim comparibus suis, michi sacramentum fecit. Hoc autem factum est in loco qui nominatur Hamme juxta Læwes. Ego autem Eadgyua habui terram cum libro de Osterlande diebus duorum regum, Æðelstani et Eadmundi, filiorum meorum. Eadredo quoque rege, filio meo, defuncto, despoliata sum omnibus terris meis et rebus. Duo quoque filii jam sæpe nominati Godonis, Leofstanus et Leofricus, abstulerunt michi duas superius nominatas terras, Culinges et Osterlande, veneruntque ad puerum Eaduuium, qui tunc noviter levatus est in regem, et dixerunt se majorem justiciam in illis terris habere quam ego. Remansi ergo illis terris et omnibus aliis privata usque ad tempora Eadgari regis. Qui cum audisset me ita dehonestatam et despoliatam, idem rex Eadgarus restituit mihi terras meas et omnia mea. Ego autem licentia et consensu illius, testimonioque omnium episcoporum et optimatum suorum, omnes terras meas et libros terrarum propria manu mea posui super altare Christi quæ sita est in Dorobernia. Si quis hanc meam donationem a jure prædictæ ecclesiæ auferre conatus fuerit, auferat ei omnipotens Deus regnum suum.

Confirmatio. Ego Æðelredus, Dei opitulante misericordia totius Anglicæ gentis regimen tenendo, privilegiis auditis veter[a]norum sapientium, cordis tactus compunctione, archipræsulis exhortatione Alfrici, ad animæ commodum deputamus nostræ, quin prædecessorum nostrorum decreto firmemus, hoc æternaliter statuentes, ut impii quique a privilegiis prædictis Christo tonanti quid auferentes, sub anathemate in æternum cum diabolo puniantur. Qui vero hanc libertatem augendo firmaverit illæsum, piissimo liberetur a Domino, cum novissima insonuerit tuba, reddens cuique secundum opera sua.

KING EADGAR. DCCCC.LXII.[1]

Sē fruma wæs ꝥ mon forstæl ænne wimman æt Iceslea Ælfsige Byrhsiges suna. Ðurwīf hatte se wimman. Ða befeng Ælfsige þone mann æt Wulfstāne Wulfgares fæder. Ða tymde Wulfstan hine to Æðelstāne æt Sunnanbyrg. þa cende he tem ⁊ let þone forberstan. ⁊ forbeh þone andagan. Æfter þam bæd Ælfsige ægiftes his mannes. ⁊ he hine agef. ⁊ forgeald

The beginning was that a woman was stolen at Ikesley, from Ælfsige Byrhsiges son. The woman was named Thurwīf. Ælfsige then traced the woman to Wulfstân, Wulfgar's father. Wulfstân then vouched her to Æthelstân at Sunbury: then he acknowledged the vouching, and let it fail, and avoided the day of decision[2]. After that Ælfsige demanded the delivery

[1] This document has many difficulties, and unfortunately I have not been successful in finding the manuscript, notwithstanding the good will of the authorities at Westminster.

[2] That is, the vouching stopped with Æthelstân, who was unwilling or unable to declare how the bond-woman came into his possession.

him mid twam pundum. Ða bæd Byrhferð ealdormann Æðelstān his wer for þam tembyrste. Ða cwæð Æðelstān ꝥ he næfde him to syllanne. Ða cleopade Eadweard Æðelstānes broðor· ⁊ cwæð· Ic hæbbe Sunnanburges bōc þe uncre yldran me læfdon· læt me ꝥ land to handa· ic agife þinne wēr þam cynge. Ða cwæð Æðelstān ꝥ him leofre wære ꝥ hit to fyre oððe flode gewurde þonne he hit æfre gebide. Ða cwæð Eadweard· Hit is wyrse ꝥ uncer naðor hit næbbe. Ða wæs ꝥ swa· ⁊ forbead Byrhferð ꝥ land Æðelstane· ⁊ he of ferde ⁊ gebeh under Wulfgare æt Norðhealum. Binnan þam wendun gewyrda· ⁊ gewāt Eadræd cyng· ⁊ gesealde ꝥ land Byrnrīce· ⁊ he feng to· ⁊ wearp Æðelstān ūt. Gemang ðam getidde ꝥ Myrce gecuran Eadgar to cyng· ⁊ him anweold gesealdon ealra cynerihta. Ða gesohte Æðelstān Eadgar cyng ⁊ bæd dōmes. Ða ǣtdemdon him Myrcna witan land buton he his wer agulde þam cynge· swa he oðrum ǣr sceolde. Ða næfde he hwanon· ne he hit Eadwearde his breðer geþafian nolde. Ða gesealde se cyng· ⁊ ge-

of the woman, and he delivered her up, and indemnified him with two pounds. Then Byrhferth the aldorman demanded his 'wêr' from Æthelstân for the failure of the vouching; then said Æthelstân that he had nothing to give him. Then cried Eadward, Æthelstân's brother, and said: "I have the charter of Sunbury, which our parents left to me: deliver the land to me; I will pay thy wêr to the king." Then said Æthelstân, that he would rather it were turned to fire or flood than he would ever abide it. Then said Eadward: "It is worse that neither of us should have it." Then that was so: and Byrhferth forbade Æthelstân the land, and he went from it, and placed himself under Wulfgar at Northhall. In the meanwhile fortune changed, and king Eadred departed; and he had given the land to Byrnrîc, and he took to it and cast Æthelstân out. In the meanwhile it befel that the Mercians chose Eadgar for king, and gave him power over all royal rights. Then Æthelstân sought king Eadgar, and prayed for judgment. Then the 'witan' of the Merbette ꝥ land Æðelstāne ealdormenn· to hæbbenne ⁊ to syllanne· for līfe ⁊ for legere· þam him leofost wære. Æfter þam getidde ꝥ Ecgferð gebohte bōc ⁊ land æt Æðelstane ealdormenn· on cynges gewitnesse ⁊ his witena· swa his gemedo wæron· hæfde ⁊ breac oð his ende. Ða betæhte Ecgferð on hālre tungan lānd ⁊ bōc· on cynges gewitnesse· Dunstāne arcebisceope· to mundgenne his lāfe ⁊ his bearna. Ða he geendod wæs· þa rād se bisceop to þam cynge· myngude þære munde ⁊ his gewitnesse. Ða cwæð se cyng him to andsware. Mine witan habbað ætre Ecgferðe ealle his āre· þurh ꝥ swyrd þe him on hype hangode ða he adranc. Nam ða se cyng þa āre þe he āhte· xx. hida æt Sendan· x. æt Sunnanbyrg· ⁊ forgef Ælfhege ealdormenn. Ða bead se bisceop his wer þam cynge. Ða cwæð se cyng ꝥ mihte beon geboden him wið clænum legere· ac ic hæbbe ealle þa spæce to Ælfhege læten. Ðæs on syxtan gere gebohte se arcebisceop æt Ælfhege ealdormenn ꝥ land æt Sendan mid xc. pundum· ⁊ æt Sunnanbyrg mid cc. mancussan goldes· ūnbecwedene ⁊ ūn-

cians judged the land from him, unless he paid his wêr to the king, as he should to the other. Then had he not whence [he could pay it], nor would he consent that Eadward his brother should. The king then improved and gave the land to Æthelstân aldorman, to have and to give, for life and for death, to whom it were to him most desirable. After that it happened that Ecgferth bought charter and land of Æthelstân aldorman, with the witness of the king and his 'witan,' as his merits were: he had and enjoyed them until his end. Then Ecgferth, in plain language, delivered over land and charter to archbishop Dunstân, as guardian to his relict and his children. When he was dead the bishop rode to the king, and reminded him of the guardianship and his witnessing. Then said the king to him in answer: "My 'witan' have deprived Ecgferth of all his property, through the sword that hung on his hip when he drowned himself." Then the king took the property that he had owned—xx. hides at Send, x. at Sunbury—and gave it to Ælfheh aldorman. Then the forbodene wið ælcne man to þære dægtide. ⁊ he him swa þa land geagnian derr. swa him sẽ sealde þe to syllenne ahte. ⁊ hi ðam se cyng sealde swa hi him his witan gerehton.

bishop solicited his 'wêr' of the king. Then said the king, "That might have been ordered him, if he had died a pure death; but I have left the whole suit to Ælfheh." In the sixth year after, the archbishop bought from Ælfheh aldorman the land at Send for xc. pounds, and at Sunbury for cc. mancusses of gold, unbequeathed to and unforbidden by any man to that day. And so he ventured to appropriate the land, as he gave it who had it to give, and the king gave it, as his 'witan' had decreed.

KING EADGAR. DCCCC.LXII.

✠ In onomate alme et individue Trinitatis. Cuncta seculorum patrimonia incertis nepotum heredibus relinquuntur; et omnis mundi gloria, adpropinquante vite hujus termino, ad nichilum reducta fatescit. Idcirco terrenis caducarum possessionibus semper mansura superne patrie emolumenta adipiscentes, Domino patrocinante, lucranda decrevimus. Quamobrem ego Eadgar, tocius Brittannie basileus, instinctu Dei monitus, magno animi conamine procuravi, ut omnia præsentis vite commoda Abbendunensi monasterio, quod ego Creatoris nostri juvamine regulari vite restauravi, per nostram largifluam donationem devote largirentur. Unde vineam circa Wæcet sitam, cum vinitoribus, rusque sibi pertinens suis giratum terminis, censum quoque regale ad cenobium præfatum per singulos annos decorandum æt Suðhamtune, unius æque navis piscationem et regale vectigal æt Hwitan clife, alterius autem æt Portmonna hyðe, unam capturam et salinum, unamque terre mansam, et ex regis nemore capture restaurationem que Brunuuic wer nuncupatur, Domino nostro Jhesu Christo ejusque genitrici Marie, ad usus monachorum inibi degentium, ob facinorum nostrorum veniam et eterne beatitudinis premium, Aþeluuoldo abbate obtinente, eterna largitus sum hereditate. His monachorum cuneus communiter locupletatus donis regularem tripudians servando custodiam in Domino jugiter voti compos hilarescat, crebraque Dominum supplicatione pro nostris intercedendo excessibus veniam impetrans sedulo deprecetur. Qui autem hanc nostram munificentie dapsilitatem augere voluerit, augeat Dominus vitam et prosperitatem ejus hic et in evum. Si quis igitur hanc nostram donationem in aliud quam constituimus transferre voluerit, privatus consortio sancte Dei ecclesie, eternis baratri incendiis lugubris jugiter cum Juda Christi proditore ejusque complicibus puniatur, si non satisfactione emendaverit congrua quod contra nostrum deliquit decretum.

Anno Dominice incarnationis DCCCC.LXII. scripta est hec carta, his testibus consentientibus quorum inferius nomina caraxantur.

✠ Ego Edgar, Anglorum basileus, hoc donum agie crucis taumate hilariter corroboravi.

✠ Ego Dunstan archiepiscopus tanti regis benivolentiam alme crucis impressione consignavi.

✠ Ego Oscutel archiepiscopus hoc ejusdem regis donum tripudians crucis designavi indiculo.

✠ Ego Osulf, gratia Dei episcopus, dilecti regis largifluam dapsilitatem crucis signaculo roboravi.

✠ Ego Byrhtelm, dono Dei episcopus, tante consulens largitati, crucis signaculum devotus impressi.

✠ Ego Alfuuold episcopus. ✠ Ego Byrhtelm episcopus. ✠ Ego Osuuold episcopus. ✠ Ego Ælfstan episcopus. ✠ Ego Aðulf episcopus. ✠ Ego Ælfhere dux. ✠ Ego Ælfheah dux. ✠ Ego Aðelstan dux. ✠ Ego Aðeluuine dux. ✠ Ego Beorhtnoð dux. ✠ Ego Byrhtferð minister. ✠ Ego Ælfuuine minister. ✠ Ego Uulfhelm minister. ✠ Ego Æðelsige minister. ✠ Ego Ælfsige minister.

* KING EADGAR. DEC. 28TH DCCCC.LXIV.

✠ Altitonantis Dei largiflua clementia, qui est Rex regum et Dominus dominantium, ego Eadgarus Anglorum basileus, omniumque regum insularum oceani que Brytanniam circumjacent, cunctarumque nationum quæ infra eum includuntur, imperator et dominus, gratias ago ipsi Deo omnipotenti, Regi meo, qui meum imperium sic ampliavit et exaltavit super regnum patrum meorum; qui licet monarchiam totius Angliæ adepti sint a tempore Æþelstani, qui primus regum Anglorum omnes nationes quæ Brytanniam incolunt sibi armis subegit, nullus tamen eorum ultra ejus fines imperium suum dilatare aggressus est; mihi autem concessit propitia Divinitas, cum Anglorum imperio, omnia regna insularum oceani cum suis ferocissimis regibus usque Norregiam maximamque partem Hiberniæ, cum sua nobilissima civitate Dublina, Anglorum regno subjugare: quos etiam omnes meis imperiis colla subdere, Dei favente gratia, coegi[1]. Quapropter et ego Christi gloriam et laudem in regno meo exaltare, et ejus servitium amplificare, devotus disposui; et per meos fideles fautores, Dunstanum videlicet arciepiscopum, et Æþelwoldum ac Oswaldum episcopos, quos in patres spirituales et consiliatores elegi, magna ex parte, secundum quod disposui, perfeci. Siquidem temporibus antecessorum meorum regum Anglorum, monasteria tam monachorum quam virginum destructa et penitus neglecta in tota Anglia erant, quæ ego ad Dei laudem, pro remedio animæ meæ reparare, et servorum et ancillarum Dei numerum multiplicare devovi. Et ipsis supradictis meis cooperatoribus strenue annitentibus, jam XL. et VII. monasteria cum monachis et sanctimonialibus constitui, et si Christus mihi tamdiu vitam concesserit, usque ad quinquagesimum remissionis numerum meæ devotæ Deo munificentiæ oblationem protendere decrevi. Unde nunc in presenti monasterium quod predictus reverendus episcopus Oswaldus, in sede

[1] I suspect that this preamble was fabricated or interpolated about 1155, when Henry II., in concert with pope Adrian IV. (Nicholas Breakspeare), was meditating the conquest of Ireland. An earlier conquest by Eadgar afforded at least the shadow of a pretext for the undertaking.

episcopali Weogreceastre, in honore sanctæ Dei genitricis Mariæ, amplificavit, et, eliminatis clericorum neniis et spurcis lasciviis, religiosis Dei servis monachis, meo consensu et favore suffultus, locavit; ego ipsis monasticæ religionis viris regali auctoritate confirmo, et, consilio et astipulatione principum et optimatum meorum, corroboro et consigno, ita ut jam amplius non sit fas neque jus clericis reclamandi quicquam inde; quippe qui magis elegerunt, cum sui ordinis periculo et æcclesiastici beneficii dispendio, suis uxoribus adherere quam Deo caste et canonice servire. Et ideo cuncta quæ illi de æcclesia possederant cum ipsa æcclesia, sive æcclesiastica sive secularia, tam mobilia quam immobilia, ipsis Dei servis monachis ab hac die perpetualiter regiæ munificen[tiæ j]ure deinceps possidenda trado et consigno, ita firmiter ut nulli principum, nec etiam ulli episcopo succedenti fas sit aut licitum quicquam [inde] subtrahere aut pervadere, aut ab eorum potestate surripere [et in] clericorum jus iterum traducere, quandiu fides Christiana i[n An]glia perduraverit. Sed et dimidium centuriatum quod Anglice vocatur Cuðburgehl[awes h]undred, ad quod jacent L. hidæ in Croppeðorne, q[uas] Offa rex Merciorum quondam familiæ in Weogereceastre donavit, liberas ab om[ni re]gali exactione, ego ipsis Dei servis cum eadem libertate tra[do et con]scribo. Insuper etiam, ad supplendum ipsum centuriatum, id est, hundred, ut ex [m]eo dono illud plenum habeant, terras ipsius æcclesiæ, quæ hactenus regiæ exactioni subjacebant, ab hac die in perpetuum liberabo et liberas esse concedo et precipio; eas videlicet quæ sunt ultra Avene flumen, quæ istis vocabulis nominantur, Uuerabreodun cum Peonedoc, Teotintun cum Myttune, Secgesbearuwe, et in monte Wiccisca, Norðwica, Eowenland, Dæiglæsford, et Dorene, et Iccacumb, et, in ripa Sturæ fluminis, Scepwæsctun, et ibi juxta eam Blacwælle, et, in occidentali parte Sabrinæ, Grimanlæge cum Wittlæge, et Cnihtawice, et Hallege cum sibi pertinentibus; et item Herefordtun juxta Avene, pro supplendo, ut supra diximus, centuriatu, id est, hundred, Deo et sanctæ Dei genitrici Mariæ, ad usus servorum ejus, monachorum scilicet, liberas dono, et quietas esse precipio deinceps et in perpetuum ab omnibus secularium rerum oneribus, duris et levibus, et ab omni servitute et exactionibus fiscalibus, magnis et modicis, notis et ignotis, tam regis quam principis et ministrorum atque exactorum eorum, exceptis pontis et arcis constructione et expeditione contra hostem. Habeatque Winsinus reverendus sacerdos, quem ipse episcopus Oswaldus, me favente et auctoritatem regiam prestante, in sede episcopali monachis preposuit, quandiu ipse vixerit, omnesque post eum sui successores, qui eidem congregationi prepositi fuerint, ipsum hundred cum omnibus debitis, quæ rex antea in eo habuit, et jus et potestatem earundem possessionum, cum tolle et teame, saca et socne, et infangeneþeof, et proprii juris debitum transgressionis, et penam delicti quæ Anglice dicitur ofersæwnesse, et gyltwite; nec sit fas aut potestas cuiquam prepositorum seu exactorum vel ministrorum meorum, nec alicui principi vel ex succedentium numero pontifici, hanc meæ munificentiæ libertatem et concessionis firmitatem in aliquo minuere, vel infringere, vel quoquo modo mutare aut pervadere, aut quocunque ingenio ipsos monachos Dei servos inquietando perturbare, ut aliqua fraudulenta occasione iterum in clericorum aut ipsius episcopi proprium transeant jus, ab ipsorum potestate quorum usui ista concessi et donavi. Providi etiam cautelæ studio ut hæc libertas firmius eis posset perdurare, ne cum regis ministris aut ejus centuriatus, id est, hundredes, exactoribus, naumachiæ expeditionem, quæ ex tota Anglia regi invenitur faciant; sed cum suo archiductore, videlicet episcopo, qui eos defendere et protegere debet ab omni perturbatione et inquietudine. Et quia idem reverendus antistes Oswaldus, per suos amicos et meos consiliarios supranominatos, videlicet Dunstanum archiepiscopum, et Æþelwoldum episcopum, et virum magnificum Bryhtnoðum comitem, me requisivit et impetravit ut ad confirmandam æcclesiasticarum possessionum libertatem sui episcopatus, ad centuriatum qui Wulferesl[aw] dicitur, quem ipsa æcclesia antiquitus libere possidebat ei co[ncede]rem alterum hundredum facere, libertate donata de terris æcclesiæ quæ adhuc hactenus regiis exactionibus subjacebant, videlicet Breodune, Bleccelea, Tyrdintune, quatinus posset ipse cum monachis suis unam naucupletionem, quod Anglice scypfylleð dicitur, per se habere, placuit mihi hoc ei annuere, tam pro ejus religiosa sanctitate quam pro ipsorum legatorum reverentia et dilectione. Quapropter ego Eadgarus Anglorum rex et basileus Deo et sanctæ Dei genitrici Mariæ ejusque ministro Oswaldo, meo fideli episcopo, libens annuo et dono hujus libertatis privilegium, sicut ab ipsis rogatus sum, scilicet ut ipse episcopus cum monachis suis de istis tribus centuriatibus, id est hundredis, videlicet Wulfereslaw, et Winburgetrowe, et tertio monachorum quod dicitur Cuðburgelawe, constituant unam naucupletionem, quod Anglice dicitur scypfylleð oþþe scypsocne, in loco quem ob ejus memoriam Oswaldeslaw deinceps appellari placuit, ubi querelarum causæ, secundum morem patriæ [et] legum jura jure discernantur: habeatque ipse episcopus omnesque sui successores ibi ad jus æcclesiasticum debita transgressionum et penam delictorum quæ nos dicimus ofersegenesse, et gyltwite, et omnia quæcunque rex in suis hundredis habet; ita tamen ne ipsi qui ibi Deo serviunt monachi de suo jure aut libertate quam ad suum hundred eis concessi quicquam perdant, sed habeant ipsi ibi omnia quæ ad suum jus, id est ad tertium centuriatum, pertinent æque integra ac si per se separatum essent, videlicet debita transgressionum et penam delictorum, et cetera quæ superius comprehensa sunt, quæ eis libere et quiete perpetualiter tenenda concessi; sintque hæc omnia et quæcunque illorum sunt sub ejus manu et potestate, qui ipsis in monastici ordinis regimine sub episcopo præpositus fuerit. Qui si se viderint injuste gravari vel vi opprimi, fas sit eis ad regiæ majestatis et archiepiscopi examen et tutelam, si tamen necesse fuerit, confugere, qui propter Deum equitatem et clementem defensionem eis impendant. Servantibus hæc vita æterna tribuatur a Domino in cælestibus. Quicunque vero imminuerit, vel in pejus mutando subtraxerit eis quicquam de iis, sit pars ejus cum Dathan et Abiron, et cum Juda traditore Domini, et Juliano apostata, æcclesiarum Dei oppressore et persecutore, æterno anathemate ligatus cum diabolo et angelis ejus infernalibus, ignibus perpetuo cruciandus, nisi resipiscat et emendet. Amen, amen, amen; fiat, fiat, fiat. Facta sunt hæc anno Dominicæ nativitatis DCCCC.LXIIII., Indictione VIII.[1], regni vero Eadgari Anglorum regis VI., in regia urbe quæ ab incolis Gleaweceastre nominatur, in natale Domini, festivitate sanctorum innocentum, feria IIII. Đis syndon þa gew . . . . . wæron . . mid þ . . . . munge getrymdon. ⁊ . . . . . . urs allinge gefæstnodon uppon allum ðam þe þis undoð oþþe gewaniað oððe gewemmað . . . oððe of þære munekan anwalde eft on clerican hand getyrnað.

✠ Ego Eadgar basileus Anglorum et imperator regum gentium, cum con[sen]su principum et archuntorum meorum, hanc meam munificentiam signo crucis Christi corroboro. ✠ Ego Ælfþryð regina consensi et signo crucis confirmavi. ✠ Ego Dunstan archiepiscopus Doruvernensis æcclesiæ Christi consensi et subscripsi. ✠ Ego Oscytel archiepiscopus Eboracensis æcclesiæ consensi et subscripsi. ✠ Ego Ælfstan episcopus consensi. ✠ Ego Æþelwold episcopus consensi. ✠ Ego Oswald episcopus consensi. ✠ Ego Osulf episcopus consensi. ✠ Ego Wynsi episcopus consensi. ✠ Ego Wulfric episcopus consensi. ✠ Ego Æscwi abbas. ✠ Ego Osgar abbas. ✠ Ego Ælfstan abbas. ✠ Ego Æþelgar abbas. ✠ Ego Ælfric abbas. ✠ Ego Kineward abbas. ✠ Ego Ælfere dux. ✠ Ego Brihtnoð dux. ✠ Ego Ordgar dux. ✠ Ego Ælfæh dux. ✠ Ego Æðelwold dux. ✠ Ego Æðelwine dux. ✠ Ego Brihtferð minister. ✠ Ego Ælfwine minister. ✠ Ego Æðelward minister. ✠ Ego Wulstan minister. ✠ Ego Earnulf minister. ✠ Ego Osulf minister. ✠ Ego Wulstan minister. ✠ Ego Leofwine minister. ✠ Ego Ælfward minister. ✠ Ego Æþelmund minister. ✠ Ego Osward minister. ✠ Ego Leofwine minister.

[1] The Indiction for 964 is 7.

KING EADGAR. DCCCC.LXVI.

✠ In nomine regnantis in perpetuum Domini nostri Jhesu Christi. Ego Eadgarus rēx Anglorum ceterarumque gentium, considerans et recolens quod etiam vas electionis veracissimis innotuit verbis, quod in novissimis temporibus instarent tempora periculosa, idcirco unusquisque de semetipso plenius poterit agnoscere quod quanto quis in hōc terreno habitaculo longiorem protraxerit vitam, tanto veraciora esse omnia quæ olim antiqui vates divinitus edocti inplenda esse predixerunt. Quod cernens ego necessarium dūxi ut, per intercessionem plurimorum, pro venia delictorum meorum et requiæ aeterna adipiscenda animæ meæ aliquid ex eis quae mihi Largitor bonorum Xp̃s Dñs donare dignatus est, hoc est decem mansas quod Cantigene dicunt x. sulunga, in illo loco ubi jamdudum solicole illius regionis nomen imposuerunt ǣt Bromleage, tibi venerabili apostolo Xp̃i Sc̃o Andreæ, et pro placabili pecunia Ælfstani antistitis, aecclesiae Hrofensi concedo, cum omnibus utensilibus quae Ds̃ cælorum in ipso telluris gramine creavit, tam in notis causis et ignotis, in modicis et in magnis, campis, pascuis, pratis, silvis, silvarumque densitatibus, donans donabo libertatem, preter expeditione et pontis arcisve instructione; quia tanti pretii emtum est suprascripta terra octuaginta mancusis auri purissimi, et sēx pondus electi argenti. Et insuper dona meo prefecto Wulfstano donando auxit xxx[ta] mancusas auri, ut fixa et immobilis permaneat sempiternaliter nostra donatio. Ita adjuro in nomine Dñi Dei nr̃i Jħu Xp̃i, qui est omnium Judex justus, ut nēc mihi nēc alicui successorum meorum regum, seu cujuslibet dignitatis, aliquid fraudare vel minuere liceat, sed absque aliqua retractione inlesa jugiter permaneat sine fine. Si quis autem propria temeritate violenter invadere presumserit, sciat sē procul dubio ante tribunal districti Judicis titubantem tremebundumque rationem redditurum, nisi prius digna satisfactione emendare maluerit.

Hæc utilitas silvarum ad eandem terram pertinet in Andrede.

Billanoran be Lindhyrste·	Billanora by Lyndhyrst and

⁊ on Glæppan felda· Scearndæn· ⁊ þarrihte wiꝺ Þorndæn· ⁊ Broccesham be eastan ea· ⁊ Tannera hole· ⁊ Trindhyrst.

in Glapfield, Sharnden, and straight on to Thornden and Brocksham, by the east water, and Tanner's hole, and Trindhyrst.

Istis terminibus circumgirata est terra suprascripta, et multis nota.

Ðis synt þara tyn sulunga landgemæro tō Bromleage. Ǽrest on eastan Cyselhyrstes gemæro· þonne ōn Croptunes gemæro· þonne þanon ōn Rugebeorges gemæro· þonne ōn suð healfe Cyssestanes gemæro forð be Weard setlan· þonne be westan Wichammes gemæru· ⁊ Beohhahammes gemæru· þonne be norðan Beringahammes gemæru· ⁊ Modingahammes gemæro· ⁊ þonon eft east ōn Cinges gemæro· þæt ōn Cyselhyrst.

These are the land-boundaries of the ten 'sulungs' at Bromley. First to the east boundary of Chiselhurst, then to Cropton's boundary, then thence to Rugebeorg's boundary, then to the south side of Keston's boundary, on by 'Weardsetl', then to the west of Wickham's boundary, and Becham's boundary, then north of Beringham's boundary, and Mottingham's boundary, and then again east to King's boundary, thence to Chiselhurst.

Acta est hæc prefata donatio anno ab incarnatione Dñi nr̃i Jhesu Xp̃i DCCCC^{mo}L^{mo}V^{to} [1] Indictione vero novem.

✠ Ego Eadgar rẽx Anglorum, sub sigillo sancte crucis ✠ corroboravi. ✠ Ego Dunstan, Dorobornensis æccłæ archiep̃s, crucis ✠ Xp̃i conclusi. ✠ Ego Ælfþryþ mater regis [2] predictum donum confirmavi. ✠ Ego Oswald, archiep̃s Eboracе civitatis, crucis ✠ Xp̃i impressi. ✠ Ego Aþelwold, Wintaniensis æccłæ ep̃s, subscripsi et confirmavi. ✠ Ego Ælfstan, Lundoniensis æcclesiæ æpiscopus, corroboravi. ✠ Ælfstan æpiscopus consignavi. ✠ Ego Eadelm æpiscopus consensi et subscripsi. ✠ Ego Sydemann æpiscopus conclusi. ✠ Ego Alfwold æpiscopus corroboravi. ✠ Ego Byrhtelm æpiscopus

[1] This date is wrong, and incompatible with the Indiction. Eadgar did not become king even of Mercia till 957.

[2] An error for *uxor regis*; Eadgar's mother was named Ælfgifu.

roboravi. ✠ Ego Byrhtferð minister. ✠ Ego Æþelweard minister. ✠ Ego Ælfwerd minister. ✠ Ego Æþelmær minister. ✠ Ego Ælfsige minister. ✠ Ego Wulfstan minister. ✠ Ego Ælfric minister. ✠ Ego Ælfheah minister. ✠ Ego Ealdred minister. ✠ Ego Leofstan minister. ✠ Ego Ælfhere dūx. ✠ Ego Æþelstan dūx. ✠ Ego Æþelwine dūx. ✠ Ego Byrhtnoð dūx. ✠ Ego Ordgar dūx. ✠ Ego Ælfric minis̄. ✠ Ego Alfwold minis̄. ✠ Ego Wulfsige minis̄. ✠ Ego Sigred minis̄. ✠ Ego Eadelm minis̄.

Dorso. ✠ Þis is þara x. sulunga boc æt Bromleage þe Eadgar cing gebocode Sc̄e Andree Cristes apostole on ece yrfe.

Dorso. ✠ This is the charter of the x. sulungs at Bromley, that king Eadgar chartered to St Andrew, Christ's apostle, in perpetuity.

---

* KING EADGAR. June 3rd DCCCC.LXVI.

✠ In nomine sancte et individue Trinitatis. Ego Edgarus rex et basileus tocius Angliæ, divino instinctus admonitu et sancte Dorobernensis ecclesie antistitis Dunstani precibus sepius exortatus, reddo et concedo sancte Dorobernensi ecclesie et monachis ibi servientibus Deo, in puram elemosinam, portum et villam de Sanduuich, eisdem monachis olim ablatam, cum omnibus libertatibus et consuetudinibus regiis ad Sanduuich pertinentibus, que ego aliquanto habui, vel aliquis antecessorum meorum, ex utraque parte aque cujuscumque terra hinc vel inde fuerit. Præterea confirmo eis omnes mansiones quas habent in villa de Sanduuich, que eis collate sunt in puram elemosinam a fidelibus. Unde volo quod nullus ibidem habeat aliquod jus, nisi tantum monachi nostri de Dorobernia. Quicumque autem hanc meam largifluam munificenciam interrumpere aut violare præsumpserit, indignationem Domini nostri et Sancte Marie et Sanctorum omnium, qui in Dorobernensi ecclesia requiescunt, senciant, nisi ante mortem emendati fuerint.

Ego Edgarus, rex tocius Angliæ, huic codicello meo signum

sancte crucis propria manu apposui ✠. Ego Kinath rex Scotorum subscripsi ✠. Ego Maccus rex insularum vidi ✠. Ego Dunstanus Dorobernensis archiepiscopus subscripsi ✠. Ego Etheluuoldus Uuintoniensis antistes consensi ✠. Ego Malcolm rex Cumbrorum subscripsi ✠. Ego Dufnal vidi ✠. Ego Oskitellus Eboracensis archiepiscopus subscripsi ✠. Ego Osuualdus Uuigorniensis episcopus consensi ✠. Ego Kineuuardus abbas Mideltun subscripsi ✠. Ego Iacob subregulus signum apposui ✠. Ego Iukil subregulus signum apposui ✠. Ego Siferch subregulus signum sancte crucis apposui, in festo Pentecostes in civitate Achmanni ✠.

---

* KING EADGAR. MAY 15TH DCCCC.LXIX.

✠ Regnante Domino nostro Jesu Christo in perpetuum. Ego Eadgarus, Dei gratia Anglorum rex, omnibus episcopis, abbatibus, comitibus, vicecomitibus, centenariis, cæterisque nostris agentibus, presentibus, scilicet, et futuris, salutem. Dignum et conveniens est clementie principali inter ceteras actiones illud quod ad salutem anime pertinet, quod pro divino amore postulatur, pio auditu suscipere, et studiose ad effectum perducere; quatenus de caducis rebus presentis seculi, que nunquam sine inquinamento et erumpna possidentur, peccatorum emundatio et vite eterne securitas adquiratur; juxta preceptum Domini dicentis: "Date elemosinam et omnia munda sunt vobis." Ergo dando elemosinam, juxta hoc ipsius dictum, oportet nos emercari peccatorum nostrorum emundacionem, ut, dum ecclesiis Christi impertimur congrua beneficia et justas bonorum vivorum peticiones efficaciter audimus, retributorem Dominum ex hoc habere mereamur. Igitur postquam dono Dei et paterna successione in regnum Anglorum inthronizatus et confirmatus fui, ubi vidi ecclesias Dei tam peccatis exigentibus quam crebris barbarorum irruptionibus dirutas, et maxime sanctam et apostolicam vitam, id est monachicum ordinem, per omnes regni mei provincias funditus deperisse, graviter dolens et consilium a sancto spiritu accipiens, Dunstano archiepiscopo et

Aðelwoldo Wyntoniensi episcopo hoc negotium indixi, ut omnia monasteria que inter terminum totius Anglie sita sunt supra vel infra circuirent, et reedificarent, possessiones que ad fiscum redacte erant de ipsis monasteriis vel ab aliis secularibus potestatibus pervase ubicumque, cartis vel testimoniis recognoscerent mea auctoritate freti, ad integrum restituerent; et tanquam docente michi Domino: "A capite incipe," imprimis ecclesiam dompni specialis patroni ac protectoris nostri beati Petri, quæ sita est in loco terribili qui ab incolis Thorneye nuncupatur, ab occidente, scilicet, urbis Lundonie, quæ olim, id est Dominice incarnationis anno DC^mo^IIII., beati Æðelbrithi hortatu, primi Anglorum regis Christiani, destructo prius ibidem abhominationis templo regum paganorum, a Sabertho, prædivite quodam subregulo, Lundonie, nepote videlicet ipsius regis, constructa est, et non ab alio, sed ab ipso Sancto Petro, apostolorum principe, in suum ipsius proprium honorem dedicata; dehinc ab Offa et Kenulpho regibus celeberrimis possessionum privilegiis et variis ornamentorum speciebus vehementer fuerat ditata, et in qua sedes regia et locus etiam consecrationis regum antiquitus erat, hanc precipi ut studiosius restruerent, et omnes possessiones ejus readunarent, et ipse de dominicatis terris meis aliquanta addidi, et cartis atque legitimis testibus corroboravi. Deinde, succedente tempore, concilio habito intra basilicam ipsam, presidente me cum filio meo Edwardo, et eodem archiepiscopo venerabili Dunstano, et universis episcopis et baronibus meis, secutus exemplum majorum meorum, renovavi, addidi, et corroboravi cartas et privilegia ejusdem loci, et ad apostolicam sedem legenda et confirmanda transmisi, atque legitima concessione in hunc modum astipulata recepi: "Johannes episcopus urbis Rome, servus servorum Dei, domino excellentissimo Edgaro, filio suo, regi Anglorum, salutem et apostolicam benediccionem. Quia literis tue Celsitudinis, fili karissime, nobis innotuisti de monasterio Sancti Petri, specialis patroni tui, quod ab antiquis Anglie regibus a potestate Londoniensis sedis episcopi, cum consilio pontificum ejusdem patrie fuerit ereptum, et ab hinc sub regimine regum vel clarissimorum abbatum semper dispositum, et postulasti a nobis ut privilegium episcoporum de eodem monasterio factum nostro privilegio, immo magis apostolorum principis roboraremus auctoritate, libentissime secundum tue benevolentie petitionem facimus. Auctoritate siquidem beati Petri apostolorum principis, qui potestatem ligandi atque solvendi a Domino accepit, cujusque nos vicarii existimus, stabilimus ut ipse locus regum, preceptis et privilegiis apostolicis fultus, per omnia tempora sine repeticione cujuscunque Londonice urbis episcopi, aut alicujus judiciarie potestatis, vel cujuscunque prepotentis hominis, cujuscunque ordinis vel dignitatis sit, semper, sicut preoptat et expetit tua benevolentia, ratus futuro tempore permaneat. Venerabiles igitur ejusdem loci fratres ydoneos ex se vel ex quacunque voluerint congregacione, abbates sive decanos sibi per successiones eligendi, ex auctoritate hujus sancte Romane sedis et nostra, sicut postulastis, amplius habeant potestatem; et ne impediantur auctoritate apostolica prohibemus, neque per violentiam extranea persona introducatur, nisi quam omnis concors congregatio elegerit. Preterea illi loco quicquid contuleris, vel collatum est, vel conferetur, divina auctoritate et nostra roboramus. Privilegia vero possessionum et dignitatum karissimi fratris nostri venerabilis Dunstani aliorumque fidelium ibidem indulta, necnon et privilegia vestra ad honorem Dei pertinencia que ibi instituere volueris, gratanti affectu annuimus, confirmamus, et confirmando in perpetuum rata inviolataque stare decernimus, et infractores eorum eterna maledictione dampnamus; observatores autem hujus firmitatis gratiam et misericordiam a Domino consequi mereantur. Causa igitur infractionis nostri privilegii ad posteros nostros perveniat. Datum Ravennæ IX. kalendas Februarii. Cognoscat ergo magnitudo seu utilitas vestra quam decrevimus, et in perpetuum mansurum jubemus atque constituimus, ut pro reverencia reliquiarum gloriosissimi apostoli Petri, et pro quiete monachorum ibidem Deo famulantium, honor et laus ejusdem ecclesie habeatur et observetur: id est, ut quisquis fugitivorum, pro quolibet scelere ad prefatam basilicam beati apostoli fugiens, procinctum ejus intraverit, sive pedes, sive eques, sive de curia regali, sive de civitate, seu de villa, seu cujuscunque condicionis sit, quocunque delicto facinoris contra nos vel succedentes reges Anglorum, vel contra alium quemlibet fidelem sancte ecclesie Dei forisfactus sit, relaxetur et liberetur, et vitam atque membra, absque ulla contradictione, obtineat." Præterea interminamur divina auctoritate et nostra, ut neque nos, neque successores nostri, neque quilibet episcopus vel archiepiscopus, nec quicunque de judiciaria potestate, in ipsam sanctam basilicam, vel in manentes in ipsa, vel in homines qui cum sua substantia vel rebus ad ipsam tradere vel devovere se voluerint, nisi per voluntatem abbatis et suorum monachorum ullam unquam habeant potestatem; sed sit hec sancta mater ecclesia peculiaris patroni nostri beati Petri apostoli libera et absoluta ab omni invasione vel inquietudine omnium hominum, cujuscunque ordinis vel potestatis esse videantur. In maneria vero vel curtes præfate basilice sic et ubi in quascunque regiones vel pagos in regno nostro quicquid a die præsenti ipsum monasterium possidere et dominari videtur, vel quod a Deum timentibus hominibus per legitima cartarum instrumenta ibidem fuit concessum, vel in antea erit additum vel delegatum, nec ad causas audiendas, nec ad fidejussores tollendos, nec ad freda vel bannos exigendos, et ad mansiones vel paratas faciendum, nec ullas redibiciones requirendas infra immunitatem Sancti Petri ingredi vel requirere quoquo tempore presumatur; sed quicquid exinde fiscus noster exauctare poterat, omnia et ex omnibus, pro mercedis nostre augmento, sub integra et firmissima immunitate concedimus ad ipsum sanctum locum, et imperpetuo confirmamus. Concedo eciam et confirmo omnes libertates et donaciones terrarum que a predictis regibus seu aliis, sicut legitur in antiquo telligrapho libertatis, ante me donatæ sunt: scilicet Hamme, Wynton, Mordun, Fentun, Aldenham, Bleccenham, Lothereslege, quas tamen venerabilis Dunstanus a me, una cum predicto loco, emerat; necnon et libertates atque empciones quas idem Dunstanus, me concedente, ab optimatibus meis mercatus est, et quas eciam coram legitimis testibus sigillo suo et anulo episcopali ibidem in usum fratrum prefate ecclesie in perpetuam perstrinxit possessionem. Nos itaque ad laudem nominis Domini, et ad honorem Sancti Petri, terras que hic caraxantur ibidem donavimus: Holewelle, Decewrthe, Wattune, Cillingtune. Hec igitur supradicta rura, cum omnibus ad se pertinentibus, et cum cenobio quod Stana vocatur, et omnibus sibi pertinentibus, scilicet Tudingtun, Halgeforde, Feltham, Ecclesforde, priscis temporibus ad eandem perhibentur ecclesiam Sancti Petri pertinere, sicut legitur, ut diximus, in antiquo telligrapho libertatis, quam rex Offa illi monasterio contulit, quando ecclesiis per universas regiones Anglorum recuperativa privilegia, Wilfredo archiepiscopo hortante, scribere jussit; quod cenobium Stanense jam olim regulari et monachorum examine pollebat, postea vero hostili quadam expedicione, fratribus dispersis solotenus est dirutum. Hanc eandem itaque libertatem prefate ecclesie Sancti Petri principis apostolorum concessi, quia locus predictus, qui templum fuerat dudum Apollinis, Dei providencia nunc mirabiliter ab ipso clavigero est consecratus et dedicatus quatinus ab omni seculari sit semper in perpetuum quieta servitute. Et ne quis presencium vel magis futurorum ambiget que sit illa libertas quam amabiliter et firmiter concedo, omnimodis cuncta illius monasterii possessio nullis sit unquam gravata oneribus, nec expedicionis nec pontis et arcis edificamine, nec juris regalis fragmine, nec furis apprehensione, et, ut omnia simul comprehendam, nil debet exsolvi nec regi, nec regis preposito, vel episcopo, vel duci, vel ulli homini, sed omnia debita exsolvent jugiter que in ipsa dominacione fuerint ad supradictum sanctum locum, secundum quod ordinaverint fratres ejusdem cenobii. Obsecramus etiam omnes successores nostros, reges et principes, per sanctam et individuam Trinitatem, et per adventum justi Judicis, ut quemadmodum ex munificencia antecessorum nostrorum ipse locus videtur esse ditatus, nullus episcoporum vel abbatum, aut eorum ordinatores, vel quelibet persona, possit quoquo ordine de loco ipso aliquid auferre, aut aliquam potestatem sibi in ipso monasterio usurpare, vel aliquid quasi per commutationis titulum, absque voluntate ipsius congregacionis vel nostrum permissum, minuere, aut calices, aut cruces, seu indumenta altaris, vel sacros codices, aurum, argentum, vel qualemcunque speciem ibidem collatam auferre, vel alias deferre presumat; sed liceat ipsi congregationi quod sibi per rectam delegacionem collatum est perpetim possidere, et pro stabilitate regni nostri jugiter exorare, quod nos pro Dei amore, et reverencia sancti apostoli, et adipiscenda vita eterna, hoc beneficium ad locum illum terribilem et sanctum, cum consilio pontificum et illustrium virorum nostrorum procerum gratissimo animo et integra voluntate visi sumus prestitisse, eo videlicet ordine ut sicut tempore predecessorum meorum ibidem chorus psallencium per turmas fuit institutus, ita die noctuque in loco ipso celebretur. Si autem quispiam hanc nostram auctoritatem vel immunitatem infringere voluerit, et alios ad hoc conduxerit, unusquisque pro seipso libras v. partibus Sancti Petri solvat, et, ut dictum est, quicquid exinde fiscus noster ad partem nostram sperare poterat in luminaribus vel stipendiis monachorum, seu etiam elemosinis pauperum ipsius monasterii perenniter per nostra oracula ad integrum sit concessum atque indultum. Et ut hec auctoritas nostris et futuris temporibus circa ipsum sanctum locum perenniter firma et inviolata permaneat, vel per omnia tempora illesa custodiatur atque conservetur, et ab omnibus optimatibus nostris et judicibus publicis et privatis melius ac certius credatur, manus nostre subscriptionibus subtus eam decrevimus roborare, et de sigillo nostro jussimus sigillare.

Signum ✠ Eadgari incliti et serenissimi Anglorum regis. Signum ✠ Eadwardi ejusdem regis filii. Signum ✠ Æðelredi fratris ejus. ✠ In nomine Christi ego Dunstanus, acsi peccator, Dorobernensis ecclesie archiepiscopus, hanc libertatem sancte crucis agalmate consignavi; ac deinde, secundum apostolici Johannis preceptum, observatores hujus libertatis, auctoritate qua perfruor, a peccatis suis absolvi; infractores vero perpetim maledixi, nisi resipiscant, et tribus annis a liminibus sancte ecclesie sequestrati penitentiam agant. ✠ Ego Oswoldus Eboracensis archiepiscopus imposui. ✠ Ego Ælfstanus Londoniensis ecclesie episcopus adquievi. ✠ Ego Æðelwoldus Wintoniensis ecclesie episcopus corroboravi. ✠ Ego Ælfstanus Roffensis ecclesie episcopus supposui. ✠ Ego Æscwius Dorcicensis ecclesie episcopus impressi. ✠ Ego Ælfegus Lichefeldensis ecclesie episcopus consolidavi. ✠ Ego Æðelsinus Scireburnensis ecclesie episcopus commodum duxi. ✠ Ego Wlgarus Wiltuniensis ecclesie episcopus confirmavi. ✠ Ego Æðulfus Herefordensis ecclesie episcopus ovanter divulgavi. ✠ Ego Æðelgarus Cisseniensis ecclesie episcopus adnotavi. ✠ Ego Sigarus Wellensis ecclesie episcopus gaudenter conclusi. ✠ Ego Aluricus Cridiensis ecclesie episcopus amendixi. ✠ Ego Sigarus Allmaniensis ecclesie episcopus consigillavi, atque cum prescriptis archiepiscopis et episcopis et abbatibus, luminibus accensis, violatores hujus munificentie, dignitatis immo apostolici, transgressores hujus decreti imperpetuum excommunicavi, nisi pretitulatam penitentiam resipiscendo peragant. ✠ Ego Folcmerus abbas. ✠ Ego Ælfric abbas. ✠ Ego Kinewardus abbas. ✠ Ego Osgar abbas. ✠ Ego Æðelgar abbas. ✠ Ego Sideman abbas. ✠ Ego Folbrycht abbas. ✠ Ego Godwin abbas. ✠ Ego Leofric abbas. ✠ Ego Wymer abbas. ✠ Ego Aldred abbas consensi, et rege suisque precipientibus, hanc libertatis singrapham scripsi, anno Dominicæ incarnationis DCCCC°LX°VIIII° Indictione XII^{ma} idus Maii, anno XIII° regni regis Eadgari. ✠ Ego Ðuredus presbiter. ✠ Ego Leoffa presbiter. ✠ Ego Wlstanus presbiter. ✠ Ego Æðelbaldus presbiter. ✠ Ego Wlfget presbiter. ✠ Ego Weremund presbiter. ✠ Ego Æðelsige presbiter. ✠ Ego Wineman presbiter. ✠ Ego Oswardus presbiter, cum supradictis et cum aliis C^{m}VII. presbiteris infractores hujus firmitatis excommunicavi. ✠ Ego Ælfere dux. ✠ Ego Marthere dux. ✠ Ego Oslac dux. ✠ Ego Birnoð dux. ✠ Ego Osred dux. ✠ Ego Fordwine dux. ✠ Ego Friðelaf dux. ✠ Ego Anulf dux. ✠ Ego Alfeh dux. Ad ultimum itaque, una cum rege et filiis ejus, nos omnes confratres et coepiscopi, et cum tota hac populosa et sancta sinodo ejusdem loci, omnes futuros abbates, decanos, atque prepositos contestamur, verum etiam in nomine Patris, et Filii, et Spiritus Sancti prohibemus, quatinus sacros illius ecclesie thesauros non distrahant, neque terras, seu redditus, vel beneficia in suis vel parentum usibus stolide expendant, neque a servis Dei, que pro illis ibidem habetur substantiam subtrahendo minuant. Quod si aliquis presumpserit, illum sicut violatorem atque transgressorem hujus nostri decreti, immo apostolici, ante summum Judicem, cum venerit seculum judicare per ignem responsurum super hac re invitamus.

---

* KING EADGAR. DCCCC.LXIII.-DCCCC.LXXV.

Her is geswutelod on þisum gewrite hu Aþelwold bisceop begeat æt his leofan cynehlaforde Eadgare cyninge þæt he· mid geþeahte his witana· geniwode Ciltancumbes freols þære halgan Þrynnesse ⁊ Sancte Petre ⁊ Sancte Paule into Wintanceastre· þan hirede on ealdan mynstre· eal swa his yldran hit ær gefreodon· ærest Cynegils cyning ⁊ his sunu Cynewald[1] cyning· þe on angynne cristendomes hit sealdan· ealswa hit lið on ælche healfe þæs portes into þære halgan stowe· ⁊ syððan ealle heora æftergengen· þæt wæs Egcbirt cynincg· ⁊ Aþulf cyning· ⁊ Ælfred cynincg· ⁊ Eadweard cynincg· ⁊ he geuðe þæt man þæt land on eallum þingon for ane hide werode·

Here is made known in this writing how bishop Æthelwold obtained from his beloved royal lord king Eadgar, that he, with the counsel of his 'witan', renewed the liberty of Chilcomb to the holy Trinity, and St Peter, and St Paul at Winchester, for the brotherhood of the Old Monastery, as his forefathers had before freed it: first king Kynegils, and his son king Kênwald, who, in the beginning of Christianity, gave it as it lies, on each side of the town, contiguous to the holy place: and afterwards, all their successors, viz. king Ecgberht, and king Athulf, and king Ælfred, and king Eadward; and he granted that the land in all things should

[1] r. Cenwalh.

swa swa his yldran hit ær gesetton ⁊ gefreodon. wære þær mare landes. wære þær læsse. ⁊ he bead. on Godes naman. þæt naðer ne þære stowe bisceop ne nanes bisceopes æftergenga þæt land næfre of þære stowe geutode. ne hit nanan woruldmen wið nanan sceatte ne wið ceape gesealde. ⁊ he bead. þurh Godes ælmichtiges myclan mægenþrymm. þæt nan his bearna ne nan heora æftergengcana þæt menster æfre leng mid preostan gesette. ac þæt hit efre mid munecan stode. swa swa he hit mid Godes ælmihtiges fultume gesette. þa þa he hit þa modigan preostas. for heora mandædon þanan út adrefde. ⁊ þerinne munecas gelogode. þæt hi Godes þeowedon æfter Sancte Benedictes tæcinge. ⁊ dæghwamlice to Gode cleopodon for ealles cristenes folces alisednesse. Ealles þæs landes is an hund hida. ac þa godan cynegas ⁊ þa wisan. ælc æfter oþran. ꝥ ylce land swa gefreodon. Gode to lofe ⁊ his þeowan to bryce into fostorlande. ꝥ hit man æfre on ende for ane hide werian sceolde. Se þe þysne freols healdan wille. God ælmihtig

be defended for one hide[1], as his forefathers had before established and freed it; should there be more land, should there be less. And he commanded, in the name of God, that neither the bishop of the place, nor any bishop's successor, should ever alienate that land from the place, nor should sell it to any secular man for any money or chattel. And he commanded, by the great majesty of God, that none of his children, nor any of their successors, ever set that monastery with priests; but that it should ever stand with monks, as he, with God Almighty's aid, set it, when he drove thence the proud priests, for their sinful deeds, and placed monks therein, that they might serve God after the teaching of S[t] Benedict, and daily cry to God, for the redemption of all Christian folk. Of all the land there are a hundred hides; but the good kings and the 'witan', each after other, so freed that same land, to the praise of God, and the use of his servants as 'foster-land', that finally it should ever be defended for one hide. Who-

[1] That is, that the contribution to the 'fyrd' should be no more than for one hide, instead of a hundred.

hine gehealde her ⁊ on ecnesse. Gif hwa þonne [freols·] þurh ænige dyrstignesse· oððe þurh deofles lare· þisne freols abrecan wille· oððe þas gesetednesse on oðer awendan durre· se he awyrged mid eallan þan awyrgednessan þe synd awritene on eallan halgan bocan· ⁊ sy he ascyred from ures Drichtnes gemaňan ⁊ ealra his halgana· ⁊ sy he gebunden þa hwile þe he libbe on þisum life mid þan ylcan bendan þe God ælmihtig þyrh hine sylfne betæchte his halgan apostolan Petre ⁊ Paule· ⁊ æfter his awyrgedan forðsiðe ligge he efre on helle grundleasan pytte· ⁊ byrne he on þan ecan fyre mid deofle ⁊ his englan a butan ælcan ende· butan he hit ær his forðsiðe gebete. Amen.

ever this freedom will observe, may God Almighty preserve him here and to eternity. But if any one, through any audacity, or through the devil's lore, will violate this freedom, or dare to avert it to other, be he accursed with all the curses that are written in all holy books, and be he severed from the communion of our Lord and all his saints, and be he bound, while he lives in this life, with the same bonds which God Almighty through himself committed to his holy apostles Peter and Paul; and after his accursed departure, may he ever lie in the bottomless pit of hell, and burn in the everlasting fire with the devil and his angels, ever without any end, unless, before his departure, he make atonement for it. Amen.

IDEM LATINE.

In hac chartella manifeste declaratur, qualiter ego Eadgarus, opitulante gratuita Salvatoris clementia, Anglorum basileus, Æðelwaldo mihi pontifice suggerente, tam optimatum meorum consilio devotus, renovavi Chiltecumbes hæreditariam libertatem, et sanctæ et individuæ Trinitati commendavi, et in veteri monasterio, in æcclesia beatorum Petri ac Pauli, ad usum monachorum inibi Deo regulariter famulantium, perpetuo jure consecravi; præcepi hanc quoque renovationem in ipsa eadem libertate fine tenus perdurare, qua illam ab aliis ditatam, et ab antecessoribus regibus omnibus meis donatam esse comperi, quorum primi extiterunt,

Kingilsus rex, et filius ejus Kinewaldus rex, qui in exordio fidei Christianæ, sanctissimo Berino episcopo verbum Dei prædicante, concesserunt ejusdem juris possessionem ad præfatum sancti loci monasterium. Deinde Egbertus rex, Aðulphus rex, Ælfredus rex, Eadgarus rex: ideoque præcipio, in nomine Domini nostri Jhesu Christi, ut nullus episcopus ejusdem loci illam terram de ipso monasterio trahere audeat, nec alicui secularium pro munere quolibet eam dare præsumat. Hoc quoque provida consideratione superaddidi, et mandavi, ut nullus filiorum vel nepotum meorum, nec aliquis successorum meorum ad prædictum sedis episcopalis cœnobium, clericos unquam introducat; sed electis eisdem monachis Christo ibidem Deo servientibus deputetur, sicut ego ipse, co-operante omnipotentis Dei auxilio, constitui, quando superbos clericos, qui Deo servire contempserunt, pro nefandis suis actibus et detestandis servitiis inde eliminatos expuli, ibique sacram cœnobitarum congregationem, qui in hymnis et laudibus Domino voluntarie servirent, congregavi. Quicunque hanc libertatem custodire voluerit, custodiat eum Deus et hic et in ævum. Si quis autem, diabolica suggestione deceptus, hanc libertatem minuere vel infringere præsumpserit, veniant super eum omnium maledictionum genera quæ scripta sunt in Novo et in Veteri Testamento; sitque cœlum ferreum super caput ejus, et tellus ahenea sub pedibus ejus; et sit ipse æterno anathemate separatus a Deo et omnibus sanctis ejus, et apostolica beatorum Petri et Pauli authoritate ligatus sit quamdiu vixerit, et post maledictum obitum suum, gehennalibus flammis, cum diabolo et angelis suis, sine fine damnatus et cruciatus intereat, nisi prius emendaverit, quod Deum omnipotentem et sanctos apostolos ejus pro nihil sperare non timuit.

BISHOP ÆTHELWOLD. DCCCC.LXIII.-DCCCC.LXXV.

✠ Her swutelað on þyssum gewrite þet Aþelwold bisceop ⁊ Wulfstan Uccea

✠ Here is made known in this writing, that bishop Æthelwold and Wulfstan hwyrfdon landa on Eadgares cyninges ⁊ on his witena gewytnesse. Se bisceop sealde Wulstane þet land æt Hwessingatune· ⁊ Wulstan sealde him þet land æt Iaceslea ⁊ æt Ægeleswurðe. Þa sealde se bisceop þet land æt Iaceslea into Þornige· ⁊ þet æt Ægelleswyrðe into Buruh· ⁊ ꝥ land æt Ægeleswyrðe headde an wyduwe ⁊ hire sune ær forwyrt· forþan þe hi drifon[1] [i]serne stacan on Alsie Wulfstanes feder· ⁊ ꝥ werð æreafe· ⁊ man teh ꝥ morð forð of hire inclifan[2]. Þa nam man ꝥ wif ⁊ adrencte hi æt Lundenebrigce· ⁊ hire sune ætberst ⁊ werð utlah· ⁊ ꝥ land eode þam kynge to handa· ⁊ se kyng hit forgeaf þa Ælfsie· ⁊ Wulstan Uccea his sunu hit sealde eft Adeluuolde bisceope· swa swa hit her bufan sægð.

Uccea exchanged lands, with the witness of king Eadgar and his 'witan'. The bishop gave to Wulfstan the land at Washington, and Wulfstan gave him the land at Jaceslea and at Aylesworth. Then the bishop gave the land at Jaceslea to Thorney, and that at Aylesworth to Peterborough: and a widow and her son had previously forfeited the land at Aylesworth, because they had driven an iron pin into Ælsie, Wulfstan's father, and that was detected: and they drew the deadly thing forth from her chamber[2]. They then took the woman and drowned her at London Bridge; and her son escaped, and became outlaw; and the land went into the hands of the king; and the king then gave it to Ælfsie, and Wulfstan Uccea his son gave it again to bishop Æthelwold, as it is here above said.

[1] See Anc. Laws and Instit. folio edit. pp. 379, 409, and Glossary, *voce* Stacung; and Grimm, Deutsche Mythol. 2nd edit. p. 1045.

[2] ⁊ ꝥ . . . . . inclifan. My translation of this passage is quite conjectural, and based on the supposition that for æreafe we should read arasod. ꝥ I understand to refer to a waxen image into which the woman had driven an iron pin, for the purpose of tormenting Alsie, whom the image was intended to represent; morð I take to mean the deadly image itself. This kind of witchcraft was known by the name of *invultuatio.* See L.L. Henrici I. 71. § 1. *ut sup.*

KING EADGAR. DCCCC.LXIII.-DCCCC.LXXV.

Her is geswitulod on ðysum gewrite hũ Eadgar cining mid rymette gedihligean[1] het þa mynstra on Wintanceastræ· syþþan he hi ðurh Godes gyfe to munuclife gedyde· ⁊ þet asmeagan het ꝥ nan ðera mynstera þær binnan þurh þet rymet wið oðrum sace næfde· ac gif oðres mynstres ãr on oðres mynstres rymette lege· ꝥ þes mynstres ealdor ðe to þam rymette fenge· ofeode þæs oðres mynstres are mid swilcum þingum swylce ðam hirede ðæ þa are ahte gecweme wære. Forðy ðonne Aþelwold bisceop· on þes cinges gewitnesse ⁊ ealles þæs hiredes his bisceopstoles· gesealde twa gegrynd butan Syðgeate into Niwan mynstre· ongẽn ðes mynstres mylne ðe stod on ðam rymette ðe se cing het gerymen into Ealdan mynstre. And se abbod Æþelgar· mid geðeahte ures cynelafordes· ⁊ þæs bysceopes Aþelwoldes· ⁊ ealles þæs hiredes· þa ylcan mylne þe se bisceop seolde· ⁊ oðre þæ hi ær ahtun binnan þære byrig· to sibbe ⁊ to sõme gesealde into nunnan

Here is made known in this writing how king Eadgar commanded the monasteries in Winchester to be separated by a space, after that, by God's grace, he had turned them to monkish life; and commanded it to be borne in mind that none of the monasteries there within should, on account of that space, have strife with the others; but if the property of one monastery lay within the space of another monastery, that the principal of the monastery which may take to that space should relinquish the property of the other monastery, for such consideration as should be acceptable to the society that owned the property. Therefore has bishop Æthelwold, in witness of the king and all the brotherhood of his episcopal see, given two plots of ground without Southgate to the New Monastery, against the monastery's mill, which stood in the space which the king commanded to be ceded to the Old Monastery. And the abbot Æthelgar, by the counsel of our royal lord, and of bishop Æthelwold, and of

[1] Qu. for gedælan?

mynstre· ⁊ Eadgyfe[1] abbedesse þæs cinges dohter betehte ongen ðone weterscype þe he into Niwan mynstre· be ðes cinges leafan geteah· ⁊ ær ðes nunhiredes wes· ⁊ him se tige sume mylne adilgade· ⁊ he gesealde þam cinge hundtwelftig mancæs reades goldes to ðance beforan Ælfdryðe ðære hlæfdian· ⁊ beforan þam bisceopan Aðelwolde wið þam lande ðæ seo eā ōn yrnð· fram þam norð wealle to þæs mynstres suð wealle an lencge· ⁊ twegræ metgyrda brad ðer ꝥ wæter ærest infylð· ⁊ þær ꝥ land unbradest is· þer hit sceol beon eahtatyne fota brad. Đyses ic geann Æþelgare abbode ⁊ þam hirede into Niwan mynstre· for his gecwemre gehyrsumnesse ā on ecnesse· ⁊ ic halsige ælc ðara ðe eftær me cynerices wealde· þurh ða halgan Đrynnesse· þet hyra nan næ undo þet ic to ðam haligum mynstrum binnan þære byrig gedon hebbe. Se þe ðis þonne awendan wylle ðe ic to sibbe ⁊ to gesehtnesse betweoh þam mynstre geradigod hæbbe· oððe þara ðinga þe on þissan þrim cyrografum ðe on ðis-

all the brotherhood, has, for peace and concord, given to the Nuns' monastery the same mill which the bishop gave, and another, which they before possessed within the town, and assigned them to the abbess Eadgyfu[1], the king's daughter, against the water-course which, with the king's leave, he has drawn into the New Monastery, and which had previously belonged to the nunnery; and the channel[2] of which had destroyed a mill of his. And he gave to the king a hundred and twenty mancuses of red gold in acknowledgment, before Ælfthryth the lady, and before the bishop Æthelwold, for the land in which the water runs, from the north wall to the south wall of the monastery in length, and two meteyards broad, where the water first falls in: and where the land is narrowest, there it shall be eighteen feet broad. This I grant to abbot Æthelgar and the convent at the New Monastery, for his ready obedience, in perpetuity. And I beseech each of those who shall rule the kingdom after me, by the holy Trinity, that

[1] Eadgar had an illegitimate daughter who died abbess of Wilton, but her name was Eadgyth.

[2] or reservoir?

sum þrym mynstrum to swytelungum gesette syndon. awende hine sẽ eca Drihten fram heofenan rice. ⁊ sii his wunung æfter his forðsiðe on helle wite. mid þam ðe symle on ælcre ungeþwærnesse blissiað. butan he hit ær his forðsiðe gebete.

no one of them undo what I have done for the holy monasteries within the city. But whoever will avert this which I have counselled for peace and concord between the monasteries, or any of the things which in these three chirographs are set down, for the guidance of these three monasteries, may the eternal Lord avert him from the kingdom of heaven, and his dwelling, after his departure hence, be in hell-torment, with those who ever rejoice in every discord; unless before his departure he atone for it.

KING EADGAR. DCCCC.LXVIII.

FREOLS BOC TO TANTUNÆ. CHARTER OF LIBERTIES TO TAUNTON.

Hac autem cartula liquido declaratur qualiter ego Eadgar Anglorum basileus Tantunes libertatem devotus renovavi ob amorem reverende Trinitatis consubstantialisque Unitatis, necnon beati Petri apostolorum principis, ejusque co-apostoli Pauli, uti episcopali cathedre Wintoniensis æcclesiæ eadem deserviret libertate qua priscis temporibus ab ejus avo, Eadwardo videlicet rege, insignita libere gloriabatur. Usus itaque saluberrimo obtimatum meorum consilio, ammodum Christo dapsilis concessi, ut episcopii homines, tam nobiles quam ignobiles, præfato rure degentes hoc idem jus in omni haberent dignitate quo sui proprii perfruuntur regalibus fiscis commorantes; omnia enim secularium rerum judicia ad usus presulum exercere eodem modo diligenti jussi examine quo regalium negotiorum discutiuntur judicia. Predicte igitur ville mercimonium censusque omnis civilis sanctæ Dei æcclesiæ Wentane civitatis, sine retractionis obstaculo, cum omnibus commodis æternaliter deserviat. Hæc autem libertas, antecessorum meorum temporibus, Ælfeago antistiti, aliisque eodem rure fruentibus concessa fuerat, quam ego renovando humillime restauravi. Qui autem hanc libertatis dapsilitatem augere voluerit, augeat Dominus ejus vitam et prosperitatem hic et in evum; si quis autem præsumptuosus, diabolo instigante, hanc libertatem infringere, minuereve, vel in aliud quam constituimus transferre voluerit, anathema sit, et in Christi maledictione permanens æterno barathri incendio, cum Iuda Christi proditore ejusque complicibus miserrimus puniatur, si non cum satisfactione ante obitum emendaverit quod contra nostrum deliquit decretum.

Dedit autem Aðelwoldus Wintoniensis æcclesiæ episcopus, pro hujus libertatis recuperatione, regi Eadgaro, ducentas auri mancusas, ejusque conjugi Ælfþryþe quinquaginta, et quoddam vas argenteum quinque libras appendens. Priscis utique temporibus, pro hac eadem libertate, date sunt Eadwardo regi sexaginta terræ mansæ, quattuor in locis dirempte, x. videlicet æt Crawancumbe, et x. æt Cumbtune, xx. æt Scealdeburnan stoce, et xx. æt Bananwylle. Hoc idem rus Eadward prefatus rex dedit famulis famulabusque Domini on Ceodre degentibus, pro commutatione illius telluris quæ Carintun nominatur. Acta est autem hujus libertatis nota renovatio, Pascali sollempnitate, sede regali æt Ceodre, anno Dominicæ incarnationis DCCCC.LXXVIII.[1], decimo vero anno ejus regalis imperii. His testibus consentientibus quorum inferius nomina ordinatim carraxantur.

Ego Eadgar Anglorum basileus hoc privilegium, in honore reverende Trinitatis atque consubstantialis Unitatis, crucis signo devotissime confirmavi. Ego Dunstan archiepiscopus confirmavi. Ego Oscytel archiepiscopus consensi. Ego Aðelwold episcopus corroboravi. Ego Ælfstan episcopus consolidavi. Ego Byrhtelm episcopus consensi. Ego Oswold episcopus corroboravi. Ego Alfwold episcopus consolidavi. Ego Osulf episcopus consensi. Ego Wynsige episcopus corroboravi. Ego Ælfþryþ regina. Ego Æþestan dux. Ego Ælfhere dux. Ego Ælfheah dux. Ego Ordgar dux. Ego Æþelwine dux. Ego Byrhtnoð dux. Ego Oslac dux. Ego Eadulf dux. Ego Ælfric abbas. Ego Osgar abbas. Ego Ælfstan abbas. Ego Æscwig abbas. Ego Æþelgar abbas.

[1] An error for 968. Eadgar died in 975.

Ego Cynewerd abbas. Ego Þyrcytel abbas. Ego Ælfheah abbas. Ego Ealdred abbas. Ego Eanulf minister. Ego Ælfwine minister. Ego Æþelweard minister. Ego Wulfstan minister. Ego Byrtferð minister. Ego Oswerd minister. Ego Osulf minister. Ego Elfwerd minister. Ego Eþelweard minister.

IDEM ANGLICE.

Her ys geswutelod on þysum gewrite· hu Eadgar cyning· mid geþeahte his witena· geniwode Tantunes freols· þære halgan þrynnesse ⁊ Scæ Petre ⁊ Scæ Paule into Wintanceastre to þam biscopstole, ealswa Eadweard cyning hit ær gefreode· ⁊ geuþe ꝥ ægþer ge twelfhynde men ge twyhynde weron on þam Godes hame þara ylcan gerihta wyrþe þe his agene men sindon on his agenum cynehamum; ⁊ man ealle spæca ⁊ gerihtu on ꝥ ylce gemet gefe to Godes handa þe man to his agenre drifð· ⁊ þes tunes cyping ⁊ seō innung þara portgerihta gange into þere halgan stowe· ealswa heo ær dyde on myra yldrena dagon· ⁊ Ælfeage biscope gehafod wæs· ⁊ gewylcum þara þe þes landes breac. Se þe þisne freols geycean wille· geyce God his gesynta to langsumun life her ⁊ on ecnesse· gif hwa þonne· þurh gedyrstignesse ⁊ deofles oþþe his lima lare· þysne freols abrecan wille· oþþe on oþer

Here is made known, in this writing, how king Eadgar renewed the liberty of Taunton, for the Holy Trinity and St Peter and St Paul, to the episcopal see of Winchester, as king Eadward had before freed it, and granted that both Twelfhynde men and Twyhynde should, in that vill of God, be worthy of the same rights that his own men are in his own royal vills; and that all suits and rights be in the same manner given into the hand of God as they were brought to his own; and let the town's market, and the produce of the town-dues go to the holy place, as they did before, in the days of my forefathers, and were levied for bishop Ælfeah, and every one of those who enjoyed the land. Whoever will increase this liberty, may God increase his prosperity in a long life here, and in eternity. But if any, through audacity, and the instigation of the devil and his limbs, will violate this liberty, awendan· buton he hit ær his fordsiþe gebete· sy he mid awurgednesse ascyred fram ures Drithnes gemanan ⁊ ealra his halgena· ⁊ on helle susle ecelice getintragod mid Iudan þe Cristes lewa wes.

or pervert it to other, unless ere his departure hence he make reparation, be he with malediction cut off from the communion of our Lord and all his saints, and ever be tormented in hell torture, with Judas, who was Christ's betrayer.

Đonne gesealde Aðelwold biscop his cynehlaforde twa und mancussa goldes ⁊ anne sylfrene lefel on fif pundum wið þe niwunge þyses freolses· ⁊ Ælfþryde his gebeddan· healf hund mancussa goldes wiþ richtes ærendes fultume. ⁊ ær wæron wiþ freolse gesealt· on Eadwardes dege cinges syxtig hide landes· x. æt Crawancumbe· ⁊ x. æt Cumbtune· ⁊ æt Bananwille xx. ⁊ xx. æt Scealdeburnan Stoce. ⁊ eft Eadward cyning gesealde ꝥ land æt Cumbtune ⁊ æt Bananwille ðan hiwon æt Ceodre· wiþ þan lande æt Carintune. Þis wes gedon æt Ceodre· on þere halgan Eastertide· þy geare weron agangene DCCCC. geara ⁊ eahta ⁊ hundseofontig[1] fram Cristes acynnednesse· ⁊ þe teoþan geãre his cynelican anwealdes· on gewitnesse þara witena þe hiora noman her wiþneoþan awritene syndon.

Then gave bishop Athelwold to his royal lord two hundred mancusses of gold and one silver cup of five pounds weight, for the renewal of this liberty; and to Ælfthryth his consort, half a hundred mancusses of gold, for aid in a just transaction. And erewhile, in the day of king Eadward, there were given for the liberty, sixty hides of land: x. at Crowcombe, and x. at Compton, and at Banwell xx., and xx. at Shalbournstoke. And again king Eadward gave the land at Compton and at Banwell to the convent at Chedder; for the land at Carhampton. This was done at Chedder, on the holy Easter tide, in which year were agone DCCCC. and seventy-eight[1] years from the birth of Christ; and in the tenth year of his kingly sway, in witness of the 'witan' whose names are here beneath written.

[1] An error for 968.

KING EADGAR. DCCCC.LXX.

☧ Omnipotentis Dei cunctorum sceptra regentis moderamine regum, immo tocius seculi creatureque cunctæ indissolubili regimine æque gubernantis habenas, ipsius nutu et gracia suffultus, Ego Eadgarus basileus dilecte insule Albionis, subditis nobis sceptris Scottorum, Cumbrorumque, ac Brittonum, et omnium circumcirca regionum quiete pace perfruens, studiosus sollicite de laudibus Creatoris omnium occupor addendis, ne nostra inertia, nostrisque diebus plus æquo servitus ejus tepescere videatur; set greges monachorum et sanctimonialium hac nostra tempestate, ipso opitulante qui se nobiscum usque in finem sæculi manere promittere dignatus est, ubique in regno nostro desertis monasteriis antiquitus Dei famulatu deficiente, nunc reviviscente, adsurgere cupimus, sub Sancti Benedicti abbatis regula viventes, quatinus illorum precatu et vigente religione sancta servitus Dei nos ipsum placatum rectorem habere queamus. Unde frequentes monitus venerabilis Aþelwoldi episcopi cordetenus pertractans, cupio honorare hoc privilegio rebusque copiosis monasterium quod in regione Elig situm dinoscitur antiquitus, ac Sancti Petri apostolorum principis honore dedicatum, decoratumque reliquiis et miraculis almæ virginis Eðeldrydæ, cujus vita venerabilis nobis modernis historia Anglorum promitur, quæ eciam incorruptibili corpore hactenus condita mausoleo marmoreo albo perdurat[1]. Locus denique prædictus, deficiente servitio Dei, nostra ætate regali fisco subditus erat; set a secretis noster Aþelwoldus Deique amator, diocesi Wyntoniensis civitatis fungens, datis nobis sexaginta cassatis in villa quæ ab accolis Heartingas nuncupatur, mutuavit locum prædictum cum appendiciis ejus, augmentavique mutuationi tres villas quæ hiis nominibus vocitantur, Meldeburna, Earningaford, Northwold, et ipse ilico monachos, meo consilio et auxilio, Deo fideliter regulari norma servientes perplures inibi collocavit, quibusque Brihtnothum quendam sapientem et bene morigeratum virum præpositi jure præfecit. Cui effectui admodum ego congaudens, letabundus pro amore

[1] See Beda, Hist. Eccles. iv. 19.

Christi et Sancti Petri, quem patronum michi sub Deo elegi, et Sancte Eþeldriðe virginis Deo dilectæ, et ejus prosapie sanctæ illic quiescentis, et pro animabus patrum meorum regum antiquorum augmentare largiter mutuationem illam hiis donis, testibus consiliariis meis, volo: hoc est decem milia anguillarum omni anno in villa quæ æt Uuyllan dicitur, pro expeditione redduntur, fratribus ad victualia modo et deinceps concedo: et intra paludes causas seculares duorum centuriatuum, et extra paludes quinque centuriatuum in Uuiclauuan in provincia Orientalium Saxonum benigne ad fratrum necessaria sanciendo largior. Quineciam omnes causas seu correpciones transgressionum juste legis in sermonibus secularibus omnium terrarum sive villarum ad monasterium predictum rite pertinencium, et quæ in futurum ævum Dei providencia loco præfato largitura est, sive emptione, seu donatione, aut aliqua justa adquisitione, stent causæ seculares emendandæ, tam clementi examine fratrum loco manencium victui vel vestitui necessaria ministrantes: adhuc insuper omnem quartum nummum reipublice in provincia Grantaceaster fratribus reddendum jure perpetuo censeo. Et sit hoc privilegium liberum quasi munus nostrum Deo devote oblatum et sanctis ejus prædictis, ad remedium animarum nostrarum, sicuti præfati sumus, ut nullus regum nec principum, aut ullius ordinis quislibet præpotens, imposterum obstinata tyrannide aliquid horum infringere præsumat, si non vult habere omnipotentis Dei maledictionem et sanctorum ejus, et meam et patrum meorum, pro quibus ista omnia libera haberi volumus æterna libertate in æternum. Amen.

Hoc privilegium hujus donationis et libertatis fecimus scribi anno incarnationis Domini nostri Jhesu Christi nongentessimo septuagessimo, Indictione tercia decima, anno regni mei æque tercio decimo, in villa regali quæ famoso vocabulo a solicolis Uulfamere nominatur, non clam in angulo, set sub divo palam evidentissime scientibus totius regni mei primatibus, quorum quedam nomina hic infra inseri ad testimonium imposterum mandavimus.

✠ Ego Eadgarus rex animo benigno hoc largiendo Deo concessi, et regia sublimitate corroboravi. Ego Dunstan archiepiscopus corroboravi. Ego Oscytel archiepiscopus consolidavi. Ego Atheluuold episcopus confirmavi. Ego Alfstan episcopus consignavi. Ego Osulf episcopus confirmavi. Ego Wulfric episcopus adquievi. Ego Uuynsyge episcopus corroboravi. Ego Alfuuold episcopus confirmavi. Ego Ælfuuold episcopus consolidavi. Ego Osuuold episcopus adquievi. Ego Byrhthelm episcopus confirmavi. Ego Eadelm episcopus consignavi. Ego Ælfric episcopus consolidavi. Ego Uulfsige episcopus corroboravi. ✠ Ælfðryð regina. Alfric abbas. Æscwig abbas. Osgar abbas ✠. Ælfstan abbas. Æthelgar abbas. Cyneuueard abbas. Đurcytel abbas. Ealdred abbas. Ordbriht abbas. Siferð abbas. Martin abbas. ✠ Æþelstan dux. Ælfhere dux. Ælfeah dux. Ordgar dux. Ætheluuine dux. Oslac dux. Malcolm dux. Byrhtnoht dux. Eadulf dux ✠. Birhtferð minister. Eanulf m. Ælfuuine m. Ætheluueard m. Uulstan m. Ælfuueard m. Ælfuuine m. Uulfgeat m. Osulf m. Osuueard m. Leofa m. Birhtric m. Ælfsige m. ✠ Ulf m. Osulf m. Heanric m. Hryngulf m. Leofstan m. Oslac m. Fræna m. Siferð m. Leofric m. Eadric m. Uulfnoð m. Ælfsige m. Ulfcytel m. Hroold m. ✠ Đurstan m. Osgod m. Gota m. Frithegist m. Đurferð m. Đurgod m. Osferth m. Oscytel m. Siferth m. Đurcytel m. Forne m. Cnut m. Đurstan m. Đurcytel m.

Hiis igitur testibus, et aliis compluribus de omnibus dignitatibus et primatibus regni mei, hæc constituta et peracta noscuntur; quæ eciam nostra usitata sermocinatione describi mandavimus hac eadem sceda, quo possint in auribus vulgi sonare, ne aliqua scrupulositate admisceri videantur, set regia auctoritate, seu potestate, nobis a Deo donata, omnis contradiccio funditus adnulletur.

IDEM ANGLICE.

Gode ælmihtigum rixiende ðe ræt ⁊ gewissað eallum gesceaftum þurh his agenne wisdom· ⁊ he ealra cininga cynedom gewylt. Ic Eadgar

God Almighty ruling, who counsels and directs all creatures, through his own wisdom; and he governs the kingdom of all kings: I Ead-cyning eac þurh his gife ofer Engla þeode nu up aræred· ⁊ he hæfð nu gewyld to minum anwealde Scottas ⁊ Cumbras ⁊ eac swylce Bryttas· ⁊ eal ꝥ þis igland him on innan hæfð· ꝥ ic nu on sibbe gesitte on minne cynestol· hohful embe ꝥ hu ic his lof arære· þe læs ðe his lof alicge to swiðe nu on urum timan· þurh ure asolcennysse· ac ic wille nu· þurh Godes wissunge· þa forlætenan mynstru on minum anwealde gehwær mid munecum gesettan· ⁊ eac mid mynecenum· ⁊ Godes lof geedniwian· ðe ær wæs forlæten· Criste wissiendum· ðe cwæð ꝥ he wolde wunian mid us oð þissere worulde geendunge· ⁊ þa munecas libban heora lif æfter regole þæs halgan Benedictes· us to þingunge· ꝥ we þone Hælend hæbben us glædne· ⁊ he us gewissige ⁊ urne eard gehealde· ⁊ æfter geendunge ꝥ ece lif us forgife. Nu is me on mode æfter mynegungum Aþeluuoldes bisceopes ðe me oft manode· ꝥ ic wille gegoodian· þurh Godes silfes fultum· ꝥ mynster on Elig· mid agenum freodome ⁊ sinderlicum wurðmynte· ⁊ siððan mid æhtum· þam to bigleofan ðe we gelogiað þær to

gar king am also, through his grace, now raised up over the English nation; and he has now reduced under my power Scots and Cumbrians, and in like manner Britons, and all that this island within it has; so that I now sit in peace on my throne, mindful in what manner I may exalt his praise; lest his praise, now in our time, lie too greatly prostrate, through our slothfulness; but I will now, through God's guidance, the forsaken monasteries in my dominion, everywhere plant with monks and also with mynchens, and God's praise renew, which was ere neglected; according to the direction of Christ, who said that he would dwell with us until the ending of this world; and that the monks live their life after the rule of the holy Benedict, to mediate for us, that we may have the Saviour propitious towards us, and that he may guide us, and preserve our country, and, after the ending, give us the life everlasting. Now it is my intention, after the admonitions of bishop Æthelwold, who has often exhorted me, that I will endow, through the support of God himself, the monastery in Ely with its

Godes þeowdome þe ðær symle wunian. Seo stow wæs gehalgod iu fram ealdum dagum þam halgan Petre to wyrðmynte · ðæra apostola yldost · ⁊ heo wæs geglengd þurh Godes sylfes wundra · þe gelome wurdon æt Æðeldryðe byrgene · þæs halgan mædenes · þe ðær gehal lið oð þis · on eallhwitre ðryh of marmstane geworht. Be hire we rædað hu heo her on life wæs · ⁊ hu heo Gode ðeowode on godre drohtnunge · ⁊ be hire geendunge · ⁊ hu heo up adon wæs ansund of hyre byrgene · swa swa Beda awrat · Engla ðeode lareow · on his lar bocum. Nu wæs se halga stede yfele forlæten mid læssan þeowdome ðonne us gelicode nu on urum timan · ⁊ eac wæs gehwyrfed ðam cyninge to handa · ic cweðe be me sylfum · ac Aðelwold bisceop · ðe is min rædbora ⁊ soð Godes freond · sealde me to gehwearfe þone ham Heartingas · on sixtigum hidum · wið þam mynsterlande ðe lið into Elig · ⁊ ic þa geeacnode into Elig mynstre þas ðry hamas ðe þus sind gehatene · Meldeburna · Earningaford · Norðwold · ⁊ he þærrihte · mid minum ræde ⁊ fultume · mid munecum ge-

own freedom and extraordinary honour, and then with possessions, for the sustenance of those whom we place there for God's service, who may there ever dwell. And the place was hallowed of old, from ancient days, to the honour of the holy Peter, chief of the apostles, and it was embellished by the miracles of God himself, which were frequent at the tomb of the holy maiden Æthelthryth, who there lies whole until now, in an all-white coffin wrought of marble. Of her we read, how she was here in life, and how she served God by a good life-course, and at her ending; and how she was taken up sound from her tomb, as Beda, the doctor of the English nation, wrote in his lore-books. Now was the holy place evilly left with less service than it pleased us, now in our time, and had also passed into the hand of the king: I said in myself; but bishop Æthelwold, who is my counsellor and a true friend of God, gave me in exchange the vill of Hartings, of sixty hides, for the monastic land adjacent to Ely; and I added to Ely the three vills which are thus named: Melbourn, Erningsette ꝥ mynster æfter regole· ⁊ him ealdor gesette us eallum fulcuðne Brihtnoð gehaten· ꝥ he under him ðane halgan regol for Gode geforþæde· æfter mynsterlicum þeawe.

Ða gelicode me ꝥ he hit swa gelogode mid Godes þeowum Gode to lofe· ⁊ ic ða geeacnode to þare ærran sylene tyn þusenda ælfixa ælce geare þam munecum· þe me for fyrdinge gefyrndagum aras binnan þam iggoðe of þam folce æt Wyllan· ⁊ ealle þa socna eac ofer ꝥ fennland into þam twam hundredum· him to scrudfultume· ⁊ on East Englan æt Wichlawan, eac ealle þa socna ofer fif hundredum· ⁊ ofer ealle þa land· gelice ða socna ðe into þam mynstre nu synd begytene· oððe ða þe him gyt becumað· þurh Cristes foresceawunge· oððe þurh ceap· oððe þurh gife· habbon hi æfre on eallum þa socne· ⁊ þone feorðan pening on folclicre steore into Grantabricge· be minre unnan· ⁊ gif ænig man þis awendan wille· þonne gange eal seo socn þe to anre niht feorme

ford, Northwold. And he straightways, with my counsel and aid, planted that monastery with monks, according to rule, and appointed them for principal Brihtnoth so called, and well known to us all; that he under him may before God further the holy rule according to monastic custom.

Then it pleased me that he had so ordered it, with God's servants, to the praise of God; and I then added to the former gift ten thousand eels every year, for the monks, which from days of old have accrued to me, within the isle, for military service, from the folk at Wells; and all the jurisdictions over the fenland in two hundreds, in aid of their clothing; and in the East Angles at Wicklow; also all the jurisdictions over five hundreds, and over all the lands; in like manner, the jurisdictions which are now acquired for the monastery, or which may yet come to it, through Christ's providence, or through purchase or through gift, let them ever have the jurisdiction in all, and the fourth penny on the public penalties in Cambridge, by my grant. And if any man will avert gebyreð into þære stowe· ⁊ beo þis priuilegium· ꝥ is sinderlic wurðmynt oððe agen freodom into ðære stowe mid eallum ðisum þingum Gode geoffrod· mid urum godum willan· Gode æfre frig ⁊ Godes halgum· for minre sawle ⁊ minra yldrena· us to alysednesse· swa ꝥ nan þara cyninga þe cumað æfter me· oððe ealdorman· oððe oðer rica· mid ænigum riccetere oððe unrihte þiss ne awende oððe gewanige· be þam ðe he nelle habban Godes awyrgednysse· ⁊ his halgena· ⁊ mine· ⁊ minra yldrena· ðe þas þing fore synd gefreode on ecum freode on ecnysse. AMEN.

this, then let all the jurisdiction which is incident to a night's sustenance go to the monastery. And be this privilege (that is, the special honour or peculiar freedom to the monastery) with all these things offered to God with our good will, ever free to God and God's saints, for the soul of myself and of my parents, for our redemption, so that none of the kings that shall come after me, or aldorman, or other potent man, by any power or injustice, may this avert or diminish, if he will not have the malediction of God, and his saints', and mine, and my parents', for whom these things privileged with an eternal privilege to eternity. Amen.

BISHOP ÆTHELWOLD. ABOUT DCCCC.LXX.

Þis synd þa madmas þe Adeluuold bisceop sealde into þam mynstre þe is Medeshamstede gehaten· Gode to loue ⁊ Sc̃e Petre· his saule to alysednesse· ꝥ is þonne an Cristes boc mid sylure berenod· ⁊ III. rode eac mid sylure berenode· II. sylurene candelsticcan and II. ouergylde· ⁊ I. sylurene storcille·

These are the treasures which bishop Æthelwold gave to the monastery which is called Medeshamstede, to the praise of God and St Peter, [and] for the redemption of his soul. These then are: one Christ's book ornamented with silver, and III. roods likewise ornamented with silver; II. silver candlesticks,

⁊ I. æren. ⁊ I. sylurene waterfet. ⁊ II. sylurene bellan. ⁊ IIII. sylurene calices. IIII. patenan. ⁊ syluren pipe. ⁊ VI. masse hacelan. ⁊ IIII. cæppan. ⁊ I. roc. ⁊ VIII. stolan. emfela handlina. ⁊ XI. subumbrale. ⁊ II. pistol claþas. ⁊ III. corporale. ⁊ III. offrinc sceatas. ⁊ XVIII. albæn. ⁊ IIII. pælles. ⁊ II. linen web to albæn. ⁊ II. blace rægl cæsternisce. ⁊ VI. uuahryft. ⁊ VIIII. setreil. ⁊ X. hangiende bellan. VII. hand bellan. ⁊ IIII. bedreaf. ⁊ VI. hornas. IIII. gerenode. ⁊ VIII. sylfrene cuppan. and II. gegylde weofod sceatas.

and II. gilded over, and I. silver censer, and I. of brass, and I. silver water-vessel, and II. silver bells, and IV. silver chalices, IV. patens, and a silver pipe, and VI. mass-robes, and IV. copes, and I. rochet, and VIII. stoles, as many hand-napkins, and XI. subumbrals, and II. epistle cloths, and III. corporals, and III. offering napkins, and XVIII. albs, and IV. palls, and II. webs of linen for albs, and II. black civic cloaks, and VI. wall-hangings, and IX. seat covers, and X. hanging bells, VII. hand bells, and IV. bed hangings (coverlets ?), and VI. horns, IV. ornamented, and VIII. silver cups, and II. gilded altar cloths.

And an twentig is þara boca þe Adeluuold biscop gesealde into Burch. ꝥ is þonne.

And of the books there are twenty which bishop Æthelwold gave to Peterborough: these are:—

Beda in Marcum.
Liber Miraculorum.
Expositio Hebreorum nominum.
Provisio Futurarum Rerum.
Augustinus de Achademicis.
Vita Sancti Felicis metrice.
Sinonima Isidori.
Vita Eustachii.
Descidia Parisiace polis.
Medicinalis.
De Duodecim Abusivis.
Sermo super quosdam Psalmos.
Commentum Cantica Canticorum.
De Eucharistia.
Commentum Martiani.
Alchimi.
Aviti.
Liber Differentiarum.
Cilicius Ciprianus de Litteris Grecorum.
Liber Bestiarum.

* KING EADGAR. DCCCC.LXXI.

In nomine Domini nostri Jhesu Christi. Quamvis decreta pontificum et verba sacerdotum inconvulsis ligaminibus, velud fundamenta moncium, fixa sunt, tamen plerumque tempestatibus et turbinibus sæcularium rerum religio sancte ecclesie maculis reproborum dissipatur ac rumpitur. Iccirco profuturum succedentibus posteris esse decrevimus, ut ea quæ salubri consilio et communi assensu diffiniuntur, nostris literis roborata firmentur. Quapropter dignum videtur ut ecclesia beatissime Dei genitricis semperque virginis Marie Glastoniæ, sicut ex antiquo principalem in regno meo obtinet dignitatem, ita speciali quadam et singulari privilegii libertate per nos honoretur. Hoc itaque Dunstano Dorobernensi atque Oswaldo Eboracensi archiepiscopis adortantibus, consenciente etiam et annuente Brithelmo Fontanensi episcopo, cæterisque episcopis, abbatibus, et primatibus, ego Edgar, divina disposicione rex Anglorum ceterarumque gencium in circuitu persistencium gubernator et rector, in nomine alme Trinitatis, pro anima patris mei, qui ibi requiescit, et antecessorum meorum, presenti privilegio decerno, statuo, et confirmo, ut predictum monasterium omnisque possessio ejus, ab omni tributo fiscalium negociorum nunc et imperpetuum libera et quieta permaneant, et habeant socam et sacam on stronde ⁊ on streame, ⁊ on wude ⁊ on felde, on griðbrice, [on burhbrice], hundred setena, [morðas], adas, ⁊ ordelas; ealle hordas bufan eorðan ⁊ beneoðan; infangeneðeof ⁊ outfangeneðeof, ⁊ flemeneferde, hamsocne, friðbrice, forsteal, tol ⁊ team, ita libere et quiete sicut ego habeo in toto regno meo. Eandem quoque libertatem et potestatem quam ego in curia mea habeo, tam in dimittendo quam in puniendo, et in quibus libet omnino negociis, abbas et monachi prefati monasterii in sua curia habeant. Si autem abbas vel quilibet monachus loci illius latronem, qui ad suspendium vel quodlibet mortis periculum ducitur in itinere obviam habuerit, potestatem habeant eripiendi eum ab imminenti periculo in toto regno meo. Confirmo etiam et corroboro ut, quod hactenus ab omnibus nostris antecessoribus diligenter observatum est, Fontanensis episcopus vel ejus ministri super hoc monasterium, vel super parochiales ejusdem ecclesias, videlicet, Strete, Mirieling, Budeclea, Schapewike, Sowy, aut super earum capellas, nec eciam super eas que in insulis continentur, scilicet, Bekeria, que parva Hibernia dicitur, Godeneya, Marteneseia, Ferramere, Padeneberga, et Adredeseia, nullam potestatem omnino habeant, nisi tantum cum ab abbate, causa dedicandi vel ordinandi, advocati fuerint; nec eorum presbiteros ad sinodum suam, vel capitulum, vel ad quodlibet placitum convocent, nec ab officio divino suspendant, et omnino nullum jus in eos excercere presumant. Monachos suos et ecclesiarum predictarum clericos, secundum antiquam ecclesie Glastonie consuetudinem et apostolicam auctoritatem, archipresulis Dunstani et omnium episcoporum regni mei assensu, abbas, a quocunque comprovinciali episcopo voluerit, ordinari faciat. Dedicaciones vero ecclesiarum, si ab abbate rogatus fuerit, Fontanensi episcopo permittimus. In Pascha quoque crisma sanctificacionis et oleum a Fontanensi episcopo ex more accipiat, et per prefatas ecclesias suas distribuat. Hoc eciam super omnia, Dei interdictione et nostra auctoritate, salva tamen sancte Romane ecclesie et Dorobernensis dignitate, prohibeo, ne persona cujuscumque potestatis, sive rex, sive episcopus, sive dux aut princeps, vel quilibet ministrorum eorum, Glastonie terminos vel supradictarum parochiarum, perscrutandi, rapiendi, placitandi gratia, vel quicquam aliud faciendi, quod contrarium possit esse ibidem Deo servientibus, intrare præsumant. Abbati tantummodo et conventui potestas sit, tam in notis [causis quam in ignotis,] in modicis et in magnis, et in omnibus omnino negociis, sicut supra memoravimus. Quisquis autem hujus privilegii mei dignitatem, qualibet occasione, cujuscumque dignitatis, cujuscumque ordinis, cujuscumque professionis, pervertere, vel in irritum deducere, sacrilega præsumpcione amodo temptaverit, sciat se proculdubio ante districtum judicem titubantem tremebundumque racionem redditurum, nisi prius digna satisfactione emendare studuerit. Acta est hec privilegii pagina et confirmata apud Londoniam, communi consilio omnium primatum meorum, anno ab incarnacione Domini nostri Jhesu Christi DCCCC.LXXII. Indiccione XIIII. Hujus doni constipulatores fuerunt, quorum nomina inferius caraxari videntur.

Ego Edgar, rex tocius Britannie, prefatam libertatem cum sigillo sancte crucis confirmavi. Ego Eilfgiua, ejusdem regis mater, cum gaudio consensi. Ego Edward clito patris mei donum cum triumpho sancte crucis impressi. Ego Kinadius rex Albanie adquievi. Ego Mascusius archipirata confortavi. Ego Dunstanus, Dorobernensis ecclesie archiepiscopus, cum trophæo sancte crucis, et cum suffraganeis presulibus, regis donum corroboravi. Ego Oswald, Eboracensis ecclesie primas, consentiens subscripsi. Ego Ethelwold, Wintoniensis ecclesie minister, et Glaston. monachus, signum sancte crucis impressi. Ego Brithelm, Fontanensis episcopus, consenciens corroboravi. Ego Elstan episcopus confirmavi. Ego Oswold episcopus concessi. Ego Winsige episcopus cum signo sancte crucis conclusi. Ego Segegar abbas confirmavi. Ego Ordgar abbas corroboravi. Ego Ethelgar abbas concessi. Ego Kynewrde abbas consensi. Ego Sideman abbas consolidavi. Ego Elpheh abbas subscripsi. Ego Aldulf, Herefordensis ecclesie catascopus, corroboravi. Ego Elfhere dux domine mee sancte Marie, Glastoniensis ecclesie libertatem omni devocione, cum sigillo sancte crucis, confirmavi. Ego Oslac dux consensi. Ego Ethelwine dux hoc donum triumphale agie crucis proprie manus depiccione impressi. Ego Oswald minister confirmavi. Ego Elfward minister corroboravi. Ego Ethelsie minister consensi. Ego Elfsie minister consensi. Hanc privilegii paginam rex Edgarus duodecimo anno regni sui sacro scripto, apud Londoniam, communi consilio optimatum suorum, confirmavit.

KING EADGAR.

CARTA DE ROMESEY[1].

✠ Christo ortodoxorum vigoris ecclesiastici monitu creberrime instruimur, ut illi opido subjecti subpeditarius famulemur, qui, tocius mundi fabricam miro ineffabilique serie disponens, microcosmum Adam videlicet tandem quadriformi plasmatum materia, almo ad sui similitudinem instinctum spiramine, universis que in infimis formaverat una probandi causa excepto vetitoque proficiens paradisiace amenitatis jocunditate, collaterana Eva scilicet comite, decentissime collocavit; larvarica, pro dolor, seductus cavillacione versipellis suasibilisque tergiversacione viraginis pellectus anathematis alogia ambro pomum momordit vetitum, et sibi ac posterum in hoc erumpnoso dejectus seculo letum promeruit perpetuum. Vaticinantibus siquidem prophetis et celitus superni Regis diuturna clamdestino præsagia dogmate promentibus, nitide orthodoxis orilogium ex deferens non ut Judeorum seditioso elingue fatetur loquacitas, sed priscorum atque modernorum limpidissimam ambiens facundiam Arrianas Sabellianasque proterendo vanias anagogico infrustrans famine, nosque ab obtusi cecitate umbraminis ad parvorum alacrimoniam patrimoniorum advocans angelus supernis elapsis liminibus in aurem intemerate virginis ut evangelica provulgant famiam stupenda cecinisse videtur carmina. Cui videlicet ecclesia catholica consona voce altiboando proclamat, "Beata es, virgo Maria, que credidisti; perficientur in te que dicta sunt tibi a Domino." Mirum dictu incarnatur verbum et incorporatur, scilicet illud de quo evangelista supereminens universorum altitudinem sensum inquit, "In principio erat verbum, et verbum erat apud Deum, et Deus erat verbum," et reliqua. Quia videlicet sumpta de virgine incarnacione antique virginis facinus demitur, et cunctis mulieribus nitidis præcluens taumatibus decus irrogatur. Intacta igitur redolentente Christi divinitate, passaque ipsius humanitate libertas addictis clementer: hinc ego Edgar altitrono amminiculante

[1] This document has reached us in a late and very corrupt form. Both the Latin and the Saxon are in many parts to me unintelligible.

Angelorum terrarumque gentium in circuitu triviatim persistentium basileus, ut hujus libertatis altitroni Moderatoris clementia merear optinere consorcium, cenobio loco celebri qui ab hujus prosapie solicolis Romesye nobili nuncupatur vocabulo situm, agie genetrici Domini nostri Jesu Christi dedicatum habetur, sanctimonialibus regulariter degentibus monastici eternam privilegii concedo libertatem, quatinus post decessum Merewenne abbatisse egregie, cujus temporibus hec libertatis restauracio, Christo suffragante, concessa est, quam sibi universa præfati cenobii congregacio elegerit concilio, secundum regularia beati Benedicti instituta abbatissam juste ex eodem sororum cuneo eligens constituat, hujus privilegii libertas deinceps usu perpetuo a cunctis teneatur, nec extraneorum quispiam, tirannica fretus contumacia, in prædicto monasterio jus arripiens exerceat potestatis, set ejusdem cenobii collegium perpetue, ut prædixi, libertatis glorietur privilegio. Sit autem præfatum monasterium omni terrene servitutis jugo eodem tenore liberum, quo a prædecessoribus nostris, catholicis videlicet regibus, uti vetuste continetur, privilegio solutum est. Ægri equidem qui ad usus sanctimonialium Domino nostro Jhesu Christo ejusque genitrici Marie priscis modernisque temporibus a regibus et religiosis utriusque sexus hominibus, et a meipso divino respectu clementia restituendo jure concessi sunt ejusdem perpetualiter sint libertatis. Si quis vero tam epilenticus philargirie seductus amencia, quod non optamus, hanc nostre munificentie dapsilitatem ausu temerario infringere temptaverit, sit ipse alienatus a consortio sancte Dei ecclesie, necnon et a participatione sacrosancti corporis et sanguinis Jesu Christi filii Dei, per quem totus terrarum orbis ab antiquo generis inimico liberatus est, et cum Juda Christi proditore sinistra in parte deputatus est, nisi prius hic digna satisfactione humilis penituerit quod contra sanctam Dei ecclesiam rebellis agere præsumpserit; nec in hac vita practica veniam, nec in theorica requiem apostata optineat illam, sed eternis baratri incendiis trusus, cum Anania et Zaphira jugiter miserrimus cruciatur. Pro silva vero huic telluri pertinente regi præfato data sunt DCCCC. meri auri mancuse in patera qùadam mirifice fabricata, et in armillis honorifice scultis, vaginaque auro nimium decorata.

Hiis metis hoc rus hinc inde giratur.

METE VEL BUNDE DE ROMESEYE.

Þis is þe landmarke to Romesye. Erest up andlang strete þare þat Þurst an seit[1]. and so to Fareburne. up andlang Fareburne. anon to Carebrok. of Carebrokes on þa Rugedich. andlang þare Rugedich to þare Laþemere. and siþen oure bi Bisshopes marke to Risbrigge. of Mearkbrok. andlang Mearkbrok to Cumeran treuwe. of Cumeran tréowe on Marchbrokeshewed. on þane brode mere. of þane mere suþrist innan þa willan. of þan willan. on Grynden brok. of Grynden brok on Stennes pæð. andlang paþe hut on Rusfeld. þanne andlang hegges ond hit comeð to Wirmesie. of Wirmesye to Bodestan. fram Bodestan suthe andlang lauen. fram þe lauen in þe dich bi wuðen. þanne andlang dich innon þe wiþige. of þan wiþie inan þe heae. andlang heae in þan dede lake. of þare dede lake to Huntesige. of Huntesige inan þan alde Tersten. andlang þar ealde Terste ond

This is the landmark at Romsey. First, up along the road where the Terstan springs forth, and so to Farebourne; up along Farebourne on to Carebrook; from Carebrook to the Rugeditch; along the Rugeditch to the Lathemere; and then over by the bishop's boundary to Rushbridge; from Markbrook; along Markbrook to Cumera's tree; from Cumera's tree to Markbrook head; to the broad mere; from the mere due south within the well; from the well to Grindenbrook; from Gryndenbrook to Stennes path; along the path out to Rushfield; then along the hedge until it comes to Wirmesey; from Wirmesey to Bodestan; from Bodestan south along the low; from the low to the ditch by the wood; then along the ditch within the withy; from the withy within the hedge; along the hedge to the dead lake; from the dead lake to Huntesey; from Huntesey

[1] scit?

þe hit comeþ in þare streit þare Þurstan seyt[1].

Ðe gyldene melle so on þane ledene speketh· and þa ye angrenene boges· an þare goleggede[2] hauseþ mid golde· waron gesald sanwel stedte. Edmond aþeling he on þare ministre ligð· and þe kyng witeþ þane sette þane Wodecalue sealde in to þare stowe· on þan gerad þat no man þare on tiþe na nede hut of þam hurede.

within the old Terstan; along the old Terstan until it comes to the road where the Terstan rises.

The golden crucifix which speaks in Latin, and the evergreen boughs . . . . were given to the same place. Edmund ætheling lies in the minster: and the king knows the 'sette' which Wodecalve gave to the place, on the condition that no man should drive or force it out of the convent.

KING EADGAR. DEC. 28TH DCCCC.LXXIV.

Rege regum, et Domino dominantium, in eternum et ultra omnipotenter ubique regnante, et ineffabili sua clementia universa celestium et terrestrium ac infernorum agmina gubernante: Ego Edgarus, per magnam ipsius Dei misericordiam tocius Anglorum regni solio sublimatus, omnibus post me futuris regibus, archiepiscopis, episcopis, abbatibus, comitibus, vicecomitibus, centenariis, ceterisque sancte ecclesie filiis, innotesco quod quidam vir dilectissimus mihi, necnon et propinquitatis consanguinitate connexus, Aylwynus aldreman nomine, instigante divina clementia, cum benivolo meo assensu ac licencia, in insula que nuncupativo usu ab incolentibus Rameseya promulgatur, in honore beate Dei genitricis ac perpetue virginis Marie, Sanctique Benedicti, omniumque sanctarum virginum, arcisterium construxit; previdens itaque incertum futurorum temporum statum, omnibus posteris meis scire profuturum decrevi quale igitur Omnipotentis gratia operante, ibidem miraculum emicuit,

[1] scyt?

[2] gold-ecgede, *gold-edged*?

sicut non incerta relatione quorumdam episcoporum meorum, immo et ipsius Aylwyni didici.

Igitur diuturno ac laborioso cruciatu podagre pedum suorum prædictus illustris vir Aylwynus multis laborans annis, usquequo nox affuit salutifera in qua piscator quidam ipsius, qui Wlfget vocabatur, cum carinula et asseclis suis, et lino, aquam que Anglico nomine Rammesmere dicitur, ingressus est, piscem videlicet gratia ad usum domini sui predicti usu consueto adquirendi. Sicut itaque noverat velle domini sui rete suo sedulo huc et illuc proiciendo aliquid capere nitebatur; sed ex predestinatione Dei omnipotentis frustra laborans, et tandem piscario labore nimium fatigatus, in carinula sua soporatus obdormivit, cui Sanctus in sompnis apparuit sic fando Benedictus: "Aurora spargente polum, tuum eiciens tragum multitudini copiose, voti compos, obviabis piscium; captorum itaque piscium majorem, quem vos haked nuncupatis, Aylwyno domino tuo ex mea parte offerens, dices ei, ut meam donationem benigne assumens, pie matri misericordie et mihi omnibusque sacris virginibus, in hac insula, monasterium, monachorum habitationem, cum officinis necessariis congruum, sine dilatione studeat fabricare; ut ei igitur hec omnia per ordinem innotescas exhortor, sermonem addens sermoni quatinus scrutetur diligencius in loco predicto quomodo noctu fessa terre sua incumbant animalia, at ubi taurum surgentem pede dextro viderit percutere terram, ibidem proculdubio xenodochii sciat se aram erigere debere. Et ut mente perspicatiori et fide constantiori meis hiis credat mandatis, hunc tuum tibi exteriorem incurvo digitum, quem et ipse mox a nexu podagre solutus, et signi certioris judicio roboratus tibi erigat reparandum."

Predictus igitur piscatorum didasculus, hiis auditis evigilans, lucisque diei spiculum in oriente conspiciens, in aquam, sicut sibi jussum fuerat, tragum suum laxare cepit, et, sicut sanctus pater predixerat, copiosam multitudinem piscium conclusit, quorum majorem eligens, ex parte Sancti Benedicti, eum domino suo obtulit, eique omnia que in sompnis didicerat revelavit, digitumque suum a sancto incurvatum ut erigat obnixe rogavit. Que omnia mente sagaci concipiens Aylwynus, digitum viri herentem erexit, piscemque suscipiens, matri Domini Jhesu Christi et Sancto Benedicto grates innumeras benedicendo exsolvit; surgensque vir insignis festinus jubet mannum preparari, et in insulam ipsam vadens, quomodo jacent sua animalia, ut preceptum erat, explorat. Mira res, et miranda, ubi vir predictus insulam est ingressus, ab intractabili statim et gemino morbo, nutu Dei funditus liberatus est, animaliaque sua in modum crucis, taurum vero in medio eorum jacere prospexit. Et sicut quondam Sancto Clementi agnus pede dextro locum fontis, sic viro isti taurus terram percuciendo locum mense futuri arcisterii significavit divinitus. Unde vir prefatus Deum laudans confestim truncatis lignis actitari capellam ibi pulchro opere precepit, ac deinde scemate condecenti, sicut mandatum sibi fuerat, regulare future congregationi monachorum construxit cenobium. Deinde revoluto quinquennio diebusque duodeviginti, precibus venerabilium amicorum meorum, Dunstani Dorobernensis, et Oswoldi Eboracensis archiepiscoporum, eandem ecclesiam in honore beate virginis Marie, sanctorumque predictorum, sexto Idus Novembris, anno ab incarnatione Domini nongentesimo septuagesimo quarto, Indictione secunda, sollempniter, ut decebat, dedicari concessi. Eodem vero anno, cum in Natali Dominico omnes majores tocius regni mei, tam ecclesiastice persone quam seculares, ad curiam meam, celebrandæ mecum festivitatis gratia, convenissent, a predictis amicissimis meis archiepiscopis itidem rogatus, omnes donationes terrarum vel possessionum, quas vel idem Aylwynus, vel quecumque alie persone, in dotalitium ejusdem ecclesie, et jus hereditatis perseverabile ad victuale subsidium monachorum Christo jugiter ibi famulantium indulserant, dando et concedendo hoc regie majestatis mee privilegio coram tota curia mea corroboravi, et tam ipsas donationes quam nomina donatorum literis meis ad future posteritatis notitiam exprimere curavi: Hoc est, primitus dona [ipsius] aldremanni, scilicet insulam in qua sedet xenodochium predictum, cum omnibus sibi pertinentibus pratis, pascuis, campis, paludibus, silvarumque densitatibus; deinde rus illud quod Upwode nominatur, cum Raveleya berewyco suo, Hemmingeford, Saltreiam, Stivecleiam,

Brinintoñ, Westoñ, Hebugeħ, Walsocnam, cum omnibus ad easdem villas pertinentibus: in Welles quoque viginti homines piscatores, sexaginta miliaria anguillarum singulis annis debentes, ad usum fratrum predictorum; Wulfina uxor ejusdem aldremanni, Brancestreiam cum omnibus ad eam pertinentibus; Dunstanus archiepiscopus Dorobornensis, Wardebusc cum omnibus sibi pertinentibus; Oswaldus archiepiscopus Eboracensis, Kingeston, id est, Wistowe, cum Raveleia et Biri, berewycis suis omnibus sibi pertinentibus; Athelstan Mannessune, Slepam et Chateriz, et de Elesworth partem orientalem, cum omnibus sibi pertinentibus; Brithnot aldremanus, Wychenton et Ysham, cum omnibus sibi pertinentibus; Aylfwoldus frater Ailwyni prescripti, Houcton, Wittoñ, Riptonam, Clintoñ, et Bithernam, cum omnibus sibi pertinentibus; Limth vidua, Graveł, Dilintoñ, Stoctoñ, et Gillinger, cum omnibus sibi pertinentibus.

Hec itaque rura, ut supra dixi, pro adipiscenda dulcedinis divine misericordia, et pro stabilitate regni mei, libenti animo, in dote perseverabili annui, cum ecclesiis, cum terris cultis et incultis, exitibus, redditibus, viis, inviis, segetibus, silvis, brueriis, secundum antiquos diu servatos confinium terminos, in pratis, pascuis, aquis, aquarumque decursibus, paludibus, piscariis, mariscis, molendinis, et theloneis, ad se pertinentibus, et cum omni utilitate que inde poterit omni tempore evenire, et cum omnibus per circuitum terminis et metis suis ab regia actione et angaria, vel a qualibet humane servitutis subactione liberrima, lege, libertate, consuetudine, tam bene et tam plene sicut ea sub mei juris dominio, suffragatore Deo, melius et liberius prenominati nobilissimi possiderunt viri, favore et consensu primatum et optimatum meorum, prenominate ecclesie firmiter perpetuo habenda concessi et confirmavi.

Ut igitur hoc donationis mee decretum fixiori firmitate et stabilitate perduret, presentis pagine privilegio decerno et statuo, ut sint libera et expedita tam predicta territoria ibidem jam data, quam ea que a fidelibus deinceps sunt danda, ab omni angaria constructionis pontis arcisve restaurationis, et ab omnibus secularibus serviciis et operibus, ita quod nullus umquam regum, vel episcoporum, seu principum procuratorum sive exactorum, ab illis pastum nec opera vel tributa exigat; sed omnia sint libera omnino et quieta quecunque superius prænotantur. Preterea ex consultu et admonitione venerabilium amicorum meorum, Dunstani Dorobernensis et Oswaldi Eboracensis archiepiscoporum, decreta utilia statui, ut quicunque majestatis regie reus, vel cujuslibet alterius offense, ad locum illum confugerit, ejus rei et membrorum ac vite impunitatem consequatur; semperque sit habitatio monachorum, ac secundum beati Benedicti traditionem, post obitum abbatis ex eadem congregatione alter qui dignus sit eligatur; aliunde vero nullus ibi preficiatur, nisi nullus, quod absit, ibi contigerit qui dignus tali officio sit, inveniri; quod si contigerit, potestatem habeant de alio noto monasterio abbatem eligendi, cujus vita sapientia et religione clarescat; laicorum autem aut clericorum nemo loci illius dominium usurpare presumat. Possessiones vero que ibi a quibuscunque donate sunt, non abbas, non alia quelibet persona licentiam habeat vendendi extraneis vel dandi, sed regum munimine locus ille semper tueatur, ipseque abbas regi Deo soli serviens spirituali et temporali commissum sibi gregem pastu diligenter foveat; liceatque ipsi congregationi quod sibi per rectam delegationem collatum est perpetuo possidere, et pro me et pro stabilitate regni mei Deum jugiter exorare. Post hujus itaque privilegii mei donationem, excommunicaverunt omnes episcopi, abbates, presbiteri, qui in plurima numerositate eodem die affuerunt, eos qui hoc constitutum infringerent vel infringi permitterent, quantum in ipsis esset.

Et ut hec auctoritas meis et futurorum post me regum temporibus, circa ipsum sanctum locum firma perhenniter permaneat et inviolata, et ut ab omnibus optimatibus meis et judicibus, privatis et puplicis, melius et certius credatur, manus mee subscriptione hanc cartulam, quinto Kalendas Januarii, decrevi roborare, et sigilli mei impressione communire.

Signum Edgari et serenissimi Anglorum imperatoris. Signum Edwardi ejusdem regis filii. Signum Athelredi fratris ejus. Ego Dunstanus Dorobernensis archiepiscopus confirmavi. Ego Oswaldus Eboracensis archipresul corroboravi. Ego Alfstanus Londoniensis episcopus consolidavi. Ego Athelwoldus Wintoniensis episcopus commodum duxi. Ego Alfnothus Dorocensis episcopus conclusi. Ego Alfstanus Rofensis episcopus consigillavi. Ego Alfgarus Wiltoniensis episcopus amen dixi. Ego Elsinus abbas, cum coabbatibus meis et presbiteris, infractores hujus firmitalis excommunicavi. Ego Elwynus alderman hoc meum desiderium ad perfectum, Deo suffragatore, usque perduxi.

KING EADGAR.

Mundane volubilitatis orbita nunquam in eodem permanet statu, sed quotidiano defectu more fluentis aque decurritur, ob id quod rerum effectus preteritarum oblivioni traditur, nisi literature characteribus exaretur, qui quasi quodam arctiore ligamento ne penitus e memoria defluat retinetur, hoc quomodo que olim gesta fuerunt innotescit posteris. Quapropter in hac chartella manifeste declaratur, qualiter ego Edgarus, opitulante gratuita Salvatoris clementia, Anglorum basileus, Æþelwaldo mihi pontifice suggerente, tum optimatum meorum concilio devotus, renovavi Chiltecumbes hereditariam libertatem, et sancte et individue Trinitati commendavi; et in Veteri monasterio in ecclesia beatorum Petri ac Pauli, ad usum monachorum inibi Deo regulariter famulantium, perpetuo jure consecravi; precepi hanc quoque renovacionem in ipsa eadem libertate fine tenus perdurare, qua illam ab aliis ditatam et ab antecessoribus regibus omnibus meis donatam esse comperi, quorum primi extiterunt Kingilsus rex, et filius ejus Kinewaldus rex, qui in exordio fidei Christiane sanctissimo Berino episcopo verbum Dei predicante concesserunt ejusdem juris possessionem ad prefatum sancti loci monasterium; deinde Egberthus rex, Aþulphus rex, Ælfredus rex, Edgarus rex. Ideoque precipio in nomine Domini nostri Jhesu Christi ut nullus episcopus ejusdem loci illam terram de ipso monasterio trahere audeat, nec alicui secularium, pro munere quodlibet, eam dare præsumat. Hoc quoque provida consideracione superaddidi et mandavi, ut nullus filiorum vel nepotum meorum, nec aliquis successorum meorum ad predictum sedis episcopalis cenobium, clericos unquam introducat; sed electis eisdem monachis Christo ibidem Deo servientibus deputetur, sicut ego ipse, cooperante omnipotentis Dei auxilio, constitui, quando superbos clericos, qui Deo servire contempserunt, pro nefandis suis actibus et detestandis servitiis inde eliminatos expuli, ibique sacram cenobitarum congregacionem, qui in hymnis et laudibus Domino voluntarie servirent, congregavi. Quicunque hanc libertatem custodire voluerit, custodiat eum Deus et hic et in evum; si quis autem diabolica suggestione deceptus hanc libertatem minuere vel infringere presumpserit, veniant super eum omnium maledictionum genera que scripta sunt in Novo et in Veteri Testamento, sitque celum ferreum super caput ejus, et tellus ahenea sub pedibus ejus, et sit ipse eterno anathemate separatus a Deo et omnibus sanctis ejus et apostolica beatorum Petri et Pauli authoritate ligatus sit quamdiu vixerit, et post maledictum obitum suum, gehennalibus flammis cum diabolo et angelis suis sine fine damnatus et cruciatus intereat, nisi prius emendaverit, quod Deum omnipotentem et sanctos apostolos ejus pro nihil sperare non timuit.

KING EADGAR.

Cum sacræ auctoritatis doctrina nos veridica sedulo ammoneat exortatione, ut non solum activæ visibilibus religiose conversando, sanctisque proficiendo virtutibus carismatis dono perfusi decentissime perfruamur, verum etiam contemplativæ invisibilia vitæ toto mentis conamine partim a recidivis semoti libentissimæ, cum puro tranquilloque animi intuitu contemplando amplectemur, dicens: "Cuncta quæ videntur temporalia sunt, quæ autem non videntur æterna." [Quapropter] ego Eadgar, Christi annuente clementia, tocius Albionis basileus, his recidivis practicæ vitæ possessiunculis æterna theoricæ emolumenta lucrando mercari desiderans, quoddam rus a supradicta Wintoniensi æcclesia injusta quondam a philargiriis abstractum rapina, Aþelwoldo obtinente presule, ab illo qui injuste possederat justo arripiens judicio, Trinitati reverendæ ejusque apostolis Petro et Paulo humillima reddens restituo devotione, XL. videlicet cassatos, loco qui celebri Alresford nominatur vocabulo. Nam rex religiosus Cynewalh nuncupatus, a Birino pontifice fidei sacramentis imbutus, idem rus, in Christiane religionis exordio, præfatæ Dei æcclesiæ magna animi largitus est devotione; hoc idem Ecgbirct, regali fretus stemmate, nova territorii consolidavit cartula. Quidam aliquando predictæ pontifex basilicæ a notis Denewulf nuncupatus, cuidam propinquorum suorum Ælfred vocitato, eatenus cum consensu æcclesiasticæ familiæ accommodavit, ut annis singulis censum tocius telluris vita comite rite persolveret: is equidem insipiens adulterans stuprum, propriam religiose pactatam abominans, scortam diligens, libidinose commisit. Quo reatu omni substantia peculiali recte privatus est, et prefatum rus ab eo abstractum rex hujus patriæ suæ ditione avidus devenire injuste optavit: cujus aviditati presul supradictus minime consentiens, datis centum viginti auri mancusis, prædictam tellurem ad usus præsulum satisfaciendo æcclesiæ Dei restituit: succedente itaque tempore supradicti adulteri et scelerati filius, falso dicens esse sibi naturale, suo injuste subiciens dominio ab ecclesia Dei presumptuosus arripuit, hereditariamque cartulam novis litterarum apicibus, rege Eadredo cum animæ suæ consentiente periculo, dæmonis instinctu fascinatus edidit. Quæ igitur cartula, et omnes qui ei ausu consenserint temerario, in Domini maledictione permaneant et nullo umquam tempore ad aliquam utilitatem perveniat. Vetus namque et hæc nova quam edidi cartula jugiter Christi omniumque judicio fidelium incolumis prevaleat; adulterina quam predixi cartula æterna dampnatione ad nichilum redacta, et imperpetuum anathematizata. Si quis igitur hanc nostram largifluam augere voluerit donationem, augeat ejus Dominus et vitam et prosperitatem, hic et in futuro: qui autem lenocinante diabolo fastu superbiæ inflatus, nostra violare vel minuere presumpserit statuta, in

Domini maledictione permaneat, et a sanctæ Dei æcclesiæ consortio, sanctorumque omnium contubernio privatus, æterna misellus dampnetur miseria, nisi resipiscens satisfaciendo restituerit quod in Domini possessione violare præsumpsit.

KING EADGAR.

Ad redemptionis suæ augmentum omni conatu cuncti student orthodoxi, ut fidei, spei, caritatisque alis veluti vestium fulgore amicti, preciosarumque splendore gemmarum adornati, sanctarum virtutum copia perspicui, criminum pondere semoti, terreni corporis ergastulo versantes, lacrimarum valle cum nimio degentes certamine, totius animi cultum celesti habitatione theorico figunt meditamine: "Nostra," inquit apostolus, "conversatio in celis est." Hinc igitur ego Eadgar, Domini largiente gratia, totius Albionis basileus, sedula procurans sollicitudine, ne catholicorum quispiam actuali degens conversatione, aliqua secularium rerum vexatione a contemplativa impeditus vita incongrue revocetur, quod olim a prædecessoribus nostris æcclesiis Domini ad sui famulatus obsequium egregia concessum fuerat libertate, renovando libentissime recupero: hujus rei gratia rura omnia prædicta[1], et superius distinctis locis ordinatim novis litterarum apicibus designata, Christi compunctus spiramine, justo utens judicio, ad usus pontificum supradictæ æcclesiæ jura religiosa regentium, pro animæ meæ salute, regnique ac successorum meorum prosperitate, æterna libertate, cum optimatum meorum consilio, devotus ammodum restitui, omnique seculari soluta gloriose ditavi servitute, ne vexatione mundanæ afflictionis, mens præsulum pro nostris facinoribus intercedentium a divina contemplatione remota deficiendo lasesceret. In nomine almæ Trinitatis et individuæ Unitatis præcipio, ut succedentium temporum episcopi ita gregem dyrocheo, id est, duplici pastu, nutriant monachorum, sicut nostris temporibus per sapientium ordinatum est providen-

[1] See preceding charter.

tiam, et alimenta ex Ciltancumbe monachis copiose tribuant, et sine ulla retractione hilariter subministrent, et nullius nimietatis inquietudine perturbent; ne a vita theorica, vel immoderata superfluitas, vel intolerabilis paupertas, cum magno animi detrimento illos amoveat, omnia in victu et vestitu secundum regulæ modificet præceptum. Certe canonici omni viciorum nævo deturpati, inani gloria tumidi, invidiæ livore tabidi, philargyriæ maculis obcecati, luxuriæ facibus libidi, gulæ omnimodo dediti, regi terreno non episcopo subjecti, præfati ruris usu veterano moderno tempore pascebantur alimentis. Ebrietatem siquidem et homicidia sectantes, conjuges suas turpiter nimia et inusitata libidine amplectentes, æcclesiam Dei raro et perpauci frequentare volebant, nec horas celebrare canonicas dignabantur; quo reatu ejectis cum præposito canonicis, et eliminata immundorum spurcicia, monachi in sede constituti sunt episcopali, qui sanctis adornati virtutibus, humilitate precipui, vigiliis, hymnis, et orationibus assidui, abstinentia macti, castitate perspicui, legitime viverent, et obsequium æcclesiæ regulariter implerent. Rura absque dubio superius notata benevola studii intentione, et quæ injuste abstracta fuerant, Durtun videlicet, Tantun, Alresford, Cleares, Ticceburn, Uorðig, Funteal, Stoke, Fermesham, æcclesiæ Dei devotus ammodum ideo restitui, ut tali et tam necessario jocundati additamento, monachorum, Christo humani generis Redemptori fideliter casteque servientium, gregem facilius libentiusque pascerent; dum præfatis ruribus sublatis, canonici turpiter contra fas inhonesteque degentes, in tam angusti rerum possessione usu pascebantur perpetuo. Alantur igitur solito monachi, ab hujus vitæ curis remoti, unde alebantur canonici, cum aviditate nimia curis vitæ recidivæ intenti: rura omnia superius notata episcoporum usui peculiariter ad votum deserviant; illa vero quæ canonici olim cum præposito sine peculiari præsulis dominio usu possederant veterano, hæc eadem monachi communiter ad necessarios usus jure possideant perpetuo, et cum antistitis consilio ac juvamine bene regant, et per præpositum fratribus cunctis necessarium, episcopoque, uti regula præcipit, cum omni humilitate subjectum, sapienter disponant. Pastum ex monachorum villis nequaquam præsul diocesim lustrando avidus exquirat: emptis necessariis fratrum indumentis, quicquid ex lucro villarum superfuerit, unito episcopi fratrumque consilio, ob æternæ beatitudinis premium, Christi erogetur pauperibus, et non loculis episcopi peculiaribus, ad anime detrimentum, reclusum custodiatur. Post unius episcopi obitum, alter ex eadem monachorum congregatione, qui dignus sit pontificatus ordine fungi, et non aliunde eligatur: si autem impedientibus peccatis vel imperitia, in eodem monasterio talis qui dignus sit inveniri nequiverit, ex alio noto monasterio monachus, non autem canonicus, ad tanti gradus dignitatem, qui dignus sit secundum meritum atque doctrinam, unanimi regis et monachorum ejusdem monasterii consilio sapienter eligatur: et non solum in hac pontificis electione, verum etiam omnibus rebus regulæ usus jugi teneatur custodia, ut in omnibus quæ egerint vel regulæ normam hilariter custodiant, vel majorum cum omni devotione imitentur exempla. Electus vero nulla superfluitate monachos perturbet vel inquietet, nec clericos sive laicos in claustra vel refectorium introducat, sed missam celebrans, monachorum reverenter fungatur officio; ac in refectorio quotiens voluerit comedens, eorum et non canonicorum vel laicorum inibi utatur obsequio; monachos, si quoslibet secum suum lustrando episcopium habere voluerit, illos sumat qui provectæ ætatis sint, quorum profectu et moribus ad Christi roboretur famulatum, et non pueros vel juvenes lascivos, quorum levitate læsus in aliquibus depravetur. Rura tam a regibus quam a diversis catholicis ad usus fratrum Domino largiflue collata, hujus sæculi militibus sive propinquis carnalibus, pro munere quolibet adulando tribuens, ad animæ suæ detrimentum nequaquam disperdat. Qui prædicta statuta benivola servare voluntate studuerit, Domini nostri Ihesu Christi benedictione in presenti sæculo perfruatur, et post ejus obitum ad æternæ beatitudinis vitam, Christo opitulante, securus perveniat. Si quis autem philargyria seductus aliquid ex his, quæ cum consilio sapientium precepta sunt, [avertere] vel minuere præsumpserit, deleatur nomen ejus de libro vitæ;

et in Iesu Christi Salvatoris mundi ejusque genitricis Mariæ omniumque sanctorum persecutione maneat, et post vitæ suæ terminum cum Juda Christi proditore ejusque complicibus inferni miseria punitus intereat, si non cum satisfactione emendaverit quod nequiter pejorando deliquit.

BISHOP OSWALD.

INDICULUM LIBERTATIS DE OSWALDES LAUUES HUNDRED.

Domino meo karissimo, regi Anglorum Edgaro, ego Oswaldus Uuigornensis ecclesie episcopus, omniumque que mihi, per ipsius clementiam, munerum tradita sunt, apud Deum et apud homines gratias ago. Igitur, si Dei misericordia suppeditet, coram Deo et hominibus perpetualiter ei fidelis permanebo, reminiscens, cum gratiarum actione, largiflue benignitatis ejus, quia per meos illud, quod magnopere expetebam, mihi concessit internuncios, id est, reverentissimum Dunstanum archiepiscopum, et venerandum Aðeluuoldum Uuintonie episcopum et virum magnificum Brihtnoðum comitem, quorum legatione et adjutorio meam et sancte Dei ecclesie querelam suscepit, et secundum consilium sapientum et principum suorum juste emendavit, ad sustentamen ecclesie, quam mihi benigne et libens regendam commisit. Quare, quomodo fidos mihi subditos telluribus que mee tradite sunt potestati per spatium temporis trium hominum, id est, duorum post se heredum, condonarem, placuit tam mihi quam ipsis fautoribus et consiliariis meis, cum ipsius domini mei regis licentia et attestatione, ut fratribus meis successoribus, scilicet episcopis, per cirographi cautionem apertius enuclearem, ut sciant quid ab eis extorquere juste debeant, secundum conventionem cum eis factam et sponsionem suam; unde et hanc epistolam, ob cautelæ causam, componere studui, ne quis maligne cupiditatis instinctu hoc sequenti tempore mutare volens, abjurare a servitio ecclesie queat. Hec itaque conventio cum eis facta est, ipso domino meo rege annuente, et sua attestatione munificentie sue largitatem roborante et confirmante, omnibusque ipsius regiminis sapientibus et principibus attestantibus et consentientibus. Hoc pacto eis terras sancte ecclesie sub me tenere concessi: hoc est, ut omnis equitandi lex ab eis impleatur que ad equites pertinet, et ut pleniter persolvant omnia que ad jus ipsius ecclesie juste competunt, scilicet ea que Anglice dicuntur ciricsceott, ⁊ toll, i. e. theloneum, ⁊ tacc, i. e. swinsceade, et cetera jura ecclesie, nisi episcopus quid alicui eorum perdonare voluerit, seseque, quamdiu ipsas terras tenent, in mandatis pontificis humiliter cum omni subjectione perseverare etiam jurejurando affirment. Super hec etiam ad omnis industrie episcopi indigentiam semetipsos presto impendant, equos prestent, ipsi equitent, et ad totum piramiticum opus ecclesie calcis, atque ad pontis edificium ultro inveniantur parati. Sed et venationis sepem domini episcopi ultronei ad edificandum repperiantur, suaque, quandocumque domino episcopo libuerit, venabula destinent venatum; insuper ad multas alias indigentie causas, quibus opus est domino antistiti sepe frunisci, sive ad suum servitium, sive ad regale explendum, semper illius archiductoris dominatui et voluntati qui episcopatui presidet, propter beneficium quod illis prestitum est, cum omni humilitate et subjectione subditi fiant, secundum ipsius voluntatem et terrarum quas quisque possidet quantitatem. Decurso autem prefati temporis curriculo, videlicet duorum post eos qui eas modo possident heredum vite spatio, in ipsius antistitis sit arbitrio quid inde velit, et quomodo sui velle sit inde ita stet, sive ad suum opus eas retinere, si sic sibi utile judicaverit, sive eas alicui diutius prestare, si sic sibi placuerit, velit; ita duntaxat, ut semper ecclesie servitia pleniter, ut prefati sumus, inde persolvantur. Ast si quid prefatorum, delicti prevaricantis causa, defuerit jurum, prevaricationis delictum, secundum quod presulis jus est, emendet, aut illo, quo antea potitus est, dono et terra careat. Si quis vero, diabolo instigante, quod minime optamus, extiterit, qui per nostrum beneficium ecclesiam Dei, fraude seu vi, sua possessione aut servitio debito privare temptaverit, ipse nostra omnique benedictione Dei et sanctorum ejus privetur, nisi profundissima emendatione illud corrigere studeat, et ad pristinum statum quod defraudavit redigat. Scriptum est enim, "Raptores et sacrilegi regnum Dei non consequentur." Nunc autem, propter Deum et Sanctam Mariam, in cujus nomine hoc monasterium dicatum est, moneo et precipio, ut nullo modo quis hoc prevaricare audeat, sed, sicut a nobis statutum est, ut prefati sumus, perpetualiter maneat. Qui custodierit, omni benedictione repleatur; qui vero infringerit, maledicetur a Domino et ab omnibus sanctis. Amen. Gratanter, reverentissime domine, quo tantis tue donis clementie, secundum quod totius Creatoris cosmi est velle, preditus sum mee operam voluntatis, ut pro te tuisque Deum jugiter interpellem, devotus impendam, meosque successores ad hoc hortari studebo, ut Domini misericordiam pro te deprecari non desinant, ut Christus pace qui perhenni regnat ethrali in arce te consortio haberi dignetur sanctorum omnium in aula celesti. Valeat in evum, qui hoc studuerit servare decretum. Harum textus epistolarum tres sunt ad pretitulationem et ad signum, una in ipsa civitate que vocatur Uuigraceastre, altera cum venerabili Dunstano archiepiscopo in Cantuaria, tertia cum Aðeluuoldo episcopo in Uuintonia civitate.

KING EADGAR AND KING ÆTHELRED. AFTER DCCCC.LXXV.

DE FALCEHAM ET BROMLEAGE[1].

✠ Ðus wæron þa land æt Bromleage ⁊ æt Fealcnaham þam cinge Eadgare gereht on Lundenbyrig· þurh Snodinglandes landbēc· þa ða preostas forstælon þam biscope on Hrofeceastre ⁊ gesealdon heo Ælfrice Æscwynne sunu wið feo dearnunga· ⁊ heo Æscwyn Ælfrices modor sealde heo ær

✠ Thus were the lands at Bromley and at Fawkham decreed to king Eadgar at London, through the charters of Snodland, which the priests stole from the bishop at Rochester, and sold them to Ælfric son of Æscwyn privately for money, and she, Æscwyn, Ælfric's mother,

[1] See Kemble, Saxons in England, ii. p. 46.

þiderin. Ða geacsode se biscop ꝥ þa becc forstolene wæron· bæd þara bōca ða geornlice. Under þam ða gewatt Ælfric· ⁊ he bæd þa lafe syððan oð man gerehte on cinges þeningmanna gemote þære stowe ⁊ þam biscope þa forstolenan becc Snodinglandes· ⁊ bote æt þære þyfðe· ꝥ wæs on Lundene. Ðær wæs se cing Eadgar· ⁊ se arcebiscop Dunstan· ⁊ Aðelwold biscop· ⁊ Ælfstan biscop· ⁊ oðer Ælfstan· ⁊ Ælfere ealdorman· ⁊ fela cynges witena· ⁊ man agæf ða into þære stowe þam biscope þa becc. Ða stōd þara wydewan āre on þæs cinges handa. Ða wolde Wulfstan se gerefa niman þa āre on þæs cinges handa· Bromleah ⁊ Fealcnaham· ða gesohte seo wydewe þa halgan stowe ⁊ þane biscop· ⁊ agæf þam cinge Bromleages bōc ⁊ Fealcnahames· ⁊ se byscop gebohte þa becc ⁊ þa land æt þam cinge on Godeshylle mid fiftigan mancessan goldes· ⁊ hundteontigan· ⁊ þrittigum pundum· þurh forespræce ⁊ costnunge into Sc̄e Andreæ. Siðþan ða lefde se biscop þare wydewan ðara lande bryces. Under þam ða gewat se cing· ongan ða syðþan Byrhtric þare wydewan

had before given them thither. When the bishop was informed that the charters had been stolen, he earnestly demanded the charters. In the meanwhile Ælfric died, and he [the bishop] afterwards demanded them of the widow, until they decreed, in the 'gemôt' of the king's thanes, the stolen charters of Snodland to the place [Rochester] and to the bishop, and compensation for the theft: that was at London. There were the king Eadgar, and the archbishop Dunstân, and Athelwold bishop, and Ælfstân bishop, and the other Ælfstân, and Ælfere aldorman, and many of the king's 'witan'. And the charters were then given up into the place to the bishop. Then stood the widow's property in the king's hand. Then Wulfstân the reeve would take the property, Bromley and Fawkham, into the king's hand. The widow then sought the holy place and the bishop, and gave up to the king the charters of Bromley and Fawkham; and the bishop bought the charters and the lands of the king at Godshill for fifty mancuses of gold, and a hundred and thirty mæg ⁊ heo to þam genedde ꝥ hy brucan þara landa on reaflace. ⁊ gesohtan þa þane ealdorman Eadwine. ⁊ ꝥ folc þe wæs Godes anspreca. ⁊ geneddan þane biscop. be alre his are. agiftes þara bōca. ne moste he beon þara þreora nānes wyrðe ðe eallum leodscipe geseald wæs on weddetale. ne teames. ne ahnunga.

pounds, through mediation and bribery, for St Andrew's. Afterwards the bishop allowed the widow the usufruct of the lands. In the meanwhile the king died; then Byrhtric, the widow's kinsman, began, and thereto compelled her, that they should possess the lands by violence, and they then sought the aldorman Eadwine, and the folk, that was God's adversary, and compelled the bishop, on peril of all his property, to give up the charters: nor might he be worthy of any of the three things which had been given to all the people in pledge: neither plea, nor vouching, nor possession.

Ðis is seo gewitnesse þæs ceapes. Eadgar cing. ⁊ Dunstan arcebisceop. ⁊ Oswald arcebisceop. ⁊ Aðelwold bisceop. ⁊ Aðelgar bisceop. ⁊ Æscwi bisceop. ⁊ Ælfstan bisceop. ⁊ oðer Ælfstan bisceop. ⁊ Sideman bisceop. ⁊ þæs cinges modor Ælfðryð. ⁊ Osgar abbud. ⁊ Ælfere ealdorman. ⁊ Wulfstan on Dælham. ⁊ Ælfric on Ebbesham. ⁊ seo duguð folces on Westan Cænt. þær ꝥ land ⁊ ꝥ læð to lið.

These are the witnesses of this purchase: Eadgar king, and Dunstân archbishop, and Oswald archbishop, and Athelwold bishop, and Athelgar bishop, and Æscwi bishop, and Ælfstân bishop, and the other Ælfstân bishop, and Sideman bishop, and the king's mother Ælfthryth, and Osgar abbot, and Ælfere aldorman, and Wulfstân at Dalham, and Ælfric at Ebbesham, and the chief of the people in West Kent, where the land and the lath lie.

DESCRIPTIO TERRÆ EPISCOPATUS WIGORNENSIS ECCLESIE, SECUNDUM CARTAM REGIS QUE EST IN THESAURO RE.....

Ecclesia Sancte Marie de Wiricestre habet I. hundret, quod vocatur Osuualdeslau, in quo jacent ccc. hidæ, de quibus episcopus ipsius æcclesiæ, ā constitutione antiquorum temporum, habet omnes redditiones socharum, et omnes consuetudines inibi pertinentes ad dominicum victum, et regis servitium et suum: ita ut nullus vicecomes ullam ibi habere possit querelam, nec in aliquo placito, nec in alia qualibet causa: hoc attestatur totus comitatus. Hæ prædictæ ccc. hidæ fuerunt de ipso dominio æcclesiæ; et siquid de ipsis cuicunque homini quolibet modo attributum vel prestitum fuisset ad serviendum inde episcopo, ille, qui eam terram præstitam sibi tenebat, nullam omnino consuetudinem sibimet inde retinere poterat, nisi per episcopum; neque terram retinere, nisi usque ad impletum tempus, quod ipsi inter se constituerant; et nusquam cum ea terra se vertere poterat.

KING ÆTHELRED. DCCCC.LXXXI.

☧ Universitatis Creatore in æternum regnante, ac justo moderamine cuncta creata, visibilia et invisibilia, miro ineffabilique modo gubernante. Ego Æthelred Anglicæ nationis cæterarumque gentium triviatim intra ambitum Britanniæ insulæ degentium, regiæ dignitatis solio ad tempus Christi mundi Redemptoris gratia subthronizatus basileus, à quodam milite, avunculo videlicet meo, qui secundæ regenerationis utero innovante gratia ineffabiliter editus, nobili Ordulf pollens floret onomate, humili devotione compunctus, subnixis deposcens precibus efflagitare Deum compunctus gratia benivolus ceperat, ut arcisterium cui notabile at Tavistoce fulget vocabulum, ubi mater ejus fraterque, ava videlicet mea et avunculus, cæterique nostræ posteritatis prosapies mausoleis somate tumulati, tuba hujus caducæ vitæ clangente ultima, terciam resurrectionis nativitatem, anima corpori Deo faciente in ictu oculi mirabiliter associata, diem judicaturi vel judicandi præstolantur extremum, ut ibi loco celebri Domino nostro Jesu Christo ejusque genetrici semperque virgini Mariæ dedicato, monachos non seculares sed regulares in omnibus sanctæ regulæ obtemperantes præceptis, licenter constitueret fiscisque naturalibus devotus locupletaret. Ejus igitur votis applaudendo, voti compos animi, et quod fides catholica poposcerat, admodum libens tripudiansque concessi, admiranda namque ejus fidei constancia. Nam illo in tempore quo præfatus miles Sancti Spiritus gratia compunctus, ad legitimos monachorum usus, ad æternæ vitæ lucrum, hoc construxerat cœnobium, cæteri quique infidelitatis nevo turpati, loca sancta dissipantes, sanctæ religionis monachos, insipidi me impote nolenteque, infantili adhuc, ut ita dicam, ætate vigente, atrociter, veluti pagani ad perpetuum sui dampnum fugabant. Ejus igitur benivolenciæ congaudens, meorum optimatum usus consilio, libertatis privilegium præfato loco sanctæ Dei genitrici semperque virgini Mariæ dicato, magna animi alacritate tripudians concedo, et secundum patroni nostri beati Benedicti traditionem, post obitum abbatis qui nunc sancto præsidet loco, abbas ex eadem eligatur congregatione, qui dignus sit tali fungi officio; aliorsum vero minime, nisi culpis promerentibus inibi inveniri nequiverit qui aptus sit animabus lucrandis. Quod si hoc, quod absit, miserabiliter evenerit, de alio noto et familiari monasterio, unanimi fratrum consilio eligatur, cujus vita probabilis sapientia prædita, cultuque religionis fulgida fidelibus clarescat. Finitis namque diebus benivoli et laudabilis viri, qui specialis lucri copia sanctum dapsilis ditaverat locum, laicorum nemo ipsius loci dominium præsumens sibi usurpet. Rex vero quæ ab eo Domino nostro Jesu Christo ejusque genitrici semperque virgini Mariæ ab æterno, usque remunerationem concessa sunt vel concedenda, nec abbas nec alicujus personæ homo licenciam habeat pro pecunia vendendi, vel gratis concedendi, vel mutandi, sed æterno Deo maneat imperpetuum, quod ei concessum vel concedendum est. Regum vero munimine deinceps ipse locus, Domino protegente, tueatur, ipsiusque loci abbas regi deserviens gregem sibi commissum dirocheo, id est, duplici pasto foveat. Sit igitur præfatum monasterium omni terrenæ servitutis jugo liberum, tribus exceptis, rata videlicet expeditione, pontis arcisve restauratione. Si quis vero tam epilempticus philargyriæ seductus amentia, quod non optamus, hanc nostræ munificenciæ dapsilitatem ausu temerario infringere temptaverit, sit ipse alienatus a consorcio sanctæ Dei ecclesiæ, necnon et a participatione sacrosancti corporis et sanguinis Jesu Christi filii Dei, per quem totus terrarum orbis ab antiquo humani generis inimico liberatus est, et cum Juda Christi proditore sinistra in parte deputatus, ni prius hic digna satisfactione humiliter pœnituerit quod contra sanctam Dei ecclesiam rebellis agere præsumpserit, nec in vita hac practica veniam, nec in theorica requiem apostata optineat ullam; set æternis baratri incendiis trusus, cum Anania et Saphira jugiter miserrimus crucietur. Anno Dominicæ incarnationis DCCCC.LXXXI. Indictione IX. scripta est hæc carta, hiis testibus consentientibus, quorum inferius nomina caraxantur.

✠ Ego Adelred rex totius Britanniæ præfatam donationem cum sigillo sanctæ crucis confirmavi. ✠ Dunstan Dorobernensis ecclesiæ archiepiscopus ejusdem regis benivolentiam consensi. ✠ Ego Alfthrith ejusdem regis mater hanc donationem confirmavi. ✠ Oswald archiepiscopus triumphale trophæum agiæ crucis impressi. ✠ Adeluuold Pictaviensis[1] ecclesiæ episcopus prædictum donum consensi. ✠ Ego Alfstan Londoniensis ecclesiæ episcopus consignavi. ✠ Ego Athelgar episcopus trophæum agiæ crucis imposui. ✠ Ego Alfstan episcopus jubente rege signum crucis infixi. ✠ Ego Alfstan episcopus consensum præbui figens crucem. ✠ Ego Athulf episcopus crucis modum manu propria subscripsi. ✠ Ego Ælfric episcopus. ✠ Ego Ælfeah episcopus. ✠ Ego Cerdic episcopus. ✠ Ego Ædelric episcopus. ✠ Ego Wulfr. episcopus. ✠ Ego Alchere dux. ✠ Ego Athelwine dux. ✠ Ego Bryhtnod dux. ✠ Ego Athelbriht dux. ✠ Ego Athelmere dux. ✠ Ego Ædwine dux. ✠ Ego

[1] Sic pro Wintoniensis.

Athelweard minister. ✠ Ego Oedelweard minister. ✠ Ego Beorthwold minister. ✠ Ego Ælfric minister. Ego Brihtwold minister. Ego Ordelm minister. Ego God minister. Ego Ælfric minister. Ego Leofwine minister. Ego Leofric minister. Ego Ælmere minister. Ego Goduuine minister. Ego Alwine minister. Ego Ælfric minister.

KING ÆTHELRED. DCCCC.LXXXIII.

Nunc mutando fragilitas mortalis vitæ marcescit, et rotunda sæculorum volubilitas inanescit, ac in carorum propinquorum amicorumque amissione conqueritur ac defletur. Ideo ego Ædelred, totius Brittanie basileus, quandam capturam in amne Derentan constructam, quæ usitato æt Ginanhecce nuncupatur vocabulo, et exiguam ruris partiunculam prædictæ capturæ piscatori atque procuratori ad usus necessarios aptam, Adelwoldo mihi episcoporum carissimo, perpetua largitus sum hereditate, ut ipse vita comite voti compos habeat, et post vitæ suæ terminum quibuscunque voluerit cleronomis immunem derelinquat. Hoc autem, in nomine alme Trinitatis et individue Unitatis, atque in veneratione sanctæ Dei genitricis semperque virginis Mariæ et omnium sanctorum angelorum, patriarcharum, prophetarum, apostolorum, martyrum, confessorum, et virginum, ut nemo successorum meorum nec aliquis hominum, altioris vel inferioris gradus, aliam capturam huic anteponere a ripa usque ad ripam ullo modo præsumat. Quod si quis, diabolico instinctus spiritu, presumpserit, anathema sit, et nisi satisfactione sui reatus cessando veniam optinuerit, in maledictione Domini persistens, æternis barathri incendiis punitus crucietur; abyssos vero gurgitum ante capturam locatos nemo retibus piscari, sine licentia episcopi, sive capturam possidentis, ullo modo audeat. Si quis vero in tribus abyssis ad capturam ipsam pertinentibus retia piscando traxerit vel statuerit, furti crimine obnoxius teneatur.

Termini vero hujus exigui telluris hi sunt:

Of Dærentan on þa ealdan þornræwe to þam æsce· on þa þornræwe þæt eft innon Dærentan.

From the Darent to the old thorn-row; to the ash on the thorn-row; then again to the Darent.

Hæc sunt nomina gurgitum qui ad piscandum extraneis cum anathemate prohibiti sunt:

Cytala pol· Lym pol· Wylles muþa.

Kettle pool, Lyme pool, Well's mouth.

Anno Dominice incarnationis DCCC[C].LXXXIII. scripta est [hæc] carta, his testibus consentientibus quorum nomina inferius caraxantur.

Ego Æþelredus rex præfatam donationem concessi. Ego Dunstan, Dorovernensis episcopus consensi. Ego Oswald archiepiscopus confirmavi. Ego Aþelwold episcopus corroboravi. Ego Ælfðryð, prefati regis mater confirmavi. Ego Ordbryht abbas confirmavi. Ego Leofric abbas consensi. Ego Ælfere dux consignavi.

OF THE LAND AT WOULDHAM. BEFORE DCCCC.LXXXVIII.

Ðus wæron þa seox sulung æt Wuldaham Sc̃e Andrea geseald into Hrofeceastre.

✠ Æðelbryht cinc hit gebocode þam apostole on ece yrfe· ⁊ betæhte hit þam biscope Eardulfe to bewitenne· ⁊ his æftergæncan. Þa betweonan þam wearð hit ũte· ⁊ hæfdon hit cynegas oð Eadmund cinc. Þa gebohte hit Ælfstan Heahstãninc æt þam cince mid hundtwelftigan mancesan goldes ⁊ þrittigan pundan· ⁊ ꝥ him sealde mæst eal Ælfeh his sunu. After Eadmunde cincge þa gebo-

Thus were the six sulungs at Wouldham given to St Andrew's at Rochester.

✠ King Æthelberht chartered it to the apostle in perpetuity, and committed it to the bishop Eardulf and his successors to administer. Then in the meanwhile it became alienated, and the kings had it until king Eadmund. Then Ælfstân Heahstân's son bought it of the king for a hundred and twenty mancuses of gold and thirty pounds; almost all of which his son Ælfeh gave him. After king code hit Eadred cinc Ælfstāne on ece yrfe. Ðа æfter Ælfstānes dæge wæs Ælfeh his sunu his yrfewærd· ⁊ ꝥ he leac on hālre tungon· ⁊ ofteah Ælfrice his breðer landes ⁊ æhta· butan he hwæt æt him geearnode. Ða for þære broðor sibbe geuðe he him Earhiðes· ⁊ Cræggan· ⁊ Ænesfordes· ⁊ Wuldahames his dæg. Ða oferbād Ælfeh his broðor ⁊ feng to his læne. Ða hæfde Ælfric suna Eadric hatte· ⁊ Ælfeh nænne. Ða geuðe Ælfeh þam Eadrice Earhiðes· ⁊ Crægan· ⁊ Wuldahames· ⁊ hæfde himsylf Ænesford. Ða gewāt Eadric ǣr Ælfeh cwideleas· ⁊ Ælfeh feng to his læne. Ða hæfde Eadric lāfe ⁊ nān bearn· þa geuðe Ælfeh hire hire morgengife æt Crægan· ⁊ stōd Earhið· ⁊ Wuldaham· ⁊ Lytlanbrōc on his læne. Þa him eft geþuhte· ða nam he his feorme on Wuldaham· ⁊ on þam oðran wolde· ac hine geyflade· ⁊ he ða sænde to þam arcebiscope Dunstane· ⁊ he com to Scylfe to him· ⁊ he cwæð his cwide beforan him· ⁊ he sette ænne cwide to Cristes cyrican· ⁊ oðerne to Sc̄e Andrea· ⁊ þane þriddan sealde his lāfe. Ða bræc syþþan Leofsunu· þurh ꝥ

Eadmund, king Eadred chartered it to Ælfstân in perpetual inheritance. Then after Ælfstân's day, Ælfeh his son was his heir; and that he declared in healthy language, and withdrew from Ælfric his brother land and possessions, unless he might merit aught from him. Then for brotherly kinship he gave him Erith, and Cray, and Ensford, and Wouldham, for his day. Then Ælfeh survived his brother, and took to his fee. But Ælfric had a son named Eadric, and Ælfeh none. Then Ælfeh gave to Eadric Erith, and Cray, and Wouldham, and held Ensford for himself. Then Eadric died before Ælfeh intestate, and Ælfeh took to his fee. Then Eadric had a relict and no child, and Ælfeh gave her her morning-gift at Cray; and Erith, and Wouldham, and Littlebrook remained in his possession. When afterwards it seemed good to him, he took up his abode in Wouldham, and would in the others, but he fell sick; and he then sent to the archbishop Dunstân, and he came to Scylf to him, and he declared his testament before him, and he wīf þe he nam· Eadrices lāfe· þæne cwide· ⁊ herewade þæs arcebiscopes gewitnesse· rād þa innon þa land mid þam wīfe butan witena dōme. Ða man ꝥ þam biscope ciðde· þa gelædde se biscop ahnunga ealles Ælfehes cwides to Earhiðe· on gewitnesse Ælfstānes biscopes on Lundene ⁊ ealles þæs hiredes· ⁊ ðæs æt Cristes cyrican· ⁊ þæs biscopes Ælfstanes an Hrofeceastre· ⁊ Wulfsics preostes þæs scirigmannes· ⁊ Bryhtwaldes on Mæreweorðe· ⁊ ealra East Cantwarena· ⁊ West Cantwarena· ⁊ hit wæs gecnæwe on Suð Seaxan· ⁊ on West Seaxan· ⁊ on Middel Seaxan· ⁊ on Est Seaxan· ⁊ se arcebiscop mid his selfes āþe geāhnode Gode ⁊ Sc̄e Andrea· mid þam bōcan on Cristes hrōde· þa land þe Leofsunu him to teah· ⁊ þæne āð nam Wulsige se scirigman· þa he nolde· to þæs cinges handa· ⁊ þær wæs gōd eaca ten hundan mannan þe þane āð sealdan.

placed one testament at Christchurch, and a second at St Andrew's, and the third he gave to his relict. Then Leofsunu, through the wife he had taken, Eadric's relict, violated the testament, and contemned the archbishop's witnessing: rode then into the land with the woman, without the decree of the 'witan'. When that was made known to the bishop, then the bishop laid claims in all Ælfeh's testament at Erith, in the witness of Ælfstân bishop of London, and of all the convent, and of that at Christchurch, and of the bishop Ælfstân of Rochester, and of the shireman Wulfsige's priest, and of Bryhtwald at Mereworth, and of all the East Kentishmen and West Kentishmen. And it was known in Sussex, and in Wessex, and in Middlesex, and in Essex. And the archbishop, with his own oath, claimed for God and St Andrew, with the charters, on Christ's rood, the lands that Leofsunu took to himself: and Wulfsige the shireman, on the part of the king, received the oath, as he [Leofsunu] declined it. And there was a good addition of ten hundred men who gave the oath.

IDEM LATINE[1].

Isto tali ordine fuerunt illæ VI. sulingæ, quæ vocantur

[1] The Latin is evidently of much later date than the Saxon, but of

Uuldeham, primum venditæ ecclesiæ Sancti Andreæ apostoli de Hrofecestra, et postea extractæ, et iterum emptæ ipsi ecclesiæ, ac tandem, per beatum Dunstanum archiepiscopum, juramento mille virorum eidem ecclesiæ acquisitæ, et jure hereditario in æternum relictæ.

✠ Rex Æthelberhtus primum hereditaverat de Uuldeham apostolum Sanctum Andream, et ecclesiam suam in Hrofecestra æterno jure, et commisit illud manerium Eardulfo episcopo Hrofensi ad custodiendum, et ejus successoribus. Igitur in manibus successorum ablatum est iterum apostolo et ecclesiæ suæ in manibus regum, ita quod plures reges, unus post alterum habuerunt illud postea, usque ad tempus regis Eadmundi. Tunc quidam probus homo nomine Ælfstanus Heahstaninc emit illud a rege Eadmundo, et dedit ei pro illo centum duodecim mancas auri, et xxx. libras denariorum. Hujus pecuniæ majorem partem dedit postea ipsi regi Ælfegus filius ipsius Ælfstani. Postea, mortuo rege Eadmundo, Eadredus rex hereditavit inde prædictum Ælfstanum in æternam hereditatem. Itaque post mortem hujus Ælfstani, præfatus Ælfegus, qui regi Eadmundo dederat majorem partem pecuniæ pro patre suo propter Uuldeham, successit huic Ælfstano in hereditatem. Qui statim conclusit, et omnino confirmavit totum quod pater suus in vita sua fecerat. Hic autem fratri suo Ælfrico et terras atque pecunias patris sui ita plene subtraxit, quod ipse Ælfricus nichil omnino inde poterat habere nisi servitio illud ab eo promeruisset, quemadmodum quilibet extraneus. Tamen præcogitatus tandem Ælfegus, propter consanguinitatis fraternitatem, concessit illi Earhetham, et Cræiam, et Æinesfordam, et Uuldeham, in diebus vitæ suæ tantum in præstito solummodo. Itaque mortuo Ælfrico Ælfegus statim omnia præstita sua, quæ fratri suo viventi præstiterat [resumpsit]. Ælfricus autem habuit filium nomine Eadricum, Ælfegus vero non habuit. Et ideo Ælfegus concessit illi Eadrico Earhetham, et Cræiam, et Uuldeham, et retinuit in manu sua Æinesford. Mortuus autem

---

which it is a useful paraphrase, elucidating some passages where the Saxon seems obscure.

ipse Eadricus absque commendatione vel distributione rerum suarum, tunc iterum Ælfegus accepit præstita sua omnia. Habebat etiam ipse Eadricus uxorem, et non liberos. Hac de causa concessit Ælfegus illi viduæ donum dotis suæ tantum quod ei dederat Eadricus, quando eam primum accepit uxorem in Cræia. Et tunc remansit Litelbroc et Uuldeham in præstito suo. Postea, quando ei visum placitum fuit, accepit firmam suam in Uuldeham, et in aliis volebat similiter facere; sed iterum infirmatus est. Et quia infirmatus valde, misit ilico ad archiepiscopum Dunstanum ut veniret ad eum, et locutus est ei in loco illo qui vocatur Scelfa. Ibi coram archiepiscopo fecit Ælfegus commendationem sive distributionem omnium rerum suarum, et constituit unam partem ecclesiæ Christi Cantuariæ, et alteram partem ecclesiæ Sancti Andreæ, et terciam partem uxori suæ. Postea fuit quidam Leofsunu, qui uxorem Eadrici nepotis Ælfegi relictam accepit sibi in uxorem; et per ipsam mulierem incepit frangere constitutiones Ælfegi, quas fecerat coram archiepiscopo, et vituperare archiepiscopum, et testimonium ejus irritum facere. Tandem, multa stimulatus cupidine, cum illa muliere sua, quasi quadam securitate illius uxoris suæ inductus, intravit in terras illas, absque consilio et judicio sapientum virorum. Quod ubi archiepiscopus audivit, sine omni mora induxit statim calumniam proprietatis in omnem distributionem Ælfegi, cui ipsemet affuit, et quæ per eum facta fuerat. Diem ergo placiti hujus rei constituit archiepiscopus apud Erhetham, per testimonium Ælfstani episcopi Lundoniæ, et Ælfstani episcopi Hrofecestræ, et totius conventus ecclesiæ Christi Cantuariæ, et omnium orientalium et occidentalium Cantiæ, et Wulfsii presbyteri, qui tunc vocatus *scirman*, id est, judex comitatus, et Brihtuualdi de Mærewurtha. Ad ultimum ita notificatum in Suthseaxa, et in Westseaxa, et in Middelseaxa, et in Eastseaxa, quod archiepiscopus Dunstanus, cum libris ecclesiastici juris, et signo crucis Christi, quam suis manibus tenebat, sui solius juramento, acquisivit æternam hereditatem Deo et Sancto Andreæ apostolo omnes terras illas, quas Leofsunu sibi usurpabat. Ipsum vero juramentum archiepiscopi accepit Uulfsi scirman, id est, judex provinciæ ad opus regis, quandoquidem ipse Leofsunu illud suscipere nolebat. Insuper ad hoc perficiendum fuit hoc quoque maximum adjumentum, temporibusque futuris maximum securitatis probamentum, quod decies centum viri electissimi ex omnibus illis supradictis comitatibus juraverunt post archiepiscopum in ipsa cruce Christi ratum, et æternæ memoriæ stabile fore sacramentum quod archiepiscopus juraverat.

---

* KING ÆTHELRED. DCCCC.XCIII.

DE ECCLESIÆ LIBERTATE [ABBANDUNENSIS].

☧ Al[tithr]oni [Tonantis onomate. Orthodoxorum vigoris æcclesiastici monitu creberrime instruimur] ut illi opp[ido subjecti supp]editantes famulemur qui totius mun[di fa]bricam [miro inef]fabilique serie disp[onens] microcosmum, Adam videlicet, tandem quadriformi plasmatum materia, almo ad sui similitudinem instinctum spiramine, universis quæ in infimis formaverat uno probandi causa excepto vetitoque, præficiens paradisiace amœnitatis jocunditate conlaterana [Eva scilic]et comite decentissime collocavit. Larvarica, pro dolor, seductus cavillatione, versipellis suasibilisque tergiversatione viraginis pellectus, anathematis alogia ambro pomum momordit vetitum, et sibi ac posteris in h[oc ær]umnoso dejectus sæculo loetum promeruit perpetuum; vaticinantibus siquidem prophetis et cælitus superni Regis diuturna clandestino præsagia dogmate promentibus nitide orthodoxis, eulogium ex supernis deferens, non ut Judæorum seditiosa elingu[e] fatetur loquacitas, sed priscorum atque modernorum lepidissimam ambiens facundiam, Arrianas Sabellianasque, proterendo nenias anagogico infrustrans famine, nosque ab obtunsi cecitate umbraminis, ad supernorum alacrimoniam patrimoniorum advocans, angelus supernis elapsus liminibus in aurem intemeratæ virginis ut evangelica promulgant famina, stupenda cecinisse videtur carmina; cui ecclesia tota, videlicet catholica, consona voce altibohando proclamat: "Beata es, virgo Maria, quæ credidisti, perficientur in te quæ dicta sunt tibi a Domino." Mirum dictu, incarnatur Verbum et incorporatur, scilicet illud de quo evangelista supereminens universorum altitudine sensuum inquit: "In principio erat verbum, et verbum erat aput Deum, et Deus erat verbum," et rl. Qua, videlicet, sumpta de virgine incarnatione antiquæ virginis facinus demitur, et cunctis mulieribus nitidis precluens taumatibus decus irrogatur. Intacta igit[ur redo]lente [Christi div]initate, passaque ipsius humanitate, libertas addictis clementer contigit servulis. Hinc ego Æþelræd altithrono amminiculante Anglorum ceterarumque gentium in circuitu triviatim persistentium basileus, non immemor angustiarum michi meæque nationi septimo regni [mei ann]o, et deinceps frequenter ac multipliciter accidentium; post decessum videlicet beatæ memoriæ michique interno amore dilectissimi Adeluuoldi episcopi, cujus industria ac pastoralis cura non solum m[ea]e, verum etiam universorum hujus patriæ tam pr[incipum] quam subditorum utilitati superno Plasmatore inspirante, consuluit, mecum plurima voluere tacitus cepi, et quæ tantorum causa periculorum existeret studiose percunctari sollicitus curavi. Tanto igitur talique studio magnopere incitatus, et archana quæque dilig[enter mal]a mecum examinans, tandem Domini compunctus gratia, ad memoriam reduxi partim hæc infortunia pro meæ juventutis ignorantia, quæ d[iv]ersis solet uti moribus, partim etiam pro quorundam illorum detestanda philargiria, qui meæ utilitati consulere debebant, accid[iss]e. Siquidem inter cætera memoriæ occurrit, me rogatu quorundam talium, Uulfgari, scilicet, episcopi defuncti, atque [abbati]s Ælfrici qui adhuc superest sacri Æbbandunensis cœnobii [pote]statem, pro munere in se . . . . beate [mem]orie episcopus Adeluuold a predecessoribus meis, Eadredo, scilicet, rege, patruo patris mei, necnon et a patruo meo rege Eaduuige, nec minus et a patre meo, rege, videlicet, E[ad]garo, ad usum monachorum Domino [nostro Jhesu Christo eju]sque genitric[i] Mariæ humilitatis et obedientiæ, ceterarumque virtutum meritis, in æternam promeruit hereditatem, et [in] perhennem adquisivit libertatem. Hæc igitur mecum vigilanti pectore volvens, et citius a tanto tamque exhorrendo anathemate liberari cupiens, anno Dominicæ Incarnationis DCCCC.XCIII., mei autem regni XVII. sinodale concilium Uuintoniæ, in die sancto Pentecosten fieri jussi, illucque episcopis, et abbatibus, ac ceteris optimatum meorum p[r]imoribus verba salutatoria et pacifica benignissime destinavi, cun[ct]osque, Christi inspirante gratia, monui, ut quæque superno Creatori digna, quæque spiritali animæ meæ saluti, seu regali meæ dignitati congrua, quæque etiam omni Anglorum populo oportuna valerent, Domino consulente, in commune tractarent, vovens etiam . . . . [v]ita comite, et retroactas ad purum cohercere neglegentias, et juxta prædecessorum meorum decreta, Jhesu Christo Domino nostro ejusque genitrici priscum restituere libertatis cyrographum. Hoc illi meo, immo Christi, monitu simul et hortatu, magnopere delectat[i vo]ti compotes, Salvatori Christo gratias egerunt, et quæque condigna salubriter instituta sanxerunt, pacto spiritali confirmaverunt. Nunc autem ego Æþelræd, Anglorum, Christo opitulante, basileus, quo debitum voti mei factis adimpleam, et ut æternæ libertatis altithroni Moderatoris clementia merear optinere consortium, pretium quod michi dux præfatus Ælfric, pro fratris sui Eaduuini prioratu contulit, quo præfata Christi sanctæque ejus genitricis hereditas iniqua servitute est venundata, perpetualiter anathematizando reicio, et gratuita Domini inspirante gratia, meorumque optimatum, tam laicorum quam ordinatorum, rogatus simul et usus consilio, eidem sanctæ Christi genitricis æcclesiæ monachisque inibi degentibus æternam privilegii, ut prædecessores mei, renovandam concedo libertatem. Hujus etenim renovandæ libertatis auctoritas, Christi auctoritate nostraque largitate, concessa et corroborata est die XVI. kalendarum Augustarum, in oratorio vici qui usitato Gillingaham nominari solet, missæque cælebratione peracta, sub horum testium præsentia, me assensum præbente, confirmata est, abbatis scilicet Ælfsini, consangineique mei Æþelmæri, necnon et avunculi mei Ordulfi, ac prioratum præfati Æbbandunensis cœnobii in manu et potestate Uulfgari abbatis michi humillima devotione subjecti, gratis sine pretio voluntariæ ren[o]vando commisi; hancque privilegii libertatem, tam sibi quam cunctæ simul ejusdem sanctæ æcclesiæ congregationi pro mille quingentis missarum sollemniis, ac mille ducentis psalteriorum melodiis, quas spontanea devotione, pro æterna animæ meæ redemptione decantaverunt, æternaliter renovandam cum sancte crucis impressione concessi, quatinus post decessum ejusdem præfati abbatis Uulfgari, cujus temporibus hæc ipsa libertatis restauratio Christo suff[rag]ante concessa est, quem sibi universa præfati cœnobii congregatio apto elegerit consilio, secundum regularia beati Benedicti instituta, abbatem juste exodem f[rat]rum cuneo eligens constituat.

Hujus privilegii libertas deinceps usu perpetuo a cunctis teneatur catholicis, nec extraneorum quispiam, tyrannica fretus contumacia, in prædicto monasterio jus arripiens exerceat potestatis, sed ejusdem cœnobii collegium perpetuæ, ut prædixi, libertatis glorietur privilegio. Sit autem præfatum monasterium omni terrenæ servitutis [jugo] eodem tenore liberum, quo a prædecessoribus nostris catholicis, a Sancto Leone videlicet papa et Cœnulfo rege catholico, vetusto continetur privilegio, Hrethuno abbate optinente, solutum. Agri equidem ad usus monachorum, Domino nostro Jhesu Christo ejusque genitrici Mariæ priscis modernisque temporibus a regibus et religiosis utriusque sexus hominibus, et a meipso meoque patri Eadgaro rege, fratreque ejus meo patruo rege Eadwigo, eorumque patruo, scilicet, Eadredo, rege fidelissimo, restituendo jure concessi sunt, ejusdem perpetuæ sint libertatis. Nam reges præfati rus quod Abbandun nuncupatur, quod rex Ceadwealla Domino nostro ejusque genitrici Mariæ priscis temporibus devoto concesserat animo, in quo prædecessores nostri, diabolica decepti avaritia, edificium sibi regale injuste construxerant, æcclesiæ Dei restituentes interdixerunt, ut regum nemo inibi pastum requireret, nec edificium in sempiternum construe[ret]. Quod ego Æðelred Anglorum basileus, optimatum meorum us[us c]onsilio, tam meis quam meorum successorum temporibus, fixum in nomine Patris, et Filii, et Spiritus Sancti, fieri in æternum precipio. Tempore siquidem quo rura quæ Domino devoto per hoc modernum privilegium restauravi animo, injuste a sancta Dei æcclesia ablata fue[ran]t, perfidi quique novas sibi hereditarias kartas usurpantes ediderunt. Sed in Patris, et Filii, et Spiritus Sancti nomine precipimus, ut catholicorum nemo easdem recipiat, sed a cunctis repudiatæ fidelibus in anathemate deputentur, veteri jugiter vigente privilegio. Si quis vero tam epilempticus phylargiriæ seductus amentia, quod non optamus, hanc nostræ munificentiæ renovatam libertatem ausu temerario infringere temptaverit, sit ipse alienatus a consortio sanctæ Dei æcclesiæ, necnon et a participatione sacrosancti corporis et sanguinis Domini nostri Jhesu Christi, per quem totus terrarum orbis ab antiquo hum[ani g]eneris inimico liberatus est, et cum Juda Christi proditore in sinistra parte deputatus, ni prius hic digna satisfactione humilis penituerit quod contra sanctam Dei æclesiam rebellis agere præsumpsit; nec in vita hac practica veniam, nec in [the]orica requiem apostata optineat ullam, sed æternis barathri incendiis trusus jugiter miserrimus crucietur.

Anno Dominice incarnationis, ut prædixi, DCCCC.XCIII., Indict. VI., humillimo rogatu prefati et devoti abbatis Uulfgari, scriptum est hujus renovatæ libertatis privilegium, his testibus consentientibus quorum inferius nomina, secundum uniuscujusque dig[nit]atem utriusque ordinis decusatim Domino disponente karaxantur.

✠ Ego Æþelred, Brittanniæ Anglorum monarchus, hoc tauma[te cruci]s roboravi.

✠ Ego Sigeric, Dorobernensis æcclesiæ archieps̄, ejusdem regis beniv[ole]ntiam subscripsi.

✠ Ego Ælfstan Lundoniensis æcłæ eps̄ hanc regis munificentiam confirmavi.

✠ Ego Ælfheah Uuintoniensis æcłæ eps̄ hanc renovationis libertatem corroboravi.

✠ Ego Ælfric Corvinensis parrochiæ eps̄, quæ præfatum adjacet monasterium, huic dono sanctam crucem impressi.

✠ Ego Ælfheah, Licetfeldensis æcłæ eps̄, testudinem sanctæ crucis depinxi.

✠ Ego Æscwig, Dorccensis æcłæ eps̄, hoc regale donum consolidavi.

✠ Ego Þeodred, Orientalium Anglorum eps̃ huic largitati assensum prebui.

✠ Ego Ælfstan, Hrofensis æclæ eps̃, huic dapsilitati crucem imposui.

✠ Ego Ordbyrht, Australium Saxonum eps̃, sigillum sanctæ crucis annotavi.

✠ Ego Wulfsige Scirburnensis æclæ eps̃ gaudenter consensi.

✠ Ego Ealdulf, Wigornensis æclæ eps̃, hilari vultu subscripsi.

Ego Aþulf, Herefordensis æclesiæ eps̃, ... di.

Ego Sigar, Wyllensis æclæ eps̃, ita posse . . . . [si]gnum duxi.

Ego Alfwold, Cridiensis æclæ eps̃, huic sc[ript]o non contradixi.

Ego Ealdred, Cornubiensis æclæ eps̃, hoc dec[retum] consentiendo laudavi.

Ego Ælfðryð, mater ejusdem regis, hujus doni fautrix extiti.

Ego Æþelstan, ejusdem regis filius, hoc stare non rennui.

Ego Ecgbyrht, ejusdem quoque regis filius, assensum præbere non distuli.

Ego Eadmund, ejusdem etiam regis filius, hoc posse fieri non interdixi.

Ego Eadred, ejusdem quidem regis filius, hoc mihi placere professus sum.

Ego Uulfgar, abb̃. Abbandunens. cœnobii, hoc sintagma triumphans dictavi.

Ego Ælfweard, Glæst. abb̃.
✠ Ego Ælfsige, Niw̃. abb̃.
✠ Ego Wulfric, Aug̃. abb̃.
✠ Ego Byrhtnoþ, Æliḡ. abb̃.
✠ Ego Lifinc, [F]ont̃. abb̃.
✠ Ego Ælfric, Meal. abb̃.
Ego Ælfere, Baþan abb̃.
Ego Leofric, Micel. abb̃.
✠ Ego Ælfhun, Middel. abb̃.
Ego Byrhthelm, Eaxc̃. abb̃.
Ego Æþelric, Æþel. abb̃.
Ego Wulfsige, Westm̃. abb̃.
Ego Germanus, Ram̃. abb̃.
Ego Kenulf, Burh. abb̃.
Ego Godeman, Jorñ. abb̃.
Ego Alfwold, Wind̃. abb̃.
✠ [Ego] . . . . [Al]bañ. abb̃.
[Ego Æþel]weard dux.
Ego Ælfric dux.
Ego Ælfhelm dux.

Ego Ælfsige mil.
Ego Æþ[e]lsige mil.
Ego [Æþel]mær mil.
[Ego By]rhtwold mil.
[Ego O]rdulf mil.
[Ego W]ulfheah mil.
[Ego W]ulfric mil.
[Ego W]ulfgeat mil.
✠ Ego Ælfwig, Westm. abb.

---

* KING ÆTHELRED. DCCCC.XCIII.

DE TERRARUM RESTITUTIONE.

✠ Regnante in perpetuum Domino nostro Jhesu Christo, omniumque regna sæculorum magni moderaminis imperio gubernante. Ego Aþelred, ipsius opitulante gratia rex Anglorum, inter varias hujus labentis seculi vicissitudines ad memoriam reduxi qualiter in tempore pueritie mee erga me gestum fuerit, dum pater meus rex Eadgar, universe terre viam ingrediens, senex et plenus dierum migravit ad Dominum; quod videlicet omnes utriusque ordinis optimates ad regni gubernacula moderanda fratrem meum Eaduuardum unanimiter elegerunt, mihique terras ad regios pertinentes filios in meos usus tradiderunt. Ex quibus, scilicet, terris quasdam pater meus dum regnaret omnipotenti Christo ejusque genitrici Sancte Marie ad monasterium quod Abbandun nuncupatur, pro redemptione anime sue, concessit: hoc est Bedeuuinde cum omnibus ad se pertinentibus, Hisseburna cum universis suis appendicibus, Burhbec omnesque sibi adjacentes redditus. Que statim terre, juxta decretum et preceptionem cunctorum optimatum de prefato sancto cenobio violenter abstracte, meeque ditioni, hisdem precipientibus, sunt subacte; quam rem si juste aut injuste fecerint ipsi sciant. Deinde cum frater meus hoc erumpnosum deseruit seculum, et sibi a Deo predestinatum percepit interminabilis vite emolumentum, ego, annuente Christo, et regalium simul et ad regios filios pertinentium terrarum suscepi dominium. Nunc autem, quia mihi videtur esse valde molestum patris mei incurrere et portare maledictum, retinendo hoc quod ipse pro sue anime redemptione Deo contulit donarium, et quia gratia Dei me ad intelligibilem perducere dignata est etatem, mihique per meorum optimatum decreta affluentem et copiosam terrarum largita est portionem, iccirco et ego ex mea propria hereditate prefatum sanctum cenobium munere congruo honorare, et oportuna possessionum largitione ditare dispono; primum pro Dei Omnipotentis ejusque sancte genitricis amore, ut ipsa pro me pia interventrix esse dignetur ad Dominum Deum nostrum; deinde pro anime genitoris mei dileccione, meeque proprie anime eterna redemptione, necnon et pro meorum causa liberorum, qui easdem prefatas sibi attrahere, sueque ditioni cogitant subicere terras. Nomina vero terrarum, quas ad prefatum libenti animo concedo monasterium, hec sunt: Unum scilicet apud Feornebeorh alterum apud Wilmaleahtun, tercium apud Cyrne. Has terrarum portiones Alfric cognomento Puer a quadam vidua Eadfled appellata violenter abstraxit, ac deinde cum in ducatu suo contra me et contra omnem gentem meam reus existeret, et he quas prenominavi portiones et universe quas possederat terrarum possessiones mee subacte sunt ditioni, quando ad sinodale concilium ad Cyrneceastre universi optimates mei simul in unum convenerunt, et eundem Alfricum majestatis reum de hac patria profugum expulerunt, et universa ab illo possessa michi jure possidenda omnes unanimo consensu decreverunt. Deinde prefatam viduam, pro amore optimatum meorum, qui ejus apud me extiterant advocati, suam hereditatem possidere clementi benignitate permisi, et ipsa tandem, in extrema sue migrationis sententia, mihi rursus earumdem terrarum possessionem benigno et libenti animo in perhennem dereliquit hereditatem. Tellurem vero ad Pyrian, quam etiam ad idem prefatum concedo monasterium, unam illarum constat esse terrarum quas Adelward Ceolflede filius mihi eternaliter possidendas pro mea donavit amicitia. Omni vulgo longe lateque satis est cognitum qualiter ipse et frater ejus contra me rei extiterint, qualiterque ambo meam inimicitiam, exigentibus suis reatibus, incurrerint. Hec prefatarum descriptio terrarum facta est per admonitionem Ordulfi avunculi mei, atque Aþelmari, consanguinitate mihi conglutinati, et Wlgati ministri mei dilecti, necnon et abbatis mei Wlfgari tota mihi devotione benigni, qui me frequenti suggestione cum ceterorum fidelium commonuit suasione quatinus Dei Omnipotentis hereditatem ex aliqua parte innovare et augere curarem: quod et feci, propter Christi, qui me in regno sublimavit, amorem, et eorum qui me amica assiduitate ad meam exortantur necessariam et eternam salutem, et propter humilem et benignam quam mihi prefatus abba fideliter et gratanter exibere solet obedientiam. Hoc quoque voluntatis mee beneficium palam cunctis innotesco, quod earumdem possessionum terras in unaquaque cui adjacent provincia, cum omnibus ad se pertinentibus, sive in prediorum municipiis, sive in tributo, sive in thelonio, sive in quocumque negotio, quod in unoquoque rure diverso modo solet exigi, plena libertate ab omni terrene servitutis jugo liberas esse concedo, quemadmodum pater meus supranominatarum portionem terrarum ab universa mundanarum rerum servitute liberas esse concessit, exceptis tribus, rata videlicet expeditione, pontis arcisve restauratione. Illud etiam cum sancte Trinitatis, et individue Unitatis, et beate Marie semper virginis auctoritate precipio, ut nullus hominum presumat hanc donationem occasione qualibet immutare, nec territorii codicem vel cirografi dictatum contra mee munificentie scripta in medium proferre; sed universa illa antiqua territoria, supradicto exigente reatu, semper in posterum pro nichilo computentur, et ad nichilum redacta omnium sputis obnoxia conculcentur, et hujus privilegii decreta stabili et inconcussa soliditate roborentur. Si quis autem, instigante diabolo, hec consulta tam mea quam divina auctoritate corroborata violare presumpserit, sive meus sit filius, sive dux, sive episcopus, sive minister, aut cujuscumque dignitatis extiterit, Omnipotens Deus, sanctaque ejus genitrix semperque virgo Maria, et omnis supernorum sancta virtus exercituum majestatem divinam incessabili voce laudantium, hunc in vita ista despiciat, et despectum in futuro seculo sine fine disperdat illum, nisi congrua satisfactione ante exitum suum emendaverit quod contra Deum sanctamque Mariam deliquit. Amen.

Hujus privilegii descriptio jugiter in prenominato conservetur monasterio, ut sit libertas externa librorum ad universas supradictarum possessiones terrarum quas Omnipotenti Deo ejusque sancte genitrici Marie ad idem cœnobium, benigno et libenti animo, concessi, et concessas eterna stabilitate commendavi.

---

* KING ÆTHELRED. DCCCC.XCIV.

✠ Ðis is se freols ðe Æþelred cynincg het gesettan to þam bisceoprice in to Wielcynne· Ealdrede bisceope.	✠ This is the freedom which king Æthelred has commanded to be established in the bishopric, for the Welsh race, under bishop Ealdred.

✠ Rector altipolorum culminis, atque Architector summæ fabricæ æthereæ aulæ, ex nihilo quidem cuncta creavit, cœlum scilicet et terram et omnia quæ in eis sunt, candida quidem angelica agmina, solem, lunam, lucidaque astra, et cætera quæ super firmamento sunt; mundi autem fabricam inenarrabili disponens ordine, ut Genesis testatur: "Et hominem sexto die formavit ad similitudinem suam." Adam, videlicet, quadriformi plasmatum materia, unde nunc constat genus humanum, quæ in terris moratur, et ima terra larvarica latibula, ubi et Lucifer cum decimo ordine per superbiam de cœlo ruit. Sed et hoc invidet pestifer Chelidrus, protoplastum a Deo conditum intellexerat ut hoc impleret, a quo ipse miser et satelliti illius de cœlo projecti sunt. Heu, quidem boni creati sunt, sed miserabiliter decepti. Ideoque invidus Zabulus totis viribus homini invidet, suadet mulieri, mulier viro; per suasionem atque per inobedientiam ambo decepti sunt fraudulenter per gustum pomi ligni vetiti, atque amœnitate Paradisi dejecti sunt in hoc ærumnoso seculo, et lethum sibi ac posteris suis promeruerunt, atque in tetrum abyssi demersi sunt. Sed hoc misericors et piissimus Pater indoluit perire tamdiu nobilem creaturam sui imaginem; misertus est generi humano; misit nobis in tempore, id est, post quinque millia annorum, proprium filium suum, ut mundum perditum iterum renovaret; ut sicut mulier genuit mortem in mundo, ita per mulierem enixa est nobis vita in mundo; et sicut per delictum Adæ omnes corruimus, ita per obedientiam Christi omnes surreximus; et sicut mors per lignum intravit, ita et vita per lignum sanctæ crucis venit, et antiquum inimicum superavit, et fortis fortem alligavit, et in imo baratro retrusit. Juste periit qui injuste decepit, atque omnes antiquas turmas a fauce pessimi leonis eripuit, et ovem perditam in humeris posuit, et ad antiquam patriam reduxit, et decimum ordinem implevit. Unde ego Æðelredus, compunctus Dei misericordia, totius Albionis cæterarumque gentium triviatim persistentium basileus, dum plerumque cogitarem de hujus seculi caduci rebus transitoriis, quomodo superni Arbitris examine cuncta quæ videntur vana sunt, et quæ non videntur æterna, et cum transitoriis rebus perpetua præmia adquirantur: Qua de re nunc patefacio omnibus catholicis, quod cum consilio et licentia episcoporum ac principum et omnium optimatum meorum, quod pro amore Domini nostri Jhesu Christi, atque sancti confessoris Germani, necnon et beati eximii Petroci, pro redemptione animæ meæ, et pro absolutione criminum meorum, donavi episcopium Ealdredi episcopi, id est, in provincia Cornubiæ, ut libera sit, eique subjecta omnibusque posteris ejus, ut ipse gubernet atque regat suam parochiam sicuti alii episcopi qui sunt in mea ditione, locusque atque regimen Sancti Petroci semper in potestate ejus sit successorumque illius. Itaque omnium regalium tributorum libera sit atque laxata vi exactorum operum, pœnaliumque causarum, necnon et furum comprehensione cunctaque seculi gravedine, absque sola expeditione, atque libera perpetualiter permaneat.

Quicumque ergo hoc augere atque multiplicare voluerit, amplificet Deus bona illius in regione viventium, paceque nostra conglutinata vigens et florens, atque inter agmina beatitudinis tripudia succedat, qui nostræ donationis muneri consentiat. Si quis vero tam epilenticus philargyriæ seductus amentia, quod non optamus, hanc nostræ elemosinæ dapsilitatem ausu temerario infringere temtaverit, sit ipse alienatus a consortio sanctæ Dei ecclesiæ, necnon a participatione sacrosancti corporis et sanguinis Jhesu Christi filii Dei, per quem totus terrarum orbis ab antiquo humani generis inimico liberatus est, et cum Juda Christi proditore sinistra in parte deputatus, ni prius hic digna satisfactione humilis pœnituerit quod contra sanctam Dei ecclesiam rebellis agere præsumpsit; nec in vita hac practica veniam, nec in theorica requiem apostata obtineat ullam, sed æternis baratri incendiis trusus jugiter miserrimus crucietur.

Anno Dominicæ incarnationis DCCCC.XCIIII., Indictione VII., scripta est hæc cartula a venerabili archiepiscopo Sigerico, Dorobernensis ecclesiæ, hujus munificentiæ cyrographa, hiis testibus consentientibus, quorum inferius nomina decusatim Domino disponente caraxantur.

✠ Ego Æðelredus, Britanniæ totius Anglorum monarchus hoc agiæ crucis taumate roboravi. ✠ Ego Sigeric, Dorobernensis æcclesiæ archiepiscopus, prefati regis benevolentiæ lætus consensi. ✠ Ego Ælfheah præsul canonica subscriptione, manu propria, hilaris et triumphans subscripsi. ✠ Ego Ealdred, plebis Dei famulus, jubente rege, signum sanctæ crucis plaudens impressi. ✠ Ego Ælfwold pontifex, agiæ crucis testudine intepidus hoc donum lepidissime roboravi. ✠ Ego Ordbricht, legis Dei catascopus hoc eulogium propria chira devotus consolidavi. ✠ Ego Ælfrich, episcopus Wiltanæ civitatis, consensi et subscripsi. ✠ Ego Wulfsye, episcopus Shyreburnensis æcclesiæ consensi et subscripsi. ✠ Ego Æðelwerd dux. ✠ Ego Ælfric dux. ✠ Ego Leofric dux. ✠ Ego Leofwyne dux. ✠ Ego Leofric abbas. ✠ Ego Ælfred abbas. ✠ Ego Ælfric abbas. ✠ Ego Brichthelm abbas. ✠ Ego Æðelmar minister. ✠ Ego Ælfric minister. ✠ Ego Ælfwine minister. ✠ Ego Leofwyne minister. ✠ Ego Osulf minister.

WYNFLÆD. BEFORE DCCCC.XCV.

✠ Her cyþ on þysum gewrite hu Wynflæd gelædde hyre gewitnesse æt Wulfamere beforan Æþelrede cyninge. ꝥ wæs þonne Sigeric arcebiscop. ⁊ Ordbyrht biscop. ⁊ Ælfric ealderman. ⁊ Ælfþryþ þæs cyninges modor. ꝥ hi wæron ealle to gewitnesse ꝥ Ælfric sealde Wynflæde ꝥ land æt Haccebuman ⁊ æt Bradanfelda ongean ꝥ land æt Deccet. Þa sende se cyning þærrihte. be þam arcebiscope. ⁊ be þam þe þær mid him to gewitnesse wæron. to Leofwine ⁊ cyþdon him þis. Ða nolde he butan hit man sceote to sciregemote. þa dyde man swa. Ða sende se cyning be Æluere abbude his insegel to þam gemote æt Cwicelmes hlæwe. ⁊ grette ealle þa witan þe þær gesomnode wæron. ꝥ wære Æþelsige biscop. ⁊ Æscwig biscop. ⁊ Ælfric abbud. ⁊ eal sio scir. ⁊ bæd ⁊ het ꝥ hi scioldon Wynflæde ⁊ Leofwine swa rihtlice geseman swa him æfre rihtlicost þuhte. ⁊ Sigeric arcebiscop sende his swutelunga þærto. ⁊ Ordbyrht biscop his. Þa getæhte man Wynflæde ꝥ hio moste hit hyre geahnian. Ða ge-

✠ Here is made known, in this writing, how Wynflæd adduced her witnesses at Wolfmere, before king Æthelred. Then it was that Sigeric archbishop, and Ordbyrht bishop, and Ælfric aldorman, and Ælfthryth the king's mother, were all to witness that Ælfric gave to Wynflæd the land at Hagborne and at Bradfield, for the land at Datchet. Then the king sent forthwith, by the archbishop, and by those who were there to witness with him, to Leofwine, and made this known to him. Then he would not [comply] unless it were carried to the shire-mote; and they did so. Then the king sent by abbot Ælfere his brief to the mote at Cuckhamslow; and greeted all the 'witan' who were there assembled. That was Æthelsige bishop, and Æscwig bishop, and Ælfric abbot, and all the shire: and prayed and commanded that they should reconcile Wynflæd and Leofwine as justly as might ever seem to them most just. And Sigeric archbishop sent his declaration thereto, and Osbyrht bishop his. They then lædde hio þa ahnunga mid Ælfþryþe fultume þæs cyninges modor· ꝥ is þonne ærest· Wulfgar abbud· ⁊ Wulfstan priost· ⁊ Æfic þara æþelinga discsten[1]· ⁊ Eadwine· ⁊ Eadelm· ⁊ Ælfelm· ⁊ Ælfwine· ⁊ Ælfweard· ⁊ Eadwold· ⁊ Eadric· ⁊ Ælfgar· ⁊ Eadgifu abbudisse· ⁊ Liofrun abbudisse· ⁊ Æþelhild· ⁊ Eadgyfu æt Leofetan oran· ⁊ hyre swustor· ⁊ hyre dohtor· ⁊ Ælfgyf . . . . . dohtor· ⁊ Wulfwyn· ⁊ Æþelgyfu· ⁊ Ælfwaru· ⁊ Ælfgyfu· ⁊ Æþelflæd· ⁊ menig god þegen ⁊ god wif· þe we ealle atellan ne magon· ꝥ . . . . . forþcom̃ eal se fulla [aþ] ge on werum ge on wifum. Ða cwædon þa witan þe þær wæron· ꝥ betere wære ꝥ man þene aþ aweg lete þonne hine man sealde· forþan þær syþþan nan freondscype nære· ⁊ man wolde biddan þæs reaflaces ꝥ he hit sciolde agyfan ⁊ forgyldan· ⁊ þam cyninge his wer. Ða let he þone aþ aweg· ⁊ sealde Æþelsige biscope unbesacen land on hand· ꝥ he þanonforð syþþan þæron ne spræce. Þa tæhte man hyre ꝥ hio sciolde bringan his fæder gold ⁊ siolfor eal ꝥ hio hæfde. Þa dyde hio swa hio dorste hyre

instructed Wynflæd that she must adduce her claims. She then adduced her claims, with the support of Ælfthryth the king's mother. That is then first, [2]Wulfgar abbot, and Wulfstan priest, and Æfic the æthelings' sewer, and Eadwine, and Eadelm, and Ælfelm, and Ælfwine, and Ælfweard, and Eadwold, and Eadric, and Ælfgar, and Eadgifu abbess, and Liofrun abbess, and Æthelhild, and Eadgyfu at Leofetan ora, and her sister, and her daughter, and Ælfgyfu . . . . daughter, and Wulfwyn, and Æthelgyfu, and Ælfwaru, and Ælfgyfu, and Æthelflæd, and many a good thane and good woman, all of whom we cannot recount; so that the full oath might come forth, both by men and by women. Then said the 'witan' who were there, that it were better that the oath should be dispensed with than given; because there would be no friendship there afterwards; and that they would desire that he should give up and pay for the reft property, and to the king his 'wêr'. He then dispensed with the oath, and gave the land over to bishop Æthelsige

[1] Sic MS. for discþen.

[2] The names which follow are those of the consacramentals.

aþe gebiorgan. Þa næs he þa gyt on þam gehealden. butan hio sceolde swerian ꝥ his æhta þær ealle wæron. Đa cwæþ hio ꝥ hio ne mihte hyre dæles ne he his. ⁊ þyses wæs Ælfgar þæs cyninges gerefa to gewitnesse. ⁊ Byrhtric. ⁊ Leofric æt Hwitecyrcan. ⁊ menig god man to eacan him.

uncontested, so that thenceforth he would not contest it. They then directed her that she should bring his father's gold and silver, all that she had. Then did she as she durst defend her oath. Then was he not yet therewith satisfied, unless she should swear that all his property was there. Then said she that she could not for her part, nor he for his. And of this was Ælfgar the king's reeve to witness, and Byrhtric, and Leofric at Whitchurch, and many a good man besides them.

KING ÆTHELRED[1]. DCCCC.XCV.

✠ Quicquid perpetualiter permanens a secularibus agitur seris litterarum firmiter muniri debetur; quia hominum fragilis memoria moriendo obliviscitur quod scriptura litterarum servando retinet. Unde ego Aþelred, gratia Dei Anglorum rex, cunctis meis volo notum adesse fidelibus, quod ego jure hereditario cuidam meo militi nomine Aþelwig quinque trato mansos, in villa que a notis vocatur Eardulfes lea, ut vita comite eos possideat, et postquam dies extremus ejus clauserit oculos, cuicumque amico voluerit in perpetuam derelinquat possessionem. Sit autem præsens donatio absoluta ab omni servili jugo, tribus tamen rebus exceptis, populari scilicet expeditione, arcis construccione, pontis restauratione. Qualiter vero præsens terra in mea advenerit manu, brevi volo enucleare sermone. Tres fratres in quodam residentes convivio, quorum unus homo, nomine Leofric, instigante diabolo, furatus est frenum; quo invento in ejusdem sinu, concito cursu qui frenum perdiderunt, et tres fratres, predicti furis domini, concito cursu bellum in invicem insurgentes inierunt: duobus vero fratribus in bello peremptis, Ælfnoð scilicet et

[1] See Palgrave, Rise and Progress, ii. p. cxxvi.

Ælfric, vix tercius Aþelwine cum predicto latrone evasit, Sancte Helene intrans ecclesiam. Circummanentibus vero hec eadem audientibus, Aþelwig meus prepositus in Bucingaham, et Winsige prepositus on Oxonaforda, inter Christianos predictos sepelierunt fratres. Leofsige igitur dux, audito hoc verbo, meam adiit presentiam, prefatos incusans prepositos, peremptis fratribus non recte inter Christianos sepultis. Ego autem nolens contristari Aþelwig, quia mihi erat carus et preciosus, una simul et sepultos cum Christianis requiescere permisi, et predictam terram eidem in hereditatem concessi perpetuam. Si quis vero, cupiditatis zelo inflatus, hunc mee donationis libellum destruere temptaverit, sit anathema maranatha, hoc est alienatio a consortio Christianorum, nisi resipuerit, et quod callide facere temptaverit penitens penituerit. Hoc autem præcipiens præcipio, ut nulla aliorum librorum scedula nostro libello præcelli videatur, sed in perpetuum delitescat et aboleatur.

Ðis sindon þara fif hida landgemæra æt Eardulfes lea.

Ærest of þære greatan dic· ꝥ to Aþelwoldes lea to ðan landgemære· of ðan gemære swa æfter dene in Sexig broc· of Sexig broce ꝥ into Uffewylle broce· of ðan broce þæt on þa grenan dic· of ðære dic be suðan ðære eorðbyrg· ꝥ on Cwicelmes hlæw· of þan hlawe ꝥ on ða portstræte· of ðære portstræte ꝥ wið lytle Ciltene an æcer bræde· ꝥ on þæne grenan weg ðe scyt to Hegforda· æfter ðan grenan wege· ꝥ foran ongen Cynewynne wylle· of ðære wylle ꝥ into þære greatan dic· ⁊lang ðære

These are the land-boundaries of the five hides at Eardulfes lea.

First from the great ditch; then to Æthelwold's lea at the land-boundary; from the boundary, so along the dean to Sexig brook; from Sexig brook, then to Uffewylle brook; from the brook, then to the green ditch; from the ditch, to the south of the earth mount; then to Cuckamslow; from the low; then to the town-road; from the town-road, then towards little Chilton, one acre wide; then to the green way that leads out to Hedgford, along the green way; then towards Kynewyn's well; from the

dic ꝥ into Bunon. ⁊lang Bunan ꝥ to ðan ealdan forda. of ðan forda ꝥ into Eardulfes lea. of ðan lea ꝥ eft to þære greatan dic.	well, to the great ditch; along the ditch, then to the Boone; along the Boone, then to the Old ford; from the ford, then to Eardulf's lea; from the lea, then again to the great ditch.

Scripta est hæc scedula anno ab incarnatione Domini DCCCC.XCV., Indictione XIIII.[1], his testibus consentientibus quorum inferius nomina caraxantur.

✠ Ego Aþelred rex, Anglorum basileus, hujus doni libertatem tocius regni fastigium tenens, libenter concesso, vel largior et consentio vel hilariter confirmo. ✠ Ego Siric. ✠ Ego Ælfstanus, Lundoniensis ecclesie præsul, corroboravi. ✠ Ego Ælfhegus, Wintoniensis ecclesie præsul, confirmavi. ✠ Ego Æscuuig, Dorccensis ecclesie presul, dictavi. ✠ Ego Ælfric, Wiltoniensis ecclesie presul, consolidavi. ✠ Ego Ealdulf, Wigoracensis ecclesie presul, adquievi. ✠ Ego Osbyrht, Australium ecclesie presul, subplevi. ✠ Ego Ælfheagus, Licetfeldensis ecclesie presul, gaudenter consensi. ✠ Ego Aðulf, Herefordensis ecclesie presul, adjuvavi. ✠ Ego Ælfuuold, Crydiensis ecclesie presul, sustentavi. ✠ Ego Wlfsige, Scyreburnensis ecclesie presul, letus desiderio donavi. ✠ Ego Aþeluuærd dux exultanter munio vel affirmo presens testis adsto. ✠ Ego Ælfric dux signum crucis imprimo vel sustento. ✠ Ego Ælfhelm dux. ✠ Ego Leofuuine dux. ✠ Ego Leofsige dux. ✠ Ego Ælfuueard abbas. ✠ Ego Ælfsige abbas. ✠ Ego Brihtnoð abbas. ✠ Ego Brihtelm abbas. ✠ Ego Leofric abbas. ✠ Ego Æluere abbas. ✠ Ego Ceanulf abbas. ✠ Ego Ælfric abbas. ✠ Ego Ælfhun abbas. ✠ Ego Germanus abbas. ✠ Ego Ælfsige minister. ✠ Ego Ordulf minister. ✠ Ego Leofric minister. ✠ Ego Uulfheah minister. ✠ Ego Uulfric minister. ✠ Ego Uulfget minister. ✠ Ego Aþelnoð minister. ✠ Ego Aþelric minister. ✠ Ego Aþelsige minister. ✠ Ego Aþelmær minister. ✠ Ego Ceolmund minister. ✠ Ego Uuihtsige minister. ✠ Ego Æðeluuig minister.

[1] The Indiction for 995 is 8.

KING ÆTHELRED. DCCCC.XCVIII.

✠ Anno incarnationis Dominicæ DCCCC. nonagesimo octavo, ego Æðelredus, totius Albionis Dei gubernante moderamine basileus, suadente archiepiscopo Ælfrico, cum consilio meorum episcoporum ac principum seu nobilium, michique fidelium assistentium, annui episcopo Wlsino ordinare monachicæ conversationis normam, castamque vitam et Deo amabilem, secundum institutionem sancti patris Benedicti, in cœnobio Scireburnensis ecclesiæ; ea ratione, videlicet, ut quisquis successor ei advenerit, sive pius sive crudelis, non habeat facultatem male tractare res monachorum; sit pastor, non tirannus, gubernet ad fratrum utilitatem, secundum pastoralem auctoritatem, non ad lupinam rapacitatem; pascat suos et se sequentes; habeat ipse solus victum inter fratres, sicut scriptum est: "Principem populorum te constitui, esto in illis quasi unus ex illis." Regat ipse juxta animarum et corporum utilitatem substantiam monasterii, ita duntaxat ut fratrum consilio non sit ignotum quicquid agatur. Et si forte, quod absit, evenerit ut pastor et grex discordantur, semper ad examen archiepiscopi reservetur, et ipse regi intimet ut justa correctio sequatur. Et quia mos minime apud nos consentit ut in episcopali sede abbas constituatur, fiat ipse episcopus eis abbas et pater, et ipsi fratres obedientes ei sint sicuti filii et monachi, cum castitate et humilitate et subjectione, secundum disciplinam almi patris nostri Benedicti, ut una bravium æternæ coronæ accipere mereantur. Et quoniam, sicut ait apostolus, "nos sumus in quos fines seculorum devenerunt," et multiplicato jam genere humano, adeo ut perplures, gratia inopiæ ruris, non habentes ubi vel arando vel fodiendo agriculturam exercentes victum adipiscantur, insuper et crescente philargiria nonnullorum, ut quisque rapiat sibi quod potuerit, optimum duxerunt priores nostri ut omnis lis terminibus certis adnulletur, ideoque territoria causa concordiæ assuescere nuper inter mundanos cœpere, ut portionem quisque propriæ telluris libere excolat. Quorum ego exempla imitatus, rus prædicti cœnobii hac cartula annotari censeo. Hoc est, in ipsa Scireburna centum agelli in loco qui dicitur Stocland, et prædium monasterii, sicut Wlsinus episcopus fossis sepibusque girare curavit; deinde novem cassatos in loco qui ab incolis Holancumb nuncupatur; item in Halganstoke xv., in Đorford vii., in Bradanford x., in Wonburna v., in Westun viii., in Stapulbreicge xx., in Wulfheardigstoke x., in Cumbtun viii., in Osanstoke ii., et massam unam juxta ripam maris, quæ dicitur æt Lim. Et quicquid Deus his auxerit ex donis fidelium continua securitate et jugi libertate possideant fratres inibi degentes, tribus exceptis quæ omnibus communia sunt, scilicet, expeditione, pontis arcisve restauratione: tamen nulli debitores sint in rogi constructione, eo quod monasterium hoc opus indigere novimus. Si forte, quod absit, hanc nostram donationem quispiam annullare temptaverit, et ad libitus proprios deflectere, sciat se æquissimo judici rationem redditurum, clangente tuba archangeli extremo examine, ubi omnis æquitas et justitia, Christo judicante, cunctis manifestabitur.

Ego Æðelredus rex Anglorum hanc libertatem concedo sæpedicto monasterio sub episcopo quemcunque elegerit semper regendo, et signaculo sanctæ crucis ✠ hanc munificentiam consigno, coram his testibus. ✠ Ego Ælfricus archiepiscopus hoc donum data michi benedictione firmavi. ✠ Ego Ealdulf archiepiscopus libens favi atque consensi. ✠ Ego Wlstanus episcopus hoc idem affirmavi. ✠ Ego Ælpheagus episcopus consensum præbui. ✠ Ego Wlsinus episcopus hoc meum desiderium ad perfectum usque perduxi. ✠ Ego Ælfwinus episcopus hilari mente concessi. ✠ Ego Æðelward dux gratanter corroboravi. ✠ Ego Ælfric dux consentaneus fui. ✠ Ego Ælfsige abbas. ✠ Ego Wlfgar abbas. ✠ Ego Leofric abbas. ✠ Ego Godwine abbas. ✠ Ego Æðelmær minister. ✠ Ordulf minister. ✠ Wulfget minister. ✠ Brihtmær minister. ✠ Leofwine minister. ✠ Brihtric minister. ✠ Wulfnoð minister.

ÆLFTHRYTH. DCCCC.XCVI.-M.VI.

Alfðryð gret Ælfric arcebiscop ⁊ Eþelwerd ealdarman eadmodlice. ⁊ ĩc cyðe inc ðet ic eom to gewitnysse ꝥ Dunstan arcebiscop getehte Aþelwolde biscope Tantun. ealswa hĩs bẽc specon. ⁊ Eadgar cyning hit agef ða. ⁊ bead ælcon his þegna þe enig land on þan lande hafde ꝥ hi hĩt ofeodon be þes biscopes gemedon. oððe hit agefon. ⁊ se cyning cwæð þa þet he nahte nan land ut to syllanne. þa he ne ðorste fram Godes ege himsylf ðet heafod habban. ⁊ ma gerad þa Risctun to þes biscopes handa. ⁊ Wulfgyþ rad þa to me to Cumbe. ⁊ gesohte me. ⁊ ic ða. for þan þe heo me gesib was ⁊ Ælfswyð for þan þe he hyre broþor wãs. abedon æt Aðelwold biscope ꝥ hi moston brucan þes landes hyra deg. ⁊ efter hyra dege eode þet lond into Tantune mid mete ⁊ mid mannum. ealswa hit stode. ⁊ wit hyt swiðe uneaðe to þan brocton. Nu cydde man me þet Aðelwold bisceop ⁊ ic sceoldon ofneadian þa boc æt Leofrice. Nu

I Ælfthryth greet Ælfric archbishop and Æthelward aldorman humbly. And I make known to you that I am to witness that archbishop Dunstan assigned Taunton to bishop Athelwold, as his charters declared. And king Eadgar then gave it up, and commanded each of his thanes, who had any land on that land, that they should hold it with the bishop's consent, or give it up. And the king said then that he had no land to give out; as he durst not, through awe of God, have the headship himself, and moreover had then surrendered Rushton into the bishop's hand[1]. And Wulfgyth then rode to me at Combe, and sought me. And I then, because she was akin to me and Ælfswyth, because he was her brother, obtained from bishop Athelwold that they might enjoy the land for their day, and that after their day the land should go to Taunton, with meat and with men, as it stood. And we brought it with great difficulty thereto.

[1] My translation is here very conjectural. The whole document is particularly obscure, and seems to require illustration from some preceding one.

ne eom ic nanre neade gecnewe þe libbe þe ma þe he wolde þeah he lyfode. ac Leofric halfde āne niwe boc. þa agef he þa. þa cydde he mid þan þet he nolde nan fals þeron dōn. Þa cydde Aðelwold bisceop hīm ꝥ hīne ne mihte nan his eftergenga bereafian. hēt þa gewritan twa gewritu. oðer himsulf hefde. oþer he Leofrice sealde.

Now it has been made known to me that bishop Athelwold and I must have extorted the charter from Leofric. Now I, who am living, am not aware of any extorting more than he would be were he alive; for Leofric had a new charter; when he gave it up he thereby manifested that he would do nothing false therein. Then bishop Athelwold declared to him that none of his successors should bereave him, and then commanded two writings to be written, one he himself had, the other he gave to Leofric.

TELLIGRAPHUS ÆTHELREDI REGIS DE LIBERTATIBUS EJUSDEM LOCI (WESTMONASTERII), ET DE TERRIS PRÆDICTIS ET ALIIS. DCCCC.XCVIII.

✠ Anno incarnationis Domini nostri Jhesu Christo nongentesimo nonagesimo octavo, ego Athelredus, totius Albionis, Dei moderante gubernatione, basileus, renovare hac cartula studui, ammonitione Ælfrici archiepiscopi attactus, quomodo pater meus Eadgarus rex venerabili et sancto viro Dunstano archiepiscopo, illud monasterium quod Anglice Westminster vocitatur, ad Dei servitium concessit [1], acceptis ab eo videlicet centum viginti mancusis optimi auri, ea ratione ut monachilem conversationem inibi, secundum sancti patris Benedicti normam, ordinaret, quod et benivolo fecit effectu. Nos quoque paterno regno potiti, pro nostro modulo libertatem præfato monasterio augmentantes, hoc privilegium scriptitare mandavimus, ne forte, quod absit, quis tirannica suffultus potestate, vim in ibi degentibus inferret. Scimus namque

[1] Referring apparently to the charter of Eadgar at p. 219, the genuineness of which this valuable document would seem to confirm.

ultimis temporibus [simultates] crebrescere, discordias ebullire, rapacitates inardescere, amicitiam titubare, caritatem refrigescere multorum, et inaudita mala evenire. Ideoque hanc largitatem benigno animo renovamus, et concedimus Sancto Petro principi apostolorum, cui locus prædictus consecratus dinoscitur antiquitus, ut omni servitute careat, tribus exceptis quæ cunctis communia sunt, scilicet, expeditione, pontis arcisve restauratione; et tamen regi emendatione monasterii solummodo administretur. Hoc quoque notum fore cupimus, quod beatæ memoriæ Dunstanus cuidam sibi fideli ac probato monacho Wulfsinus vocabulo, quem quasi filium pura dilectione amavit, illud monasterium ad regendum regulariter commisit, et nos postea abbatem illum illic constituimus. At post annos aliquot episcopum illum elegimus ad sedem Sciréburnensis ecclesiæ, firmo sibi jure concesso, ut secundum suum regimen locus ille ordinetur et disponatur; et post dies ejus sit tam liberum sicuti cætera monasteria. Rura etiam ejusdem monasterii qualiter adquisita sint hic notare non omittimus. Hoc est primitus circa illud monasterium, quinque mansas quas pater Dunstanus a patre meo emebat, septuaginta mancusis auri. Iterum, quando frater meus Sanctus Edwardus regni sceptra obtinuit, habuit quidam miles ipsius Bryhtmer vocitatus tres mansas juxta Logereslea; tunc, variante rerum ordinatione, dimisit Brihtmer dominum suum regem, cum tellure prædicta, et alterius dominium elegit; et Dunstanus nil moratus terram illam emebat triginta libris a meo fratre, et addidit monasterio sæpe nominato. Item, ut ego regni gubernacula Dei nutu possedi, dedi quinque mansas prænominato monasterio in loco qui Hamstede vocitatur a ruricolis. Item Sanctus Dunstanus mercatus est decem mansas a beato Aðelwoldo episcopo, et x. a quodam Wulnoðo milite regis octoginta libris probati argenti, et addidit monasterio. Item tres cassatos emebat ipse a quodam Eadnoðo regis ministro xii. libris, in loco qui Codanhlaw nuncupatur, et dedit monasterio sæpe nominato. Tunc etiam temporis erat quidam minister regis in Middilsexan mansitans, Ælfwine vocitamine, qui adiens limina sanctorum apostolorum Petri et Pauli, Romæ scilicet, et gratia inopiæ petiit a beato

Dunstano quoddam amminiculum, qui commodans ei xxx. libras argenti, suscepit ab eodem octo mansas cujusdam telluris in Hanawella, ea ratione, ut rediens Roma, pecunia reddita archiepiscopo, rus redivit ad se; sed ille demum domum reversus nequaquam quivit accommodata persolvere, et Sanctus Dunstanus permisit ei diebus suis terra illa uti, et post ejus obitum redire ad cœnobium præscriptum, quod et factum audivimus. Item Sanctus Dunstanus emebat x. cassatos ab Ælfheago duce ducentis auri, in loco qui Sunnanburig dicitur, et accommodavit eos, insita ei largitate, cuidam viduæ diebus suis, Æðelflæd nomine, et post ejus finem redeat rus illud ad Westminster. Et illa possessio in Scepertune redeat ad jus Sancti Petri in præfato monasterio post dies Æðelflædi. Item Ælfhelm Polga, pro animæ suæ remedio, quinque mansas largitus est cœnobitis in Westminster conversantibus, in loco qui Bricandun vulgari vocitamine dicitur. Item Ælfwine, præfectus meus in Kent, tres cassatos cœnobio præfato, pro animula sua conjugisque, largitus est, in loco qui vulgo Sillingtune dicitur. Et illud prædiolum in Paddingtone, post dies Wulfrici ad libertatem propriam redeat ad monasterium prædictum. Sciendum etiam quod illud prædium in Cofanlea, post dies Ælfrici, ad arbitrium episcopi Wulfsini reverti debet. Quisquis fidelium hanc nostram munificentiam amplificare propriis donis satagerit, augmentet illi omnipotens Deus gaudium perhenne, ubi perpetuitas viget. Si quis autem demere seu atque temere violentia conatus fuerit, caveat opido ne obseretur ei introitus cœlestis paradisi ab eo janitore, cui Christus tradidit claves regni cœlorum, cui et locus ille honorifice consecratus antiquitus dinoscitur. Scripta est namque hæc sceda, me jubente, hiis testibus, quorum onomata infra habentur, consentientibus[1], quando ad classem proficiscens illud monasterium visitarem.

[1] The witnesses' names are wanting.

KING ÆTHELRED. M.V.[1]

*　*　*　*　*　*　*　*
*　*　*　*　*　*　*

Emit Æðelmarus a me cum triginta libris duodecim mansiones de villulis quas matrona quædam nomine Leoftæt suis perdidit ineptiis et amisit, tres semis, videlicet, manentes et Maranaclive, etc.

KING ÆTHELRED. M.XII.

*　*　*　*　*　*　*　*
*　*　*　*　*　*　*

Erat eadem villa cuidam matronæ nomine Æðelflæde, derelicta a viro suo, obeunte illo, quæ etiam habebat germanum quendam, vocabulo Leofsinum, quem de satrapis nomine tuli, ad celsioris apicem dignitatis dignum duxi promovere ducem constituendo, scilicet, eum, unde humiliari magis debuerat, sicut dicitur, "Principem te constituerunt, noli extolli," et cætera. Sed ipse hoc oblitus, cernens se in culmine majoris status sub rogatu famulari sibi pestilentes spiritus promisit, superbiæ, scilicet, et audaciæ, quibus nichilominus ipse se dedidit in tantum, ut flocci penderet quin offensione multimoda me multoties graviter offenderet; nam præfectum meum Æficum, quem primatem inter primates meos taxavi, non cunctatus in propria domo ejus eo inscio perimere, quod nefarium et peregrinum opus est apud Christianos et gentiles. Peracto itaque scelere ab eo, inii consilium cum sapientibus

[1] This and the following extract are from charters belonging to the second division of the work, or the Grants of Land, but are here inserted on account of the manner in which the lands became forfeit to the crown, by the delinquency of the holder. The cases here cited are *ineptiæ* (perhaps incontinence), and harbouring a relative guilty of murder; in conformity with the law of king Eadmund I., where it is said: "If any one of his kinsmen harbour him, be he forfeit to the king of all he owns." According to the Saxon Chronicle Ætic was murdered by Leofsige in the year 1002.

regni mei petens, ut quid fieri placuisset de illo decernerent, placuitque in commune nobis eum exulare et extorrem a nobis fieri cum complicibus suis. Statuimus etiam inviolatum fœdus inter nos, quod qui præsumpsisset infringere, exhereditari se sciret omnibus habitis, hoc est, ut nemo nostrum aliquid humanitatis vel commoditatis ei subministraret. Hanc optionis electionem posthabitam nichili habuit soror ejus Æðelflæd omnia quæ possibilitatis ejus erant, et utilitatis fratris omnibus exercitiis studuit explere; et hac de causa aliarumque quam plurimarum, exheredem se fecit omnibus.

EADMUND ÆTHELING[1]. ABOUT M.VI.

✠ Her swutelað on ðisum gewrite ꝥ Eadmund æðeling bæd ðone hired æt Scireburnan ðæt he moste ofgan ðæt land æt Holancumbe. Ða ne dorste se hyred hym ðæs wyrnan· ac cwæðon ꝥ hy ðæs wel uðon· gyf se cing ⁊ se bisceop ðe heora ealdor wæs ðæs geuðon. Ða gewerð hym· ⁊ se æðeling ⁊ se prafost ⁊ ða yldostan munecas comon to ðam cinge· ⁊ him forecyddon· ⁊ his leafe bædon· ⁊ ðæt ærende abead Wulfstan archebisceop. Ða cwæð se cing ꝥ he nolde ðæt ꝥ land mid ealle ut aseald wære· ac ꝥ hi elles swilce foreword worhton ðæt ꝥ land eft into ðære halgan stowe agifen wære to ðam fyrste

✠ Here is made known in this writing, that Eadmund ætheling prayed the convent at Sherborne that he might have the land at Holcomb. Then the convent durst not refuse him this, but said that they would well give it, if the king and the bishop, who was their principal, would grant it. It was then agreed between them: and the ætheling and the provost and the senior monks came to the king, and made it known to him and besought his leave: and archbishop Wulfstân announced the errand. Then said the king that he would not that the land should be sold outright, but that they should else make such an agreement,

[1] Afterwards king Eadmund Ironside.

ðe hym ealle gewurde. Ða geweorð hi ðæt se æðeling sealde ðam hyrede xx. punda wið ðam lande ælswa hit stod mid mete ⁊ mid mannon ⁊ mid ællon þingon· ⁊ bruce his dæg· ⁊ ofer his dæg eode ꝥ land eft into ðære halgan stowe· mid mete ⁊ mid mannun ⁊ mid eallum þingum· swa swa hit ðonne wære.

that the land should be given back to the holy place at the term they should all settle. They then agreed that the ætheling should give the convent xx. pounds for the land as it stood, with meat and with men, and with all things, and enjoy it for his day, and that after his day the land should revert to the holy place, with meat and with men, and with all things, as it then might be.

Ðises wæs to gewitnesse Wulfstan archebisceop· ⁊ Lyfing ƀ. ⁊ Æðelric ƀ. ⁊ Æðelsie ƀ. ⁊ Eadric ealdorman· ⁊ Æðelmær ealdorman· ⁊ Æðelfand Æðelmæres suna· ⁊ Leofsuna abbud æt Cernel· ⁊ Ælfget Hengðes sunu· ⁊ Siwerd· ⁊ Brihtric reada· ⁊ ealle ða ildostan þægnas on Dorsæton· ⁊ Ealdwine pr̃. ⁊ Wulfric pr̃. ⁊ Leofwine æðelinges discðen· ⁊ Ælfget ⁊ Ælwerd his cnihtas· ⁊ ealle ðe geoðre hiredmen.

Of this was to witness: Wulfstân archbishop, and Lyfing bp., and Æthelric bp., and Æthelsie bp., and Eadric aldorman, and Æthelmær aldorman, and Æthelfand son of Æthelmær, and Leofsuna abbot of Cerne, and Ælfget Hengthes son, and Siwerd, and Brihtric the Red, and all the senior thanes in Dorsetshire, and Ealdwine priest, and Wulfric pr̃., and Leofwine the ætheling's sewer, and Ælfget and Ælwerd his pages, and all the other household men.

BISHOP GODWINE AND LEOFWINE. BEFORE M.XI.

✠ Her cyð on þysum gewrite hu Godwine biscop on Hrofeceastre ⁊ Leofwine Ælf-

✠ Here is made known, in this writing, how Godwine bishop of Rochester, and Leofeages sunu wurdon gesybsumode ymbe ꝥ land æt Snoddinglande on Cantwarabyrig. Ða ðа se biscop Godwine com to þam biscopstole· þurh hæse his cynehlafordes Æðelredes cynges· æfter Ælfstanes biscopes forðsiðe· þa gemætæ he on ðam mynstre þa ylcan swutelunga þe his foregenga hæfde· ⁊ þærmid on ðat land spæc. Ongan þa to specenne on þat land· ⁊ elles for Godes ege ne dorste· oð þæt seo spræc wearð þam cynge cuð. Ða ða him seo talu cuð wæs· þa sende he gewrit ⁊ his insegl to þam arcebisceope Ælfrice· ⁊ bead him þat he ⁊ hys þegenas on East Cent ⁊ on West Cent hy on riht gesemdon· be ontale ⁊ be oftale. Þa þæt wæs ðæt se bisceop Godwine com to Cantwarabyrig to ðam arcebiscope· þa com ðider se scyres man Leofric· ⁊ mid him Ælfun abbod ⁊ þegenas· ægðer ge of East Cent ge of West Cent· eal seo duguð· ⁊ hy þær ða spæce swa lange handledon· syððon se bisceop his swutelunge geeowod hæfde· oð hy ealle bædon þone biscop eaðmodlice ðæt he geunnan sceolde þæt he moste mid bletsunga þæs landes brucan æt Snoddinglande his dæg· ⁊ se bi-

wine son of Ælfeah were agreed respecting the land at Snodland in Canterbury. When bishop Godwine came to the episcopal see, by command of his royal lord king Æthelred, after the death of bishop Ælfstân, he found in the monastery the same title-deeds which his predecessor had, and therewith laid claim to the land. He began then to lay claim to the land, and for awe of God durst not otherwise; until the suit became known to the king. When the case was known to him, he sent his writ and his signet to the archbishop Ælfric, and commanded him that he and his thanes in East Kent and in West Kent should justly decide between them, by plaint and by defence. Then it was that bishop Godwine came to Canterbury to the archbishop; then came thither the shiresman Leofric, and with him abbot Ælfûn, and thanes both from East Kent and West Kent, all the chief people; and they there handled the suit so long after the bishop had produced his title, until they all prayed the bishop humbly that he would grant that he (Leofwine) might, with his blessing, enjoy sceop þa ðæs getiðode on ealra þæra witena þanc ðe þær gesomnode wæran· ⁊ he behet ðæs truwan· þæt land æfter his dæge unbesacen eode eft into ðære stowe þe hit utlæned was· ⁊ ageaf ða swutelunga ðe he to þam lande hæfde þe ær of ðære stowe geutod wæs· ⁊ þa hagan ealle ðe he be westan þære cyrcan hæfde into ðære halgan stowe. And þises loces ærendracan wæran· Ælfun abbod· ⁊ Wulfric abbod· ⁊ Leofric sciresman· ⁊ Siweard· ⁊ Wulfstan æt Sealtwuda· ⁊ Ælfelm Ordelmes sunu. Đonne is her seo gewitnes ðe æt þisum loce wæs· þæt is ærest se arcebiscop Ælfric· ⁊ se biscop Godwine· ⁊ Wulfric abbod· ⁊ Ælfun abbod· ⁊ Ælfnoð æt Orpedingtune· ⁊ se hired æt Cristes cyrcan· ⁊ se hired æt Sc̃e Augustine· ⁊ seo burhwaru on Cantwarebyrig· ⁊ Leofric sciresman· ⁊ Lifing æt Meallingan· ⁊ Siweard· ⁊ Sired his broðor· ⁊ Leofstan æt Mærseham· ⁊ Godwine Wulfeages sunu· ⁊ Wulfstan æt Sealtwuda· ⁊ Wulfstan iunga· ⁊ Leofwine æt Dictune· ⁊ Leofric Ealdredes sunu· ⁊ Goda Wulfsiges sunu· ⁊ Ælfhelm Ordelmes sunu· ⁊ Sidewine æt Wealeswyrðe· ⁊

the land at Snodland for his day. And the bishop assented thereto, for the sake of all the 'witan' who were there assembled. And he (Leofwine) pledged his faith for this, that the land, after his day, should revert uncontested to the place whence it had been alienated; and gave up the titles that he had to the land which had before been alienated from the place, and all the messuages which he had west of the church, to the holy place. And of this compact the delegates were: Ælfûn abbot, and Wulfric abbot, and Leofric shiresman, and Siweard, and Wulfstân at Saltwood, and Ælfelm Ordelm's son. Now here are the witnesses who were at this compact: That is first, the archbishop Ælfric, and the bishop Godwine, and Wulfric abbot, and Ælfûn abbot, and Ælfnoth at Orpington, and the convent at Christchurch, and the convent at St Augustine's, and the burghers of Canterbury, and Leofric shiresman, and Lifing at Malling, and Siweard, and Sired his brother, and Leofstân at Mersham, and Godwine Wulfeah's son, and Wulfstân at Saltwood, and Wulfstân the Young, and Leofwine

Wærelm· ⁊ Æðelred portgerefa on Byrig· ⁊ Guðwold.˙ Gif hwa ðis þence to awendenne ⁊ ðas foreword to abrecenne· awende him God fram his ansyne on þam miclan dome· swa þat he si ascyred fram heofena rices myrhðe· ⁊ sy eallum deoflum betæht into helle. Amen.

at Ditton, and Leófric Ealdred's son, and Goda Wulfsige's son, and Ælfhelm Ordelm's son, and Sidewine at Wallsworth, and Wærelm, and Æthelred portreeve at Bury, and Guthwold. If any one meditate to avert this, and to break this agreement, may God avert his countenance from him at the great doom, so that he be cut off from the joy of heaven's kingdom, and be delivered over to all the devils in hell. Amen.

KING CNUT. M.XVIII.

✠ Ego denique imperator Knuto, a Christo Rege regum regiminis Anglici in insula potitus, audiens beneficia prædecessorum meorum regum, scilicet regalia privilegia, similiter cernens libertatem monasteriorum intra Cantiam positorum, archipræsulisque Liuingi admonitione, placuit cordi amborum præsentem chartulam corroborare; videlicet, æcclesia Salvatoris in Dorobernia sita, omnium æcclesiarum regni Angligeni mater et domina, cum omnibus ad illam pertinentibus, sit libera, nec quisquam hominum in ea et in rebus suis aliquid juris vel consuetudinis, præter archiepiscopum et monachos ibidem Deo famulantes, exigat vel obtineat. In sempiternum hoc nostrum decretum inviolabile tempore meo et successorum meorum, pro spe salutis æternæ, stabile perseveret: his testibus quorum signa subtus annotantur.

Ego Knuto gubernator Anglici orbis propria manu confirmo ✠. Ego Liuingus metropolitanus archipræsul libenter annuo ✠. Ego Emma regina signo crucis confirmo ✠. Ego Wolstanus Eboracensis consolidavi ✠. Ego Ealdelmus episcopus gratum habens ✠. Ego Ælfgarus episcopus concedo ✠. Ego Leofricus episcopus confirmo ✠. Ego Hald-enne princeps regis [dono] pro viribus assensum præbeo ✠. Et ego Turkillus dux concedo ✠. Facta est autem ista concessio anno Dominicæ incarnationis millesimo xviii.

---

* KING CNUT. M.XVIII.

☧ In nomine Poliarchis Ihesu Christi, Salvatoris mundi tociusque creature Creatoris, cujus divino dominatui quæque dominaciones debito servicio subnixe deserviunt, cujus etiam omnipotentatui universi potentatus obsecundari examussim preproperant, quia bonitas ejus bonitas est incomprehensibilis, et miseracio interminabilis, dapsilitas bonitatis ineffabilis, longanimitas quoque super pravorum nequicias quantitatis prolixitate cujuslibet longior, qui cotidianis admonicionibus religiosam conversacionem ducentes monet, ut pie sectando justiciæ culturam non eam deserendo linquant, quin pocius perseverabili instancia in ejus cultura, ut permaneant paterno affectu hortatur, qui nihilominus eadem affectione mandet peccatoribus ut resipiscant a suis iniquitatibus convertentes, quia eorum execratur mortem. Ejus amoris stimulo et fide suffultus, cujus largiflua miseracione, ego Cnut rex tocius Albionis insule aliarumque nacionum plurimarum in cathedra regali promotus, cum consilio et decreto archiepiscoporum, episcoporum, abbatum, comitum, aliorumque omnium meorum fidelium, elegi sanciendum atque perpeti stabilimento ab omnibus confirmandum, ut monasterium quod Beadriceswurthe nuncupatur sit per omne ævum monachorum gregibus deputatum ad inhabitandum, et ab omni dominatione omnium episcoporum comitatus illius funditus liberum, ut in eo Domino servientes monachi sine ulla inquietudine pro statu regni Dominum prævaleant precari. Placuit etiam mihi hanc optionis electionem roborare privilegio isto in quo videre præcepi libertatis donum, quod jam olim Eadmundus rex Occidentalium Saxonum largitus est suo equivoco, pro nanciscenda ejus gracia ⁊ mercede eterna, scilicet, Eadmundo regi et martyri, quod bone voluntatis voto augere cupimus, quatinus ejus promereri precibus merear porcionem ejus beatitudinis post hujus cursum vite. Tali libertate concedo fundo frui illi, in quo idem sanctus pausat, ut quotiens populus universus persolvit censum Danis, vel ad naves seu ad arma, persolvant inhabitantes in ipso fundo eadem ad usus quos elegerint fratres illius loci. Sitque nobis remedio hoc, mihi quippe eque regine mee Ælgife ac filiis nostris, omnibusque qui pridem ei hoc contulerunt. Huic libertati concedo additamentum, scilicet, maritimos pisces qui mihi contingere debent annualiter per thelonei lucrum et piscationem quam Ulfkytel habuit in Wylla, et omnia jura quarumcunque causarum in villis que monasterio adjacent, et quæ adiciende sunt per gratiam Dei. Dedi quoque, regine mee assensu concedens ei, pro sua elemosina dare quatuor milia anguillarum cum muneribus que pertinent ad illas pro annuali censu, in villa que cognominatur Lacyngahyðe. Si quislibet, quod absit, istam libertatem quoquolibet conatu nititur servitutis jugo subigere, vel prava intentione transmutare, ut rursus clericos in eo collocet loco, sit addictus captivitati eterne, carens sempiterna libertate, et mancipatus servitio diaboli, ejusque consortio sit inextricabilibus habenis constitutus, nisi satisfactio ejus erratui subveniat, quod prorsus optamus.

✠ Ego Cnut rex gentis Anglorum aliarumque nationum nihilominus hoc privilegium jussi componere et compositum cum signo Dominice crucis confirmando impressi. ✠ Ego Ælgifa regina omni alacritate mentis hoc confirmavi. ✠ Ego Wlfstanus archiepiscopus confirmavi. ✠ Ego Godwinus episcopus corroboravi. ✠ Ego Ælfwinus episcopus assensum dedi. ✠ Ego Ælfsinus episcopus consignavi. ✠ Ego Æð[el]ricus episcopus conclusi. ✠ Ego Ælfwinus episcopus roboravi. ✠ Ego Brihtwaldus episcopus. ✠ Ego Iric dux. ✠ Ego Godwinus dux. ✠ Ego Ulf dux. ✠ Ego Eglaf dux. ✠ Ego Hakun dux. ✠ Ego Leofwinus dux. ✠ Ego Godricus dux. ✠ Ego Ælfwinus abbas. ✠ Ego Leofwinus abbas. ✠ Ego Wlfredus abbas. ✠ Ego Oskitellus abbas. ✠ Ego Leofricus abbas. ✠ Ego Ælfwardus abbas. ✠ Ego Æðelstanus abbas. ✠ Ego Oslacus miles. ✠ Ego Đord miles. ✠ Ego Đurkil miles. ✠ Ego Đrim miles. ✠ Ego Broðor miles. ✠ Ego Ælfricus miles. ✠ Ego Ælwinus miles. ✠ Ego Ælfwinus. ✠ Ego Ælfricus. ✠ Ego Leofsius. ✠ Ego Leofricus. ✠ Ego Ælfricus. ✠ Ego Leofricus.

IDEM ANGLICE INTERPRETATUM, ET EIDEM CARTÆ PRINCIPALI INSERTUM.

On ælmihtiges Drihtnes naman. Ic Cnut kyning kyðe eallum mannum ymbe þone ræd þe ic mid minum rædgyfum gerædd hæbbe· for minre sawle þearfe ⁊ for ealles þeodscypes gesundfulnysse þis· ꝥ ic ann ece freodomes þam halgan kyninge Sancte Eadmunde swa forð swa he fyrmest hæfde into þære stowe þe he on restað· ⁊ swa wille ic ꝥ se freodom stande on his geweald unawend· buton elces bisceopes anwealde þære scire ecelice freo· ⁊ swa fela syðe swa menn gyldað heregyld oððe to scipgylde· gylde se tunscipe· swa swa oðre menn doð· to þære muneca neode þe þær binnan sceolon for us þeowian· ⁊ we gecuron ꝥ hit næfre ne sceolde ænig mann gewendan to oðres hades mannum· buton he wolde beon ascyred fram Godes gemanan ⁊ eallum his þam halgum· ⁊ ic geann þam munecan to fodan ealne þone fixnoð þe Ulfkytel ahte æt Wyllan· and min gafol fisc· þe me arist

In the name of the Almighty Lord. I Cnut king make known to all men, with respect to the resolution which I have adopted with my counsellors, for my soul's need and for the well-being of all the nation, this—That I grant perpetual freedom to the holy king St Eadmund, as complete as he best had it, at the place in which he rests. And I will so that the freedom stand in his control unperverted, exempt from every bishop's power, to that shire eternally free. And as often as men pay the army-tax, or for ship-tax, let the township pay, so as other men do, for the need of the monks who shall for us therein serve. And we have resolved that no man shall ever turn it to men of another order, unless he would be cut off from the communion of God and all his saints. And I give to the monks for food all the fishing that Ulfkytel owned at Wells, and my toll-fish, which accrue be sæ lande. ⁊ min cwen Ælfgyfu ann þam halgum feower þusend æla. mid hera lacon þe herto gebyriað. æt Lakynge hyðe. ⁊ ic ann heom ealra heora tun socne of ealle heora lande þe hi nu habbað ⁊ git begitan sceolon on Godes este.

to me from the maritime lands. And my queen Ælfgyfu gives to the saint four thousand eels, with the gifts which are incident thereto, at Lakenheath. And I give to them 'tûn-socn' of all their lands which they now have, and, by favour of God, may yet acquire.

KING CNUT. M.XIII.-M.XX.

✠ Cnut cing gret Lifing arceƀ. ⁊ Godwine ƀ. ⁊ Ælmær aƀƀ. ⁊ Æþelwine scīrman. ⁊ Æþelric. ⁊ ealle mine þegnas twelfhynde ⁊ twihynde. freondlice. ⁊ ic cyðe eow ꝥ se arceƀ. spæc to me ymbe Xp̃es circean freols. ꝥ heo hæfð nu læsse munde þonne hio hwilan ǽr hæfde. þa lyfde ic him ꝥ he moste niwne freols settan on minan naman. Ða cwæð he to me ꝥ he freolsas genoge hæfde. gif hi aht forstodan. Ða nam ic me sylf þa freolsas ⁊ gelēde hi uppan Xp̃es agen weofod on þæs arceƀ. gewitnysse. ⁊ on Ðurkilles eorles. ⁊ on manegra goddra manna ðe me mid wæron. to þan ylcan forewеardan þe hit Æþelbyrht cing gefreode. ⁊ ealle mine

✠ I Cnut king greet Lyfing archbishop, and Godwine bishop, and Ælmær abbot, and Æthelwine shireman, and Æthelric, and all my thanes, twelfhynd and twihynd, amicably. And I make known to you that the archbishop spake to me concerning the liberty of Christchurch: that it has now less immunity than it had a while before. I then allowed him that he might establish a new liberty in my name. He then said to me that he had liberties enough, if they stood for aught. I myself then took the liberties and laid them upon Christ's own altar, in witness of the archbishop, and of earl Thurkill, and of many good men who were with me, foregencgan· ꝥ næfre nan man ne sy swa dyrsti· sy he gehadod sy he læwode· ꝥ ænig þinga gelytlie þe on ðam freolse stænt. Gif hit hwa þænne dō· sy his lif her gescert ⁊ his wunung on helle grunde· butan he hit ðe stiðlicor gebete ǣr his ænde be þæs arcebisceopes tæcinge.

with the same immunities with which king Æthelbyrht and all my predecessors had privileged it; that never any man should be so daring, be he in orders, be he lay, that he diminish any of the things which stand in that liberty. And if any one so do, be his life here shortened, and his dwelling in the ground of hell, unless he the more make amends before his end, by the archbishop's teaching.

KING CNUT. M.XIX.

✠ Rector altipolorum culmine atque Architector summe fabrice etheree aule, ex nichilo quidem cuncta creavit, cœlum, scilicet, et terram, et omnia que in eis sunt; candida quidem angelica agmina, solem, lunam, lucidaque astra, et cetera que super firmamento sunt; mundi autem fabricam inenarrabili disponens ordine, ut Genesis testatur: "Et hominem sexto die formavit ad similitudinem suam," Adam, videlicet, quadriformi plasmatum materia, unde nunc constat genus humanum que in terris movetur, et ima terra larvarica latibula, ubi et Lucifer cum decimo ordine per superbiam de celo ruit. Sed et hoc invidet pestifer Chelidrus prothoplastum a Deo conditum intellexerat ut hoc impleret, a quo ipse miser et satellites illius de celo projecti sunt. Heu! quidem boni creati sunt, sed miserabiliter decepti. Ideoque invidus Zabulus totis viribus homini invidet, suadet mulieri, mulier viro, per suasionem atque per inobedientiam ambo decepti sunt fraudulenter per gustum pomi ligni vetiti, atque ab amenitate Paradisi dejecti sunt in hoc erumpnoso seculo, et letum sibi ac posteris suis promeruerunt, atque in tetrum abyssi demersi sunt. Sed hoc misericors et piissimus Pater indoluit perire tandiu nobilem creaturam sui imaginem; misertus est generi humano, misit nobis in tempore, id est, post quinque millia annorum, proprium filium suum, ut mundum perditum iterum renovaret; ut sicut mulier genuit mortem in mundo, ita per mulierem enixa est nobis vita in mundo; et sicut per delictum Adæ omnes corruimus, ita per obedientiam Christi omnes surreximus; et sicut mors per lignum intravit, ita et vita per lignum sancte crucis venit, et antiquum inimicum superavit, et fortis fortem alligavit, et in imo barathro retrusit: juste periit qui injuste decepit, atque omnes antiquas sanctas turmas a fauce pessimi leonis eripuit, et ovem perditam in humeris posuit, et ad antiquam patriam reduxit, et decimum ordinem implevit. Unde ego Cnuth, rex Anglorum ceterarumque gentium persistencium in circuitu, patefacio omnibus hanc cartulam legentibus et auscultantibus, quod Adelbertus dux revelavit michi quod mei præpositi in Defonia provincia imponebant jugum servitutis prediis sancte æcclesie Dei et ejus genitricis Marie, omniumque sanctorum, que est in Exencestria, diruto monasterio a paganis, et crematis privilegiis que antiqui reges concesserant supradicto cenobio. Quamobrem ego Cnuth, Deo favente, tocius Albionis primicerius, pro peticione supradicti ducis, et pro remedio anime mee mearumque culparum emendatione, atque incolumitate mei regni, hanc cartulam concedo Adelwoldo abbati ejusque fratribus et suorum successoribus in supradicto monasterio commorantibus ad perpetuam libertatem, ut liberum permaneat ipsum monasterium cum omnibus prædiis illi concessis, et cum omnibus rebus ad eum rite pertinentibus, id est, campis, pratis, pascuis, silvis, venationibus, piscariis, ab omni regali atque seculari gravedine, majora atque minora, exceptis assiduis orationibus, nisi sola expeditione et pontis constructione; et si aliquid pro expeditione, aut pro aliquo regali tributo reddatur, detur monasterio. Quicumque ergo hoc augere atque multiplicare voluerit, amplificet Deus bona illius in regione viventium, paceque nostra conglutinata vigens et florens, atque inter agmina beatitudinis tripudia succedat, qui nostræ donationis muneri consentiat. Si quis vero tam epilenticus philargyrie seductus amentia, quod non optamus, hanc nostræ elimosyne dapsilitatem ausu temerario infringere tentaverit, sit ipse alienatus a consortio sanctæ Dei ecclesie, necnon a participatione sacrosancti corporis et sanguinis Jhesu Christi filii Dei, per quem totus terrarum orbis ab antiquo humani generis inimico liberatus est, et cum Juda Christi proditore sinistra in parte deputatus, nisi prius hic digna satisfactione humilis pœnituerit quod contra sanctam Dei æcclesiam rebellis agere præsumpsit, nec in vita hac practica veniam, nec in theorica requiem apostata obtineat ullam, sed æternis barathri incendiis trusus, jugiter miserrimus crucietur. Anno Dominice incarnationis M°XIX°, Indictione secunda, scripta est hujus munificencie singrapha, hiis testibus consencientibus quorum inferius nomina, secundum uniuscujusque dignitatem utriusque ordinis decusatim, Domino disponente, carraciantur.

Ego Cnhut, Britannie Anglorum monarchus, hoc taumate donum agie crucis roboravi. Ego Lyuingh, Dorovernensis basilice primas, huic regali dono assensum præbui. Ego Wlstan, Eboracensis cathedre archipontifex, signum sancte crucis letus impressi. Ego Ælfsige episcopus præbui. Ego Godwyne episcopus consensi. Ego Ælfwine episcopus adquievi. Ego Leofsige episcopus annui. Ego Brichtwolf episcopus jussi. Ego Æðelfred episcopus roboravi. Ego Æðelwine episcopus præbui. Ego Eadnoð episcopus subscripsi. Ego Brihtwolf episcopus impressi. Ego Đurcil dux. Ego Hacun dux. Ego Leouuine dux. Ego Halfdan dux. Ego Yric dux. Ego Æðelred dux. Ego Eilaf dux. Ego Godwine dux. Ego Haram dux. Ego Syhrod dux. Ego Brihtrig abbas. Ego Ælfsige abbas. Ego Ælfstan abbas. Ego Ælfhere abbas. Ego Leofric abbas. Ego Æðelwold abbas. Ego Germanus abbas. Ego Æðeric abbas. Ego Aua abbas. Ego Æðelwine abbas. Ego Luxihs abbas. Ego Ælfnoð abbas. Ego Filnoð abbas. Ego Ælfwine minister. Ego Haldan minister. Ego Swesa minister. Ego Leofric minister. Ego Ælfgar minister. Ego Odda minister. Ego Ælfwig minister. Ego Eadwig minister. Ego Osferð minister. Ego Leofsige minister. Ego Eadsið minister. Ego Ælfgar minister. Ego Ælfrich minister. Æðelmar minister. Eadwyne minister. Leofnoð minister. Wulfsighe minister. Eadwig minister. Wyne minister. Ælua minister. Æðelwine minister. Sewlf minister. Ælfric minister. Sodda minister. Æðelnoð minister. Æðelmar minister.

EARL GODWINE. M.XVI.-M.XX.

✠ Her swutelað on þysan gewrite þa foreward ðe Godwine worhte wið Byrhtric þa he his dohter awogode[1]. Ðæt is ærest· ꝥ he gæf hire anes pundes gewihta goldes· wið þon ðe heo his spæce· underfenge· ⁊ he geuðe hire þæs landes æt Stræte mid eallan ðon þe þærto herð· ⁊ on Burwara mersce oðer healf hund æcera· ⁊ þærto þrittig oxna ⁊ twentig cuna· ⁊ tyn hors· ⁊ tyn þeowinen. Ðis wæs gespecen æt Cincgestune· beforan Cnute cincge· on Lyfinges arcebiscopes gewitnesse· ⁊ on þæs hiredes æt Cristes circan· ⁊ Ælfmeres abbodes· ⁊ þæs hiredes æt Sc̃e Augustine· ⁊ Æðelwines sciregerefan· ⁊ Siredes ealdan· ⁊ Godwines Wulfeages suna· ⁊ Ælfsige cild· ⁊ Eadmer æt Burham· ⁊ Godwine Wulfstanes sunu· ⁊ Kar[l] þæs cincges cniht.

✠ Here is made known, by this writing, the compact that Godwine made with Byrhtric, when he wooed his daughter[1]. That is first, that he should give her one pound weight of gold, in consideration that she would receive his suit; and he should give her the land at Street, with all which thereto belongs; and at Burwash a hundred and fifty acres, and thereto thirty oxen, and twenty cows, and ten horses, and ten serfs. This was agreed at Kingston, before king Cnut, with the witness of archbishop Lyfing and the convent at Christ-church, and of Ælfmær abbot, and the convent at St Augustine's, and of Æthelwine the shire-reeve, and of Sired the Old, and of Godwine son of Wulfeah, and of Ælfsige child, and of Eadmer at Burnham,

[1] Godwine's second wife. See Will. Malmesb. p. 342, edit. E. H. Soc.

And ða man ꝥ mædan fette æt Byrhtlingan, ða eode þyses ealles on borh· Ælfgar Syredes sunu· ⁊ Frerð preost on Folcestāne· ⁊ of Doferan Leofwine preost· ⁊ Wulfsige preost· ⁊ Eadræd Eadelmes sunu· ⁊ Leofwine Wærelmes sunu· ⁊ Cenwold Rust· ⁊ Leofwine Godwines sunu æt Hortune· ⁊ Leofwine se Reade· ⁊ Godwine Eadgeofe sunu· ⁊ Leofsunu his broðer. And swa hwæðer heora læng libbe fō to eallan æ[h]tan· ge on þam lande ðe ic[1] heom gæf· ge o[n] ælcon þingan. Ðyssa þinga is gecnæwe ælc dohtig man on Kænt ⁊ on Suð Sexan· on þegenan ⁊ on ceorlan· ⁊ ðyssa gewrita synd þreo· ǣn is æt Cristes cyrcan· oðer æt Sc̃e Augustine· ⁊ þridde hæfð Byrhtric self.

and of Godwine son of Wulfstân, and of Karl the king's page. And when they fetched the maiden from Brightling, then for all this went as security Ælfgar son of Syred, and Frerth the priest at Folkestone; and from Dover Leofwine priest, and Wulfsige priest, and Eadred son of Eadelm, and Leofwine son of Wærelm, and Cênwold Rust, and Leofwine son of Godwine at Horton, and Leofwine the Red, and Godwine son of Eadgifu, and Leofsunu his brother. And let whichsoever of them live the longer succeed to all the possessions, both in the land which I have given them, and in every thing. Of these things is cognizant every good (doughty) man in Kent and in Sussex, of thanes and churls. And of these writings there are three: one is at Christchurch, another at St Augustine's, and the third Byrhtric himself has.

ARCHBISHOP WULFSTÂN. M.XX.

Wulfstan arcebisceop[2] gret Cnut cyning his hlaford and Aelfgyfe þa hlæfdian eadmodlice· and ic cyðe inc leof ꝥ we habbað gedon swa swa

Wulfstân archbishop greets Cnut king, his lord, and Ælfgyfu the lady, humbly. And I make known to you, beloved, that we have done,

[1] Byrhtric.

[2] Of York.

us swutelung fram eow com æt ðam b. Æðelnoðe[1]. ꝥ we habbað hine nu gebletsod. Nu bidde ic for Godes lufon and for eallan Godes halgan ꝥ gewitan on Gode þam æðe. ⁊ on þam halgan hade. ꝥ he mote beon þære þinga wyrðe ðe oðra beforan wæron. Dunstan ðe gód wæs ⁊ mænig oðer. ꝥ þes mote beon eallswa rihta ⁊ gerysna wyrðe ꝥ inc byð bam þearflic for Gode. ⁊ eac gerysenlic for worolde.

with respect to bishop Æthelnoth, so as the declaration from you came; viz. that we have now blessed him. I now pray, for love of God, and for all God's saints, who depart in God the lenient, and in the holy state, that he may be worthy of the things which others were before, [as] Dunstân the Good was, and many another; so that this [man] may be as worthy of rights and regards as may be desirable for you both, and fitting before the world.

KING CNUT. M.XXIII.

✠ In nomine Dei summi et Salvatoris nostri Ihesu Christi. Certis astipulationibus nos sancti et justi patres frequentativis orationibus admonent, ut Deum quem diligimus et credimus intima mentis affectione cum bonorum operum diligentia incessanter eum timeamus et amemus, quia retributionem omnium actuum nostrorum, in die examinationis juxta uniuscujusque meritum reddet. Ideoque subtilissima mentis certatione illum imitari satagamus, licet mortalis vitæ pondere pressi et labentibus hujus seculi possessionibus simul infœcati, tamen miserationis ejus largitate caducis opibus æterna cœlestis vitæ præmia mercari queamus. Quapropter ego Cnut, divina favente gratia Anglorum ceterarumque adjacentium insularum basileus, propriis manibus meis, capitis mei coronam auream pono super altare Christi in Dorobernia, ad opus ejusdem æcclesiæ; et concedo eidem æcclesiæ, ad

[1] Of Canterbury.

victum monachorum, portum de Sanduuic et omnes exitus ejusdem aquæ, ab utraque parte fluminis, cujuscunque terra sit, a Pipernæsse usque ad Mearcesfleote, ita ut natante nave in flumine cum plenum fuerit, quam longius de navi potest securis parvula, quam Angli vocant [1]'taper eax' super terram projici, ministri æcclesiæ Christi rectitudines accipiant; nullusque omnino homo habet aliquam consuetudinem in eodem portu, exceptis monachis æcclesiæ Christi. Eorum autem est navicula et transfretatio portus et theloneum omnium navium cujuscunque sit, et undecunque veniat, quæ ad prædictum portum et ad Sanduuic venerint. Si quid autem in magno mari extra portum quantum mare plus se retraxerit, et adhuc statura unius hominis tenentis lignum quod Angle nominant 'spreot', et tendentis ante se quantum potest, monachorum est. Quicquid etiam ex hac parte medietatis maris inventum et delatum ad Sanduuic fuerit, sive sit vestimentum, sive rete, arma, ferrum, aurum, argentum, medietas monachorum erit, alia pars remanebit inventoribus. Quod si alter deinceps codicellus emerserit, qui priscæ tempestatis stilo digestus huic nostræ confirmationi visus fuerit aliquatenus refragari, illiusmodi litteraturæ membranula suricum morsibus corrodenda, aut certe potius ignivomi vaporis incendio adnichiletur; ejusque præsentator cujuscumque extiterit personæ, pro purgamento favillæ deputetur, et ignominiosissima confusione subsannetur, et ab omnibus in circuitu præsentibus uni animo detestetur. Hujusque privilegii rata confirmatio semper in posterum prævaleat, et tam Dei omnipotentis auctoritate quam mea, simul et omnium concorditer optimatum corroboratione confirmata contra universa refragatorum cogitamenta cunctis succedentibus ævi temporibus stabilis et inconcussa, columnaris status similitudine perseverantissimo jure consolidetur. Si autem, quod non optamus, aliquis, tumido supercilio inflatus, hanc nostram corroborationem infringere vel minuere temptaverit, noverit se anathematizatum esse a Deo et sanctis ejus, ni ante mortem digna satisfactione emendaverit quod injuste deliquit. Scripta est hæc scedula anno ab incarnatione Domini nostri Ihesu Christi

[1] O. Nor. tapar-öxi, *securis malleata.*

millesimo xxiii., his testibus concordantibus quorum nomina inferius lucide karaxantur.

✠ Ego Cnut rex Anglorum hanc litteraturæ confirmationem indeclinabiliter confirmo. ✠ Ego Æðelnoðus Dorobernicus archipræsul hanc prærogativam vexillo sancto confirmavi. ✠ Ego Ælfricus Eboracensis æcclesiæ archiepiscopus ejusdem regis benevolentiam cum sanctæ crucis signo corroboro. ✠ Ego Ælfwinus Lundoniensis æcclesiæ pontifex consensi. ✠ Ego Ælfsinus Wentoniæ episcopus assensum præbui. ✠ Ego Byrhtwoldus Corviniensis æcclesiæ episcopus condonavi. ✠ Ego Æðelricus Dorccensis æcclesiæ episcopus consolidavi. ✠ Ego Ælmær bisceop. ✠ Ego Godwine bisceop. ✠ Ego Bryhtwine b̄. ✠ Ego Æðelstan b̄. ✠ Ego Ælmær abb̄. ✠ Ego Brihtmær abb̄. ✠ Ego Brihtwig abb̄. ✠ Ego Wulfnoð abb̄. ✠ Ego Godwine dux. ✠ Ego Eglaf dux. ✠ Ego Đrym dux. ✠ Ego Yric dux. ✠ Ego Đord minister. ✠ Ego Agemund m̄. ✠ Ego Ægelric m̄. ✠ Ego Ælfwine m̄. ✠ Ego Brihtric m̄. ✠ Ego Leofric m̄. ✠ Ego Siræd m̄. ✠ Ego Godwine m̄. ✠ Ego Eadmær m̄.

IDEM ANGLICE.

✠ On þas hegestes Godes ⁊ ures Hlauordes Hælendes Xp̄es naman. Ure halige ⁊ ure rihtwise fæderes mid soðre gefæstnunge· ⁊ mid gelomrædre menunge us gemenegið· ꝥ we ðone ælmihti God ðe we lufiað ⁊ we on beleuað mid inweordre gelustfulnesse ure heorten· ⁊ mid geornfulnesse godre wurke unatirendlice ondræden ⁊ luuian· forði ðe he scel geldan edlean alre ure weorke on domes dæge æfter æghwilces mannes earnunge· ⁊ forði mid

✠ In the name of God the highest and of our Saviour Jesus Christ. Our holy and our righteous fathers, with true confirmation and with frequent admonition admonish us, that we, with inward joyfulness of our heart, and with diligence in good works, should untiringly dread and love the Almighty God whom we love, and in whom we believe; because he shall pay the reward of all our works on doomsday, according to each man's desert; and there-þan hehlicastan gewinne ures modes swinke we him to gefolgienne· þeah ðe we gesæmde beon mid þare berdene ðæs deadlices liues· ⁊ ðare gewitendre æhte ðises middaneardes beon awemde· þeahhwæðere we magen gebecgen ða ece meden ðas heouenlices liues mid ðam riosenden welan· ⁊ forði ic Cnut· þurh Godes geue Ænglelandes kining· ⁊ ealre þare eglande ðe ðærto licgeð· legge up an Cristes weouod in Cantwareberig mines heouodes kinehelm mid minen agenen handen· to ðas ilcen menstres freme· ⁊ ic ann ðam ilikan menstre· to ðare munece bigleoue· ða hæuene on Sandwic· ⁊ ealle ða lændinge ⁊ ða gerihte of ðam ilkan wætere· of ægðer healue ðas streames· age land se ðe hit age· fram Pipernæsse to Mærcesfleote· swa ꝥ ðonne hit bið full flod ⁊ ꝥ scip bið aflote· swa feorr swa mæg an taper æx beon geworpen ut of ðam scipe up on ꝥ land· ða gereflanges of Cristes circean underfōn ða gerihte· ne næfre nān man a nanes kennes wisan næfð nænne anwæld on ðare ilicere hæuene· butan ða munekes of Cristes circean· ⁊ heore is ꝥ scip ⁊ se ouer-

fore with the highest struggle of our mind, let us strive to follow him; for though we be loaded with the burthen of this deathlike life and with the transitory possessions of this world we are polluted, yet we may buy the eternal meed of the heavenly life with perishable riches. And therefore, I Cnut, by God's grace king of England and of all the islands thereto adjacent, lay upon Christ's altar in Canterbury the kingly crown of my head, with my own hands, for the same monastery's benefit. And I give to the same monastery, for the subsistence of the monks, the haven of Sandwich, and all the landings and dues of both sides of the stream, let own the land whoever owns it, from Pepperness to Marfleet; so that when it is full flood, and the ship is afloat, as far as a 'taper-axe' can be cast out from the ship upon the land, let the ministers of Christchurch receive the dues. Nor shall ever any man, in any kind of way, have any power in the same haven, except the monks of Christchurch. And theirs shall be the ship and the ferry over the haven, and the toll of all ships, be it whosesoever færeld ðare hæuene. ⁊ se tolne of ealle scipen bi ðas ðe hit beo. ⁊ cume ðanon ðe hit cume. ðe to ðare ilicare hæuene æt Sandwic cumð. ⁊ gif aht is in ðare micelre sæ wiðutan ðare hæuene. swa micel swa seo sæ heo mæst wiðteohð. ⁊ git anes mannes lenge ðe healt anne spreot on his hand. ⁊ strecð hine swa feor swa he mæg aræcan into ðere sæ. ꝥ is ðare muneke. ⁊ eal ꝥ ðe of ðas healue ðare middel sæ wurð gefunden ⁊ to Sandwic gebroht. bi hit scrud. bi hit net. oððe wæpne. oððe isen. gold oððe seoluer. ꝥ healue dæl sceal bion ðare muneke. ⁊ ꝥ oðer dæl scel beliuan ðam þe hit findæð. ⁊ gif ænig oðer gewrit heoneforð wurð forðgebroht. ðe beo heortoforen gemaked. ðe on æniges kinnes wisen beo geðuht ðissere ure gefæstnunge to wiðcweðene. ꝥ gewrit beo geworpen musen to gnagene. oððe on fere to forbærnenne. ⁊ se ðe hit forð brængð. beo swilces hades swilc he beo. bio he gehealden for æsce geswap. ⁊ mid ealre ðare unwurðreste scame beo he gescænt. ⁊ of eallan ðan mannan ðe ðær gehænde beoð mid âne mode wurð he gescunned. ⁊ seo strange ge-

(ship) it may be, and come whencesoever it may come, which shall come to the said haven at Sandwich. And if there is aught in the great sea without the haven, as far as the sea at the utmost recedes, and yet the length of a man holding a pole in his hand, and stretching himself as far as he can reach into the sea, that is the monks'; and all that which is found on this side of the middle sea, and brought to Sandwich, be it a garment, be it a net, or a weapon, or iron, gold or silver, the half part shall be for the monks, and the other part shall remain for him who finds it. And if any other writing shall henceforth be brought forth, that shall have been heretofore made, which, in any kind of way, may seem to gainsay this our confirmation, be that writing cast to the mice to gnaw, or into the fire to be burnt: and whosoever shall bring it forth, be he of whatever condition he may, be he kept for sweeping ashes, and with all the most disgraceful shame be he shent; and of all the men who are there at hand, with one mind be he shunned. And be the strong confirmation of this charter fæstnunge ðissere landboc æfre mã heoneforð beo gestranged. ⁊ ægðer mid ðæs Almihtiges Godes ealderdōme ⁊ mīnre ⁊ ealre minre þegene gefæstnunge togænes ealre ðare wiðcweðendre smæigunge on ecnesse staðelfæst ⁊ unawægendlic mid þurhwuniende rihte beo gefæstned. ⁊ gif ænig is ꝥ gewilnað oððe to brekenne oððe to gelitligene mid toðundene modignesse ðas ure gefæstnunge. wite he hine selfne amansumod fram Gode ⁊ fram eallan his halgan. butan he toforan ðam deaðe. mid wurðe behriwsunge. gebete ꝥ he unrihtwislice forgelte.

Ðeos landbōc wæs gewriten on ðan þusende ⁊ þri ⁊ twentehte gære fram ures Hlauordes Hælendes Cristes akennednesse. mid ðare geðwærunge ðissere manne ðe here naman heræfter beoð gewritene.

evermore henceforth strengthened; and both with the authority of Almighty God, and the confirmation of myself and of all my thanes, against the machinations of all the gainsayers, to eternity stable and immovable, with perpetual right be it confirmed. And if there is any who, swollen up with pride, desires either to violate or diminish this our confirmation, let him know himself excommunicated from God and from all his saints, unless before death, with worthy penitence, he amend the sin he has unrighteously committed.

This charter was written on the thousandth and three and twentieth year from the birth of our Saviour Jesus Christ, with the consent of these men, whose names are hereafter written.

KING CNUT. M.XXIII.

CARTA REGIS CANUTI, DE QUIBUSDAM IMMUNITATIBUS ECCLESIÆ SANCTI PAULI PER IPSUM CONCESSIS.

✠ Ic Cnud cyng grete mīne biscopes. ⁊ mīne eorles. ⁊ ealle mīne þegenas. on þan

✠ I Cnut king greet amicably my bishops and my earls, and all my thanes, in scīran þær mīne preostas on S. Paules mynstre habbað land inne. freondlice. ⁊ ic ciðe eow ꝥ ic wylle ꝥ hig beon heora sacc here ⁊ socna weorðe. tolles ⁊ teames. binnan tīd ⁊ buton tīd. ⁊ swa full ⁊ swa forð swa hig hæfdon on æniges cynges deage fyrmest on ællan þingan. binnan burh ⁊ butan. ⁊ ic nelle geðafian ꝥ nān man æt ænigum þingan heom misbeode. ⁊ þyses is to gewitnesse Ægelnoð arcebiscop. ⁊ Ælfric arcebiscop. ⁊ Ælwi biscop. ⁊ Ælfwine biscop. ⁊ Duduce biscop. ⁊ Godwine eorl. ⁊ Leofric eorl. ⁊ Osgod Clape. ⁊ Đored. ⁊ oðre genoge. God hine aweorge þe þis awænde.

the shires where my priests of St Paul's monastery possess land. And I make known to you that I will that they be worthy of their saca and socn, toll and team, within tide and without tide, as fully and as freely, as they most fully had in any king's day, in all things, within town and without. And I will not consent that any man, in any things, misuse them. And of this are witness: Ægelnoth archbishop, and Ælfric archbishop, and Ælwi bishop, and Ælfwine bishop, and Duduc bishop, and Godwine earl, and Leofric earl, and Osgod Clapa, and Thored, and others enough. May God curse him who shall pervert this.

WULFRIC. M.XXIII.

✠ Her swutelað on þysum gewrite ymbe þa forwerda þe Wulfric ⁊ se arcebisceop geworhtan þa he begeat þæs arceƀ. swuster him to wife. ꝥ is þæt he behet hyre ꝥ land æt Ealretune ⁊ æt Ribbedforda hire dæg. ⁊ he behet hire ꝥ land æt Cnihtewican. ꝥ he wolde hit hire begytan

✠ Here is made known in this writing concerning the compacts which Wulfric and the archbishop made, when he got him the archbishop's sister to wife. That is, that he promised her the land at Alderton, and at Ribbesford, for her day; and he promised her the land at Knightwick, þreora manna dæg æt þam hirede on Wincelcumbe· ⁊ sealde hyre ꝥ land æt Eanulfintune· to gyfenne ⁊ to syllenne þan þe hire leofest wære· on dæge ⁊ æfter dæge· þær hire leofest wære· ⁊ behet hire L. mances goldes· ⁊ xxx. manna· ⁊ xxx. horsa. Nu wæs þyses to gewitnesse Wulfstan arceƀ. · ⁊ Leofwine ealdorman· ⁊ Æðelstan ƀ. · ⁊ Ælfword aƀƀ. · ⁊ Briteh munuc· ⁊ manig god man to eacan heom· ægðer gehadode ge leawede· ꝥ þas forewerda þus geworhte wæran. Nu syndon to þysum forwordan twa gewrita· oðer mid þam arceƀ. on Wigerceastre· ⁊ oðer mid Æðelstane ƀ. on Herforda.

that he would get it for her, for three men's day, from the convent at Winchcombe; and he gave her the land at Eanulfintun, to give and to sell to whom to her might be most desirable, for her day and after her day, where to her might be most desirable; and he promised her L. mancuses of gold, and xxx. men, and xxx. horses. Now of this were for witness: Wulfstân archbishop, and Leofwine aldorman, and Æthelstân bishop, and Ælfword abbot, and Briteh monk, and many a good man besides them, both ordained and lay, that these compacts were thus made. Now of these compacts there are two writings; one with the archbishop in Worcester; and the other with bishop Æthelstân in Hereford.

EADWINE, A MONK[1].

Ic Eadwine munek, cildremeistre on Niwan munstre· grette þe wel Alfsie biscop. Ic kyþe þe laford ꝥ nu for þrum gearan ic læi innan minan portice anbutan non-

I Eadwine monk, childmaster in the New monastery, greet thee well, bishop Ælfsie. I make known to thee, lord, that now three years since I lay within my

[1] I am unable to assign a date to this strange narrative. Ælfsige, to whom it is addressed, was bishop of Winchester from 1015 to 1032; while Ægelwine did not succeed to the see of Durham till 1056. From 1020 to 1048 Eadmund was bishop of Durham.

tide· end me ateude þer se halga Cuthbert openlice. Ic þes swyþe bliþe wes· ic eode to minen abboden Ælfwine ⁊ bed hine ꝥ ic moste norþ faran to þam halgan ⁊ hine gesecan· ac min abbod Ælfwine me þes forwurnde ⁊ eac forbied. Ic þa feng on mine agenne red ⁊ eode me þider norð· ⁊ me þer Ægelwine bisscup mid wurscupe underfeng· ⁊ me geuþe God ⁊ þe halga ꝥ ic hine mid minen handen gewochs· ⁊ his heafod mid gambe gekamde· ⁊ his her mid scearan gescherf[1]· ⁊ hine eall mid niwan scrude hie scrudde· ⁊ his ealde claþes him fram genam· sume ic þer let· ⁊ sume her habbe. Nu laford buþohte ic me ꝥ ic nefde mines abbodes leaue· ⁊ ic þerfore ham gæwende ⁊ kom me into Ealden mynstre· ⁊ gesohte Crist· ⁊ Sancte Peter· ⁊ Sancte Suiðun· ⁊ þe wolde· ac þu nere æt ham· ac ic funde Leofwine þane decanum ⁊ ealle þa gebroðþra· ⁊ hi me wurþlice underfengen· ⁊ me to minen abboden geþingade· ⁊ he me blyþelice underfeng· si Gode lof.

Nu willic þe kyþan· hla-

cell, about noontide, and there the holy Cuthbert manifestly appeared to me. At this I was very blithe: I went in to my abbot, Ælfwine, and prayed him that I might go north to the saint and seek him; but Ælfwine my abbot refused me this, and also forbade. I then took my own counsel, and went thither north, and bishop Ægelwine received me with worship; and God and the saint granted me that I washed him with my hands, and combed his head with a comb, and sheared his hair with shears[1], and clothed him all with new clothing, and took from him his old clothes; some I left there, and some I have here. Now, lord, I bethought me that I had not my abbot's leave, and I therefore wended home, and came to the Old monastery, and sought Christ, and S[t] Peter, and S[t] Swithin, and would thee; but thou wast not at home: but I found Leofwine the dean and all the brothers, and they received me worthily, and interceded for me to my abbot, and he received me blithely, praise be to God!

I will now make known to

[1] On opening the coffin in the year 1104, there were found an ivory comb and scissors of silver.

ford Ælfsie biscup· hu þys gecuþdreðene fyrmest wæs gestaþolod bytwyx Ealden mynstre ⁊ Niwan mynstre· eal swa ic sylf hi gehyrde· þa þe ic gung wæs· whu se lafard Sanct Ælwold leig seoch· ⁊ him kom to þe halga Dunstan of Cantuwarabyre for hine to gesydde· ⁊ ealdor Æþelgar abbod þyder eode· ⁊ munekes mid him· þet wes Boia þe ealde· ⁊ Æluric decanus· ⁊ Ælfnoð þe metere· ⁊ Ælfwine þe nu abbod his· ⁊ þer coman munkes of Ealden mynstre· ꝥ wes Ealdwig· ⁊ Wlstan cantor· ⁊ Godwine decanus· ⁊ managa oþre mid him. Boia þe ealde munuk set a cneuwa ætforan Sc̄e Aþelwolde· ⁊ bed hine ꝥ he scolde sette gode lagan bytwyx þam twam mynstre on muneke dagan eal swa Friþestan biscup hefd geset a pruste dagan· ꝥ wes ꝥ þa tweien hiredes weren eall to anan on eallan godcunnesse· ⁊ ꝥ wes gif eni prust forðferde on aþere stede· hi scolde ealle togædere cuman ⁊ ꝥ lic buburian· ⁊ ealne þeuwdom don þe to Gode bulumpe· ⁊ a cyrhalgan dei· þe byþ binnan Ealdan mynstre scolden cuman þa prustes of Niwen

thee, lord bishop Ælfsie, how this agreement was first established between the Old monastery and the New monastery, as I myself heard it, when I was young, how the lord St Ælwold[1] lay sick, and St Dunstan came to him from Canterbury, to sit with him, and the elder abbot Æthelgar went thither, and monks with him: that was Boia the Old, and Ælfric dean, and Ælfnoth the purveyor, and Ælfwine who is now abbot. And there came monks from the Old monastery: that was Ealdwig, and Wulstan chanter, and Godwine dean, and many others with them. Boia the Old, monk, knelt before St Athelwold, and prayed him that he would set good laws betwixt the two monasteries in monks' days, as bishop Frithestân had done in priests' days: that was that the two fraternities should be all as one in all holiness: and it was then, that if any priest died in either place, they should come altogether and bury the corpse, and do all the service which pertains to God. And on the church-hallowing day which is in the Old monastery, the priests should

[1] Bishop of Winchester, 963–984.

mynstre to Ealden mynstre· ⁊ þer bun to euensange· ⁊ to messen· ⁊ to gerurde· ⁊ þa prustes of Ealden mynstre scolden cumen to Niwan mynstre æt Sc̃e Iudoces messe deie· eal on þa ylcan wisan· ⁊ gyf ænie prusten mistimide on aþaran mynstre· ne fore he nawider ac gesohte he his nagaburas ⁊ him þingadan. Þa þis gehurde Sanc Æþelwold þa he rede ꝥ hit swa were nu on his timan ⁊ on þeren munechen deie· ⁊ cweð Godes curs eallan þam þe efre þis unduden· ⁊ geaf to tacne ꝥ hit staþelfest bun scolde twa brune messehagala· ana into Ealden mynstre· ⁊ ana . . . . .

come from the New monastery to the Old monastery, and there stay to evensong, and to mass, and to refection. And the priests of the Old monastery should come to the New monastery on St Judoc's mass-day, all in the same wise. And if any priest misconducted himself in either monastery, he went nowhither, but he sought his neighbours, and they mediated for him. When St Æthelwold heard this, he then advised that it should now be so in his time and in monks' days; and pronounced God's curse on all those who should ever undo this; and gave, as a token that it should be so established, two brown mass-vestments, one to the Old monastery, and one . . . . .

KING CNUT. M.XXXII.

✠ Her geswutelað on þisum gewrite ꝥ Cnut cyng let ꝥ land æt Folcstan into Cristes cyrcean on Cantwarbyrig· þa Eadsige his preost gecyrde into munuke· to þam forewearde ꝥ Eadsige munuc hit hæbbe his lifes timan for his gehyrsumnysse þe he him wel gehyrde· ⁊ he hit ne mæg naðer ne gifan· ne syllan· ne

✠ Here is made known, in this writing, that king Cnut conceded the land at Folkeston to Christchurch in Canterbury, when Eadsige his priest turned monk, under the agreement, that Eadsige the monk have it for his lifetime, for his obedience with which he has well obeyed him; but he may neither give forspecan· ne forspillan ut of ðam halgan minstre· ac æfter his dæge ga ꝥ land þam hirede on hand ðe þonne Criste þeniað innan ðam halgan mynstre· mid sake ⁊ socne· ⁊ mid eallon ðam þingon ðe þær fyrmest to læg· forðam ðe his witan him sædon ꝥ hit hwilon ær læg ðiderin on Æðelstanes dæge kynges· ⁊ on Odan arcebiscopes· ⁊ hit wearð syððan ut gedon mid mycelan unrihte. Nu geuðe he þis land into Cristes cyrcæan his sawle to ecære alysednisse· ⁊ gif ænig man sy swa dyrstig ongæn God ꝥ þis awendan wille awænde hine God ælmyhtig from heofonrices myriðe into hellegrunde· buton þas he æt his ænde hit ðe dæpper gebete. Ðis wæs gedon innon Suðrige on Kyngestune· on þone halgan dæg Pentecosten. And þises wæs to gewitnesse· Ælfgifu Imma· Ælfsige bisceop on Winceastre· ⁊ Ægelric ƀ. on Suðsexean· ⁊ Ælmer abbud æt Sc̃e Augustine· ⁊ Wulnoð abbud æt Westminstre· ⁊ Ælfwine abbud æt Niwan minstre· ⁊ Wulfsi abbud æt Certesige· ⁊ Ulf eorl· ⁊ Eglaf eorl· ⁊ Leofric eorl· ⁊ Harold eorl· ⁊ Yric eorl· ⁊ Ðored steallare· ⁊ Agamund·

nor sell it, nor promise it nor waste it away from the holy monastery; but after his day let this land go into the possession of the brotherhood who shall then serve Christ within the holy monastery, with sac and socn, and with all the things which were first attached thereto; because his 'witan' said to him, that it a while before was attached thereto, in the day of king Æthelstân, and of archbishop Oda; and it was afterwards alienated with great injustice. He now gives the land to Christchurch for the eternal redemption of his soul. And if any man be so audacious towards God that he will avert this, may God Almighty avert him from the joy of heaven's kingdom into the ground of hell; unless at his end he the more deeply make amends. This was done in Surrey, at Kingston, on the holy day of Pentecost. And of this were to witness Ælfgifu Imma, Ælfsige bishop of Winchester, and Ægelric bishop of Sussex, and Ælmer abbot of St Augustine's, and Wulnoth abbot of Westminster, and Ælfwine abbot of the New monastery, and Wulfsi abbot of Chertsey, and Ulf earl, and Eglaf earl, and Osgod Clapa· ⁊ Tofig· ⁊ Ægelwine Ælfhelmes sunu· ⁊ Siword æt Cylleham· ⁊ Ægelric Bigga· ⁊ Ælfword Kæntisce· ⁊ Eadmær æt Burham· ⁊ ealle þæs kyninges rædgyfan· gehadode ⁊ læwede· ðe þær gesamnode wæron. And þissera gewrita synd þreo· ān is innon Cristes cyrcean· oðer æt Sc̃e Augustine· ⁊ þe ðridde is inne mid þæs kynges haligdome.

and Leofric earl, and Harold earl, and Yric earl, and Thored constable, and Agamund, and Osgod Clapa, and Tofig, and Ægelwine Ælfhelm's son, and Siword at Chilham, and Ægelric Bigga, and Ælfword Kæntisce, and Eadmær at Burham, and all the king's councillors, ordained and lay, who were there assembled. And of these writings there are three: one is in Christchurch, another at St Augustine's, and the third is in the king's treasury.

IDEM LATINE.

✠ Hic declaratur in hac scriptura quia Cnut rex terram illam quæ Folkestane dicitur concessit æcclesiæ Christi Cantuariæ, quando Eadsinus presbyter suus monachus ibi effectus est; ea videlicet conventione, ut idem Eadsinus monachus habeat terram illam quamdiu vixerit, propter obædientiam qua bene regi servivit. Et ipse non potest eandem terram donare, nec vendere, nec verbis forisfacere, nec extirpare de eadem ecclesia Christi; sed post ejus obitum eat terra in dominium conventus, qui tunc servierit æcclesiæ Christi, cum sake et socne, et cum omnibus rebus quæ prius ad eandem terram pertinebant; quoniam barones regis dicebant ei quia olim eadem terra æcclesiæ Christi fuit in diebus Æðelstani regis et Odonis archiepiscopi, et juri ejusdem æcclesiæ sublata fuerat cum magna injustitia. Nunc ergo concedit ipse hanc terram æcclesiæ Christi, pro æterna redemptione animæ suæ. Et si aliquis hominum fuerit tam audax contra Deum, qui hanc regis munificentiam mutare voluerit, avertat illum Deus Omnipotens a gaudiis regni cœlestis in profundum inferni; nisi ante finem perfectius emendaverit. Hoc fuit factum in Suðrie apud Kyngestune, in die sc̃o Pentecosten. Et huic rei fuit testis Ælgiua Imma domina· ⁊ Ægelnoðus archiepiscopus· ⁊ Ælfwinus episcopus Lundoniæ· ⁊ Ælfsinus episcopus Wintoniæ· ⁊ Egelricus episcopus de Suðseaxe· ⁊ Ælmerus abbas de Sancto Augustino· ⁊ Wlnoðus abbas de Westmonasterio· ⁊ Ælfwinus abbas de Novomonasterio· ⁊ Wlfsinus abbas de Certesie· ⁊ Ulf comes· ⁊ Eglaf comes· ⁊ Lifricus comes· ⁊ Haroldus comes· ⁊ Yrcus comes· ⁊ Ðoredus steallara· ⁊ Agamundus· ⁊ Osgodus Clapa· ⁊ Tofig· ⁊ Ælwinus filius Ælfelmi· et Siwordus de Cilleham· ⁊ Ægelricus Bigga· ⁊ Ælwordus de Cantia· ⁊ Eadmerus de Burhham· ⁊ omnes conciliarii regis, tam ordinati quam laici, qui ibi fuerant congregati. Et horum brevium tria sunt: unum in æcclesia Christi, alterum in monasterio Sancti Augustini, et tertium in thesauro regis cum reliquiis sanctorum.

KING CNUT. M.XXXII.

✠ Regnante in perpetuum Domino, qui sua ineffabili potentia omnia disponit atque gubernat, vicesque temporum hominumque mirabiliter discernens, terminumque incertum, prout vult æquanimiter imponens, et de secretis naturæ mysteriis misericorditer docet, ut de fugitivis et sine dubio transitoriis mansura regna Dei suffragio adipiscenda sunt. Quapropter ego Cnut, rex Anglorum cæterarumque gentium in circuitu persistentium gubernator et rector, cum consilio et decreto archipræsulis nostri Æðelnoti, simulque cunctorum Dei sacerdotum, et consensu optimatum meorum, ob amorem cœlestis regni, et indulgentiam criminum meorum et relaxationem peccaminum fratris mei regis Eadmundi, concedo æcclesiæ sanctæ Dei genitricis semperque virginis Mariæ Glastoniæ jura et consuetudines in omni regno meo, et omnes forisfacturas omnium terrarum suarum; et sint terræ ejus sibi liberæ et solutæ ab omni calumpnia et inquietatione, sicuti meæ michi habentur. Verum illud præcipue ex Omnipotentis Patris, et Filii, et Spiritus Sancti auctoritate, et perpetuæ Virginis interdictione prohibeo, et universis regni mei præpositis et primatibus, super suam salutem præcipio, ut nullus omnino illam insulam intrare audeat, cujuscumque ordinis sit aut dignitatis; set omnia, tam in æcclesiasticis quam in sæcularibus causis tantummodo abbatis judicium et conventus expectent, sicuti prædecessores mei sanxerunt et privilegiis confirmaverunt, Kentwines, Ines, Cuðredus, Ælfredus, Eadwardus, Aðelstanus, et gloriosissimus Eadmundus, et incomparabilis Eadgarus. Si quis autem, quovis deinceps tempore, sub aliqua occasione, interrumpere atque irritum facere hujus privilegii testimonium nisus fuerit, sit a consortio piorum ultimi examinis ventilabro dispertitus. Si quis vero benevola intentione hæc facere, probare, et defendere statuerit, beatissimæ Dei genitricis Mariæ et omnium sanctorum intercessione, amplificet Deus portionem ejus in terra viventium. Scripta est hujus privilegii donatio et promulgata in lignea basilica, sub præsentia regis Cnutonis, anno ab incarnatione Domini M.XXXII. [Indictione secunda].

KING CNUT AND QUEEN ÆLFGIFU EMMA. M.XXXII.

✠ Her swutelað on ðysan gewrite hū Cnut cyncg ⁊ Ælfgifu seo hlæfdige geūðan Eādsige heora preoste· ða he gecyrde to munece· ꝥ he moste ateōn ꝥ land æt Apoldre· swa him sylfan leofast wære. Ða sealde he hit into Cristes cyrican ðam Godes þeōwum· for his sawle· ⁊ he hit gebohte ðæt æt ðam hirede his dæg ⁊ Eadwines mid feower pundum· on ꝥ forwyrd ꝥ man gelæste ælce geare into Cristes cyrican III. wæga cæses of þam lande ⁊ þreo gebind æles· ⁊ æfter his dæg ⁊ Eadwines

✠ Here is made known, in this writing, how king Cnut and Ælfgifu the lady granted to Eadsige their priest, when he turned monk, that he might dispose of the land at Appledore as to himself should be most desirable. Then gave he it to Christchurch, for the servants of God, for his soul. And he bought that at . . . . of the convent, for his day and Eadwine's, for four pounds, with the agreement that there should be paid every year to Christchurch III. weys of cheese from the land, and gange ꝥ land into Cristes cyrican· mid mete ⁊ mid mannum· eal swa hit ðænne gegōdod sy· for Eādsiges sawle. ⁊ he gebohte ꝥ land æt Werhornan æt ðam hirede his dæge ⁊ Eadwines eac mid feower pundan· ðænne gæð ꝥ land forð mid ðam oðran· æfter his dæge ⁊ Eadwines· into Cristes cyrican· mid þære tilðe ðe þar ðænne on sy· ⁊ ꝥ land on his dæg æt Berwican ðe he geearnode æt his hlāforde Cnute cynge· ⁊ he geunn eac þæs landes æt Orpedingtune on his dæge for his sawle into Cristes cyrican· ðam Godes þeowum to scrūdland· þe he gebohte mid hundeahtigum marcan hwites seolfres be hustinges gewihte· ⁊ he geun eāc ðæs landes æt Palstre ⁊ æt Wihtriceshamme æfter his dæge ⁊ Eadwines forð mid ðam oðrum ðam Godes þeowum to fosterlande for his sawle. Đises cwides he geunn ðam hirede to þam forwyrdan· ꝥ hi æfre hine wel healdan· ⁊ him holde beon on life ⁊ æfter life· ⁊ gif hi mid ænegan unrǣde wið hine ðas forwyrd tobrecen· ðonne stande hit on his āgenan gewealde hu he siððan his āgen ateōn wille. Đises is to gewitnesse·

three bundles of eels. And after his day and Eadwine's, let the land go to Christchurch, with meat and with men, as it may then be enriched; for Eadsige's soul. And he bought the land at Warehorne from the convent, for his day and Eadwine's, also for four pounds; then will that go along with the other, after his day and Eadwine's, to Christchurch, with the tilth which may then be thereon. And the land, for his day, at Berwick, which he received from his lord, king Cnut. And he gives also the land at Orpington, for his day, for his soul, to Christchurch, as clothing-land for God's servants, which he bought for eighty marks of white silver by husting's weight. And he also gives the land at 'Palstre' and at Wittersham, after his day and Eadwine's, along with the others, to God's servants, as fosterland, for his soul. This bequest he gives to the convent on the condition that they ever will maintain him, and be kind to him in life and after life. But if they, by any evil counsel, break this compact with him, then let it stand in his power how he will afterwards dispose of his property. Of this is witness:

Cnut cyng ⁊ Ælfgyfu seo hlǽfdige. ⁊ Æðelnoð arceƀ. ⁊ Ælfstân aƀƀ. ⁊ se hired æt Sc̃e Augustine. ⁊ Brihtrīc geonga. ⁊ Æðelrīc bigenga. ⁊ Đorð Đurcylles nefa. ⁊ Tofi. ⁊ Ælfwine pr̃. ⁊ Eadwold pr̃. ⁊ ealle þæs cynges rǽdesmen.

Cnut king and Ælfgyfu the lady, and Æthelnoth archbp., and Ælfstân abbot, and the convent at St Augustine's, and Brihtric the Young, and Æthelrīc Bigenga, and Thorth Thorkell's son, and Tofi, and Ælfwine priest, and Eadwold priest, and all the king's councillors.

And ðissa gewrita syndon III.. ân is æt Cristes cyrican. ⁊ ân æt Sc̃e Augustine. ⁊ ân hæfð Eâdsige mid him sylfan.

And of these writings there are III.: one is at Christchurch, and one at St Augustine's, and one Eadsige has with himself.

KING CNUT. M.XX.-M.XXXVI.

✠ Cnut cyngc gret Eadsige bisceop. ⁊ Ælfstan abbod. ⁊ Egelric. ⁊ ealle mine þegenas on Cent freondlice. ⁊ ic cyðe eow ðat ic wylle ðæt Æðelnoð arcebisceop werige[1] his landare into his bisceoprice nu ealswa he dyde ær Ægelric wære gerefa. ⁊ siððan he gerefa wæs. forð oð ðis. ⁊ ic nelle na geðafian ðat man þam bisceope ænige unlage beode. beo gerefa se ðe beo.

✠ I king Cnut greet bishop Eadsige, and abbot Ælfstan, and Ægelric, and all my thanes in Kent, amicably. And I make known to you that I will that archbishop Ætholnoth defend[1] his land-property for his bishopric now as he did before Ægelric was reeve, and after he was reeve, on until this day. And I will not consent that any illegality be offered to the bishop, be the reeve who he may.

[1] See page 116, *note*.

ARCHBISHOP ÆTHELNOTH AND TOKIG. ABOUT M.XXXIII.

✠ Her swuteliað on ðisse Cristes bēc Æþelnoðes arcebisceopes forword ⁊ Tokiges embe ꝥ land æt Healtune. ꝥ wæs ꝥ Tokig com to Hrisbeorgan to ðam arcebisceop syþþan Æðelflæd his wif forðfaren wæs· ⁊ cydde him Wulfnoðes cwyde· ꝥ he ꝥ land becweden hæfde into Cristes cyrcean æfter his dæge ⁊ his wifes· ⁊ bæd þone arcebisceop ꝥ he ꝥ land habban moste his dæg· ⁊ æfter his dæge ꝥ hit lage into Cristes cyrcean mid eallum þingum ðe he þæron getilian mihte unbesacen· ⁊ cwæð ꝥ he wolde þam biscope þances kepan ⁊ his mannum. And se arcebisceop him þæs tiðude· ⁊ sæde ꝥ he riht wið hine gedon hæfde· ꝥ he sylf him for ðam cwyde secgean wolde· þeh he hit ær ful georne wiste. And þises wæs to gewitnysse· Æþelstan æt Bleddehlæwe· ⁊ Leofwine his sunu· ⁊ Leofric æt Eaningadene· ⁊ feala oðra godra cnihta· þeh we hi ealle ne nemnon· ⁊ eall þæs arcebiscopes hired· ge gehadude ge læwede.

✠ Here is made known, in this Christ's book [1], the compact of archbishop Æthelnoth and Tokig, concerning the land at Halton. That was, that Tokig came to Risborough to the archbishop, after Æthelflæd his wife had departed, and made known to him Wulfnoth's bequest: that he had bequeathed that land to Christchurch after his day and his wife's; and prayed the archbishop that he might have the land for his day, and that after his day it might be attached to Christchurch, with all the things which he might cultivate thereon, uncontested. And said that he would keep it gratuitously for the bishop and his men. And the archbishop granted him this, and said that he had done rightly towards him in voluntarily speaking to him about the bequest, though he knew it all full well before. And of this was witness Æthelstân at Bledlow, and Leofwine his son, and Leofric at Eaningadene, and many other good 'cnihts', though we name them not all, and all of the archbishop's family, both ordained and lay.

[1] The Gospels.

KING CNUT. M.XXXV.

✠ Ego Cnut rex, per Dei gratiam totius Angliæ regni atque Danorum, pontificibus meis revelo et ducibus meis optimatibus, cum eis etiam insimul Danis et Anglis, quod ad monasterium vetus quod est in Wintonia eternaliter concedo, Christo ad laudem, sanctoque Petro atque Paulo, sanctisque inibi quiescentibus, quatinus monasterium illud liberum permaneat ab omni servitio seculari, exceptis operibus illis quæ cunctis populis communes sunt, scilicet expeditio, sive sit in navali collectione, sive in pedestri, pontisque instauratione, murique fabrica, et quicquid interea ab omnibus generaliter pernecessarium fuerit; viguit autem libertas ista longo tempore ad prædictum monasterium, in diebus priorum regum qui ante nos regnaverunt. Proinde generaliter omnibus divulgo augmentum quod huic libertati adicere curavi, pro anime meæ redemptione, omniumque ante vel post me regnantium regum; id sunt scelera quæ dicuntur Anglice hamsocne, et forsteallas, et myndbrycas, omnisque correctionis, sive magni sive parvi, super universos quibus obedire debent qui monasterio illo ad manum Dei præsunt. Nunc ego annuo et concedo hanc libertatem Domino meo, qui bona mihi plurima concessit, quibus in hoc seculo perfunctus sum, et beato Petro, qui potestatem habet in cælo et in terra ligandi itemque solvendi ad eternum incolum contra crimina quæque nefaria. Proinde præcipio per magnam majestatem Dei, ut nullus successorum meorum hanc commutare præsumat libertatem. Si quis forte per quamlibet temeritatem, aut per diabolicam instigationem, hanc libertatem perfringere voluerit, sive hanc institutionem in aliud mutare præsumpserit, sit maledictus omnibus maledictionibus quæ in universis sanctis ascripte sunt libris; sitque segregatus a communione Domini nostri Ihesu Christi, omniumque sanctorum suorum, ligatusque perseveret quamdiu vixerit eisdem vinculis[1] quæ per seipsum Dominus suis tradidit apostolis Petro atque Paulo; et post maledictum exitum suum crucietur jugiter in profundissimo puteo, ardeatque in inferno

[1] MS. incolis.

cum diabolo et cum maledictis spiritibus secum sine fine habitantibus, nisi ante mortem suam emendaverit quod injuste commiserat.

IDEM ANGLICE.

Cnut cing· þurh Godes gyfe ealles Englelandes ⁊ ealre Dene· cyðe minan biscopan ⁊ minum eorlum ⁊ ellan minan þegnan· ægðer ge Deniscan ge Engliscan· hwæs ic gea͂n into Ealdan mynstre on Winceastre· Gode to lufe ⁊ Sc̃e Petre ⁊ Sc̃e Paule ⁊ þam halgan þe þær binnan restað· þæt his ꝥ ic wylle ꝥ þæt mynster sig frig ælces woruldlican weorces buton þam þe eallam folce gæmene is· þæt is fyrdfara· sig hit on scip fyrde sig hit on land fyrde· ⁊ bryggeweorc· ⁊ wealgewuorc· ⁊ loc hwet sig gemæne neod ealles folces. Nu stod þis ær into þam mynstre on þaræ cininga dagum þe us ætforan wære. Nu switelige ic her· on þisan gewrite· hwæt se eaca is þe ic þærto geunnen hæbbe· mynre sawle to onlysednesse ⁊ ealra minra forgenga ⁊ efterfyliendra· þet syndan hamsocne· ⁊ forsteallas· ⁊ myndbræcas· ⁊ ælces wytes· smales ⁊ greates· ofer eallæ þa men þe þam ealdre hyran sculan þe þæt mynster bewat Godes handa.

I, Cnut, king, through God's grace, of all England and of all the Danes, make known to my bishops and my earls, and all my thanes, both Danish and English, what I grant to the Old monastery in Winchester, to the praise of God, and St Peter, and St Paul, and of the saints that there within rest. That is, that I will that that monastery be free of every worldly work, except that which to all the folk is common, that is: military service, be it naval service, be it land-service, and bridge-work, and wall-work, and what may be the common need of all people. Now thus it stood before with regard to the monastery, in the days of the kings who were before us. Now I here declare, in this writing, what the augmentation is which I have thereto granted, for the redemption of my soul and those of all my predecessors and successors: That is, hâmsocn, and forestals, and mundbræcs, and every penalty, small and great,

Nu gean ic þyses frylsas mine Dryhtene to wyrðmynte· þe me ealla ða god forgeaf þæ ic on þyssere worulde gebiden hæbbe· ⁊ þam eadigan Sc̃e Petre· þe þa myhta hæfð on heofenan ⁊ on eorðan to gewryðenne ⁊ eft to onlysenne þa fæstan cnotten fyranlicra synna. Gyf hwa þonne· þurð ænige dyrstnysse· oððe þurð deofles lare· þysne freols abrecan wylle· oððe þas gesetednysse on oþer awendan durre· sig he awyrged mid eallan þan awyrgednyssan þæ synd awritene on eallan halgan bocan· ⁊ sig he ascyred fram ures Drihtnes gemanan· ⁊ ealre his halgana· ⁊ syg he gebunden· þa hwile þe he libbe on þissan life· mid þam ylcan bendan þe God elmihtig þurh hine sylfne betæhte his halgan apostolan Petre ⁊ Paule· ⁊ efter his awyrgedan forðsige ligce he æfre on helle grundleasan pytte· ⁊ byrne he on þam ẽcan fyre· mid deofle ⁊ mid þam ãwyrgedum gastan· þe him midwuniað æfre buton ende· buton he hit ær his forðsiþe gebete.

over all the men who have to obey the elder who has charge of that monastery from the hand of God. I now grant these liberties, for the honour of my Lord, who has given me all the good which has in this world awaited me, and of the blessed St Peter, who has the power in heaven and on earth to bind, and again to loosen the fast knots of nefarious sins. If therefore any one, through any audacity, or through the devil's lore, will break this liberty, or may dare to turn to other this settlement, be he accursed with all the curses which are written in all the holy books, and be he severed from the communion of our Lord and all his saints; and be he bound, while he lives in this life, with the same bonds which God Almighty through himself has delivered to his holy apostles, Peter and Paul; and, after his accursed departure hence, lie he ever in the groundless pit of hell, and burn he in the eternal fire, with the devil and with the accursed spirits, which dwell with him ever without end; unless, ere his departure hence, he make amends.

Hæc siquidem libertas renovata fuit anno Dominice incarnationis M.XXXV. omnibus Anglorum episcopis et ducibus, abbatibus et principibus consencientibus, atque maledictionem æternam imponentibus huic libertati violatoribus; pacem quoque et vitam æternam optantes huic ipsi libertati piis fautoribus, quorum seniorum et principum vocabula stilus presens hoc ordine luculenter demonstrat. Ego Cnut, rex Anglorum multarumque in circuitu adjacentium insularum, hoc nostre donum renovationis hac scedula demonstrari congruum duxi. Ego Ælfgyfu regina ejusdem regis donationem ovanter divulgavi. Ego Æðelnoðus Dorovernensis ecclesie archiepiscopus confirmavi. Ego Ælfricus archiepiscopus Eboracensis æcclesiæ corroboravi. Ego Ælfwinus Wintoniensis æcclesiæ episcopus conscripsi. Ego Ælfwius Lundoniensis æcclesiæ episcopus consolidavi. Ego Bryhtwoldus Wiltoniensis ecclesie episcopus consigillavi. Ego Godwinus dux. Ego Leofric dux. Ego Asgod minister. Ego Alfwine minister. Ego Þurcil minister. Ego Ordgar minister.

KING CNUT.

Cnud rex Anglorum dedit æcclesiæ Christi brachium Sancti Bartholomei apostoli cum magno pallio, et sui capitis auream coronam, et portum de Sandwic, et omnes exitus ejusdem aque ab utraque parte fluminis, ita ut natante nave in flumine cum plenum fuerit, quam longius de navi potest securis parvula super terram proici, debet a ministris æcclesiæ Christi rectitudo navis accipi; nullusque omnino hominum aliquam consuetudinem in eodem portu habet, exceptis monachis æcclesiæ Christi. Eorum quoque est transfretatio portus et navicula, et theloneum naviculæ et omnium navium quæ ad Sandwic venerint a Pepernessa usque Norðmutha. Si quid autem in magno mari reptum fuerit delatum Sandwic, medietatem æcclesia Christi habebit, reliqua vero pars inventoribus remanebit.

KING CNUT.

✠ Ego Knut, per Dei misericordiam basileus, Ægelnodo archiepiscopo, et omnibus episcopis, abbatibus, comitibus, vicecomitibus, et omnibus fidelibus totius Angliæ, salutem et amiciciam. Sciatis me dedisse Deo, et Sancto Augustino et fratribus, ut habeant eorum saca et socna, et pacis fracturam, et pugnam in domo factam, et vie assaltus, et latrones in terra sua captos, latronumque susceptionem vel pastionem super illorum proprios homines, infra civitatem et extra, theloneumque suum in terra et in aqua, atque consuetudinem que dicitur theames, et super omnes allodiarios quos eis habeo datos. Nec volo consentire ut aliquis in aliqua re de hiis se intromittat, nisi eorum prepositi quibus ipsi hæc commendaverint; quia habeo has consuetudines Deo datas et Sancto Augustino, pro redemptione anime mee et successorum meorum, ita ut eas libere et pleniter habeant et possideant inperpetuum. Et qui hanc donacionem meam infringere vel irritam facere temptaverit, a Deo Omnipotente et omni sancta ecclesia excommunicatus sit. Amen.

EÂNWEN. BEFORE M.XXXVI.

✠ Her swutelað on ðissum gewrite ꝥ an scīrgemōt sæt æt Ægelnoðes stāne be Cnutes dæge cinges. Ðær sæton Æðelstān ƀ.. ⁊ Ranig ealdorman· ⁊ Edwine þæs ealdormannes· ⁊ Leofwine Wulsiges sunu· ⁊ Ðurcil Hwīta· ⁊ Tofig Pruda com þær on þæs cinges ærende· ⁊ þær wæs Bryning scīrgerefa· ⁊ Ægelweard æt Frome· ⁊ Leofwine æt Frome· ⁊ Godrīc æt Stoce· ⁊ ealle þa þegnas on

✠ Here is made known, in this writing, that a shire-moot sat at Ægelnoth's stone, in the day of king Cnut. There sat Æthelstân bishop, and Ranig aldorman, and Eadwine the aldorman's son, and Leofwine Wulfsige's son, and Thurkil White; and Tofig Prud came there on the king's errand; and there were Bryning shire-reeve, and Ægelweard at Frome, and Leofwine at Frome, and God-

Herefordscire. Ða com þær farende to þam gemōte Edwine Enneawnes sunu· ⁊ spæc þær on his āgene modor æfter sumon dǣle landes· ꝥ wæs Weolintūn ⁊ Cyrdesleah. Ða acsode þe bisceop· hwa sceolde andswerian for his modor. Ða andsweorode Ðurcil Hwīta· ⁊ sæde ꝥ he sceolde gif he þa talu cuðe. Ða he þa talu na ne cuðe· þa sceawode man þreo þegnas of þam gemōte ðær þær heo wæs· ⁊ ꝥ wæs æt Fæliglæh· þæt wæs Leofwine æt Frome· ⁊ Ægelsig þe Reada· ⁊ Winsig Scægðman. And þa þa heo to hire comon· þa acsodon heo hwylce talu heo hæfde ymbe þa land þe hire sunu æfter spæc. Ða sæde heo ꝥ heo nān land hæfde þe him aht to gebyrede· ⁊ gebealh heo swiðe eorlice wið hire sunu· ⁊ gecleopade ða Leoflæde hire magan to hire· Ðurcilles wīf· ⁊ beforan heom to hire þus cwæð· Her sit Leoflæd min mæge þe ic geann ægþer ge mines landes· ge mines goldes· ge ræglæs· ge reafes· ge ealles þe ic āh· æfter minon dæge. And heo syððan to ðam þegnon cwæð· Dōð þegnlice ⁊ wel· abeodað mīne ærende to þam gemōte beforan eallum þam gōdan man-

ric at Stoke, and all the thanes in Herefordshire. Then came there to the moot Eadwine Eanwen's son, and there raised a claim against his own mother to a portion of land, namely at Wellington and Cradley. Then asked the bishop, who would answer for his mother? Then answered Thurkil White, and said that he would, if the claim were known to him. As the claim was not known to him, three thanes were selected from the moot, [who should ride] to where she was, and that was at Fawley. These were Leofwine at Frome, and Ægelsige the Red, and Winsige Scægthman. And when they came to her, they asked what claim she had to the lands for which her son was suing. Then said she that she had no land that in any way belonged to him, and was very bitterly incensed against her son; and then called Leoflæd her kinswoman to her, Thurkil's wife, and, before them all, thus spoke to her: "Here sits Leoflæd my kinswoman, to whom I give not only my land, but my gold, and garments, and robes, and all that I own, after my day." And she then said to the num· ⁊ cyðaþ heom hwæm ic mines landes geunnen hæbbe· ⁊ ealre mīnre ǽhte· ⁊ mīnan āgenan suna næfre nān þing· ⁊ biddað heom beōn þisses to gewitnesse. And heo þa swæ dydon· ridon to þam gemōte ⁊ cyðdon eallon þam gōdan mannum hwæt heo on heom geled hæfde. Ða astōd Ðurcil Hwīta up on þam gemōte· ⁊ bæd ealle þa þegnas syllan his wīfe þa landes clæne þe hire mage hire geūðe· ⁊ heo swa dydon· ⁊ Ðurcil rād ða to Sc̄e Æþelberhtes mynstre· be ealles þæs folces leāfe ⁊ gewitnesse· ⁊ let settan on āne Cristes bōc.

thanes, "Do nobly and well: announce my errand to the moot before all the good men, and declare to them to whom I have given my land and all my property; and to my own son never anything; and of this bid them be witness." And they then so did, rode to the moot, and declared to all the good men what she had imposed on them. Then Thurkil White stood up in the moot, and prayed all the thanes to grant to his wife clean the lands which her kinswoman had given her; and they did so. And Thurkil then rode to St Æthelberht's monastery, with the leave and witness of all the folk, and caused it to be set in a Christ's book.

KING HAROLD HAREFOOT. M.XXXVIII.

INSTRUMENTUM DE SANDWICO, QUEM QUIDEM PORTUM A MONACHIS ECCLESIÆ CHRISTI CANTUAR. ABSTULIT HAROLDUS REX, ET POSTEA EIS RESTITUIT, CUM OMNIBUS LIBERTATIBUS ET PRIVILEGIIS, EADSIGO ARCHIEPISCOPO ILLUD IMPETRANTE.

Her kyþ on þison gewrite ꝥ Harold king let berīdan Sandwic of Xp̄es cyrcean him sylfan to handa· ⁊ hæfde hit him wel neh twelf monað· ⁊ twegen hæringc tīman swa

Here is made known, in this writing, that king Harold caused Sandwich to be seized from Christchurch into his own hand, and held it well nigh a twelvemonth, and, at þeah fullice· eall ongean Godes willan· ⁊ agen ealra þara halgena þe restað innon Xp̄es cyrcean· swa swa hit him syððan sorhlice þær æfter agiode· ⁊ amanc þisan siþan wearð Ælfstān abƀ. æt Sc̄e A. ⁊ begeat mid his smeh wrencan· ⁊ mid his golde ⁊ seolfre· eall dyrnunga æt Steorran· þe þa wæs þæs kinges rædesman· ꝥ him gewearð se þridda pænig of þære tolne on Sandwic. Þa gerædde Eadsige arceƀ. þa he þis wiste· ⁊ eall se hired æt Xp̄es cyrc̄.. betweonan heom ꝥ man sende Ælfgar munuc of Xp̄es cyrc̄. to Harolde kingce· ⁊ wæs se king þa binnan Oxnaforde swyðe geseocled· swa ꝥ he læg orwene his līfes. Þa wæs Lyfingc ƀ. of Defenanscire mid þam kincge· ⁊ Þancred munuc mid him. Ða com Xp̄es cyrc̄. sand to þam ƀ. ⁊ he forð þa to þam kincge· ⁊ Ælfgar munuc mid him· ⁊ Oswerd æt Hergerdesham· ⁊ Þancred. ⁊ sædon þam kinge ꝥ he hæfde swyðe agylt wið Crist ꝥ he æfre sceolde niman ænig þing of Xp̄es cyrc̄. þe his foragengceon dydon þider inn. Sædon þam kinge þa embe Sandwic· ꝥ hit wæs him to handa geriden. Ða læg se king ⁊ asweartode eall

all events, fully two herring-seasons: all against God's will, and against all the saints' who rest within Christchurch, as it afterwards sorrowfully to him fell out. And during this time Ælfstân was abbot at St Augustine's, and obtained, with his subtle devices, and with his gold and silver, all secretly, from Steorra, who was then the king's adviser, that the third penny of the toll at Sandwich should fall to him. Then did Eâdsige, the archbishop, and all the convent at Christchurch, when they knew this, resolve among them, that Ælfgar, a monk of Christchurch, should be sent to king Harold; and the king was then in Oxford very sick, so that he lay hopeless of life. Then was Lyfing, bishop of Devonshire, with the king, and Tancred, a monk, with him. Then came the messenger from Christchurch to the bishop, and he then forth to the king, and the monk Ælfgar with him, and Oswerd at Harrietsham, and Tancred, and said to the king that he had greatly sinned against Christ, that he should ever take anything from Christchurch that his predecessors had thereto given.

mid þare sage. ⁊ swor syþþan under God ælmihtine ⁊ under ealle halgan þarto. ꝥ hit næfre næs na his rǣd na his dæd ꝥ man sceolde æfre Sandwic don ut of Xp̃es cyrc̃. Ða wæs soðlice gesyne ꝥ hit wæs oðra manna geþeaht næs na Haroldes kinges. ⁊ soðlice Ælfstanes abbodes rǣd wæs mid þam mannan þe hit of Xp̃es cyrc̃. ut geræddon. Ða sende Harold king Ælfgar munuc agen to þam arceƀ. Eadsige. ⁊ to eallon Xp̃es cyrc̃. munecan. ⁊ grette hig ealle Godes gretincge ⁊ his. ⁊ het ꝥ hig sceoldan habban Sandwic into Xp̃es cyrc̃. swa full ⁊ swa forð swa hig hit æfre hæfdon on ænies kinges dæge. ge on gafole. ge on streame. ge on strande. ge on witun. ge on eallon þam þingan þe hit æfre ænig king fyrmest hæfde ætforan him. Ða Ælfstan aƀƀ. þis ofaxode. þa com he to Eadsige arceƀ. ⁊ bæd hine fultumes to þam hirode embe þone þriddan penig. ⁊ hi begen þa to eallon gebroþran. ⁊ bædon þone hired ꝥ Ælfstan aƀƀ. moste beon þæs þriddan peniges wurðe of þære tolne. ⁊ gyfan þam hirede x. pd̃.. ac hy forwyrndon heom ealle togædere endemes. ꝥ he hit na sceolde

They then spoke to the king about Sandwich, that it had been seized into his hand. Then the king lay and all blackened at that speech, and afterwards swore by God Almighty, and by all the saints besides, that it never was either his rede or his deed that Sandwich should ever be taken away from Christchurch. Then was it truly seen that it was the thought of other men, not of king Harold; and indeed abbot Ælfstân's counsel was with those men who had counselled it away from Christchurch. Then king Harold sent the monk Ælfgar again to archbishop Eâdsige and to all the monks of Christchurch, and greeted them all with God's greeting and his; and commanded that they should have Sandwich for Christchurch, as fully and as freely as they ever had it in any king's day, both in rent, and in stream and on strand, and in mulcts, and in all things which any king most freely had before him. When abbot Ælfstân was informed of this, he came to archbishop Eâdsige, and prayed his influence with the convent with reference to the third penny, næfre gebidan· ⁊ wæs þeah Eadsige arceƀ. swiðor his fultum þonne þæs hiredes. ⁊ þa he ne mihte na forð hermid· þa gyrnde he ꝥ he moste macian foran gen Mildryþe æker ænne hwerf wið þon wodan to werianne[1]· ac eall se hired him forwyrnde þæs forð ūt mid ealle· ⁊ se arceƀ. Eadsige let hit eall to heora agene ræde. Ða gewearð se aƀƀ. Ælfstan æt· mid micelan fultume· ⁊ let delfon æt Hyppeles fleote an mycel gedelf· ⁊ wolde ꝥ scip ryne sceolde þærinne licgean eall swa hig dydon on Sandwic. Ac him na speow nan þingc þæron· forþam he swingð eall on idel þe swincð ongean Xp̄es willan· ⁊ se aƀƀ. let hit eall þus· ⁊ se hired fengc to heora agenan· on Godes gewitnesse· ⁊ Sc̄a Marian· ⁊ ealra þara halgena þe restað innan Xp̄es cyrcean· ⁊ æt Sc̄e Augustine. Þis is eall soð. gelyfe se þe wylle. Na gebad Ælfstan aƀƀ. næfre on nanan oþre wisan þone þriddan penig of Sandwic. Godes bletsung si mid us eallon a on ecnysse. Amen.

and they both then [went] to all the brothers, and prayed the convent that abbot Ælfstân might be entitled to the third penny of the toll, and give x. pounds to the convent; but finally they altogether refused them, so that he should never expect it; and yet was archbishop Eâdsige rather a supporter of him than of the convent; and when he could not effect anything herewith, then desired he that he might make a wharf over against Mildred's field, as a protection against the ford; but all the convent refused him this out and totally; and the archbishop left it all to their own discretion. Then the abbot Ælfstân set to work, with a great aid, and caused to be dug at Hyppels fleet a great delve, and intended that a ship-current should lie therein, as they had done in Sandwich. But he sped nothing therein, because he toils all in vain who toils against the will of Christ. And the abbot left it all thus, and the convent took to their own, in the witness of God and St Mary, and all the saints who rest within Christchurch and at St Augustine's. This is all true, believe it he who will. Abbot

[1] Of this passage I can only venture on a very doubtful interpretation, by assuming a substantive 'woda', equivalent to wæd, *a ford, vadum.*

Ælfstân never, in any other wise, expected the third penny from Sandwich. God's blessing be with us all for evermore. Amen.

---

* KING HARTHACNUT. M.XXXIX.-M.XLII.

✠ In nomine sancte Trinitatis et individue Unitatis. Descriptio immunitatis Hardcnut Anglorum regis super monasterio Sancti Eadmundi martyris. Quum divina scriptura multis in locis attestante liquet omnino cursum presentis vite in valle lacrimarum constitutum fore, perspecta volubili rota transeuntis mundi nulli cujuslibet sciencie perspicaci vigore pollenti hic investiganda est aut apetenda felicitas veri gaudii, cum quantalibet dignitas carnis nostræ non tantum calcabili feno comparata assimiletur prophetica voce, verum etiam ejus momentaneo flori quo nil in universitate rerum materialium visibili fragilius aut labilius invenietur haberi. Cum ergo ita se rei veritatem proculdubio liqueat habere, adeo proh dolor, hebetate mentis involvimur ceca caligine, ut odio digna amplecti solicite studeamus, et quæ diligenda merito forent omnino vitemus et postponamus, dum relinquenda jugiter tenere concupiscimus, et ad perpetuitatem celestis glorie, ad quam divina admonitione sanctorumque patrum crebra institutione invitamur cotidie, nullius affectu desiderii satagimus anelare. In cujus rei serie si quis voluerit perspicaci diligencia animadvertere, quamplurima nobis comperiet adversa digne pervenire, dum irretiti transitoria pompa ambitionis mundane salubria animarum nostrarum remedio et utilitatem præsumimus vitare et fugere, ponderose usquequam carnis superati proh nephas! fragilitate; sed juxta vocis Dominice testimonium: "In quo valet proficere aliquis hominum lucrator universarum mundanarum rerum, si contigerit anime sue pati mortale detrimentum." Quinetiam expediret valde meditari jugiter et recolere verba exhortationis Dominice, quibus conscientiarum testis ipse convertentibus ad eum se promittit appropinquare et non deesse, interminans ab eo elongantes de terra vivencium dolendos fore; quod si nil est dulcius, jocundius, atque felicius quam cum eodem Domino rerum gaudere perpetualiter in celestibus, facile e contrario agnosci datur prorsus nil esse difficilius, miserius, atque lugubrius, quam cum diabolo membrisque ejus suppliciis addici gehennalibus, cujus exactionis si effugere conamur passionem, ne pigeat evangelicis verbis mentis sollicitam adhibere intentionem, cujus instigamur salutifera admonitione, non solum tales de mammona iniquitatis nobis amicos præparare, quorum fulti auxilii levamine corporaliter hinc deficientes recipi mereamur in eterna beatitudine; sed etiam sanctam ecclesiam nostrarum facultatum quantitate ditare, et quieti Domino famulancium inibi providere. Si vero id necessarium fore credatur Christiane fidei impressione insignitis omnibus prout facultate virium devocius insudare debeant hiis ac hujusmodi similibus ceterorum bonorum operum excerciciis et fructibus, cum precipue tam bonæ devotionis liberalis munificentia nobis inesse debet regibus, quorum ditioni, non quorumlibet meritorum qualitate, sed solius divine clementie providencia et dispositione ad regendum concessus est subjectus populus, et ad tuendum a malis imminentibus sexus utriusque ordo ecclesiasticus. Denique quoniam juxta quantitatem commissi talenti durius nos esse exigendos non ignoramus in conspectu Judicis adorandi et tremendi, et pro cursu transacte vite, adepturos locum remunerationis aut pene; ideo expedit ut in suscepti officii cura ita strenue vigilare studeamus, quatinus hic cum fructu bonorum operum tranquilla pace degentes de triumphoque sanctæ Dei ecclesie hostium nostrorum gaudentes ab eodem Domino ditari mereamur auditu: "Boni euge," et perpetualiter foveri in promissa sanctorum consortio requie. Cujus adeptionis ardore inhianter succensus, ego Hardcnut, rex Anglorum vocatus, gratum mecum duxi notificare omnibus, tam præsentibus quam futuris, utriusque sexus fidelibus, præcellentissimum Cnut, genitorem meum, cum assensu, laude, et consilio suorum archiepiscoporum, episcoporum, abbatum, monachorum, clericorum, et regni sui devotorum procerum, et ceterorum minoris ordinis gregariorum militum, sicut in ordine ejusdem continetur regalis præcepti, eo tenore constituisse monachos in loco Sancti Eadmundi, uti nulli regum aut hominum umquam in futuro liceat ponere inibi ordinem alium. Quo vitalibus auris exempto, meque in ejusdem regni solio, divina opitulante clementia, substituto, et Londoniæ præsidenti in generali curie placito, Ægelnothus, Cantuariensis archiepiscopus, cum ejusdem comitatus præsule, Ælfrido nomine, et cum præfati sancti viri vocato abbate, in præsencia mea palam astitit, et utrumque a me cum eisdem petiit, ut descriptam prius a venerabili patre meo, ut dixi, ejusdem loci confirmationem proprie firmitatis auctoritate roborarem, et quod adhuc supererat proficere minime differrem; ad hæc me quid sibi vellet, et quo tenderet hujus rationis prolatio requirente; illi e contra indicaverunt repente se id velle a nostræ principalitate serenitatis ab omnibusque æcclesiasticis personis atque proceribus ibidem congregatis humiliter petere, quatinus pro remedio anime patris et matris atque mee, et prospera regni stabilitate nostri, hanc libertatis immunitatem Sancti Eadmundi locoque ejus habitatoribus dignarer concedere, ne inibi famulantes Domino cenobite pastorum æcclesiasticorum, aut ad se pertinencium personarum ullo deinceps tempore quaterentur seu inpedirentur molestia aut opressione. Dixerunt igitur se id pluribus modis, quamdiu vitalibus auris fruerentur, velle fieri, tum quia ipsi ambo interfuerunt paternæ confirmationi, tum quia meritis præfati sancti pro petito beneficio hujus sperabant a Domino mihi sibique perpetuam remunerationem provenire, tum quia verebantur ne perversioris intentionis et animi nostri successores sentirentur et invenirentur atque sui. Quo patefacto nostro generaliter auditui, licet non pocior esset eis voluntas petendi, quam michi desiderium exequendi, tamen perquisito inde consilio communi, universali concordia inprimis a devotissima matre Ymma, deinde ab omnibus opportunum responsum accepi, hoc probabile, utile, dignumque effectum esse a nullo eorum abnegari posse. Quapropter Dei Omnipotentis succensus amore, et ejusdem martyris patrocinio gaudens et honore, cum favore laudeque æcclesiasticorum pastorum mundanorumque principum, taliter descriptum constituo roboroque præceptum, ut nullus archiepiscoporum aut episcoporum, aut aliqua secundi ordinis eorum disciplinatui adherencium personarum audens, quoquomodo hujus nostræ constitutionis violare judicium præsumat quicquam consuetudinis sive dominationis amodo in eodem monasterio et villa super monachos, clericos, aut laicos, proclamare, usurpare, justiciam aliquam facere, aut missas celebrare, nisi monitus fuerit ab ipsius loci abbate, aut ipsi abbati pro homicidio aut adulterio placuerit aliquem suorum ad eum mittere. Si quis vero posterorum, quod non putamus futurum, hoc aggressus fuerit temere calumpniari aut infringere decretum, præsencium ecclesiasticorum prolate excommunicationi subjaceat, et cum Juda traditore ignis Tartarei penas indesinenter luat et sustineat, et insuper regio fisco xxx. auri talenta persolvat. Et super conservatores Domini veniat benedictio, adjutorium, et consolatio vite, et rerum congrua tranquillitas, corporis et mentis jugis protectio, salus, et sanitas, ut et hic prosperam vitam ducant, cum fructu Deo placitorum operum, atque post carnis obitum perpetuum divine contemplationis adepti gaudium feliciter in sorte maneant et consortio sanctorum.

Ego Hardcnut, rex Anglorum aliarumque nationum, hoc privilegium jussi componere, et compositum propria manu impressione Dominice crucis confirmavi. Ego Ymma regina, mater ipsius Hardcnut, gaudenter assensum præbui. Ego Ægelnothus, Dorobernensis archiepiscopus[1], signo crucis consignavi. Ego Ælfricus, Eborum archiepiscopus consignavi. Ego Ælwinus, Wynton. episcopus, consignavi. Ego Ælfricus, Elmhamensis episcopus[1], consignavi. Ego Lyuingus, Wigornensis episcopus, consignavi. Ego Wlsinus, Lichefeldensis episcopus, consignavi. Ego Ælwardus, London. episcopus, consignavi. Ego Brihtwaldus, Wilton. episcopus, consignavi. Ego Grimketel, Suthsex̄. episcopus, consignavi. Ego Eadmundus, Lyndisfarnensis episcopus, consignavi. Ego Sigeward abbas consignavi. Ego Elias abbas consignavi. Ego [Godwinus] comes assensum præbui. Ego Þuri comes consensi. Ego Leofricus comes

[1] Died in 1038, a year, at least, before Harthacnut's accession.

consensi. Ego Sywardus comes consensi. Ego Reom comes consensi.

BISHOP ALFWOLD. M.XL.

✠ Her cyð on þisum gewrite hu þa forword wæron geworhte on Excestre ætforan Godwine eorl ⁊ ætforan ealre scire· betwyx Alfwolde bisceope· ⁊ þam hirede æt Sciređurnan· ⁊ Care Tokies suna· æt þam lande æt Holacumbe. ꝥ wæs ꝥ hi wurdon sehte þæt þa gebroðra eallæ geeodon of þam lande butan anum se his Ulf gehatan· þe hyt becweden wæs· ꝥ he hyt hæbbe his dæg· ⁊ ofer his dæg ga þæt land swa swa hit stent· mid mete ⁊ mid mannum· unbesacun ⁊ unbefliten into þam halgan mynstre to Scireburnan. Đyses is to gewitnesse Godwine eorl· ⁊ Alfwold bisceop on Dorsæton· ⁊ Lyfing ƀ. be norðan· ⁊ Ælfwine abbot on Bucfæsten· ⁊ Sihtric abbot on Tæfingstoce· ⁊ Odda· ⁊ Ælfric his broðor· ⁊ Ordgar· ⁊ his twegen gebroðra· Ælfgær ⁊ Escbern· ⁊ Dodda cild· ⁊ Alon· ⁊ Æðelmær Cola sunu· ⁊ Osmær· ⁊ Leofwine æt Exon· ⁊ Ælfweard Alfwoldes sunu· ⁊ Wiking· ⁊ Ælfgær

✠ Here is made known, in this writing, how the compacts were made at Exeter, before earl Godwine and before all the shire, betwixt bishop Alfwold and the convent at Sherborne, and Care Toki's sons, concerning the land at Holcomb. That was, that they were agreed that the brothers should all go from the land save one who is named Ulf, to whom it was bequeathed: that he should have it for his day, and after his day the land should go as it stands, with meat and with men, without litigation and without contention, to the holy monastery at Sherborne. Of this are witness: Godwine earl, and Alfwold bishop in Dorsetshire, and Lyfing ƀ. in the north, and Ælfwine abbot in Buckfastleigh, and Sihtric abbot in Tavistock, and Odda, and Ælfric his brother, and Ordgar and his two brothers, Ælfgar and Escbern, and Dodda child, and Alon, and Æthelmær Cola's son, and æt Mynheafdon· ⁊ Wulfweard æt Winesham· ⁊ Hunewine Heca sunu· ⁊ Ælfwig æt Hægdune· ⁊ Godman preost· ⁊ Lutsige on Wiht. And seðe þis awendan wylle oððe ætbredan þænce þære halgan stowe· si he awend fram Gode on domesdæg ⁊ fram eallum his halgum· ⁊ si he besenct on middan þam weallendan bryne helle wites· mid Iudan Cristes læwan ā ecelice fordemed· buton he hit her ǽr þe deoppor gebete. Ðyssera gewrita syndon twa· ān ys æt Sciretburnan· ⁊ þæt oðer æt Cridiantune· sprecað buta ān.

Osmær, and Leofwine at Exon, and Ælfweard Alfwold's son, and Wiking, and Ælfgar at Minehead, and Wulfweard at Winsham, and Hunewine Heca's son, and Ælfwig at Haydon, and Godman priest, and Lutsige in Wight. And whoever will avert this, or think to withdraw it from the holy place, be he averted from God in doomsday, and from all his saints, and be he cast down amid the boiling fire of hell-torment, with Judas Christ's betrayer, ever eternally condemned, unless he here the more deeply make amends. Of these writings there are two: one is at Sherborne, and the second at Crediton. One speaks for both.

KING EADWARD THE CONFESSOR. M.XLII.[1]

✠ Ic Eadward cyngc cyðe on þissan gewrite eallum leaffullum mannum hwet ic geredd habbe wið mine arcebiscopes· ⁊ biscopes· ⁊ abbodes· ⁊ eorles· ⁊ wið ealle mine þegenas. ꝥ is ꝥ ic wille ꝥ Sc̄e Eadmundes mynster·

✠ I king Eadward make known in this writing to all faithful men what I have resolved with my archbishops, and bishops, and abbots, and earls, and with all my thanes. That is, that I will that the monastery of St Eadmund,

[1] A half-effaced marginal note says that this charter was "lecta coram baronibus de Scaccario et allocata."

mines meges. ⁊ se tūn þe þat mynster inne is. beo ecelice on þan ilce freodome ðe Cnut cyng ⁊ Harðecnut cyngc min broðer þiderin geuðen. ne neofre se stede ne worðe geloged mid oðres hādes mannum þanne mid munecum. ne nān þere biscope ðe æfre ma sceal beon on Norðfolce oððe on Suðfolce ne habbe næfre nān insting on þat mynster. ne swa wīd swa þes tūnes mærce gæð þe þat mynster inne stent. ⁊ þa muneces cysan heom ealdor of heom silfum. swa swa riht is. And ic wille ꝥ seo socne ⁊ seo sace þe ic heom geunnen habbe. stande unawend æfre. swa hwær hi nu habben land. oððe men. oððe get begeoten sculon. þurh Godes fultum ⁊ gōdre manne. Nu bidde ic ealle Godes freond. ægðer ge þa ðe nu libbað. ge þa ðe æfter us cumen sculon. ꝥ hi. for Godes eige. næfre ne beon on stede ne on stealle þær æfre undon worðe ꝥ ure foregengles geuðen. ⁊ we nu geunnen habben into ꝥ halige minstre. And gif þonne æfre ænig man swa dysig worðe. þurh þes deofles lāre. ꝥ he þis wiðcweðen wylle ⁊ awegen. seo he amansumed ⁊ on helle susle be-

my kinsman, and the town in which that monastery is, enjoy perpetually the same freedom that king Cnut and king Harðacnut my brother granted thereto; and that the place be never occupied by men of another order than monks; and that none of the bishops, who shall ever more be in Norfolk or Suffolk, have ever any authority in that monastery, or so widely as the town's mark goes, in which that monastery stands; and that the monks choose them a principal from themselves, as is just. And I will that the socn and the sac, which I have granted them, stand immutable, wheresoever they now have land or men, or may yet acquire, through the aid of God and of good men. Now I pray all friends of God, both those who now live, and those who shall come after us, that they, for awe of God, never be in *stead or stall* where be ever undone what our predecessors granted, and what we have now granted to the holy monastery. And if then any man ever be so foolish, through the devil's lore, that he will gainsay and elude this, be he excommunicated and sunk in hell-torseinct· buten he ǽr his lífes ende þe deopere bete.

ment, unless, ere his life's end, he the more deeply make amends.

EARL GODWINE. M.XXXVIII.-M.L.

✠ Her swutelað on ðisum gewrite [embe ða forew]eard ðe Godwine eorl worhte betweonan Ælfstāne abbod ⁊ þam hirede æt Sc̃e Augustine ⁊ Leofwine preoste· embe Sc̃e . . . . . . ne. Ðæt is ꝥ Leofwine cende ꝥ he bohte ða âre æt Cnute cinincge· ⁊ se abbot cænde ꝥ Cnut cing gelogode ða halig . . . . e . . . . . ra eama wergeld wæs into Sc̃e Augustine unawendedlice ðam Godes þyowan bi to libbanne· ða hwile . . . . se seht ðe Godwine eorl worhte betweonan ðam arcebisceop ⁊ þam hirede æt Sc̃e Augustine ⁊ Leofwine preoste . . . . . . man Leofwine preoste II. suling landes· ân æt Langtune· ⁊ oðer æt Gildinge· ⁊ v. pund penega . . . . elmæssan· ⁊ healf to midlængtene on ful · . . . . . his dæge ga land ⁊ feoh into Sc̃e Augustine . . . . ⁊ magum . . . . geborenan mæn· si abbot se ðe si.

Nu is þises to gewitnesse· Eadsi arcebisceop· ⁊ Siword

✠ Here is made known, in this writing, concerning the compacts that earl Godwine made between abbot Ælfstân and the convent at St Augustine's, and Leofwine the priest concerning St . . . . That is, that Leofwine declared that he bought the property of king Cnut; and the abbot declared that king Cnut placed the holy . . . . . . wergeld was to St Augustine immutably to the servants of God to live on, while . . . . the agreement that earl Godwine made between the archbishop and the convent at St Augustine's, and Leofwine the priest . . . . to Leofwine the priest II. sulungs of land, one at Langton, and another at Yalding, and v. pounds of pennies . . . . . alms, and half at Midlent, on full . . . . his day let the land and cattle go to St Augustine's . . . . .

Now of this is witness Eadsige archbishop, and Siword

bisceop· ⁊ Godwine eorl· þe ðone .... se hired on Cristes ciricean· ⁊ se hired æt Sc̃e Augustine ...... [Nu si]nd þisse gewrite þreo· ān is æt Cristes cyricean· ⁊ oðer æt Sc̃e Augustine· ⁊ þridde hæfð Leofwine preost.

bishop, and Godwine earl, who .... the convent at Christchurch, and the convent at St Augustine's. Now of these writings there are three: one is at Christchurch, and the second at St Augustine's, and the third Leofwine the priest has.

GODRIC. M.XLIII.

✠ Her swutelað on þisum gewrite hu Godric æt Burnan begeat ꝥ land æt Offaham. ꝥ is ðonne ꝥ he sealde Eadgyuan his sweostor ān marc goldes ⁊ XIII. pd̄. ⁊ LXIII. peñ. on geceapodne ceap[1]· to gyfanne ⁊ to syllanne· on dæge ⁊ æfter dæge· þam þe him leofust sy. Þes ceap wæs geceapod on Wii ætforan ealra scyre. Þises is to gewitnesse Eadsige arceƀ. ⁊ Siward ƀ. ⁊ Godric decanus· ⁊ eall se hired æt Cristes cyricean· ⁊ Wulfric aƀƀ. ⁊ se hired æt Sc̃e Augustine· ⁊ Ægelric Bygga· ⁊ Þurgar Ælfgares sunu· ⁊ Eadric Ælfrices sunu· ⁊ Osweard æt Hergeardes ham· ⁊ Leofwine preost· ⁊ Godwine portgerefa· ⁊ Wulf-

✠ Here is shown, in this writing, how Godric at Bourne got the land at Offenham. That is, then, that he gave to Eâdgife his sister one mark of gold, and XIII. pounds, and LXIII. pence in bought 'chap'[1], to give and to sell, in life and after life, to whom it to him may be most agreeable. This 'chap' was bought in Wye, before all the shire. Of this is witness Eâdsige archbp, and Siward bp, and Godric dean, and all the convent at Christchurch, and Wulfric abbot, and the convent at St Augustine's, and Ægelric Bygga, and Thurgan Ælfgar's son, and Eâdric Ælfric's son, and Osweard at 'Hergeardesham', and Leofwine priest, and

[1] i. e. 1 mark in gold, and the rest in *ceap*, or goods, cattle, &c.

sige þæs cynges gerefa. ⁊ manig gōd man þarto.

Nu synd þissa gewrita þreo. ān is æt Cristes cyricean. ⁊ oþer æt Sc̄e Augustine. ⁊ þridde hæfð Godric mid him.

Godwine portreeve, and Wulfsige the king's reeve, and many a good man thereto.

Now of these writings there are three: one is at Christchurch, and a second at St Augustine's, and the third Godric has with him.

KING EADWARD THE CONFESSOR. M.XLIII.

✠ Pace regnante, largiflua Christi omnipotentis bonitas semper ab omnibus est laudanda omnique laude preferenda, quia nullo bonitatis termino valet concludi in seculorum secula, utpote quia idem Deus ipse sit sue proprie bonitatis bonitas, distribuens gratis non tantum dignis, verum etiam indignis partem sue bonitatis: est quippe Rex regum et Dominus dominancium omniumque subsistencium, visibilium atque invisibilium Creator, et sue creationis discretissimus Dispositor, attingens a fine usque ad finem, suaviterque disponens omnem creaturum ut competit divine dominationi ejus. Nam quosdam libero arbitrio quibusdam prefecit dignitate hujus seculi et operibus diversis, quibus rursum mandat ut ipsi sua sufficientia et bonorum habundantia illorum relevare et sustentare debeant inopiam, qui minus secularibus habundant negotiis, ut pro hoc majori possint mercede ab eo donari. Unde ego Eadwardus Anglorum rex omnibus post me futuris regibus, archiepiscopis, episcopis, abbatibus, ducibus, omnibusque Christi fidelibus, notum fieri volo, quod venerabilis dux Leofricus, divina inspirante gratia monitisque gloriosi ac Deo dilecti summi pontificis Alexandri, monasterium sancte Dei genitricis Marie, Sanctique Petri, et omnium sanctorum, in villa quæ dicitur Couentre, extruxit, largisque muneribus adornavit, atque subscripta maneria ad victuale subsidium abbatis et monachorum in eodem loco Deo perpetue servientium, mea larga donacione et concessione, ibidem contulit; videlicet, medietatem ejusdem ville in qua fundata est ipsa ecclesia, deinde Souðam, Greneburgan, Icketonam, Hunitonam, Neowenham, Hulhtune, Chadeleshunte, Herdewyk, Cestretune, Waspertune, Suohham, Byrtingabirig juxta Aven, Merston, item Merstuna in Gloecestria, medietatem ville de Lintune, Sowe, Salewarp, Eatuna juxta fluvium Dee, Kildesbig, Winewican, Burhbeca, Barwalle, Scrapetoft, Pakinton. Pro reverencia itaque et honore sancte Dei genitricis Marie sanctique advocati mei apostoli Petri, do et concedo abbati Leofwino et omnibus futuris ibidem post eum abbatibus, in tota possessione monasterii, sakam et socnam et thelonium suum, in terra et in aqua, in urbe et extra, et omnes leges et consuetudines, tam plene et tam libere sicut eas prefatus dux honorificencius et liberius de me tenuit. Precipio itaque ut omnia que ad ipsam ecclesiam pertinent sint omnino libera, terre culte et inculte, cum exitibus atque redditibus predictorum, necnon maneria et ecclesie, cimiteria, decime redditus, et servicia debita, oblaciones, luminaria, causarum discussiones, emendationes ecclesiastice, vel seculares, et quicquid illi loco collatum est sub integra immunitate, concedimus et perpetuo firmamus. Et ne quis præsentium vel magis futurorum ambiget que sit illa libertas quam amabiliter et firmiter concedo, omnimodis cuncta illius ecclesie possessio nullis sit unquam gravata oneribus, nec expeditionis, nec pontis et arcis edificatione, nec juris regalis fragimine, nec furis apprehensione. Et, ut omnia simul comprehendam, nil debet exsolvi nec regi, nec regis preposito, vel episcopo, vel ulli homini, sed omnia debita exsolvantur jugiter que in ipsa ditione fuerint ad supradictum sanctum locum, secundum quod ordinaverint fratres ejusdem cœnobii. Ut autem cunctis hec transgredientibus ad damnationem suam evidenter possit ostendi literas summi pontificis papæ Alexandri, quas ab eo suscepimus, directas tam posteris quam præsentibus hic manifestari curavimus:

"Alexander episcopus, servus servorum Dei, dilecto filio Eadwardo regi Anglorum salutem et apostolicam benedictionem. Scriptorum vestrorum eloquia incolumitatem vestram significantia læti suscepimus, gratias itaque Omnipotenti

Deo retulimus, qui cordis vestri sinceritatem ad omnia utilia sanctæ matris æcclesiæ compungit. Proinde juxta scripta vestra monasterio Sanctæ Mariæ de Coventria, ubi servorum Dei constituta est congregatio a reverendæ memoriæ Leofrico duce nuper exstructo, hujusmodi privilegia præsentis authoritatis nostræ indulgemus, concedimus, atque confirmamus, statuentes ut ipse locus, regiis præceptis et privilegiis apostolicis fultus, per omnia tempora sine convexatione cujuscunque diocesani episcopi, aut alicujus judiciariæ potestatis cujuscumque ordinis vel dignitatis sit; sed semper, sicut præoptat et expetit benevolentia tua regalis, futuro tempore permaneat. Fratres igitur ejusdem loci idoneos, ex se vel ex qua voluerint congregatione, abbates sive decanos sibi per successiones eligendi habeant potestatem, et ne impediantur auctoritate apostolica prohibemus. Præterea quicquid illi loco contuleris, vel collatum est, vel conferetur, divina et nostra auctoritate roboramus; necnon privilegia vestra ad honorem Dei pertinentia, quæ ibi instituere volueris, gratanti affectu annuimus, confirmamus, et confirmando imperpetuum stare decrevimus, et infractores eorum æterna maledictione damnamus."

Anno incarnationis Dominice M°XLIII° scripta est hec singrapha, hiis consentientibus ierarchis qui subter notati: videlicet,

✠ Ego Edwardus rex hanc meam libertatem regali stabilimento affirmavi. ✠ Ego Ælfgyfa, mater ejusdem regis, assensum accommodavi. ✠ Ego Eadgið regina, ejusdem collateralis regis, ejusdem donacioni regali consensi. ✠ Ego Eadsinus, Dorobernensis ecclesie archiepiscopus, adquievi. ✠ Ego Ælfricus, Eboracensis ecclesie archipresul, corroboravi. ✠ Ego Alfwoldus, Londoniensis episcopus, subposui. ✠ Ego Ealdredus, episcopus Wygornensis, impressi. ✠ Ego Duduco, episcopus Willensis, adnotavi. ✠ Ego Wlfinus, episcopus Lichesfeldensis, consolidavi. ✠ Ego Æðelstanus, episcopus Herfordensis, stabilivi. ✠ Ego Liuingus, episcopus Cridiensis, adposui. ✠ Ego Eadnoðus, episcopus Dorcensis, consensum præbui. ✠ Ego Brihtwinus, episcopus Scirbernensis, confirmavi. ✠ Ego Berhtwold, episcopus Wiltuniensis, conclusi. ✠ Ego Manni abbas. ✠ Ego Siward abbas. ✠ Ego

Ælfwinus abbas. ✠ Ego Godwinus abbas. ✠ Ego Ælfstanus abbas. ✠ Ego Godwinus dux. ✠ Ego Haroldus dux. ✠ Ego Leofricus dux. ✠ Ego Siward dux. ✠ Ego Sweyn dux. ✠ Ego Tostig dux. ✠ Ego Radulphus More. ✠ Ego Esgar. ✠ Ego Rodbord minister. ✠ Ego Hulfketel minister. ✠ Ego Godwine minister. ✠ Ego Frewine minister. ✠ Ego Leofric minister. ✠ Ego Morcere minister. ✠ Ego Alfgar minister. ✠ Ego Godric minister. ✠ Ego Leofric minister. ✠ Ego Siwerd minister. ✠ Ego Æðelsi minister.

ÆGELRIC BIGGE. M.XLIV.

✠ Her swutelað on þisum gewrite embe þa forewyrd þe Ægelric worhte wið Eadsige arcebisceop æt þam lande æt Cert. þe Ceolnoð arcebisceop gebohte æt Hæleþan þam þegene mid his agenan sceatte. ⁊ Æþelulf cing hit gebocode Ceolnoðe arcebisceope on ece yrfe. þis synd þænne þa forewyrd. ꝥ Ægelric hæbbe ꝥ land æt Cert his dæg. ⁊ æfter his dæge ga þænne ꝥ land þam arcebisceope Eadsige on hand. swa gegodod swa heom bam gerisan mage. ⁊ syððan heora begra dæg agan si. Ægelrices ⁊ þæs arcebisceopes Eadsiges. þænne ga þis foresprecene land into Cristes cyricean mid mete ⁊ mid mannan eal swa hit stande. for Ægelrices sawle. ⁊ for Eadsiges arcebi-

✠ Here is declared, in this writing, concerning the compacts which Ægelric made with archbishop Eâdsige respecting the land at Chart, which archbishop Ceolnoth bought of Hæletha the thane with his own money, and king Æthelwulf chartered it to archbishop Ceolnoth in perpetual heritage. These then are the agreements: that Ægelric have the land at Chart for his day; and after his day then let the land go into the hand of archbishop Eâdsige, so improved as may be fitting for them both; and after the day of them both, Ægelric and the archbishop Eâdsige, shall be agone, then let this aforesaid land go to Christchurch, with meat and with sceopes· þam Godes þeowan to fostre ⁊ to scrude· þe þærinne Godes lof dreogan sceolan dæges ⁊ nihtes. ⁊ Ægelric gifð þa landboc þe þærto gebyreð on his life Criste ⁊ þam hirede· him to ecere ælmessan. ⁊ bruce Ægelric ⁊ Esbearn his sunu þara oðra landa heora twegra dæg· to þam ilcan forewyrdan þe Ægelnoð arcebisceop ⁊ Ægelric ær geworhtan· ꝥ is Stuting· ⁊ Melentun· ⁊ se haga binnan port þe Ægelric him sylfan getimbrod hæfde. ⁊ æfter heora twegra dæge fo se arcebisceop Eadsige þærto· gyf he leng libbe þænne hi· oððe loc hwa his æftergencga þænne beo· butan sum heora freonda þa land furþor· on þæs arcebisceopes gemede· ofgan mage to rihtan gafole· oððe to oðran forewyrdan· swa hit man þænne findan mage wið þone arcebisceop þe þanne libbe. ⁊ þises is to gewitnesse Eadweard cyncg· ⁊ Ælfgyfu seo hlæfdige· ⁊ Ælfwine ƀ. ⁊ Stigand ƀ. ⁊ Godwine ƀ. ⁊ Godric decanus· ⁊ eal se hired æt Cristes cyricean· ⁊ Wulfric abbud· ⁊ eal se hired æt Sc̃e Augustine· ⁊ Ælfwine abbud· ⁊ Siweard abbud· ⁊ Wulfnoð abbud· ⁊ Godwine eorl· ⁊ Leofric eorl· ⁊ Atsur

men, as it may stand, for the souls of Ægelric and of the archbishop Eâdsige, for the sustenance and clothing of God's servants who therein have to celebrate the praise of God day and night. And Ægelric gives the charter which appertains thereto, in his life, to Christ and the convent, in perpetual alms. And let Ægelric and his son Esbearn enjoy the other lands for the day of those two, under the same agreements that archbishop Ægelnoth and Ægelric erewhile made; that is, Stouting, and Melton, and the 'haga' within the town, which Ægelric had built for himself. And after the day of those two, let the archbishop Eâdsige succeed thereto, if he live longer than they, or whoever his successor may then be; unless one of their friends, with the archbishop's consent, may desire to hold on the land at a fair rent, or on other conditions, as it may then be arranged with the archbishop who may then live. And of this is witness: Eadward king, and Ælfgyfu the lady, and Ælfwine bp, and Stigand bp, and Godwine bp, and Godric dean, and all the convent at Christchurch, and Wulfric

Roda. ⁊ Ælfstan steallære. ⁊ Eadmær æt Burhham. ⁊ Godric æt Burnan. ⁊ Ælfwine se Reada. ⁊ mænig man þær to eacan. ge gehadude ge læwede. binnan burgan ⁊ butan. ⁊ gif ænig man on uferan dagan. gehadud oððe læwede. þisne cwyde wille awendan. awende hine God ælmihtig hrædlice of þisan lænan life into helle wite. ⁊ þær ā wunige mid eallan þam deoflan þe seo laðlice wunung betæht is. buton he þe deoppor hit gebete. ǣr his ende. wið Crist sylfne ⁊ wið þone hired. Nu synd þissa gewrita þreo. ān is innan Cristes cyricean. ⁊ oþer æt Sc̄e Augustine. ⁊ ꝥ þridde hæfð Ægelric mid him sylfan.

abbot, and all the convent at St Augustine's, and Ælfwine abbot, and Siweard abbot, and Wulfnoth abbot, and Godwine earl, and Leofric earl, and Atsur Roda, and Ælfstân constable, and Eâdmær at Burham, and Godric at Bourne, and Ælfwine the Red, and many a man besides, both ordained and lay, within town and without. And if any man in future days, ordained or lay, shall desire to avert this bequest, may God Almighty quickly avert him from this transitory life into hell-torment, and may he there ever dwell with all the devils to whom the loathly dwelling is committed; unless he the more deeply make atonement, ere his end, to Christ himself and to the convent. Now of these writings there are three: one is in Christchurch, and the second at St Augustine's, and the third Ægelric has with himself.

A LATER COPY OF THE ABOVE IN THE KENTISH DIALECT.

DONATIO ETHELRICE BIGGE DE MANERIO DE CHERT, STUTING, ET MELETUNE. ANNO DOMINI MILLESIMO QUADRAGESIMO QUARTO.

Hyer suotelet on þisen ywrite embe þo uorewarde ðe Eðelrich wrogte wið Edsige archebiscop at ðan londe at Chert ðe Chelnoð archebiscop bogte at Heleðen þan þeyne mid his ogene sheatte. ⁊ Eðeluf king hit ybokode Ceolnoð archebiscope on eche yrue. Ðis sind þanne þe uorewerde. ðet Eðelrich habbe ðet land at Chert his dey. and æfter his dage go þet land ðan archebiscope Eadsige an hand· suo ygoded suo hem bam yrisen mage· and siððen hire beyre day agon sy· Eðelrices and ðas archebiscopes Edsiges· þanne go þis uorespekene land into Cristes chereche· mid mete and mid mannen al suo hit stondet· uor Eðelriches saule· and for Edsiges archebiscopes· ðan Godes þeuwen to uostre and to shrude· þe ðerinne Godes lof þreugen shulle dages and nigtes. And Eðelrich geft ðo landboc ðe ðerto yberð on his liue Criste and ðan hirde him to echðes elmesse. And bruke Eðelrich and Esbarn his sune ðare oðre land here tueyre dey to þan yleke uorewerde þe Eðelnoð archebiscop and Eðelric er ywrogten. Ðat is Stutinge and Meletune· ⁊ se hage binne port ðe Eðelrich him self ytimbred hauede· and efter hire tueyre dage uo se archebiscop Edsige ðerto· gef he leng libbe þanne hy· oðer hwo his eftergengle ðanne by· bute sum of hyre frende ðet lond furðer on þas archebiscopes ymede ofgon mage to rigten gauelle· oðre to oðre uorewarde suo hit man ðanne uinden mage wið ðane archebiscop ðet þan libbe. And ðisses is to ywitnesse Edward king· and Elfgiue sy leuedi· and Elfwine biscop· and Stigand biscop· and Godwine biscop· ⁊ Godrich decan· and al se hired at Cristes cherche· and Wolfrið abot· and al se hired at Seynt Austines· [⁊ manie abottes and hierles·] ⁊ manie oðre men yhodede and lewede· binne burg and bute. And gef eny man on ure dagen· yhoded oðer lewed· ðisne quyde wille awende· awende hine God almigti raðlice of ðis [lene] liue into helle wite· and ðer a wonie mid alle ðan deulen ðe se lodliche woninge his bitagt· bute he þe diepper hit ybete er his ende wið Crist selfne· and wið þan hird. Nu send ðis ywrite ðrie. On is at Cristes chereche· oðer at Seynt Austine· and ðat þridde hauet Eðelrich mid him selue.

KING EADWARD THE CONFESSOR. M.XLIV.

✠ In nomine sancte et individue Trinitatis. Ego Eadwardus, Anglorum, Dei gratia, basileus, omnibus post me futuris regibus, archiepiscopis, episcopis, abbatibus, comitibus, vicecomitibus, omnibusque baronibus ac ministris, cunctisque presentibus et futuris, salutem, et hujus rei noticiam. Summum in regibus ac principibus bonum est justiciam Dei colere et ecclesiarum quieti prospicere, et de illarum perpetua securitate sollerter tractare; quia qui eam exaltant et honorant, cum ea et in ea et per eam exaltantur et honorantur. Et quoniam in locis plurimis inquietudines plurimas, molestias, persecutiones, scandala atque gravamina monachos a nonnullis pertulisse cognovimus, decet ut nostre excellencie regia provisio de ipsorum ventura quiete, salubri meditetur dispositione, ut in ipsis manentes tranquilla mente in servitute Dei, ipsius subveniente gracia, permaneant; unde presentes et posteri sciant universi, quod antiqui gloriosi reges, Ælfredus, videlicet, et Eadwardus filius ejus, ecclesiam S. Petri de Gant, que in monte Blandinio sita est, nimio affectu dilexerunt, honoraverunt; et donationem illam, Leuesham, scilicet, cum omnibus sibi pertinentibus, quam Elðrudis, prefati Ælfredi neptis, ecclesie eidem libere contulit, regia concessione et libertate perpetua munierunt. Quorum boni operis intentione perpendens, ne eorum statuta unquam ducantur in irritum, aut ullis, quod absit, posteris turbentur temporibus, ego quidem hujus libertatis patrocinator, donis eorum favens, pro eorum et mea omniumque successorum meorum regum, atque Baldwini comitis, cognati mei, necnon et omnium fidelium prosperitate et salute, Deo et beato apostolo Petro, pio fautori nostro, et abbati Richardo, monachisque prefate ecclesie de Gant, concedo, atque mea regia autoritate confirmo, manerium de Leuesham, cum omnibus sibi pertinentibus, videlicet, Greenwic, Wulewic, Modingeham, atque Cumbe, et cum vallibus etiam in Andreda eisdem maneriis adjacentibus, scilicet, Æschore, Æffehaga, Wingindene, Scarendene, Sandherste, et cum ecclesiis, cimiteriis, decimis, redditibus, in campis et silvis, in pratis et pascuis, in aquis et paludibus, in piscariis et piscationibus, in molendinis et in omnibus suis appendiciis. Præterea addidi loco illi prelibato infra Londoniam, partem terre de terra illa, videlicet, que Wermanecher Anglice nuncupatur, cum huervo eidem terre pertinenti, et cum omnibus rectitudinibus et consuetudinibus que ad illam pertinent. Concedo eis etiam, in omnibus terris suis prenominatis, consuetudines hic Anglice scriptas, scilicet, infangeneþeof, mondbruce, mischenninge, uðleaw, ferdwite, wearwite, blodwite, hleastynge, sceawinge, hamsocne, forstall, aliasque omnes leges et consuetudines que ad me pertinent. Donavi etiam Richardo, religioso abbati, et omnibus futuris post eum ibidem abbatibus, et fratribus ejusdem loci, in omni predicta monasterii possessione, sacam et socam, theloneumque suum in terra et in aqua, et consuetudinem que dicitur teames, latrones latronumque captiones vel emissiones, et pacis fracturam, et pugnam in domo factam, et domus invasionem, et omnes assultus in suo jure, in via et extra, in festo et extra, in urbe et extra, in aqua et extra, tam plene et tam libere sicut eas habebam in manu mea; nullis itaque unquam graventur oneribus expeditionum nec pontium vel castrorum restructione, nec regalium sive episcopalium ministrorum exactione. Defendo insuper, et ex nomine sancte Trinitatis prohibeo, ut nullus regum succedentium, episcoporum, principum, comitum, vicecomitum, procuratorum, sive aliorum regum clientium, vel episcoporum, ministrorum, pastum, censum, vel impensionem, seu aliud quidlibet ab ecclesia illa, vel a terris præscriptis ad eam pertinentibus, per vim aut per consuetudinem, exigat, sed omnimodam libertatem mea regia corroboratione perpetualiter possideant, quatinus ipsa religiosa concio, pro remedio anime mee, et successorum meorum regum Anglie, omniumque benefactorum ejusdem ecclesie, ac fidelium salute, pervigiles persolvat deprecationes, oleumque bone actionis, more sapientium virginum, sub habitu religionis, servans Christo Domino et ejus beato apostolo Petro, indefesse deserviat. Si quis autem contra hanc auctoritatis nostre paginam senserit, quicunque ille fuerit, cujuscunque etatis vel potestatis, gradus et ordinis, et eam infringere voluerit, vel alios ad hoc conduxerit, unusquisque pro seipso libras v. partibus Sancti Petri persolvat, et quicquid exinde fiscus noster, in murdris, geldis, danegeldis, omnibusque aliis rebus vel stipendiis, que in terris illis surrexerint, ad partem nostram sperare poterat, in luminaribus, sive fratrum ipsius monasterii victus aminiculis perenniter per nostra oracula ad integrum sit concessum atque indultum. Quicunque successorum meorum hanc donationis libertatem firmiter atque inviolabiliter custodierit, eterna coronetur claritate, celestisque regni perfruatur felicitate. Si quis vero eam, quod absit, destruere voluerit, sive eandem possessionem a donatione et servicio sepedicte ecclesie et abbatum ejusdem loci et monachorum subtrahere conatus fuerit, vel per partes quasi hereditatis jure auferre præsumpserit, sicut contradictor et convulsor hujus nostri decreti ac temerator, cum Iuda traditore Domini eterno anathemati subjaceat, nisi Deo et beato suo apostolo Petro digna penitentia satisfecerit. Non enim superiorem vel inferiorem aliquem decet hominem illud sibi in jus hereditatis vendicare quod per regiam corroborationem ad illud, cujus esse debeat, provida ratione fuerit redactum.

Anno igitur Dominice incarnationis M.XLIIII., Indictione XII., et VII. concurrentibus, atque XI. epactis rotantibus, hec regalis concessio et donatio facta est sub astipulatione primatum, quorum nomina karaxata videntur.

Ego Eadwardus, rex tocius Britannie, hanc propriam donationem regali stabilimento affirmavi ✠. Ego Ælfgyfu, ejusdem regis mater, assensum accomodavi ✠. Ego Eadsinus, Dorobernensis ecclesie archiepiscopus, hanc pietatem divulgavi ✠. Ego Ælfricus, Eboracensis civitatis archipresul, hanc territoriam scedulam diligenter assignavi ✠. Ego Ælweardus, Londoniensis episcopus, consolidavi ✠. Ego Godwinus, Rofensis episcopus, gaudenter impressi ✠. Ego Ælwynus, Wintoniensis episcopus, corroboravi ✠. Ego Beorhtwoldus, Wiltuniensis episcopus, coadunavi ✠. Ego Liuingus, Cridiensis episcopus, confirmavi ✠. Ego Æðelstanus, Herefordensis episcopus, consignavi ✠. Ego Wulstanus, Wigorniensis episcopus, hanc divulgavi ✠. Ego Eadnoðus, Dorccensis episcopus, condixi ✠. Ego Duduco, Wellensis episcopus, conscripsi ✠. Ego Grimkillus, episcopus Australium Saxonum, consensi ✠. Ego Wulsinus, episcopus Licetfeldensis, commodum duxi ✠. Ego Britwinus, episcopus Sciréburnensis, conclusi ✠. Ego Godwinus dux Amen dixi ✠. Ego Leofricus dux testificavi ✠. Ego

Siwardus dux testificavi ✠. Ego Haroldus dux testificavi ✠. Ego Leofwinus dux testificavi ✠. Ego Swegenus dux testificavi ✠. Ego Tostig dux testificavi ✠. Ego Gyrdus dux testificavi ✠. Ego Eadwinus abbas Westminsteriensis ✠. Ego Wulfuoldus abbas Certesige ✠. Ego Ælsi abbas Sancti Augustini ✠. Ego Godwine abbas Wincelcumbe ✠. Ego Manny abbas Eoueshamensis ✠. Ego Ælfricus abbas Perscorensis ✠. Ego Hugelinus camerarius ✠. Ego Esgar stallere ✠. Ego Roldbertus filius Wimarc stallere ✠. Ego Ordgar minister ✠. Ego Osgod minister ✠. Ego Odda minister ✠. Ego Ælfgar minister ✠. Ego Karl minister ✠. Ego Đured minister ✠. Ego Æþelwig minister ✠. Ego Ædridg minister ✠. Ego Ordulf minister ✠. Ego Duduco minister ✠. Ego Siward minister ✠.

KING EADWARD THE CONFESSOR. M.XLII.-M.XLV.

✠ Edward king gret Ælfword biscop ⁊ Esgar stallare ⁊ alle mine burgþeignes on Lundone freondlice. Ic kiðe eow ꝥ ic ann ⁊ ic wille ꝥ Sc̄e Peter ⁊ ða gebroðera on Westminstre habben ðat land and ðane wearf ðarto ðe Ulf portegerefa ⁊ his wif Kinegið· for here saule alesednisse into ðare halagen stowe gæfon· swa full ⁊ swa forð swa hi best it ahton. And icc ann heom eft ealswa ꝥ hy habben ðerto fulne freodom on eallum þingun ðe ðer uppaspringað· be lande ⁊ be strande· forðan icc nelle nateswon geðafian ðat ænig mann ænig atbrede

✠ I king Eadward greet bishop Ælfweard, and Esgar constable, and all my burgh thanes in London amicably. I make known to you that I grant and will that St Peter and the brothers in Westminster have the land and the wharf thereto, which Ulf the portreeve and his wife Kinegith, for their souls' redemption, gave to the holy place, as fully and as freely as they best possessed it. And I also again grant them that they may have thereto full freedom in all things which shall there spring up, by land and by strand; for I will on oððe geutige heora geofa ⁊ heora almesse· oððe ðat ðer ænig mann ænigne onstingc habbe on ænigum þingum oððe on ænigum timan· butan se abbod ⁊ ða gebroðera to ðæs minstres neode. God eow ealle gehealde ⁊ gife eow ece gesælðe. Amen.

no account allow that any man take away or alienate their gifts and their alms; or that any man have there any authority in any things, or at any time, except the abbot and the brothers, for the monastery's need. God preserve you all, and give you eternal bliss. Amen.

---

* KING EADWARD THE CONFESSOR. M.XLV.

In nomine sanctæ et individuæ Trinitatis. Ego Eadward[us, Dei gratia Anglorum rex, futuris][1] post me regibus, episcopis, abbatibus, comitibus, vicecomitibus, et omnibus [omnino Christianis, salutem. Cum piæ voluntatis] desiderium, et laudandæ devotionis intentio regalibus sit semper studiis adjuv[anda cura est sollicitudinis adhibenda, ut ea] quæ pro quiete religiosæ conversationis sunt ordinata; nec dissimulatio negliger[e nec ulla valet presumptio perturbare, sed] sicut hoc quod ratio exigebat oportuit definiri, ita quod definitum est non debet viola[ri. Quapropter noverit præsentium futurorumque] universitas, quod fidelissimus noster Wlnothus abbas, et monachi monasterii ter beati ap[ostolorum principis Petri], peculiaris patroni nostri, adierunt serenitatem nostram humiliter obsecrantes, ut sicut antiqui et gloriosi Anglorum reges, Eadgarus, Eadwardus, Ætheldredus, Eadmundus, Cnutus, et reliqui, qui usque ad nostra tempora idem Westmonasterium supradicti sancti apostoli, decretorum suorum sanctionibus [co]ntra iniquorum pervasionem munierant, atque episcoporum et apostolicorum consensu et auctoritate postulatione regia plen[issime roborari] poposcerant; ita nos, Dei nostri voluntatem in omnibus sequentes, et illos prædecessores nostros in hoc fidel[iter]

[1] The words between brackets are wanting in MS. Cott. Aug. II. 58.

imi[tantes nostram illi mon]asterio adderemus, immo nostra sanctione illorum roboraremus. Et quoniam in ipsis diebus nostris inter [Robertum episcopum clerumque Lond]oniæ, et abbatem præfati monasterii monachosque orta quædam contentio fuerat, episcopo et cler[o sibi volentibus in sup]radic[to mona]sterio Sancti Petri contra leges atque decreta supramemorata quasdam consuetudines et obson[ia usur]pare [et abbatie mon]achisque contra sese defendentibus regum et apostolicorum, et maxime Sc̃i Dunstani, qui prius fuerat Lundoniensis [episcopu]s, et poste[a Cantuarien]sis archiepiscopus, prolata privilegii auctoritate, hujus conventionis causa coram episcopis et optimatibus regni nostri, et in præsentia [nostra ventilata et fini]ta. Nos demum justiciæ faventes, diffinitæ causæ consensus nostri vigorem præstaremus; igitur fidelium nostrorum atque pal[atino]rum usi consili[o et hoc] prospicien[tes ipsi] ecclesiæ et habitantibus in ea sive pertinentibus ad eam utile fore, non solum in presenti sed et in futuro, regum qui fuer[unt ante nos de]cr[et]a, sed et Sc̃i Dunstani privilegium, et Anglicorum episcoporum seu Romanorum apostolicorum privilegia sancti et egr[eg]ii apostoli Petri monasterio indulta, per hanc præceptionis nostræ paginam decernimus in perpetuum servanda. Et ut sine ulla perturbatione vel inquietudine episcopi Lundoniensis clericorumve ejus fratres ibidem Omnipotenti Deo valeant famulari, et pro nobis ipsis et stabilitate regni nostri attentius deprecari, omnino generales eorum accessus ad monasterium prohibemus fieri, et communes stationes ab eisdem, ne inde prava consuetudo surrepat aliquando in eodem sepefato monasterio celebrari, qualiter sicut est in ejus monasterii privilegiis constitutum, in perpetuis temporibus maneat inviolatum. Si quis autem contra hanc præceptionis et auctoritatis nostræ paginam senserit, quicunque ille fuerit, cujuscunque nominis et honoris, etatis et potestatis, gradus et ordinis, et eam vel in magno vel in minimo infringere voluerit, et id quod cupit non efficiat, et ad erarium nostræ domus XII. libras ex auro purissimo coactus addat, et insuper reus majestatis habeatur, et prophanus ab omnibus, nisi satis pro emendatione fecerit, computetur. Ut igitur hoc decretum a nobis promulgatum pleniorem obtineat vigorem, nostra manu subter apposito signo roboravimus, atque fidelibus nostris præsentibus roborandum tradidimus; nostræque imaginis sigillo insuper assignari jussimus. Ego Eadwardus, Xp̃i gratia largiente, Anglorum rex, sigillo etiam sc̃æ crucis ✠ signo hoc privilegium, ut si quis illud infregerit, ab eo qui pro nobis crucifixus est æterna perditione damnetur. ✠ Ego Ælfgyfa Imma, mater ejusdem regis, assensum accommodavi. ✠ Ego Eadgytha, ejusdem collaterana regis, eidem donationi regali consensi. ✠ Ego Eatsinus, Dorobernensis æcclesiæ archiepiscopus, hanc donationem confirmavi. ✠ Ego Ælfricus, Eboracensis æcclesiæ archiep̃s, pietatem hanc corroboravi. ✠ Ego Ælfuuinus ep̃s consensi et subscripsi. ✠ Ego Brihtuuoldus ep̃s consensi et subscripsi. ✠ Ego Lyuingus ep̃s cs̃s. et subscrip̃. ✠ Ego Æthelstanus ep̃s cs̃s. et subscr̃. ✠ Ego Eadnothu[s ep̃s cs̃s.] et subscr. ✠ Ego Ægelricus ep̃s consensi et subsc̃. ✠ Ego Duduco ep̃s cs̃s. et subscr̃. ✠ Ego Grymcillus ep̃s cs̃s. et subscr̃. ✠ Ego [Ælf]uuinus abbas cs̃s. et subscr̃. ✠ Ego Ætheluuardus abbas cs̃s. et subscr̃. ✠ Ego Siuuardus ab̃b̃. cs̃s. et subscr̃. ✠ Ego Ælf[sta]nus ab̃b̃. [cs̃s.] et subscr̃. ✠ Ego Godwinus comes. ✠ Ego Leofricus comes. ✠ Ego Siuuardus comes. ✠ Ego Suueinus comes. ✠ Ego Osgodus minister. ✠ Ego Ord[ga]rus minist̃. ✠ Ego Odda minist̃. ✠ Ego Ælfstanus minister. ✠ Ego Ordulfus min[ister]. Wulfwius regie dig[nit]at[is c]ancellarius relegit et sigillavit. Datum Kł. Augusti, anno v^{to}, regnante serenissimo et glori[osissimo] Eaduua[rdo Anglorum re]ge, ab incarnatione autem Domini M.XL^{mo}V^{to}, Indictione XII^{a}, concurr̃. VII^{tem} atque XVIII^{to} epact[æ. Actum] Londoniæ palatio regi[o i]n Dei no[mine fœlic]iter. Amen.

PRIOR EADMÆR, AND OTHERS.

Aadmerus prior, et Ægeluuordus, et Ansfridus, et ceteri monachi ecclesie Sancti Augustini, confirmamus conventionem quæ facta est inter Algodum monetarium, filium Ælfredi Manne sune, et Ædelgiue, et Dunstanum filium ejus, de domibus predicti Ælgodi, et de terra que ad illas domos pertinet. Hec autem est conventio: quinquaginta solidos predicta Eadgiua dedit Algodo pro domibus suis et terra quæ ad illas domos pertinet; et ipse Algodus et tota progenies sua de illa terra omnibus modis exeant, et ipsa Eadgiua et Dunstanus filius ejus eo modo introeant, ut ita libere et quiete domos et terram illam possideant sicut Algodus vel Hacmannus unquam melius vel liberius possederunt: et si alicui seu dare vel vendere voluerit, dent vel vendent ea sive in progenie seu extra suam progeniem; et singulis annis, in medio Quadragesime, octo denarios super sepulcrum Sancti Augustini ponant, quia terra Sancti Augustini est et in potestate nostra. Hujus conventionis veraces testes sunt isti, Ernulf prior, etc.

KING EADWARD THE CONFESSOR. M.L.

TRANSLATIO SEDIS CATHEDRALIS DE CRIDETUN IN EXONIAM[1].

Igitur cum universa in sapiencia a Deo bene condita sint, videlicet, celum, arvum, et que in eis continentur, dignum quippe equumque dinoscitur fore quamquam impossibilitas egre humanitatis humanos actus pluris calamitatibus conturbet, quo nos qui rectores hominum a Deo constituti dicimur instinctu superne Clemencie, juxta modulum nostre censure prudenter equitatem civilis exquirere studeamus sciencie, atque præcipue res ecclesiastice benigne discutiendo tractare ea que cernuntur nostris non equa optutibus rectius constituere, sicque sancita ad profectum innocencie, sive utriusque vice corroborando gubernare. Equidem gloriosum est nimiumque laudabile destructas edes sanctorum locorum ad divinum adminiculum exposcendum reedificare, sacraque altaria venustis velis cum nitore pii cordis velare, et unamquamque nocturnam sive diurnam sinaxim armoniacis modulis resonare. Quapropter ego Eadwardus, Dei gratia Anglorum

[1] The copy in Hickes (Diss. Epist. p. 16), from the archives of Exeter cathedral, varies in the names of the witnesses.

rex, consilio imbutus bone voluntatis, quoniam provisum est michi, secundum quod præcipitur in divinis decretis, cathedram pontificalem consolidare Exoniæ civitatis, in monasterio beati Petri apostolorum principis, quod est situm infra menia ejusdem urbis, auctoritate superni Regis meaque, meeque conjugis Eadgyde ac universorum episcoporum ducumque meorum, per hoc privilegium testamenti atque cautionem cyrographi in perpetuo tempore constituto presulem Leofricum, ut sit ibi pontifex, et post illum ceteri affuturi ad laudem et gloriam sanctæ et individue Trinitatis, Patris, et Filii, et Spiritus Sancti, et ad honorem Sancti Petri apostoli. Dono etiam possessiones omnes ad eundem locum pertinentes quecumque sint, tam in ruribus, quam in pascuis, pratis, silvis, aquis, liberis, servis, ancillis, legibus, censu, pagis, Deo Sanctoque Petro fratribusque canonicis ibi famulantibus, ut habeant jugiter subsidium hubesum corporis, quo valeant Christo militare, sine ulla molestia animi. Hoc tamen notum pape domino inprimis Leoni facio, ipsiusque attestatione confirmo, deincepsque cunctis Anglorum magnatibus, quod Cornubiensem diocesim, que olim in beati Germani memoria, atque Petroci veneratione episcopali solio assignata fuerat, ipsam cum omnibus sibi adjacentibus parochiis, terris, villis, opibus, beneficiis, Sancto Petro in Exonia civitate trado, scilicet, ut una sit sedes episcopalis, unumque pontificium, et una æcclesiastica regula, propter paucitatem atque devastationem bonorum et populorum, quoniam piratici Cornubiensem ac Cryditonensem ecclesias devastare poterant; ac per hoc in civitate Exoniæ tuciorem munitionem adversus hostes habere visum est, et ideo ibi sedem esse volo. Hoc est ut Cornubia cum suis ecclesiis et Devonia cum suis simul in uno episcopatu sint, et ab uno episcopo regantur. Itaque hoc privilegium ego Eadwardus rex manu mea super altare Sancti Petri pono, et presulem Leofricum per dexterum brachium ducens, meaque regina Eadgyda per sinistrum, in cathedra episcopali consisto, presentibus meis ducibus et consanguineis, nobilibus necnon capellanis, et affirmantibus laudantibusque archiepiscopis Eadsino et Alerico, cum ceteris aliis, quorum nomina describentur in meta hujus cautionis. Enimvero si quis hoc testamentum privilegii affirmare post meum vite transitum, et bona ecclesie augere tuendo voluerit, adaugeat Omnipotens Deus dies vitæ ejus, atque centuplicato fructu nono decimo coronet eum eterno præmio in gaudio ethereo. Si autem, quod absit, aliquis compilator fraudis, vel cavillator fautoris, nevo fomitatus inique cupidinis, hanc cautionem seu decretum hujus episcopi destituere aut permutare contempnendo presumpserit, vel ejusdem minuere et subtrahere substanciam temptaverit, eternis mancipatus habenis cum diabolo ejusque ministris, sit separatus a Christo ipsiusque sanctis, dissegregatione perpetue anathematis fiat. Anno igitur incarnacionis Dominicæ M.L^{mo}, Indictione tertia, Epacteque XXV., et Concurrentes VII., hec cautio scripta est edictione solida karecterata karecteribus, testium jubente piissimo rege Anglorum Eadwardo gubernante eodem feliciter tocius monarchiam majoris Britannie.

Ego Eadwardus rex hoc donum cautione hac affirmo. Ego Eadsinus archiepiscopus Christi ecclesie manu mea subscripsi. Ego Elericus archiepiscopus Eboracensis ecclesie confirmavi. Ego Stigandus episcopus dignum duxi. Ego Herimanus episcopus corroboravi. Ego Rodbertus episcopus testis fui. Ego Ealdredus episcopus consolidavi. Ego Doduca episcopus consensi. Ego Godwinus dux. Ego Leofricus dux. Ego Siwerdus dux. Ego Haraldus dux. Ego Radulfus dux. Ego Tosti nobilis. Ego Ægelwerdus abbas adjuvi. Ego Ælwinus abbas consensi. Ego Lintricus abbas assensi. Ego Ræinbaldus presbiter commendavi. Ego Godwinus presbiter aspiravi. Ego Godmannus presbiter interfui. Ego Petrus presbiter laudavi. Ego Odda nobilis. Ego Rymhtrucus nobilis. Ego Ordsanus minister. Ego Celericus minister. Ego Touinus minister. Ego Radulphus minister. Ego Dodda minister. Ego Eadulfus minister. Ego Ordulfus minister. Ego Ecgulfus minister. Ego Eabpisus minister. Ego Celfpendus minister.

In dorso. Ðis is se freols to þam ƀ.rice on Defenanscire· ⁊ on Wealan ðe Eadweard cyningc dihte ⁊ gesette mid

This is the freedom to the bishopric of Devonshire and Wales, which king Eadward appointed and established his witena ræde· for his sawle alysednisse· into þam bisceopstole on Exanceastre Leofrice ðe ⁊ his æftergengean on æce yrfe.

with the advice of his 'witan', for the redemption of his soul, for the episcopal see at Exeter, in perpetual heritage to bishop Leofric and his successors.

QUEEN ÆLFGIFU EMMA. BEFORE M.LII.

✠ Ic Ælfgyfu seo hlæfdige· Eadweardes cyninges modor· geærndede æt Cnute cyninge minum hlaforde þæt land æt Niwantune· ⁊ þæt þærto hyrð into Xp̃es cyrcean· þa Ælfric se þegen hit hæfde forworht þan cyninge to handan· ⁊ se cyning hit geaf þa into Xp̃es cyrcean þan hirede to fosterlande for uncre beigra sawle.

✠ I Ælfgifu the lady, king Eadward's mother, obtained from king Cnut, my lord, the land at Newton, and what thereto belongs, for Christchurch, when Ælfric the thane had forfeited it to the hands of the king; and the king then gave it to Christchurch, as 'fosterland' for the convent; for the souls of us both.

KING EADWARD THE CONFESSOR. M.LIII.

✠ Eadward king gret Wulwi biscop· ⁊ Gyrð eorll· and alle mine þeinges on Oxnefordescire freonlice· ⁊ ic kiðe ou ꝥ ic habbe gegifan Criste ⁊ Sc̃e Petre into Westmunster þet cotlif ðe ic wæs geboran inne be naman Gihtslepe· ⁊ ãne healfe hide æt Mersce· scotfre ⁊ gafolfreo·

✠ I king Eadward greet bishop Wulfwig, and earl Gyrth, and all my thanes in Oxfordshire, amicably; and I make known to you that I have given to Christ and St Peter in Westminster the village in which I was born, by name Islip, and a half hide at Marsh, scot-free and rent-mid eallan þam þingan þe þerto belimpað. on wude ⁊ on felde. on mæde ⁊ on watere. mid ciricen ⁊ mid ciricsocnen. swa full ⁊ swa forð. and swa freo swa hit me siluan on hande stod. ⁊ swa swa Ælgifa Imme min moder. on minre frumbyrde dæiæge. to forme gyfe it me gæf. ⁊ to gecinðe becwæð. ⁊ ic an heom þerofer saca ⁊ socna. toll ⁊ team. ⁊ infangeneþeof. ⁊ blódwite. ⁊ weardwite. ⁊ hamsocne. ⁊ foresteall. griðbrice ⁊ mundbrice. ⁊ ealle ða gerihte þe to me belimpað. Nu grete ic wel minne leofne mæi Wigod on Wallungeforde. and ic beode þe þat þu. on minre stede. beride þas land þam hælge to hande. for ic nelle naðeswon geðafian ꝥ þær ænig mann ænige onsting habbe on ænigum þingum oððe on ænigum timan butan se abƀ. ⁊ ða gebroðra to þæs munstres nitwurðlicre þearfe. ⁊ hwa se þas ælmesse holdlice healde. healde hine God ⁊ Godes moder on ece blisse. ⁊ hwa swa hio awende. sieo he awænded fram Gode to þare helware stiðe pinnesse. buton he hit on þissere yrfðe þe stiðlikere gebete. God eow gehealde ⁊ Sc̃e Petres holde.

free, with all the things which thereto belong, in wood and in field, in mead and in water, with church and with church-socn, as full and as complete, and as free as they stood in my own hand, and so as Ælfgifu Emma, my mother, on my birthday, gave it to me for a first gift, and naturally bequeathed it. And I give them thereover sac and socn, toll and team, and infangenetheof, and blôdwite, and wardwite, and hamsocn, and forsteall, grithbryce and mundbryce, and all the rights which to me belong. I now greet well my beloved kinsman Wigod at Wallingford, and I enjoin thee, that thou, in my stead, perequitate these lands into the possession of the saint; for I will on no account allow that any man have any authority there, in any things, or at any times, save the abbot and the brothers, for the monastery's necessary requirements. And whoso shall faithfully hold this alms, may God and God's mother hold him in everlasting bliss. And whoso avert it, be he averted from God to the rigid torture of hell's inmates, unless he, on this earth, the more rigidly make amends. God and St Peter's favour preserve you.

BISHOP WULFWIG, EARL LEOFRIC, AND GODGYFU HIS WIFE. M.LIII.

CHARTA DE PACTO INTER WULFWIUM EPISCOPUM, LEOFRICUM COMITEM, ET GODIVAM EJUS UXOREM, DE MONASTERIO STOWENSI ORDINANDO.

✠ Her swutelað on þisan gewrite hu ða forewearde geworhte syndon þe Wlwig ƀ. ⁊ Leofric eorl· ⁊ Godgife þæs eorles wīf geworhtan ymbe ꝥ mynster æt Sancte Marian stowe. ꝥ is ǽrost ꝥ hig bædan þone bisceop ꝥ hig mostan ꝥ mynster gódian· ⁊ lande þiderin tolecge be his fullre leáfe. Ða tyðede heom se bisceop· ⁊ wæs swyðe bliðe ꝥ he ænigne fultum hæfde ꝥ him þærto fylstan wolde. Nu habbað hig hit gesett mid preostan· ⁊ willað þær habban þeowdóm eallswa man hæfð on Paules byrig binnan Lundene. ⁊ þa land þe hig þiderin lecgeað beon þa ðam gebroðran þe þær binnan beoð to fódnoðe ⁊ to scrude. ⁊ se ƀ. habbe into his feorme ælc þæra þinga ðe Æðeric ƀ. ⁊ Ædnoð ƀ. hæfdan ætforan him· of þam ðe mid rihte gebyrað into his bisceoprice· ꝥ is þa twegen déles ælc þæra þinga ðe kymð into þam mynstre· ⁊ þæ preostas habban þone þriddan dǽl forutan þam

✠ Here is declared, in this writing, how the compacts are made, which bishop Wulfwig, and earl Leofric, and Godgifu, the earl's wife, made concerning the monastery at St Mary's stow. That is, first, that they prayed the bishop that they might endow the monastery, and assign lands to it, with his full leave. Then the bishop permitted them, and was very blithe that he had any support that would assist him thereto. They have now supplied it with priests, and will there have service as it is had in St Paul's within London. And the lands which they assign thereto shall be for food and clothing to the brothers who shall therein be. And let the bishop have for his subsistence everything which bishop Ætheric and bishop Ædnoth had before him, of that which rightfully pertains to his bishopric: that is, two parts of everything that comes into the monastery, and the priests twam mæssan· þonne habbe se b. eall ꝥ þærto kymð· ehta dagas to ðære ǽrre Sanctæ Marian mæssan· ⁊ ehta dagas to þære æftran Sancta Marian mæssan· butan þam mete ānum· þonne habban þa preostas þone þriddan dǽl of ðam mete ðe þærto kymð. ⁊ þa land ðe se b. ⁊ se eorl ⁊ Godgife ⁊ gode menn þiderin geunnað beon þa æfre into þæra halgan stowe ðam gebroðran to neode· ⁊ ꝥ mynster to gōdianne· ꝥ nān b. þe æfter him kymð þærof nane feorme ne crafige· butan of þam ðe him mid rihte to gebyrað into his b.rice· eallswa oðre bisceopas ǽr ætforan him hæfdon. And þis is gedon be Eadwardes cynges fulra leafe· ⁊ on his gewitnesse· ⁊ on Eadgyðe his gebeddan· ⁊ on Stigandes arcebisceopes· ⁊ on Kynsiges arcebisceopes· ⁊ on Heremannes bisceopes· ⁊ on Dodika bisceopes· ⁊ on Leofrices bisceopes· ⁊ on Ealdredes bisceopes· ⁊ on Heka bisceopes· ⁊ on Ægelmeres bisceopes· ⁊ on Alfwoldes bisceopes· ⁊ on Wilelmes bisceopes· ⁊ on Leofwines bisceopes· ⁊ on Sigeweardes eorles· ⁊ on Haroldes eorles· ⁊ on Raulfes eorles· ⁊ on Ælfgares eorles· ⁊ on Manniges

the third part; except at the two masses, then let the bishop have all that thereto comes, eight days at the first St Mary's mass, and eight days at the second St Mary's mass, except the meat alone; then let the priests have the third part of the meat which thereto comes. And the lands which the bishop, and the earl, and Godgifu, and good men give thereto, be they ever to the holy place, for the need of the brothers, and to endow the monastery, so that no bishop who shall come after him shall crave subsistence therefrom, except from that which rightfully belongs to his bishopric, as other bishops before him had. And this is done with full leave of king Eadward, and with his witness, and of Eadgyth his consort's, and Stigand archbishop's, and Kynsige archbishop's, and Hereman bishop's, and Dodeca bishop's, and Leofric bishop's, and Ealdred bishop's, and Heca bishop's, and Ægelmær bishop's, and Alfwold bishop's, and William bishop's, and Leofwine bishop's, and Sigeward earl's, and Harold earl's, and Ralph earl's, and Ælfgar earl's, and Mannig abbot's, and Ælfwine abbot's, aƀƀ.. ⁊ on Ælfwines aƀƀ.. ⁊ on Leofsiges aƀƀ.. ⁊ on Leofrices aƀƀ.. ⁊ on oðres Leofsiges aƀƀ.. ⁊ on Brihtmæres aƀƀ.. ⁊ on Esgeres stealres. ⁊ on Raulfes stealres. ⁊ on Lifinges stealres. ⁊ on eallra þæs kynges hūscarlan. ⁊ on his mæssepreostan. ⁊ on Đurgodes lagen. ⁊ on Sigferðes. ⁊ on Godrices. ⁊ on Owines. ⁊ on Sigrices. ⁊ on eallra ðara burhwara gewitnesse on Lincoln. ⁊ on ealra þæra manna þe seceað gearmarket to Stowe. ⁊ se ðe ða geferædne mid gōde geece. God ælmihtig geece his līfdagas her on līfe. ⁊ on þam toweardan life ꝥ he mote wununga habban mid Godes gecorenan. ⁊ se þe hig todræfe ⁊ þa land ūt of þære halgan stowe geutige. adrefed wurðe he fram Gode. ⁊ fram Sancta Marian. ⁊ fram eallan his halgan on þan myclan dōmes dæg. Nu syndon þisse gewrita þreo. ān is mid þæs kynges haligdōme. ⁊ oðer is mid Leofrīce eorle. ⁊ ꝥ þridde is mid þam bisceop on þa halgan stowe.

and Leofsige abbot's, and Leofric abbot's, and the other Leofsige abbot's, and Brihtmær abbot's, and Esger constable's, and Ralph constable's, and Lifing constable's, and of all the king's hûs-carls, and his mass-priests, and Thurgod Lagen, and Sigeferth, and Godric, and Owine, and Sigeric, and in witness of all the burghers of Lincoln, and of all the men who attend the yearly market at Stow. And whoso shall increase the fellowship with good increase, may God Almighty increase his life-days here in life, and in the life to come, that he may have a habitation with God's chosen. And whoso shall disperse it, and alienate the land from the holy place, be he driven from God, and from St Mary, and from all his saints on the great domsday. Now of these writings there are three: one is in the king's sanctuary, and the other with earl Leofric, and the third is with the bishop at the holy place.

BRIHTMÆR. M.LIII.

✠ Her suotelen on ðisen yurite embe ðo uorewerde ðe

✠ Here is shown, in this writing, concerning the com-

Briðmer at Gerschereche wrogte wið Stigant archebiscop· ⁊ wið Godric ðane den· ⁊ wið alle þem hird at Xp̃es chereche at Cantwarberi. Ðet is ðanne ðet he uðe Criste into Cristes chereche ðane hōmestal ðet he on set· ⁊ alre Halgene chereche· efter his dage· ⁊ efter Eadgefan his ybedden· and efter his childrene dage· Edmeres and Eðelwynes· swo hi hit alðer best ygodeden uor hire saule alesednesse· and swo ðet se hyred sholde witen ðet se þendom ne [1]adeswen ðe into ðare cheriche belimpeht ne ne atfalle al be ðan ðe se chereche were ygodod.

Hierto byreð ywitnesse Lyefstan portireue and [3]biscop· and Eylwine Stikehare· and manye oðre þar þeyne binne burg and bute.

pact that Brihtmær at Grasschurch[2] made with archbishop Stigand, and with Godric the thane, and with all the convent at Christchurch at Canterbury. That is then, that he has given to Christchurch the homestall on which he resides, and the church of All-Hallows, after his day and after Eadgifu his consort's, and after the day of his children, Eadmer and Æthelwine, as they shall have best endowed it, for their souls' redemption, and so that the convent should know that the service, for all which the church was endowed, come not to naught nor fall off.

Hereto bear witness: Leofstân portreeve and bishop[3], and Eylwine Stikehare, and many others of the thanes, within burgh and without.

[1] adwæsce? [2] Now Gracechurch.
[3] The bishop's name (Willelm) has evidently been omitted.

GODWINE SON OF EARWIG.

Her swutelað an [ðissum gewrite] ꝥ Godwine Earwiges sunu hæfð gelæd fulle lade æt ðan unriht wīfe ðe Leofgar bisceop hyne tihte· and ꝥ wæs læd æt Licitfelda.

Here is made known, in this writing, that Godwine, Earwig's son, has fully cleared himself about the unchaste woman, of which bishop Leofgar accused him: and that was done at Lichfield.

OSWULF AND ÆTHELITH. M.LIII.–M.LXVI.

Hec est cartula que demonstrat convencionem illam quam fecerunt Oswulfus et Æþiliþa uxor sua cum domino abbate Leofstano et monachis ecclesie Sancti Albani, quando introierunt in fraternitatem illorum. Dederunt autem inprimis Oswulfus et Æþeliða uxor sua domino abbati Leofstano et monachis ecclesie Sancti Albani ad introitum fraternitatis eorumdem propter caritatem xx[ti] sol., obtuleruntque Deo ac sancto ejus martyri Albano cum magna devocione illam terram que dicitur æt Stodham, sicuti ipsi illam ea die melius possiderent. Idque factum est cum consensu ac licencia regis Eadweardi atque regine Eadgyþe, scilicet, ut et ipsi participes essent istius doni et retribucionis ejusdem consortes in regno celorum. Ipsi autem, scilicet Oswulfus et Æþeliþa, hoc donum Deo et Sancto fecerunt Albano pro animabus eorum cunctorumque consanguineorum suorum, quatinus in futuro judicio veniam mereantur percipere peccatorum; specialius tamen illa nobilis matrona, videlicet Æþeliþa, hanc donacionem fieri obtinuit a presente domino suo, hoc est Oswulfo, pro anima prioris domini sui Ulfi, qui sibi illam tribuit villam. Postea autem rogaverunt ambo dominum abbatem Leofstanum ut dedisset eis ligna ad edificandam in eadem villa ecclesiam in honore Domini nostri Jhesu Christi et Sancti Albani, ut et hec ecclesia sibi in specialissimum fieret proprietatis signum, et ut ex illa die ob nullius eventum cause eam ullo modo amplius Sanctus perdere posset Albanus; ea tamen condicione, ut quamdiu illi viverent terram illam in suum usum haberent, cum licencia domni abbatis Leofstani simul et monachorum; et hoc tali pacto, quod ob istius rei agnicionem, unoquoque anno ad victum proprie monachorum, xx. solidos darent, quamdiu superstites ipsi fuissent. Hujus rei testes sunt:

Wufwius episcopus, Bondius stabulator, Burhredus, Edwinus ejusdem filius, Godricus tribunus, Ælfstanus vicecomes, Leofwinus de Cadendune, ceteraque innumerabilis multitudo utriusque sexus ac diverse etatis, qui ad dedicacionem supradicte ecclesie fuerunt; coram quibus omnibus utique dixerunt: "Notum vobis cunctis omnibusque hominibus esse volumus, quod nos hodie, videlicet ego Oswulfus et Æþeliþa uxor mea, Deo sanctoque ejus martyri Albano, istam terram, videlicet Stodham, damus in perpetuam hereditatem, in presencia domini Wulfwii episcopi et fratrum ecclesie Sancti Albani qui hic assunt modo nobiscum." Ad quorum vocem, imposito silencio, coram omni populo, episcopus Wulfwius alta voce respondens dixit: "Quicunque hoc dono Sanctum privaverit Albanum, sciat se in futuro, Dei judicio, cum Iuda, Salvatoris nostri proditore, perpetualiter condemnaturum fore; nosque illum tamen tamque presumptuosum ex auctoritate Dei Omnipotentis, Patris, et Filii, et Spiritus Sancti, et sanctorum canonum, et nostri ministerii, excommunicamus, et a consorcio tocius Christianitatis, et a liminibus sancte æcclesie sequestramus, donec terram illam sancto martyri reddat Albano." Cui cuncti qui aderant "Amen" responderunt.

BISHOP ÆTHELSTÂN[1].

✠ Her swutelað on ðissum gewrite [ꝥ] Æþelstan bisceop gebohte æt Leofrice æt Blacewellan fif hide landes æt Intebyrgan. be Æþelredes cinges leafe. ⁊ be Ælfeges arcebisceopes gewitnesse. ⁊ be Wulfstanes arcebisceopes. ⁊ be ealra þæra witena þe ða on Englalande lifes wæron. mid ten pundan reodes goldes ⁊ hwites seolfres. unforboden ⁊ unbesacen. to geofene ⁊ to syllanne. ær dæge ⁊ æfter dæge. sibban oððe fremdan.

✠ Here is made known, in this writing, that bishop Æthelstân bought of Leofric at Blackwell five hides of land at Inkberrow, by leave of king Æthelred, and with the witness of archbishop Ælfeah, and of archbishop Wulfstân, and of all the 'witan' who were then living in England, for ten pounds of red gold and white silver, unforbidden and uncontested, to give and to sell, during life and after life, to relatives or strangers, where

[1] Of Hereford, ob. 1056.

þær him leofost wære. ⁊ se cyng het þone arcebisceop Wulfstan þærto boc settan· ⁊ Aþelstane bisceope boc ⁊ land betæcan unnendere heortan. Þa æfter þysan manigum gearum· soc Wulfstan ⁊ his sunu Wulfric on sum þæt land· þa ferde se bisceop to sciregemote to Wigeranceastre· ⁊ draf þær his spræce. Þa sealde Leofwine ealdorman· ⁊ Hacun· ⁊ Leofric· ⁊ eal seo scir his land clæne· þa he hit unforbodan ⁊ unbesacan bohte· ⁊ settan dæg to þæt man to ðam lande scolde faran· ⁊ þa ilcan þe him ær landgemære læddon hatt . e . . . . an· ⁊ cwædan gif ða landgemære ealswa wæron swa man heo on fruman lædde· þat se bisceop þat land ful rihte ahte. Ða com se bisceop þærto· ⁊ se þe him land sealde· ⁊ þa þe him ær [to wit]nesse wæron· ⁊ com Wulfstan ⁊ his sunu· ⁊ þa þe hyra geferan wæron· ⁊ heo ealle þa þa landgemære geridan· eal swa heo man on fruman þam bisceope lædde· ⁊ heo ealle cwædan þe [ðær] wæron þæt se bisceop ful riht þæt land ahte· þa se þar geanwyrde þæs þe him land sealde. Spæcon ða Leofrices freond ⁊ Wulfstanes freond· þæt hit

to him might be most desirable. And the king commanded the archbishop Wulfstân to draw up a charter to that effect, and to deliver charter and land to bishop Æthelstân, with benignant heart. Then, many years after this, Wulfstân and his son Wulfrîc contested some of the land; then the bishop went to the shire-moot at Worcester, and there preferred his case. Then Leofwine aldorman, and Hacun, and Leofric, and all the shire gave him his land clean, as he had bought it unforbidden and uncontested; and set a day for going to the land with the same persons who had before drawn the land-boundaries . . . . and they said, if the land-boundaries were as they were drawn at first, that the bishop full rightfully possessed the land. Then came the bishop thereto, and he who had sold him the land, and those who were his witnesses; and Wulfstân and his son came, and those who were their companions, and they all then rode along the land-boundaries, as they were at first drawn for the bishop; and they all who were there said that the bishop had full right betere wære ꝥ heora seht togæ[dere wur]de. þonne hy ænige [sa]ce hym betweonan heoldan. sohtan þa hyra seht. þæt wæs þæt Leofric sealde Wulfstane ⁊ his suna an pund ⁊ twegra þegna að. ⁊ wære himsylf þridde. þæt he [þ]am ilcan wolde beon gehealden. gif seo spæc to Leofrice eode. swa swa heo þa wæs to Wulfstane gegan. Ðis wæs ure ealra seht. Wulfstan ⁊ his sunu sealdon þa þæt land clæne Leofrice. ⁊ Leofric. ⁊ Wulfstan. ⁊ Wulfric þam bisceope clæne land ⁊ unbesacan. ær dæge ⁊ æfter. to gyfanne þær him leofost wære. Her swutelað seo gewitnes ⁊ se borh þe þær æt wæron. Ðæt wæs ærest se bisceop. ⁊ L[eofri]c. ⁊ Wulfstan. ⁊ Brihtwine. ⁊ Cynsige. ⁊ Wynstan. ⁊ Ægelwig munuc. ⁊ Ælwine mæssepreost. ⁊ Ælmær mæssepreost. ⁊ Wulfric mæssepreost. ⁊ Cyneword æt Pebbewurðy. ⁊ Ælewig [æt Secca]nham. ⁊ Eadwig his mæg. ⁊ Wulfric æt Cloddesheale. ⁊ Sæword æt Uptuny. ⁊ Wulfric æt Bynningtune. ⁊ Wulfsig Madding. ⁊ mænig god cniht to eacan þysan.

to the land; as he would there answer for who had sold him the land. Then said Leofric's friends and Wulfstân's friends that an amicable agreement would be better than that they should carry on any suit between them: they then framed their agreement. That was, that Leofric should give to Wulfstân and his son one pound, and the oath of two thanes, and should be himself the third, that he would be holden to the same, if the suit should go to Leofric as it had gone to Wulfstân. This was the agreement of us all. Wulfstân and his son should then give the land clean to Leofric, and Leofric, and Wulfstân, and Wulfrîc to the bishop, the land clean and uncontested, before his day and after, to give as shall to him be most agreeable. Here are declared the witness and the security who were there present. That was, first the bishop; and Leofric, and Wulfstân, and Brihtwine, and Kynsig, and Wynstân, and Ægelwig monk, and Ælwine mass-priest, and Ælmær mass-priest, and Wulfric mass-priest, and Kyneword at Pebworth, and Ælewig at Sec-[ca]nham, and Eadwig his

Nu syndan þissa gewrita þreo· an on Wigernaceastre æt Sc̃a Marian· þær þæt land to herð· ⁊ oðer on Hereforda æt Sc̃e Æþelbrihte· ⁊ þridde ā mid þam þe þæt land on hande stande. God ælmihtig þone gehealde þe þis wille rihtlice healdan. ⁊ gif ænig man þonne seo þe þis awendan wille· God ælmihtig· ⁊ Sc̃a Maria· ⁊ ealle his leofan halgan þæne aniðerige ægþær ge her on life· ge þær he længast wunian sceal· buton he hit þe deoppor ær gebete· swa bisceop him tæce.

✠ CYROGRAPHUM.

kinsman, and Wulfric at Clodesheal, and Sæword at Upton, and Wulfric at Bynnington, and Wulfsig Madding, and many a good 'cniht' besides these.

Now of these writings there are three: one at St Mary's in Worcester, where the land belongs, and a second at St Æthelbriht's in Hereford, and a third with him in whose hand the land is. May God Almighty preserve him who will hold to this rightly. But if there be any man who will avert this, may God Almighty, and St Mary, and all his beloved saints, lower him, both here in life, and where he longest shall abide; unless he before the more deeply make amends, as the bishop may teach him.

✠ CHIROGRAPH.

BISHOP SIWEARD.

✠ Siwardus episcopus Godwino comiti, et Hermanno episcopo, et Kinewardo, et ceteris omnibus nobilibus de Bearrucscira, salutem. Audivi Brihtwinum terram de Lechamstede sibi omnino appropriare, sed injuste id agit; nam, me permittente, ea potitus est eo tenore, ut post suum decessum, monachorum libere in manum redeat; quod conventione dispositum est illustrium virorum plurimorum præsentia, eo die quo Brihtnodus ejus frater defunctus Abbendonie sepultus fuit, qui tercius a patre, nam mater ejus inter se et patrem media, ejusdem terre possessione functus est, quibus tantummodo, Cnutonis regis tempore, trino vite spacio hominum possessores fieri, inde a monachis Abbendonensibus concessum fuerat; hec haud aliter haberi, fide quam Deo et regi meo domino debeo interposita, juro; sed et si adhuc his quis discrederit, judicio quo censura vestra potuerit jure definiri, in veritate que protestatus sum, ero paratus.

CONVENTIO INTER STIGANDUM ARCHIEPISCOPUM ET CONVENTUM BATHÆ. M.LX.

Her swutelað on þisum gewrite ꝥ Ælfwig abbud and eall seo geferræden on Bað-an hæfð gelæten to Stigande archeƀ. xxx. hyda landes æt Dyddanhamme· his dæg· wið x. marcan goldes and wið xx. pundon sęolfres· ⁊ æfter hys dæge ga hyt eft into þam halegan mynstre· mid mete ⁊ mid mannum· swa full ⁊ swa forð swa hyt þænne byþ· ⁊ I. marc goldes to eacan· ⁊ VI. merswīn· ⁊ xxx. þusenda hæringys· ælce eare. Þisys ys to gewitnysse Eadweard ciningc· ⁊ Eadgyð seo hlæfdige· ⁊ Ealdryd archeƀ.· ⁊ Hereman ƀ.· ⁊ Gisa ƀ.· ⁊ Harold eorl· ⁊ Tosstig eorl· ⁊ Æþelnoð aƀƀ.· ⁊ Ægylwig aƀƀ.· ⁊ Ægylsige aƀƀ.· ⁊ Ordric aƀƀ.· ⁊ Esęgar steallere·

Here is made known, in this writing, that Ælfwig abbot and all the brotherhood at Bath have let to Stigand archbishop xxx. hides of land at Diddenham, for his day, for x. marks of gold and for xx. pounds of silver; and after his day to revert to the holy monastery, with meat and with men, as fully and as freely as it then shall be; and I. mark of gold in addition, and VI. porpoises, and xxx. thousand herrings, every year. Of this are witness: Eadward king, and Eadgyth the lady, and Ealdred archbishop, and Hereman bishop, and Gisa bishop, and Harold earl, and Tostig earl, and Æthelnoth abbot, and Ægylwig aƀƀ., and Ægylsige

⁊ Roulf steallere. ⁊ Bondig steallere. ⁊ manega oþre gode menn. þe heora naman her awritene ne syndon. ⁊ gyf ænig mann si swa dyrstig ꝥ wylle þis awendan. si he amansumod fram Criste. ⁊ fram Sanctæ Marian. ⁊ fram Sc̃e Petre þam halegan apostele. ⁊ fram eallum Cristes halegum æfre on æcnysse. buton he hyt eft þe raþor gebete.

abb., and Ordric abb., and Esegar constable, and Roulf constable, and Bondig constable, and many other good men, whose names are not here written. And if any man be so daring that he will avert this, be he excommunicated from Christ, and from St Mary, and from St Peter the holy apostle, and from all Christ's saints to all eternity, unless he the more speedily amend it.

KING EADWARD THE CONFESSOR. M.LX.

HEC EST TRANSLATIO CARTE REGIS EDWARDI IN LINGUA SAXONICA TRANSLATA IN LATINUM, DE COLLOCACIONE EPISCOPATUS HEREFORDENSIS CUIDAM WALTERO FACTA, ET DE DIVERSIS PRIVILEGIIS ET LIBERTATIBUS, SCILICET SOK ET SAK, ET ALIIS LIBERTATIBUS, EIDEM WALTERO ET EPISCOPATUI HEREFORDENSI CONCESSIS.

Edwardus rex saluto Haroldum comitem, et Osebarnum, et omnes meos ministros in Herefordensi comitatu amicabiliter. Et ego notifico vobis quod ego concessi Waltero episcopo istum episcopatum hic vobiscum, et omnia universa illa quæ ad ipsum cum justicia pertinent, infra portum et extra, cum saka et cum socna, tam plene et tam plane sicut ipsum aliquis episcopus ante ipsum prius habuit in omnibus rebus. Et si illic sit aliqua terra extra dimissa quæ illuc intus cum justicia pertinet, ego volo quod ipsa reveniat in ipsum episcopatum, vel ille homo ipsam dimittat eidem in suo precio, si quis ipsam cum eo invenire possit. Et ego nolo ullum hominem licenciare quod ei de manibus rapiat aliquam suam rem quam ipse juste habere debet; et ego ei sic concessi.

---

*KING EADWARD THE CONFESSOR. M.LX.

☧ In onomate summi Kyriou omnia jura regnorum gubernantis, et ab alto celi fastigio cuncta cernentis. Ego Æadwardus totius Albionis Dei moderante gubernatione basileus, archiepiscopis, episcopis, abbatibus, centenariis, cunctisque sanctæ fidelibus æcclesiæ clericis et laicis, insuper et omnibus post me futuris regibus, salutem, perpetuamque pacis felicitatem. Summum regibus ac principibus bonum est justiciam Dei colere, sanctam æcclesiam ejus exaltare et honorare, quia qui eam exaltant et honorant, cum ea, et in ea, et per eam, exaltantur et honorantur. Prevenit cor meum gratia Dei, ut quod ab antecessoribus meis regibus collatum est ejus æcclesiæ, mea firmetur auctoritate. Æcclesia namque beatæ Dei genitricis semperque virginis Mariæ, Sanctique Benedicti, omniumque sanctarum virginum, quæ Rameseie nuncupatur, quæ olim, id est tempore præcellentissimi regis Æadgari, a quodam insigni viro Æilwino onomate, utpote in ejusdem regis gloriosi munificentiæ kartula, quam ibidem donaverat, data, ac sigillo regio confirmata, legitur, almipotentis Christi mirabilius cooperante gratia, est constructa, ac terrarum copiosis ditata muneribus; imprimis eam ita liberam et quietam, tam ab omni exactione episcopali quam a sæculari esse volo, ut neque nos, neque successores nostri, neque quilibet episcopus, nec quicunque de judiciaria potestate in ipsam sanctam basilicam, vel in manentes in ipsa, vel in homines qui cum suis terris, vel qualibuscunque substantiis, ad ipsam tradere vel devovere se voluerint, nisi per voluntatem abbatis et omnium suorum monachorum, ullam unquam habeant potestatem; sed sit hæc sancta mater æcclesia specialis dominæ nostræ perpetuæ virginis Mariæ, ac patroni nostri Sancti Benedicti, et omnium sanctarum virginum, libera et absoluta ab omni invasione vel inquietudine omnium hominum cujuscunque ordinis vel potestatis esse videantur. Præterea inperpetuum confirmo, ut monachi ejusdem æcclesiæ per successiones, secundum regulam Sancti Benedicti, eligere ex se idoneos abbates habeant potestatem; et quisquis fugitivorum, de quocunque loco, pro quacunque causa, cujuscunque conditionis sit, ipsum sanctum locum vel procinctum ejus intraverit fugiens, membrorum suorum ac vitæ impunitatem consequatur. Possessiones vero quæ ibi a quibuscunque donatæ sunt, non abbas, non alia quælibet persona licentiam habeat vendendi vel extraneis dandi; sed regum munimine deinceps locus ipse tueatur, ipseque abbas, regi soli serviens, atque ei soli os ad os respondens, commissum sibi gregem spirituali et temporali pastu habundanter foveat. Concedo etiam et confirmo omnes donationes terrarum, vel libertatum, aut aliarum rerum quæ a regibus Eadgaro videlicet et Hardecnuto, seu aliis fidelibus, ante me donatæ sunt: Hoc est Uppwude cum Ravelega[1] berewico suo, et cum insula in qua prædictum stat arcisterium, omnibusque sibi pertinentibus, Hemmingeforde cum omnibus ad se pertinentibus, Sautrey[2] cum omnibus ad se pertinentibus, Hellingh[3] cum omnibus ad se pertinentibus, Wallsocne cum omnibus ad se pertinentibus. In Welles xx^ti^ piscatores ibidem singulis annis ad usum fratrum LX. millia anguillarum reddentes; Brancestrei cum omnibus ad se pertinentibus, et cum omni maris projectu, quod nos Anglice 'shipwrec'[4] appellamus, Ripton[5] cum omnibus ad se pertinentibus, Tinell[6] cum omnibus ad se pertinentibus, Kyngestune cum Raffleya[7] et Byrig, berewicis suis, omnibusque sibi pertinentibus, Wardeburc cum omnibus ad se pertinentibus, Scepton[8] cum omnibus ad se pertinentibus, Chaterih[9] cum omnibus ad se pertinentibus, et unam mansionem orientalem de Elesworð cum [omnibus] ad se pertinentibus, Houcton[10] cum omnibus ad se pertinentibus, Witton[11] cum omnibus ad se pertinentibus, Elinton[12] cum omnibus ad se pertinentibus, Biðerne cum omnibus ad se pertinentibus, Briumton[13] cum omnibus ad se pertinentibus, Wichinton[14] cum omnibus ad se pertinentibus, Isham cum omnibus ad se pertinentibus, Weston[15] cum omnibus ad se pertinentibus, Grauell[16] cum omnibus ad se pertinentibus,

The variations are from the 'Inspeximus.'

[1] Kæflea. [2] Saltreðe. [3] Hellingeia. [4] sæ upwurp. [5] Riptunæ. [6] Styveclea. [7] Ræflea. [8] Slæpe. [9] Ceateric. [10] Hohtunæ. [11] Wittunæ. [12] Elintunæ. [13] Brynintunæ. [14] Hwiccintunæ. [15] Westunæ. [16] Græflea.

Bilinchon[1] cum omnibus ad se pertinentibus, Stocton[2] cum omnibus ad se pertinentibus, Gillinge cum omnibus ad se pertinentibus; necnon et illas quas optimates mei meo tempore addiderunt, scilicet Æðericus, Dorecensis æcclesiæ episcopus, Clinton[3], et Beornewelle, et Hemingeton[4], et unam mansionem in Ælleswrð occidentalem, et Gretton[5], et Ðerefelde[6], et Sucklingdon[7], et Westmulnæ orientalem, et Offerton[8] in Hoylandia, et III. hidas in Broctune, et III. hidas in Bodekesham, et cum omnibus ad se pertinentibus; Ædnotus[9] episcopus, successor ejus, Over[10] et Barton[11] et Snapwell[12] cum omnibus ad se pertinentibus; Æðnoðus[9] filius Godrici, Accle cum omnibus ad se pertinentibus. Eylwynus[13] Suerte Crangfeldæ et Kemestan[14], et Cloppham cum omnibus; Leofsius diaconus, Wipsinton[15] et Langetehill[16], et Mærtune, et Watlinworð, cum omnibus sibi pertinentibus; Leofsius nepos ejus, Mæringe cum omnibus ad se pertinentibus; Ælfsius de Lampaðe[17], Burewelle cum omnibus ad se pertinentibus; Iohol de Lincolnia, Querinton[18] cum omnibus ad se pertinentibus; Hardeknut vero, frater meus, Hemingeford et Gilling cum omnibus sibi pertinentibus. Postremo ego ipse, propter spem retributionis æternæ, et pro remissione delictorum meorum, et pro animabus patris et matris meæ, et omnium parentum meorum, ad laudem Omnipotentis Dei, ibidem ad usus fratrum inibi Deo servientium, de meo jure quod mihi soli competebat, absque ullius reclamatione vel contradictione ista addidi: Imprimis Ringstede cum omnibus ad se pertinentibus, et cum omni maris ejectu, quod shipwrec[19] appellamus, et Winebodesham cum hundredo et dimidio infra Bichamdia, et cum LX^{ta}IIII^{ta} soccamannis ad hundredos pertinentibus, et cum foro de Dunham ad Winebodesham pertinenti. Relaxamus igitur istis et omnibus supra nominatis terris consuetudines omnes et exactiones regalium et episcopalium ministrorum, sicut antecessores mei reges prius

1 Dilintunæ.
2 Stoctunæ.
3 Æðelintunæ.
4 Hemmingtunæ.
5 Grytttune.
6 Ferefelde.
7 Scytlingedune.
8 Osfyrðtunæ.
9 Eadnoð.
10 Ovræ.
11 Bertunæ.
12 Cnapenwelle.
13 Ailwinæ.
14 Cæmbestunæ.
15 Wipsintunæ.
16 Langestille.
17 Langwaðe.
18 Cuernintune.
19 sæ uppwurp.

fecerunt, ut nullis graventur oneribus expeditionum, nec pontium, vel castrorum restructione, nec furis apprehensione, et emissione, nec sanguinis effusione; et omnia quæ ad locum ipsum pertinent, sint omnino libera, cellæ, æcclesiæ, cimiteria, terræ, pascua, silvæ, venationes, aquæ, piscationes, cum redditibus, servitiis, debitis, oblationibus, luminaribus, decimis, donariis, censu, morthidis, legibus, consuetudinibus, causarum discussionibus, emendationibus, sive æcclesiasticis sive sæcularibus, et cum omnibus quæcunque maris procellosis tempestatibus in aquam vel in terram eorum ejecta fuerint, quod Anglice shipwrech[1] promulgatum est onomate, et omnibus quæcunque scriptis vel testimonio bonorum hominum rememorari potuerint, quæ a regibus concessa vel concedenda sunt, ut nullus ex iis subtrahere, vel diminuere, aut disperdere, qualibet occasione, judicio vel potestate presumat. Renovamus etiam et confirmamus privilegia antiquorum regum, atque ob reverentiam dominæ nostræ perpetuæ virginis Mariæ, Sanctique Benedicti, sanctarumque virginum, omnibusque futuris ibidem abbatibus, in tota possessione monasterii, sacam et socam, theloneumque suum, in terra et in aqua concedo, et consuetudines, ut ab omnibus apertius et plenius intelligantur Anglice scriptas, scilicet mundbryce, feardwitæ, fihtwite, blodwite, mischennynge, fryðsocne, hamsocne, forstall, forhpheang, þiefphang, hangwite, gryðbryce, utleap, infangeneþeof, scipbryce, toll et team, aliasque omnes leges et consuetudines quæ ad me pertinent, tam plene et tam libere sicut eas in manu mea habebam. Et, ut omnia concludam, nullus succedentium regum, episcoporum, principum, comitum, vicecomitum, procuratorum, seu aliorum regum clientium, vel alia quælibet magna vel parva persona, per vim aut per consuetudinem, pastum, censum, vel impensionem, non opera, non tributa, exenia, seu munuscula, vel aliud quidlibet ab eorum possessionibus exigat, sed omnimodam libertatem perpetualiter in terra et in aqua, in urbe et extra, in domo et extra, in villa et extra, in via et extra, in placito, in soca et saca, in theloneo, et in omnibus suis appendiciis habeant. Quisquis igitur fidelium hanc nostram

[1] sæ uppwurp.

munificentiam amplificare propriis donis sategerit, augmentet illi Omnipotens Deus gaudium perhenne, ubi perpetuitas viget. Si quis vero, quod absit, eam destruere voluerit, vel hujus nostri decreti contradictor, convulsor, et temerator extiterit, perpetuo anathemati subjaceat, nisi Deo et ejus gloriosæ matri digna pœnitentia satisfecerit. Scripta est namque hæc sceda, me jubente, et sigillata his testibus, quorum onomata infra habentur, consentientibus, II. Kal. Decembris.

✠ Ego Eadwardus, rex Deo largiente Anglorum, signum venerandæ crucis impressi. ✠ Ego Stigandus archiepiscopus concessi, et confirmando signo sanctæ crucis consignavi. ✠ Ego Æðelredus archiepiscopus gratanter corroboravi. ✠ Ego Wlfstanus episcopus vexillo sanctæ crucis prænotavi. ✠ Ego Gyso episcopus consentaneus fui. ✠ Ego Walterus episcopus consensum præbui. ✠ Ego Reinbaldus cancellarius consigillando commodum duxi. ✠ Ego Switgarius notarius scripsi. ✠ Ego Ælsius abbas. ✠ Ego Eadwinus abbas. ✠ Ego Ægelwinus abbas. ✠ Ego Baldewinna abbas. ✠ Ego Alwinus abbas hoc meum desiderium ad perfectum adduxi, et a rege hilariter suscepi. ✠ Ego Leofricus dux. ✠ Ego Haroldus dux. ✠ Ego Leofwinus dux. ✠ Ego Eadwinus dux. ✠ Ego Hugelinus cubicularius. ✠ Ego Eadgarus stallere. ✠ Ego Robertus filius Wittman. ✠ Ego Wigodus de Lincolne.

KING EADWARD THE CONFESSOR. M.LX.

Oportet nos quos Deus præfecit temporaliter rectores populo suo ad omnes facere justiciam, maxime autem ad matrem nostræ salutis æcclesiam, per quam Christiani facti perveniamus ad æternam Domini misericordiam, qui judicabit reges terræ, et secundum opera sua reddet unicuique. Quapropter ego Æduuardus rex Anglorum pro villa Fiskertuna data in Burch Sancto Petro, jubeo fieri nostræ confirmationis testamentum contra omnem, scilicet, calumniam iniquorum. Hanc quippe villam, cum Leofgyua femina Lundonica haberet omnino propriam et liberam, beato Petro in prædictum locum post obitum suum donavit eam, sicut fideli testimonio nobis probatum est, perpetuo possidendam, ea scilicet plena libertate qua ipsa possidebat. Hæc obiit in via Ierosolimæ, quod ubi Leofricus abbas de Burch cognovit, ad nos causam suam retulit, et per idoneos testes justam comprobavit, nostrumque assensum inde postulavit. At regina mea Ædgyth, cum terram vendicasset, dicendo quod hanc sibi eadem femina decrevisset, idem abbas per me et principes meos reginæ fratres, Haroldum et Tostinum, ipsius potentiam flexit, datisque ei in gratiam xx. marcis auri et ornamentis æcclesiæ quæ ad alias xx. marcas apportiantur, terram monasterio suo liberrimam et integerrimam restituit. Hanc igitur donationem ego rex Æduuardus cum ipsa regina ita annuo, concedo, et confirmo, quatinus tota illa possessio Fiskertuna in æternum sit propria et dominica ipsius Sancti Petri in Burch, ad usus sibi servientium, atque ita maneat libera in terris, aquis, silvis, pratis, pascuis, cunctisque rebus et justitiis pertinentibus, cum saca et socna, ut nullus inde quicquam repetat preter arcis et expeditionis subsidium. Hinc ergo contestor omnes posteros meos, reges et judices, per Dominum omnium judicem, justitiæ amatorem, et tocius injustitiæ vindicem, ne quis unquam audeat quicquam tam ex his quam de omni jure Sancti Petri detrahere aut diminuere; quia re vera sicut illi consequuntur æternam vitam qui æcclesiam Dei amplificant, ita illis manent sempiterna tormenta qui eam in aliquo spoliant: qui autem hæc violaverit, omnium sacerdotum et ministrorum Dei ore anathema sit. Anno ab incarnatione Domini millesimo LX° confirmatum est hoc testamentum, cui testes conspicui subscribendo annotantur.

Ego Æduuardus rex constitui. Ego Ædgyth regina concessi. Ego Stigandus archiepiscopus collaudavi. Ego Aldredus archiepiscopus comprobavi. Ego Wlfuuius Lincolie antistes corroboravi. Ego Haroldus dux favi. Ego Tostinus dux testis fui. Signum Raulfi regis dapiferi. Signum Asgæri regis dapiferi. Signum Marlesuuein. Signum Godrici filius Ædgyfe. Signum Ulf de Lincolia. Signum Askyl Tokes sune. Signum Iaulf Maltes sune.

KING EADWARD THE CONFESSOR. M.LX.-M.LXI.

✠ Eadward king gret Harold erl· ⁊ Aylnoð abbot· ⁊ Godwine schyrereuen· ⁊ alle mine þeynes on Sumerseten frendliche. And ich kyþe eow þat ich habbe geunnen Gisan minan preste þes bissopriche her mid eow and alre þare þinge þas þe ðær mid richte gebyrað· on wode ⁊ on felde· mid saka ⁊ mid sokna· binnon porte ⁊ buton· swo ful ⁊ swo forð swo Duduc bissop oð any bissop hit firmest him toforen hauede· on ællen þingan. And gif her ani land sy out of þan bissopriche gedon· ich wille ꝥ hit cume in ongeæn· oðer ꝥ man hit ofgo on hise gemoð swo man wið him bet finde mage. And ich bidde eou allen ꝥ ge him fulstan to driuan Godes gerichte lock huen hit neod sy, and heo eowwer fultumes biþurfe. And ich nelle nanne man geþefien ꝥ him uram honde teo anige þare þinge þas þe ich him unnen habben.

✠ I king Eadward greet earl Harold, and abbot Aylnoth, and Godwine shire-reeve, and all my thanes in Somersetshire, amicably. And I make known to you that I have given to Gisa my priest the bishopric here with you, and all the things which thereto rightfully belong, in wood and in field, with sac and socn, within town and without, as fully and as freely as bishop Duduc or any other bishop best had it before him, in all things. And if there be any land taken from the bishopric, I will that it come in again, or that it be settled at his gemôt, as may be best for him. And I pray you all that ye aid him in promoting God's rights, where it may be needful, and he may require your support. And I will not consent that any man withdraw from his hand any of the things which I have given him.

IDEM LATINE.

✠ Edwardus rex Haroldo comiti, Ailnodo abbati, Godwino vicecomiti, et omnibus ballivis suis Somerset. salutem. Sciatis nos dedisse Gisoni presbytero nostro episcopatum hunc apud vos, cum omnibus pertinentiis, in bosco et plano, et saca et socna, in villis et extra, ita plene et libere in omnibus sicut episcopus Dudocus aut aliqui predecessorum suorum habuerunt. Et si quid inde contra justitiam fuerit sublatum, volumus quod revocetur, vel quod aliter ei satisfaciat. Rogamus etiam vos ut auxiliari eidem velitis ad Christianitatem sustinendam, si necesse habuerit. Nolumus autem ut ullus hominum ei auferat aliquid eorum quæ ei contulimus.

KING EADWARD THE CONFESSOR AND QUEEN EADGYTH. M.LXI.

Ðis is se freols ðe Eadweard cyngc ⁊ Eadgyth seo hlæfdige geuðon into þam haligum mynstre æt Hortune· Criste to lofe· ⁊ Sancta Marian· ⁊ eallon Cristes halgon.

✠ Regnante in perpetuum Domino nostro Jhesu Christo. Rixiendum urum Drihtne Hælendum Criste on ecnysse· þam heahstan ⁊ þan untosprecendlican· ealra þinga ⁊ ealra tida Scyppend· se ðe manegum þingum his mihtum setteð ⁊ wealdeð· eac swilce ðam upahafenlican ⁊ þam unasecgendlican rice ꝥ ðe he þises lifes eadigysse ⁊ gesælignesse nænigum þingum ne forlæte. Forþan ic Eadwerd Englalandes cyngc· mid Godes

This is the liberty which king Eadward and Eadgyth the lady have granted to the holy monastery at Horton, to the praise of Christ, and St Mary, and all Christ's saints.

✠ Regnante in perpetuum Domino nostro Jhesu Christo. Reigning our Lord Jesus Christ in eternity, the highest and the unutterable, of all things and of all tides Creator, who by his might sets and governs many things; in like manner the heavenly and the ineffable realm, so that he the happiness and prosperity of this life in no respects neglects. Therefore I Eadward, king of England, with the grace of God and with gyfe ⁊ mid minra witena geþeahte ⁊ ræde· ic forgyfe þisne freols into þære haligan stowe æt Hortune· Gode to lofe ⁊ Sc̃a Marian to wurðmynte· þe seo stowe ys foregehalgod· ⁊ me on gemende ys mid þisum eorðlicum þingum þa ecanlican gestreon to begytende· sicut Salomon dixit, "Redemptio animæ propriæ diuitiæ": swa swa Salomon cwæð· þæt we sceoldon mid urum spedum urum sawlum þa ecan gesælignysse begytan. Forðan ic cuðlice mid geþeahte· geþafunge· ⁊ leafe ealra minra biscope ⁊ eorla· ⁊ butan þan ealra minra selostra witena· ic forgef þisne freols for mine agene sawle· ⁊ for mine leofostra frenda· ꝥ eall ꝥ land ðe lið into þan haligan mynstre æt Hortune· ꝥ hit sy fæstlice ⁊ unawendedlice â ecelice gefreod ealra cynelicra ⁊ ealdordomlicra þeowdoma· ge þeoffengces ge æghwylcere uneaðnesse ealles woroldlices broces· buton fyrdsocne ⁊ burhgeweorce ⁊ bryggeweorce. Gif hwa þanne si ꝥ he hine for Godes lufon to ðan geeadmedan wylle ꝥ he þas mine gyfe geycan wylle oððe gemenigfyldan· geyce him ælmihtig God eall gód her on worolde· ⁊ his dagas gesund-

the counsel and advice of my 'witan', grant this liberty to the holy place at Horton, to the praise of God, and the honour of St Mary, to whom the place is specially hallowed; and I have in mind, with these earthly things, to obtain the everlasting treasures, sicut Salomon dixit: "Redemptio animæ propriæ divitiæ": as Solomon said, that we should with our riches obtain eternal happiness for our souls. Therefore I publicly, with the counsel, consent, and leave of all my bishops and earls, and, besides that, of all my best 'witan', give this liberty for my own soul, and my dearest relatives', that all the land which is adjacent to the holy monastery at Horton be firmly and immutably ever eternally freed from all royal and aldormannic services, both from 'theoffeng' and from every annoyance from all worldly trouble, except 'fyrdsocn', and burghwork, and bridgework. But if any there be that, for love of God, will so far condescend that he will increase or multiply this my gift, may Almighty God increase to him all good here in the world, and make his days fullie. Gif þonne hwylc mann to ðam geþristlæce· oððe mid deofles searwum to ðam beswicen sy ꝥ he þis on ænegum þingum· lytlum oððe mycelum· þence to abrecende oððe to awendende· wite he þonne þæt he þæs riht agyldende sy beforan Cristes þrymsettle· þonne ealle heofonwara ⁊ eorðwara on his andwerdnysse beoð onstyred ⁊ onhrerede· buton he hyt ær her on worolde mid rihte gebete. Đis wæs gewriten on ðam geare þe wæs agan fram Cristes acennednysse ân þusend geara ⁊ ân ⁊ sixtig geara· ⁊ an þam tacncircule ꝥ seofanteoðe gear.

Ic Eadwerd cyngc· mid ðære halgan Cristes rodetacne· þis het swiðe geornlice getrymman ⁊ gefæstnian þisne freodom· on ælmihtiges Godes naman ⁊ on ealra his halgena. Ic fæstlice bebeode ꝥ hine nænig minra æfterfylgendra eft ne onwende· ne on nænigum dælum· læssum ne on marum· hyne ne onmyrdon· ac þeos freols â ecelice forð þurhwunige· swa lange swa God wylle þæt Cristen geleafa mid Angelcynne untosceacan wurðe.

prosperous. But if any man be so daring, or with the devil's wiles so deceived, that in any things, little or great, he think of violating or perverting this, then be it known to him that he will have to make just retribution before the throne of Christ, when all heaven's inhabitants and earth's inhabitants shall, in his presence, be troubled and agitated, unless he previously here in the world make just compensation. This was written in the year that was agone from the birth of Christ one thousand and sixty-one, and of the lunar cycle the seventeenth year.

I, king Eadward, with the sign of Christ's holy rood, command to be very earnestly confirmed and established this freedom, in the name of Almighty God and of all his saints. I steadfastly enjoin that none of my successors again change it, nor in any part, little or great, obstruct it; but that this liberty ever eternally continue on as long as God will that Christian belief remain with the Angle race unimpaired.

KING EADWARD THE CONFESSOR. M.LV.-M.LXIV.

✠ Eadweard cyngc gret Tostig eorl ⁊ ealle mine þegenas on Eoferwicscire freondlice. ⁊ ic cyðe eow ꝥ hit is min unna ⁊ min fulle leafe ꝥ Ealdred arcebiscop ꝥ he dihte privilegium to þam landan þe ligcað innto Sc̃e Iohannes mynstre æt Beferlict. ⁊ ic wille ꝥ ꝥ mynstre ⁊ seo circ þe ðider innto hirð. ꝥ hit beo swa freols swa ænig oðer mynster is æt eallan þingan. ⁊ loc hwilc bisceop ðærofer byð þæt hit beo him underþeod. ⁊ þæt he beo þærto geheald ⁊ mund under me. ꝥ þær nan mann nan þing on ne teo butan he. ⁊ þæt he na geþafige ꝥ man þanon ut do ænig þæra þinga ðæs þe þær mid rihte to gebyrað. swa swa he wille beon wið Godd geborgen. ⁊ Sc̃s Iohannes. ⁊ eallra ðæra halgena þe seo halige stoww is foregehalgod. ⁊ ic wille ꝥ þær æfre beo mynstrelif ⁊ samnung þa hwile þe ænig mann leofað.

✠ I king Eadward greet earl Tostig and all my thanes in Yorkshire amicably; and I make known to you that it is my grant and my full leave that archbishop Ealdred draw up a privilege for the lands which are adjacent to St John's monastery at Beverley. And I will that that monastery, and the church which thereto belongs, be as free as any other monastery is in all things; and that whatever bishop be thereover, that it be subject to him, and that he be thereto guardian and patron under me, so that no man there, excepting himself, bring anything in, and that he allow not that any of the things be taken away which thereto rightfully belong, as he will be secure towards God, and St John, and all the saints to whom the holy place is specially hallowed. And I will that there ever be there a monastery and brotherhood while any man lives.

KING EADWARD THE CONFESSOR. M.LXII.

✠ In nomine Domini nostri Ihesu Christi, qui unus Deus in Trinitate ab omnibus se colentibus veneratur, et puro cordis affectu adoratur. Ego Ædwardus, Dei dono Anglorum rex, in hujus mundi decursu hujus seculi filiorum qui justi inveniuntur studens exaltare cornu utpote regalis imperii jure rite roborati, accedant ad eum per callem justiciæ qui dat petentibus juste et relligiose vivere. Hec tamen beata commutatio digne censetur in hoc seculo ut cui felicitas tantum deliberaverit animi quod mundialium gravedine cupiditatum postposita, velut granum frumenti a spinis suffocantibus aliquando vero dumetis arescentibus, decipiat in hunc tenorem emergi, ut divina virtute firmatus vigeat suo Creatori et Domino. Istis etenim inter transitorias mundi procellas cuidam meorum comitum onomate Haroldo quandam terram, que antiquitus ab incolis illius loci nuncupatur Waltham, hereditario jure concessi, cum omnibus ad se pertinentibus campis, pascuis, pratis, silvis, et aquis. Ex hinc sibi tantam Deus sue pietatis graciam contulit ut inter momentanea mundi desideria cogitaret feliciter desudando celestia; quineciam illi qui omnia in omnibus operatur ut vult talem divine pietatis dulcedinem ut supra memoravi concessit ei, ut non solum Dei cultor efficiatur, verum eciam canonice regule strenuus institutor fieri credatur; nam hec divinitus fidei declaratione et operum exhibitione ceterarumque ecclesiarum rerum plenitudine probavit eventus. Quis autem finis ejus desiderii post hec evenerit, sapiencia per Salomonem declarando prompsit, dum ait: "Justis dabitur desiderium bonum." Enimvero rationali consilio ditatus ac sue non immemor conditionis, in præscripto loco monasterium ad laudem Domini nostri Ihesu Christi et sancte crucis construxit. Primum concedens ei terram que vocatur Northlande, unde ecclesiam ville antiquitus dotatam invenit; post fundatum dehinc sacre fidei monasterium ad normam sancte Dei ecclesiæ dedicari fecit honorifice ob memoriam mei et conjugis mee, nomine Ædiðæ, patris ac matris, pro se suisque omnibus vivis et defunctis sibi consanguinitate conjunctis.

Hoc enim perplurimis, sanctorum apostolorum, martyrum, confessorum, virginum, reliquiis ornavit. Hoc non solum terris, quarum vocabula post hec sunt recitanda, verum etiam libris angelicis[1], vestibus, ac diversis ornamentorum generibus, templo Domini congruentibus qui divinis cultibus clare ac dulcedine imbutus attentius sancte celebrationis templum excolere cepit ac venerari. Quid plura? sue denique conditionis non immemor, ibidem quorumdam catervulam fratrum, secundum auctoritatem sanctorum patrum, canonice regule subjectam constituit, que Deo et sanctis ejus die noctuque laudes hymnizando decantet.

Hec sunt vocabula prædiorum ad præfatum pertinencia monasterium: Passefelda, cum omnibus ad se pertinentibus campis, pascuis, pratis, silvis, et aquis; Walde, cum omnibus ad se pertinentibus campis, pascuis, pratis, silvis, et aquis; Upminster, cum omnibus ad se pertinentibus campis, pascuis, pratis, silvis, et aquis; Walhfare, cum omnibus ad se pertinentibus campis, pascuis, pratis, silvis, et aquis; Tippedene, cum omnibus ad se pertinentibus campis, pascuis, pratis, silvis, et aquis; Alwartune, cum omnibus ad se pertinentibus campis, pascuis, pratis, silvis, et aquis; Wodeforda, cum omnibus ad se pertinentibus campis, pascuis, pratis, silvis, et aquis; Lambehide, cum omnibus ad se pertinentibus campis, pascuis, pratis, silvis, et aquis; Nesingan, cum omnibus ad se pertinentibus campis, pascuis, pratis, silvis, et aquis; Brikendune, cum omnibus ad se pertinentibus campis, pascuis, pratis, silvis, et aquis; Melnho, cum omnibus ad se pertinentibus; Alricheseia, cum omnibus ad se pertinentibus; Wrmeleia, cum omnibus ad se pertinentibus; Nethleswelle, cum omnibus ad se pertinentibus; Hicche, cum omnibus ad se pertinentibus campis, pascuis, pratis, silvis, et aquis; Lukintone, cum omnibus ad se pertinentibus; Westwaltham, cum omnibus ad se pertinentibus.

Has omnes supradictas terras ego Ædwardus rex, pro redimendis peccatis meis et antecessorum, sive etiam successorum meorum, consilio archiepiscoporum et episcoporum, necnon et principum terre mee, ecclesie Sancte Crucis, et

[1] euangelicis?

fratribus ibidem in Dei nomine congregatis sive congregandis concedo, cum sacha et soche, tol et team, et infangeneðof, et flemenesfyriðe, et gridbreche, forstal, hamsokne, blodwite, ordel, et oreste. Si vero aliquis successorum meorum, quod absit, de terris istis quicquam subtraxerit vel subtrahi permiserit, et inde requisitus emendare noluerit, ei Deus justus judex regnum pariter et coronam auferat. Nos autem archiepiscopi et episcopi, ad hanc confirmationem congregati, ex præcepto domini nostri regis, ejusdem hortatu, excommunicamus, et maledictione perpetua condempnamus omnes transgressores hujus consularis donationis et regularis concessionis.

Đis synd ða landgemæra into Passefelde.

Þæt is ærest· of þare ealdan hæcce æt Freoðene felde into Presta hlype; into þam bece to Staun dune· ⁊ of Staun dune to Scealdeforda· ⁊ of Sceldeforda to Coleboge welle· of þere welle eft into þære ealdan hæcce· ⁊ swa eft into Freoðene felda.

Đis synd þa landgemæra into Welde.

Ærest of Dellen norð into þere gemyðe· east into Hafegeæte· of Hafegeæte east into þam Wulfpytte· of þam pytte suð into þam purce· of þam purce suð to Freobearnes hlype· ⁊ swa into Mannes lande· ⁊ þanon eft into Dellen.

Đis synd þa landgemære into Upmynstre.

Ærest at Tigelhyrste suð to þare marcdice· of þare dice west in Ingceburne· ⁊ of þare burne norð into Beccengare·

These are the land-boundaries to Passfield:

That is first, from the old hatch at Freethen field to Presta hlyp; to the brook at Standon; and from Standon to Shalford; and from Shalford to Colebog well; from the well again to the old hatch, and so again to Freethen field.

These are the land-boundaries to Weld:

First from Dellen north to the mouth, east to Hafegate; from Hafegate east to the wolf-pit; from the pit south to the Purk, from the Purk south to Freebarn's leap, and so to Mannes land, and thence again to Dellen.

These are the land-boundaries to Upminster:

First at Tilehurst south to the boundary ditch; from the ditch west to Ingbourne; and from the bourne north to Bec-

⁊ of Beccengare norð andlang þare strate wald into Stangare. of Stangare norð into Mannes lande. of Mannes lande eft into Tigelhyrste.

Ðis synd þa landgemære into Walhfare.

Ærest of þam æssce to þære ældan hlype. of þare hlype to þare ealden wude hæcce. of þære hæcce to þare ealden strate. ⁊ of þare strate to Sandæcere. ⁊ of þam æcere to Beadewan eá. of þare eá to Wine broce. of þam broce norð eft to þan æssce.

Ðis synd þa landgemære into Tippedene.

Ærest in Tippaburne. of þare burne up to þam heðe. ⁊ of þam heðe to Þetdene gemære wið Æffan hecce. ⁊ swa into þære eá. andlang ðære eá. þæt eft in Teppeburne.

Ðis synd þa landgemare into Ælwartone.

Ærest æt Werdhæcce. of Werdhacce to Eácrofte. of Eácrofte into Beolle pole. of þam pole into Leofsiges mad. of Leofsiges mad into Omermad. of Omermad into Æðerices hlype. of þare hlype into Wulfhlype. of Wulfhlype into Þesfalde. of Þesfalde into Stanweges hacce. of Stanweges hacce into Sateresbyrig.

cengar; and from Beccengar north along the road-weald to Stangar; from Stangar north to Mannes land; from Mannes land again to Tilehurst.

These are the land-boundaries to Walhfare:

First from the ash to the old leap; from the leap to the old wood hatch; from the hatch to the old road, and from the road to Sandacre, and from the acre to Beadewan river; from the river to Winbrook; from the brook north again to the ash.

These are the land-boundaries to Tipden:

First to Tippebourne; from the bourne up to the heath; from the heath to Thetden's boundary opposite Æffa's hatch, and so to the river; along the river, then again to Teppebourne.

These are the land-boundaries to Elverton:

First at Werdhatch; from Werdhatch to Eacroft; from Eacroft to Beolle pool; from the pool to Leofsige's meadow; from Leofsige's meadow to Omermeadow; from Omermeadow to Ætheric's leap; from the leap to Wulfleap; from Wulfleap to Thesfald; from Thesfald to Stanway hatch; from Stanway hatch to Sætersborough.

Ðis synd þa landgemare into Wudeforda.

Ærest in Angrices burne to Ealdermannes hæcce· to þær cynges hæcce· of þær cynges hæcce eft into Angrices burne.

Ðis synd þa landgemære into Lambehyðe.

Ærest æt Brixges stane· ⁊ swa forð þurwh þane graf to þam mæredice· ⁊ swa to Bulce treo· ⁊ fram Bulce treo to Hyse· ⁊ fram Hyse to Ælsyges hæcce· ⁊ swa est to þare strate· ⁊ swa andlang strete eft to Brixes stan.

Ðis synd þa landgemære into Nassingan.

Þat is harst· of Cerlen hacce andlang mearce to Scelden mære· ⁊ of Scelden mere to þare burnan· ⁊ of þare burnan to Buterwyelle· ⁊ of Buterwelle to Þuroldes gemaren· ⁊ of Þuroldes gemaren eft andlang marce to Cerlen hacce· ⁊ seo mæd þe þarto gebyrað lið ut be Ligean.

These are the land-boundaries to Woodford:

First to Angric's bourne to Alderman's hatch; to the king's hatch; from the king's hatch again to Angric's bourne.

These are the land-boundaries to Lambeth:

First at Brixton, and so on through the grove to the boundary dike, and so to Bulke tree; and from Bulke tree to Hyse; and from Hyse to Ælsige's hatch; and so east to the road; and so along the road again to Brixton.

These are the land-boundaries to Nazing:

That is first, from Cerlen hatch, along the mark to Skelden boundary; and from Skelden boundary to the brook; and from the brook to Buterwell; and from Buterwell to Thurold's boundary, and from Thurold's boundary again along the mark to Cerlen hatch: and the meadow thereto belonging lies out by the Lea.

Ego Ædwardus, nutu divino rex, omnia prædia que Haroldus comes monasterio apud Waltham subjecit, vel quæ adhuc se daturum decernit, sublevans statuo, ut ab omni servitutis jugo sint semper libera, et a shiris et hundredis, et extra curiam Sanctæ Crucis omnibus placitis et omnibus geldis. Scriptum est autem istud privilegium anno Dominice incarnationis M.LXII., Indictionibus ter quinis, Epactis septenis, Concurrente I. Hiis testibus consentientibus.

Ego Ædwardus, Anglorum basileus, hac inscriptione ✠ salutifere crucis deliberando assigno. ✠ Ego Eadgyða, Dei munere Christi regina, hec eadem confirmando testimonium do. ✠ Ego Stigandus, Dorobornensis archipræsul, hec eadem affirmo. ✠ Ego Ealdredus, Eboracensis archiepiscopus, hoc consolido. ✠ Ego Ælfwoldus episcopus ad hec testimonium perhibeo. ✠ Ego Heremannus episcopus testimonium exhibeo. ✠ Ego Leofricus episcopus testimonium adhibeo. ✠ Ego Willielmus episcopus hec affirmo. ✠ Ego Ailmarus episcopus hec consolido. ✠ Ego Leofwinus episcopus testimonium perhibeo. ✠ Ego Wlfwinus episcopus hec eadem confirmo. ✠ Ego Ælwinus episcopus testimonium exhibeo. ✠ Ego Ælfricus episcopus hec affirmo. ✠ Ego Walterus episcopus hec eadem corroboro. ✠ Ego Gyso episcopus hec omnia prescripta confirmo. ✠ Ego Ægelnoðus abbas. ✠ Ego Ælfwinus abbas. ✠ Ego Wlffricus abbas. ✠ Ego Leoffricus abbas. ✠ Ego Leofstanus abbas. ✠ Ego Ælwig abbas. ✠ Ego Hordricus abbas. ✠ Ego Ægelsinus abbas. ✠ Ego Leofstanus abbas. ✠ Ego Eadmundus abbas. ✠ Ego Sichtricus abbas. ✠ Ego Haroldus comes operando consolido. ✠ Ego Ælfgarus comes. ✠ Ego Tostinus comes. ✠ Ego Leofwinus comes. ✠ Ego Gyrð comes. ✠ Ego Esgarus regie procurator aule. ✠ Ego Rodbertus regis consanguineus. ✠ Ego Radulphus regis aulicus. ✠ Ego Bundinus regis palatinus. ✠ Ego Hesbernus regis consanguineus. ✠ Ego Regenbaldus regis cancellarius. ✠ Ego Petrus regis capellanus. ✠ Ego Baldewinus regis capellanus. ✠ Ego Brihtricus princeps. ✠ Ego Ælfstanus princeps. ✠ Ego Wigodus regis pincerna. ✠ Ego Herdingus regine pincerna. ✠ Ego Adzurus regis dapifer. ✠ Ego Yfingus regis dapifer. ✠ Ego Godwinus regine dapifer. ✠ Ego Doddo princeps. ✠ Ego Ælfgarus princeps. ✠ Ego Brixinus princeps. ✠ Ego Ægelnoðus princeps. ✠ Ego Esbernus princeps. ✠ Ego Eadwig princeps. ✠ Ego Eadricus princeps. ✠ Ego Ægelmundus princeps. ✠ Ego Siwardus princeps. ✠ Ego Alwoldus princeps.

✠ Ego Ælphig princeps. Hec ego subscripsi Swidar, sub nomine Christi ✠.

---

* KING EADWARD THE CONFESSOR. M.LXV.

✠ In nomine sanctæ et individuæ Trinitatis. Edwardus, divina gratia largiente, Anglorum rex. Quum religiosi antecessores nostri dignitatem æcclesiarum clarissimam interdum fore perspexerunt terrenarum opulentia rerum, tam quæ authoritatis robur habere quanta fulciebatur copia divitiarum, digne tenuitatem æcclesiasticam larga amplificare studuerunt manu, tam in possessione prædiorum quam cæteris reddi-tibus legalium constitutionum. Etenim vero, cum ipsi fideles qui sumus in Christo ab apostolo vocemur et simus æcclesia quam prope quam numerosa multitudine gentium in unitate corporis sui ad æcclesiam Dei nuncupamus, sua Christiana consecravit gratia videbimur adulterini et non filii, si in ejus non sedules nos non exhibuerimus dilatanda gloria. Quapropter ego Edwardus, Christi pietate rex Anglorum, dolens Eboracum metropolim nostro tempore dejecta, ad antiquam celsitudinem qua illustrabatur; a piis regibus nostris prædecessoribus, in pristinum cupiens reparare dignitatis statum, nostro fideli domino archiepiscopo ejusdem æcclesiæ metropolitanæ Edwardo regali domino, dono nostro contulimus ad integrum quicquid a pio patre nostro Aldredo Anglorum rege ejus antecessori Oswaldo, prædictæ sedis pontifici, est collatum; et post cum Romæ peteret pallium a beato papa Formoso, per privilegii descriptionem ei est traditum donum, scilicet, Wiricestriæ episcopatus, per nostrum tamen consilium deponendum, in archiepiscopatus dignitate exaltanda supplementum vicarium, quod etiam idem Oswaldus, et post eum Adulphus et Wlstanus archipræsules regio munere adepti sunt et tenuerunt quietum et solidum, donec Anglia dirupta est et discissa invasione Danorum, et cum cæteris ornamentis æcclesiarum prædictæ civitatis, illud papæ Formosi privilegium constat esse incensum. Hic autem charissimus noster

Ealdadus episcopi curam suscipiens, ejusdemque æcclesiæ jura requirens et sciens a beato papa Nicholao Romæ pallio donatus, ad nos super æcclesiæ sibi commissa dignitate apostolica scripta signata detulit, quibus cum sua fidelitate commoniti justam petitionem papæ et suam nolumus refutare quod absit, præsertim cum super eadem re apostolicum præsentavit privilegium. Donavimus igitur, consilio reginæ meæ et aliorum fidelium, ei ejusque posteris ordinationem Wirecestriæ episcopatus, cum nostro tamen disponendam consilio, quatenus in exequenda episcopali cura eo specialius utatur vicario utque a beato papa Nicholao in ejus scriptum habetur privilegio. Quod si quis e regibus posteris nostris infringere temptaverit, iram Dei incurrat, et sit anathema, secundum supradictum apostoli decretum, nisi resipiscat. Ut autem hoc meæ descriptionis privilegium perpetuo inviolatum servetur, manus nostræ signum, sigillique auctoritas subter insignitur; item regiæ uxoris meæ testimonio munitur; episcoporum quoque interminatio cum singulorum nomine et caractere exprimitur abbatum; et principum regni nostri contestificatione fulcitur.

✠ Ego Edwardus, Dei gratia Anglorum rex, hoc scriptum confirmavi. ✠ Ego Eadiða, Dei pietate Anglorum regina, jussu domini mei regis, voluntarie huic descriptioni faveo. ✠ Ego Stigandus archiepiscopus subscribo. ✠ Ego Hermannus episcopus subscribo. ✠ Willelmus episcopus. ✠ Leofric episcopus. ✠ Robertus stalre. ✠ Osbernus capellanus. ✠ Raimboldus. ✠ Petrus. ✠ Haraldus Dei gratia dux. ✠ Tosti. ✠ Ælgarus dux. ✠ Girð dux. ✠ Leofwinus dux. ✠ Brihtric. ✠ Ulf. ✠ Suen. ✠ Ælnoð. ✠ Walder subscripsimus.

Actum Wintoniæ, in publica curia, natalis Christi in die festivitatis Sancti Sylvestri, anno Domini M.LXV., anno autem regni nostri XXI. Per omnia benedictus Deus. Amen.

✠ Ego Ælfnoð abbas. ✠ Aselnodus abbas. ✠ S. Leofricus abbas. ✠ Ego Ealdredus subdiaconus scriptum recognovi.

KING EADWARD THE CONFESSOR. M.LXVI.

✠ In nomine sanctæ et individuæ Trinitatis. Ego Edwardus Æðelredi regis filius, gratia Dei Anglorum rex, futuris post me regibus, et omnium dignitatum gradibus, omniumque etatum hominibus salutem, et hujus rei noticiam. Scire vos volo quoniam tempore avorum meorum patrisque mei multa et gravia bellorum pericula afflixerunt gentem Anglorum, et ipsos tam a suis quam ab extraneis concitata, adeo ut pene periclitata sit hereditaria regum successio, magnumque interstitium inter fratrem meum Edmundum, qui patri meo mortuo successit, meque habitum sit, invadentibus regnum Suuegeno et Cnutho filio ejus, regibus Danorum, ac filiis ipsius Cnuthi, Haroldo et Hardecnutho, a quibus eciam alter meus frater Alfredus crudeliter occisus est, solusque, sicut Joas occisionem Otholiæ, sic ego illorum crudelitatem evasi. Tandem respectu misericordiæ Dei post plures annos ego Edwardus ad paternum regnum reaccessi, et eo potitus sine ullo bellorum labore, sicut amabilis Deo Salomon, tanta pace et rerum opulentia abundavi, ut nullus antecedencium regum similis mei fuerit in gloria et divitiis. Sed gracia Dei non me, ut assolet, ex opulencia superbia et contemptus invasit, immo cepi cogitare, cujus dono et auxilio ad regni culmen evasi, quoniam "Dei est regnum, et cui vult dare illud," et quia "mundus transit et concupiscencia ejus;" qui autem totum se subdit Deo feliciter regnat et perpetualiter dives est. Itaque deliberavi ire ad limina sublimium apostolorum Petri et Pauli, et ibi gracias agere pro collatis beneficiis, et exorare ut eam pacem firmaret Deus perpetuam mihi et posteris meis. Preparavi ergo et dinumeravi expensas necessarias itineri, et honorabilia dona que ferrem sanctis apostolis. Sed gravis super hac re mæror habebat optimates meos, utpote memores malorum que sub aliis regibus pertulerant, ne tanto domino et pio patrie rege absente, regnum noviter sedatum, aliqua turbaretur hostilitate, et metuentes id quod et sanctus Ezechias, ne si forte in via aut egritudine aut alio incommodo deficerem, hereditariis regibus carerent, maxime quod nullum habebam filium. Itaque communi habito consilio, rogabant me ut ab hac intencione desisterem, pollicentes se satisfacturos Deo pro voto meo, tam in missarum et oracionum oblacione quam in elemosinarum larga distribucione. Sed cum obnixe contradicerem, tandem utrisque placuit, ut mitterentur legati duo ab utraque parte, Ealdredus et Heremannus episcopi, et abbates Wulfricus et Ælfwinus, qui apostolico meam voluntatem et votum et illorum peticionem indicarent; et secundum ejus sentenciam, quam mihi mandaret, promisi me omnino facturum. Factum est ergo quod voluimus, et venientes Romam legati nostri, ex voluntate Dei, invenerunt collectam synodum in eadem urbe. Cumque exposuissent meam voluntatem et suam peticionem coram CC.L. episcopis et alia multitudine sanctorum patrum, tunc apostolicus, ex consultu sanctæ synodi, hanc epistolam mihi scripsit: "Leo episcopus, servus servorum Dei, dilecto filio Eaduuardo Anglorum regi, salutem et apostolicam benedictionem. Quoniam voluntatem tuam laudabilem et Deo gratam agnovimus, gratias agimus ei per quem reges regnant et principes justa decernunt. Sed quia prope est Dominus in omni loco omnibus invocantibus eum in veritate, et sancti apostoli cum suo capite conjuncti unus spiritus sunt, et pias preces equaliter audiunt; et quia constat periclitari regionem Anglicam ex tua discessione, qui freno justicie sediciosos ejus motus cohibes, ex auctoritate Dei et sanctorum apostolorum et sanctæ synodi, absolvimus te a peccato illius voti, pro quo Dei offensam times, et ab omnibus negligenciis et iniquitatibus tuis; ea nimirum potestati usi, quam Dominus in beato Petro concessit nobis, dicens, "Quecunque solveritis super terram, soluta erunt et in cœlis." Deinde precipimus tibi, sub nomine sancte obedienciæ et penitenciæ, ut expensas quas ad iter istud paraveras, pauperibus eroges, et cenobium monachorum, in honore Sancti Petri apostolorum principis, aut novum construas, aut vetustum emendes et augeas, et sufficienciam victualium fratribus de tuis redditibus constituas, quatinus dum illi assidue inibi Deum laudaverint, et sanctis augeatur gloria et tibi indulgencia. Cui loco quicquid contuleris, vel collatum est, vel conferetur, ut ratum sit apostolica auctoritate precipimus, et ut semper habitatio monachorum sit, et nulli laicæ personæ nisi regi subdatur; et quecunque privilegia inibi instituere volueris ad honorem Dei pertinencia, concedimus, et robustissima auctoritate confirmamus, et infractores eorum eterna malediccione damnamus." Hec et alia apostolici mandata cum referrent nobis legati, interea revelavit beatus Petrus cuidam probabilis vitæ monacho incluso, nomine Wlfsino, voluntatem suam esse ut restruerem locum qui dicitur Westmonasterium, quod a tempore Sancti Augustini, primi Anglorum episcopi, institutum, multaque veterum regum munificentia honoratum, propter vetustatem et frequentes bellorum tumultus, pene videbatur destructum. Cumque hanc visionem mihi meisque retulisset, et apostolicæ literæ equalia precepta detulissent, contuli voluntatem meam cum voluntate Dei, et, cum tocius regni eleccione, dedidi me ad restruccionem ejusdem loci. Itaque decimari precepi omnem substanciam meam, tam in auro et argento quam in pecudibus et omni genere possessionum, et, destruens veterem, novam a fundamentis basilicam construxi, et constructam dedicari feci v. Kal. Januarii, in qua collocavi ipsa die reliquias quas Martinus papa, et Leo, qui eum consecravit, dederunt Aluredo regi, et quas ipse a Carlomanno rege Francorum dari sibi impetravit, cujus filiam pater ejus Æðelwlfus rex, post mortem primæ conjugis, duxerat uxorem, quæque ab ipso ad successorem ejus Ethelstanum, deinde ad Edgarum, ad ultimum ad nos pervenerunt, scilicet: Duas partes crucis Domini, et partem unius clavi, partemque tunicæ ejus inconsutilis, et de vestimentis Sanctæ Marie, et reliquias apostolorum Petri et Pauli, Andreæ, Bartholomei, Barnabæ, et aliorum plurimorum sanctorum, et quinque capsas aliis sanctorum reliquiis plenas; et statui ut quicunque reus majestatis regiæ vel cujuslibet alterius offensæ ad locum in quo pausant istæ reliquiæ confugerit, ejus rei, et membrorum, ac vite impunitatem consequatur. Eodem die renovavi, confirmavi, et emendavi privilegia que famosissimus avus meus Eadgarus, patruusque meus, Deo amabilis rex et martyr gloriosus Eaduuardus, ejusdem Eadgari filius, et sanctissimus pater Dunstanus Cantuariensis archiepiscopus, ac piissimus rex Æðelredus, pater meus, illi loco contulerunt; meam quoque auctoritatem adjeci, augmentans decreta utilia admonicione venerabilium archiepiscoporum Stigandi et Ealdredi, et aliorum optimatum meorum, videlicet, ut ille locus in perpetuum ab seculari servicio sit liber, et secundum beati Benedicti tradicionem, post obitum abbatis, ex eadem congregacione eligatur alter qui dignus sit, aliorsum vero nullus, nisi culpis promerentibus inibi inveniri nequiverit qui dignus sit tali officio fungi. Quod si evenerit, quod absit, potestatem habeant, de alio noto et familiari loco, abbatem eligendi, cujus vita sapiencia et religione clarescat. Laicorum autem vel clericorum nemo ipsius loci dominium usurpare presumat. Possessiones vero quæ ibi a quibuscunque donatæ sunt, nec abbas nec alia quelibet persona licenciam habeat vendendi vel extraneis dandi, sed regum munimine deinceps locus iste tueatur, ipseque abbas regi soli serviens commissum sibi gregem spirituali et temporali pastu abundanter foveat. Concessi eciam et confirmavi donaciones que ab eisdem regibus ante me donatæ sunt: hoc est, circa ipsum monasterium XVII. hidas et dimidiam; in Heandune XX., in Heamstede V., in Greneford XII. et unam virgam, in Hanewelle VIII., in Scepertune VIII., in Sunnabyri VII., in Ealdenham X., in Deccewyrðe IIII. et unam virgam, in Wattune IIII. et dimidiam, in Holewelle VI. et dimidiam, in Hamme II., in Winitune IIII., in Kynlevedene V., in Fentune IIII., in Mordune X., in Æwelle II., in Pereham VII., in Collingtune III., in Cillingtune IIII.; necnon et illas quas optimates mei meo tempore addiderunt, scilicet, Leofcild, Mulesham cum omnibus ad se pertinentibus; Agelricus, Kylewendun cum omnibus ad se pertinentibus; Wlfwinus, Mapulderstede cum omnibus ad se pertinentibus; Cuðmundus, Kynelevedene et Raeine et Laecedune cum omnibus ad se pertinentibus; Alfricus, Wenstede cum omnibus ad se pertinentibus; Atsere Swerte, Lygetun cum omnibus ad se pertinentibus; Ingulf, Paclesham cum omnibus ad se pertinentibus; Atsere, Leosne cum omnibus ad se pertinentibus; Tostig, Cleigate cum omnibus ad se pertinentibus; Ælfwine, Gottun Ægete cum omnibus ad se pertinentibus; Wlstanus, Deneham cum omnibus ad se pertinentibus; Siwardus, dimidiam hydam in Agmodesham, et unam in Weodune; Leofsi de Londonia, II. hydas et dimidiam in Wurmelea. Postremo ego ipse, pro spe retribucionis eternæ, et pro remissione delictorum meorum, et pro animabus patris mei et matris meæ, et omnium parentum meorum, ad laudem Omnipotentis Dei posui, in dotalicium et in perpetuam hereditatem, super altare, varia ornamentorum genera, quibus ecclesiæ serviretur, vel in quotidianis vel in solennibus ministeriis; et ad usus fratrum inibi Deo servi-encium, de meo jure quod mihi soli competebat, absque ullius reclamacione vel contradiccione, ista, inprimis Langtun cum omnibus ad se pertinentibus, Gihtslepe cum omnibus ad se pertinentibus, Stana cum omnibus ad se pertinentibus, Windlesore cum omnibus ad se pertinentibus, Huuaethamp-stede cum omnibus ad se pertinentibus, Stithenæce cum omnibus ad se pertinentibus, Æscewelle cum omnibus ad se pertinentibus, Dene cum omnibus ad se pertinentibus, Suðbure cum omnibus ad se pertinentibus, Pertun cum omnibus ad se pertinentibus, Roteland cum omnibus ad se pertinentibus. Post mortem Edgiðe regine conjugis meæ, Perscoram cum omnibus ad se pertinentibus, Deorhyrste cum omnibus ad se pertinentibus. Relaxavi igitur istis et omnibus supranominatis terris consuetudines omnes et exacciones regalium et episcopalium ministrorum, sicut antecessores mei reges prius fecerunt, ut nullis graventur oneribus expedicionum, nec poncium vel castrorum restruccione, nec furis apprehensione. Et omnia que ad locum ipsum pertinent sint omnino libera, cellæ, ecclesiæ, cimiteria, terræ, pascuæ, silvæ, venaciones, aquæ, piscaciones, cum redditibus, serviciis, debitis, oblacionibus, luminaribus, decimis, donariis, censu, morthidis, legibus, consuetudinibus, causarum discussionibus, emendacionibus, sive ecclesiasticis sive secularibus, et omnibus quecunque scriptis et testimonio bonorum hominum rememorari poterunt, que a regibus concessa vel concedenda sunt, ut nullus ex his subtrahere, vel diminuere, aut disperdere, qualibet occasione, judicio, vel potestate, presumat. Donavi eciam religioso abbati Eadwino, qui tunc illi loco preerat, et omnibus futuris post eum ibidem abbatibus, in tota possessione monasterii, sacam et socam, theloneumque suum in terra et in aqua, et consuetudinem que dicitur teames, latrones, latronumque capciones vel emissiones, et pacis fracturam, et pugnam in domo factam, et domus invasionem, et omnes assultus in suo jure, in via et extra, in festo et extra, in urbe et extra, et omnes leges et consuetudines tam plene et tam libere sicut eas habebam in manu mea. Et, ut omnia concludam, nullus succedentium regum, per vim aut per consuetudinem, pastum ab eorum possessionibus exigat, sed omnimodam libertatem perpetualiter habeat. Post hanc donacionem excommunicaverunt omnes episcopi et abbates tocius Anglie, ac monachi ac clerici, secundum apostolici Leonis preceptum, eos qui hoc constitutum infringerent vel infringi permitterent, quantum in ipsis esset. Si quis vero hanc nostram donacionem augere et amplificare voluerit, augeat Deus dies ejus prosperos hic et in futuro: si autem evenerit ut aliquis, aut regum succedencium vel alicujus personæ homo, quod non optamus, diabolica temeritate fuerit elatus vel seductus, quatenus hoc nostrum statutum infringere vel minuere aut in aliud mutare velit, sciat se perpetuo anathemate damnatum, nisi tamen digna satisfaccione emendaverit. Sin autem emendacione fuerit indignus, ipse quidem cum Juda traditore Gehenne ignibus cremabitur. Sed hæc carta nichilominus in sua libertate permanebit quamdiu Christiani nominis timor et amor in hac nostra gente perseveraverit. Ad ultimum, cartam istam conscribi et sigillari jussi, et ipse manu mea signum sancte crucis impressi, et idoneos testes annotari precepi. Ad corroborandam itaque hanc donacionis libertatem, ego Edwardus, Deo largiente Anglorum rex, signum venerande crucis impressi ✠. Ego Eadgiða regina huic donacioni regis consenciens subscripsi ✠. Ego Stigandus archiepiscopus consensi et subscripsi ✠. Ego Ealdredus archiepiscopus consensi et subscripsi ✠. Ego Walterus episcopus consensi et subscripsi ✠. Ego Leofricus episcopus consensi et subscripsi ✠. Ego Willielmus episcopus consensi et subscripsi ✠. Ego Heremannus episcopus consensi et subscripsi ✠. Ego Wulstanus episcopus consensi et subscripsi ✠. Ego Siwardus episcopus consensi et subscripsi ✠. Ego Wulfwinus episcopus consensi et subscripsi ✠. Ego Giso episcopus consensi et subscripsi ✠. Ego Ælfwinus abbas consensi et subscripsi ✠. Ego Leofricus abbas consensi et subscripsi ✠. Ego Eadwinus abbas consensi et subscripsi ✠. Ego Ægelsius abbas consensi et subscripsi ✠. Ego Wulfwoldus abbas ✠. Ego Reinbaldus cancellarius ✠. Ego Ægelwinus abbas consensi et subscripsi ✠. Ego Baldwinus abbas consensi et subscripsi ✠. Ego Leofwinus dux ✠. Ego Gyrð dux ✠. Ego Haroldus dux ✠. Ego Eadwinus dux ✠. Ego Raulfus minister ✠. Ego Rotbertus minister ✠. Ego Æsgarus minister ✠. Ego Eadnoðus minister ✠. Ego Bondius minister ✠. Ego Wigodus minister ✠. Ægelnoðus ✠. Wulfricus ✠. Siwardus ✠. Godricus ✠.

Acta apud Westmonasterium v. Kalendarum Januarii, die sanctorum Innocentium, anno Dominicæ incarnationis M.LXVI. Indictione tertia, anno regni serenissimi Edwardi regis vigesimo quinto. Swiðgarus notarius, ad vicem Reinbaldi, regiæ dignitatis cancellarii, hanc cartam scripsi et subscripsi in Dei nomine feliciter. Amen.

KING EADWARD THE CONFESSOR. M.LXVI.

✠ In nomine sanctæ et individuæ Trinitatis. Propter eos qui justiciam Dei contemnunt, et suam volunt constituere, quoniam justiciæ Dei non sunt subjecti, procurandum est his qui ecclesiarum Dei privilegia constituunt, ut multiplices cartas et multitudinem testium atque maledictionum congerant, quibus etsi non semper, tamen aliquotiens pessimorum hominum impia protervia et perniciosa præsumptio tutius proteratur, retundatur, ac reverberetur, necnon fortissimo defensionis robore funditus eradicetur. Quapropter ego Ædwardus, gratia Dei Anglorum rex, notum facio omnibus futuris post me seculi generationibus, quoniam præcepto Leonis papæ pro pœnitentia et remissione peccatorum meorum, renovavi et melioravi basilicam Sancti Petri, quæ sita est prope mœnia principalis Anglorum urbis Londoniæ, et ab occidentali ora ejusdem urbis dicitur Westmonasterium, quæ ædificata quidem fuerat antiquitus sub Melito, Londoniæ primo episcopo, socio et contemporaneo Sancti Augustini, primi Cantuariæ archiepiscopi, et per ipsum beatum Petrum, angelico famulante servitio, sanctæ crucis impressione et sacri crismatis perunctione dedicata; sed per frequentes incursiones barbarorum, et maxime Danorum, qui, patre meo Æðeldredo vivente, irruptionem in Angliam fecerant, et eo mortuo cum fratre meo Eadmundo dimidium regnum sub amicitiarum pactione tenuerant, fratremque meum alium Ælfredum miserabiliter interceptum enecaverant, neglecta et penitus destructa videbatur. Cum ergo renovassem eam, et multa privilegia regiæ potestatis et apostolicæ auctoritatis per beatum Leonem papam in ea constituissem, defuncto ipso Leone, et confirmato in ejus loco Nicholao, placuit mihi renovare, meliorare, et confirmare consuetudines et donaciones pecuniarum, quas antecessores mei reges Sancto Petro instituerant, propter summam devotionem quam habuit semper Anglorum gens erga eum et ejus vicarios. Itaque, propter hoc negotium et alia quamplura, legatos misi Romam, episcopum unum Aldredum, et duos electos ad ordinandum episcopos, Ghysonem, scilicet, et Walterum, ut a domno papa sacrarentur. Venientes autem Romam, ab apostolico Nicholao honore quo decebat sunt suscepti; invenerunt ibi ad sinodum congregatam multitudinem magnam episcoporum, abbatum, monachorum, clericorum, cæterorumque fidelium. Cumque audiente sinodo suæ legationis causam perorarent, hujus summam epistolæ domno papæ obtulerunt. "Summo universalis ecclesiæ patri Nicholao, Edwardus, gracia Dei Anglorum rex, debitam subjectionem et omnimodum servitium. Glorificamus Deum, quia curam habet suæ electæ ecclesiæ, quoniam in loco boni predecessoris vos optimum successorem constituit. Quapropter justum judicamus apud vos, velut ad solidam petram acuere et probare omnes bonas intenciones nostras, et vestram noticiam atque societatem in bono habere, quatinus eas donaciones et privilegia quæ obtinuimus apud predecessorem vestrum renovetis et augeatis nobis, videlicet, ut quod ille injunxit nobis sub nomine obædientiæ ac pœnitentiæ, propter votum quod voveram ire Romam, et, in remissionem omnium peccatorum meorum, construere cœnobium monachorum in honore apostoli Petri, ratum faciatis, et privilegia possessionum et dignitatum ejusdem loci confirmetis, renovetis, atque augeatis, et imperpetuum immutabilia stare decernatis. Ego quoque pro modulo meo augeo et confirmo donaciones et consuetudines pecuniarum quas habet Sanctus Petrus in Anglia, et ipsas pecunias collectas cum regalibus donis mitto vobis, ut oretis pro me et pro pace mei regni, et continuam ac solempnem memoriam haberi instituatis tocius gentis Anglorum coram corporibus sanctorum apostolorum. Valete." His igitur litteris a summo pontifice susceptis, cum feliciter ad votum suum omnibus peractis a Roma redirent, consulente sancta synodo, transmissam a domino papa mihi detulerunt epistolam. "Nicholaus episcopus, servus servorum Dei, gloriosissimo ac piissimo omnique honore dignissimo, spirituali quoque filio nostro, Edwardo Anglorum regi, visitationem omnimodam, salutem mellifluam, et benedictionem apostolicam. Omnipotenti Deo referimus grates, qui vestram prudentissimam excellentiam in omnibus ornavit ac decoravit erga beatum Petrum apostolorum principem, et nobiscum habere dilectionem, et in omnibus apostolicis consentire censuris. Literas igitur vestræ nobilitati transmittimus, et per eas societatem sanctorum apostolorum et nostram vobis damus, orantes misericordiam illius qui est Dominus omnium, et Rex super omnia solus, ut ipse vos participem faciat ex omnibus, si qua sunt coram Deo, bonis operibus nostris, et fratres nos ac socios in sua dilectione constituat in omni tempore amplius, ac non minorem partem nostri obsequii vobis reconsignet in suo regno quam nobismet ipsis provenire optamus. Erimus eciam deinceps pro vobis sine dubio orantes assidue ut ipse Deus vobis subjiceat hostes et inimicos qui contra vos voluerint surgere, et confirmet vos in paterno solio et propria hereditate; ac beatus Petrus sit vobis custos et adjutor semper in omni tribulatione. Claret enim Anglorum reges pro reverentia et devocione quam exhibuerunt beato Petro, gloria et honore floruisse, ac ipsius patrocinio famosos triumphos obtinuisse, cujus beati apostoli meritis vestro desiderio et voluntati Omnipotens Deus præstet effectum, et confirmet vobis paterni regni imperium, et tribuat pacis incrementum, et post præsentis vitæ decursum perducat ad æternum permanentis gloriæ imperium. Renovamus ergo et confirmamus et augemus vobis privilegia vestra: scilicet, ut absoluti sitis ab illo voto quod timebatis, et ab omnibus aliis peccatis et iniquitatibus vestris, auctoritate illius qui me, licet indignum, suæ sanctæ sedi præesse voluit. Preterea illi loco quem sub nomine sanctæ penitentiæ, construendum et meliorandum suscepistis, quoniam, ut fertur, primam antiquitus consecrationem a beato Petro accepit, cujus, licet indigni, vicarii simus, et quia regia antiquitus sedes est, ex auctoritate Dei et sanctorum apostolorum atque hujus Romanæ sedis et nostra concedimus, permittimus, et solidissime confirmamus, ut amplius imperpetuum regiæ constitutionis et consecrationis locus sit, atque repositorium regalium insignium, et habitacio perpetua monachorum, qui nulli omnino personæ nisi regi subdantur; habeantque potestatem, secundum regulam Sancti Benedicti, per successiones eligere ex se idoneos abbates; neque introducatur per violentiam extranea persona, nisi quam concors congregacio sibi præesse elegerit. Absolvimus eciam eum locum ab omni servitio et dominacione episcopali, ut nullus episcopus illuc introeat ordinaturus aut precepturus aliquid, nisi ex petitione et consensu abbatis et monachorum; et habeat idem locus liberum procinctum, id est, ambitum, et cymeterium mortuorum circa se absque episcopali vel cujuscunque respectu vel exactione, et omnia que ad libertatem et exaltationem illius loci ad honorem Dei pertinentia per nostram auctoritatem accedere possunt, hilari et promtissima voluntate, concedimus. Possessiones autem quas antiqui reges seu quicunque alii homines vos quoque ac vestri barones ad eundem locum contulistis, et cartas quæ ex eis factæ sunt, divina et nostra auctoritate roboramus, et ratas ac stabiles esse decernimus; et infractores earum, vel invasores, aut diminutores, aut dispersores, venditores etiam, æterna maledictione cum Juda proditore dampnamus, ut non habeant partem in beata resurrectione, sed a beato Petro se judicandos sciant, quando sedebit cum suis coapostolis judicans duodecim tribus Israel. Vobis vero et posteris vestris regibus committimus advocationem et tuitionem ejusdem loci et omnium tocius Angliæ æcclesiarum, ut vice nostra, cum consilio episcoporum et abbatum, constituatis ubique quæ justa sunt, scientes pro hoc vos recepturos dignam mercedem ab eo cujus regnum et imperium nec desinet nec minuetur in sæculum. Valete." Hanc igitur epistolam apostolici privilegii placuit inserere huic nostræ confirmacioni, ut secundum quod Sancto Leoni prius placuerat michique preceperat, concordante ad hoc successore ejus Nicholao, et eadem aut majora mihi præcipiente, sciant omnes futuræ generationes, me, pro voti prædicti absolutione, peccatorumque meorum omnium remissione, et æternæ vitæ remuneratione, pro animabus regum, tam successorum quam predecessorum meorum, et omnium parentum meorum, et pro pace et stabilitate regni mei, et prosperitate tocius Anglorum populi, loco illi omnimodam libertatem quantum ad potestatem terrenam concessisse, et quod illi de æcclesiastica hoc de regia libertate statuo. Ejus igitur amoris stimulo, et fide plenissima ac devotissima suffultus, cujus largiflua miseracione in cathedra regali promotus sum, cum consilio et decreto archiepiscoporum, episcoporum, comitum, aliorumque omnium meorum optimatum, prospiciens hoc ipsi æcclesiæ et habitantibus in ea, sive pertinentibus ad eam utile fore, non solum in presenti sed etiam in futuro elegi sanctiendum atque perpeti stabilimento ab omnibus confirmandum, ut pro Christi honore et amore, et pro reverencia summi apostolorum principis Petri, cujus patrocinio meipsum commisi, et pro devocione et veneracione sanctarum reliquiarum quas eidem loco contuli, beatorum videlicet apostolorum, martyrum, confessorum, et virginum, ut Omnipotens Dominus, per istorum suffragia sanctorum, depulsis cunctis adversitatibus, cum pacis et honoris sui stabilitate, ac perpetuæ tranquillitatis sullimatione, locum illum custodiat, disponat, et protegat, et pro magnifica dignitate, sive regali excellencia, ipsius æcclesiæ, et pro quiete monachorum ibidem Deo famulantium, tantus honor eidem æcclesiæ habeatur imperpetuum et observetur, ut neque nos, neque successores nostri, neque quilibet episcopus, nec quicunque de judiciaria potestate in ipsam sanctam basilicam, vel in manentes in ipsa, vel in homines qui cum suis terris vel qualibuscunque substanciis ad ipsam tradere vel devovere se voluerint, nisi per voluntatem abbatis et suorum monachorum, ullam unquam habeant potestatem. Sed sit hæc sancta mater æcclesia peculiaris patroni nostri domini et magni apostoli ter beati Petri, libera et absoluta ab omni invasione vel inquietudine omnium hominum cujuscunque ordinis vel potestatis esse videantur. Præterea aliud constituo atque imperpetuo confirmo, ut quisquis fugitivorum, de quocumque loco, pro quacumque causa, cujuscunque condicionis sit, ipsum sanctum locum vel procinctum ejus fugiens intraverit, immunis sit omnino, ac plenam libertatem consequatur. Placuit etiam mihi hanc optionis electionem et libertatis donum gratissimo animo et integra voluntate augere, et privilegio isto corroborare, et insuper dono meo inviolabiliter confirmare omnes donaciones terrarum vel ecclesiarum aut aliarum rerum, quæ ibi ab antecessoribus meis regibus seu a quibuscunque ante me donatæ sunt, necnon et illas quas vel ego, vel optimates mei, vel etiam quilibet de civibus intra Londoniam donaverant, tam terras quam consuetudines, et omnia jura qualiumcunque causarum in omnibus terris que vel in Londonia vel in aliis quibuscunque locis prædicto monasterio adjacent, vel adjiciendæ sunt per gratiam Dei. Huic libertati concedo additamentum, in qua, ut ab omnibus apertius et plenius intelligatur, nomina consuetudinum Anglice præcepi ponere: scilicet, mundbryche, burhbryce, miskænninge, sceawinge, hlæstinge, friðsokne, flymenafyrmðe, wergeldþeof, uðleap, forfænge, fyhfænge, fyrdwite, fihtwite, weardwite, hængewite, hamsokne, forsteal, infangeneþeof, saka, socna, toll et team, aliasque omnes leges et consuetudines quæ ad me pertinent. Renovavi eciam privilegia antiquorum regum, et ex nomine sanctæ Trinitatis et omnium sanctorum, nostra etiam regia auctoritate, cum consensu atque consultu primatum meorum, interdixi, et cartam in presencia mea fieri jussi, ut nullus unquam succedentium regum, episcoporum, principum, comitum, vicecomitum, procuratorum, seu aliorum regum clientium, vel alia quælibet magna vel parva persona, pastum, censum, vel impensionem, castrorum vel pontium reædificationem, xenia, seu munuscula, vel aliud quidlibet ab æcclesia illa, vel a terris ad eam pertinentibus, per vim aut per consuetudinem exigat; non opera, non tributa, vel expeditiones, ad se trahat; sed exclusa penitus exactione vel angaria cunctarum consuetudinum, omnia, sicut in manu mea habueram, melius, plenius et liberius, ita cum omnimoda libertate sint concessa eidem ecclesie, in terra et in aqua, in urbe et extra, in domo et extra, in villa et extra, in via et extra, in placito, in soka et saka, in theloneo, in furis apprehensione et emissione, in sanguinis effusione, in campis et silvis, in pratis, in pascuis, in aquis, in piscariis, in molendinis, et omnibus suis appendiciis, quatinus ipsa religiosa concio, pro remedia animæ meæ et omnium benefactorum ejusdem æcclesiæ, pervigiles persolvat deprecationes, et, more sapientium virginum, oleum bonæ accionis servans, sub habitu religionis, Christo Domino et ejus beato apostolo indefesse deserviat. Si quis autem contra hanc præceptionis et auctoritatis nostræ paginam senserit, quicunqne ille fuerit, cujuscunque nominis et honoris, ætatis et potestatis, gradus et ordinis, et eam vel in magno vel in minimo infringere voluerit, et alios ad hoc conduxerit, unusquisque pro seipso libras quinque partibus Sancti Petri persolvat; et quicquid exinde fiscus noster ad partem nostram separare poterat, in luminaribus vel stipendiis monachorum, seu et elemosinas pauperum ipsius monasterii perenniter per nostra oracula ad integrum sit concessum atque indultum. Hanc igitur cartam meæ donationis et libertatis in die dedicationis predictæ æcclesiæ recitari jussi, coram episcopis, abbatibus, comitibus, et omnibus optimatibus Anglie, omnique populo audiente et vidente; et secundum apostolici Leonis ejusque successoris Nicholai constitutum, excommunicari feci eos qui decretum nostrum infringerent vel infringi permitterent, quantum in ipsis esset. Quisquis autem successorum meorum hanc donationis libertatem firmiter atque inviolabiliter custodierit, æterna coronetur claritate, cœlestisque regni plena perfruatur felicitate. Si quis vero, quod absit, eam destruere voluerit, vel hujus nostri decreti contradictor, convulsor, et temerator extiterit, cum Juda proditore æterno anathemati subjaceat, nisi Deo et beato suo apostolo Petro digna pœnitencia satisfecerit. Ut ergo hec auctoritas nostris et futuris temporibus circa ipsum sanctum locum perenniter firma et inviolata permaneat, vel per omnia tempora illesa custodiatur atque conservetur, et ab omnibus optimatibus nostris et judicibus, publicis et privatis, melius et certius credatur, manus nostre subscriptionibus subter eam decrevimus roborare, et idoneos testes annotare, atque sigillo nostro jussimus sigillare.

✠ Ego Edwardus, Dei gratia Anglorum rex, hoc privilegium jussi componere, et compositum cum signo Dominicæ crucis confirmando impressi. ✠ Ego Eadgyða regina, omni alacritate mentis, hoc corroboravi. ✠ Ego Stigandus, sanctæ metropolis æcclesiæ Cantuariensis episcopus, confirmavi. ✠ Ego Ealdredus, archiepiscopus Eboracensis æcclesiæ, consignavi. ✠ Ego Willielmus, episcopus Londoniensis æcclesiæ, ad omnia suprascripta consentiens subscripsi. ✠ Ego Heremannus episcopus consensi et subscripsi. ✠ Ego Wlfwinus episcopus consensi et subscripsi. ✠ Ego Walterus episcopus consensi et subscripsi. ✠ Ego Leofricus episcopus consensi et subscripsi. ✠ Ego Giso episcopus consensi et subscripsi. ✠ Ego Wlstanus episcopus consensi et subscripsi. ✠ Ego Siwardus episcopus consensi et subscripsi. ✠ Ego Godwinus episcopus consensi et subscripsi. ✠ Ego Ægelsius abbas consensi et subscripsi. ✠ Ego Eadwinus abbas consensi et subscripsi. ✠ Ego Ægelwius abbas consensi et subscripsi. ✠ Ego Leofricus abbas consensi et subscripsi. ✠ Ego Baldewinus abbas consensi et subscripsi. ✠ Ego Wlfwoldus abbas consensi et subscripsi. ✠ Ego Eadmundus abbas. ✠ Ego Reinbaldus regis cancellarius relegi et sigillavi. ✠ Ego Osbernus regis capellanus. ✠ Ego Petrus regis capellanus. ✠ Ego Rodbertus regis capellanus. ✠ Ego Haroldus dux. ✠ Ego Eadwinus comes. ✠ Ego Girð comes. ✠ Ego Leofwinus comes. ✠ Ego Markerus comes. ✠ Ego Esgarus minister. ✠ Ego Bondius minister. ✠ Ego Radulphus minister. ✠ Ego Rodbertus minister. ✠ Ego

Eadnoðus minister. ✠ Ego Ægelnoðus minister. ✠ Ego Wygodus minister. ✠ Ego Wlfricus miles. ✠ Ego Siwardus miles. ✠ Ego Godricus miles. ✠ Ego Colo miles. ✠ Ego Wlfwardus miles. Omnes consentientes subscripsimus. Stabilita apud Westmonasterium v. Kł. Januarii, die sanctorum Innocentium, anno Dominicæ incarnationis MºLXºVIº Indictione tertia. Anno regni Edwardi, nobilissimi et clementissimi regis, vigesimo quinto. Ego Ælfgeatus notarius ad vicem Reinbaldi, regiæ dignitatis cancellarii, hoc privilegium scripsi et subscripsi, in Dei nomine feliciter. Amen.

KING EADWARD THE CONFESSOR.

✠ Eadward kingc gret Alfwold b.· ⁊ Harold eorl· and Alfred scyrgereuan· and ealle mine þegenes on Dorsætan freondlice. ⁊ ic ciþe eow ꝥ Urk min huskarl habbe his strand eall forne gen hys agen land ofer eal wel ⁊ freolice· upp of sæ ⁊ ut on sæ· ⁊ eall ꝥ to his strande gedryuen hys· be minum fullan bebode.

✠ I king Eadward greet bishop Alfwold, and earl Harold, and Ælfred shire-reeve, and all my thanes in Dorsetshire, amicably. And I make known to you that Urk my 'hûscarl' may have his strand, all in front of his own land, over all well and freely, up from sea and out on sea, and all that is driven to his strand, by my full command.

KING EADWARD THE CONFESSOR.

CARTA BEATI REGIS EDWARDI DE WYNDESORA ET STANES, CUM LIBERTATIBUS IN EISDEM.

✠ Eadward kyngc gret alle mine bisceopes· ⁊ mine eorles· ⁊ mine þegenes· on Barroccscire· ⁊ on Middelsexen freondlice. ⁊ ic kyþe

✠ I king Eadward greet all my bishops, and my earls, and my thanes, in Berkshire, and in Middlesex, amicably. And I make known to you eow ꝥ ic habbe gegefan Criste ⁊ Sancte Petre into Westmynstre Windlesoran ⁊ Stane· ⁊ eall ꝥ ðærto herþ· binnan burh· ⁊ butan· mid saca· ⁊ mid socne· mid tolle· ⁊ mid teame· ⁊ mid infangenumþeofe· on wude· ⁊ on felde· be strande· ⁊ be lande· on stræte· ⁊ of stræte· ⁊ on eallan þingan swa full· ⁊ swa forþ swa hit mesylfan [fyrmest on hande] stod. ⁊ ic nelle geþafian ꝥ þær ani man ænine onstync ðærofer habbe on ænige þingan· butan se abƀ. ⁊ þa mynecas to Sancte Petres neode. God eow gehealde.

that I have given to Christ and St Peter at Westminster, Windsor and Staines, and all that thereto belongs, within burgh and without, with sac and with socn, with toll and with team, and with infangentheof, in wood and in field, by strand and by land, on road and off road, and in all things as full and as free, as it first stood in my own hand. And I will not permit any man there to have any authority thereover in any things, except the abbot and the monks, for St Peter^s need. May God preserve you.

KING EADWARD THE CONFESSOR.

Eadward kyng gret Aylmer bisscop· ⁊ Girð erl· ⁊ Toly· ⁊ ealle mine þeynes on Est Angle frendlice· ⁊ ic kiðe ihu ꝥ ic habbe unnen Baldewine abbot one munetere wiðinnen Seynt Eædmundesbiri· alswo freelike on alle þinge to habben alswo me mīne on hande stonden· ower on oni mīre burge alre frelikest. God se ihu alle frend.

I king Eadward greet bishop Aylmær, and earl Gyrth, and Toli, and all my thanes in East Anglia, amicably: and I make known to you that I have granted to abbot Baldwine one minter within St Edmundsbury, to have in all things as freely as mine have stood in my service, or in any of my towns, most freely. God be the friend of you all.

KING EADWARD THE CONFESSOR.

Eadward kyng gret Aylmer bisscop and Ælfger erl· and alle mine þeynes on Suffolc and on Norfolc frendlike· and ic kiðe ou ðat ic wille [⁊] ðat it is mine fulle unna ðat Ælfrich Modercope mot bugan to ðo tueyen abboten at Seynt Eadmunde· and at Sc̄e Æðeldred· be Godes leue and be mine.

I king Eadward greet bishop Aylmer and earl Ælfgar, and all my thanes in Suffolk and in Norfolk, amicably: and I make known to you that I will, and that it is my full grant, that Ælfric Modercop may put himself under the two abbots, at St Eadmund's and at St Æthelred's, by God's leave and by mine.

KING EADWARD THE CONFESSOR.

✠ Eadweard cyngc gret mine biscopas· ⁊ mine eorlas· ⁊ ealle mine þegenas· on þan sciran þar mine preostas on Paules mynstre habbað land inne· freondlice. And ic cyðe eow ꝥ ic wille ꝥ hig beon heora saca ⁊ heora socne wurðe· ægðer ge binnan burh ge butan· ⁊ swa gōdera lagana wurðe nu swa full and swa forð swa hig betst wæran on æniges cynges dæge· oððe on æniges biscopes· on eallan þingan. ⁊ ic nelle ꝥ hig underfon ani ma preostas into heora mynstre þonne heora lande are aberan mage ⁊ hig sylfe willan. ⁊ ic nelle geþafian ꝥ heom ænig man æt ænigan þingan misbeode.

✠ I king Eadward greet my bishops, and my earls, and all my thanes, in the shires where my priests at St Paul's monastery have land, amicably. And I make known to you that I will that they be worthy of their sac and their socn, both within town and without, and worthy of as good laws now, as fully and as widely, as they best were in any king's day, or in any bishop's, in all things. And I will not that they receive any more priests into their monastery than their land-property may bear, and they themselves will. And I will not permit that any man in anything misuse them.

IDEM LATINE.

[Ego] Edweardus rex saluto meos episcopos, et meos comites, omnesque meos thanos (vel ministros), in præfecturis illis ubi mei sacerdotes in Pauli ecclesia terram possident, amice. Et ego notum vobis facio, quod volo ut ipsi sint eorum sacæ et socnæ digni et intra burgum et extra : item tam bonorum jurium digni per hæc tempora, adeo plene et eatenus sicut ipsi, quando eorum status fuit optimus fuerint in alicujus regis diebus, aut in alicujus episcopi, in omnibus. Et nolo ut recipiant plures sacerdotes in eorum ecclesiam quam facultates suas pati possint, et ipsimet voluerint. Et non permittam ut aliquis in aliquo eos vexet.

KING EADWARD THE CONFESSOR.

✠ On almichtin Drichtines name. Ic Eadward kyng kiðe alle man þe red ðat ic mid alle mine redgiuen red habbe· for mine soule þerfe ⁊ for alle mine þedschipes sundfulnisse. Ðat is þat ic an eke fredomes þan halegen kinge Seynt Eadmunde· so forð so he firmest hauede· into þere stowe þe he onresteð. And ic wille him þat se fredom stonde on his welde· þat so fele siðe so men gildeð here gilde to heregild oþer to schipgild· gilde se tunschipe so oþere men don to þe abbotes nede ⁊ þere muneke þe þer binnen schulen for hus seruen. And þe abboteriche þat Cnut kyng þer ches· ⁊ siðon Hard-

✠ In the name of the Almighty Lord. I king Eadward make known to all men the counsel on which I have resolved with all my counsellors, for my soul's need and for the well-being of all my people. That is, that I grant perpetual freedom to the holy king St Eadmund, as free as he best had it, at the holy place in which he rests. And I will that the freedom so stand in his power, that as often as men pay their payment to the military tax or the ship-tax, let the township pay, as other men do, for the need of the abbot and the monks who have there to serve for us. And the abbacy cnut king mine broðer also it staþelfaste. ⁊ ic suðon eac swilke mid ðere schirebiscopes rede. ⁊ mid mine wedde. ⁊ alle mine bischopes. ⁊ alle mine witene it fultremede þat ic nefre ne schulle ani man wenden to oðere hodes manne. buten he wolde ben aschired from Godes manne ⁊ alle his halegen. And ic an þan halegen kinge þat lond at Mildenhale. mid mete ⁊ mid manne. ⁊ mid sokne. so it me on hande stod. ⁊ þe half nigende hundredes sokne into Đinghowe. And ic an hem al here tune sokne of hale here londe. þe he nu habbeð oðer giet bigiton schullen. on Godes est ⁊ on mines and on alle folkes. God how healde.

which king Cnut there chose, and afterwards king Hardecnut, my brother, likewise established, and I also since, with the counsel of the shire-bishop, and with my pledge, and that of all my bishops and all my 'witan', have confirmed so that no man shall ever turn it to men of another order, unless he would be cut off from God's communion and all his saints. And I give to the holy king the land at Mildenhall, with meat and with men, and with socn, as it stood in my hand; and the VIII. and a half hundred socn at Thingoe. And I give them all their town-socn of all their lands, which they now have or may yet obtain, through God's favour, and mine, and all the people's. God preserve you.

IDEM LATINE.

✠ In Omnipotentis Dei nomine. Ego Eadwardus rex indico omnibus hominibus de consilio quod consiliatus sum cum omnibus consiliariis meis, pro remedio anime mee, et pro incolumitate totius gentis mee. Hoc est, quod annuo eternam libertatem Sancto regi Edmundo, in loco in quo requiescit, ita pleniter sicut unquam plenius habuit; et hoc volo, ut libertas ita stet in ejus potestate, ut quociens homines censum persolverint exercitui vel navibus, tociens ville illius habitatores censum persolvant, velud alii homines, ad necessitatem abbatis et monachorum qui ibi debent pro nobis servire. Et abbaciam quam Knout rex ibi elegit, ac postea frater meus Hardeknout rex simili modo stabilivit, pignore meo et omnium episcoporum meorum, cunctorumque procerum meorum, necnon comitatum, ejusdem episcopi consilio corroboravi, ut nunquam aliquis debeat transmutare ad alterius ordinis viros, nisi velit separari a communione Dei et omnium sanctorum ejus. Annuo etiam Sancto regi Edmundo terram at Mildenhale, cum victu et hominibus; et jura regalia VIII° et dimidiam placitorum[1] ad Ðynghowe, quod Anglice dicitur nygend half hundred; et omnium villarum suarum jura regalia annuo in omnibus terris quas modo habent, et quas adhuc adquisituri sunt, in Dei amore ac mei et tocius populi.

KING EADWARD THE CONFESSOR.

✠ Ego Eadwardus rex Anglorum notifico in his literis omnibus Dei fidelibus, quod consiliatus sum cum meis archiepiscopis et episcopis et abbatibus et comitibus, et cum omnibus meis baronibus, videlicet, volo et præcipio quod monasterium cognati mei Sancti Edmundi, et villa in qua situm est illud monasterium, sit perpetualiter in eadem libertate quam Cnut rex et Hardecnut rex, meus frater, ei concesserunt, et quod ille locus nunquam sit locatus cum aliis personis quam cum monachis; nec aliquis episcopus qui est vel unquam erit, in Norfolc vel Suffolc, habeat unquam potestatem aliquam in eodem monasterio, nec infra fines ejusdem ville crucibus designatos. Et monachi qui ibi degunt eligant sibi abbatem de seipsis, sicuti eidem monasterio et eædem ville concessi. Permaneat in perpetuum, ubicunque habent monachi terras sive homines, seu in futurum acquirent, per Dei auxilium et bonorum hominum. Nunc igitur rogo omnes Dei amicos qui nunc vivunt seu futuri sunt, quod pro timore Dei nunquam sint in loco seu in concilio ubi prædicta libertas sit mutata vel adnichillata, quam antecessores nostri et nos Sancto Edmundo et monasterio suo concessimus. Quod si aliquis fuerit ita vesanus, per incitamenta diaboli, quod velit

[1] MSS. Cantab. et Harl. 645. f. 125[b]. 'dimidii hundredorum.'

hanc libertatem mutare, sive in aliquo adnichillare vel depravare, sit ille anathematizatus, et in Gehennam ignis demersus, nisi in vita sua resipuerit.

KING EADWARD THE CONFESSOR.

Ego Eaduuardus, Dei gratia rex Anglorum, Eadsio archiepiscopo, et Godino comiti, et omnibus suis baronibus Cantie salutem. Sciatis me dedisse Deo ac Sancto Augustino et fratribus ut habeant eorum saca et socna, et pacis fracturam, et pugnam in domo factam, et vie assaltus, et latrones in terra sua captos, latronumque susceptionem vel pastionem, super illorum proprios homines, infra civitatem et extra, theloneumque suum in terra et in aqua, atque consuetudinem que dicitur teames, et super omnes allodiarios quos eis habeo datos. Nec volo consentire ut aliquis in aliqua re de hiis se intermittat nisi eorum prepositi quibus ipsi hec commendaverint; quia habeo has consuetudines Deo datus et Sancto Augustino, pro redempcione anime mee, ita pleniter et libere sicut melius habuerint tempore predecessoris mei Knuti regis; et nolo consentire ut aliquis hec infringat, sicuti meam amicitiam vult habere.

KING EADWARD THE CONFESSOR.

A COPPIE MADE OF A GRAUNT BY KING EDWARD CALLED THE CONFESSOR, BEFORE THE CONQUEST, AND REMAYNETH OF RECORD IN THE EXCHEQUER.

Iche Edovard kinge have yeven
Of my forreste the keepinge
Of the hundreth of Chelmer and Dawncing
To Randolph Peperking and his kinling,
Withe hart and hinde, do and bokke,
Hare and fox, catt and brooke,

Wylde foule with his flock,
Partriche, feasant hen and feasant cock,
With greene and wyld, stob and stock,
To kepen and to yeomen, by all her might,
Bothe by daie and eke by night,
And houndes for to houlde,
Good and swyfte and bowlde,
Four grey houndes and vi. raches,
For hare and fox and wild cattes:
And therefore I make him my booke,
Wittnes the busshop Wolston,
And booke ylearned many a one,
And Swayne of Essex our brother,
And teken to him many other,
And our stuard Howelyn,
That besought mee for him.

KING EADWARD THE CONFESSOR.

✠ Eadward cyng gret Stigand ercebiscop. ⁊ Ægelmær biscop. ⁊ Gyrð eorl. ⁊ Toli scirreue. ⁊ ealle his þeines inne Norðfolce ⁊ inne Suðfolce. ⁊ ealle his oðre witen ofer eall Ænglande. hadede ⁊ leawede. freondlice. ⁊ ic cyðe eow ꝥ ic habbe gegeofen Criste. ⁊ Sancte Marie. ⁊ Sancte Benedicte. ⁊ Ælfwine abbod into Ramesege. saca ⁊ socna. tol ⁊ team. ⁊ infangenþeof. fihtwite ⁊ ferdwite. foresteall ⁊ hamsocne. griðbryce ⁊ scipbryce. ⁊ þa sǽ upwarp on eallen þingen. æt Bramcæstre ⁊ æt Ringstyde. swa wel

✠ King Eadward greets archbishop Stigand, and bishop Ægelmær, and earl Gyrth, and Toli shire-reeve, and all his thanes in Norfolk and in Suffolk, and all his other 'witan' over all England, ordained and lay, amicably. And I make known to you that I have given to Christ, and St Mary, and St Benedict, and to abbot Ælfwine in Ramsey, sac and socn, toll and team, and infangenetheof, fihtwite and ferdwite, foresteal and hamsocn, grithbryce and scipbryce, and the sea-upwarp, in

⁊ swa freolice swa ic hit meseolf betst habbe· bi þa sæ rime ahwær in Engelande· ⁊ ealle þa gerihte ðа ic meseolf ǽr ahte. And ic wylle ꝥ seo socne wiðinnen Bicham dic ligce into Ramesege to Sancte Benedicte on eallen þingen swa full ⁊ swa forð swa ic heo meseolf ahte· ⁊ ealle þa gerihte ðа æni kingc mæi ahen. ⁊ ealle þa men þa beon motwurði· ferðwurðe· ⁊ faldwurði in ꝥ oðer healfe hundred· swa hwilc man swa þa men ahe· Sancte Marie ⁊ Sanctus Benedictus ⁊ se abbod ⁊ ða gebroðra into Ramesege habben ða socne on eallen þingen ofer heom· ⁊ þat market æt Dunham· bi wætere ⁊ bi lande· mid inlade ⁊ mid ǘtlade· ⁊ mid eallen þan gerihte ðe þærto hereð· swa wel ⁊ swa freolice swa ic hit meseolf betst ahte. ⁊ ic nelle geþafien ꝥ ani man þis gelytlige mid ænige þinge. And in ælcer scire þær Sanctus Benedictus hafð land inne his saca ⁊ his socne· tol ⁊ team· ⁊ infangeneþeof· wiðinne burh ⁊ wiðuten· ⁊ on ælce styde· be lande ⁊ be strande· be wude ⁊ be felde· swa hwylc man swa ða socne ahe· Sanctus Benedictus habbe his freodom on eallen þingen swa

all things, at Branchester and at Ringstead, as well and as freely as I myself best have them, by the sea-shore everywhere in England; and all the rights which I myself before possessed. And I will that the socn within Bicham dike belong to St Benedict in Ramsey, in all things, as free and as far as I myself possessed it, and all the rights that any king can have. And all the men that are moteworthy, fyrd-worthy, and faldworthy, in that hundred and half, whatever man own the men, let St Mary, and St Benedict, and the abbot, and the brothers in Ramsey have the socn over them in all things; and the market at Downham, by water and by land, with ingress and with egress, and with all the rights which thereto belong, as well and as freely as I myself best possessed them. And I will not permit that any man diminish this in anything. And in every shire where St Benedict has land, I grant him his sac and his socn, toll and team, and infangentheof, within burgh and without; and in every place, by land and by strand, by wood and by field, whatsoever man may wel ⁊ swa freolice swa ic hit meseolf betst ahe ahwær in Engelande· ⁊ ealle þa gyltes þa belimpeð to mine kinehelme inne Iol ⁊ inne Easterne· ⁊ inne ða hali wuca æt Gangdagas· on ealle þingan· al swa ic heo meseolf ahe· ⁊ tol freo ofer ealle Engleland· wiðinne burhe ⁊ wiðutan· æt gerescepinge ⁊ on æfrice styde· be wætere ⁊ be lande. And ic forbeode· Godes forbode ⁊ min· ꝥ nan man þis geofe ne lytlige ne awende. And gif æni man hit awanige mid æfrænige þinge of ðan þe ic habbe her geunnen on þeosen gewrite· si he gesyndred fram Criste ⁊ fram eallen his halgan. Amen.

possess the socn, let St Benedict have his freedom in all things, as well and as freely as I myself best possess it anywhere in England; and all the forfeitures which belong to my crown, in Yule, and in Easter, and in the holy week of the Rogations, in all things as I myself possess them; and toll-free over all England, within burgh and without, at the yearly marketing, and in every place, by water and by land. And I forbid, with God's forbiddance and mine, any man to diminish or change this gift. And if any man impair anything of that which I have granted in this writing, be he sundered from Christ and from all his saints. Amen.

Ðis writ wæs gemaced æt Windlesoren on feorð Easter dæei· on Eadgyðe gewitnysse ðære cwene· ⁊ Godwines eorles· ⁊ Haroldes eorles.

This writing was made at Windsor, on the fourth day of Easter, with the witness of Eadgith the queen, and of earl Godwine, and of earl Harold.

IDEM LATINE.

✠ Eadwardus rex Anglorum Stigando archiepiscopo, Ailmaro episcopo, Girð comite, Toli vicecomiti, et omnibus ministris suis de Norðfolke et Suðfolke, et universis aliis fidelibus suis per totam Angliam constitutis, tam clericis quam laicis, salutem. Notifico vobis me concessisse Deo, et Sancte Marie, et Sancto Benedicto, et Ælfwino abbati de Ramesia sacam et socam, tol et team, et infangeneþef, fihtwite et ferdwite, foresteall et hamsokne, griðbriche et schipbriche, et se upwarp, in omnibus rebus apud Bramcestre et apud Ringstede, ita bene et libere sicut ipse ea melius et liberius habeo in littore marino alicubi in Anglia, omnesque rectitudines et jura que ibi ego ipse unquam habui. Volo etiam ut soca que est infra Bichamdich in omnibus ad Sanctum Benedictum Ramesiensem pertineat ita plene et perfecte sicut eam ipse habui; et omnes rectitudines quas rex ibi potest habere. Volo preterea ut Sancta Maria, et Sanctus Benedictus, et abbas et fratres Ramesiæ habeant socam in omnibus super omnes homines qui sunt motwrði, ferdwrði, et faldwrði in illo hundredo et dimidio, cujuscunque homines sint. Concedo eis etiam mercatum de Dunham, per aquam et terram, cum inductione et eductione, et cum omnibus rectitudinibus que ad illud pertinent, ita bene et libere sicut illud ipse unquam melius habui; et nolo pati ut aliquis hoc in aliquo imminuat. In omni quoque comitatu ubi Sanctus Benedictus habet terram, concedo eis sacam et socam suam, tol et team, et infangeneðef, infra burgum vel civitatem et extra, ubique in terra et aqua, in bosco et plano, cujuscunque fuerit soca, habeat Sanctus Benedictus libertatem suam in omnibus, ita bene et plene sicut ego ipse alicubi habeo in tota Anglia; habeant et omnes forisfacturas que pertinent ad regiam coronam meam in Natali Dominico, in Pascha, et in sancta ebdomada rogationum, in omnibus rebus sicut ipse habeo, et per totam Angliam, infra civitatem et extra, in omni foro et annuis nundinis, et in omnibus omnino locis, per aquam et terram, ab omni telonii exactione liberi sint. Prohibeo itaque Dei prohibitione et mea ne aliquis hanc concessionem meam mutet aut minuat. Si quis vero aliquid horum que in hoc scripto continentur temerare presumpserit, segregatus sit ille a Christo et ab omni sanctorum ejus consortio. Hæc carta facta fuit apud Windleshoram, in IIII. die ebdomade paschalis, sub testimonio Eadgiðæ regine, Godwini et Haroldi comitum.

KING EADWARD THE CONFESSOR.

✠ CONDITOR celi terreque Deus, universitate totius creature de nichilo perfecta, primum hominem de limo formavit, eumque ad imaginem suam configuravit, cui et omnium operum suorum dominari præcepit, ea videlicet ratione, ut homo rationabilis irrationabili uteretur creatura, per quam Deo ipse serviens obediret, et obediendo Creatorem honoraret. Deinde succedente generatione in generationem templa et ecclesias fieri constituens, de primiciis et decimis ac de substancia sue largitionis eas in nomine suo honorari precepit; insuper et per ewangelium nos instruens ait: "Thesaurizate vobis thesauros in celo," et reliqua. Quapropter ego Eadwardus, Regis regum gratia, rex et Anglorum princeps, post longam exiliationem, solius miserentie Dei nutu, in regno meo reversus, et in solio patrum meorum residens, ecclesiam quam, hortatu beati Augustini, rex Æthelberht, in honore apostolorum Petri et Pauli, a fundamento constituit diversisque donis ditavit, in qua ipsius regis et omnium episcoporum Cancie ac regum corpora poni possent, cum omnibus appendiciis vel adjacenciis suis, liberam esse annuo et statuo. Quum quidem in eadem ecclesia supradictus rex conditus jacet, ejusque stirpis progenita Deo dilecta requiescit virgo Mildretha; ego eciam ejusdem regis stemate ortus, et regno ejus Deo juvante, potitus, Tanatos insulam trado, quam Hegbertus rex jure hereditario concessit venerabili regine Domneue, matri scilicet Sancte Mildrethe, quantum cerva cursu suo lustraverat, pro interemptione duorum fratrum ejus Æthelredi atque Æthelbryti, quos, jussu ejusdem principis, Deo odibilis Thunur iniqua stravit morte: quem mox celestis ulcio terribiliter subsecuta est ipsum perimendo; sed et omnes donationes possessionum vel facultatum quas prisco sive moderno tempore prædecessores mei reges eidem ecclesie contulerunt, et ego regia potestate contrado, atque firma astipulatione, cum consensu et testimonio episcoporum, ducum, principum, et satellitum meorum, abbati Ælfstano ac monachis ibidem, sub regula beati Benedicti abbatis, Deo militantibus, ad habenda et perfruenda sibi perpetua libertate constituens attribuo. Si cui vero hec largicio displicet, vel si quis, quod absit, hanc minuerit, percutiat eum Deus amencia et cecitate ac furore mentis, omnique tempore calumpniam maledictionis Dei sustineat, nec sit qui eum liberet, nisi penitens resipiscat, et digna emendatione satisfaciat. Hec autem traditio regalis in eodem loco servetur inconvulsa et incontaminata, Deo teste, qui dixit: "Michi vindictam, et ego retribuam"; contradicentibus vero ad ruinam et ad condempnationem in die ire furoris Domini, cum eis qui dixerunt Domino Deo: "Recede a nobis, scienciam viarum tuarum nolumus."

KING EADWARD THE CONFESSOR.

PERMISSION TO TOLE, WIDOW OF URK, TO BEQUEATH HER LAND AND OTHER POSSESSIONS.

✠ Eadward kyng gret Heremann B.· ⁊ Harold eorl· ⁊ ealle mine ðegenas on Dorsætan freondlice· ⁊ ic cyþe eow ꝥ hit is min fulla unna ꝥ Tole min man Urces lafe ꝥ heo becweþe hire land ⁊ ehta into Sancte Petre et Abbodesbyrig· swa hire leofest sy· be minan fullan geleafan· swa full ⁊ swa forþ swa ða forewirda ær geworhte wæran· ꝥ hit sceolde æfter heora begra dæge· hire ⁊ Urces hire hlafordes· for heora sawle gan into ðam haligan mynstre. Nu wille ic ꝥ heora cwide stande swa swa hit geforewird wes on godre manna gewitnesse ðe

✠ I king Eadward greet bishop Hereman, and earl Harold, and all my thanes in Dorsetshire, amicably: and I make known to you that it is my full grant, that Tole my vassal, Urk's relict, bequeath her land and possessions to St Peter's at Abbotsbury, as to her may be most agreeable, by my full leave, as fully and as freely as the compacts before made were: that it should, after the day of them both, of her and Urk, her lord, for their souls, go to that holy monastery. I now will that their bequest stand as it was agreed with the witness of the good men who ðarwid wæran. ⁊ ic wille ꝥ swilc freols beo into þam mynstre swilce is into elcan oðre ðær þe best is on eallan þingan. ⁊ ic mesylf wille beon geheald ⁊ mund þerofer· ⁊ ofer þa are þe ðar into hirþ. ⁊ ic nelle nanan menn geþafian ðe ðar geutige ænig þæra ðinga ðæs ðe hig ðider inn gedon habbaþ.

were thereby. And I will that such be enjoyed by that monastery as is by every other where it best is in all things. And I myself will be guardian and protector thereover, and over the property that thereto belongs. And I will not allow any man to take away any of the things which they have thereto given.

QUEEN EADGYTH. M.LXVI.

✠ Eadgið se hlauedi· Eadwardes kinges lefe· gret al þat hundred at Wedmore frendlice. And ich cyðe eow þat ich habbe gegefen Giso ƀ. þat land at Merketun· ⁊ alch þare þinga þæs ðe ðar mid richte tobirid into his canoncan æt Sancte Andrea æt Wyllan· mid saca and mid socna· swo full ⁊ swo forð swo hit me sylfen on honde stod· for Eadwardes kinges sawle ⁊ for mine sawlę. And ic bidde eow ꝥ ge deme me rihtne dom of Wudemann· þe ic hors bitachite· and mi gauil hauið ofhealden· twa gear· eiþer ge hunig ⁊ eac feoch· ⁊ eac feoð. God eow gehealde.

✠ Eadgith the lady, relict of king Eadward, greets all the hundred at Wedmore amicably. And I make known to you that I have given to bishop Gisa the land at Markton, and everything which thereto rightfully belongs, for his canonry at St Andrew's at Wells, with sac and with socn, as fully and as freely as it stood in my own hand, for the soul of king Eadward and for mine. And I pray you that you judge me a just judgment on Wudeman, to whom I intrusted a horse; and he has withheld my rent for two years, both honey and money also; and is hostile to me. May God preserve you.

BISHOP LEOFRIC. M.L.-M.LXXIII.

✠ Her swutelia𝛿 on þissere Cristes bec hwæt Leofric bisceop hæf𝛿 gedon innto Sc̃e Petres minstre on Exanceastre· þær his bisceopstol is. ꝥ is ꝥ he hæf𝛿 geinnod ꝥ ær geutod wæs· þurh Godes fultum· ⁊ þurh his forespræce· ⁊ þurh his gærsuma. ꝥ is ærest· ꝥ land æt Culmstoke· ⁊ ꝥ land æt Brancescumbe· ⁊ æt Sealtcumbe· ⁊ ꝥ land æt Sc̃e Maria circean· ⁊ ꝥ land æt Stofordtune· ⁊ æt Swearcan wille· ⁊ ꝥ land æt Morceshille· ⁊ Sidefullan hiwisc· ⁊ ꝥ land æt Brihtricesstane· ⁊ ꝥ land æt Toppeshamme· þeah 𝛿e Harold hit mid unlage utnam· ⁊ ꝥ land æt Stoke· ⁊ ꝥ land æt Sydebirig· ⁊ ꝥ land æt Niwantune· ⁊ æt Nor𝛿tune· ⁊ ꝥ land æt Clift[1] þe Wid hæfde. Đonne ys þis se eaca on landum þe he hæf𝛿 of his agenum ꝥ mynster mid gegodod· for his hlaforda sawlum ⁊ for his agenre· þam Godes þeowum to bigleofan þe for heora sawlum þingian sceolon. ꝥ ys ærost· þat land æt Bemtune· ⁊ æt Esttune· ⁊ æt Ceommenige· ⁊ ꝥ land æt Doflisc· ⁊ æt Holacumba· ⁊ æt Suþwuda. ⁊ he

✠ Here is declared, in this Christ's book, what bishop Leofric has given to St Peter's monastery in Exeter, where his episcopal see is. That is, that he has, through God's support and through his advocacy, and through his treasure, recovered what had before been alienated: That is first, the land at Culmstock, and the land at Branscomb, and at Salcomb, and the land at St Mary's church, and the land at Staverton, and at Swarcwell, and the land at Morkeshill, and 'Sidefullan hiwisc', and the land at Brihtricesstân, and the land at Topsham, although Harold unlawfully took it away, and the land at Stoke, and the land at Sidbury, and the land at Newton, and at Norton, and the land at Clift[1] that Wid had. Now this is the addition in lands, from his own, with which he has endowed the monastery, for the souls of his lords, and for his own, for the sustenance of God's servants who have to intercede for their souls. That is first, the land at Bemton, and at Easton, and at Ceom-

[1] Clyst?

ne funde þa he to þam mynstre feng nan mare landes þe ðiderynn gewylde wære. þonne twa hida landes æt Ide. ⁊ þæron næs orfcynnes nan mare buton VII. hruðeru. Ðonne ys ðis seo oncnawennis ðe he hæfð God mid gecnawen ⁊ Sanctum Petrum into þam halgan mynstre. on circlicum madmum. ꝥ is ꝥ he hæfð ðiderynn gedon II. bisceop-roda. ⁊ II. mycele gebonede[1] roda. butan oðrum litlum silfrenum swurrodum. ⁊ II. mycele Cristes bec gebonede. ⁊ III. gebonede scrin. ⁊ I. geboned altare. ⁊ V. silfrene caliceas. ⁊ IIII. corporales. ⁊ I. silfren pipe. ⁊ V. fulle mæssereaf. ⁊ II. dalmatica. ⁊ III. pistelroccas. ⁊ IIII. subdiacones handlin. ⁊ III. cantercæppa. ⁊ III. canterstafas. ⁊ V. wællene[2] weofodsceatas. ⁊ VII. ofbrædelsas. ⁊ II. tæppedu. ⁊ III. berascin. ⁊ VII. setlhrægel. ⁊ III. ricghrægel. ⁊ II. wahræft. ⁊ VI. mæsene sceala. ⁊ II. gebonede hnæppas. ⁊ IIII. hornas. ⁊ II. mycele gebonede candelsticcan. ⁊ VI. læssan candelsticcan gebonede. ⁊ I. silfren storcylle mid silfrenum storsticcan. ⁊ VIII. læflas. ⁊ II.

menig, and the land at Dawlish, and at Holcomb, and at Southwood. And he found, when he succeeded to the monastery, no more land that had been given thereto, than two hides of land at Ide, and thereon of cattle there were no more than VII. oxen. Then this is the acknowledgment by which he has acknowledged God and St Peter in the holy monastery, in ecclesiastical gifts. That is, that he has placed therein: II. episcopal roods, and II. great burnished roods, besides other little silver neck-roods, and II. great Christ's books (Gospels) burnished, and III. burnished shrines, and I. burnished altar, and V. silver chalices, and IV. corporals, and I. silver pipe, and V. full mass-robes, and II. dalmaticas, and III. epistle rochets, and IV. subdiacon's handcloths, and III. chanter-copes, and III. chanter-staves, and V. woollen altar-sheets, and VII. coverlets, and II. tapets, and III. bear-skins, and VII. seat-coverings, and III. mantles, and II. wall-hangings, and VI. brazen dishes, and II. burnished bowls, and IV. horns, and II. large

[1] My translation of this word is conjectural. = Dan. bone, *to rub, polish*?

[2] wyllene?

guðfana. ⁊ I. merc. ⁊ VI. midreca. ⁊ I. firdwæn. ⁊ I. cyste. ⁊ þær næron ær buton VII. upphangene bella. ⁊ nu þa sind XIII. upphangene ⁊ XII. hand bella. ⁊ II. fulle mæssebec. ⁊ I. collectaneum. ⁊ II. pistelbec. ⁊ II. fulle sangbec. ⁊ I. nihtsang. ⁊ I. Ad te leuaui. ⁊ I. tropere. ⁊ II. salteras. ⁊ se þriddan saltere swa man singð on Rome. ⁊ II. ymneras. ⁊ I. deorwyrðe bletsing boc. ⁊ III. oðre. ⁊ I. Englisc Cristes boc. ⁊ II. sumerræding bec. ⁊ I. winterræding boc. ⁊ Regula canonicorum. ⁊ Martyrlogium. ⁊ I. canon on Leden. ⁊ I. scriftboc on Englisc. ⁊ I. full spelboc wintres ⁊ sumeres. ⁊ Boeties boc on Englisc. ⁊ I. mycel Englisc boc be gehwilcum þingum on leoðwisan geworht[1]. ⁊ he ne funde on þam mynstre þa he tofeng boca na ma buton ane capitulare. ⁊ I. forealdodne nihtsang. ⁊ I. pistelboc. ⁊ II. forealdode rædingbec swiðe wake. ⁊ I. wac mæssereaf. ⁊ þus fela Leden boca he beget into þam mynster. Liber pastoralis. ⁊ Liber dialogorum. ⁊ Libri IIII. prophetarum. ⁊ Liber Boetii de Consolatione.

burnished candlesticks, and VI. less candlesticks burnished, and I. silver censer with silver incense-stick, and VIII. cups, and II. banners, and I. flag, and VI. boxes, and I. carriage, and I. chest. And there were before only VII. hung-up bells, and now there are XIII. hung up, and XII. hand-bells; and II. complete mass-books, and I. Collectaneum, and II. Epistle books, and II. complete hymn-books, and I. 'Night-song', and I. Ad te levavi, and I. Troparium, and II. Psalters, and the third psalter as they sing at Rome, and II. Hymnariums, and I. valuable Benedictional, and III. others, and I. English Gospels, and II. Summer reading-books, and I. Winter reading-book, and Regula Canonicorum, and Martyrologium, and I. Canon in Latin, and I. Confessional in English, and I. complete Homilarium, for winter and summer, and a Book of Boethius in English, and I. Great English book of divers things, composed in song-wise[1]. And he found in the monastery, at his accession, no more than one Capitularium, and I. worn-out Night-song, and I.

[1] This appears to be the MS. since printed under the title 'Codex Exoniensis.'

⁊ Isagoge Porphirii· ⁊ i. Passionalis· ⁊ Liber Prosperi· ⁊ Liber Prudentii psichomachie· ⁊ Liber Prudentii ymnorum· ⁊ Liber Prudentii de martyribus· ⁊ Liber Ezechielis prophetæ·⁊ Cantica canticorum· ⁊ Liber Isaye prophetæ on sundron· ⁊ Liber Isidori etimologiarum· ⁊ Passiones apostolorum· ⁊ Expositio Bede super euuangelium Lucæ· ⁊ Expositio Bede super Apocalipsin· ⁊ Expositio Bede super vii. Epistolas canonicas· Liber Isidori de Novo et Veteri Testamento· ⁊ Liber Isidori de miraculis Christi· ⁊ Liber Oserii· ⁊ Liber Machabeorum· ⁊ Liber Persii· ⁊ Sedulies boc· ⁊ Liber Aratoris· ⁊ Diadema monachorum· ⁊ Glose Statii· ⁊ Liber officialis Amalarii. ⁊ ofer his dæg he ann his capellan þiderbinnan forð mid him silfum on eallum þam þingum þe he silf dide mid Godes ðeninge· on ꝥ gerad ꝥ þa Godes þeowas þe þærbinnan beoð æfre his sawle gemunon mid heora gebedum ⁊ mæssesangum to Criste· ⁊ to Sc̃e Petre· ⁊ to eallum þam halgum þe ꝥ halige minster is foregehalgod· ꝥ his sawle beo Gode þe anfengre. ⁊ se þe þas gyfu ⁊ þisne unnan wille Gode

Epistolarium, and ii. worn-out Reading-books, very fragile, and i. fragile mass-robe. And thus many Latin books he got for the monastery: Liber Pastoralis, and Liber Dialogorum, and Libri iiii. Prophetarum, and Liber Boethii de Consolatione, and Isagoge Porphyrii, and i. Passionalis, and Liber Prosperi, and Liber Prudentii Psychomachiæ, and Liber Prudentii Hymnorum, and Liber Prudentii de Martyribus, and Liber Ezechielis Prophetæ, and Cantica Canticorum, and Liber Isaiæ Prophetæ separately, and Liber Isidori Etymologiarum, and Passiones Apostolorum, and Expositio Bedæ super Evangelium Lucæ, and Expositio Bedæ super Apocalypsin, et Expositio Bedæ super vii. Epistolas Canonicas, Liber Isidori de Novo et Veteri Testamento, and Liber Isidori de Miraculis Christi, and Liber Oserii and Liber Machabæorum, and Liber Persii, and Sedulius' book, and Liber Aratoris, and Diadema Monachorum, and Glosæ Statii, and Liber officialis Amalari. And after his day he gives his chapel there within, along with himself, with all the things

⁊ Sc̃e Petre ætbredan· si him heofena rice ætbroden· ⁊ si he ecelice geniðerod into helle wite.

which he himself used at God's altar-service, on the condition that the servants of God which shall therein be, ever remember his soul in their prayers and mass-songs to Christ, and to St Peter, and to all the saints to whom the holy monastery is specially hallowed, that his soul may be to God the more acceptable. And whoso will withdraw this gift and this grant from God and St Peter, may the kingdom of heaven be withdrawn from him, and may he be eternally cast down into hell-torment.

AFTER M.LXVI.

ÞIS IS ÞEO BOC BE ÞAM GERIHTAN ÞE LIGAÞ INTO TANTUNÆ.

Her swutulað on þisum gewrite hwylce gerihta langon[1] into Tantune on þam timan þe Eadwerd cing wes cucu ⁊ dead. Þæt is ærest· of þam lande æt Nigon hidon seo mann redden into Tantune cirhsceattas· ⁊ burhgerihtu· heorðpenegas· ⁊ hundredpenegas· ⁊ teoþung of ælcere hide eahta penegas· hamsocn ⁊ forsteall· griþbrice ⁊ handfangenþeof· aþ ⁊ ordel· fyrdwite· ⁊ eall swa oft swa him ma[2] bude to gemote he come· ofþe hine man badode. Dunna wes þæs biscopes mann to þam timan

THIS IS THE CHARTER OF SERVICES INCIDENT TO TAUNTON.

Here is made known, in this writing, what services were incident to Taunton at the time when king Eadward was quick and dead. That is first: from the land at Nine hides, the tenant renders to Taunton church-shots, and burgh-services, hearth-pennies, and hundred-pennies, and tithing for every hide eight pennies, 'hamsocn' and forsteall, 'griðbrice' and 'handfangeneþeof,' oath and ordeal, 'fyrdwite'; and that he come to the 'gemôt' as often as he is bidden, or some one be answerable for him. Dunna

[1] lagon?

[2] Sic MS.

þe Eadward cing wæs cucu ⁊ dead· of ðam lande æt Acō̃n· ⁊ of Taā̃[1] lande· ⁊ of twam Cedenon· ⁊ he geaf to gerihton v. circsceattas· ⁊ heorð-penegas· ⁊ hundredpenegas· hamsocne ⁊ forsteall· griðbrice ⁊ handfangenneþeof· aþ ⁊ ordel· ⁊ þriwa secan gemō̃t on xii. monþum· ⁊ of Eaforda þa ilcan gerihtu. And Ealdreð wæs þæs biscopes mann of þam lande æt Hele· ⁊ dyde þe ilcan gerihta þæ ma[2] dyde of Nigon hidon. And of þam fif hidon æt Baggabeorgan iii. circsceattas· ⁊ burgerihta· heorð-penegas· ⁊ hundredpenegas· ⁊ handfangeneþeof· aþ ⁊ ordel· hamsocn ⁊ forsteall· griðbrice· ⁊ þreo motlæþu ungeboden on xii. monþum. Of Lidigerde i. circsceatt· ⁊ eall þe geilcan gerihta þe ma[2] dyde of Baggabeorge. Of Hylle i. circsceatt· ⁊ burhgerihtu· heorðpenegas ⁊ hundreðpenegas· hamsocne ⁊ forsteall· griðbrice ⁊ handfangeneþeof· aþ ⁊ ordel· ⁊ iii. gemō̃t on geare· buton he hit gebicge oþþe gebidde. Of þære oþre healfre hide æt twam Holaforda ii. circsceattas· ⁊ eall þæ geylcan gerihta þe ma[2] deð of Cedenon.

was the bishop's tenant, at the time that king Eadward was quick and dead, of the land at Acon, and of Taâ-land, and of the two Cedenons; and he gave as services v. church-shots, and hearth-pennies, and hundred-pennies, hamsocn and forsteall, griðbrice and handfangeneþeof, oath and ordeal, and thrice in xii. months to attend the gemôt; and from Eaford the same services. And Ealdred was the bishop's tenant for the land at Hele, and did the same services that were done at Nine hides. And for the land at Bagborough, iii. church-shots, and burgh-dues, hearth-pennies and hundred-pennies, and handfangeneðeof, oath and ordeal, hamsocn and forsteall, griðbrice, and three attendances at the gemôt, without summons, in xii. months. For Liddiard, one church-shot, and all the same services which are done for Bagborough. For Hylle, one church-shot, and burgh-services, hearth-pennies and hundred-pennies, hamsocn and forsteall, griðbrice and handfangeneþeof, oath and ordeal, and three gemôts

[1] MS. of ta á.

[2] Sic MS.

yearly, unless he buy it or beg it off. For the hide and a half at the two Holfords, II. church-shots, and all the same services that are done at Cedenon.

Ðises ys gewitnes.

Gisa bisceop. ⁊ Ælfsie abƀ.. ⁊ Wulgeat abƀ.. ⁊ Ælfnod mynster prauost. ⁊ Wulfwerd Wita. ⁊ Godwine Eadwies sunu. ⁊ Ælmer þæs abbodes broþor. ⁊ Ælgelric æt healf wege. ⁊ Heardinc Eadnoðes sunu. ⁊ Garmund. ⁊ Ælfric Tigel. ⁊ Ordgar se wite. ⁊ Ælfwerd Leofsunes sunu. ⁊ Brichtric se calewa. ⁊ Dodda æt Curi. ⁊ Ælmer Werl. ⁊ Sæwold æt Iliacum. ⁊ Wulfric æt Paules Hele. ⁊ Ealdred æt Sulfhere. ⁊ Wulger æt Hiwerc. ⁊ Æilwine Wunge.

Of this is witness:

Gisa bishop, and Ælfsie abbot, and Wulgeat abbot, and Ælfnoth monastery provost, and Wulfweard White, and Godwine Eadwie's son, and Ælmær the abbot's brother, and Ægelric at Halfway, and Heardinc Eadnoth's son, and Garmund, and Ælfric Tigel, and Ordgar the White, and Ælfweard Leofsunu's son, and Brihtric the Bald, and Dodda at Curry, and Ælmer Werl, and Sæwold at Iliacum, and Wulfric at Paul's Hele, and Ealdred at Sulfhere, and Wulger at Hiwerc, and Æilwine Wunge.

FULDER.

☧ Her swutelaðon ymb þa foreward þe wæron geworhte betwux þam hirede on Wihgeraceastre ⁊ Fuldre. ꝥ is ꝥ he hæbbe ꝥ land æt Ludintune III. gear. for þam ðreom pundum þe he lænde. ⁊ þone bryce þe on þam lande

☧ Here is made known concerning the compacts that were made between the convent at Worcester and Fulder: that is, that he have the land at Luddington, for the three pounds which he lent, and the usufruct of what shall be beo III. gear· ⁊ binnon þrym gearum agife ꝥ land þam hirede mid swa myclum swa se hired him on hand sette· ꝥ synd XII. þeowe men· ⁊ II. gesylhðe oxan· ⁊ I. hund sceapa· ⁊ half hundred foðra cornes. And se ðe þas foreward tobreke· he gewurðe hit him næfre forgifen· ac beo he fordemed into helle wite· ⁊ þær mid deofle wunige oð to domes dæge.

on that land, for III. years, and in three years that he give back the land to the convent with as much as the convent gave him in hand; that is, XII. serfs, and II. plough-oxen, and one hundred sheep, and a half hundred fothers of corn. And whoever shall break these compacts, be it never forgiven him, but be he condemned into hell-torment, and there dwell with the devil till doomsday.

EARL WALTHEOF. M.LXVI.–M.LXIX.

Godgiue vidua dedit Sancto Petro, in loco qui dicitur Burch, duas villas, Righale et Beolmesthorp, pro redemptione animæ suæ, per consensum regis Æduuardi. Postea accepit eam Siuuardus comes in conjugio; post tempus non multum mortua est, et deprecatus est Siuuardus comes abbatem Leofricum et fratres, ut quamdiu viveret posset habere supradictas villas; et post illius decessum reverterentur ad monasterium. Mortuoque Siuuardo comite, facta est conventio ante regem Æduuardum inter Waltheof, filium supradicti comitis, et Leofricum abbatem, et accepit ipse Waltheof v. marcas auri, tali tenore, ut ipse Waltheof haberet Righale in vita sua, et Beolmesthorp quieta remansit in monasterio Sancti Petri, per jussionem regis Æduuardi. Hoc actum est ante regem publice: sed post mortem regis fracta est conventio ab ipso Waltheofo. Sed postea, pœnitentia ductus, veniente ipso ad monasterium præfatum, concessit ambas terras Sancto Petro, eo tenore, ut ipse quamdiu viveret teneret; et post obitum illius ambas simul in monasterio dimitteret; nec ipse aliquomodo istam conventionem frangere, nec terras proprio reatu perdere, potest. Sed si quis istud instinctu diabolico evertere cupit, sciat se excommunicatum cum ipso diabolo in inferno mercedem accipere. Fiat, Fiat.

THE PRIOR AND BROTHERHOOD OF BATH. AGREEMENT WITH SÆWI AND THEODGYFU.

Her swutelaþ on þisse Cristes boc þa forewordan þe þe prior on Baþan ⁊ ealle þa gebroþran habbaþ gemaked wið Sæwi ⁊ wiþ Þeodgyfu his wif. ꝥ is ꝥ we habbaþ heom geunnen· of Godes healf· ⁊ of S. Mar̃.· ⁊ of Sc̃e Petres· ⁊ of ure· þa broþerrǽddene ⁊ þa bedrǽddene for life ⁊ for deþe· ⁊ gelænd heom ꝥ land of þære stræt þe ure wæs· heore hus on to rymende· þa hwile þe hi libbeþ. ⁊ hi us þar togenes gifeþ ꝥ hi us hyrsumien wylleþ ⁊ holde beon· mid eallan þam þe hi magan ⁊ cunnen· ⁊ æfter heore tweire dæie· Sæwies ⁊ Đeodgyfe· hi gyfeþ heore hus ⁊ heore land ⁊ ure Criste ⁊ Sc̃e Petre· to þam ꝥ me hi fægere underfo· ⁊ holdlice for heore sawla beo. Her is to gewitnesse· Osward preost· ⁊ Will. ðe clerec· ⁊ Hugo þe portgerefe· ⁊ Beoring· ⁊ Leoffric· ⁊ Heaþewulf· ⁊ Burehhard· ⁊ Wylwi·

Here is made known, in this Christ's book, the agreement which the prior of Bath and all the brothers have made with Sæwi and with Theodgyfu his wife. That is, that we have granted to them, on behalf of God, and of St Mary, and of St Peter, and of ourselves, brotherhood and tabling, for life and for death, and have bestowed on them the land of the road that was ours, on which to enlarge their house, as long as they live. And they give us on their part, that they will obey and be faithful to us, in all that they may and can; and after the day of them both, Sæwi and Theodgyfu, they give their house and their and our land to Christ and St Peter, in order that they may be worthily and kindly received, for their souls. Hereof is to witness: Osward priest, and William the clerk, and

⁊ Geosfræi· ⁊ Ælfword þe smiþ· ⁊ Edwi Scredes sune· ⁊ Roðð. þe Frenccisce.

Hugo the portreeve, and Beoring, and Leofric, and Heathewulf, and Burehhard, and Wylwi, and Geoffrey, and Ælfword the smith, and Eadwi the Red's son, and Robert the Frenchman.

PRIVILEGIUM OSBERNI, EXONIENSIS EPISCOPI, DE PULSANDIS CAMPANIS, MONACHIS SC̄I NICHOLAI CONCESSUM.

Wita ða þe nu beoð· ⁊ ða te cumene sy· þat yc Osbern Execestre biscop gef leaua ðam munche on Sancte Nicholaus minstre to hringinde hyre tyde be dage ⁊ be nihte· hwanne hi efre willat· swa swa belimpð to hire andebernisse· bute an Cristes massenіht· ⁊ giester sunneue· ⁊ Sancte Petres and Paules massedæe. And þeos leaua þurch hyre abbed Henri· ⁊ to foran him ⁊ his munchun· ⁊ to foran eallum mynum canunche innan minum capitule· of myne ⁊ hyre ealre helf swa fastlice ys ysett· þat nan man after þys ðas ysettinge undon ne mage. And for þyse leaue· twygys elce gere· þat is an Palmsunnendeg· ⁊ Cristes upstigan deg· to processiun mid þam canunche hy gan sceule.

Know those who now are, and those who are to come, that I Osbern, bishop of Exeter, give leave to the monks of St Nicholas' monastery to ring their hours by day and by night, whenever they will, as belongs to their regulation; except on Christmas night, and Easter Sunday eve, and S[t] Peter's and S[t] Paul's mass-day. And this leave through their abbot Henry, and before him and his monks, and before all my canons in my chapter, is of my and all their part so firmly established, that no man after this establishing may undo it. And for this leave, twice every year, that is, on Palm Sunday, and Christ's Ascension-day, they shall go in procession with the canons.

ORDRIC TREASURER OF ST. EADMUND'S.

Đis forward was makid wid Ordric hordere. Þat is þat aelc man in Sc̃e Eadmundesbyri husfast on his owe land sal gifen to þe halegenes bideripe[1] þe hordor on peni at Petermasse onginninge heruest· an sea þat sit on oderes land sea sceal gifen oan halpeni· for þat he aalle scolden sceren ðe halegenes corn. Fram þis sceal naefre no maen bescyr buton Sancte Eademundes þewes· ⁊ sea cnytes agenn ure[2]· and þe preostes inne þeo singen at þo wyuedes. God seonde heore frieond þe worden Sancte Eadmund.

This compact was made with Ordric treasurer. That is, that every man in St Eadmundsbury, holding a house on his own land, shall give, on the saint's 'bederîp'[1], to the treasurer one penny at Petermass, at the beginning of harvest; and he who resides on another's land shall give one halfpenny, or else they should all cut the saint's corn. From this no one shall ever be exempt, save St Eadmund's serfs, and our own servants, and the priests there who sing at the altar. God be the friend of them who honour St Eadmund.

KING WILLIAM THE CONQUEROR.

✠ Willelm cyngc gret̃ ealle mine þegenas on Eoferwicscire· Frencisce ⁊ Englisce freondlice. ⁊ ic cyðe eow ꝥ ĩc hæbbe gegyfen Sc̃e Iohanne æt Beuerlic sac ⁊ socna ofer eallum þam landum þe wæron gyfene on Ædwærdes dæg cynges innto Sc̃e Iohannes mynstre· ⁊ eac ofer þæm

✠ I king William greet all my thanes in Yorkshire, French and English, amicably. And I make known to you that I have given to St John at Beverley sac and socn over all the lands which were given in the day of king Eadward to St John's monastery, and also over those lands which

[1] Compulsory reaping.

[2] MS. agen nure: the sense is doubtful to me.

landum ðe Ealdred ærcebiscop hæfð siðþan begitan on minan dagan þider inn. on witword oððe on caupland. beo hit all freo wið me ⁊ wið æghwilcum men. butan ðam biscope ⁊ ðam mynster preosten. ⁊ ne beo nan man swa deort þe hit undo ꝥ ic hebbe gecyðet Criste ⁊ Sc̃e Iohanne. ⁊ ic wylle ꝥ ðær beo æfre mynsterlif ⁊ canonica samnung ða hwile þe ænig man leofað. Godes bletsunge beo mid eallum cristenum mannum ðe filstað to þes halgan weordscipe. Amen.

archbishop Ealdred has since acquired for it, in my days. In 'witword' or in 'caupland' be it all free, as regards me and every man, save the bishop and the monastic priests. And let no man be so bold, that he undo what I have declared to Christ and St John. And I will that there ever be monastic life and canonical congregation while any man lives. God's blessing be with all Christian men who promote the honour of the saint. Amen.

KING WILLIAM THE CONQUEROR.

Ðis mycel is gegolden of þære cyricean[1] W. cyninge. syððan he þis land ahte. wiðutan þam hidgelde. þe nan̄ man wiðutan Gode ānum atellan ne mæg. Ðæt is ærest. of þam æscene. þe is oðre namon hrygilebuc gecleopad. x. pund. ⁊ of þam xv. hrodan vi. marc. ⁊ of þam oðran æscene. ⁊ of þam hlæfle. ⁊ of þære crucan. ⁊ of þam hnæpfe xi. marc. ⁊ of þære hlangan scrine viii.

This much has been paid by the church[1] to king William, after he possessed this land, without the hide-gild, which no man but God alone may tell. That is first: from the flagon, which is by another name called hrygilebuc, x. pounds, and from the xv. roods vi. marks, and from the other flagon, and from the cup, and from the jar, and from the bowl xi. marks, and from the long

[1] Of Worcester.

pund. ⁊ of þam III. hornan III. marc. ⁊ of þam candelstæfe X. pund. ⁊ of þære hæcce XXXIII. marca. ⁊ þærto eakan XL. marca. ⁊ sixte half marc goldes.

chest VIII. pounds, and from the III. horns III. marks, and from the candlestick X. pounds, and from the crosier XXXIII. marks; and thereto in addition XL. marks and sixty half-marks of gold.

DE CIRISCEATTO.

De Cirisceatto dicit vicecomitatus, quod episcopus de omni terra que ad ecclesiam suam pertinet, debet haberi in die festivitatis Sancti Martini, unam summam annone, qualis melior crescit in ipsa terra, de unaquaque hida libera et villana. Et si dies ille fractus fuerit, ille qui retinuerit reddet ipsam summam, et undecies persolvat; et ipse episcopus accipiat inde forisfacturam qualem ipse debet habere de terra sua. ¶ De cirisceato de Perscora dicit vicecomitatus, quod illa ecclesia de Perscora debet habere ipsum cirisceattum de omnibus CCC. hidis, scilicet de unaquaque hida, ubi francus homo manet, unam summam annone, et, si plures habet hidas, sint libere. Et si dies fractus fuerit, in festivitate Sancti Martini, ipse qui retinuerit det ipsam summam, et undecies persolvat abbati de Perscora, et reddat forisfacturam abbati de Westminstre, quia sua terra est.

COMMEMORATIO PLACITI INTER WULFSTÂN EPISCOPUM ET WALTERUM ABBATEM DE EOVESHAM.

Hec commemoratio placiti, quod fuit inter W. episcopum et Walterum abbatem de Eovesham: hoc est, quod ipse episcopus reclamabat super ipsum abbatem sacam, et socam, et sepulturam, et circsceat, et requisitiones, et omnes consuetudines faciendas ecclesiæ Wigornensi in hundredo de Oswaldeslawe, et geldum regis, et servitium, et expeditiones in terra et in mari, de XV. hidis de Hantona, et de IIII^or^ hidis de

Benningewrde, quas debebat abbas tenere de episcopo, sicut alii feudati ecclesiæ ad omne debitum servitium regis et episcopi libere tenent. De hac re fuit magna contentio inter episcopum et abbatem, qui abbas diu resistens injuste hoc defendebat. Ad ultimum tamen hæc causa ventilata et discussa fuit per justitiam, et breve et preceptum regis Willelmi senioris, quod misit de Normannia, in presentia Gosfridi Constantiensis episcopi, cui rex mandaverat ut interesset predicto placito, et faceret discernere veritatem inter episcopum et abbatem, et fieri plenam rectitudinem. Ventum est in causam. Conventus magnus factus est in Wirecestra vicinorum comitatuum et baronum ante Gosfridum episcopum. Discussa est res; facta est supradicta reclamatio W. episcopi super abbatem. Abbas hanc defendit, episcopus legitimos testes inde reclamavit, qui tempore regis Edwardi hoc viderant, et predicta servitia ad opus episcopi susceperant. Tandem ex precepto justitiæ regis, et decreto baronum, itum est ad juditium: et quia abbas dixit, se testes contra episcopum non habere, judicatum est ab optimatibus, quod episcopus testes suos nominaret, et die constituta adduceret, et per sacramentum dicta episcopi probarent, et abbas quascunque vellet reliquias afferret. Concessum est ab utraque parte. Venit dies statuta. Venit episcopus W. et abbas Walterus, et ex precepto Gosfridi episcopi; affuerunt barones qui interfuerant priori placito et juditio. Attulit abbas relliquias, scilicet corpus Sancti Ecguuini. Ibi affuerunt ex parte episcopi probabiles personæ, paratæ facere predictum sacramentum, quarum unus fuit Edricus, qui fuit, tempore regis Edwardi, stermannus navis episcopi, et ductor exercitus ejusdem episcopi ad servitium regis; et hic erat homo Rodberti Herefordensis episcopi, ea die qua sacramentum optulit, et nichil de episcopo W. tenebat. Affuit etiam Kinewardus, qui fuit vicecomes Wirecestrescire, qui hoc vidit, et hoc testabatur. Affuit etiam Siwardus dives homo de Scropscyre, et Osbernus filius Ricardi, et Turchil de Warewicscyre, et multi alii seniores et nobiles, quorum major pars jam dormiunt. Multi autem adhuc superstites sunt, qui illos audierunt, et adhuc multi de tempore regis Willelmi idem testificantes.

Abbas autem videns sacramentum et probationem totam paratam esse, et nullo modo remanere si vellet recipere, accepto ab amicis consilio, episcopo demisit sacramentum, et totam querelam recognovit, et omnem rem sicut episcopus reclamaverat, et inde, concordiam se facturum cum episcopo, conventionem fecit. Et inde sunt legitimi testes apud nos, milites, homines Sanctæ Mariæ, et episcopi, qui hoc viderunt et audierunt, parati hoc probare per sacramentum et bellum contra Rannulfum fratrem ejusdem Walteri abbatis, quem ibi viderunt, qui cum fratre suo tenebat illud placitum contra episcopum, si hanc conventionem negare voluerit, factam inter episcopum et abbatem. Habemus etiam sacri ordinis viros, sacerdotes et diaconos, paratos illud affirmare juditio Dei.

¶ Willelmus rex Anglorum V. vicecomiti, et Osberno filio Escrop, et omnibus Francis et Anglis de Wiriceastrescyre, salutem. Volo et precipio, ut episcopus Wł. ita pleniter habeat socam, et sacam, et servitia, et omnes consuetudines ad suum hundred, et ad terras suas pertinentes, sicut melius habuit in tempore regis Edwardi; et de terris quas ipse diratiocinavit abbatem de Eovesham de suo feudo tenere, scilicet IIII^or^ hidas ad Benninguurde, et domos in civitate, precipio, ut, si abbas illas vult habere, sibi inde serviat, sicut alii sui feudati. Et de xv. hidis de Hantona, unde episcopus diratiocinavit socam, et geldum, et expeditionem, et cetera mea servitia ad suum hundred, et cirichescot, et sepulturam ad suam villam pertinere, precipio, ne ullus ei contra teneat, sed sic habeat omnia de illis ad meum opus et suum, sicut coram Gosfrido episcopo, et coram vobis, secundum meum preceptum, testante vicecomitatu, diratiocinatum et juratum est, teste ipso Gosfrido episcopo et R. de Ivereio.

INDICIUM DONATIONIS ÆCCLESIÆ WESTBYRIÆ, QUAM WLSTANUS EPISCOPUS USIBUS MONACHORUM HUJUS ÆCCLESIÆ DEDIT. M.XCIII.

☧ Largiente gratia Salvatoris nostri Domini Jesu Christi

ego Wlstanus Uuigornensis æcclesiæ Prelatus antistes, æcclesiam sitam in villa que vocatur Uuestbiria, a beato Osuualdo quondam constructam, et terris et opibus et monachis ibidem Deo servientibus honorificenter jampridem ditatam, postea vero a piratis devastatam, et vetustate et præpositorum negligentia destructam, ad laudem ipsius Domini et Redemptoris nostri Jesu Christi, ejusque sanctæ genitricis Mariae omniumque apostolorum, studui reparare. Et quia terra quæ jure ad æcclesiam pertinebat, impedita et direpta erat a laicis hominibus, inito congruenti consilio, auxilio bonorum hominum, partem prædictæ terræ, legali jure recuperatam, partem pecunie meæ redemptam prætio, juri et ditioni æcclesiæ restitui, scilicet, II. hidas et dimidiam hidam et dimidiam virgam in Uuestbiria, partem etiam terræ quæ concluditur ambitu ipsius monasterii, et VII. acras terræ in orientali parte monasterii, partem quoque silvulæ Æscgraf, et XII. acras prati, liberas dedi ab omni tributo et vectigali, omnique servitio regali et episcopali, prò remedio animæ meæ, et redemptione animarum omnium episcoporum prædecessorum sive successorum meorum, quicumque hanc nostram elemosinam illesam servaverint, aut in aliqua re augendo emendaverint. Hanc libertatem ideo dedi, quia, hac terra excepta et libera permanente, omne regale servitium, quod de meis circumjacentibus terris jure debetur, expleri potest, et persolvendum locavi et statui. In Heanbiria etiam, et in Ceorlatune, et in Uuica II. hidas et dimidiam hidam, et XXVIII. acras terræ; æcclesias quoque in Henbiria et in Stoke, cum omnibus decimis, tam de frugibus quam de pecudibus sive de armentis, similiter liberas ab omni servitute regali et episcopali, concessi, sicut semper liberæ fuerunt ab antiquis temporibus. In Bereuuica etiam I. hidam et dimidiam hidam; et in Hæseldene I. virgam liberam, preter regis servitium. Has terras, cum omnibus sibi pertinentibus silvis et planis, pratis et pascuis, aquis et piscaturis, et ipsam æcclesiam, et ibi Deo servientibus dedi ad sustentationis necessaria, ipsumque monasterium cum omnibus rebus quibus illud ditavi, terris, ornamentis, et cunctis ecclesiasticis ministeriis, Deo et Sanctæ Mariae ad Uuigornensem ecclesiam, utilitatibus monachorum, qui ibi Deo serviunt, in sede episcopali deserviendum dedi. Hujus donationis legitimam sponsionem, consilio et testimonio meorum bonorum hominum et amicorum fidelium confirmavi, offerens illud super altare Sanctæ Mariae, die nativitatis ipsius sanctæ et intemeratæ virginis et Dei genitricis, anno Dominicæ incarnationis M.XCIII., regni autem regis Willelmi junioris V., Ordinationis meæ XXXI. anno, eodem die completo, Indictione I.; desiderans et adjurans, ut hæc possessio et confirmatio firma et stabilis in æternum, ad usus monachorum in Uuigornensi æcclesia Deo servientium permaneat, prohibens pontificali nostra et divina auctoritate, ne quis hoc violare presumat. Si quis vero, diabolicæ cupiditatis instinctu, hoc infringere presumpserit, exterminatus ab æterna cælesti hereditate, consors factus proditoris Judæ, nisi in via satisfactionis redierit, perpetualiter crucietur exitialibus flammis Gehennæ, anathematizatus cum angelis Satanæ, sine fine luiturus pœnas presumptionis sue.

Hujus donationis et confirmationis testes hi sunt:

Thomas prior, cum fratribus Uuigornensis æcclesiæ.

Alricus archidiaconus. Ordricus dapifer. Fretheric capellanus. Alfwinus filius Berhtmari. Alfuuinus presbiter. Alricus camerarius. Aldredus. Alstanus cunestabula. Mauricius Freauuinus clerici episcopi.

EXCOMMUNICATIO CUNCTA SUPRADICTA CONCLUDENS.

Cuncta namque mortalia, velut umbra tenuis, veloci fine recedunt, ideoque quæ in laude Dei geruntur, necesse est ut litterarum seriei commendentur. Quapropter ego supplex Wlstanus, hujus sancti locelli custos et presul, elemosinas terrarum, a Christicolis huc collatas, in unum coaugmentare feci, ne a succedentibus oblivioni tradantur, veritus, quia humana cupiditas, prona in malum, plus ea quæ mundi, in maligno positi, quam quæ Dei sunt amplectitur. Hanc cupiditatem, ut stercora, reiciens, cunctos Deum obtestor amantes, quo nulla, Deo favente, a nobis conjuncta, iniquo turbare audeant conamine. Si autem quis, diabolica instigatus machinatione, hæc audaci disperserit lesione, cum Juda, Christi proditore, sciat se penas subiturum infernales, cum Dathan quoque et Abiron fluviis submersurum herebicis, si hic cum condigna non emendaverit satisfactione.

⁊ ic bidde ⁊ eac on Godes noman halsige· ꝥ ælc mann hine sylfne georne wið þisne curs warnige· ⁊ þissere stowe hold sy ⁊ getreowe· ⁊ se þe elles do· hæbbe him wið Gode gemæne· swa swa þes curs swutelað.

And I pray, and eke, in the name of God, implore, that every man earnestly take heed against this curse, and be faithful and true to this place; and whoever shall do otherwise, let him have to account with God, as this curse declares.

OF BISHOP WULFSTÂN.

Her geswutelað hu Wlstan bisceop becom to biscoprice.

Beforan Gestihtiende ure Drihtene Hælende ⁊ Xpe· to fultumiende þære eadigan fæmnan Sc̃a Marian ⁊ Sc̃e Oswaldes. Aldred bisceop ærest gesette Wulstan bisceop to ciricwearde þære ciricean on Wihgeraceastre· for his clænnysse ⁊ fægrum þeawum· ⁊ hine syþþan wurðodon cyningas ⁊ eorlas ⁊ ealdormen· ⁊ rice ⁊ heane hine georne biddende [wæron] ꝥ he heom fore to Gode geþingode· heore life ⁊ sawle hæle ⁊ reste. And þæræfter hine God geuferade ꝥ he wearð prior ⁊ fæder þæs bufan cweðenan

Here is made known how bishop Wulstân attained to the bishopric.

Before our Lord, the all-disposing Saviour, Christ, and with the support of the blessed virgin St Mary, and St Oswald. Bishop Aldred first appointed bishop Wulstân as sacristan of the church in Worcester, for his purity and excellent morals; and him afterwards honoured kings, and earls, and aldormen, and high and low were earnestly praying him that he would intercede for them to God, for their life and soul's health and rest. And therefore God promoted him so that he became prior and mynstres. Betwyxs þissum him getyþade Leofric eorl· mid erndunga Godyfan his wifes· II. land· Blækewællan ⁊ Wulfweardig lea· þe wæron bereafode þurh Densce men· ⁊ wiðerwearde deman ut of þam mynstre. Syððan Ælfgar eorl him begeat ⁊ geaf ꝥ land æt Ickacumbe· ⁊ þæræfter he wæs sona to bisceope gesett ⁊ gehadod· ⁊ us is nu swyðe earfoðe to gehreccenne hu wel he þone bisceopdom Gode likigende ⁊ eallum mannum geheold ⁊ gestihte· oðð his lifes ende· ꝥ is twa ⁊ þrittig wintra· ⁊ IIII. monðas· ⁊ III. wucan. Syððan Ælfstan prior his broðer begeat ꝥ land æt Lenc· ⁊ æt Dunhamstyde· ⁊ æt þecesleage. And æfter þam þe he bisceop wæs he begeat æt Willelme cyninge æt Cullaclif II. hida landes· ⁊ æt Ælfestune xv. hida· ⁊ Myttun· ⁊ Eastun· ⁊ twegen linde hrycgeas· ⁊ Penhyll· ⁊ Grimanleah· ⁊ II. hina wican· ⁊ hit eal to me his priore beteahte· þe þone anweald æfter Ælfstane underfeng· ⁊ gyt him mare geuðe· þa mylne æt Norðwican· ⁊ I. feorðen dæl landes· þærto [sume][1] þara munecena comon to

father of the above-said monastery. During this time, eorl Leofric granted him, at the desire of his wife Godyfu, II. lands, Blackwell and Wolverley, of which the monastery had been despoiled by Danish men and hostile judges. Afterwards earl Ælfgar acquired and gave him the land at Iccomb; and after that he was soon appointed and ordained bishop; and it is now very difficult for us to relate how well he held and ordered the bishopric, pleasing to God and all men, until his life's end; that is, two and thirty winters, and IV. months, and III. weeks. After that, prior Ælfstân his brother acquired the land at Lench, and at Dunhamstead, and at Thatchley. And after he was bishop, he acquired, from king William, at Cullaclif II. hides of land, and at Alveston xv. hides, and Mytton, and Aston, and two linden ridges, and Penhill, and Grimley, and II. peasant villages; and committed it all to me, his prior, who undertook the rule after Ælfstân; and gave him yet more: the mill at Northwick, and a fourth

[1] [Sume] is supplied from conjecture; the MS. is here too faint to be legible.

grindanne· ⁊ þæt mynstre æt Westbyrig on Gleawecestrescire. Ðæt mynster se halga Oswald ærur arærde· ⁊ hit mid landum gegodade· ⁊ þær munekas gesette· ac hit wearð æfter his forðsiðe· þurh yfelemen ⁊ wicingas eall awest· swa þæt þær næs butan I. preost· se þær seldan mæssan gesang. Ac syððan se arwurða bisceop Wulstan to biscoprice feng he hit eft geedstaðalade· ⁊ hit mid reafum ⁊ lande gegodade· ⁊ to Sc̃e Marian mynstre beteahte· ⁊ þær munekas gelohgode swa fela swa hit aberan mæg· oððæt hit gyt God geyce swa his willa si.

part of the land: thereto some of the mynchens came to grind: and the monastery at Westbury in Gloucestershire. That monastery St Oswald erewhile reared, and endowed it with lands, and set monks there; but, after his departure hence, it was by evil men and wikings all laid waste, so that there was but I. priest, who seldom sang mass there. But after the venerable bishop Wulstân succeeded to the bishopric, he re-established it, and endowed it with robes and land, and assigned it to St Mary's monastery, and placed as many monks there as it could contain, until that God may yet increase it as his will may be.

DE MINISTERIO CELLARII (CŒNOBII *scil.* WIGORN.).

Ad ministerium cellarii pertinet firma que datur per annum. ¶ In septimanam recipiet X. sextarios frumenti fannatos, et X. mittas brasii, et II. sextarios pisorum et VIII. pondera caseorum, et IIII. sextarios avene ad prebendam, et I. marcam argenti in coquinam, et ad servientes sex centos panes de grossa annona, et in festivitate Sancti Martini dabunt firmarii LII. porcos, valentes totidem horas, ad occidendum, vel totidem horas. ¶ In Nativitate Domini dabitur de unaquaque villa que firmam dat, I. sextarius frumenti, I. sextarius brasii, I. sextarius avene, et XVII. denarii, X. auce, V. galline, CC. ova, et I. denarius ad butirum. In Pascha similiter, et contra II. aucas I. agnus. In Assumptione et in Natali Sancte Marie, sicut in Natali Domini fiet. ¶ In Quadragesima, pro caseo dabitur omni ebdomade I. sextarius mellis. ¶ Ad pisces emendos in Quadragesima, de unaquaque hida villanorum dabuntur XII. denarii, et pro conductu IIII. denarii. ¶ Ad lac in coquinam, et ad pabula equorum hospitum, Tidbertun, Lippard, et Herderewica. ¶ Ad vasa et utensilia officinarum, mansure et domus quas possidemus in civitate. ¶ Ad ligna emenda, Hinewica major et minor, et Wantesford, et Wrbenhala, et de prepositis qui firmant in festivitate Sancti Martini XII. solidi, et in tertia ebdomade Paschæ similiter XII. solidi, et de supradicta marca argenti omni ebdomade IIII. denarii. ¶ De Cliva, et Hallega, et Grimelega, et Fepsintun, tertia pars decumationis. ¶ De Grimelega, et Hallega, et Bradewas, ligna IIII. navigiorum ad servientes in aula, in Natali Domini. ¶ De Grimelega et Bradewas C. discos in Natali Domini, et in festivitate Sancte Marie similiter. ¶ De Stoca et Wlfward due vacce pingues ad occidendum in festivitate Sancte Marie. ¶ Ad karitatem fratrum. De duodecim villis que firmant, scilicet Lindelugga, Neweham, Bradewas, Grimelega, Croppetorn, Uerabire, Tetintun, Scepwast, Blachewelle, Segesbere, Cliva, Alveston, dantur XII. sextarii mellis. De Wlfwarde II. De Horselega II. De Dunhamstude IIII. De Stoctune I. De dimidia hida de Scepwash I. sextarius mellis, et de supradicta marca argenti, omni ebdomade IIII. denarii. ¶ Et molendinum ad Salewarpam. Et, ex dono domini Samsonis episcopi, et domini Teowaldi episcopi, decimatur vini tertia pars de Fladeberia, Rippelega, Saltemare. ¶ Et sunt ad ministerium II. piscarie et dimidia, scilicet Ætsieswera, quam dedit nobis Walterus Puhere, secunda Scadewella, tertia apud Hallega, quarta apud Bevereburna, quinta apud Bevereie, dimidia apud Grimelega. ¶ De molendinis de Cliva, XL. sticcæ anguillarum. De Herforte XXX. De Croppethorne XXX. De Salewarpa XXX. ¶ Ex dono domini Teolwaldi episcopi, XX. solidi in Pentecoste, ex processione ad caritatem fratrum.

DE RIBETFORDE.

Simili modo[1] villam, quæ Ribbetford dicitur, cujus villani captatorias sepes piscium et alias venatorias instaurare debita lege debebant, operaque nostra, ubicunque eis præcipiebatur, exercebant, prius Dani, pòst Turstanus Flandrensis monasterio vi abstulit, sicque ejus usque nunc dominatum perdidimus, ipseque non multo post et ipsam et omnem terram suam perdidit, exilioque multatus est. Sic qui parum Deo injuste abstulit, omnia sua juste perdidit.

DE WITLÆGE.

Villam etiam, quæ dicitur Witlæhge, Aldred episcopus et Wulstanus tunc temporis prior, obtentu Edrici, cognomento Silvatici, presbitero ejus Earnwio præstiterunt, quam postea Rawulfus de Beornegia vi monasterio et sibi abstulit; sed parvo post non solum illam sed etiam omnem suam terram perdens, carcerali custodia multatus est, Deo sibi dignam ultionem reddente.

DE GRIMMANHYLLE ET EARESBYRIG.

Has equidem villas, Grimmanhyll et Earesbyrig nuncupatas, temporibus regis Eadwardi monasterio subjacentes, et per inedicibile temporis spatium, jure et propria dominatione monasterii habitas et possessas, Urso vicecomes invasit, postquam vicecomitatum . . . . susceperat. Extitit enim tunc ex parte ambitiosus captor terrarum fere ubicumque potuit, sed post modicum temporis per Dei misericordiam, semetipsum justius aliquantulum optemperavit. Cui denique villæ supra nominatæ (nec sine nimio timore) concessæ fuerunt, ab his, videlicet, qui tunc temporis res monasterii gubernandas habuerunt. Nam illis et valere et nocere, si vellet, potuit; atque hoc plurimum ipsi metuentes, concesserunt, ... que ab illis

[1] See pp. 262, 267.

habere voluit. His itaque ipse susceptis utens ut propriis, omne debitum servitium exinde tamen indeficienter persolvit regis. Nos autem hac de causa terris prenotatis, et, ut premonstratur, a sancto loco alienatis, has etiam nunc terras, quas diximus, litteris supponere curavimus, quoniam minus servitium, quam inde debetur, nos jam habere sentimus.

DE ODDUNCGALEA.

Erat quidam clericus, Kinethegen vocatus, genere et sapientia clarissimus, et per totam hanc diocesin, bonitatis scientiæque suæ fama nominatissimus. Hic sepe veniens ad Goduuinum, virum venerabilem, et hujus monasterii tunc temporis decanum, terram unius cassati, quæ ab incolis Oddungcalea dicitur, in usus proprios quesivit; cuique quod petebat minime denegare volebat (nam illum strenuum magnæque prudentiæ virum esse sciebat), concessit sine dilatione, ea tamen ratione, ut v. solidos pro eadem terra persolveret anni cujusque revolutione. Quam conventionem ipse, quamdiu vivebat, mente devotissima persolvebat: verum eodem subtracto ex hac luce, qui de ejus genere superstites fuere, hanc eandem terram sibi usurpavere, nec postmodum servitium aliquod pro eo nobis exhibere voluere. Tali modo hac terra caruimus, et servitio quod pro illa habere debuimus.

DE CROHLEA.

Tempore illo, quo Dani hujus patriæ possessores fuerunt, villa, quæ dicitur Crohlea, a dominico victu monachorum hoc modo ablata est, licet servitio æcclesie adhuc, Deo largiente, mancipata sit. Nam Simund quidam, genere Danus, miles Leofrici, comitis Merciorum, possessor existens alterius Crohlea, prædictæ jam vicinæ, ut illius generis homines erant soliti, nostre tunc propriæ villæ dominatum avare cupiebat. Quam cum adipisci nullo modo posset, vi et potentia sua et domini sui, eam tot damnis et placitis pejoravit, ut fere eam colonis destitueret. Hinc facto placito, precibus domini sui, predicti comitis, Ægeluuinus, prior istius monasterii, ei terram ipsam concessit possidendam vitæ suæ spatio, ea tamen conventione, ut pro ea ipse ad expeditionem terra marique (quæ tunc crebro agebatur) monasterio serviret, pecuniaque placabili, sive caballo, ipsum priorem unoquoque anno recognosceret.

DE STÆFFORDSCIRE.

Villa quæ dicitur Suuinford, sita in Stæffordscire, et aliæ villæ, sitæ in Uuigereceastrescire, quæ ita nominantur, Clent, et Terdebiggan, ad jus monasterii quondam pertinere domini Wlstani episcopi didicimus relatione, qui pius pater quomodo adquisitæ, et quomodo iterum ablatæ fuerunt, hoc modo sepius narrare solebat. Dixit enim quendam decanum loci istius exstitisse, Ægelsium nomine, nobilem valde et prudentem, tam in monasticis quam in secularibus actionibus, in tantum ut etiam inter consiliarios regis connumeraretur, et esset inter eos satis conspicabilis. Hinc factum est, ut in divitiis et pecuniarum abundantia plurimos majoris ordinis precelleret. Unde et ab ipso rege Athelredo has predictas villas emit cc. libris argenti in jus perpetuum monasterii, ipseque quoad vixit tempore eas possedit. Mortuo autem rege Athelredo, facta est magna turbatio patriæ, certantibus de regno Eadmundo filio ejus, et Cnut rege Danorum. Manente vero regni, ut jam dixi, discidio, defunctus est ipse Ægelsinus decanus. Quo mortuo, quidam malignus homo, Æyic nomine, qui fuit vicecomes in Stæffordscire illis temporibus, easdem villas invasit, et quia non erat qui justitiam sanctæ ecclesiæ faceret, regno utique, ut sepedixi, turbato, nec adhuc sub uno rege stabilito, a possessione hujus monasterii ipse Dei inimicus eas villas alienavit. Unde huc usque sub manu vicecomitis de Stæffordscire sunt omnes eædem villæ, licet quædam in hac vicecomitatu sint sitæ.

DE WEREUUICSCIRE.

Tempore quo Cnut, rex Danorum, hac patria devicta, vectigal importabile toti Anglorum regno imposuerat, ablatæ sunt hæ villulæ in Uuareuuicscire a monasterii possessione, vi et fraude malignorum Danorum, quorum potentia eo tempore terrori erat indigenis hujus patriæ. Nomina autem terrarum hæc sunt: Ludingtun et Dræitun, et III. hidæ ad Lockeslea, et Lappawurðin, et dimidia Mylekote. Constituerunt enim, ut siquid vectigalis ad III^{am} constituti diei deesset, quisquis prius pecuniam pro ea solveret, ejus possessioni subjaceret. Hac calliditate inventa, quisquis aliquam terram de monasterio concupierat, pecunia data vicecomiti, vectigali refutato etiam satis tempestivo, quod male concupierat, pro libitu injuste rapiebat. Sed Deus hanc sui rapinam absque ultione non dimisit. Nam unusquisque eorum, qui huic fraudi operam dederunt, digna ultione percussi, aut luminibus privati, aut paralisi dissoluti, aut in insaniam versi sunt, plurimi etiam semetipsos interfecerunt. Eo quoque tempore Eduuinus, frater Leofrici comitis, isto modo invasit has villas, quæ his nominibus appellantur: Bikemersc in Uuareuuicscire, et Wicbald in hoc vicecomitatu, et alias de quibus jam diximus in Scropscire. Sed ipse diu hac rapina gavisus non est. Nam ipse non multo post a Grifino, rege Brittorum, ignominiosa morte peremptus est. Ad cujus XXX^{mum} diem pius pater Wlstanus, tunc tempore prior hujus monasterii, et Wilstanus præpositus, qui postea fuit abbas Gloeceastre, cum venissent ad Alritune, expetentes terras monasterii, vix pratum solummodo ad Marnanclive adquirere potuerunt, villas vero nullo modo adquirere valuerunt; sed usque hodie injuste retentae sunt, quod Deus emendet cum sibi placuerit. Ægeluuius quoque, abbas Eoueshammii, prosperis successibus in tantum accrescens in sæculo, ut sub rege Willelmo seniore judex factus esset provinciæ, cum dimidiam partem, quæ ante a monasterio ablata fuerat, ipsius villæ, quæ Mylekota dicitur, ab ipso, qui eam possederat, suis ingeniis, ut solebat, adquisisset, instabat quantum poterat, ut etiam medietatem ejus, quæ adhuc monasterio subjacebat, adquireret. Tandemque, adquisitis fautoribus quibusdam etiam ex consiliariis episcopi pecunia sua, spondens quoque, se nominatam pecuniam unoquoque anno pro ea persolvere, insuper etiam et ejus terræ medietatem, quæ ante ablata fuerat, post certum annorum spatium, se promisit velle monasterio redintegrare, suorum precibus et consiliis victus, quievit episcopus. Accepta vero terra, abbas vix anno uno conventionem tenuit. Fracta autem conventione, et ipse morte multatus est. Post cujus obitum, ut jam diximus, Odo episcopus, frater regis, eandem terram, sicuti et omnes alias quas tenebat, preter abbatiam, invasit; sicque a monasterii dominio deviavit.

MEMORIALE TERRÆ DE OFFCOLM ALIENATÆ, POST QUOMODO RESTITUTA EST PATEBIT SEQUENTER.

Nobilissimi Edwardi regis Anglorum, ac Eadgythe regine licencia testimonioque, venerabilis Egelwardus abbas Glaston., cum tocius congregacionis sue consensu, prestitit Eadgythe Hemmingþ relicte quandam villam Uffaculma nuncupatur, in diebus ejus tantum, et ipsa ei septem marcas auri in numis donavit, que eciam filium suum, eo quod mulier esset, coram comite Godewyno universisque majoribus provincie Exon., quod post illius obitum humum suam Sancta Maria non esset amisura, fidem abbati memorato cum jurejurando dare precepit. Et ut hec convencio stabilis esset ac firma, sedecim ei tradidit vades: Leauricum, videlicet, prefate civitatis episcopum, et Godewinum comitem; aliorum vero vadum nomina alibi pleniter scribuntur. Quo facto mox coram populo assistente, cartulas tres scribere jusserunt, quarum unam memoratus episcopus secum retinuit, alteram vero abbati, terciam autem mulieri tradunt, in quibus hec convencio et ex communicacio ista scripta est quam episcopus hora eadem coram omnibus fecit, videlicet, ut omnis per quem hec statucio violaretur, privaretur et ipse regno celesti, et infernalibus subderetur penis, nisi sese resipiscendo, ad penitenciam converteret congruam. Hanc igitur Walterus, cum sibi duxisset uxorem, didicit ab ea, quod prefata tellus sub tali sibi convencione esset prestita, quam et ipse postmodum multis coram testibus ore confessus est suo, Sancte exstitisse Marie; attamen post ejus mortem, non prece, nec precio, nec vi illam ab eo abstrahere potuimus, dónec eum Dominus infirmitatis flagellis corriperet; nam cum dies Sancte Nativitatis Marie illuxisset, celebris, ut assolet, et populus ex diversis partibus ad nostrum, orandi gracia, conveniret monasterium, affuit et ipse Walterus cum suis, quem statim die eodem languor immensus tetigit. Qui cum sese jam moriturum crederet, convocavit ad se uxorem[1], fratrem, dapiferumque suum, et alios quamplures, quorum nomina penes nos habentur scripta, quos ad ecclesiam Sancte Dei genitricis cum ciroteca sua mittens, ut per eam, nobis presentibus, sepedictam humum quam diu injuste tenuerat, super altare quod in ea est, Deo offerrent. Quod cum fieret, hora mox eadem, unum ex nobis monachum ad eandem terram saysiendum destinarunt. Illis autem post hec domum revertentibus, ipsius germanus frater ab eo quod fecerant si vellet concedere quesivit: qui cum se hoc velle fateretur, "Accipe tunc," inquid, "hanc cirotecam, quam ex tuis jussionibus Deo optulimus, et prioris manibus trade"; adherat namque prior tunc ibidem una nobiscum omnibus. Quod cum fecisset, tunc eciam et duo aurea feretra, que jam defuncta femina cum supradicta tellure nobis promiserat, reddidit. Sequenti vero nocte mittens ad nos, semel ac secundo et tercio, monachicum habitum obnixis precibus sibi dari petiit: cujus precibus tandem devicti, ad ejus hospicium usque perreximus; attamen antequam eum habitu monachico induere voluimus, ab ipso inquirere cepimus, si monachus fieri vellet; et si nobis verbis respondere non posset, saltem labia moveret pro signo, et pugnum suum clauderet. Qui cum hoc perfecisset, cepit eciam ad se, ut potuit, cucullum trahere. Tunc omnes astantes simul et uxorem ejus, si vellent concedere quod eorum dominus fieret monachus, interrogavimus. Illi autem omnes pariter flentes ut ullam moram pateremur, nos precari cepere, quia "ecce jam moritur" inquiunt. Hec vero ipsis dicentibus atque

[1] A second wife.

precantibus, unus ex astantibus cum cultello accessit, et camisiam qua erat indutus per mediam cecavit. Nos autem denique omni eum habitu monacico induimus, cujus eciam comam detondimus, ad coronam fecimus; ejus vero capillos, si necesse fuerit, adhuc ostendere possumus, quos tunc de ejus capite rasimus. Quo facto, nobis ad monasterium revertentibus, duos ad custodiendum illum fratres ibidem reliquimus, donec die illuscesscente cum tranquillitate ad infirmariam nostram deferri potuisset; non enim in nocte eum a loco suo movere voluimus, propter suam nimiam qua detinebatur infirmitatem. Ac vero ipse interim de infirmitate sua convalescens, et fratre eum suo rursus interrogante si habitus monachilis ei placeret, respondit omni modo sibi placuisse; sed et gracias egit Domino quod illum sibi concesserat suscepisse. At sui contra, videntes quod convalesceret, gavisi sunt valde, et timentes si eum amisissent, nunquam se postmodum talem sibi dominum invenire posse, (quid plura?) projectis foras monachis nostris, et iterum suis eum induunt vestimentis, testes: Hubertus capellanus, Emma uxor Walteri, Raimierus frater ejus, Wluric dapifer, Ludo de Ucreto, Radulphus de Contivilla, et aliis (*sic*).

PART II.

WILLS.

II. WILLS.

ARCHBISHOP WULFRED, OSUULF ALDORMAN, AND BEORNTHRYTH HIS WIFE. DCCC.IV.-DCCC.XXIX.[1]

✠ Ic Osuulf aldormonn· mid Godes gæfe· ond Beorndryð mīn gemecca· sellað to Cantuarabyrg· to Cristes cirican þæt lond æt Stānhāmstede· xx. swuluncga· Gode allmehtgum and þere halgon gesomnuncgæ· fore hyhte and fore aedleane þæs aecan and þæs towardon lifes ⁊ for uncerra saula hela· ⁊ for uncerra bearna. Ond mid micelre eaðmodnisse biddað þæt wit moten bion on þem gemanon þe þær Godes þiowas siondan· ⁊ þa menn þa þær hlafordas wæron[2]· ⁊ þara monna ðe hiora lond to þære cirican saldon. Ond þættæ mon unce tide ymb tuælf monað mon geuueorðiæ on godcundum gōdum and eac on ælmessan suæ mon hiora doeð.

✠ I Osulf, by the grace of God aldorman, and Beornthryth . my consort, give to Christ's church at Canterbury the land at Stanstead, xx. sulungs, to God Almighty and to the holy convent, in the hope, and for the reward of the eternal and future life; and for the health of the souls of us both, and of our children. And with great humility we pray that we may be in the community of those who are servants there of God, and the men who there have been lords[2], and of the men who have given their lands to the church. And that a twelvemonth after our time, there be given in divine goods and also in alms, as is done from their own.

[1] See p. 96.

[2] That is, at Christchurch. The lords (hlafordas) are probably the archbishops. On this subject see Lingard, Anglo-Saxon Church, ii. pp. 64 *sq.*

Ic þonne Uulfred· mid Godes gæfe arcebisceop· þas forecuædenan word fulliae· ⁊ bebeode þæt mon ymb tuælfmonað hiora tīd boega þus geuueorðiæ to anes dæges to Osuulfes tide· ge mid godcundum godum ge mid ælmessan· ge æc mid higna suesendum. Þonne bebeode ic þæt mon þas þing selle ymb tuælf monað of Liminum þe þis forecuaedene lond to limpað of þæm ilcan londe æt Stānhāmstede· cxx. huaetenra hlāfa· ⁊ xxx. clenra· ⁊ ān hriðer dugunde· ⁊ IIII. scep· ⁊ tua flicca· ⁊ v. goes· ⁊ x. henn fuglas· ⁊ x. pund caeses· gif hit fugul daeg sie. Gif hit þonne festen dæg sie· selle mon uuege cæsa ⁊ fisces ⁊ butran ⁊ aegera þaet mon begeotan maege· ⁊ xxx. ombra gōdes Uuelesces aloð þet limpað to xv. mittum· ⁊ mittan fulne huniges· oððа tuegen uuines· suæhuaeder suae mon þonne begeotan maege. Ond of higna gemænum gōdum þær aet hām· mon geselle c.xx. gesuflra hlāfa to ælmessan· for hiora saula· suæ mon aet hlaforda tīdum doeð. Ond þas forecuædenan suæsenda all agefe mon þæm reogolwarde· ⁊ he brytniæ

[1] Cleansed from the bran?

I now Wulfred, by the grace of God archbishop, fulfil these aforesaid words, and ordain that a twelvemonth after the time of them both, it may thus be, on one day, at Osulf's anniversary, both with divine goods and with alms, and also with refection to the convent. Now I ordain that these things be given a twelvemonth after from the Liminges, to which this aforesaid land belongs, [i. e.] from the said land at Stanstead, c.xx. wheaten loaves, and xxx. clean[1], and one good ox, and IV. sheep, and two flitches, and v. geese, and x. henfowls, and x. pounds of cheese, if it be a fowl-day. But if it be a fast-day, let be given a wey of cheese, and of fish, butter, and eggs, what can be got; and xxx. ambers of good Welsh ale, which are equal to xv. mittas; and a mitta full of honey, or two of wine, whichsoever may then be got. And of the common goods of the convent at the monastery, let be given c.xx. 'gesufl'-loaves, in alms, for their souls, as is done at lords' tides[2]. And let all these aforesaid provisions be delivered to the rule-ward, and let him distribute

[2] See Lingard, *ut sup.* p. 65.

swæ higum maest red sie ⁊ þaem sawlum soelest. Aec mon þaet weax agæfe to ciri-can· ⁊ hiora sawlum nytt ge-doe þe hit man fore doeð. Aec ic bebeode minum aefter-fylgendum þe þaet lond hæb-ben aet Burnan þaet hiae simle ymb XII. monað foran to þære tide gegeorwien ten hund hlāfa ⁊ swæ feola sufla· ⁊ þæt mon gedele to ælmessan aet þere tīde· fore mīne sawle ⁊ Osuulfes ⁊ Beornþryðe æt Cristes cirican. ⁊ him se reogolweord on byrg gebeode foran to hwonne sio tīd sie. Æc ic bidde higon þette hie þas godcundan gōd gedon aet þere tīde for hiora sawlum· þaet æghwilc messepriost ge-singe fore Osuulfes sawle twa messan· twa fore Beornþryðe sawle· ⁊ æghwilc diacon arede twa passione fore his sawle· twa fore hire· ond æghwilc Godes þiow gesinge twa fiftig fore his sawle· twa fore hire· þaette ge fore weorolde sien geblitsade mid þem weorold-cundum gōdum· ⁊ hiora saula mid þem godcundum gōdum. Æc ic biddo higon þæt ge me gemynen aet þere tīde mid suilce godcunde gōde suilce iow cynlic þynce; ic þe þas

them as may be most advisa-ble to the convent and best for the souls. Also let the wax be given to the church; and for their souls do for them the useful which is [usually] done for them. Also I ordain to my successors, who may have the land at Bourn, that they always, about a twelvemonth before that time, prepare ten hundred loaves and as many 'sufls', and that they be dealt in alms at that time, for my soul, and Osulf's, and Beornthryth's, at Christ's church. And let the rule-ward in the town announce beforehand when the time is. Also I pray the community that they perform these divine goods at that time, for their souls: that every masspriest sing for Osulf's soul two masses, two for Beornthryth's soul; and every deacon read two Passions[1] for his soul, two for hers; and every ser-vant of God sing two Fifties[2] for his soul, two for hers, that ye before the world may be blessed with worldly goods, and their souls with divine goods. Also I pray the com-munity that ye remember me at that time with such divine

[1] Narratives of Christ's passion from the Gospels.

[2] A Quinquagenarium, one of the three divisions of the Psalter.

gesettnesse sette· ge hueder ge for higna lufon ge þeara saula þe haer beforan hiora namon awritene siondon. Valete in Domino.

good as may to you seem fitting; I who have settled this settlement, both for love of the convent and of the souls of those whose names are here before written. Valete in Domino.

ÆTHELNOTH REEVE AND GÆNBURG HIS WIFE. DCCC.IV.–DCCC.XXIX.

✠ Æðelnoð se gerefa to Eastorege ⁊ Gænburg his wif aræddan hiora erfe beforan Wulfrede arcebiscope· ⁊ Æðelhune his mæsseprioste· ⁊ Esne cyninges þegne· suæ hueðer hiora suæ leng lifes were foe to lande ⁊ to alre æhte. Gif hio bearn haðđe[1]· þon foe æt[2] ofer hiora bæga dagas to londe ⁊ to æhte· gif hio þonne bearn næbbe· ⁊ Wulfred lifes sie· þonne foe he to þæm londe ⁊ hit forgelde· ⁊ þæt wiorð gedæle fore hiora gastes· suæ ælmeslice ⁊ suæ rehtlice suæ be him seolfa on his wisdom geleornie· ⁊ þas wrece mænig[3] mon uferran dogor on nænge oðre hælfe oncær reade si mynne suæ * * * * * * * * * * Ðis gewrit hafað * *

✠ Æthelnoth the reeve at Eastry and Gænburg his wife have disposed of their inheritance before Wulfred archbishop, and Æthelhun his masspriest, and Esne king's thane, that whichever of them live the longer succeed to the land and to all the property. If she have a child, then let it succeed to the land and to the property, after the days of them both; but if she have no child, and Wulfred be living, then let him take to the land, and pay for it, and divide the worth, for their souls, as charitably and as rightly as he of himself in his wisdom may learn. * This writing hath * *

[1] hæbbe? [2] hit? [3] nænig?

Ðisses londs earan þrie sulong æt Hegyðeþorne. ⁊ gif hiora oðra oððа bæm suð forgelimpe biscop þæt land gebycge suæ hie[1] þonne geweorðe.	Of this land there are three sulungs at Hegythethorn: and if one of them or both die, let the bishop buy the land as it may then be[2].

ARCHBISHOP WULFRED. DCCC.XXIV.

✠ In nomine altithroni Regis æterni, ego Uulfred, gratia Dei arc̃.episc̃., de meis multifariis necessitatibus frequenti meditatione mentis meæ cogitans; quapropter, pro remedio et salute animæ meæ, speque et amore futuræ æternique remunerationis in cælis, illa devota familia, quæ Deo Omnipotenti servitura est in Dorovernia civitate, aliquam partem meæ propriæ hereditariæ terræ, hoc est IIII. aratrorum quod ab incolis terre illius nominatur æt Sceldesforda, cum illa prata quæ mihi ab eadem familia ante tradita fuerat, hoc est XXX. jugerum, post obitum meum dabo et concedo sivimet ipsis habendum feliciterque perfruendum in propriam possessionem, posterisque suis semper derelinquendum, qui cum gratia Dei ad eandem famulatum futuri sunt; et numquam hæc mea donatio hujus terræ ab ista prædicta familia tradatur, nec pro alia commutatur, nec pecunia venundatur; sed semper in posterum ad necessitatem istius congregationis, cum omnibus usis ejus in propria possessione permaneat, his notis terminibus circumjacentibus: In oriente terra regis quæ pertinet ad Eastrægge; in meridiæ Osberhting lond; iterum in meridiæ et in occidente terra quæ pertinet ad Uuigincggaham; in aquilone vero Sceldesford et dimidium rivuli paludis; seu etiam cum illa munificentia hujus terræ omnibusque bonis quas illis fecerim. Postquam nostra communis congregatio per Dei gratiam facta est, ad istam meam familiam flagitabo ut me cum divinis spiritalibusque bonis semper memorare concedant, talemque adjutorium pro re-

[1] hit?

[2] Much of the foregoing translation is conjectural.

frigerio anime meæ in elemosynis salmodiisque ac celebratione missarum faciant qualem illis videtur quod perficere possint. Acque condicione interposita, hanc prædictam agellum donabo, ut omnia nostra acta et dicta a nobis ante condicta firma immutataque perpetualiter maneant et semper ad meliora quod ad bonum condictum habuimus Deo auxiliante unusquisque augescere contendat. Insuper etiam illam terram quod Cynehard diac̃. habuit, et ille mihi donavit, sivique in propriam hereditatem a regibus Ecgberhto et Æðeluulfo donata fuerat, hoc est LXXXV. segetum cum libello ejusdem agelli, ista prædicta familia in Dorovernia, post dies meos, pro nostrorum amborum animarum salute, donabo, hacque condicione, ut semper vespere matutinaque tempore, quando fratres ad ecclesiam beati Petri apostoli ad consuetam canticum ingrediuntur, pro supplicatione animæ illius, illud dominicum orationem 'Pater noster' decantent, seu etiam illum curtem quem Dodda monachus in monasterio habuit, et sivi in propriam possessionem optinebat post migrationem sp̃s mei ae scto pro nostrorum animarum salute, hoc est mei Cynehardi et Doddan, huic eadem familiæ ad proprium usum liberaliter feliciterque perfruendum concedo, ad quacumque utilitate ei placuerit, vel necesse fuerit sua propria bona intus condere valeant, vel ad refectionem civorum, quando alicui oportunitas vel necessitas temporis contigerit; seu etiam quando presbyter aut diaconus familiæ illius corporali infirmitate gravatus fuerit, congruo honore ibi requiescere possit; pro hancque donate commoditate hujus villæ istam meam devotam familiam rogabo, quod fideles remuneratores intercessoresque animarum nostrarum apud omnipotentem Deum existere concedatis, hoc ipsumque posteris vestris observare perpetualiter præcipite.

✠ Ego Uulfred gratia Dĩ arc̃.episc̃.

✠ Ego Ciolnoth divina gratia arc̃.episc̃.

✠ Ego Beagmund pr̃ ab̃.

✠ Ego Uuerhard pr̃ ab̃.

✠ Ego Æðelhun pr̃.

✠ Ego Abba pr̃.

✠ Ego Hunred pr̃.

✠ Ego Osmund pr̃.

✠ Ego Wigmund pr̃.

✠ Ego Badanoð diac̃.

✠ Ego Heaberht diac̃.

. . . . ðwulf diac̃.

✠ Ego Brunhard pr̃.
✠ Ego Osfereð pr̃.
. . . . mund pr̃.
. . . . ferð pr̃.
. . . .
. . . . wulf.

✠ Ego Cichus.
✠ Ego Ealheard.
✠ Ego Osmod.
✠ Ego Freoðogeard.
. . . .
. . . . red.

Dorso. Wlredus archiepiscopus dedit fratribus ecclesie Christi Scealdeuorde et prata xxx[ti] juger̃, quæ ab ipsis antea habebat, et agellum LXXXV. segetum, quem Wigardus diaconus ei donavit, et curtem Doddæ. Anno DCCC°XXIIII.

EADWALD OSHERING AND CYNETHRYTH. DCCC.XXX.

✠ Ðis is geðinge Eadwaldes Osheringes ⁊ Cyneðryðe Eðelmōdes lafe aldormonnes· ymb ðet lond et Cert· ðe hire Eðelmōd hire hlabard salde. Wes hit becueden Osbearte his broðar suna· gif he Cyneðryðe oferlifde· ⁊ siððan neniggra meihanda ma ðes cynnes· ac hia hit atuge yfter hira dege swe hit him boem rehtlicast ⁊ elmestlicast were. Ðonne hebfað Eadwald ⁊ Cyne[ðryð] ðas wisan ðus fundene· mid hira friandum. Gib Eadweald leng lifige ðonne Cyneðryð· geselle et ðem londe et Cert x. ðusenda· gif he gewite er ðonne hia· his barna sue hwelc sue lifes sie agefe ðet feoh ond atee sue hit soelest sie for ða hit begetan. Nis

✠ This is the agreement of Eadwald son of Oshere and Cynethryth relict of Æthelmôd aldorman, concerning the land at Chart, which Æthelmôd her lord gave to her. It was bequeathed to Osbert, his brother's son, if he outlived Cynethryth; and afterwards to no more relations of the family; but she might dispose of it after their day as might be most righteous and charitable for both. Now have Eadwald and Cynethryth devised this course with their friends. If Eadwald live longer than Cynethryth, let him give from the land at Chart x. thousand; if he depart before her, let whichever of his children be living give and dispose of that

Eðelmode enig meghond neor ðes cynnes ðanne Eadwald. his modar his broðar dohtar. mest cyn ðet he ðet lond hebbe ⁊ his beorn yfter him and sue ateon sue him nytlicas ðynce for ða ðe hit mid reohte begetan.

money as it may be best for those who acquired it. There is no relative nearer of kin to Æthelmôd than Eadwald; his mother [being] his brother's daughter, it is most natural that he have the land, and his children after him, and so dispose of as to them may seem most beneficial for those who lawfully acquired it.

✠ Ego Ceolnoð mid Godes gefe ercebisc̄. þis mid Xp̄s rodetacne festnie ⁊ write.

✠ I Ceolnoð, by God's grace archbishop, this with the sign of Christ's rood confirm and write.

✠ Ego Ðelwald episc̄. cs̄.
✠ Ego Whelm. episc̄. cs̄.
✠ Ego Osmund pr̄ cs̄.
✠ Ego Eðelwald pr̄ cs̄.
✠ Ego Biarnhelm pr̄ cs̄.
✠ Ego Biarnheah pr̄ cs̄.
✠ Ego Eardulf pr̄ cs̄.
✠ Ego Eðelmund pr̄ abb̄. cs̄.
✠ Ego Sefreð pr̄ cs̄.
✠ Ego Biarnhelm pr̄ cs̄.
✠ Ego Eadgar pr̄ abb̄. cs̄.
✠ Ego Elfstan pr̄ cs̄.
✠ Ego Sigefreð pr̄ cs̄.

✠ Ego Sigefreð ar̄. dc̄. cs̄.
✠ Ego Ealhstan ar̄. dc̄. cs̄.
. . . . ar̄. dc̄. cs̄.
✠ Ego Cialbart sb̄ dc̄. cs̄.
✠ Ego Wealdhelm sb̄ dc̄. cs̄.
✠ Ego Tirwald sb̄ dc̄. cs̄.
✠ Ego Oba cs̄.
✠ Ego Biarnhelm pr̄ abb̄. cs̄.
✠ Ego Sigemund pr̄ cs̄.
✠ Ego Herefreð pr̄ cs̄.
✠ Ego Wanhelm pr̄ cs̄.
✠ Ego Winibeald cs̄.
✠ Ego Wermund cs̄.

WERHARD. DCCC.XXX.

✠ Anno Dominice incarnationis DCCC.XXX., ego Werhardus, Dei gratia presbiter, his literis intimare cupio quomodo volo, post obitum meum, substantiam meam et terras dividere, quas, donante Deo, et Wulfredo archiepiscopo, propinquo meo, auxiliante, adquisivi. Inprimis autem, cum magna humilitate et humili devotione, reddo ecclesie Christi et monachis, fratribus meis ibidem Deo servientibus, omnes terras infra Canciam et extra, quas hactenus tenui, donante prefato archiepiscopo, et consentiente predicta familia Christi. Precepit enim hoc mihi idem archiepiscopus ita facere, eo quod easdem terras ad opus jam sepedicte familie emisset, et cum magno labore adquississet, pro remuneratione eterne salutis. Hæc autem sunt nomina terrarum quas reddo: Hergas c. et IIII^or hidas, Otteford c. hidas, Gravenea XXXII. hidas, Burnan XLIIII. hidas, Oeswalun X. hidas, Bereham, quam idem archiepiscopus et monachi ecclesie Christi michi dederunt pro commutatione terre de Clive, XXXVI. hidas; unum jugum quod jacet in australi parte Limene, et ab incolis nominatur Lambaham, pertinet autem ad Burnan, et reddit XL. pensas casei, et agnos et lanam absque caseo; aliud jugum apud Northuuda, et reddere debet c.xx. mensuras, quas Angli dicunt 'ambres', de sale; marascos omnes in australi parte Limene et in aquilone cum prefatis terris devote reddo. Mansionem quoque quæ est in aquiloni parte Doroberniæ muris, et clausulam quam Angli dicunt 'teage', que pertinet ad predictam mansionem. Hanc autem redditionem ideo ex parte reddo, quia ipse dominus meus archiepiscopus ita precepit michi, et in scripto quod ipse scribere fecit antequam infirmaretur de divisione rerum suarum, hoc idem notari precepit. In quo etiam scripto constituit elemosinam quam cotidie fieri precepit, in illis terris quas ipse adquisivit, pro anima sua et pro animabus omnium illorum qui ecclesie Christi aliquid auxilii impendissent, et hoc intentissime fieri precepit, ita ut diceret, inter Deum et sequentes nos archiepiscopos sit de facienda aut negligenda ista elemosina a me ordinata: apud Hergam V. pauperes, apud Otteford v., apud Clive II., apud Gravenea II., apud Oeswalun VII., in civitate Dorobernia VI., unicuique detur cotidie ad manducandum quod convenienter sit satis; et per annum cuique pauperi ad vestitum XXVI. denarii. Cotidie quoque precepit missam celebrari pro animabus supramemoratorum. In anniversario suo precepit dari MCC. pauperibus ad manducandum, cuique panem unum et caseum, aut lardum et denarium unum. Hoc est preceptum archiepiscopi Wulfredi. Ego quoque Werhardus presbiter concedo ecclesie Christi prenominate XXXII. hidas de patrimonio meo, quas dare possum cui volo, in civitate Dorobernia, pro salute anime mee et Wulfredi archiepiscopi, de patrimonio meo quas dare possum cui volo, nomine Hysc. Aliam quoque terram nomine Mesgeldesuurthe[1], quam Ceolnothus archiepiscopus et monachi sepe nominate ecclesie Christi mihi dederunt, eidem ecclesie redono. Adhuc addo terram octo hidarum nomine Cuniland. Super hec XXX. hidas cum villa nomine Twitham, in provincia Middlesexan. Videant ergo fratres et domini mei monachi ecclesie Christi, ut memores sint anime mee; quia libenti animo reddidi quod reddere debui, et quod meum fuit, devotissimo animo Christo contuli.

EALHBURG AND EADWEALD. CIRCA DCCC.XXXI.

✠ Đis sindan geðinga Ealhburge ⁊ Eadwealdes et ðem lande et Burnan· hwet man elce gere ob ðem lande to Cristes cirican ðem hiwum agiaban scel for Ealhburge· ⁊ for Ealdred· ⁊ fore Eadweald· ⁊ Ealawynne· XL. ambra mealtes· ⁊ XL. ⁊ CC. hlaba· I. wege cesa· I. wege speces· I. eald hriðer· IIII. weðras· X. goes· XX. hen fugla· IIII. foðra weada. ⁊ ic Ealhburg bebiade Eadwealde minem mege· an Godes naman· ⁊ an ealra his haligra· ðet he ðis wel healde his dei· ⁊ siððan forð bebeode his erbum to healdenne ða hwile ðe hit

✠ These are the agreements of Ealhburg and Eadweald concerning the land at Bourne: That every year there shall be given from the land to the convent at Christchurch, for Ealhburg, and for Ealdred, and for Eadweald, and Ealawyn, XL. ambers of malt, and CCXL. loaves, I. wey of cheeses, I. wey of bacon, I. old ox, IV. wethers, X. geese, XX. hen-fowls, IV. fothers of wood. And I Ealhburg enjoin Eadweald my son, in the name of God and of all his saints, that he will hold this for his day, and enjoin it thenceforth to his heirs as long as it

[1] Mogelwurð. *MS. Bodl.*

cristen se. ✠ ⁊ suelc mon se ðet lond hebbe eghwylce sunnan dege xx. gesufl ra hlafa to ðare cirican for Ealdredes saule ⁊ for Ealhburge. ✠ Đis is sia elmesse ðe Ealhhere bebead Ealawynne his daehter et Đenglesham· et III. sulungum elce gere· c. peñ. to Cristes cirican ðem higum. ⁊ suelc man se ðisses landes bruce agebe ðis fiah an Godes gewitnesse ⁊ an ealra his haligra. ⁊ suilc man sue hit awege· ðonne se hit on his sawale· nas on ðes ðe hit don het.

is Christian. ✠ And let such man as may have the land, give every Sunday xx. 'gesufl' loaves to the church, for Ealdred's soul, and for Ealhburg's. ✠ This is the alms that Ealhhere enjoined to Ealawyn his daughter at Thenglesham: from III. sulungs, every year to the convent at Christchurch, c. pennies. And let such man as may enjoy this land, give this money in witness of God and of all his saints. And such man as may avert it, be it then on his soul, not on his who enjoins it to be done.

ABBA REEVE AND HEREGYTH HIS WIFE. DCCC.XXXV.

✠ Ic Abba geroefa cyðe ⁊ writan hate hu min willa ís þæt mon ymb min ærfe gedoe æfter minum dæge. Ærest ymb min lond þe ic hæbbe ⁊ me God lah· ⁊ ic æt minum hlafordum begeat· is min willa· gif me God bearnes unnan wille· þæt hit foe to londe æfter me· ⁊ his bruce mid minum gemeccan· ⁊ sioððan swæ forð min cynn þa hwile þe God wille þæt ðeara ænig sie þe londes weorðe sie ⁊ land gehaldan cunne. Gif

✠ I Abba reeve make known and order to be written how my will is what shall be done with my inheritance after my day. First concerning my land which I have, and God has lent me, and I have obtained from my lords, it is my will, if God will grant me a child, that it succeed to the land after me, and enjoy it with my consort, and my kin so on afterwards, as long as God will that there be any one of them that is land-me þonne gifeðe sie þæt ic bearn begeotan ne mege. þonne is min willa þæt hit hæbbe min wiīf ða hwile þe hia hit mid clennisse gehaldan wile. ⁊ min broðar Alchhere hire fultume. ⁊ þæt lond hire nytt gedoe. ⁊ him man sælle an half swulung an Ciollandene. to habbanne ⁊ to brucanne. wið ðan þe he þy geornlicar hire þearfa bega ⁊ bewiotige. ⁊ mon selle him to ðem londe IIII. oxan. ⁊ II. cȳ. ⁊ L. scæpa. ⁊ anne horn. Gif min wiīf þonne hia nylle mid clennisse swæ gehealdan. ⁊ hire liofre sie oðer hemed to niomanne. þonne foen mine megas to ðem londe. ⁊ hire agefen hire agen. Gif hire þonne liofre sie a . . . . ynster to gāngenne. oððа suð to faranne. þonne agefen hi twægen mine mægas. Alchhere ⁊ Æðelwald. hire twa ðusenda. ⁊ fon him to ðem londe. ⁊ agefe mon to Liming L. eawa ⁊ V. cȳ. fore me. ⁊ mon selle to Folcanstāne in mid minum lice X. oxan. ⁊ X. cȳ. ⁊ C. eawa. ⁊ C. swina. ⁊ higum ansundran L. pend̄.. wið þan ðe min wiif þær benuge innganges swæ mid minum lice swæ sioððan yferran dogre. swæ hwæder swæ hire liofre sie. Gif higan þonne

worthy and can hold land. But if it be not granted me that I may beget children, then it is my will that my wife have it as long as she will hold it in celibacy, and my brother Alchhere aid her and make the land useful to her. And let be given to him half a sulung in Ciollandene, to have and to enjoy, in consideration that he the more diligently attend to and watch over her needs. And let be given to him with the land IV. oxen and II. cows, and L. sheep, and one horn. But if my wife will not so hold herself in celibacy, and it be to her more desirable to contract another marriage, then let my brothers succeed to the land, and give back to her her own. But if it be more desirable to her to enter a monastery, or to journey south, then let my two brothers, Alchhere and Æthelwold, give her two thousand, and succeed to the land. And let be given to Lyminge L. ewes, and V. cows, for me. And let be given to Folkestone, together with my body, X. oxen, and X. cows, and C. ewes, and C. swine; and to each of the convents L. pence, provided that my wife obtain oððe hlaford þæt nylle hire mynsterlifes geunnan· oððа hia siolf nylle· ⁊ hire oðer ðing liofre sie· þonne agefe mon ten hund peñd. in mid minum lice me wið legerstowe ⁊ higum ansundrân fif hund peñd. fore mine sawle. ⁊ ic bidde ⁊ bebeode swælc monn se þæt min lond hebbe· þæt he ælce gere agefe ðem higum æt Folcanstāne L. ambra maltes· ⁊ VI. ambra gruta· ⁊ III. wega spices ⁊ ceses· ⁊ CCCC. hlafa· ⁊ an hriðr· ⁊ VI. scep. ⁊ swælc monn seðe to minum ærfe foe· þonne gedæle he ælcum messepreoste binnan Cent mancus goldes· ⁊ ælcum Godes ðiowe peñd. ⁊ to Sc̃e Petre min wærgeld twa þusenda. And Freoðomund foe to minum sweorde· ⁊ agefe ðeræt feower ðusenda· ⁊ him mon forgefe ðeran ðreotene hund pending. And gif mine broðar ærfeweard gestrionen ðe londes weorðe sie· þonne ann ic ðem londes. Gif hie ne gestrionen oððа him sylfum ælles hwæt sæle· æfter hiora dege ann ic his Freoðomunde, gif he þonne lifes bið. Gif him elles hwæt

admission there, either with my body or afterwards, as may be most agreeable to her. But if the convents or the lord will not permit her a monastic life, or she herself will not, and another thing be more agreeable to her, then let ten hundred pence be given in with my body for a resting-place, and to each of the convents five hundred pence for my soul. And I pray and enjoin whatsoever man that may have my land, that he give every year to the convents at Folkestone L. ambers of malt, and VI. ambers of groats, and III. weys of bacon and cheese, and CCCC. loaves, and one ox, and VI. sheep. And whatsoever man may succeed to my inheritance, let him distribute to every mass-priest within Kent a mancus of gold, and to every servant of God a penny, and to St Peter my wêrgeld, two thousand[1]. And let Freothomund succeed to my sword, and give therefrom four thousand; and let be given him besides thirteen hundred pence. And if my brothers beget an

[1] That is, 2000 thrymsas = 1200 shillings, the wêr, or pecuniary value, of a thane, whether ecclesiastic or lay (mæsse þegn or woruld þegn). In Kent, as in Mercia and E. Anglia, it appears that the þryms was a current money.

sæleð· þonne ann ic his minra swæstar suna swælcum se hit geðian[1] wile ⁊ him gifeðe bið. ⁊ gif þæt gesele þæt min cynn to ðan clane gewite· þæt þer þeara nān ne sie ðe londes weorðe sie· þonne foe se hlaford to· ⁊ ða higon æt Kristes cirican· ⁊ hit minum gaste nytt gedoen. An ðas redenne ic hit ðider selle þæt se monn seðe Kristes cirican hlaford sie se min ⁊ minra erfewearda forespreoca and mundbora· ⁊ an his hlaforddome we bian moten[2].

✠ Ic Cialnoð mid Godes gefe ærcebiscop ðis write ⁊ ðeafie· ⁊ mid Kristes rodetacne hit festniæ.

✠ Ic Beagmund pr̃ ðis ðeafie ⁊ write.

✠ Ic Wærhard pr̃ ab̄. ðis ðeafie ⁊ write.

✠ Ic Abba geroefa ðis write ⁊ festnie· mid Cristes rodetacne.

✠ Ic Æðelhun pr̃ ðis ðeafie ⁊ write.

heir who may be land-worthy, I then give them the land. If they do not beget, or to themselves something else befall; after their day I give it to Freothomund, if he be then living. If aught else befall him, then I give it to my sister's son whichsoever will accept it, and it shall be given him. And if it happen that my kin so cleanly depart that there be none of them that is land-worthy, then let the lord succeed to the land, and the convent at Christchurch, and make it beneficial for my soul. On this condition I give it thither, that the man who is lord of Christchurch be the advocate and protector of me and my heirs, and that we may be in his lordship[2].

✠ I Ceolnoth, by God's grace archbishop, write and consent to this, and with the sign of Christ's rood confirm it.

✠ I Beagmund pr̃. consent to it and write.

✠ I Werhard pr̃. ab̄b̄. consent to it and write.

✠ I Abba reeve write and confirm this with the sign of Christ's rood.

✠ I Æthelhun pr̃. consent to it and write.

[1] geþicgan?

[2] See page 459, *note* [2].

✠ Ic Abba pr̃ ðis ðeafie ⁊ write.

✠ Ic Wigmund pr̃ ðis write ⁊ ðeafie.

✠ Ic Iop pr̃ ðis ðeafie ⁊ write.

✠ Ic Osmund pr̃ ðis ðeafie ⁊ write.

✠ Ic Wealhhere diac̃. ðis write ⁊ ðeafie.

✠ Ic Badanoð diac̃. ðis write ⁊ ðeafie.

✠ Ic Heaberht diac̃. ðis write ⁊ ðeafie.

✠ Ic Norðwulf subdiac̃. ðis write ⁊ ðeafie.

✠ Ic Wealhhere subdiac̃. ðis write ⁊ ðeafie.

✠ Ic Ciolwulf subdiac̃. ðis write ⁊ ðeafie.

Indorsed.

✠ Heregyð hafað ðas wisan binemned ofer hire deg ⁊ ofer Abban· ðæm higum æt Cristes cirican of ðæm londe et Cealflocan· ðæt is ðonne ðritig ombra alað· ⁊ ðreo hund hlafa· ðeara bið fiftig hwite hlafa· an weg spices ⁊ ceses· an ald hriðr· feower weðras· an suin oððe sex weðras· sex gos fuglas· ten henn fuglas· ðritig teapera gif hit wintres deg sie· sester fulne huniges· sester fulne butran· sester fulne saltes. And Heregyð bibeadeð ðem mannum ðe efter hire to londe foen· on

✠ I Abba pr̃. consent to this and write.

✠ I Wigmund pr̃. write this and consent.

✠ I Iop pr̃. consent to this and write.

✠ I Osmund pr̃. consent to this and write.

✠ I Wealhhere deacon write this and consent.

✠ I Badanoth deacon write this and consent.

✠ I Heaberht deacon write this and consent.

✠ I Northwulf subdeac̃. write this and consent.

✠ I Wealhere subdeac̃. write this and consent.

✠ I Ciolwulf subdeac̃. write this and consent.

✠ Heregyth has in this manner appointed after her day and after Abba's: To the monastery at Christchurch, from the land at Challock, viz. thirty ambers of ale, and three hundred loaves, of which fifty shall be white loaves; one wey of bacon and cheese, one old ox, four wethers, one swine or six wethers, six goose-fowls, ten hen-fowls, thirty tapers, if it be winter, a sesterful of honey, a sesterful of butter, a sesterful of salt. And Heregyth enjoins the men who succeed to the

Godes noma· ðæt hie ful gere witen ðet hie ðiss gelæsten ðe on ðissem gewrite binemned is ðem higum to Cristes ciri-can· and ðæt sie simle to higum beodlese[1] ymb twelf monað agefen. And se mann se to londe foe agefe hire erfehonda[1] XIII. pund pend-ingæ· ⁊ hio forgifeð fiftene pund· for ðy ðe mon ðas feorme ðy soel gelæste.

land after her, in the name of God, that they be full well mindful that they perform this which is appointed in this writ for the convent at Christ-church: and that there be ever a table-gathering[1] for the convent after a twelve-month. And let the man who succeeds to the land give to her administrator[1] XIII. pounds of pennies; and she will give fifteen pounds, in order that this refection may be the better provided.

Indorsed in a more modern hand.

Anno DCCC°XXX°V°.

LUFA. DCCC.XXXII.-DCCC.LXX.

✠ Ic Lufa mid Godes gefe ancilla Dī wes soecende ⁊ smeagende ymb mine saul ðearfe· mid Ceolnoðes ærce-biscopes geðeahte ⁊ ðara hioua et Cristes cirican· willa ic gesellan of ðem ærfe ðe me God forgef ⁊ mine friond to gefultemedan· ælce gere· LX. ambra maltes· ⁊ CL. hlafa· L. hwite hlafa· CXX. elmes hlafes· an hriðer· an suin· IIII. weðras· II. wæga spices ⁊ ceses· ðem higum to Cristes circcan· for mine saule· ⁊

✠ I Lufa, by God's grace handmaid of God, was seek-ing and meditating concern-ing my soul's need, [and], with the counsel of archbishop Ceolnoth and the brotherhood at Christchurch, I will to give from the heritage which God has given me and my friends have helped me to, every year LX. ambers of malt, and CL. loaves, L. white loaves, CXX. alms loaves, one ox, one swine, IV. wethers, II. weys of bacon and cheese, to the brother-

[1] My translation of this word is conjectural.

minra frionda ⁊ mega· ðe me to gode gefultemedan. ⁊ ðæt sie simle to Adsumsio Scǣ Marie ymb xii. monað. End sue eihwelc mon swe ðis lond hebbe minra ærbenumena ðis agefe· ⁊ mittan fulne huniges· x. goes· xx. henfuglas.

hood at Christchurch, for my soul, and my friends' and kinsmen's who have helped me to good. And be that always on the Assumption of St Mary, after a twelvemonth. And let what man soever of my heirs, who may have this land, give this and a mitta full of honey, x. geese, and xx. hen-fowls.

✠ Ic Ceolnoð mid Godes gefe ercebisc̄. mid Cristes ródetacne ðis festnie ⁊ write.

✠ I Ceolnoth, by the grace of God archbp, confirm and write this with the sign of Christ's rood.

✠ Beagmund pr̄ geðafie ⁊ mid write.

✠ Beagmund priest approves and consigns.

✠ Beornfrið pr̄ geðafie ⁊ mid write.

✠ Beornfrith priest approves and consigns.

✠ Wealhhere pr̄. ✠ Osmund pr̄. ✠ Deimund pr̄. ✠ Æðelwald diac̄. ✠ Werbald diac̄. ✠ Sifreð diac̄. ✠ Swiðberht diac̄. ✠ Beornheah diac̄. ✠ Æðelmund diac̄. ✠ Wighelm diac̄. ✠ Lubo.

✠ Ic Luba eaðmod Godes ðiwen ðas forecwedenan god· ⁊ ðas elmessan gesette ⁊ gefestnie ob minem erfelande et Mundlingham ðem hiium to Cristes cirican. ⁊ ic bidde ⁊ an Godes libgendes naman bebiade ðæm men ðe ðis land ⁊ ðis erbe hebbe et Mundlingham· ðet he ðas god forðleste oð wiaralde ende. Se man se ðis healdan wille· ⁊ lestan ðet ic beboden hebbe an ðisem gewrite· se him seald ⁊ gehealden sia hiaben-

✠ I Lufa, a humble handmaid of God, these aforesaid goods and these alms appoint and confirm from my heritable land at Mundlingham to the brotherhood at Christchurch. And I pray and, in the name of the living God enjoin the man who may have this land and this heritage at Mundlingham that he perform these benefits forth to the end of the world. To the man who will hold this which I have enjoined in this lice bledsung. Se his ferwerne oððe hit agele· se him seald ⁊ gehealden helle wite· bute he to fulre bote gecerran wille Gode ⁊ mannum. Uene ualete.

Indorsed. ✠ Lufe þincg gewrit.

writing, be given and holden the heavenly blessing. To him who refuses it or neglects it, be given and holden hell-torment, unless he will turn to full compensation to God and men. Bene valete.

Indorsed. ✠ Lufe's deed of gift.

BADANOTH. DCCC.XXXVII.

✠ Ic Badanoð Beotting cyðo· ⁊ writan hato hu min willa is ðet min ærfelond fere· ðe ic et Æðeluulfe cyninge begæt ⁊ gebohte· mid fullum friodome on æce ærfe· æfter minum dege ⁊ minra ærfewearda· ðet is mines wifes ⁊ minra bearna. Ic wille ærist me siolfne Gode allmehtgum forgeofan to ðere stowe æt Cristes cirican· ⁊ min bearn ðær liffest gedoan· ⁊ wiib ⁊ cild ðæm hlaforde ⁊ higum ⁊ ðære stowe befestan ober minne dei to friðe ⁊ to mundbyrde ⁊ to hlaforddome on ðæm ðingum ðe him ðearf sie· ⁊ hie brucen londes hiora dei· ⁊ higon gefeormien to minre tide swæ hie soelest ðurhtion megen· ⁊ higon us mid heora godcundum godum swæ gemynen swæ us arlic ⁊ him ælmeslic

✠ I Badanoth Beotting make known and order to be written how my will is that my heritable land shall go, which I obtained and bought of king Æthelwulf, with full freedom, in perpetual inheritance, after my day and my heirs', that is my wife's and my children's. I will first give myself to God Almighty in the place at Christchurch, and my children most willingly there place, and wife and children commit to the lord, and to the convent and to the place, after my day, for peace aud protection and patronage, in those things that may to them be needful; and let them enjoy the land for their day, and give refection to the convent on my anniversary, as they may best perform it; and the convent siæ. ⁊ ðonne ofer biora dei wifes ⁊ cilda· ic bebeode· on Godes noman· ðæt mon agefe ðæt lond inn higum to heora beode him to brucanne on ece ærfe swæ him leofast sie. ⁊ ic biddo higon· for Godes lufe· ðæt se monn se higon londes unnen to brucanne· ða ilcan wisan leste on swæsendum to minre tide· ⁊ ða godcundan lean minre saule mid gerece· swæ hit mine ærfenuman ær onstellen.

Ðonne is min willa ðæt ðissa gewriota sien twa gelice· oðer habben higon mid boecum· oðer mine ærfeweardas heora dei. Ðonne is ðes londes ðe ic higum selle xvi. gioc ærðe londes ⁊ medwe· . . . . all on æce ærfe to brucanne· ge minne dei ge æfter· swæ to ationne swæ me mest red ⁊ liofast sie.

✠ Ceolnoð arc̃.episc̃. ðiss writo ⁊ festniæ mid Cristes rodetacne.

✠ Ælchhere dux ðiss writo ⁊ ðeafiæ.

so remember us with their divine benefits as may to us be honourable and in them charitable. And then, after my wife and children's day, I enjoin, in the name of God, that the land be given to the convent for their table, for them to enjoy in perpetual inheritance, as may to them be most agreeable. And I pray the convent, for the love of God, that the man to whom the convent grants the usufruct of the land, may observe the same custom of refection at my anniversary, and, at the same time, have care for the divine reward of my soul, as my heirs may previously appoint.

Now it is my will that of these deeds there be two alike: one let the convent have with the charters, the other my heirs, for their day. Now of the land which I give to the convent, there are xvi. yokes of arable land and meadow, ... all in perpetuity to enjoy, both in my day and after, so to dispose of as may to me be most advisable and agreeable.

✠ Ceolnoth archbp writes this and confirms with the sign of Christ's cross.

✠ Ælchhere dux writes this and confirms.

✠ Bægmund prб. aб. ðiss writo ⁊ ðeafiæ.

✠ Hysenoð pr̃ ðiss writo ⁊ ðeafiæ.

✠ Bægmund presb. aбб. writes this and confirms.

✠ Hysenoth pr̃. writes this and confirms.

✠ Wigmund pr̃. ✠ Badenoð pr̃. ✠ Osmund pr̃. ✠ Suiðberht diac̃. ✠ Ðyddel. ✠ Cichus. ✠ Sigemund. ✠ Eðelwulf. ✠ Tile. ✠ Cyneberht. ✠ Eðelred. ✠ Badanoð.

DUNN. DCCC.LV.

In nomine Domini. Dunn hafað þas bóc geseald his wife ⁊ ðæt land ðe þæran gewriten is· an Godes est· ðæt hio hæbbe hire dæg ⁊ his bruce· ⁊ æfter hire dæg geselle hit· on ðæs halgan apostoles naman Sc̃e Andreas· ðam hirode[1] in· mid unnan Godes ⁊ his halgena· for unc buta ⁊ ealle uncre eldran[2]· butan hi hit mid unnan hiredes ofgan to rihtan gafole· swa swa hyt hy geðingian magan· butan ælcen bræde cððe beswice· ⁊ hi ðonne se hired hit geearnian mid heora godcundnæsse ofeṙ twelf monoð. ⁊ stande simle mid cwide seo bóc on ðæs hiredes handa.

In nomine Domini. Dunn has given this deed to his wife, and the land that is therein written, under favour of God: that she have it for her day, and enjoy it; and that after her day she give it, in the name of the holy apostle St Andrew, to the convent[1], with the permission of God and his saints, for us both and all our parents[2], unless, with the consent of the convent, they hold it at a fair rent, as they may settle it, without any fraud or deception; and then the convent earn it with their godliness, after a twelvemonth. And let stand ever, with this bequest, the charter in the hands of the convent.

[1] At Rochester.

[2] From here to the end the sense seems obscure.

EALHBURH. DCCC.LX.

In nomine Domini. Ealhburh hafæþ geset myd hyre freonde þeahtunga· ꝥ man ælce gere agyfe þam hywum to Scæ̃ Agustine of þam lande æt Bradanburnan XL. ambura mealtes· ⁊ eald hryðer· ⁊ IIII. weþeras· ⁊ XL. ⁊ CC. hlafes· ⁊ ane wæge spices ⁊ cyses· ⁊ IIII. foþro wudes· ⁊ XX. henfugla. Swylc man se ꝥ land hæbbe þa ðingc agyfe for Ealdredes saule· ⁊ for Ealhburge· ⁊ þa hiwan asingan ælce dæge· æfter hyra ferse þæne sealm for hia· Exaudiat te Dñs. Swæ hwylc man· swa þis abrece· si he asceaden fram Gode ⁊ fram eallum hallgum· ⁊ fram þan halgan were on þysum life· ⁊ on ecnesse. Þoñ synt her æfť þara manna naman to gewitnesse þisse gesetednesse. ꝥ is þoñ Drihtnoþ abƀ. pr̃· ⁊ Osmund prƀ· Æþelred pr̃· Wynhere diacon· Beahmund· Cenheard· Hyse· Adda· Cada· Bearnferþ· Bearnhelm· Ealdred· Ealhburh· Ealhwaru· Hoshere· Leofe· Wealdhelm· Dudde· Ofa· Ofe· Wighelm· Wullaf· Eadweald. Gif hit þoñ swa gegæþ swa we na ne wyscað· ꝥ hwylc brocon becume þurh hæþen folc oþþe

In nomine Domini. Ealhburh has settled, with the counsels of her friends, that there be given every year to the convent of St Augustine, from the land at Bradbourn, XL. ambers of malt, and an old ox, and IV. wethers, and CCXL. loaves, and one wey of bacon and cheese, and IV. fothers of wood, and XX. hen-fowls. Let whatever man have the land, give these things, for Ealdred's soul, and for Ealhburh's; and let the convent sing for her every day, after their hymn, the psalm 'Exaudiat te Dominus.' Whatsoever man violate this, be he severed from God and from all saints, and from the holy covenant, in this life and to eternity. Now hereafter are the names of the men in witness of this testament. That then is: Drihtnoth abbot priest, and Osmund priest, Æthelred pr., Wynhere deacon, Beahmund, Cenheard, Hyse, Adda, Cada, Bearnferth, Bearnhelm, Ealdred, Ealhburh, Ealhwaru, Hoshere, Leofe, Wealdhelm, Dudde, Ofa, Ofe, Wighelm, Wullaf, Eadweald. But if it so happen, as we wish not, that any hwylce oðre earfoþnesse· ꝥ hit man ne mæge þæs geres gelæstan· agife on oþrum geare be tweofealdum. gif þoñ git ne mæge· sylle on ðriddum geare be ðryfealdum. gyf he þoñ git ne mæge ne nelle· agife land ⁊ bec þam hiwum to Sc̃æ Agustine.

affliction come through heathen folk, or any other calamity, so that it may not be performed this year, let be given twofold in the second. But if it yet cannot be, let be given in the third year threefold. If he then cannot or will not, let him give up the land to the convent at St Augustine's.

ÆLFRED ALDORMAN[1]. DCCC.LXXI.-DCCC.LXXXIX.

✠ Xp̃. Ic Elfred dux hatu writan ⁊ cyðan an ðissum gewrite· Elfrede regi ⁊ allum his weotum ⁊ geweotan· ⁊ ec swylce minum megum ⁊ minum gefeorum· þa men þe ic mines erfes ⁊ mines boclondes seolest onn. Ðæt is þonne Werburg min wif ⁊ uncer gemene bearn. ꝥ is þonne æt ærestan an Sonderstede ⁊ on Selesdune xxxii. hida· ⁊ on Westarham xx. hida· ⁊ on Cloppaham xxx. hida· ⁊ on Leangafelda vii. hida· ⁊ on Horsalege x. hida· ⁊ on Netelamstede vii. hida. Ic Elfred dux sello Werburge ⁊ Alhdryðe uncum gemenum

✠ Xp̃. I Ælfred aldorman command to be written and made known, by this writing, to king Ælfred and all his 'witan' and witnesses, and also to my kinsmen and my intimate friends, those persons to whom I most gladly give my inheritance and my 'bôc-land'. Now these are, Werburg my wife and our common child. That is then, in the first place, at Sanderstead and at Selsdon xxxii. hides, and at Westerham xx. hides, and at Clapham xxx. hides, and at Lingfield vii. hides, and at Horsley x. hides, and at Nettlehampstead vii. hides.

[1] To this aldorman belonged the splendid MS. of the Gospels, in the Royal Library at Stockholm, described at the end of Rask's Anglo-Saxon Grammar, with a facsimile.

bearne· æfter minum dege· þas lond mid cwice erfe· ⁊ mid earðe· ⁊ mid allum þingum þe to londum belimpaþ. ⁊ twa ðusendu swina ic heom sello mid þem londum· gif hit heo[1] gehaldeð mid þare clænnisse þe uncer word gecwædu seondan. ⁊ hio gebrenge æt Sancte Petre min twa wergeld· gif þet Godes wille seo þæt heo ꝥ færeld age. Ond æfter Werburge dæge seo Alhdryðe þa lond unbefliten on Sonderstyde· ⁊ on Selesdune· and on Leangafelda. Ond gif heo bearn hæbbe· feo þæt bearn to þæm londum æfter hire. Gif heo bearn næbbe· feo þonne an hire rehtfæderen [cynnes] sio neste hond to þem londe· ond to þem erfe. ⁊ swa hwylc minra fædrenmega swa þæt sio ꝥ hine to þan gehagige· ꝥ he þa oþoro lond begeotan mæge ⁊ wille· þonne gebycge he þa lond æt hire mid halfe weorþe. Ond swe hwylc mon swa þæt sio þæt þes londes bruce ofer minne dæg on Cloppaham. þanne geselle he cc. peninga eghwylce gere to Ceortesege for Elfredes sawle· to feorm-fultume. Ond ic sello Æðelwalde minum suna III. hida boclondes· II. hida on Hwæte-

I Ælfred aldorman give to Werburg and to Alhdryth our common child, after my day, these lands, with the live stock, and with the crop, and with all things that pertain to the lands. And two thousand swine I give them with the lands, if she[1] holds them in celibacy, as our verbal agreements are. And let her bring to St Peter my two wêrgelds, if it be God's will that she make that journey. And after Werburg's day, be the lands at Sanderstead, and at Selsdon, and at Lingfield, uncontested, Alhdryth's. And if she have a child, let the child succeed to the lands after her. If she have no child, let the nearest hand of her direct paternal [kin] succeed to the land and to the stock. And whichsoever of my paternal kinsmen it may suit so that he be able and willing to obtain the other lands, then let him buy those lands of her for half the value. And let whatsoever man it may be who shall enjoy the land at Clapham after my day, give cc. pence every year to Chertsey, for Ælfred's soul, in aid of their sustenance. And I give to my son Æthelwald III.

[1] Werburg.

dune· anes hides an Gatatune· ⁊ him sello ðærto c. swina. ⁊ gif se cyning him geunnan wille þes folclondes to þæm boclonde· þonne habbe ⁊ bruce. Gif hit þæt ne sio· þonne selle hio him swa hwaðer swæ hio wille· swa þet lond on Horsalege· swa þet an Leangafelda. Ond ic sello Berhtsige minum mege an hide boclondes on Læncanfelda· ⁊ ðærto c. swina. ⁊ geselle hio c. swina to Cristes cirican for me ⁊ for mine sawle· ⁊ c. to Ceortesege· ⁊ þone oferecan mon gedæle gind mynsterhamas to Godes ciricum in Suðregum· ⁊ in Cent· þa hwile þe hio lestan willen. Ond ic sello Sigewulfe minum mege· ofer Werburge dæg· þæt lond an Netelhæmstyde. Ond Sigulf geselle of ðem londe c. peninga to Cristes cirican. Ond eghwylc þara erfewearda ðe æfter him to ðæm londe foe· ðonne ageofen hio þa ilcan elmessan to Cristes cirican· for Ælfredes sawle· þa hwile ðe fulwiht sio· ⁊ hit man on þæm lande begeotan mæge. Ond ic sello Eadrede minum mege ðet lond on Fearnlege æfter Æðelredes dæge· gif he hit to him geearnian wile· ⁊ he geselle of þem londe xxx.

hides of bôcland, II. hides at Wheaton, one hide at Gatton; and I give him thereto c. swine. And if the king will give him the folkland to the bôcland, then let him have and enjoy it. If that may not be, then let her give him whichsoever she will, either the land at Horsley, or that at Lingfield. And I give to Berhtsige my kinsman one hide of bôcland at Lankfield, and thereto c. swine. And let her give c. swine to Christchurch for me and for my soul; and c. to Chertsey; and let the surplus be divided among the monastic dwellings at God's churches in Surrey and in Kent, as long as they shall last. And I give to Sigewulf my kinsman, after Werburg's day, the land at Nettlehamstead. And let Sigulf give from that land c. pence to Christchurch. And let each of the heirs who shall succeed to the land after him, give the same alms to Christchurch, for Ælfred's soul, as long as baptism may be, and it may be obtained in the land. And I give to Eadred my kinsman the land at Farleigh after Æthelred's day, if he will himself merit it; and let him give from the [sestra] cornes æghwelce gere to Hrofescestre. Ond sio ðis lond gewriten ⁊ unbefliten æfter Eadredes dæge in Ælfredes reht meodrencynn ða hwile ðe fulwihte sio on Angelcynnes ealonde.

Ðeos foresprec ⁊ þas gewriotu ðe her beufan awreotene stondaþ· ic Ælfred willio· ⁊ wille ꝥ hio sion soðfæstlice forðweard getrymed me ⁊ minum ærfeweardum. Gif ðæt ðonne God ællmæhtig geteod habbe· ond me þæt on læne gelið þet gesibbra ærfeweard forþcymeð wepnedhades· ⁊ acenned weorðeþ· ðanne ann ic ðæm ofer minne dæg alles mines erfes to brucanne swa him leofust sio. And swa hwylc mon swa ðas god· ⁊ ðas geofe· ⁊ ðas gewrioto· ⁊ ðas word· mid rehte haldan wille· ond gelestan· gehalde hine heofenes Cyning in þissum life ondwardum· ⁊ eac swa in þæm towardan life. Ond swa hwylc mon swa hio wome· ⁊ breoce· gewome him God almahtig his weorldare ond eac swa his sawle are.

Her sindon ðæra manna naman awritene ðe ðeosse wisan geweotan sindon.

✠ Ic Æðered ar.bisc̃. mid ðære halgan Cristes rodetacne

land xxx. sesters of corn every year to Rochester. And be this land written and uncontested, after Eadred's day, in Ælfred's direct maternal kin, while baptism shall be in the island of the Angle race.

This provision and these writings, which here above stand written, I Ælfred desire and will that they be uprightly henceforth confirmed to me and my heirs. But if God Almighty shall have decreed it, and that loan be in store for me that a nearer heir come forth of the male sex, and is born, then give I to him, after my day, all my inheritance to enjoy as may be most agreeable to him. And whatsoever man this property, and this gift, and these writings, and these words, will righteously hold and fulfil, may heaven's King preserve him in this present life, and also in that to come. And whatsoever man shall corrupt and violate them, may God Almighty corrupt his worldly honour, and also his soul's happiness.

Here are the names of the men written who are witnesses of this disposition.

✠ I Æthered archbp, with the holy sign of Christ's rood,

ðas word ⁊ ðas wisan fæstnie ⁊ write.

confirm these words and this disposition.

✠ Ælfred dux. ✠ Beorhtuulf dux. ✠ Beornhelm abb̄. ✠ Earduulf abb̄. ✠ Werburg. ✠ Sigfred pr̃. ✠ Beonheah pr̃. ✠ Beagstan pr̃. ✠ Wulfheah. ✠ Æðelwulf pr̃. ✠ Earduulf pr̃. ✠ Beornoð diac̃. ✠ Wealdhelm diac̃. ✠ Wine sb̄ diacon. ✠ Sæfred. ✠ Ceolmund m̃. ✠ Eadmund m̃. ✠ Eadwald m̃. ✠ Siguulf m̃.

KING ÆLFRED[1]. DCCC.LXXX.-DCCC.LXXXV.

✠ Ic Ælfred cingc· mid Godes gife ⁊ mid geþeahtunge Æðeredes ercebisceopes ⁊ ealra Westseaxena witena gewitnesse· smeade ymbe minre sawle þearfe· ⁊ ymbe min yrfe þæt me God ⁊ mine yldran forgeafon· ⁊ ymbe þæt yrfe þæt Aðulf cingc min fæder us þrim gebroðrum becwæð· Aðelbolde· ⁊ Æðerede· ⁊ me· ⁊ swylc ure swylce lengest wære· þæt se fenge to eallum. Ac hit gelamp þæt Æðelbold gefor· ⁊ wyt Æþered· mid ealra Westseaxena witena gewitnesse· uncerne dæl oðfæstan Æðelbyrhte cincge· uncrum mæge· on þa gerædene þe he hit eft gedyde unc swa gewylde swa hit þa wæs þa wit hit him

✠ I Ælfred king, with God's grace and with the counsel of Æthered archbishop, and with the witness of all the West Saxons' 'witan', have meditated concerning my soul's need, and concerning my inheritance that God and my parents have given me, and concerning the inheritance that king Athulf my father bequeathed to us three brothers, Æthelbald and Æthered and me, and that whichsoever of us should live the longest should succeed to all. But it happened that Æthelbald died, and we two, Æthered and I, with the witness of all the West Saxons' 'witan', intrusted our portion to king Æthelbyrht, our bro-

[1] The Latin translation in Camden, Angl. Hibern. Scriptt., is quite unworthy of republication. It is printed in Cod. Diplom. v. p. 127.

oðfæstan· ⁊ he þa swa dyde· ge þæt yrfe ge þæt he mid uncrum gemanan begeat· ⁊ þæt he sylf gestrynde. Þa hit swa gelamp þæt Æðered tofeng· þa bæd ic hine· beforan urum witum eallum· þæt wyt þæt yrfe gedældon· ⁊ he me ageafe minne dæl. þa sæde he me þæt he naht eaðe ne mihte todælan· forðon he hæfde ful oft ǽr ongefangen· ⁊ he cwæð þæs ðe he on uncrum gemanan gebruce ⁊ gestrynde· æfter his dæge he nanum menn sel ne uðe þonne me. ⁊ ic þæs þa wæs wel geþafa. Ac hit gelamp þæt we ealle on hæðenum folce gebrocude wæron. Ða spræce wyt ymbe uncre bearn· þæt hy sumre are beþorftan· sælde unc on þam brocum swa unc gesælde. Þa wæron we on gemote æt Swinbeorgum· þa gecwædon wit· on Westseaxena witena gewitnesse· þæt swaðer uncer leng wære· þæt he geuþe oþres bearnum þara landa þe wyt sylfe begeaton· ⁊ þara landa ðe unc Aðulf cingc forgeaf be Æðelbolde lifiendum· butan þam ðe he us þrim gebroðrum gecwæð· ⁊ þæs uncor ægðer oðrum his wedd sealde· swaðer uncer leng lifede þæt se fenge ægþer

ther, on the condition that he should restore it to us so as it then was when we intrusted it to him; and he then did so, not only the inheritance, but that which he with our common property had acquired, and what he himself had gained. Then it so happened that Æthered succeeded, when I prayed him, before all our 'witan', that we should divide the inheritance, and he should give me my share. Then said he that he could not easily divide anything, for that he had already very often undertaken it; and he said that what he had enjoyed and acquired with our* common property, he would, after his day, give to no one in preference to me. And therewith I was well content. But it befell that we were all afflicted by the heathen folk. We then spoke of our children, that they would need some property, let befall us, through these afflictions, whatever might. We were then at the moot at Swinburgh, when we said, with the witness of the West Saxons' 'witan', that whichever of us two lived the longer, that he should give to the other's children the lands ge to lande· ge to madmum ⁊ to eallum his æhtum· butan þam dæle þe uncer gehwæþer his bearnum becwæð. Ac hit gelamp þæt Æðered cingc gefor· þa ne cyðde me nan mann nan yrfe gewrit· ne nane gewitnesse· þæt hit ænig oðer wære butan swa wit on gewitnesse ær gecwædon. Þa gehyrde we nu manegu yrfe geflitu. Nu þa lædde ic Aðulfes cinges yrfe gewrit on ure gemot æt Langandene· ⁊ hit man ærædde beforan eallum Westseaxena witum. Þa hit aræd wæs· þa bæd ic hy ealle for minre lufan· ⁊ him min wedd bead· þæt ic hyra næfre nænne ne oncuðe forþon ðe hy on riht spræcon· ⁊ þæt hyra nan ne wandode ne for minan lufan ne for minum ege· þæt hy þæt folcriht arehton· þylæs ænig man cweðe· þæt ic mine mægcild· oððe yldran oððe gingran· mid wo fordemde. ⁊ hy þa ealle to rihte gerehton ⁊ cwædon þæt hy nan rihtre riht geþencan ne mihtan· ne on þam yrfe gewrite gehyran. Nu hit eall agan is on þæron oð þine hand· þonne ðu hit becweðe ⁊ sylle swa gesibre hand swa fremdre· swaðer ðe leofre sy. ⁊ hi ealle me þæs hyra wedd sealdon ⁊ hyra

which we two had ourselves acquired, and the lands which king Athulf gave to us in Æthelbald's lifetime, excepting those which he bequeathed to us three brothers; and then each of us gave the other his pledge, that whichever of us lived the longer, should succeed to the land and to the treasures, and to all his possessions, except that part which either of us had bequeathed to his children. But it befell that king Æthered died, when no man made known to me any testament or any witness that it was any other except so as we two with witness had before said. We then heard, for the first time, of contentions about the inheritance. I now laid king Athulf's testament before our moot at Langden, and it was read before all the West Saxons' 'witan'. When it was read, I prayed them all, for love of me, (and offered them my pledge, that I would never inculpate any one because he had spoken according to right, and) that none of them, either from love or awe of me, should fear to interpret according to folkright; lest any man should say, that I wrongfully handsetene· þæt be hyra life hit nænig man næfre ne onwende on nane oþre wisan butan swa swa ic hit sylf gecweðe æt þam nyhstan dæge.

adjudged to my brother's children, either elder or younger. And they all declared according to right, and said, that they could neither conceive right more right, nor hear of than in that testament. "Now all therein has passed to thy hand: do thou bequeath and give it either to a kindred hand or to a stranger, whichever to thee is most agreeable." And of this they all gave me their pledge and their sign manual, that while they lived no man should ever avert it in any other wise, except as I myself should declare at my last day.

Ic Ælfred· Westseaxena cingc· mid Godes gife ⁊ mid þisse gewitnesse· gecweðe hu ic ymbe min yrfe wille æfter minum dæge. Ærest ic an Eadwearde minum yldran suna þæs landes æt Strætneat on Triconscire· ⁊ Heortingtunes· ⁊ þa bōcland ealle ðe Leofheah hylt· ⁊ ꝥ land æt Carumtune· ⁊ æt Cylfantune· ⁊ æt Burnhamme· ⁊ æt Wedmor. ⁊ ic eom fyrmdig to þam hiwum æt Ceodre[1]· ꝥ hy hine ceosan on þa gerad ðe we ær gecweden hæfdon· mid þam lande æt Ciwtune· ⁊ ðam þe þærto hyrað. ⁊ ic him an þæs landes æt Cantuctune· ⁊ æt Bedewindan·

I Ælfred, king of the West Saxons, with God's grace, and with this witness, declare how I will with regard to my inheritance after my day. First to Eadward, my elder son, I give the land at Stratton in Cornwall, and Hartington, and all the bôclands that Leofheah holds, and the land at Carhampton, and at Chillington, and at Burnham, and at Wedmore. And I am desirous that the inmates at Chedder should choose him[1], on the condition of which we have already spoken, with the land at Chewton, and that which thereto belongs. And I give him the land at Quan-

[1] Charters of Eadwig, Eadgar, and Eadmund are dated from the royal palace at Chedder. The 'hiwan' here mentioned are probably either the vassals attached to the palace, or the inmates of an abbey there, both having legal power to choose their lord (hlaford).

⁊ æt Pefesigge. ⁊ Hysseburnan. ⁊ æt Suttune. ⁊ æt Leodridan. ⁊ æt Aweltune. And ealle þa bocland ðe ic on Cent hæbbe ⁊ æt þam nyþeran Hysseburnan. ⁊ æt Cyseldene. agyfe man into Wintanceastre. on þa gerad ðe hit min fæder ær gecwæð. ⁊ ꝥ min sundorfeoh þæt ic Ecgulfe oðfæste on þam neoþeran Hysseburnan. ⁊ þam gingran minan suna ꝥ land æt Eaderingtune. ⁊ ꝥ æt Dene. ⁊ ꝥ æt Meone. ⁊ ðæt æt Ambresbyrig. ⁊ æt Deone. ⁊ æt Stureminster. ⁊ æt Gifle. ⁊ æt Cruærn. ⁊ æt Hwitancyrican. ⁊ æt Axanmuðan. ⁊ æt Brancescumbe. ⁊ æt Columtune. ⁊ æt Twyfyrde. ⁊ æt Mylenburnan. ⁊ æt Exanmynster. ⁊ æt Suðeswyrðe. ⁊ æt Liwtune. ⁊ þa land þe þærto hyran. ꝥ synd ealle ðe ic on Wealcynne hæbbe butan Triconscire. And minre yldstan dehter þæne hā̄m æt Welewe. ⁊ þære medemestan æt Clearan. ⁊ æt Cendefer. ⁊ þære gingestan[1] þone hā̄m æt Welig. ⁊ æt Æsctune. ⁊ æt

tock, and at Bedwin, and at Pewsey, and at Husseboum, and at Sutton, and at Letherhead, and at Alton. And let all the bôclands that I have in Kent, and at the Nether Husseboum, and at Chiselden, be given to Winchester, on the condition that my father before said; and my separate property in Nether Husseboum, which I intrusted to Ecgulf. And to my younger son the land at Adrington, and that at Dean, and that at Meon, and that at Amesbury, and at Downe, and at Stourminster, and at Gidley, and at Crewkern, and at Whitchurch, and at Axmouth, and at Branscomb, and at Collumpton, and at Twyford, and at Milbourn, and at Axminster, and at Southsworth, and at Litton, and the lands which thereto belong, that is, all which I have among the Welsh race, excepting Cornwall. And to my eldest daughter the hâm (vill) at Wellow, and to the middlemost that at Clere, and at Candever, and to the youngest[1]

[1] Ælfthryth, the youngest, had the village of Lewisham in Kent, with its appurtenances, Greenwich and Woolwich, which, in the year 916, she gave to the abbey of St. Peter in Ghent. The charters and confirmations of these gifts still exist in manuscript, and have been lately brought to light by Prof. Warnkönig. *Note from* Lappenberg, Eng. under the A. S. Kings, ii. p. 82.

Cippenhamme. ⁊ Æðelme mines broþer suna þone ham æt Ealdingburnan. ⁊ æt Cumtune. ⁊ æt Crundellan. ⁊ æt Beadingum. ⁊ æt Beadingahamme. ⁊ æt Burnham. ⁊ æt Þunresfelda. ⁊ æt Æscengum. ⁊ Æþelwolde mines broðor suna þone ham æt Godelmingum. ⁊ æt Gyldeforda. ⁊ æt Stæningum. ⁊ Osferðe minum mæge þone ham æt Beccanlea. ⁊ æt Hryðeranfelda. ⁊ æt Diccelingum. ⁊ æt Suðtune. ⁊ æt Lullingmynster. ⁊ æt Angemæringtun. ⁊ æt Felhhamme. ⁊ þa land þe þærto hyran. ⁊ Ealhswiðe þone ham æt Lambburnan. ⁊ æt Waneting. ⁊ æt Eðandune. ⁊ minum twam sunum an þusend punda. ægðrum fif hund punda. ⁊ minre yldstan dehter. ⁊ þære medemestan. ⁊ þære gingstran. ⁊ Ealhswiðe. him feowrum feower hund punda. ælcum an hund punda. ⁊ minra ealdormanna ælcum an hund mangcusa. ⁊ Æþelme. ⁊ Aðelwolde. ⁊ Osferðe. eac swa. ⁊ Æþerede ealdormenn an sweord on hundteontigum mancusum. ⁊ þam mannum þe me folgiað. þe ic nu on Eastertidum feoh sealde. twa hund punda agyfe man him. ⁊ dæle man him betweoh. ælcum swa him to

the hâm at Welig, and at Ashton, and at Chippenham. And to Æthelm, my brother's son, the hâm at Aldingbourn, and at Compton, and at Crondal, and at Beden, and at Bedingham, and at Burnham, and at Thundersfield, and at Eashing. And to Æthelwold, my brother's son, the hâm at Godalming, and at Guildford, and at Steyning. And to Osferth my kinsman the hâm at Beckley, and at Rotherfield, and at Ditchling, and at Sutton, and at Lullington, and at Angmering, and at Felpham, and the lands which thereto belong. And to Ealhswith, the hâm at Lambourn, and at Wantage, and at Edington. And to my two sons a thousand pounds, to each five hundred pounds; and to my eldest daughter, and to the middlemost, and to the youngest, and to Ealhswith, to them four hundred pounds, to each a hundred pounds. And to each of my aldormen a hundred mancuses. And to Æthelm and Æthelwold and Osferth the same. And to Æthered aldorman a sword of a hundred mancuses. And to the men who follow me, to whom I have now at Eastertide gebyrian wille· æfter þære wisan þe ic him nu dælde. ⁊ þam ercebisceope c. mancusa· ⁊ Esne bisceope· ⁊ Wærferðe bisceope· ⁊ þam æt Sciremburnan. Eac swa gedæle for me· ⁊ for minne fæder· ⁊ for þa frynd þe he fore þingode ⁊ ic fore þingie· twa hund punda fiftig mæssepreostum ofer eall min rice· fiftig earmum Godes þeowum· fiftig earmum þearfum· fiftig to ðære cyrican ðe ic æt reste. ⁊ ic nat naht gewislice hwæðer þæs feos swa micel is· ne ic nat þeah his mare sy· butan swa ic wene. Gif hit mare sy· beo hit him eallum gemæne þe ic feoh becweden hæbbe. ⁊ ic wille þæt mine ealdormenn ⁊ mine þenigmenn þær ealle mid syndan· ⁊ þis þus gedælan. Þonne hæfde ic ær on oðre wisan awriten ymbe min yrfe· þa ic hæfde mare feoh ⁊ ma maga· ⁊ hæfde monegum mannum þa gewritu oðfæst· ⁊ on þas ylcan gewitnesse hy wæron awritene· þonne hæbbe ic nu forbærned þa ealdan þe ic geahsian mihte. Gif hyra hwylc funden bið, ne forstent þæt naht· forþam ic wille þæt hit nu þus sy· mid Godes fultume. ⁊ ic wille þa menn þe þa land habbað· þa word

given money, let two hundred pounds be given, and let it be dealt among them, to each as shall be fitting, after the wise in which I lately dealt to them. And to the archbishop c. mancuses, and to bishop Esne, and to bishop Wærferth, and to the [bishop] at Sherborne. In like manner distribute for me, and for my father, and for the friends for whom he interceded and I intercede, two hundred pounds, fifty to mass-priests over all my realm, fifty to poor servants of God, fifty to the poor needy, fifty to the church at which I shall rest. But I know not for certain whether there is so much money, nor know I if there be more of it, but so I ween. If it be more, be it in common to them all to whom I have bequeathed money. And I will that my aldormen and my thanes be all there together, and this thus distribute. Now I had previously written in another wise concerning my inheritance, when I had more money and more kinsmen, and had intrusted the writings to many men, and with this same witness they were written; but now I have burned those old ones gelæstan þe on mines fæder yrfe gewrite standað. swa swa hy fyrmest magon. ⁊ ic wille gif ic ænigum menn ænig feoh unleanod hæbbe. þæt mine magas þæt huru geleanian. ⁊ ic wille þa menn þe ic mine bócland becweden hæbbe. ꝥ hy hit ne asyllan of minum cynne ofer heora dæg. ac ic wille [ofer] hyra dæg þæt hit gange on þa nyhstan hand me. butan hyra hwylc bearn hæbbe. þonne is me leofast þæt hit gange on þæt stryned on þa wæpned healfe. þa hwile þe ænig þæs wyrðe sy. Min yldra fæder hæfde gecweden his land on þa spere healfe. næs on þa spinl healfe. þonne gif ic gesealde ænigre wifhanda ꝥ he gestrynde. þonne forgyldan mine magas. ⁊ gif hy hit be þan libbendan habban wyllan. gif hit elles sy. gange hit ofer hyra dæg. swa swa we ær gecweden hæfdon. Forðon ic cweþe þæt hi hit gyldan. forþon hy foð to minum þe ic syllan mot. swa wif handa swa wæpned handa. swaðer ic wylle. ⁊ ic bidde. on Godes naman ⁊ on his haligra. ꝥ minra maga nan. ne yrfewearda. ne geswence nan nænig cyrelif[1] þara þe ic fore-

that I could discover. If any of them be found, it stands for naught, for I will that it be now thus, with the aid of God. And I will that the men who have the lands, fulfil the words which stand in my father's testament, as they best may. And I will, if to any man I have not paid any money, that my kinsmen at all events pay it. And I will that the men to whom I have bequeathed my bôclands, give them not from my kin after their day; but I will that after their day it go to the next of kin to me, unless any of them have children; then it is to me most desirable that it go to the one begotten on the male side, while there shall be any worthy of it. My grandfather had bequeathed his lands to the spear-side, not to the spindle-side: now if I have given to any female hand what he acquired, then let my kinsmen make compensation; and let them, if they will, have it in their lifetime; if it be otherwise, let it go after their day, so as we had before spoken. I say that they should make compensation, because they succeed to that of mine which I may give either to

[1] See Kemble, Saxons in England, i. p. 504. From cyre, *choice*, and lif.

geald. ⁊ me Westseaxena witan to rihte gerehton. þæt ic hi mot lætan swa freo swa þeowe. swaðer ic wille. ac ic. for Godes lufan ⁊ for minre sawle þearfe. wylle ꝥ hy syn heora freolses wyrðe. ⁊ hyra cyres. ⁊ ic on Godes lifiendes naman beode. þæt hy nan man ne brocie. ne mid feos manunge. ne mid nænigum þingum ꝥ hy ne motan ceosan swylcne mann swylce hy wyllan. ⁊ ic wylle þæt man agyfe þam hiwum æt Domrahamme hyra landbec ⁊ hyra freols. swylce hand to ceosenne swylce him leofast sy. for me. ⁊ for Ælflæde. ⁊ for þa frynd þe heo fore þingode. ⁊ ic fore þingie. And sec man eac on cwicum ceape ymbe minre sawle þearfe. swa hit beon mæge. ⁊ swa hit eac gerysne sy. ⁊ swa ge me forgyfan wyllan.

the female hand or to the male hand, whichsoever I will. And I pray, in the name of God and his saints, that no one of my kinsmen or heirs oppress any dependent of those for whom I have paid, and the West Saxons' 'witan' have rightfully adjudged to me, so that I may let them be either free or servile, whichever I will; but I, for love of God, and for my soul's need, will that they be entitled to their freedom and their choice: and, in the name of the living God, I command that no man oppress them either by exaction of money, or by anything, so that they may not choose such man (lord) as they will. And I will that there be given to the convent at Damerham their charters and their liberty to choose such hand (lord) as may be most desirable to them, for me and for Ælflæd, and for the friends for whom she has interceded and I intercede. And for my soul's need, let there be provided in living cattle, as it may be, and also as it may be becoming, and as ye may be willing to give me.

CEÔLWIN. BEFORE DCCCC.V.

Ceólwin cýð on ðis gewríte þæt hi an þæs landes æt Aweltune ðara xv. hida ðæ

Ceolwin makes known by this writing, that she gives the land at Alton, the xv.

hire hlaford hire læfde· ⁊ him man on agene æht gereahte on Ælfredes cynges gewitnesse. Đenne an hio his ðæm hīwum to Wintanceāstre æfter hire dēge into hære beddarn æt ðam bisceopstole· mid swelcan yrfe swelcan hi ðenne to gehagað· on ða gerað ðe hi gemunen hi ⁊ Osmodes saulæ· swa him rihtlic ⁊ cynlic þince· to his gemunde dege· ðæt beoð seofan nihtan ær gangdagan. ⁊ hio he[1] bebot on Godæs naman ⁊ Sancte Petres ðet ða hīwan hit næfre ūtt ne syllan of hira bæddern wið nanan feo· buton hi hit wið oðre land sullan· ðæ him gehændre beo ⁊ behefre. ⁊ hiwan habbað hire behaton ðet hi finden ðet Wulfstan hire broðor sunu hæbbe an hiwissce ægefœles[2] landæs ða wīle ðe hæ libbe.

hides that her lord left her, and it was acquired by him in legal possession, in witness of king Ælfred. She now gives it, after her day, to the convent at Winchester, for their refectory at the episcopal see, with such property as may then be fitting; on the condition that they remember the souls of her and Osmôd, as to them may seem just and becoming, on his commemoration-day, which is seven nights before the Rogations. And she enjoins them, in the names of God and St Peter, that the convent never give it from their refectory for any money, unless they give it for other land which may be more at hand and convenient. And the convent has promised her to settle so that Wulfstân, her brother's son, have a hide of rent-free land as long as he shall live.

IDEM LATINE.

Ceolwen indicat in hac carta quia ipsa concedit terram de Aweltuna, hoc est xv. hidas quas ei vir suus reliquit, et pro qua ei pretium datum fuit sub testimonio Ælfredi regis: has ergo concedit conventui Wintoniæ, post decessum suum, ad refectorium sedis episcopalis, cum tali pecunia quæ tunc competens erit, ea ratione, ut memores sint ejus et animæ Osmodi, sicut illis justum videbitur, ad anniversarium ejus,

[1] Sic MS. [2] ægafoles.

hoc est septimo die ante Rogationes. Ipsa quoque præcipit, in nomine Domini et Sancti Petri, quod conventus idem eandem terram numquam vendat pro aliqua pecunia, nisi forte pro alia terra quæ eis vicinior sit, vel utilior. Idem vero conventus spopondit ei quod procurent Wlfstano, filio fratris sui, quod habeat aliquam hidam liberam quamdiu vivet.

Ðes londes gemæro sindon to Aweltune· Ærest of þam westmæstan æwylle an gerihta upp to ðam ealdan herepaðe be westan Wodnesbeorge· þonne ōn ænne stān æt Ceorlacumbes heafoð· þonne on ænne stān on Woncumb neoþeweardne ís ufeweard hol· þonne ofer Randūne to þæm ealdan dīc on æfen þær liggeþ on oðre healfe an lytel crundol· þonne on þane gemænan garan beūton ðæm dīc· oð þæt eft geð inna þet read geāt· þonne on anne micelne stān æt þera hlinca east heafdum· þonon on oþerne micelne stān on þam wege middan on þære denæ bytnan þe ligged ūtt on Woddes geat· þonne on ænne crundol on þam suð hliðe nioþeweardum· þonne up ofer þa dune ōn ænne þorn stent inne on þem dīc be eastan Ciceling wege· þonne andlang þæs hlinces of Moxes dune on þane ealdan walweg to Weascing wege nioþeweardan ōn þone dīc· þonon

The boundaries of this land at Alton are: First from the westmost spring right up to the old high way to the west of Wanborough; then to a stone at Charlcomb's head; then to a stone down on Woncomb, above which there is a hollow; then over Randon to the old dike, even with which there lies, on the other side, a little crundel; then to the common gore without the dike, until it again goes within the red gate; then to a great stone at the east heads of the links; thence to another great stone on the midway to the bottom of the dell that lies out to Woddes gate; then to a crundel on the south hill downwards; then, up over the down, to a thorn which stands within the dike to the east of Chickeling way; then along the link from Moxes down to the old walway at Washing way, down to the dike; thence to Wigley; thence to a link's head on Beorhtnoth's boundary; thence straight on to on Wicleāge· þonon on anes hlinces heafod on Beorhtnoðes gemære· þonon on gerihto to Ruwan hlince· þonne ⁊lang þæs hlinces to Heaþobrihtting leāge nioþoweardre· þonne ōn anne ealdne holne weg andlang þæs sledes to Ewelforda· þonne andlang þæs broces [be ðam ealden eadenne] eft to þæm æwelle· fram Moxes dune suðeweardre on þa dīc· þonne andlang dīc· ꝥ wið eastan Cealfa mære· þonne ōf þære dīc on þone midmæstan scrippan· þonne on þa wæres leāge ufeweārde· þonne andlang rode on þone litlan garan middeweardne· þonan andlang gewyrpes to herpoðe· þonne to þære dice hyrnan· þonne andlang dīc to Creodan hylle· þonne to herpoðe ongean þa xx. æceras· þonne ōf þæm andlang hærpaðes to Tesan mede· ⁊ se heðfeld eal gemæne·

Rubric. Ceolwenne cweðe of Aweltunæ.

Ruwan link; then along the link down to Heathobrihting lea; then to an old hollow way along the slade to Ewelford; then along the brook [by the old river bed], again to the spring; from Moxes down southward to the ditch; then along the ditch; then to the east of Cealfa mære; then from the ditch to the midmost 'scrippa'; then up to the weir's lea; then along the road to the little gore midward; thence along the bank to the high road; then to the corner of the ditch; then along the ditch to Creoda's hill; then to the high road towards the xx. acres; then from them along the high road to Tesan mead; and the heath field all in common.

Rubric. Ceolwin's bequest of Alton.

WULFGAR. AFTER DCCCC.XXXI.

✠ Ic Wulfgar an þæs landes æt Collingaburnan ofer minne dæg Æffan hiere dæg· ⁊ heo tilige uncer begea sawla þearfe

✠ I Wulfgar give the land at Collingbourn, after my day, to Æffe, for her day; and let her till it for the gemænelice þæron. ⁊ feormige þrie dagas þa Godes þeowas þær min lic reste. on þone gemynddæg. ⁊ selle þam mæssepreoste fif peningas. ⁊ þara oðra ælcum twegen. ⁊ ofer hiere dæg to Winteceastre þam niwan hierede for mine sawle. to habbenne ⁊ to brucenne. ⁊ na of þam mynstre to sellanne. ⁊ ic an þæs landes æt Ingepenne ofer minne dæg Æffan to brucenne ⁊ to bewitanne. ⁊ þæt heo hæbbe ælce gere to þam tune ealra gearwæstma þa þrie dælas. ⁊ þone feorþan to Cynetanbyrig þam Godes þeowum. for mine sawle. ⁊ for mines fæder. ⁊ for mines ieldran fæder. Þonne ofer hiere dæg in to Cynetanbyrig to þære halgan stowe. for Wulfgares sawle þe ic hit in selle. ⁊ for Wulfrices. ⁊ for Wulfheres. þe hit ærest begeat. to habbenne ⁊ to brucenne. ⁊ næfre ut to sellanne. Þonne an ic þæs landes æt Cræft ofer minne dæg Wynsige ⁊ Ælfsige. ⁊ ealles þæs þe ic þæron begite. ⁊ ic an þæs landes æt Denforda ofer minne dæg Æþelstane ⁊ Cynestane. gif hie me oþ ꝥ on ryht gehieraþ. ⁊ ic an þæs landes æt Butermere ofer minne dæg Byrhtsige twegen hida. ⁊

common need of both our souls, and, during three days, supply with food the servants of God where my body may rest, on the commemoration-day; and give to the mass-priest five pence, and to each of the others two; and after her day, to Winchester, to the New monastery, for my soul, to have and to enjoy, and not to be given from the monastery. And I give the land at Inkpen, after my day, to Æffe, to enjoy and to administer; and let her have every year, at the vill, of all the yearly produce the three parts, and the fourth [be given] to God's servants at Kintbury, for my soul, and for my father's, and for my grandfather's. Then, after her day, [let it be given] to the holy place at Kintbury, for my, Wulfgar's, soul, who give it, and for Wulfric's, and for Wulfhere's, who first acquired it, to have and to enjoy, and never to alienate. Then I give the land at Craft, after my day, to Wynsige and Ælfsige, and all which I thereon get. And I give the land at Denford, after my day, to Æthelstân and Kynestân, if they until then duly obey me. And I give the land at But-

Ceolstanes sunum anes· gif hie me oð ðæt on ryht gehieraþ. ⁊ ic cweþe on wordum be Æscmere on minum geongum magum swelce me betst gehieraþ.

Dorso. And ic wille ꝥ Æffe feormige of þæm þrim dælum æt Ingepenne þa Godes þeowas æt Cynetanbyrig· þrie dagas on twelf monþum· ænne dæg for me· oþerne for minne fæder· þriddan for minne ieldran fæder. ⁊ ic an þæs landes æt Hamme Æffan ofer minne dæg· ⁊ heo tilige þæron uncer begea sawla þearfe· ⁊ feormige þrie dagas þa Godes þeowas þær min lic reste· on Eastron· ⁊ ofer hiere dæg in to Winteceastre to þam ealdan hierede to Sc̃e Trinitate· to habbenne ⁊ to brucenne· ⁊ næfre ut to sellanne.

Dorso. Her swutelaþ ꝥ Wulfgar geuþe Hamme in to ealdan mynstre· æfter Æffan dæge hys wifes.

termere, after my day, to Byrhtsige, II. hides; and to Ceolstân's sons one, if they until then duly obey me. And I bequeath, in words, Ashmore to such of my young kinsmen who shall best obey me.

Indorsed. And I will that Æffe supply provisions, from the three parts at Inkpen, to the servants of God at Kintbury, three days in twelve months, one day for me, the second for my father, the third for my grandfather. And I give the land at Ham to Æffe, after my day; and let her till thereon, for the soul's need of both, and, at Easter, supply with provisions, for three days, the servants of God where my body may rest; and after her day to Winchester, to the Old monastery of the Holy Trinity, to have and to enjoy, and never to alienate.

Indorsed. Here is made known that Wulfgar gave Ham to the Old monastery, after the day of Æffe his wife.

ÆTHELGIFU. DCCCC.XLIV.-DCCCC.XLVI.

✠ Ego Eðelgiue aperio domino meo regi, et reginæ dominæ meæ, et omnibus amicis meis, quomodo testamentum meum dispono. Id est, imprimis, domino meo regi xxx. mancusas auri, et duos equos, et omnes canes meos; et dominæ meæ reginæ xxx. mancusas auri, et terram Westwicam; et Sancto Albano terram quæ vocatur Gatesdene, eo tenore ut fruantur ea fratres communiter; et xxx. mancusas auri, et xxx. boves, xx. de Getesdene, et x. de Acersce; et xx. vaccas, x. de Getesdene, et x. de Acersce; et cc.l. oves, et gregem porcorum, et subulcum cum ipsis; et duos ciphos argenteos, et duo cornua, et unum librum, et unam cortinam, et unum bancale, concedo cum consensu domini mei regis. Et illam terram apud Longaforde Elfnoto dies suos, eo tenore ut singulis annis det ad Hiccam pastum trium dierum; et post dies suos supradictam terram. Et Leofwino nepoti meo unam hidam apud Cliftune, et illam dimidiam quam Winemannus habuit; et Elfwoldus terram Mundene dies suos habeat, eo tenore quod dabit annis singulis, in Quadragesima ad Brahcingum sex modios de brais, et ad hoc farinam et pisces, et tandumdem ad Wellingum. Et Leofsinus habeat Standune, et post ipsum Ifwoldus, et post mortem amborum, Sanctus Albanus prædictam terram habeat, pro suis animabus, dominorumque suorum. Et Leofsius terram Offanlege, et omne quod liber docet, et terram Ciwingum, ad porcos ibi nutriendos, eo tenore ut annis singulis, pro firma de istis duabus villis, omnem congregationem Sancti Albani tribus diebus pascat, aut pro firma dabit hoc quod ego testificata sum testimonio optimatum domini mei. Et terram apud Weodune, et pro illa similiter faciat quod testificata sum. Et terram Offanlege dabit filio suo, si de desponsata muliere filium habet; sin autem, dabitur Sancto Albano, præter illam ubi Tatulwus sedet, et Eðelferdus, et Eðelswið, illa dabitur filiæ dominæ suæ Elfgiue, si adhuc vivit; si non, tota Sancto Albano reddatur. Et Alfwoldus medietatem terræ apud Lundoniam habeat; et filius ejus Elfheah medietatem. [Et dabitur] Leofrune terra Watford, et apud Weotune duos homines et octo boves, etc.

✠ Ego Edwardus[1] rex concessi. ✠ Ego Đeodred præsul. ✠ Ego Wulgarus episcopus concessi. ✠ Ego Burgricus episcopus. ✠ Ego Ælfredus episcopus. ✠ Ego Wulfhelmus

[1] Edmundus.

episcopus. ✠ Ego Æðelgarus episcopus. ✠ Ego Coenwaldus episcopus. ✠ Ego Wulfhelmus episcopus. ✠ Ego Cynsius episcopus. ✠ Ego Æðelwaldus episcopus. ✠ Howell subregulus. ✠ Eadgarus etheling. ✠ Wulgarus comes. ✠ Ego Oda archiepiscopus. ✠ Ego Ælfhelgus pontifex. ✠ Ego Ælfricus antistes. ✠ Ego Wulsius episcopus. ✠ Æðelstanus dux. ✠ Æðelwaldus dux. ✠ Æðelmundus dux. ✠ Aðelmus dux. ✠ Æðelstanus dux. ✠ Eadricus dux. ✠ Uhtredus dux. ✠ Scule dux. ✠ Haldene dux.

LEOF ÆTHELWOLD ALDORMAN. DCCCC.XLVI.-DCCCC.LV.

Her geswutelad þæt Eadred cing geuþe þæt land æt Wilig· þa twelf hida· to scrudfultume· þam hirede into Ealdan mynstre.

Leof Æþelwold ealdarman cyþ his leófan cynehlaforde Eadred cynge hu ic wille ymbe þa landare þe ic æt mine hlaforde geearnode. Ærest Gode ⁊ þære halgan stowe æt þam bisceopstole æt Wintanceastre· þam bisceope ⁊ þam hiwum· þæt land æt Wilig· þa twelf hida· to scrudfultume· þæt hi me on heora gebeddredenne hæbben· swa swa ic him to gelyfe. ⁊ þam cinge minne hæregeatwa· feower sweord· ⁊ feower

Here is made known that king Eadred granted the land at Wiley, the twelve hides, to the convent at the Old monastery.

I Leof Athelwold aldorman make known to my royal lord king Eadred how I will with regard to the landed property which I have acquired from my lord. First to God and the holy place at the episcopal see of Winchester, for the bishop and the convent, the land at Wiley, the twelve hides, as a clothing-aid, that they may have me in their prayers, as I trust they will. And to the king my heriots[1]: four swords,

[1] Had these Wills been known to Mr. Hallam, he would not have written that the heriot subsisted in England as early as the reign of Canute; that is, after 1014. See View of the Middle Ages, p. 173, edit. 1855. Cnut appears only to have defined the heriot due from each rank of freemen. Anc. LL. and Inst. p. 177, fol. edit.

spæra. ⁊ feower scyldas. ⁊ feower beagas. twegen on hundtwelftigum mancosun. ⁊ twegen on hundeahtatigum. ⁊ feower hors. ⁊ twa sylfrene fata. ⁊ minum breðer Eadrice þæt land æt Oceburnan. ⁊ æt Æcscesdune. ⁊ æt Cegham. ⁊ æt Wessingatune. ⁊ Æþelstane minæ breðer þet land æt Bradanwætere. ⁊ þet æt Niwantūne. ⁊ Ælfsige mine breðer suna þet land æt Carcel. ⁊ Ælfstanes suna mines broþor þæt land æt Cleran. ⁊ eall þæt yrfe þæ ic hæbbe on lænelendum. þonne wylle ic þæt þæt sie gedeled for mine sawle swa swa ic nu þam freondum sæde þæ ic to spræc.

and four spears, and four shields, and four torques, two of a hundred and twenty mancuses, and two of eighty; four horses, and two silver vessels. And to my brother Eadric the land at Ockbourne, and at Ashton, and at Keyham, and at Wessington. And to Æthelstân my brother the land at Broadwater, and that at Newton. And to Ælfsige, my brother's son, the land at Carcel. And to my brother Ælfstân's son the land at Clere, and all the property which I have in 'lænlands'. Then I will that there be distributed for my soul, as I have now said to the friends to whom I spoke.

BYRHTRIC AND ÆLFSWYTH. DCCCC.L.

✠ Đis is Byrhtrices ⁊ Ælfswyðe his wifes nihsta cwide. þe hi cwædon on Meapaham. on heora maga gewitnesse. ꝥ wæs Wulfstan Ucca. ⁊ Wulfsie his broðor. ⁊ Sired Ælfredes sunu. ⁊ Wulfsie se blaca. ⁊ Wine preost. ⁊ Ælfgar on Meapaham. ⁊ Wulfeh Ordeges sunu. ⁊ Ælfheh his broðor. ⁊ Byrhtwaru Ælfrices laf. ⁊ Bryhtric hyræ mæg. ⁊ Ælfstan bisceop.

✠ This is the last testament of Byrhtric and Ælfswith his wife, which they declared at Meopham, with the witness of their kinsmen: that was, Wulfstân Ucca, and Wulfsie his brother, and Sired Ælfred's son, and Wulfsie the Black, and Wine priest, and Ælfgar of Meopham, and Wulfeh Ordeh's son, and Ælfheh his brother, and Byrhtwaru Ælfric's relict, and

Ærest his kyne hlaforde ænne beah on hundeahtotigan mancysan goldes· ⁊ an handsecs on ealswa miclan· ⁊ feower hors· twa gerædede· ⁊ twa sword gefelsode· ⁊ twegen hafocas· ⁊ ealle his header hundas. ⁊ þære hlæfdian ænne beah on þrittigan mancysan goldes· ⁊ ænne stedan· to forespræce· ꝥ se cwyde standan moste. ⁊ for his sawle ⁊ his yldrena· in Sc̃e Andreæ[2]· twa sulung æt Denetune· ⁊ hio for hire sawle ⁊ hire yldrena· twa æt Langanfelda· ⁊ þider in for hy þrittig mancus goldes· ⁊ ænne sweor beah on XL. mancysan· ⁊ ane cuppan seolfrene· ⁊ healfne bænd gyldennæ· ⁊ ælce geare to heora gemynde· twegra daga feorme of Hæslholte· ⁊ II. of Woðringaberan· ⁊ II. of Bærlingan· ⁊ II. of Hærigeardeshamme. ⁊ to Cristes circan LX. mancys goldes· XXX. þam biscope· XXX. þam hirode· ⁊ ænne sweorbeah on LXXX. mancys· ⁊ twa cuppan seolfrene· ⁊ ꝥ land æt Meapaham. ⁊ to Sc̃e Augustine þrittig mancys goldes· ⁊ twa cuppan seolfrene· ⁊ healfne bænd gyldenne. ⁊ ꝥ land æt

Byrhtric her kinsman, and bishop Ælfstân.

First to his royal lord one torque of eighty mancuses of gold, and one hand-seax of as much, and four horses, two caparisoned, and two belted swords, and two hawks, and all his tall-deer hounds. And to the lady, one torque of thirty mancuses of gold, and one steed[1], for her mediation that the will might stand. And for his soul and his parents', two sulungs at Denton to St Andrew's[2]; and she, for her soul and her parents', two at Longfield, and thereto, for her thirty mancuses of gold, and one neck-torque of XL. mancuses, and one silver cup, and half a golden band; and every year, on their commemoration, provision for two days from Hazleholt, and II. from Wathringbury, and II. from Birling, and II. from Harrietsham. And to Christchurch LX. mancuses of gold, XXX. to the bishop, XXX. to the convent; and one neck-torque of LXXX. mancuses, and two silver cups, and the land at Meopham. And to St Augustine's thirty mancuses of gold, and two silver cups, and half a golden band. And to

[1] equum emissarium.

[2] At Rochester.

Dærentan Byrhtwara hire dæg· ⁊ æfter hire dæge into Sc̃e Andreæ· for unc ⁊ uncre yldran. ⁊ Bærlingas Wulfehe· ⁊ he selle x. hund pænega into Sc̃e Andreæ· for unc ⁊ uncre yldran. ⁊ Wulfsie Woþringanbyras innon ꝥ gecynde. ⁊ Sirede Hæslholt innon ꝥ gecynde. ⁊ Wulfege· ⁊ Ælfege his breðer Herigeardeshamme innon ꝥ gecynde· Wulfege ꝥ inland· ⁊ Ælfege ꝥ utland. ⁊ Wulfstane Uccan Wolcnesstede innon ꝥ gecynde· ⁊ an handsecs on þrim pundan. ⁊ þa tyn hyda on Strættune into þæm mynstre to Wolcnesstede. ⁊ ꝥ land æt Fealcnaham· æfter Byrhwara dæge· into Sc̃e Andreæ· for Ælfric hire hlaford ⁊ his yldran· swa heora cwide wæs. ⁊ Bromleah· æfter Brihtwara dæge· into Sc̃e Andrea· swa Ælfric hire hlaford hit becwæð· for hine ⁊ his yldran. ⁊ Snodingcland eac into Sc̃e Andrea· æfter hire dæge· swa Ælfere hit becwæð Ælfrices fæder· ⁊ he seoððan· on gewitnesse Eadgife þære hlæfdian· ⁊ Odan arcebisceopes· ⁊ Ælfeges Ælfstanes suna· ⁊ Ælfrices his broðor· ⁊ Ælfnoðes Pilian· ⁊ Godwines æt Fecham· ⁊ Eadrices æt Ho· ⁊ Ælfsies preostes on Crog-

Byrhtwaru, the land at Darenth for her day; and after her day, to St Andrew's, for us (two) and our parents. And Birling to Wulfeh; and let him give x. hundred pence to St Andrew's, for us and our parents. And to Wulfsige, Wothringbury, within that generation. And to Sired, Hazleholt, within that generation. And to Wulfeh, and Ælfeh his brother, Harrietsham, within that generation, to Wulfeh the inland, and to Ælfeh the outland. And to Wulfstân Ucca, Wolcnesstede, within that generation; and one hand-seax of three pounds. And the ten hides at Stratton to the monastery at Wolcnesstede. And the land at Fawkham, after Byrhtwaru's day, to St Andrew's, for Ælfric her lord and his parents, according to their testament. And Bromley, after Byrhtwaru's day, to St Andrew's, as Ælfric her lord bequeathed it, for him and his parents. And Snodland also to St Andrew's, after her day, as Ælfere, Ælfric's father, bequeathed it, and he afterwards, with the witness of Eadgifu the lady, and archbishop Oda, and Ælfeh Ælfstân's son, and Ælfric his brother, and Ælf-dæne. ⁊ Wulfstane LX. mancos goldes to dælanne for unc ⁊ uncre yldran· ⁊ oðer swilc Wulfsige to dælanne· ⁊ hæbbe heom wið God gemæne· gif hy hit ne don. ⁊ Wulfsige Tydiceseg· ⁊ þa boc innon ꝥ gecynde· ⁊ II. spuran on III. pundan. ⁊ ic bidde· for Godes lufan· minne leofan hlaford· ꝥ he ne þafige ꝥ ænig man uncerne cwide awænde· ⁊ ic bidde ealle Godes freond ꝥ hi þarto filstan. Hæbbe wið God gemæne þe hit brece· ⁊ God him sy symle milde þe hit healdan wille.

noth Pilia, and Godwine of Fetcham, and Eadric of Hoo, and Ælfsi the priest at Croydon. And to Wulfstân LX. mancuses of gold, to distribute for us (two) and our parents; and another such to Wulfsige to distribute; and be it between them and God if they do it not. And to Wulfsige, Tydiceseg, and the charters, within that generation; and two spurs of III. pounds. And I pray, for the love of God, my dear lord, that he will not allow any man to pervert this our testament; and I pray all God's friends that they give support thereto. Let him have to account to God who violates it; and may God be ever merciful to him who will observe it.

IDEM LATINE.

DE DANITUNA, ET DE LANGAFELDA, ET DE DÆRENTE, ET DE FALCHEHAM, ET DE SNODILANDE, ET DE BROMLEGA.

✠ Hæc est ultima commendatio, sive rerum suarum pro Deo distributio, quam fecerunt simul Brihtricus et Ælfsuuitha uxor ejus, appropinquante die mortis eorum, in villa quæ vocatur Meapeham, testibus his præsentibus de propriis parentibus suis, videlicet, Uulfstano cognomine Ucca, et Uulfsio fratre ejus, et Siredo filio Ælfredi, et Uulfsio cognomine Blaca, et Wine presbytero, et Ælfgaro in Meapaham, et Wulfeg filio Ordegi, et Ælfego fratre ejus, et Brihtwara Ælfrici relicta, et Bryhtrico consanguineo, et Ælfstano episcopo.

Primum naturali domino suo regi armillam auream, quæ habebat octoginta mancas auri, et unum handseax tantundem auri habentem; et quattuor equos, duos ex eis optime faleratos; et duos gladios optime adornatos, et duos accipitres, et omnes canes suos venaticos. Et dominæ suæ reginæ armillam unam quæ habebat triginta mancas auri, et unum equum emissarium, eo pacto ut adjuvaret eum apud regem, quatinus ista commendatio sive distributio rerum suarum firma et stabilis esset post mortem suam. Et pro anima sua et omnium antiquorum suorum, dedit ecclesiæ Sancti Andreæ duas sullingas terræ in Danituna. Et ipsa Ælfsuuitha similiter dedit eidem ecclesiæ Sancti Andreæ, pro anima sua et omnium parentum suorum, duas sullingas terræ quæ vocantur Langafelda. Et præter hæc dedit eidem ecclesiæ xxx. mancas auri, et unam torquem auream de xl. mancis auri, et unam cuppam argenteam, et dimidiam vittam capitis auream. Et omni anno, in diebus anniversariorum suorum, ordinaverunt servitoribus ecclesiæ Sancti Andreæ, firmam duorum dierum, de terra illa quæ vocatur Hæsleholt, et duorum dierum de Uuotringeberia, et duorum dierum de Berlinges, et duorum dierum de Herigetesham. Et ecclesiæ Christi Cantuariæ dederunt sexaginta mancas auri, xxx. archiepiscopo, xxx. conventui fratrum, et unam torquem auream, quæ habebat octoginta mancas auri, et duas cuppas argenteas, et terram illam quæ vocatur Meapeham. Et ecclesiæ Sancti Augustini dederunt xxx. mancas auri, et duas cuppas argenteas, et dimidiam vittam auream. Et terram illam quæ vocatur Dærente dederunt Brihtuuara, in diebus vitæ ejus tantum, et post mortem ejus ecclesiæ Sancti Andreæ, pro se et antecessoribus suis. Et Berlinges dederunt cuidam nomine Wulfego, tali pacto, ut ipse daret inde, omni anno, decies centum denarios, pro se et pro antecessoribus suis, ecclesiæ Sancti Andreæ. Et cuidam Wulfsio dederunt Wotryngebyri, sibi suæ progeniei in hereditatem futuram. Et Siredo Hæselholt. Et Wulfego et Ælfego fratri suo Hergetesham, in hereditatem futuram. Et cuidam Wulfstano cognomine Ucca terram quæ vocatur Wolcnestede. Et illas x. hydas terræ quæ sunt in Strættuna dederunt monasterio de Wolcnestede. Et post mortem Bryhtware, terram de Falckeham dederunt ecclesiæ Sancti Andreæ, et Bromlegam similiter, post mortem ejus, sicut Ælfricus, dominus ejus, dederat eam eidem ecclesiæ. Similiter dederunt et Snodilande eidem ecclesiæ, post mortem

Brihtware, sicut Ælferus filius Ælfrici eum primus dederat ipsi ecclesiæ, et ipse postea, per testimonium Eadgyue reginæ, et Odonis archiepiscopi, et Ælfegi filii Ælfstani, et Ælfrici fratris ejus, et Ælfnoði cognomine Pilia, et Goduuini de Fecham, et Eadrici de Ho, et Ælfsi presbyteri de Croindene. Et cuidam Wulfstano dederunt LX. mancas auri, dividere pauperibus pro animabus suis. Et cuidam Wulfsio tantundem, dividere pro animabus eorum: et cum Deo agant judicium, nisi fideliter fecerint. Ego Brihtricus, pro Dei amore, rogo dominum meum dulcissimum, ut ista nostra donatio inviolabilis permaneat, nec eam a quoquo violari permittat. Similiter rogamus et petimus omnes amicos Dei, quatinus nobis adjutores in hac re existant. Et quicunque eam aliquatenus violare presumpserint, ab ipso Domino Christo judice æternum recipiant judicium. Et qui eam inviolabilem conservaverint, Deum sibi sentiant affore propicium.

ÆLFGAR. ABOUT DCCCC.LVIII.

✠ In nomine Domini. Ðis is Ælfgares quide. Ðat is erst þat ic an mine louerd tueye suerde fetelsade and tueye bege· ayðer of fifti mancusas goldes· and þre stedes· and þre scheldes· and þre speren. And me kidde Ðeodred bisscop and Edric alderman· þa ic selde mine louerd þat suerd· þat Eadmund king me selde on hundtuelftian mancusas goldes· and four pund silueres on þan fetelse· þat ic moste ben mine quides wirde. And ic nefre forwrouht ne habbe on Godes

✠ In nomine Domini. This is Ælfgar's testament. That is first, that I give my lord two belted swords, and two torques, each of fifty mancuses of gold, and three steeds, and three shields, and three spears. And bishop Theodred and aldorman Eadric informed me, when I gave my lord the sword that king Eadmund gave me of a hundred and twenty mancuses of gold, and four pounds of silver on the belt, that I might be worthy of my testament. And I never, with God's wit-

witnesse wid mine louerd· buten it so mote. And ic an Aðelflede mine douhter þe lond at Cokefeld and at Ditton· and þat at Lauenham ouer min day· on þe red þat heo be þe bet for mine soule· ⁊ hire moder soule· ⁊ for hire broðer soule· ⁊ for hire seluen. And þanne ouer ure aldre day ic an þat lond at Cokefeld into Beodricheswrðe to Seynt Eadmundes stowe. And ic wille þat Aþelfled unne ouer hire day þe londes at Ditton into suilke halegen stowe suilk hire redlikest þinge· for ure aldre soule. And ouer ure aldre day ic an þat lond at Lauenham mine douhter childe· gif þat God wille þat heo ani haued· buten Aðelfled her wille him his unnen. And gif heo non ne habbe· gange it into Stok for ure aldre soule. And ic an þat lond at Babingþirne Aðelflede mine douhter· and after hire day mine oðer douhter hire day· and ouer hire boðre day· mine douhter berne· gif heo bern habbe. And gif heo bern ne habbe· þanne go it into Sancte Marie stowe at Berkynge· for ure aldre soule. And ic an þat lond at Illeyge mine ginger douhter hire day·

ness, have done wrong towards my lord, that it may not so be. And I give to Æthelflæd, my daughter, the land at Cokefield, and at Ditton, and that at Lavenham, after my day, on the condition that she be the better[1] for my soul, and her mother's soul, and for her brother's soul, and for herself. And then, after our parents' day, I give the land at Cokefield to St Eadmund's place at Bedericksworth. And I will that Æthelflæd give, after her day, the land at Ditton to such holy place as may to her seem most advisable, for our parents' souls. And after our parents' day, I give the land at Lavenham to my daughter's child, if God wills that she have any; unless Æthelflæd will previously give it to him. And if she have none, let it go to Stoke, for our parents' souls. And I give the land at Babbingthorn to Æthelflæd, my daughter; and after her day, to my second daughter, for her day; and after the day of them both, to my daughter's child, if she have a child. And if she have no child, then let it go to St Mary's place at Barking, for the souls of our

[1] the more fervent or zealous.

⁊ ouer hire day Berðnoðe his day· gif he leng libbe þanne heo. Gif heo bern habben· þanne an ic it hem· gif heo non ne habbeð· þanne an ic it Aðelfled mine douhter ouer here day· and after hire day into Cristes kirke at Caunterbiri· þen hirde to brice. And þe lond at Colne and at Tigan ic an min gingere douhter· ⁊ ouer hire day· gif heo bern habbe· hire bern· and gif heo ne habbe· bequeðe it Bernoðe his day· and ouer his day into Stok for ure aldre soule. And ic an þat lond at Piltendon and at Mereseye into Stok. And ic an þat Aðelfled bruke þe lond þer wile þe hire lef beð· one raða heo it on rihte helde· and on þe red þat heo do þan hirde so wel so heo best may into Stok for mine soule and for ure aldre. And ic an þat lond at Grenstede into Stok for mine soule· and for Aðelwardes· ⁊ for Wifwiðe. And ic [an] Aðelfled þere brice wile hire lif beð· on þe red þat heo do for ða soule so wel so heo best may· nu his me God uðe ⁊ min lauerd. And ic an þat lond at Tidweldington Ælfwold ouer mine day þe he formige ilke ihere þen hird at Paulesbiri for ure

parents. And I give the land at Illey to my younger daughter, for her day; and after her day, to Berthnoth, for his day, if he live longer than she. If they have children, then I give it to them; if they have none, then I give it to Æthelflæd my daughter, after their day; and after her day, to Christchurch at Canterbury, for the use of the convent. And the land at Colne, and at Tye, I give to my younger daughter; and, after her day, if she have children, to her children; and if she have none, I bequeath it to Berthnoth, for his day; and after his day, to Stoke, for the souls of our parents. And I give the land at Peldon, and at Mersey, to Stoke. And I grant that Æthelflæd enjoy the land there, while it shall be agreeable to her, on condition that she hold it righteously, and on condition that she do as she best can to the convent at Stoke, for my soul and for our parents'. And I give the land at Greenstead to Stoke, for my soul, and for Æthelweard's, and for Wifwith's. And I give to Æthelflæd the usufruct for her life, on the condition that she do for the souls so well as she best aldre soule. And ic an þat lond at Cotham Berðnoðe and mine gingere douhter here day· and after here day wende lond into Mereseye Aðelfled mine douhter. And ic an þat wudelond at Aisfeld into Stok also Eakild self it her bouhte. And ic [an] mine moder þat lond at Ryssebroc· gif heo leng liuid þan hic· þanne after unker boðer day· ic an hit Winelme· gif heo Aðelfled on richte hirð. And ic wille bidden suilc louerd so þanne beð· for Godes luuen and for alle hise halegen· werken min bern þat he werken· þat he nefre ne mugen forwerken mine quide· ðe ic for mine soule cueden habbe. And gif hit wo awende· habbe him wid God gemæne and wid þe holi saintes þe ic it to becueðen habbe· þat he it nefre ne bete buten on helle wite se þis quide awende· boten it me seluen wende er min ende. And ic Aðelgar an an hide lond þes ðe Aeulf hauede be hundtuelti acren· ateo so he wille.

can, now God and my lord have given it me. And I give the land at Tidweldington to Alfwold, after my day, [on the condition] that he, every year, give entertainment to the convent at Paulsbury, for our parents' souls. And I give the land at Cotham to Berthnoth and my younger daughter, for their day; and after their day, let the land revert to Mersey, for Æthelflæd my daughter. And I give the woodland at Ashfield to Stoke, as Eakild himself ere bought it. And I give to my mother the land at Rushbrook, if she live longer than I; then after the day of us both, I give it to Winelm, if she rightly obey Æthelflæd. And I will pray such lord as shall then be, for love of God, and for all his saints, that, do my children as they may, they never fordo my bequest which I have bequeathed for my soul. And if any one avert it, let it be between him and God, and with the holy saints to whom I have bequeathed it; so that he never atone, save in hell-torment, who shall avert this bequest; except that I myself alter it ere my end. And I give to Æthelgar a hide of land which Æulf had, of a hundred and twenty acres; dispose of it as he will.

ÆTHELWYRD. DCCCC.LVIII.

✠ Đis is Æðelwẏrdæs cwide· mid geþæhte Odan ærcebiscopæs ⁊ þæs hioredæs æt Cristæs cirican. Đæt is þonne þæt Æðelwyrd bruce þæs landæs on Geocham his dæg on freodome· be Godes leafe· ⁊ be þæs ærcebiscopæs· ⁊ be þæs heoredæs· þonne yftær his dæge Eadric· gif he libbe· his dæg· wið þon gofole þe hit gecwæden is· þæt sint v. pund· ⁊ ælce gære ane dæg feorme in hiowum· þæt is þonne XL. sæstra ealað· LX. hlafa· weðær ⁊ flicce· ⁊ an hriðres læuw· II. cesas· IIII· hænfugulas· ⁊ v. pænningas to beðe[2]. ⁊ þis sio gelæst to Sc̃e Michaelæs tide. ⁊ bio he ælces wites wyrðe. ⁊ gif hwilc forwyrht man hiowan gesæce· bio se þingad swa hit medlic sio be þæs geltes meðe. Gif hit þonne gebærige þet Æðel-wyrd læng libbe ðonne Ead-ric· þonne fo Æðelgyfu to· wið þan ilcan gofole ðe hit hier beufan gecwædæn is· hire dæg. Gif hit þonne geberige þæt Æðelwyrd læng libbe ðonne Eadric oððe Æðelgyfu· ⁊ he þa unætnessa abidan

✠ This is Æthelwyrd's testament, with the counsel of archbishop Oda and the convent at Christchurch. That, then, is, that Æthelwyrd enjoy the land at Ickham for his day in freedom, by God's leave, and the archbishop's, and the convent's; then after his day, Eadric, if he live, for his day, in consideration of the rent which is here said: that is, v. pounds, and every year one day's provision to the convent; that is, then, XL. sesters of ale, LX. loaves, a wether, and a flitch, and one ox's liver[1], II. cheeses, IV. hen-fowls, and v. pence 'to beðe'[2]. And be this performed at St Michael's tide. And be he entitled to every 'wite'. And if any culprit seek the convent, let him find mediation as may be moderate, according to the degree of the crime. But if it happen that Æthelwyrd live longer than Eadric, then let Æthelgyfu succeed, in consideration of the same rent which is here above said, for her day. But if it happen

[1] For lifer? Low Ger. *leuer*.

[2] This expression I am unable to explain. In the poem of Judith (Anal. A. S. p. 146) it occurs with a slight variation—to behðe.

scel· agefe man land in yfter his dæge in mid him selfum for hine ⁊ for ðam þe him land fram com.

that Æthelwyrd live longer than Eadric or Æthelgyfu, and he has to abide that affliction, let the land be given in with himself[1], for himself and for those from whom the land came to him.

Ðisæs is Oda ærcebisscop gewita· ⁊ Byrhtere mæssepreost· Cænwig mæssepr̃.· Wealdred mæs̃.prẽ.· Sigefreð diac̃.· Osweald diac̃.· Freðegod diac̃.· Sigered diac̃.· Heared diac̃.· Sired pr̃.· Byrhtmund· Eadsige· Eadelm· Byrhtsige· Æðelm· Byrhtsige· Byrhtwig· Liofric· Sielm· Wulfred· Cænric· Eadweard.

Of this is Oda archbishop witness, and Byrhtere mass-priest, Cænwig mass-priest, Wealdred mass-priest, Sigefred deacon, Oswald deacon, Frethegod deacon, Sigered deacon, Heared deacon, Sired priest, Byrhtmund, Eadsige, Eadhelm, Byrhtsige, Æthelm, Byrhtsige, Byrhtwig, Liofric, Sielm, Wulfred, Cænric, Eadward.

Ðisæs wes gewita Eadelm abbod æt Sc̃e Augustine· ⁊ Byrhtsige diac̃.· Eorlebyrht mæs̃.prẽ.· Roðin mæs̃.prẽ.· Bærhtram mæs̃.prẽ.· Beornmund prẽ.· ⁊ ða III. Ælfstanas· Æðelweald· Eadmund· Wenelm· Cynsige· Eadric· Liofing· Eadsige· Wulfelm· Sigefreð· Liofric· Liofstan· Eadstan· Eadmund· . . . . . stãn cyninges þægen· Byrhtric· Wihtgar· Wulfstãn· ⁊ ða III. geferscipas innan burhwara· ⁊ utan burhwara· ⁊ micle mættan.

Of this were witness, Eadelm abbot of St Augustine's, and Byrhtsige deacon, Eorlebyrht mass-priest, Rothin mass-priest, Bærhtram mass-priest, Beornmund priest, and the III. Ælfstâns, Æthelweald, Eadmund, Wenelm, Cynsige, Eadric, Liofing, Eadsige, Wulfelm, Sigefred, Liofric, Liofstân, Eadstân, Eadmund, ... stân king's thane, Byrhtric, Wihtgar, Wulfstân, and the III. fellowships, of inner townsmen and outer townsmen, and many of the commonalty.

[Ðeos is] seo gerednæs þe

[This is] the covenant that

[1] his body.

Eadric hæfð wið þane hired to Cristes cirican. Ðæt is ðonne þæt Eadric gesealde þam hirede to gerisenum v. pund· twa þæm ældæstum· and þreo eallum hirede· an þæt gerad· ðæt he hebbe land mid fulre unnan ælde ⁊ gegeðe· mid eallan þan netwyrðan þingum· læssan ⁊ maran· ðe to þæm lande belimppað· unbesprecæn wið æghwylcne lifes man.

Eadric has with the brotherhood at Christchurch. That then is, that Eadric should give the brotherhood, as a gratuity, v. pounds, two to the principals, and three to all the brotherhood, on the condition that he have the land with the full consent of old and young, with all the useful things, less and greater, which appertain thereto, uncontested, against every living man.

A LATER COPY OF THE ABOVE.

✠ Ðis is Aþelwirdes quide· mid Odes archibiscopes and þe hiredes at Cristeschereche yrede. Þet is þanne þet Aþelwird bruke þas londes on Ycham his day on uredome· be Godes ylaue· and by þes archebiscopes· and by þes hirdes· þanne hefter his daye Eadrich· gef he libbe· hit bruke his day· wiht þen gauele þe hit ycueþen is· þet sind· v. pund· and eche gere enne dey ferme into þan higen· þet his þanne· XL. sestres eleþ· LX. loues· weþes and fliththe· and ane weþere shap· II. cheses· IIII. henfugeles· and v. paneges to beþe· and þis by ylest to Seyntes Micheles tide· and by he eches wites worþe· and gef hwilche woworþe man þa hygen hit ofsake· be se þinged suo hit meþlic sy by þes geltes meþe. Gif hit þanne yberege þet Eþelwird leng libbe þanne Eadrich· þanne fo Eþelgife to wiht þan ylcke gauele þe hier buuem yqueþen is hire dey. Gef hit þænne ybyrige þet Eþelwird leng libbe þanne Edrich oþer Eþelgiue· and he þo unnetnesse ybyde· þanne ageue he land and boc efter his dage in mid him seluen uor hine and for þo þe· him land uram com.

Ðises is Ode archebiscop ywytnesse and Brigthere messeprest· and þo þri yuershipes· binne burg and bute· þet is al se hird at Cristescheriche· and Seynt Austynes· and at Seynt Gregories· and manie oþre yhodede and liauuede of binne burg and bute.

BISHOP THEODRED.

✠ In nomine Domini nostri Ihesu Christi. Ic Ðeodred Lundeneware biscop wille bequeðen mine quiden mines erfes þe ic begeten habbe ⁊ get bigete. Godes þances ⁊ his halegen. for mine soule ⁊ for min louerde þat ic under bigeat. ⁊ for mine eldrene. and for alle þe mannes soule þe ic foreþingiæ. and ic almesne underfongen habbe. ⁊ me sie rithlike for to bidden. Ðat is þan erst ꝥ he an his louerd his heregete. þat is þanne tua hund marcas arede goldes. ⁊ tua cuppes siluerene. ⁊ four hors so ic best habbe. ⁊ to suerde so ic best habbe. ⁊ four schelda. ⁊ four spere. ⁊ þat lond þat ic habbe at Dukeswrðe. ⁊ þat lond þat ic habbe at Illyngtone. ⁊ þat lond þat ic habbe at Earmingtone. And ic an Eadgiue fifti marcas redes goldes. And into Sancte Paules kirke mine to beste messehaclon ðe hic habbe. mid alle ðe þinge ðe þereto birið. mid calice ⁊ on cuppe. and mine best massebóc. ⁊ alle mine reliques þe ic best habbe into Paules kirke. And ic an þat land at Cic into Seynte Paules kirke ðen

✠ In nomine Domini nostri Jhesu Christi. I Theodred, bishop of the Londoners, will bequeath my bequest of my property, which I have acquired and yet may acquire, by the grace of God and his saints, for my soul, and for my lord, under whom I acquired it, and for my parents, and for the souls of all the men, for whom I intercede, and of whom I have received alms, and who righteously pray for me. That, then, is first, that he gives his lord his heriot, which then is, two hundred marks of red gold, and two silver cups, and four horses, the best I have, and two swords, the best I have, and four shields, and four spears, and the land which I have at Dukesworth, and the land which I have at Illington, and the land which I have at Ermington. And I give to Eadgifu fifty marks of red gold. And to St Paul's church the two best mass-hackles which I have, with all things which thereto belong, with chalice and one cup; and my best mass-book, and all my relics, the best I have, to St Paul's church. And hewen to bedlonde· mid al ðe þeron stant· buten þe men ðe þer aren· fre men alle for mine soule. And ic an þat lond at Suðereye· mid alle ðe fiscode ðe þerto bireð· ðen hewen into Sancte Paules kirke· and frie men ðo men for ðe bisscopes soule. ⁊ Đeodred biscop an þat lond at Tillingham into Sancte Paules kirke þo hewen to hare· and fre men ðo men for mine soule. And ic an þat lond at Dunemowe ouer myne day into Saynte Paules kirke ðen hewen. And ic an þat lond at Mendham Osgote mine sustres sune ouer mine day· buten ic will þat se minstre and hide londes at Myndham to þere kirke. And ic an þat lond at Scotford ⁊ Mydicaham into Myndham kirke ðo Godes hewen. And ic an Osgot þat lond at Silham ⁊ at Isestede ⁊ at Chikeringe ⁊ at Æysfeld ⁊ at Wrtinham· ⁊ alle þe smale londe þat ðereto bereð. And ic an þat lond at Horham ⁊ at Elyngtone into Hoxne into Seynte Æðelbrichtes kirke ðen Godes hewen. And ic an þat lond at Luðinglond Offe mine sustres sune ⁊ his broðer· ⁊ fre men þo men halue· ⁊ at Mindham also for þe bisscopes

I give the land at Chiche to St Paul's church, as table land for the convent, with all that thereon stands; except the men who are there, let all be freed for my soul. And I give the land in Surrey, with all the fishing thereto belonging, to Saint Paul's church; and let the men be freed for the bishop's soul. And bishop Theodred gives the land at Tillingham to St Paul's church, in property to the convent; and let the men be freed for my soul. And I give the land at Dunmow, after my day, to the convent at St Paul's. And I give the land at Mendham to Osgot, my sister's son, after my day; except that I will that the monastery and the hide of land at Mendham [go] to the church. And I give the land at Shotford and at Mydicaham to Mendham church, for God's servants. And I give to Osgot the land at Silham, and at Isestede, and at Chikering, and at Aysfield, and at Wurtinham, and all the small lands that thereto belong. And I give the land at Horham and at Ellington to St Æthelbriht's church at Hoxne, for God's servants. And I give the land at Luthsoule. And ic an Osgote mine mey Eadulfes sune þat lond at Bertune ⁊ at Bucham ⁊ at Pakenham. And ic an þat lond at Newetune ⁊ at Horningges hæð· ⁊ at Ikewrð· ⁊ at Wepstede into Seynt Eadmundes kirke· þen Godes hewen to are· for Ðeodred biscopes soule. And ic an þat lond at Waldringfeld Osgote mine sustres sune· ⁊ min hage þat ic binnin Gypeswich bouhte. And ic [an] Wlstan þat lond at Wrtham so it stant. And ic an into eueri bisscopes stole fif pund to delen for mine soule. And ic an þen archebiscop fif markes goldes. And ic an þat men dele at mine biscopriche binnen Lundene ⁊ buten Lundene x.ʳ pund for mine soule. And ic an at Hoxne at mine biscopriche þat men dele x. pund for mine soule. ⁊ ic wille þat men nieme þat erfe þat at Hoxne stand þat ic þerto bigeten habbe· ⁊ dēle it man on to· half into þe minstre[1]· ⁊ dēle for mine soule. And lete men stonden so mikel so ic þeron fond. And fre men ðo men alle for mine soule. ⁊ ic wille þat men lete stonden at Lundenbyri so mikel so ic þeron fond·

ingland to Offa, my sister's son, and his brother; and let half the men be freed; and also at Mendham, for the bishop's soul. And I give to Osgot my kinsman, Eadulf's son, the land at Barton, and at Buckenham, and at Pakenham. And I give the land at Newton, and at Horningsheath, and at Ickworth, and at Whepstead, to St Eadmund's church, in property to God's servants, for bishop Theodred's soul. And I give the land at Waldingfield to Osgot, my sister's son; and my vill in Ipswich which I bought. And I give to Wulstân the land at Wortham, as it stands. And I give to every bishop's see five pounds to distribute for my soul. And I give to the archbishop five marks of gold. And I give to be distributed at my bishopric, within London and without London, x. pounds for my soul. And I give at Hoxne, at my bishopric, x. pounds to be distributed for my soul. And I will that the property which stands at Hoxne, which I have thereto acquired, be taken and divided into two, half to the monastery, and half for my soul.

[1] After 'minstre' some words are evidently omitted.

⁊ nime þat ic þerto bigat. ⁊ dēle on to. half into þe minstre. ⁊ half for mine soule. ⁊ fre men alle þo men. ⁊ do men þat ilke at Wunemannedune ⁊ on Sceon. And let men stonden at Fullenham so it nu stant. buten hwe[1] mine manne fre wille. ⁊ on Denesige let stonden so mikel so ic þeron fond. ⁊ dēle it man on to. half into þe minstre ⁊ half for mine soule. And ic an into Glastingbiri v. pund for mine soule. And ic an Ðeodred min wite massehakele þe ic on Pauie bouhte. ⁊ al þat þerto bireð. ⁊ simbel calice. ⁊ þere messeboc ðe Gosebricht me biquað. And ic an Ordgar þere gewele massehakele ðe ic on Pauie bouhte. ⁊ þat þerto bireð. And ic an Gundwine þer oðer gewele massehakele þat is ungerenad. and þat ðe þerto bireð. And ic [an] Spratacke þe rede messehakele ⁊ al þat þe þerto bireð. And wo so mine cuyde oftē. God him oftē heueneriches. buten he it er his end it bete.

And let stand as much as I found thereon. And let all the men be freed for my soul. And I will that so much be let stand at London as I found therein; and let be taken what I thereto acquired, and divided into two, half to the monastery, and half for my soul; and let all the men be freed; and let the same be done at Wunemannedan, and at Sheen. And let it stand at Fulham as it now stands, unless the convent will free my men. And in Dengeye let stand as much as I found therein, and let it be divided in two, half to the monastery, and half for my soul. And I give to Glastonbury v. pounds for my soul. And I give to Theodred my white mass-hackel, which I bought in Pavia, and all that thereto belongs, and a festival chalice, and the mass-book which Gosebriht bequeathed to me. And I give to Ordgar the yellow mass-hackel, which I bought in Pavia, and what thereto belongs. And I give to Gunwine the other mass-hackel, which is without ornament, and what thereto belongs. And I give to Spratack the red mass-hackel, and all that thereto belongs. And whoso abstracts from my testament, may God abstract from him the kingdom of heaven, unless, ere his end, he make atonement.

[1] hewen?

ALFHILD.

ISTUD EST CYROGRAPHUM ALFILDE COMITISSE, UXORIS ALFWOLDI COMITIS, QUOMODO IN FATA CONCESSURA RESIGNAVIT ECCLESIE RAMESENSI RIPTONAM ET WENINTONAM ET ELINTONAM, ET BYTHERNAM.

In nomine Domini Dei summi. Ego Alfild notum facio omnibus amicis meis quomodo disposui de rebus et possessionibus meis, quas vir meus Alfwoldus comes, frater Æilwini aldermanni, mihi et liberis meis concessit. Imprimis igitur concedo Deo, et Sancte Marie, et Sancto Benedicto Ramesie, terram de Ryptona, et terram de Wenintona, et terram de Elintona, sicut prædictus vir meus Alfwoldus eas adhuc vivens viva voce eidem ecclesie concessit. Concedo etiam Ædnotho, filio filie mee, ut si fratres Ramesie eum in monachum suscipere voluerint, terram de Bytherna simul cum eo cedat Ramesie in possessionem: quod si noluerint, nichilominus concedo eandem terram præfate ecclesie, pro anime mee salute. Concedo præterea Almaro, capellano meo, terram de Cloptona in diebus suis libere tenendam; post dies vero ejus remaneat simul cum ceteris terris ecclesie Ramesensi. Rogo autem Deum Omnipotentem ut quicunque, vel parentum meorum vel hominum ceterorum, contra hoc venire presumpserit, vel quicquam horum inmutare, iram Judicis eterni cum reprobis angelis incurrat, nisi vivens delictum suum digne emendaverit. Amen.

ÆTHERIC. DCCCC.LXX.

✠ Her cyð Æðeric on þissum gewrite hwam he geann· ofor his dæig· þæra æhta ðe him God alæned hæfð. Ðæt is ærest sona· minum hlaforde syxti mancusa goldes· ⁊ mines swyrdes mid fetele· ⁊ þarto twa hors· ⁊ twa targan· ⁊ twegen francan. And	✠ Here, in this writing, Ætheric makes known to whom he gives, after his day, the possessions which God has lent him. That is immediately first, to my lord sixty mancuses of gold, and my sword with belt, and thereto two horses, and two targets,

ic geann Leofwinne minan wife ealles þæs ðe ic læfe hire dæig. ⁊ ofor hire dæg gange ꝥ land on Boccinge into Cristes circean. þam hirede. for uncera saule. ⁊ for mines fæder þe hit ǽr begeat. eall buton ânre hide. ic gean into þære cyrcean þam preoste þe þar Gode þeowað. And ic geann ðæs landes æt Regene be westan into Sc̃e Paule. þam bisceope to geleohtenne. ⁊ þaron Godes folce cristendõm to dǽlenne. ⁊ ĩc geann þarto twegra hida þe Eadric gafelað ælce geare mid healfum punde ⁊ mid anre garan[1]. And ic geann be eastan stræte ægðer ge wudas ge feldas Ælfstâne bisceope into Coppanforda. ⁊ þæs heges on Glæsne. And ic geann þæs landes æt Norðho. healf into Sc̃e Gregorie on Suðbyrig. ⁊ healf into Sc̃e Eadmunde on Bedericeswyrðe. Nu bidde ic þone bisceop Ælfstân ꝥ he amundige mine lafe ⁊ þa þincg þe ic hire læfe. ⁊ gif him God lifes geunne lencg þonne unc. ꝥ he gefultumige ꝥ ælc ðara þinga stande ðe ic gecweden hæbbe.

and two 'francas'. And I give to Leofwyn my wife all that I leave, for her day; and after her day, let the land at Bocking go to the convent at Christchurch, for our souls, and for my father's, who before acquired it, all save one hide, which I give to the church, for the priest who there serves God. And I give the land to the west of Rayne to St Paul's, to light the bishop, and therein to impart Christianity to God's folk; and I give thereto two hides which Eadric rents every year for half a pound, together with agricultural work[1]. And I give, on the east of the road, both woods and fields, to bishop Ælfstân for Copford, and the hedge at Glæsen. And I give of the land at Northhoo, half to St Gregory at Sudbury, and half to St Edmund's at Bedericksworth. Now I pray the bishop Ælfstân that he protect my relict, and the things which I leave to her; and if God grant him a longer life than us, that he aid that all the things may stand which I have bequeathed.

[1] mid anre garan. This cannot be correct, gara being masculine: I therefore adopt the later reading, although far from confident as to the sense or integrity of either text. See next page.

A LATER COPY OF THE PRECEDING.

✠ Her kiðeð Aðeric on þis write hwam he an ouer his day þe ahte þe him God alent haued. Þat is sone erst· mine louerd syxti markes goldes ⁊ mine suerdes mid fetele· ⁊ þerto tueye hors ⁊ tueye targen ⁊ tue frangen. And ic an Lefwine mine wife al þat ic leue hire day· and ouer hire day go þat lond at Bockinge into Cristes kirke þen hirde for unker boðere soule· ⁊ for mine fader þe it her begat· al buten an hide ic an into þe kirke þe prest þe þer God þeweð. ⁊ ic an þat lond at Regene be westen strete into Seynte Paule· þe bisscop to lihten· and þeron Godes folke cristendom to delen. And ic an þerto þe tueye hide þe Edric gauelið ilke iher mid half pund ⁊ mid acre garen. And ic an be esten strete· buðe wudes ⁊ feldes Alfstane bisscop into Coppingforde· ⁊ þe heges on Glesene. And ic an þat lond at Norðhoo half into Seynte Gregorie on Subyr̃. and half into Seynt Eadmunde on Bidricheswrð. Nu bidde ic þene bisscop Alfstan þat he amunigie mine laue[1]· ⁊ þat þing þat ic her leue· and gif him God liues unne leng þan unc· þat he fultume þat alle þinge stonde þe ic queðen habbe.

BRIHTRIC GRIM. DCCCC.LXIV.-DCCCC.LXXX.

Her is geswutulad þet Brichtrīc Grīm gean þes landes æt Rimtune intō ealdan mynstre æfter his dege· mid þere hide þe he syþþan begeāt into þan lande· ⁊ agyfþ þa bōc ðe Eadred cyning hīm gebōcode into þam ealdan mynstre to þere ealdan bǣc þe Æþestan cyning ær gebocode· on þet gerad þet he hæbbe þone bryce þes landes swa lange

Here is made known, that Brihtric Grim gives the land at Rempton to the Old monastery, after his day, with the hide that he afterwards acquired to that land, and gives up the charter that king Eadred chartered to him, to the Old monastery, in addition to the charter which king Æthelstân previously chartered; on the condition that he have the

[1] MS. louerd.

swa his tyma sy. ⁊ gange syððan into þære stōwe swa gewered swa hit stande. mīd mete ⁊ mid mannum. ⁊ mid ælcum þīngan. his sawle to frōfre. ⁊ þyses īs to ywitnesse. Dunstan arcebisceop. ⁊ Aþelwold bisceop. ⁊ Ælfstan bisceop. ⁊ Æþelgar abbod. ⁊ se hired on Glestingabyrig. ⁊ þa twegen hiredas. on ealdan mynstre ⁊ on nīwan mynstre. on Wintanceastre.

usufruct of the land as long as his time may be; and let it afterwards go to that place so provided as it stands, with meat and with men, and with everything, for his soul's comfort. And of this are to witness: Dunstân archbishop, and Athelwold bishop, and Ælfstân bishop, and Æthelgar abbot, and the convent of Glastonbury, and the two convents at the Old monastery and at the New monastery in Winchester.

ÆLFLÆD'S WILL, RECITING QUEEN ÆTHELFLÆD'S[1]. CIRCA DCCCC.LXXII.

✠ Ðis is Æþelflæde cwyde. ꝥ is ærest. ꝥ ic gean minum hlaforde þes landes æt Lamburnan. ⁊ þæs æt Ceolsige. ⁊ æt Readingan. ⁊ feower beagas on twam hund mancys goldes. ⁊ IIII. pellas. ⁊ IIII. cuppan. ⁊ IIII. bleda. ⁊ IIII. hors. ⁊ ic bidde minne leofan hlaford. for Godes lufan. ꝥ min cwyde standan mote. ⁊ ic nan oðer nebbe geworht on Godes gewitnesse. ⁊ ic gean þæs landes æt Domarhame into Glæstingabyrig for Ædmundes kinges sawle. ⁊ for Eadgares cinges. ⁊ for mire sawle. ⁊ ic gean þes landes

✠ This is Æthelflæd's testament. That is first, that I give to my lord the land at Lambourn, and that at Cholsey, and at Reading, and four torques of two hundred mancuses of gold, and IV. palls, and IV. cups, and IV. bowls, and IV. horses. And I pray my dear lord, for love of God, that my testament may stand; and I have made no other, in God's witness. And I give the land at Damerham to Glastonbury, for king Eadmund's soul, and for king Eadgar's, and for my soul. And I give the land at Ham

[1] Wife of King Eadmund I. Sax. Chron. a. 925.

æt Hamme into Cristes cyrcan æt Cantwarebyrig· for Eadmundes cinges sawle· ⁊ for mire sawle. ⁊ ic gean þes landes æt Wudaham Beorhtnoðe ealdormen ⁊ mire swuster hyre dæg· ⁊ ofer hire deg into Sc̃a Marian cyrcan æt Byorcingan. ⁊ ic gean þes landes æt Hedham Bæorhtnoðæ ealdormen ⁊ mire swuster hæora dæg· ⁊ æfter hæora dæge into Paulusbyrig æt Lundænæ to bisceophamæ. ⁊ ic gean þæs landæs æt Dictunæ into Ylig to Sc̃æ Æðeldryð ⁊ to hire geswustran. ⁊ ic gean þara twegra landa æt Cohhanfeldæa ⁊ æt Ceorlesweorþe Bærorhtnoðæ æaldermen ⁊ miræ swust̃ hire dæg· ⁊ ofer hire dæg into Sc̃æ Eadmundes stowe to Bydericeswyrðe. ⁊ ic gean þæs landes æt Fingringahõ Bæorhtnoðe æaldermæn ⁊ mire swust̃. hiræ dæg· ⁊ ofer hire dæg into Sc̃æ Pætres cyrcan æt Myresige. ⁊ ic gean þæs landes æt Polstede Bæorhtnoðe æaldormæn ⁊ mire swust̃. hire deg· ⁊ ofor hira dæg into Stocy. ⁊ ic gæan þæs landæs æt Hwifersce into Stocy ofer minnæ deg. ⁊ ic gean Bæorhtnoðæ æaldermen ⁊ mire swust̃. þæs landes æt Strætforda hiræ dæg· ⁊ ofer hire dæg ic

to Christchurch at Canterbury, for king Eadmund's soul, and for my soul. And I give the land at Woodham to Beorhtnoth aldorman and my sister, for her day, and after her day, to St Mary's church at Barking. And I give the land at Hadham to Beorhtnoth aldorman and my sister, for their day, and after their day, to Paulsbury at London, for an episcopal dwelling. And I give the land at Ditton to St Ætheldryth and to her sisters. And I give the two lands at Cockfield and at Charlesworth to Beorhtnoth aldorman and to my sister, for her day, and after her day, to St Eadmund's place at Bedericksworth. And I give the land at Fingringhoe to Beorhtnoth aldorman and my sister, for her day, and after her day, to S[t] Peter's church at Mersey. And I give the land at Polstead to Beorhtnoth aldorman and to my sister, for her day, and after her day, to Stoke. And I give the land at Wiversh to Stoke, after my day. And I give to Beorhtnoth aldorman and my sister the land at Stratford, for her day, and after her day, I give it to Stoke. And I will that his gæan into Stocy. ⁊ ic willæ ꝥ Lauanham ga into Stoce ofær þes æaldermannes dæg· ⁊ mire swust̃. ⁊ ic gean þæs landes æt Byligesdynæ into Stocy ofter þæs æaldermannes dæg· ⁊ mire swust̃. ⁊ ic gean þara landa æt Peltandune· ⁊ æt Myresige· ⁊ æt Grenstede into Stocy ofer minnæ dæg· ⁊ ofer Bæorhtnoðes æaldormannæs· ⁊ ofær mire swust̃. ⁊ ic gean þæs landes æt Ylmesæton Bæorhtnoðe æaldormen ⁊ mire swust̃. hira dæg· ⁊ ofær hira dæg ic his gæan Æadmundæ. ⁊ ic an þæræ are hide æt Þorpæ into Hedlæge· for mire sawle ⁊ for mira eldrena ofer . . . . ⁊ ic gean ðæra x. hida æt Wicforda Sibrihte minum mægæ ofer minne dæg. ⁊ ic gean Æcgwinæ minum geræfan þara IIII. hida æt Hedham ofer minne dæg· swa hit on æald dagum gestōd. ⁊ ic gean Brihtwolde minum cnihtæ þara twegra hida on Dunninclande ofer minnæ dæg. ⁊ ic an Alfwolde minum preoste twegra hida on Dunninglande ofær minnæ dæg. ⁊ ic gean Æþælmære minum præoste twægra hida on Dunninglande ofær minne dæg. ⁊ ic gæan Ælfgæate minum megæ twegra hida on

Lavenham go to Stoke, after the aldorman's and my sister's day. And I give the land at Bilson, after the aldorman's and my sister's day. And I give the lands at Peldon, and at Mersey, and at Greenstead to Stoke, after my day, and after Beorhtnoth aldorman's, and after my sister's. And I give the land at Elmsett to Beorhtnoth aldorman and my sister, for their day, and after their day, I give it to Eadmund. And I give the one hide at Thorp to Hadleigh, for my soul and for my parents', after * * * * * * *. And I give the x. hides at Wickford to Sibriht my kinsman, after my day. And I give to Ægwine my reeve the IV. hides at Hadham, after my day, as it stood in old days. And I give to Brihtwold my page the two hides in Donyland, after my day. And I give to Alfwold my priest two hides in Donyland, after my day. And I give to Æthelmær my priest two hides in Donyland, after my day. And I give to Ælfgeat my kinsman two hides in Donyland, after my day. And I give the land at Waldingfield to Crawe my kinswoman, after my day. And I will that half

Dunninglande ofar minnæ dæg. ⁊ ic gæan ðæs landæs æt Wæaldingafælda Crawa mira magan ouær minnæ dæg. ⁊ ic wille ꝥ man frigæ hæalue mine men on elcum tune· for mine sawlæ· ⁊ ꝥ man dele æal healf ꝥ yrue ꝥ ic hæbbæ on ælcum tune· for mire sawle.

my men be freed, in every vill, for my soul, and that half of all the cattle which I have in every vill be distributed for my soul.

Ælflæd gæswytelaþ on þis gewrite hu hæo wile habban gefadad hiræ æhta for Gode ⁊ for worldæ. Ærest ꝥ ic an minum hlaforde þara VIII. landa· æfter minum dege· ꝥ is erest æt Douercortæ· ⁊ æt Fulanpette· ⁊ æt Ælesforde· ⁊ æt Stanwegun· ⁊ æt Byrætune· ⁊ æt Læxadyne· ⁊ æt Ylmesætun· ⁊ æt Bucyshealæ· ⁊ twægra beha on twera punda gewihte· ⁊ twa sopcuppan· ⁊ an sæolfran fæt. ⁊ þæ leof æadmodlice bidde· for Godes luuan· ⁊ for mines hlafordæs sawle lufan· ⁊ for minræ swystor sawlæ lufan· ꝥ þu amundie þa halgan stowæ et Stocæ þe mine yldran on restaþ· ⁊ þa are þæ hi þiderin sæadon a to freogon Godæs rihte. ꝥ is þonne ꝥ ic gean æalswa mine yldran his er geuþan· ꝥ is þonne ꝥ lond æt Stoce into þæræ halagan stowæ· ⁊ æal ꝥ ꝥ þær to tune gehyrð· ⁊ þonæ wuda æt

Ælflæd makes known by this writing how she will have disposed of her property, before God and before the world. First, that I give to my lord, after my day, these VIII. lands: that is first, at Dovercourt, and at Fulpit, and at Aylesford, and at Stanway, and at Berdon, and at Latchingdon, and at Elmsett, and at Buxhall, and two torques of two pounds weight, and two sop-cups, and one silver vessel. And thee, dear, I humbly pray, for love of God, and for love of my lord's soul, and for love of my sister's soul, that thou protect the holy place at Stoke, in which my parents rest, and the property which they gave in thither, for the perpetual freedom of God's rights. That is then, that I give, as my parents before gave it, the land at Stoke to the holy place, and all that which there in the vill be-

Hæþfælda þæ min swistur geuþæ· ⁊ mine yldran. Þonne synd þis þa land þæ minæ yldran þærto bæcwædon· ofær minre swystor dæg· ⁊ ofær minne· ꝥ is ðonne Stredfordæ· ⁊ Fresantun· ⁊ Wiswyþetun· ⁊ Lauanham· ⁊ Byliesdyne· ⁊ Polstyde· ⁊ Wifermyrsc· ⁊ Grænstyde· ⁊ Peltandune· ⁊ Myræsegæ· ⁊ ꝥ wudæland æt Totham· þæ min fæder geuþæ into Myresiæ· ⁊ Colne· ⁊ Tigan. Þonne synd þis þa land þe minæ yldran becwædon into oþrum halgum stowum. ꝥ is þonne· into Cantwarabyrig to Cristæs circan· þan hired to bræce· þes landes æt Illanlege· ⁊ into Paules mynstre into Lundene þæs landes æt Hedham to biscophame· ⁊ þæs landes æt Tidwoldingtune· þan hirede to brece into Paules mynstre· ⁊ into Beorcingan· þan hirede to brece· þes landes æt Bobbingþyrnan. ⁊ ic gean Ælfþræðe minæs hlauordæs medder Wuduhamæs æftær minum dæge· ⁊ æfter hiræ dege gange hit into Sc̄a Marian stowæ into Beorcingan· æal swa hit stænt mid mæte ⁊ mid mannum. ⁊ ic gæan into Sc̄æ Eadmunde þara twegra landa Ceorlesweorþe ⁊ Cochanfelde· þam hirede to brece·

longs, and the wood at Heathfield, which my sister gave, and my parents. Now these are the lands which my parents thereto bequeathed, after my sister's day, and after mine: that is then, Stratford, and Freston, and Wiston, and Lavenham, and Bilson, and Polstead, and Wyvermarsh, and Greenstead, and Peldon, and Mersey, and the woodland at Totham which my father gave to Mersey, and Colne, and Tye. Now these are the lands which my parents bequeathed to other holy places. That is then, to Christchurch at Canterbury, for the use of the convent, the land at Illey; and to St Paul's monastery in London, the land at Hadham, for an episcopal vill; and the land at Tidwoldington, for the use of the convent, to St Paul's monastery; and to Barking, for the use of the convent, the land at Babbingthorn. And I give to Ælfthryth, my lord's mother, Woodham, after my day; and after her day let it go to St Mary's place at Barking, as it stands, with meat and with men. And I give to St Eadmund's the two lands, Charlesworth and Cockfield, for the use of the convent, as my parents ere gave them;

æalswa mine yldran his er geuþan. ⁊ þæs landes æt Hnyddinge æftær Crawan dæge miræ magan. ⁊ ic gæan into Myresie æfter minum dæge ealswa min hlaford ⁊ min swester geuþan. ꝥ is Fingringaho. ⁊ þara six hida þæ ꝥ mynstær on stent. ⁊ ic gæan. æftær Crawan dege. þes landes æt Wealdingafelda into Suðbyrig to Sc̃æ Gregoriæ ealswa min swestar hit er foræwyrde. ⁊ ic gean into Elig Sc̃æ Petre. ⁊ Sc̃æ Æþeldryþe. ⁊ Sc̃e Wihtburhe. ⁊ Sc̃æ Sexburhe. ⁊ Sc̃e Eormenhilde. þer mines hlafordes lichoma rest. þara þreo landa þe wit buta geheotan Gode ⁊ his halga. ꝥ is æt Rettendune. þe wæs min morgangyfu. ⁊ æt Sægham. ⁊ æt Dictune. ealswa min hlaford ⁊ min swæstar his er geuþan. ⁊ þaræ anre hide æt Cæfle þe min swystar begeat. ⁊ þes beahges gemacan þe man sæalde minum hlaforde to sawlescæatte. ⁊ ic gean Æðelmere æaldormen þes landes æt Lellinge ofer mine dæg. mid mete ⁊ mid mannum. æalswa hit stent. on þet gerad ꝥ he beo on minum life min fulla freond ⁊ forespreca. ⁊ mira manna. ⁊ æfter minum dege beo þara halgan stowe ⁊ þeræ

and the land at Nedging, after the day of Crawe my kinswoman. And I give to Mersey, after my day, as my lord and my sister gave: that is Fingringhoe, and the six hides on which the monastery stands. And I give, after Crawe's day, the land at Waldingfield to St Gregory's at Sudbury, as my sister before arranged it. And I give to St Peter's, and to St Ætheldryth, and to St Wihtburh, and to St Sexburh, and to St Eormenhild, at Ely, where my lord's body rests, the three lands, which we both promised to God and his saint: that is, at Rettendon, which was my morning-gift, and at Soham, and at Ditton, as my lord and my sister before gave them; and the one hide at Cheveley, which my sister acquired; and the fellow of the torque which was given to my lord as soul-shot. And I give to Æthelmær aldorman the land at Lelling, after my day, with meat and with men, all as it stands, on the condition that he be in my lifetime the full friend and advocate of me and my men; and, after my day, be the full friend and advocate of the holy place and the property at are ful freond ⁊ forespræca æt Stocæ. þe mine eldran on restaþ. ⁊ ic gean þes landes æt Lissingtune Æðelmere mines . . . . mid mete ⁊ mid mannum. ealswa hit stent. ⁊ hine eadmodlice bidde ꝥ he min fulla freond ⁊ mundiend beo on minum dege. ⁊ efter minum dege gefelste ꝥ min cwide ⁊ mira yldran standan mote.

Ðis synd þa landmearca to Byligesdyne. Of ða burnan æt Humelcyrre. fram Humelcyrre [ꝥ hit cymð] to Heregeres heafode. fram Heregeres heafode. æfter ðam ealdan hege. to ðære grene æc. þonne forð ꝥ hit cymð to þare stanstræte. of þare stanstræte ⁊lang scrybbe ꝥ hit cymð to Acantune. fram Acyntune ꝥ hit cymð to Rigindune. fram Rigindune æft to þara burnan. ⁊ þære is landes fif hida.

Ðis sind þa landgemæra to Hwifermirsce ⁊ to Polstede. Of Loppandyne to Scelfleage. fram leage to Mercyl. ⁊lang Mercyle into Sture. ⁊lang Sture to Leofmannes gemære. ⁊lang Leofmannes gæmære to Amulburnan. fram Amulburnan to Norðfelda. ðonne forð to Bindhæcce. fram Bindhæcce to Tudanhæcce. fram

Stoke, in which my parents rest. And I give the land at Liston to Æthelmær my * * * * * * with meat and with men, all as it stands, and humbly pray him that he be my full friend and protector in my day, and after my day give his aid that my testament and my parents' may stand.

These are the land-boundaries at Bilson. From the bourn to Humelcyrre; from Humelcyrre [till it comes] to Heregeres head; from Heregeres head, along the old hedge, to the green oak; then on till it comes to the stone road; from the stone road along the shrubbery till it comes to Acton; from Acton till it comes to Rigdon; from Rigdon again to the bourn. And there are five hides of land.

These are the land-boundaries at Wyvermarsh and at Polstead. From Lopton to Shelley; from Shelley to Mercyl; along Mercyl to the Stour; along the Stour to Leofman's boundary; along Leofman's boundary to Amulburn; from Amulburn to Northfield; then on to Bindhatch; from Bindhatch to

Tudanhæcce to Giddincgforda· fram Giddingforda to Huntstede· fram Huntstede to Hwitincgho· fram Hwitingho to Wudemannes tune· fram Wudemannes tune to Cæresege gæmære· fram Cæresige gemære to Hædleage gemære· fram Hædleage gæmære to Hligham gemære· fram Hligham gemære eft to Loppandyne. To Hwifræme . . . . landes . . . . . .

Dorso. Ælflæd. Ceorlesworðe ⁊ Cokefelda.

Tudanhatch; from Tudanhatch to Gidding; from Gidding to Huntstead; from Huntstead to Whittinghoo; from Whittinghoo to Woodmanston; from Woodmanston to Kersey boundary; from Kersey boundary to Hadleigh boundary; from Hadleigh boundary to Ligham boundary; from Ligham boundary again to Lopton * * * * * * * * * * * * * * *

Indorsed. Ælflæd. Charlesworth and Cockfield.

ÆLFHEAH ALDORMAN. DCCCC.LXV.-DCCCC.LXXV.

Her is geswutelod an ðis gewrite hu Ælfheah ealdorman his cwidæ gecwæðen hæfð be his cynehlafordæs geþafuncge. Þæt is þonnæ æræst· þæt he geān his Drihtne· for his sawlæ þearfæ· þæs landæs æt Ællændune· ⁊ þæs æt Crundelom to ealdan mynstære to Winticeastræ· and þæra twæntiga hida æt Ceorlatunæ into Mealdælmæsbyrig· and þæra fiftyna hida æt Suðtune into Baðan. And he geān his cynehlafordæ þæra hundtwæntiga hida æt Wyrðæ· and þæs landæs æt Coccham· and æt

Here is made known, by this writing, how Ælfeah aldorman has declared his testament, with the permission of his royal lord. That then is first, that he gives to his Lord, for his soul's need, the land at Ellendon, and that at Crondall, to the Old monastery at Winchester; and the twenty hides at Charlton to Malmesbury, and the fifteen hides at Sutton to Bath. And he gives to his royal lord the twenty hides at Worth, and the land at Cookham, and at Thatcham, and at Chelsworth, and at Inglesham, and at þæcham. and æt Ceolæswyrðæ. and æt Incgenæsham. and æt Ægelesbyrig. and æt Wændofron. and þreo hund mancusa goldes. and annæ dīcs an þrym pundom. and anæ sōppcuppan an þrym pundan. ⁊ an handsex. and þæræ lecge[1] is hundeahtati mancussa goldæs. ⁊ seax swurð. and seax hors mid geredan. and swa fæla spæra and scylda. And he geān Ælfrið ðæs cyninges wīfæ his gefæðeran þæs landæs æt Scyræburnan ealswa hit stænt. and þam yldran æþælingæ þæs cyngæs suna and hiræ. þritiga mancussa goldæs and anæs swurdæs. and þam gincgran ðæs landes æt Wolcnæsstedæ. And he gean Ælfhære his breðær þæs landæs æt Færndunæ. and æt Ealdincburnan. and Godwinæ his suna þæs æt Tudincgatunæ. and Ælfwerdæ æt Wyritunæ. and Æþelwerdæ his mege æt Wicuman. and Ælfwine his swustur suna þæs æt Froxafelda. Þonnæ an ic Ælfsiþæ minon wifæ. gyf heo leng beoð þonne ic. and it swa gehylt swa ic hiræ truwan to hæbbe. ealra þara oðæra landa þæ ic læfæ. And heo þanne gæornlicæ of þam God

Aylesbury, and at Wendover; and three hundred mancuses of gold, and one dish of three pounds, and one sop-cup of three pounds, and one hand-seax; and in the hilt there are eighty mancuses of gold; and six swords, and six horses with trappings, and as many spears and shields. And he gives to Ælfthryth, the king's wife, his gossip, the land at Sherborne, as it stands; and to the elder ætheling, the king's son and hers, thirty mancuses of gold and one sword; and to the younger the land at Wolcnesstede. And he gives to Ælfhere, his brother, the land at Farndon, and at Aldingbourn; and to Godwine, his son, that at Teddington; and to Ælfweard, [that] at Wyritun; and to Æthelweard, his kinsman, [that] at Wicuman; and to Ælfwine, his sister's son, that at Froxfield. Then I give to Ælfsith, my wife, if she shall live longer than I, and so conducts herself as I trust she will, all the other lands which I leave. And let her earnestly thank God therefore, and pray earnestly for our souls; and let her enjoy the land at Batcomb

[1] From leccan, *prehendere*?

geþæncæ· and for uncre sawle geornlicæ beo· and brucæ heo þæs landæs æt Batancumbæ hyræ dæg· and æfter hire dæge ga hit an Ælfwærdes hand uncres suna· gif hæ lifæs beo· gyf hæ næ beo fon mine broðorn to þa hwilæ þæ hi beon· and æfter hyra dege ga into Glæstingabyrig for urnæ fædær· and for uræ modor· and for us eallæ. And ic wullan þæt man gefreogen ælcne witeþeowne man on ælcum þæra landæ þæ ic minon freondon bæcwedden hæbbæ. And þisseræ geþafuncga þæ sæ cyning geuþæ is to gewitnæssæ Ælfþryþ þæs cynincges wif· and Aþelwold bisceop· ⁊ Ælfhære ealdorman· ⁊ Æþelwine ealdorman· ⁊ Ælfwinæ· ⁊ Æscwig abbod.

for her day; and after her day, let it go into the hand of Ælfweard, our son, if he be living; if he be not, let my brothers succeed to it, as long as they live; and after their day, let it go to Glastonbury, for our father, and for our mother, and for us all. And I will that every penal serf be freed on each of the lands that I have bequeathed to my friends. And of this permission which the king has granted me, are to witness Ælfthryth, the king's wife, and Athelwold bishop, and Ælfhere aldorman, and Æthelwine aldorman, and Ælfwine, and Æscwig abbot.

WULFWARU.

✠ Ic Wulfwaru bidde minne leofan hlaford Æðelred kyning him to ælmyssan· ꝥ ic mote beon mines cwydes wyrðe. Ic kyðe þe leof her on þisum gewrite hwæs ic geann into Baðum· to Sc̃e Petres mynstre· for mine earman sawle· ⁊ for minra yldrena ðe me min ar of com·

✠ I Wulfwaru pray my dear lord king Æthelred in charity, that I may be worthy of my testament. I make known to thee, dear, here, by this writing, what I give to St Peter's monastery in Bath, for my poor soul and for my parents', from whom my property and my possessions

⁊ mine æhta. ꝥ is ðonne ꝥ ic geann þæder into þære halgan stowe anes beages is on sextigum mancussum goldes· ⁊ ânre blede is on þriddan healfon punde· ⁊ twega gyldenra roda· ⁊ anes mæssereafes mid eallum ðam ðe þærto gebyreð· ⁊ ânes hricghrægles þæs selestan ðe ic hæbbe· ⁊ ânes beddreafes mid wahhryfte ⁊ mid hopp-scytan· ⁊ mid eallum ðam ðe þærto gebyreð. ⁊ ic geann Ælfere abbode ðæs landes æt Ferscesforda· mid mete ⁊ mid mannum· ⁊ mid ealre tylðe swa ðærto getilod bið. ⁊ ic geann Wulfmære minum yldran suna ðæs landes æt Clatfordtune· mid mete ⁊ mid mannum· ⁊ mid eallre tilðe· ⁊ ðæs landes æt Cumtune· mid mete ⁊ mid mannum· ⁊ mid ealre tilðe. ⁊ ðæs landes æt Budancumbe ic geann him healfes· mid mete ⁊ mid mannum· ⁊ mid ealre tilðe· healf ic his geann Alfware minre gyngran dehter· mid mete ⁊ mid mannum· ⁊ mid eallre tilðe· ⁊ dælon hi þæt heafodbotl him betweonan swa rihte

came to me. That then is, that I give thither, to the holy place, one torque of sixty mancuses of gold, and one bowl of two pounds and a half, and two golden roods, and one mass-robe with all which thereto belongs, and one dorsal[1], the best I have, and one bed-furniture, with wall-hanging and with cover-let, and with all which thereto belongs. And I give to abbot Ælfere the land at Freshford, with meat and with men, and with all the tilth which shall be thereon produced. And I give to Wulfmær, my elder son, the land at Claverton, with meat and with men, and with all the tilth; and the land at Compton, with meat and with men, and with all the tilth. And of the land at Budcombe I give him half, with meat and with men, and with all the tilth; half of it I give to Alfwaru, my younger daughter, with meat and with men, and with all the tilth; and let them divide the chief dwelling between them, as they most justly can, so that each of them

[1] At p. 429 I have rendered this word by *mantle*, but I since find it thus explained: "manteau très riche d'ornemens, qui n'étoit porté que par les gens de haute condition." Roquefort, *voce* Dossal. A dorsal is also a wall-hanging of tapestry, used chiefly in the church, at the back of the stalls.

swa hi rihtlicost magon· ꝥ heora ægðer his gelice micel habbon. And Ælfwine minum gyngran suna ic geann ðes landes æt Leage· mid mete ⁊ mid mannum· ⁊ mid eallre tilðe· and ðes landes æt Healhtune· mid mete ⁊ mid mannum· ⁊ mid eallre tilðe· ⁊ ðes landes æt Hocgestune· mid mete ⁊ mid mannum· ⁊ mid eallre tilðe· ⁊ þrittiga mancussa goldes. ⁊ ic geann Godan minre yldran dehter ðes landes æt Wunfrod· mid mete ⁊ mid mannum· ⁊ mid eallre tilðe· ⁊ twegea cuppena on feower pundum· ⁊ ânes bendes on þritigum mancussum goldes· ⁊ twegea preonas· ⁊ ânes wîfscrudes ealles. And Alfware minre gyngran dehter ic geann ealles ðæs wîfscrudes þe ðer to lafe bið. And Wulfmære minum suna· ⁊ Ælfwine minum oðrum suna· ⁊ Alfware minre dehter· heora þreora ælcum· ic geann twegea cuppena on godum feo. And ic geann Wulfmære minum suna ânes heallwahriftes· ⁊ anes beddreafes. Ælfwine minum oðrum suna ic geann anes heallreafes· ⁊ ânes burreafes· mid beodreafe· ⁊ mid eallum hræglum swa þærto gebyreð. And ic geann

may have equally much of it. And to Ælfwine, my younger son, I give the land at Leigh, with meat and with men, and with all the tilth, and the land at Holton, with meat and with men, and with all the tilth, and the land at Hoxton, with meat and with men, and with all the tilth; and thirty mancuses of gold. And I give to Gode, my elder daughter, the land at Windford, with meat and with men, and with all the tilth, and two cups of four pounds, and one band of thirty mancuses of gold, and two brooches, and one female attire complete. And to Alfwaru, my younger daughter, I give all the female attire that shall be left. And to Wulfmær, my son, and Ælfwine, my second son, and Alfwaru, my daughter, to each of these three, I give two cups of good price. And I give to Wulfmær, my son, one hall-wall-hanging and one bed-furniture. To Ælfwine, my second son, I give one hall-hanging, and one chamber-hanging, with table-covering, and with all the cloths which thereto belong. And I give to my four pages, Ælmær, and Ælfwerd, and minum feower cnihtum· Ælmære· ⁊ Ælfwerde· ⁊ Wulfrice· ⁊ Wulfstāne· ānes bendes on twentigum mancussum goldes. And ic geann eallum minum hired wīfmannum to gemanum ānes gōdes casteneres[1] wel gerenodes. And ic wylle ꝥ ðа ðe to minre are fon ꝥ hi fedon twentig freotmanna· tyne be eastan· ⁊ tyne be westan. And æfre ælce geare ealle gemænelice ane feorme into Baðum· swa gōde swa hi bezte þurhteon magon· to swylcre tide swylce heom eallum þince ꝥ hi bezt ⁊ gerisenlicost hi forðbringan magon. Swylc heora swylce þis gelæste· hæbbe he Godes milze ⁊ mine· and swylc heora swylce ðis gelæstan nelle· hæbbe he hit him wið þone Hehstan gemæne· ꝥ is se soða God· ðe ealle gesceafta gesceop ⁊ geworhte.

Wulfric, and Wulfstân, one band of twenty mancuses of gold. And I give to all my household women in common one good chest, well supplied. And I will that those who succeed to my property, feed twenty freedmen, ten in the east, and ten in the west. And ever, in every year, all in common, with one refection in Bath, as good as they best can supply it, at such time as may seem to them all that they can best and most conveniently accomplish it. Such of them as shall perform this, may he have God's mercy and mine; and such of them as will not perform it, may he have to account with the Highest, that is the true God, who created and wrought all creatures.

ÆRNKETEL AND WULFRÛN.

Ego Ærnketel et Wlfron uxor mea Æthelredo regi domino nostro, et omnibus suis de Eboraco et de Notingeham notum facimus nos concessisse, et præsenti cyrographo confirmasse Deo, et Sancte Marie, et Sancto Benedicto de Rameseia, post dies nostros, terram nostram de Hikelinge, et terram de Kinildetune, cum firma et servitio, sicut habetur in dominio nostro. Volumus autem ut post dies nostros corpora nostra

[1] Ohg. chastanâri, *arca*, *capsa*.

ibidem, si Deo placuerit, sepulta requiescant; et ubicunque alter nostrum vitam finierit, fratres Ramesie venientes cum custamento, tam suo quam amicorum nostrorum, corpus defuncti Ramesiam deferant tumulandum. Et ego Ærnketel volo quod in precium sepulture mee et anime salutem, proveniant ecclesie Ramesensi xv^{cim} libre de argento et auro et catallis, que die defunctionis mee apud me contigerit inveniri: pro salute vero anime præfate uxoris mee et corporis sepultura, remanebit eidem ecclesie terra de Lochamtona cum catallis omnibus quæ in ea invenientur. Ego autem Wlfroun singulis annis vite mee, ad festum Sancti Benedicti, quod est in estate, x. mittas de brasio, et v. de grut, et v. mittas farine triticee, et VIII. pernas, et XVI. caseos, et duas vaccas pingues de terra mea Hikelinge, pro respectu decerno eidem ecclesie procurari; in Capite vero Quadragesime VIII. isicios. Quicunque ergo hanc donationem infringere presumpserit vel permutare, animadversionis eterne in die judicii coram Deo reus existat, nisi condigna penitencia temeritatem suam correxerit. Nec liceat cuiquam episcopo vel monacho has terras pro auro vel argento permutare, set sint semper in possessione ecclesie cui eas per hoc cyrographum studuimus confirmare.

WULFGYFU.

In nomine Domini. Ego Wlfgiua comitissa omnibus notum facio hoc quod Omnipotenti Deo concedere volo post dies meos pro anima mea. Villam, scilicet, de Bramcestria do Deo et Sancto Benedicto Ramesie: hoc volo ut firmiter stet, et a nullo hominum immutetur. Hoc scriptum fuit in tribus partibus divisum, quarum una remansit in manibus Athelstani episcopi, alteram mecum retinui, tertiam optuli Ramesie. Deus optimus custodiat omnes quicumque hoc custodire voluerint; et qui hoc inmutare attemptaverit, Deus illum ad justiciam et emendacionem revocet. Amen.

ÆTHELGYFU.

Ego Æthelgiua comitissa do et concedo ecclesie Ramesensi, ad honorem Dei et Sancti Benedicti, et ad anime mee subsidium sempiternum, terram meam de Stowe et de Brunne, ita libere et quiete possidendam sicut ego ipsa eam unquam liberius et quiecius possedi; et novum molendinum, et unam marcam auri, cujus medietas in usus monasterii necessarios cedat; de altera vero medietate refectio fratribus procuretur. Do etiam duos cyphos argenteos de XII. marcis ad pondus Hustingie Londonensis, ad serviendum fratribus in refectorio, quatinus dum in eis potus edentibus fratribus ministratur, memoria mei eorum cordibus arctius inculcetur. Estote, fratres karissimi, memores mei erga eum cujus gratia indigeo: Deus autem sit nobis propicius; et ego vobis fida soror ero quamdiu duraverit tempus meum.

WYNFLÆD. ABOUT DCCCC.XCV.

✠ Wynflæd cyð hu hio wile ymbe þæt hio hæfð ofer hyre dæg. Hio becwið into cyrcan hyre ofring f. . u· ⁊ hyre beteran ofring sceat· ⁊ hyre rode· ⁊ into beodern hiwun twa selefrene cuppan· ⁊ hyre to saulsceatte ælcon Godes þeowe mancos goldes· ⁊ butan þam Ceoldryþe I. mancus· ⁊ Oðelbryhte ⁊ Else ⁊ Æþels . . . þe· ⁊ an pund to Wiltune ðam hiwum· ⁊ Fugele anne mancus. ⁊ hio becwið Æðelflæde hyre dehter hyre agrafenan beah ⁊ hyre mentelpreon· ⁊ ꝥ land æt

✠ Wynflæd makes known how she wills concerning what she has, after her day. She bequeaths to the church her offering-[vessels] . . . . and her better offering-vestment, and her rood; and to the refectory for the convent, two silver cups, and for her soul-shot, to every servant of God a mancus of gold; and besides that, to Ceoldryth one mancus, and to Othelbyrht, and Else, and Æthels . . . and one pound to the convent at Wilton, and to Fugel one mancus. And she bequeaths to Æthel-

Ebbelesburnan· ⁊ þa boc on ece yrfe· to ateonne swa hyre leofosð sy. ⁊ hio [a]n [h]yre þara manna ⁊ þæs yrfes ⁊ ealles þæs þe þær þenne on bið· butan þæt man scel for hyre saulle þær ofdon ægþer ge an mannon ge an yrfe. ⁊ æt Ceorlatune hio hyre an ealswa þere manna ⁊ þæs yrfes b[ut]an ðam freotmannon· ⁊ þæt man finde of þam yrfe æt Ceorlatune [healfes] pundes wyrþne saulsceat to Mylenburnan· ⁊ healfes pundes wyrþne saulscet fram Cinnuc to Gyfle. ⁊ Eadmære þæt land æt Coles[h]ylle· ⁊ æt Inggeneshamme· ⁊ hio an him eac þæs landes æt Faccancu[mbe]· hyre morgengyfu wes· his dæg· ⁊ ofer his dæg· gyf Æþelflæd leng lybbe þonne he· þonne fo hio to þam lande æt Faccancumbe· ⁊ ofer hyre dæg ga hit eft an Eadwoldes hand. ⁊ gif God wille þæt Eadwold weorþe to þam gewexen an his fæder dæge þæt he land healdan mæge· þenne bid ic Eadmær þæt he him læte þara twega landa· oþer to . . . . . . oþþe æt Colleshylle· oð[er] æt Eadburggebyrig· ⁊ ofer his dæg buta. ⁊ hio wile þæt man finde æt Inggenesham[me h]ealfes pundes wyrþne saul-

flæd her daughter her graven torque, and her mantle brooch, and the land at Ebbesborne, and the charters, in perpetuity, to dispose of as to her shall be most agreeable. And she gives to her the men and the cattle, and all that shall then be thereon, except what, for her soul, there shall be taken away, either in men or in cattle. And at Charlton she also gives her the men and the cattle, except the freedmen; and that, from the property at Charlton, there be found soul-shot of half a pound worth for Milbourn, and soul-shot of half a pound worth from Chinnock for Gidley. And to Eadmær the land at Coleshill and at Inggenesham: and she gives him also the land at Faccancumb (it was her morning-gift), for his day; and after his day, if Æthelflæd live longer than he, then let her succeed to the land at Faccancumb; and after her day, let it revert into Eadwold's hand. And if God will that Eadwold should be so grown up in his father's day that he can hold land, I then pray Eadmær that he relinquish to him one of the two lands, either the one at sceat to Waneting for hy· ⁊ æt Colleshylle· ⁊ finde man of þam yrfe LX. penegga wyrð to Scrifenanhamme· LX. to Colle[s hy]lle· LX. to Cillariðe. ⁊ freoge man Wulfware· folgyge þam þe hyre leofo[st . . .]ttryþe ealswa. ⁊ freoge man Wulfflæde on þæt gerad þæt hio folgige Æþelflæde ⁊ Eadgyfe. ⁊ hio becwið Eadgyfe ane crencestran· ⁊ ane sem[estran]· oþer hatte Edgyfu· oþer hatte Æþelgyfu. ⁊ freoge man Gerburge ⁊ Miscin ⁊ his . . . . . el· ⁊ Burhulfes dohtur æt Cinnuc· ⁊ Ælfsige ⁊ his wif· ⁊ his yldran dohtor· ⁊ Ceolstanes wif. ⁊ æt Ceorlatune freoge man Pifus ⁊ Edwyn[e]· ⁊ . . . . . . n wif. ⁊ æt Faccancumbe frioge man Ædelm· ⁊ Man· ⁊ Iohannan· ⁊ Sprow ⁊ his wif· ⁊ En[e]fætte· ⁊ Gersande· ⁊ Snel. ⁊ æt Colleshylle freoge man Æþelgyþe· ⁊ Bican wif· ⁊ Æffan· ⁊ B[e]dan· ⁊ Gurhannes wif· ⁊ freoge man Wulfwara swystor Bryhsiges wif· ⁊ i . . . . . . þysne wyrhtan· ⁊ Wulfgyþe Ælfswyþe dohtor. ⁊ gif þær hwylc witeþeowman sy butan þyson þe hio geþeowede· hio gelyfð to hyre bearnon þæt hi hine willon lyhtan for hyre saulle. ⁊

. . . . or at Coleshill, or the other at Eadburgsbury, and after his day, both. And she wills that there be found at Inggenesham soul-shot of half a pound worth, for her for Wantage, and at Coleshill; and let there be found from the property LX. pence worth for Shrivenham, LX. for Coleshill, LX. for Childrey. And let Wulfwaru be freed, and follow whom it is most agreeable to her; and . . . thryth also. And let Wulfflæd be freed, on the condition that she follow Æthelflæd and Eadgyfu. And she bequeaths to Eadgyfu one weaveress and one sempstress, the one is named Eadgyfu, the other is named Æthelgyfu. And let Gerburg be freed, and Miskin, and his . . . . . and Burhulf's daughter at Chinnock, and Ælfsige, and his wife, and his elder daughter, and Ceolstân's wife. And at Charlton, let Pifus be freed, and Eadwine, and . . . . wife. And at Faccancumb, let Æthelm be freed, and Man, and Johanna, and Sprow and his wife, and Enefæt, and Gersand, and Snel. And at Coleshill, let Æthelgyth be freed, and Bicca's wife, and Æffe, and Beda, and Gurhan's

Ælfwolde hyre twegen wesend hornas· ⁊ an hors· ⁊ hyre reade ge[t]eld. [⁊] hio becwyð Eadmære ane hlidfæsþe cuppan· oþre Æðelflæde· ⁊ bit þæt hi findon betweox him twa smicere scencingcuppan into beodern for hi· oþþe hyre ahgene ieredan cuppan geiccon· hy sy . . . . ec . . an anon punde. þonne wolde hio þæt man dyde innon ægþere cuppan healf pund penega. ⁊ agyfe man Eadwolde his ag[e]ne II. sylerenan cuppan· ⁊ hio becwið him hyre goldfagan treowenan cuppan· þæt he ice his beah mid þam golde oþþe hi mon æt him gehweorfe mid XVI. mancussum reades goldes· swa micel þær is to gedong. ⁊ hio becwiþ him twa mydrecan· ⁊ þær an innan an bedreaf eal þæt to anum bedde gebyreð. ⁊ agyfe Eadmær Eadwolde swa micel yrfe ⁊ swa fela manna swa [hio] him ær æt Hafene becwæð. ⁊ [h]e his fæder syððan swa he wille. ⁊ be þan lande æt Cinnuc hit agon þa hiwan æt Sceaftesbyrig ofer hyre dæg· ⁊ hio ah þæt yrfe ⁊ þa men· þenne an hio þan hiwum þara gebura þe on þam gafollande sittað· ⁊ þera þeowra manna hio an hyre

wife; and let Wulfwaru's sister, Byrhsige's wife, be freed, and . . . . wright, and Wulfgyth, Ælfswyth's daughter. And if there be any penal serf whom she has held in servitude, besides these, she trusts to her children that they will release him for her soul. And to Ælfwold [she gives] her two buffalo horns, and one horse, and her red tent. And she bequeaths to Eadmær one covered cup, another to Æthelflæd, and prays that they find between them two fair skinking-cups for the refectory, for her, or enlarge her own ornamented cups: they are . . . . . of one pound. Then she would that there be put into each cup half a pound of pennies. And let be given up to Eadwold his own two silver cups; and she bequeaths to him her gold-decorated wooden cup, that he may enlarge his torque with the gold, or let it be exchanged with him for XVI. mancuses of red gold; so much there is laid on. And she bequeaths to him two boxes, and therein one bed-furniture, all that belongs to a bed. And let Eadmær give up to Eadwold as much cattle and syna dehter Eadgyfe· ⁊ þæs yrfes butan þam saulsceatte þe man to Gifle syllan sceal. ⁊ hio wile ꝥ man læte on þan lande standan vi. oxsan ⁊ iiii. cy mid feower cealfon. ⁊ of [þ]am þeowan mannan æt Cinnuc hio becwið Eadwolde Ceolstan Etstanes sunu· ⁊ Æffan sunu· ⁊ Burhwynne Mærtin ⁊ his wif. ⁊ hio becwiþ Eadgyfe þær angean Ælfsige þene coc· ⁊ Ælfware Burgan dohtor· ⁊ Herestan ⁊ his wif· ⁊ Ecelm ⁊ his wif ⁊ hiora cild· ⁊ Cynestan· ⁊ Wynsige· ⁊ Byrhtrices sunu· ⁊ Edwynne· ⁊ Buneles sunu· ⁊ Ælferes dohtor. ⁊ hio becwið Æþelf[læde] Elhhelmmes dehter Ælfferes dohtor þa geonran· ⁊ hyre twili brocenan[1] cyrtel· ⁊ oþerne linnenne oþþe linnen web. ⁊ Eadgyfe twa mydrecan· ⁊ þær an innan hyre betsþe bedwahrift ⁊ linnenne ruwan· ⁊ eal þæt bedræf þe þærto gebyreð· ⁊ . . . . ⁊ hyre betstan dunnan tunecan· ⁊ hyre beteran mentel· ⁊ hyre twa treowenan gesplottude cuppan· ⁊ hyre ealdan gewiredan preon is an vi. mancussum. ⁊ sylle man hyre iiii.

as many men as [she] previously bequeathed to him at Hafen. And . . . . his father afterwards as he will. And concerning the land at Chinnock, let the convent at Shaftesbury possess it after her day, and she keeps possession of the cattle and the men: then gives she to the convent the boors who reside on the 'gafol'-land; and the serfs she gives to her son's daughter Eadgyfu, and the cattle, except the soul-shot which is to be given to Gidley. And she wills that there be left standing on the land vi. oxen and iv. cows with iv. calves. And of the serfs at Chinnock she bequeaths to Eadwold, Ceolstân, Eastân's son, and Æffa's son, and to Burhwyn, Mærtin and his wife. And she bequeaths to Eadgyfu, on the other hand, Ælfsige the cook, and Ælfwaru Burga's daughter, and Herestân and his wife, and Ecghelm and his wife, and their child, and Kynestân, and Wynsige, and Bryhtric's son, and Eadwyn's and Bunel's son, and Ælfere's daughter. And she bequeaths to Æthel[flæd], Elhhelm's

[1] broccen roc, *melotes, vestis ex pelle agnorum caprarumve facta.* Ettm.
[2] cinewiððe, *redimiculum.*

mancussas of hyre sa[ulesceatte] . . . . . . bege· ⁊ an lang healwahrift· ⁊ oþer sceort· ⁊ þrio sethrægl. ⁊ hio an Ceoldryþe hyre blacena tunecena swa þær hyre leofre beo· ⁊ hyre betsð haliryft· ⁊ hyre betsþan bindan· [⁊ ÆÐelf]læde þisse hwitan hyre cinewaðenan cyrtel· ⁊ cuffian· ⁊ bindan. ⁊ finde Æþelflæd syþþan an hyre nunscrude· loce hwæt hio betsð mæge· Wulfflæde ⁊ Æþelgife· ⁊ ice mid golde· þæt hyra ægþer hyru hæbbe LX. peneng[a wyr]þ· ⁊ Ceolwynne ⁊ Edburge· þæt sy XXX. penega wyrþ. ⁊ þær synt twa micle mydercan· ⁊ an hrægleysð· ⁊ an lytulu tow myderce· ⁊ eac twa ealde mydercan. Þenne an hio Æþelflæde on ælcum þingum þe þær unbecweden bið· on bocum ⁊ an swilcum lytlum· ⁊ hio gelyfð þæt hio wille hyre saulle geþencan. ⁊ þær synt eac wahriftu sum þe hyre wyrþe bið· ⁊ þa læstan hio mæg syllan hyre wimmannon. ⁊ hio becwið Cynelufe hyre dæl þera wildera horsa þe mid Eadmæres synt. ⁊ hio an ÆÐelflede hyre hy[sa . . . . cu]ppe ⁊ þara andlumena· ⁊ ealra þera getæsa þet þær

daughter, Ælfhere's younger daughter, and her double lamb's-wool kirtle, and another of linen or linen web. And to Eadgyfu two boxes, and therein her best bed-wall-hanging, and a linen rug, and all the bed-clothes which thereto belong . . . . and her best dun tunic, and her better mantle, and her two wooden spotted cups, and her old wire brooch of VI. mancuses. And let IV. mancuses be given her from her soul-shot . . . . and one long hall-wall-hanging, and another short one, and three seat-coverings. And she gives to Ceoldryth whichever she prefers of her black tunics, and her best holy veil, and her best binder, [and to Æthelf]læd her white striped[1] kirtle, and cuffs, and binders. And let Æthelflæd afterwards find one of her nun-habits, the best she can, for Wulfflæd and Æthelgifu, and eke with gold, so that each of them may have at least LX. pence worth; and to Ceolwyn and Eadburg what may be XXX. pence worth. And there are two large boxes, and one clothes chest, and one little hanaper, and also two old

[1] Translation conjectural.

binnan beoð. ⁊ eac ðes worþiges. gif his hyre se cing an swa swa Eadweard cing ær his Byrhtwynne hyre meder geuþe. ⁊ hæbbe Eadwold ⁊ his sweostor hyre taman hors gemæn[e . . . . . his agene toforan.

boxes. Then she gives to Æthelflæd all the things that are there unbequeathed, as books and such little things; and she believes that she will be mindful of her soul. And there are also wall-hangings, one which will be of worth to her; and the least she may give to her women. And she bequeaths to Cynelufu her share of the wild horses that are with Eadmær. And she gives to Æthelflæd her . . . . cup and the utensils, and all the desirable things that are there within; and also this estate, if the king will give it her, as king Eadward before gave it to Byrhtwyn her mother. And let Eadwold and his sister have her tame horses in common . . . . . his own previously.

KING ÆTHELRED. DCCCC.XCVII.

LICENCE TO THE WIDOW OF ÆTHERIC THAT HIS WILL MAY STAND GOOD.

✠ Her swutelað on þison gewrite hu Æðelred kyning geuðe ꝥ Æðerices cwyde æt Boccinge standan moste. Hit wæs manegon earon ǽr Æðeric forðferde. ꝥ þam kincge wæs gesæd ꝥ he wære on þam unræde ꝥ man sceolde on East Sexon Swegen underfōn. ða he ǽrest þyder mid flotan com. ⁊ se cincg hit on mycele gewitnysse Sigerice arcebisceope cyðde. ðe his forespeca ða wæs for þæs landes þingon æt Boccinge.

✠ Here is made known, in this writing, how king Æthelred has granted that Ætheric of Bocking's testament might stand. It was many years before Ætheric deceased, that it was said to the king that he was of that evil counsel, that Sweyn should be received in Essex, when he first came thither with a fleet. And the king, before a great number of witnesses, made it known to archbishop Sigeric, who was then his advocate, on ac-ðe he into Cristes cyrcean becweden hæfde. Ða wæs he ðisse spæce· ægðer ge on life ge æfter· ungeladod ge ungebett· oð his laf his hergeatu ðam cincge to Cocham brohte· ðær he his witan wīdan gesomnod hæfde. Ða wolde se cing ða spæce beforan eallon his witan uphebban· ⁊ cwæð· ꝥ Leofsige ealdorman· ⁊ mænige men ðære spæce gecnæwe wæron. Ða bæd seo wuduwe Ælfric arcebisceop ðe hire forespeca wæs· ⁊ Æðelmær· ꝥ hig ðone cincg bædon ꝥ heo moste gesyllan hire morgengyfe into Cristes cyrcean· for ðone cincg ⁊ ealne his leodscype· wið ðan ðe se cing ða egeslican onspæce alete· ⁊ his cwyde standan moste· ꝥ is swa hit her beforan cwyð· ꝥ land æt Boccinge into Xp̃es cyrcean· ⁊ his oðre landare into oðran halgan stowan· swa his cwyde swutelað. Ða God forgylde ðam cincge· getiðode he ðæs for Xp̃es lufan ⁊ Sc̃a Marian· ⁊ Sc̃e Dunstanes· ⁊ ealra þæra haligra ðe æt Xp̃es cyrcean restað· ðæs costes ðe heo ðis gelæste· ⁊ his cwyde fæste stode. Ðeos swutelung wæs þærrihte gewriten· ⁊ beforan ðam cincge ⁊ ðam witon geræedd. Ðis syndon ðæra

count of the land at Bocking, which he had bequeathed to Christchurch. Then was he, for this charge, both during life and after, unabsolved and without having made atonement, until his relict brought his heriot to the king at Cookham, where he had assembled his 'witan' from afar. Then would the king, before all his 'witan', prefer the charge, and said that Leofsige aldorman and many men were cognisant of the charge. Then the widow prayed archbishop Ælfric, who was her advocate, and Æthelmær, that they would pray the king that she might give her morning-gift to Christchurch, for the king and all his people, provided the king would abandon the terrible accusation, and that his testament might stand; that is, as it is here before said, the land at Bocking to Christchurch, and his other landed property to other holy places, as his testament declares. Then, may God requite the king, he consented to this, for love of Christ, and St Mary, and St Dunstân, and all the saints who rest at Christchurch, on the condition that she perform this, and manna naman ðe ðises to gewitnesse wæron.

his testament should stand fast. This declaration was straightways written, and read before the king and the 'witan'. These are the names of the men who of this were witnesses :—

Ælfric arceƀ.· ⁊ Ælfheh ƀ. on Wintaceastre· ⁊ Wulfsige ƀ. on Dorsæton· ⁊ Godwine ƀ. on Hrofeceastre· ⁊ Leofwine ealdorman· ⁊ Ælfsige aƀƀ.· ⁊ Wulfgar aƀƀ.· ⁊ Byrhtelm aƀƀ.· ⁊ Lyfincg aƀƀ.· ⁊ Alfwold aƀƀ.· ⁊ Æðelmær· ⁊ Ordulf· ⁊ Wulfget· ⁊ Fræna· ⁊ Wulfric Wulfrune sunu· ⁊ ealle ða þegnas ðe ðær wīdan gegaderode wæron· ægðer ge of West Sexan· ge of Myrceon· ge of Denon· ge of Englon. Ðissa gewrita syndon þreo· ān is æt Xp̄es cyrcean· oðer æt ðæs cinges haligdome· þridde hæfð seo wuduwe.

Ælfric archbp., and Ælfeh bp. of Winchester, and Wulfsige bp. of Dorchester, and Godwine bp. of Rochester, and Leofwine ealdorman, and Ælfsige abbot, and Wulfgar abbot, and Byrhtelm abbot, and Lyfincg abbot, and Ælfwold abbot, and Æthelmær, and Ordulf, and Wulfget, and Fræna, and Wulfric Wulfrun's son, and all the thanes who were there gathered from afar, as well of West Saxons as of Mercians, as of Danes and of Angles. Of this writing there are three: one is at Christchurch, the second in the king's treasury, the third the widow has.

LEOFWINE. DCCCC.XCVIII.

✠ In nomine Domini nostri Ihesu Christi. Ðis is Leofwines cwide Wulfstānes suna. Ðæt is þonne ærest ꝥ ic gean Criste ⁊ Sc̄e Petre for minre saule into Westmynster ealra

✠ In nomine Domini nostri Jhesu Christi. This is the testament of Leofwine, son of Wulfstân. That then is first, that I give to Christ and St Peter at Westminster, for my þara þinga ðe me Crist to gefultumian wyle· æt þam lande æt Cynlauedyne ⁊ æt Mearcyncgceollan· on wuda ⁊ on felda. ⁊ ic gean of Purlea into Nutlea healfere hide landes on east healf stræte· for mine sawle· þam Godes þeowan. ⁊ minre faðan Leofware þæs heafod botles on Purlea· ⁊ ealles þæs ðe me þær to locað. ⁊ gif Eadwold længc libbe· hire suna· þonne heo· fō he þærto. Gif heo þonne læng beo· ⁊ ꝥ God wylle· sylle hit on þa hand þe hire æfre betst gehyre on uncer bega cynne. ⁊ ic gean minum hlaforde Wulfstane bisceope þæs landes æt Bærlingum. Ðys wæs gedon þæs geares fram ures Drihtnes gebyrdtide anno Domini DCCCC.XCVIII. Indict. XI. Epac. XX. Concurr. V. Ciclos VIII. Dies XIII. (I.) Lunæ. XVII. Kal. Maii. Dies Pasce XV. Kal. Maii. Lunæ ipsius XVI.

soul, all the things to which Christ will help me from the land at Cynlavedyne and at Mearcyngcol, in wood and in field. And I give from Purley to Notley a half hide of land on the east side of the road, for my soul, for God's servants. And to my paternal aunt Leofwaru the chief dwelling at Purley and all that there look to me. And if Eadwold her son live longer than she, let him succeed thereto. But if she live the longer, and God wills it, let her give it to the hand that ever best obeys her in the kin of us both. And I give to my lord bishop Wulfstân the land at Birling. This was done in the year from our Lord's birth-tide, anno Domini DCCCC.XCVIII., Indict. XI., Epact. XX., Concurr. V., Cycl. VIII., Dies XIII. (I.) Lunæ, XVII. Kal. Maii, Dies Paschæ XV. Kal. Maii, Lunæ ipsius XVI.

QUEEN ÆTHELFLÆD[1]. M.

✠ Her swutelað on ðam cwide ðe Egelfled gecweden

✠ Here is made known, in this writing, what Æthelflæd

[1] First wife of Æthelred II. In the Chronicles she is variously named, but Æthelflæd (Ægelflæd) is no doubt correct. See Lappenberg, Engl. under the A. S. Kings, ii. p. 163.

hæfd Gode to lofe and hire saule to þerfe. and hire hlafordes. ꝥ is ðonne ða feower hida landes æt Lagefare. ⁊ twa hida æt Cochamstede. ðe hy gean for hire saule and for hire hlafordes into S. Paules mynstre on Lundene. ðan gebroðran to bigleofan. ðam ðe ðær dæghwamlice Gode ðeniað. be ðes cynges fulle geleuen Æðelredes. on ðera manna gewitnesse ðe heora naman her standað. ꝥ is ðonne Egelnoð arcebiscop. ⁊ Wulfstan arcebiscop. ⁊ Ælfun biscop on Lundene. ⁊ Ælfric abbot. ⁊ Wigard abbot. ⁊ Ælsi abbot on Cowwaford. ⁊ Ælfere ealdorman. ⁊ Briðnoð ealdorman. ⁊ Eadric ealdorman. ⁊ Ælfsige cynges þegn. ⁊ Ufegeat sciremann. ⁊ Frena cynges þegn. ⁊ swa hwilc man swa ðisne cwide awende. sy he Iudas gefere ðe urne Drihten belewde on helle wite.

has bequeathed to the glory of God, and for the need of her soul and her lord's. That is then the four hides of land at Lagefare, and two hides at Cuckhamstead, which she gives, for her soul and her lord's, to St Paul's monastery in London, for the sustenance of the brotherhood, those who daily there serve God, with the full leave of king Æthelred, in witness of the men whose names here stand. Now these are: Ægelnoth archbishop, and Wulfstân archbishop, and Ælfhun bishop of London, and Ælfric abbot, and Wighard abbot, and Ælsi abbot of Cowford, and Ælfhere aldorman, and Brihtnoth aldorman, and Eadric aldorman, and Ælfsige king's thane, and Ufegeat shireman, and Frena king's thane. And whatever man shall set aside this testament, be he the companion of Judas, who betrayed our Lord, in hell-torment.

WULFRIC. M.II.

ENDOWMENT OF THE ABBEY OF BURTON.

✠ In nomine Domini. Her swutelað Wulfric his leofan hlaforde his cwide. ⁊ eallon

✠ In nomine Domini. Here Wulfric declares his testament to his dear lord, and to his freondon. Ðæt is ꝥ ic geann minum hlaforde twa hund mancessa goldes· ⁊ twa seolfor hilted sweord· ⁊ feower hors· twa gesadelode ⁊ twa ungesadelode· ⁊ þa wæpna ðe þærto gebyriað. ⁊ ic geann ælcum bisceope v. mancessa goldes· ⁊ ðam twam arcebisceopan· heora ægðron tyn mancusas goldes. ⁊ ic geann into ælcum munucregole I. pund· ⁊ ælcon abbode ⁊ ælcon abbatissan v. mancusas goldes. ⁊ ic geann Ælfrice arcebisceope þæs landes æt Dumeltun forð mid ðon oðran for mine sawle· wið þon ðe he freond ⁊ fultum ðe betere sy into þære stowe þe ic geworht hæbbe. ⁊ ic geann Ælfhelme ⁊ Wulfage þæra landa betwux Ribbel ⁊ Mærse ⁊ on Wirhalum· ꝥ heo hig dælan him betweonan swa hig efnost magon· butan heora ægðer his ágen habben wille· on ꝥ geräd ðonne sceaddgenge sy· ꝥ heora ægðer sylle III. þusend sceadda into þære stowe æt Byrtune. ⁊ ic geann Ælfhelm Rolfestũn ⁊ Heorelfestũn. ⁊ ic geann Wulfage þæs landes æt Beorelfestune ⁊ æt Merchamtũne. ⁊ ic geann Ælfhelme þæs landes æt Cunugesburh· wið þon ðe he do ꝥ þa munucas habben ælce

all his friends. That then is, that I give to my lord two hundred mancuses of gold, and two silver-hilted swords, and four horses, two saddled, and two not saddled, and the weapons which thereto belong. And I give to every bishop v. mancuses of gold, and to the two archbishops, to each of them, ten mancuses of gold. And I give to every monastic rule I. pound, and to every abbot and every abbess v. mancuses of gold. And I give to archbishop Ælfric the land at Dumbleton, along with the others, for my soul, on condition that he may the better be a friend and support to the place which I have built. And I give to Ælfhelm and to Wulfeah the lands between the Ribble and the Mersey, and in Wirral, that they may share them between as they most equitably may, unless either of them will have his own; on the condition that, when the shad season is, each of them give III. thousand shad to the convent at Burton. And to Ælfhelm I give Rolleston and Harleston. And I give to Wulfeah the land at Beorelfestun, and at Merchamtun. And I give to Ælfhelm the geare þriddan dæl ðæs fisces. ⁊ he þa twa dæl. ⁊ ic gean Wulfage þæs landes æt Alewaldestūne. ⁊ ic gean Ufegeate ðæs landes æt Norðtūne. on ꝥ gerād ꝥ he freond ⁊ fultum þe betere sy into þære stowe. ⁊ ic gean minre earman dehter þæs landes æt Elleforde ⁊ ðæs æt Aclea. mid eallon þam þe þær nu tohyrð. þa hwīle ðe hire dæg bið. ⁊ ofer hire dæg ga ꝥ land into ðære stowe æt Byrtūne. ⁊ heo hit nage mid nānon þinge to forwyrcenne. ac hæbbe heo þone bryce þa hwīle ðe heo hit geearnian cann. ⁊ gā hit syððan into ðære stowe æt Byrtūne. forðon þe hit wæs mīnes godfæder gyfu. ⁊ ic wile ꝥ Ælfhelm sy hire mund ⁊ ðæs landes. ⁊ ꝥ æt Tomwurðin hire to nānon þeowdōme ne nānon geborenan men. butan ꝥ heo ðone ealdordōm hebbe. ⁊ ic geann Wulfgare minan cnihte þæs landes æt Baltryðeleage. ealswa his fæder hit him begeat. ⁊ ic becweðe Morcare ꝥ land æt Walesho. ⁊ ꝥ æt Ðeogendeþorpe. ⁊ ꝥ æt Hwītewille. ⁊ ꝥ æt Clune. ⁊ ꝥ æt Barleburh. ⁊ ꝥ æt Ducemannestune. ⁊ ꝥ æt Moresburh. ⁊ ꝥ æt Eccingtūne. ⁊ ꝥ æt Bectūne. ⁊ ꝥ æt Done-

land at Congresbury, on condition that he do so that the monks may have every year a third of the fish, and he the two parts. And I give to Wulfeah the land at Alwalton. And I give to Ufegeat the land at Norton, on the condition that he may the better be a friend and support to the convent. And I give to my poor daughter the land at Elford and that at Oakley, with all that thereto now belongs, the while that her day shall be; and after her day, let the land go to the convent at Burton. And she may not, on any account, impair it; but let her have the use of it the while she may be deserving of it, and let it afterwards go to the convent at Burton; because it was my godfather's gift. And I will that Ælfhelm be her guardian, and of the land. And [I give to her] that at Tamworth, without any service to any born man, but that she have the lordship. And I give to Wulfgar, my page, the land at Baltrytheleag, all as his father acquired it. And I bequeath to Morcare the land at Walesho, and that at Theddlethorp, and that at Whitwell, and that at Clun, cestre. ⁊ ꝥ æt Morligtūne. ⁊ ic geann his wīfe Aldulfestreo ealswa hit nu stont mid mete ⁊ mid mannum. ⁊ ic geann Ælfhelme mīnan meage þæs landes on Paltertūne ⁊ þæs ðe Sægð me becwæð. ⁊ ic geann Æþelrice ꝥ land æt Wibbetofte. ⁊ ꝥ æt Twongan. his dæg. ⁊ ofer his dæg ga ꝥ land for mine sawle. ⁊ for his moder. ⁊ for his. into Byrtōne. And þis sind þa ðe ic geann into Byrtone. ꝥ is ǣrest Byrton ðe ꝥ mynstre on stent. ⁊ Stræton. ⁊ Bromleage. ⁊ Bedingtūn. ⁊ Gageleage. ⁊ Witestūn. ⁊ Laganford. ⁊ Styrcleage. ⁊ Niwantūn æt þære wīc. ⁊ Wædedūn. ⁊ ꝥ little land ðe ic āh on oðer Niwantūne. ⁊ Wyneshylle. ⁊ Suttūn. ⁊ Ticenheale. ⁊ æt Scenctūne. ⁊ æt Wicgestāne. ⁊ æt Halen. ⁊ æt Remesleage. ⁊ ꝥ æt Sciplea. ⁊ ꝥ æt Suðtūne. ⁊ ꝥ æt Actune. twegra manna dæg. ealswa ða foreword sprecað. ⁊ Deorlāfestūn ⁊ ꝥ þærto hereð. ꝥ is Rudegard ⁊ mīn litle land on Cotewaltūne. ⁊ Lege mid eallon þam ꝥ þærto hereð. Acofre mid þam ꝥ þærto hereð. ꝥ is Hilum ⁊ Celfdum. ⁊ Cætesðurne. ⁊ ꝥ heregeatland æt Suttūne. ⁊ Morlege. ⁊ Brægesheale.

and that at Barleyborough, and that at Ducemannestun, and that at Moresborough, and that at Eckington, and that at Beckton, and that at Doncaster, and that at Morleston. And I give to his wife Aldulfestreo, as it now stands, with meat and with men. And I give to Ælfhelm, my kinsman, the land at Paltertun, and that which Sægth bequeathed to me. And I give to Æthelric the land at Wibtoft, and that at Twonge, for his day; and after his day, let the land go, for my soul, and for his mother's, and for his, to Burton. And these are the lands which I give to Burton. That is first, Burton, on which the monastery stands, and Stretton, and Bromley, and Bedington, and Gageley, and Witestun, and Longford, and Strickley, and Newton, at the wick, and Watton, and the little land which I own in the other Newton, and Winshill, and Sutton, and Ticknall, and at Shenkton, and at Wigston, and at Halen, and at Remsley, and that at Shipley, and that at Sutton, and that at Acton, for two men's day, all as the compacts say; and Darliston, and what thereto

Mórtún ⁊ eal seo socna ðe þærto hereð. ⁊ ꝥ land þiderinn æt Wyllesleage. ⁊ Oggodestún. ⁊ Winnefeld. ⁊ Snodeswíc into Mortúne. ⁊ ꝥ æt Taðawyllan. ⁊ ꝥ land æt Æppelby ðe ic gebohte mid mínum feo. ⁊ æt Westúne. ⁊ Burhtún. ⁊ seo híd æt Scearnforda into Wiggestáne. ⁊ ꝥ æt Hereburgebyrige. ⁊ Ealdeswurðe. ⁊ Ælfredingtúne. ⁊ Eccleshale. ⁊ æt Waddúne. ⁊ án hida æt Sceon. ⁊ ic geann ðon hirede in Tamwurdin ꝥ land æt Langandúne ealswa hi hit me ǽr to leton. ⁊ habban hi þone bryce healfne. ⁊ healfne þa munecas into Byrtúne. ge on mete. ge on mannon. ge on yrfe. ge on ælcon þingon. ⁊ se bisceop fó to his lande æt Bubandúne. ⁊ fón þa munucas into Byrtúne to ðan þe on þam land is. ge on mannon ge on eallon þingon. ⁊ ꝥ land þam bisceope æt þære syle. And ic wille ꝥ se cyng beo hlaford ðæs mynstres ðe ic getimbrede. ⁊ þære landára ðe ic þyderinn becweden hæbbe. Gode to lofe ⁊ to wurðmynte. for minan hlaforde ⁊ for mínre sawlan. ⁊ Ælfric arcebisceop ⁊ Ælfhelm mín broðor ꝥ hig ben mund ⁊ freond ⁊ forespreocan into

belongs, that is, Rudyard and my little land at Cotwalton, and Leigh, with all that thereto belongs; Oakover, with that which thereto belongs, that is, Hilum and Celfdum, and Cætesthurn, and the heriot-land at Sutton, and Morley, and Breadsall, Morton and all the 'socna' which thereto belong, and the land besides at Willesley. And Oxton, and Wingfield, and Snodeswic to Morton; and that at Tathwell, and the land at Appleby, which I bought with my money, and at Weston, and Burton; and the hide at Sharnford ; to Wigston; and that at Hereburgebury, and Aldsworth, and Alfreton, and Eccleshall, and at Waddon, and one hide at Sheen. And I give to the convent at Tamworth the land at Longdon, as they before relinquished it to me; and let them have half the usufruct, half the monks of Burton, of meat, and of men, and of cattle, and of all things. And let the bishop succeed to his land at Bubdon; and let the monks of Burton succeed to that which is on the land, both of men and of all things; and the land at the 'syl' to the bishop. And I will that the king be ðære stowe wið ælcne geborenne man· heom to nā̃nre ā̃genre æhta· butan into Sanctus Benedictus regole. ⁊ ic geann mī̃nre goddohtor Morcares ⁊ Ealdgyðe ꝥ land æt Strættū̃ne· ⁊ þone bule ðe wæs hire ealdermoder. ⁊ into þæn mynstre æt Byrtū̃ne ā̃n hundred wildra horsa· ⁊ XVI. tame hencgestas· ⁊ þærto eall ꝥ ic hæbbe on libbandan ⁊ on licgendan· butan þan ðe ic becweden hæbbe. And God ælmihtig hine awende of eallum Godes dreame· ⁊ of ealre cristenra gemanan se ðe þis awende· butan hit mī̃n ane cynehlaford sy· ⁊ ic hopige to him swa gō̃dan ⁊ swa mildheortan ꝥ he hit nylle sylf dō̃n· ne eac nā̃num oðrum geþafian. Ualete in Christo.

lord of the monastery that I have built, and of the landed property which I have bequeathed thereto, to the praise and honour of God, for the honour of my lord, and for my soul; and that archbishop Ælfric, and Ælfhelm, my brother, be patrons, and friends, and advocates of that place against every born man; not as their own private property, but for St Benedict's rule. And I give to my goddaughter, [the daughter] of Morcare and Ealdgyth, the land at Stretton, and the 'bulla' that was her grandmother's. And to the monastery at Burton, a hundred wild horses, and XVI. tame steeds; and thereto all that I have in living or lying, except that which I have bequeathed. And may God Almighty avert from all God's joy, and from all Christians' communion, him who shall avert this, unless it be my royal lord; and in him, so good and so merciful, I hope that he himself will not do it, nor also permit any other. Valete in Christo.

Rubric. Ðis is seo freolsbō̃c to þan mynstre æt Byrtū̃ne ðe Æðelred cyng æfre ecelice gefreode· Gode to lofe ⁊ eallon his halgan to weorð-

Rubric. This is the Charter of Freedom to the monastery at Burton, which king Æthelred for ever freed, to the praise of God, and the honour unge. swa swa hit Wulfric gestaðelode for hine ⁊ for his yldrena sawle. ⁊ hit mid munecon gesette. ꝥ þær æfre inne þæs hādes menn under heora abbude Gode þeowian æfter Sanctus Benedictus tæcinge.

of all his saints, as Wulfric established it for the souls of himself and his parents, and supplied it with monks, that therein for ever the men of that order, under their abbot, may serve God, after the teaching of St Benedict.

ARCHBISHOP ÆLFRIC. DCCCC.XCVI.–M.VI.

✠ Her sutelað hu Alfric arcebisceop his cwyde gedihte. ꝥ is ærest. him to saulsceate he becwæð into Xp̄es cyrcan ꝥ land æt Wyllan. ⁊ æt Burnan. ⁊ Risenbeorgas. and he becwæð his laford his beste scip. ⁊ þa segelgeræda þarto. ⁊ LX. healma. ⁊ LX. beornena. ⁊ he wilnode. gif hit his lafordes willa wære. ꝥ he gefæstnode into Sc̄e Albane ꝥ land æt Cyngesbyrig. ⁊ fenge sylf wið þam eft to Eadulfingtune. And he becwæð ꝥ land æt Dumeltun into Abbandune. ⁊ Ælfnoðe þarof III. hida his dæg. ⁊ suððan to þan oþaran to Abbandune. ⁊ X. oxan. ⁊ II. men he him becwæð. ⁊ filgan hi þam lafordscype þe ꝥ land to hyre. And he cwæð þæt land æt Wealingaforda. þe

✠ Here is made known how archbishop Ælfric has ordered his testament. That is first: for his soul-shot, he has bequeathed to Christchurch the land at Wells, and at Bourn, and at Risborough. And he has bequeathed to his lord his best ship, and the sailing-gear thereto, and LX. helms, and LX. coats of mail. And he has desired, if it were his lord's will, to confirm to St Alban's the land at Kingsbury, and himself to take again that at Eadulfingtun. And he has bequeathed the land at Dumbleton to Abingdon; and to Ælfnoth III. hides thereof, for his day, and afterwards, with the other, to Abingdon; and X. oxen and II. men he has bequeathed to him; and let them follow the lordship to which the he gebohte. Celewærde. ⁊ hofer his dæg into Ceolesige. ⁊ he becwæð into Sc̃e Albane ꝥ land æt Tiwan. ⁊ standan þa forword betweonan þan abƀ'e ⁊ Ceolrice. ðe ær wið ðæne arcebiscop geforwyrd wæran. ꝥ is ꝥ Ceolric habbe ðæne dæl þæs landes þe he hæfð his dæg. ⁊ eac þæne dæl þe se arceƀ. for his sceatte him to let. ꝥ wæs ehtoðe healf hid wið v. pundun ⁊ L. mancusum goldes. ⁊ ga hit ofer his dæg eall togædere into Sc̃e Albæne. ⁊ heora forewyrd wæron. ꝥ Osanig æfter Ceolrices dæge gange eac þyder in. ⁊ ꝥ land on Lundene. þe he mid his feo gebohte. he becwæð into Sc̃e Albæne. ⁊ his bec ealle he cwæð eac þyder in. ⁊ his geteld. And he becwæð ꝥ man fenge on þe feoh ðe man hæfde. ⁊ ærest ælcne borh agulde. ⁊ sudðan tilode to his hergeatwæn þæs ðe man habban sceolde. And anes scipes he geuþe þam folce to Cent. ⁊ oþres to Wiltunescı̃re. ⁊ elles on oðrum þingum. gif þæs hwæt wære. he bæd ꝥ Uulfstan bisceop ⁊ Leofric abbud dihton swa heom best þuhte. And þe land be westan æt Fittingtune ⁊ æt Niwantune he be-

land belongs. And he has bequeathed the land at Wallingford, which he bought, to Celeweard; and after his day, to Cholsey. And he has bequeathed to St Alban's the land at Tewin, and let stand the agreements between the abbot and Ceolric, which were before agreed on with the archbishop: that is, that Ceolric have the part of the land which he has, for his day, and also the part which the archbishop let to him for his money, that was seven and a half hides, for v. pounds and L. mancuses of gold: and after his day, let it go altogether to St Alban's. And their agreements were, that Oseney, after Ceolric's day, should also go thither. And the land in London which he bought with his money, he has bequeathed to St Alban's; and all his books he has also bequeathed thither; and his tent. And he has bequeathed that the money held by any one be received; and first every loan be paid, and afterwards there be found for his heriot what should be necessary. And one ship he has given to the folk in Kent, and another to Wiltshire. And with respect to other things cwæð his sweostrun ⁊ heora beornun. ⁊ Ælfheages land Esnes suna ga a on his cyn. And he becwæð Uulfstane ærcebiscope ane sweor rode. ⁊ anne ring. ⁊ anne psaltere. ⁊ Alfheage biscope anne rode. And he forgeaf. on Godes est. Centingan þæne borh þe hy him sceoldan. ⁊ Middelsexon ⁊ Suðrion ꝥ feoh ꝥ [he] heom fore sceat. And he wyle ꝥ man freoge æfter his dæge ælcne witefæstne man þe on his timan forgylt wære. Gif hwa þis awende. hæbbe him wið God gemaene. Amen.

besides, if there should be aught, he has prayed that bishop Wulfstân and abbot Leofric would order so as to them might seem best. And the land in the west at Fittington, and at Newton, he has bequeathed to his sisters and their children. And let Ælfheah Esne's son's land go ever in his kin. And he has bequeathed to archbishop Wulfstân one neck-rood, and one ring, and one psalter; and to bishop Ælfheah one rood. And he has forgiven, under God's favour, to the Kentish people the loan which they owed to him; and to the Middle Saxons and the Southerns the money that he advanced to them. And he wills that, after his day, every penal serf, who had been condemned in his time, be freed. If any one prevent this, let him have to account with God. Amen.

IDEM LATINE.

Hic notificatur quomodo Ælfricus archiepiscopus suarum rerum testamentum in extremo condidit. In primo æcclesiæ Christi Cantuariæ terram apud Wellam, et apud Burnam, et Hrisenburgam contulit. Domino suo meliorem suarum navium unam, cum sibi pertinentibus armamentis; et LX. galeas cum totidem loricis. Et hoc apud ipsum dominum suum erat interveniens, ut concederet loco Sancti Albani terram apud Cingesbiri, et ipse in commutationem reciperet Eadulfingtun. Abbendonensi æcclesiæ, terram apud Dumeltun, ubi Alfnodo cuidam III. hidas concessit tenere tantum suis diebus, et postea rediret cum reliqua terra Abbendonensis æcclesiæ potestati: insuper et decem boves cum duobus hominibus. Cuidam quoque viro nomine Celewardo terram quam emerat apud Walingaford, ut quamdiu viveret possideret, et post ejus decessum æcclesia de Ceolsiga ipsius dominatu terre potiretur. Æcclesiæ Sancti Albani terram apud Tiwan et Osanig, cum terra de Lundonia quam emerat idem archiepiscopus. Quæ omnia quidam Ceolricus tunc tenebat, sed secundum quod archiepiscopo in conventione habebat post vite illius viri finem ad prædictam æcclesiam martiris universa redirent. Libros etiam suos universos illic delegavit, precepitque ut de suis propriis expensis quicquid in mutuo ab aliquo acceptum erat restitueretur, et cetera in ejus exequiis expenderentur. Populo Cantie unam navem, et alteram genti Wiltescire jussit largiri. Reliqua universa que sua videbantur esse domnum Wlfstanum episcopum et Leofricum abbatem rogavit, quatinus sua providentia, quo melius consulerent, dispertirent. Sororibus suis et earum filiis terram de Fittinctune et Niwentune contulit; et terram quæ erat Alfeagi filii Esni restituit iis quibus proprie pertinuerat habere. Domno Wlfstano archiepiscopo I. philacterium, cum I. anulo et codice psalterii; sed et Alfheago episcopo unam crucem in suam memoriam dedit. Debita que sibi debebantur a multis passim condonavit. Siquis vero, secundum patriæ Anglie morem, in aliquam incurrisset servitutem tempore sue potestatis, libertate sibi penitus contributa, relaxatus ejus jussu est. De his quicumque aliter quam ut dictata sunt perverterit, inde cum Deo concertamen habeat. AMEN.

ÆLFGYFU. M.XII.

Ðis ys Ælfgyfæ gegurning to hiræ cinehlafordæ. Þæt ís þæt heo hyne bítt· for Godæs lufun and for cynescypæ· þæt heo mote beón hyre cwydes wyrðæ. Þonnæ cyð heo þæ leóf bæ þinre geþafiunga hwæt heo for þæ ⁊ for þyræ sawlæ to Godæs ciricean dón wýlæ.

This is Ælfgyfu's petition to her royal lord. That is, that she prays him, for love of God, and for his kingship, that she may be worthy of her testament. Then she makes known to thee, dear, by thy permission, what she for thee and for thy soul wills to þæt īs æræst· þæt heō ānn into Ealdan mynstær· þær heo hiræ licaman ræstan þæncþ· þæs landæs æt Hrisanbeōrgan eall swa hit stænt· buton þæt heo wylæ bæ þinre geþafunga þæt man freōge on ælcum tunæ ælne witæþæownæ mann þæ undær hiræ geþeowuð wæs· and twa hund mancussa goldæs to þam mynstær· and hire scrīn mid hiræ haligdomæ. And heo an innto Nigean mynstær þæs landæs æt Bleddanhlæwe· and hund mancussa goldæs· and annæ offring disc into Nunna mynstær. And þæs landæs æt Hwætædunæ into Rummæsigæ Xp̃. ⁊ Sanctan Marian· and æt Cæstæleshammæ into Abbandunæ· and æt Wicham into Baþum. And ic ānn minæn cinæhlafordæ þæs landæs æt Weowungum· and æt Hlincgeladæ· and æt Hæfæresham· and æt Hæðfælda· and æt Mæssanwyrðæ· and æt Gyssic· and twegea bæagas· æigþær ȳs ōn hundtwælftigum mancussum· and anræ sōpcuppan· and syx horsa· and swa fela scylda and spæra. and þam æþelingæ þæs landæs æt Niwanhām· and anæs beages on þritægum mancussum. And þæræ hlæfdigan

do to God's church. That is first, that she gives to the Old Monastery[1], where she intends her body to rest, the land at Risborough, all as it stands, except that she wills, with thy permission, that, in every vill, every penal serf be freed, who under her was reduced to serfdom: and two hundred mancuses of gold to the monastery, and her shrine with her relics. And she gives to the New Monastery[1] the land at Bledlow, and a hundred mancuses of gold; and one offering-dish to the Nuns' Monastery[1]. And the land at Wheaton to Christ and St Mary at Rumsey; and at 'Cæstælesham' to Abingdon; and at Wickham to Bath. And I give to my royal lord the land at Weowung, and at Linchlade, and at Haversham, and at Heathfield, and at Mæssanworth, and at Gussage; and two torques, each of a hundred and twenty mancuses, and one sop-cup, and six horses, and as many shields and spears. And to the ætheling, the land at Newnham, and one torque of thirty mancuses. And to the lady, one neck-torque of a hundred and twenty man-

[1] At Winchester.

anes swyrbeages on hundtwelftigum mancussum· and anæs beages on þritegum mancussum· ⁊ ãnre sõpcuppan. And ic ãnn Aþelwoldæ bisceopæ þæs landæs æt Tæafersceat· and bidde hinæ þæt hæ symlie þingiæ for minæ modor an for me. And ic ãnn bæ minæs hlafordæs geþafiungæ þæs landæs æt Mundingwillæ· and æt Beorh þan stædæ Ælfwerdæ· and Æþelwærdæ· and Ælfwaræ· him to gemanan hira dǽg· ⁊ ofær hira dæg into Ealdan mynstær· for minnæ cynehlaforð and for mæ. And syllan hi ælcæ geãre twa dǽg fæorman into þam twam mynstrum þa wilæ þæ hi his brucæn. And ic ãn Ælfwaræ miræ swystær eallæs þæs þæ ĩc hiræ ãlenæð hæfdæ· and Æþælfledæ minæs broþur wifæ þæs bændes þæ ic hire ãlæneð hæfdæ· and ælchum abbodæ fif pund pæniga to hira mynstres bote. And leof be þinre geþafiunga· þæt ic motæ bætæcen þam bisceope· and þam abbodæ· þonæ ofæreacan to þære stowe botæ· and earmum mannum for me to dælænne· swa swa him þincæ þæt mæ for Godæ þearfliicustþ sĩ. And ic biddæ minnæ cinelaford· for Godæs

cuses, one torque of thirty mancuses, and one sop-cup. And I give to bishop Athelwold the land at Teafersceat, and pray him that he constantly intercede for my mother and for me. And I give, by my lord's permission, the land at Mundingwell, and at the place at Beorh, to Ælfweard, and to Æthelweard, and to Ælfwaru, in common to them, for their day, and after their day, to the Old Monastery, for my royal lord and for me. And let them give, every year, two days' subsistence to the two monasteries, while they enjoy it. And I give to Ælfwaru, my sister, all that I had lent her; and to Æthelflæd, my brother's wife, the band that I had lent her; and to every abbot five pounds of pence, for the reparation of their monastery. And, dear, [I would,] with thy permission, that I might give over, to the bishop and the abbot, the surplus, for the reparation of the place, and to be distributed to poor men, for me, as may to them seem most needful for me before God. And I pray my royal lord, for love of God, that [he] abandon not my men who seek him, and appear worthy to him.

lufum· þæt [he] næ forlæte minæ mænn þe hinæ gesæcen· and him wyrðæ syn. And ic ann Ælfwerdæ anræ sōp-cuppan· ⁊ Æþelwerdæ anæs geræenodes drincæhornæs.

And I give to Ælfweard one sop-cup, and to Æthelweard one ornamented drink-horn.

MANTAT AN ANCHORITE[1]. M.XVII.-M.XXXV.

Mantat Ancer Godes wrǣcca greteð Cnut cing ⁊ Emma hlæfdie swiðe bliþe-like mid Godes blisse. And ic ciðe ꝥ ic habbe ure almesse Crist betaht ⁊ his allen halgan· ure sawle to frofre ⁊ to blisse þære it lengest wunian sculen. Ðæt is ærest· þæt land æt Twiwell into Ðornige· þær ure bān resteð· þæt land æt Cunintun prestes ⁊ diaknes· þa þe hit æt me earnodon on mine life. And hi habbað God behaten ⁊ me on hande gesealde ꝥ hi sculen elke geare don for us twa hundred messen ⁊ twa hundred sauters· ⁊ þerto eaken fele holy beden. Nu bidde ic inc· for Godes lufa ⁊ for ure wreccan bene· þat þis none man ne awende· þat þat god ꝥ inc ne wæs nen

Mantat the Anchorite, God's wretch, greets king Cnut and Emma the lady very blithely with God's bliss. And I make known that I have committed our alms to Christ and all his saints, for the comfort and bliss of our soul, where it shall longest endure. That is first: the land at Twiwell to Thorney, where our bones will rest; and the land at Conington to the priests and deacons who have merited it of me in my life. And they have promised to God and pledged to me that they will every year say for us two hundred masses and two hundred psalters, and, in addition thereto, many holy prayers. I now pray you, for love of God, and for the prayer of us

[1] The object of this not very intelligible document seems to be to pray that his bequest may stand good. The document itself is barbarous and the MS. defective.

bescoran man nytter þænne. ⁊ þat inc sceal ben cuðe on þan towarden liue. Gehealde inc here on liue heofan engle kinge. ⁊ geleade inc on his lihte mid him þer yt wiðuten sorhge euer wunian. Amen.

wretch, that no man set aside this * * * * * * * and that shall be well known to you in the life to come. May heaven's angels' King preserve you here in life, and lead you into his light, where without sorrow may ye ever dwell. Amen.

WULFSIGE. M.XXX.

✠ Her switeleð on þise write wam Wlsi an hi aihte. Ðat is erst for his soule ꝥ lond at Wiken into Seynt Eadmundesbiri þa tueye deles. ⁊ Ælfric biscop ðe þridde del. buten ane girde ⁊ XII. swinemesten þat schal habben Wlwine hire day. ⁊ after hire day into Seynt Eadmundesbiri. ⁊ alle þo men fre for unker boðer soule. And ic an mine kynelouerd II. hors. ⁊ helm. ⁊ brinie. ⁊ ān swerd. ⁊ a gold wreken[1] spere. And ic an mine lauedy half marc goldes. an mine nifte ann ore wichte goldes. And habbe Standhand alle þing ðe ic him bicueðen habbe. ⁊ mine broðer bern here owen land. ⁊ II. hors mid sadel garun. ⁊ I. brinie. ⁊ on

✠ Here is made known, by this writing, to whom Wulfsige gives his property. That is first, for his soul, the land at Wicken, two parts to St Eadmundsbury, and to bishop Ælfric the third part, save one rod, and mast for XII. swine, which Wulfwin shall have for her day, and after her day, to St Eadmundsbury. And be all the men free, for the souls of us both. And I give to my royal lord II. horses, and a helm, and a coat of mail, and one sword, and a gold-'wreken' spear. And I give to my lady a half mark of gold; and to my niece one ore-weight of gold. And let Standhand have all the things which I have bequeathed to him; and to my brother's

[1] wrigen, *covered?*

hakele. And se ðe mine cuiðe awende. God almithtin awend his asyne from him on domes day. buten he it her ðe raðere bete.

children their own land, and two horses with saddle-equipments, and I. coat of mail, and one hackel. And whoever my testament averts, may God Almighty avert his countenance from him on doomsday, unless he for it here the more speedily atone.

ÆTHELSTÂN ÆTHELING[1].

✠ On Godes ælmihtiges naman. Ic Æðelstan æðeling geswutelige on ðisum gewrite hu ic mine are ⁊ mine æhta geunnen hæbbe. Gode to lofe. ⁊ minre saule to alysednysse. ⁊ mines fæder Æðelredes cynges. ðe ic hit æt geearnode. Ðæt is ǽrest. ꝥ ic gean ꝥ man gefreoge ælcne witefæstne man ðe ic on spræce ahte. ⁊ ic gean in mid me þær ic me reste. Criste ⁊ Sc̄e Petre þæs landes æt Eadburgebyrig. ðe ic gebohte æt minon fæder mid twam hundred mancosan goldes be gewihte. ⁊ mid v. pundan be gewihte seolfres. ⁊ ꝥ land æt Merelafan. ðe ic gebohte æt minum fæder

✠ In the name of Almighty God. I Æthelstân ætheling make known, by this writing, how I have given my property and my possessions, to the praise of God, and the redemption of my soul, and my father, king Æthelred's, from whom I acquired them. That is first, that I give, that every penal serf, which I have possessed by litigation, be freed. And I give in with me, where I shall rest, to Christ and St Peter, the land at Edburgbury, which I bought of my father for two hundred mancuses of gold by weight, and for five pounds by weight of silver. And the land at Marlow, which I

[1] Æthelstân was the third son of Æthelred II. by his first wife Ælflæd or Ægelflæd.

mid þridde healf hund mancosan goldes be gewihte. ⁊ ꝥ land æt Mordune. þe min fæder me to let. ic gean into þære stowe. for uncer begra saule. ⁊ ic hine þæs bidde. for Godes lufan. ⁊ for Sc̃a Marian. ⁊ for Sc̃e Petres. ꝥ hit standan mote. ⁊ þæs swurdes mid þam sylfrenan hylte ðe Wulfric worhte. ⁊ þone gyldenan fetels. ⁊ þone beh þe Wulfric worhte. ⁊ þone drenchorn þe ic ær æt þam hirede gebohte on Ealdan mynstre[1]. ⁊ ic wille ꝥ man nime ꝥ feoh þe Æðelwoldes laf me ah to gyldenne. þe ic for hyre are gesceoten hæbbe. ⁊ betæce Ælfsige bisceope into Ealdan mynstre. for mine saule. ꝥ synd xii. pund be getale. ⁊ ic gean into Cristes cyrican on Cantwarabyrig þæs landes æt Holungaburnan. ⁊ þæs þe þærto hyrð. buton þære anre sulunge þe ic Siferðe geunnen hæbbe. ⁊ þæs landes æt Garwaldintune. ⁊ ic ann þæs landes æt Hryðerafelda into Nunnan mynstre[1]. Sc̃a Marian þances. ⁊ ænne sylfrene male on v. pundon. ⁊ into Niwan mynstre[1] ænne sylfrene hwer on v. pundon. on þære halgan þrynnesse naman. þe seo

bought of my father for two hundred and fifty mancuses of gold by weight; and the land at Mordon, which my father relinquished to me, I give to that place, for the souls of us both; (and I pray him, for love of God, and St Mary, and St Peter, that it may stand;) and the sword with the silver hilt, which Wulfric wrought, and the golden belt, and the torque which Wulfric wrought, and the drinking-horn, which I bought of the brotherhood at the Old Monastery[1]. And I will that the money which Æthelwold's widow has to pay me, which I have disbursed for her honour, be taken and delivered to bishop Ælfsige at the Old Monastery, for my soul, that is xii. pounds by tale. And I give to Christchurch at Canterbury the land at Hollingbourn, and what thereto belongs, except the one sulung which I have given to Siferth; and the land at Garwaldington. And I give the land at Rotherfield to the Nuns' Monastery[1], freely to St Mary; and one silver crucifix of v. pounds. And to the New Monastery[1], one silver

[1] At Winchester.

stow is forehalig. ⁊ ic gean to Sceaftenesbyrig· to þære halgan rode ⁊ to Sc̃e Eadwearde þara VI. punda ðe ic Eadmunde minon breðer[1] gewissod hæbbe. ⁊ ic gean minon feder Æðelrede cynge þæs landes æt Cealhtune· buton þam VIII. hidan þe ic Ælmære minon cnihte geunnen hæbbe· ⁊ þæs landes æt Norðtune· ⁊ þæs landes æt Mollintune· ⁊ þæs seolferhiltan swurdes þe Ulfcytel ahte· ⁊ þære byrnan þe mid Morkære is· ⁊ þæs horses þe Đurbrand me geaf· ⁊ þæs hwitan horses þe Leofwine me geaf. ⁊ ic gean Eadmunde minon breðer þæs swurdes þe· Offa cyng ahte· ⁊ þæs swurdes mid þam pyttedan hiltan[2]· ⁊ anes brandes· ⁊ ænne seolfor hammenne blædhorn· ⁊ þara landa þe ic ahte on East Englan· ⁊ þæs landes æt Peacesdæle. ⁊ ic wille ꝥ man gelæste ælce geare âne dægfeorme þam hirede into Ælig of þysse âre· on Sc̃e Æðeldryðe mæssedæg. ⁊ gesylle þærto þam mynstre an hund penega· ⁊ gefede

ewer of v. pounds, in the name of the Holy Trinity, to whom the place is especially holy. And I give to Shaftesbury, for the holy rood, and for St Eadward, the VI. pounds which I have indicated to Eadmund my brother[1]. And I give to my father, king Æthelred, the land at Chalton, except the eight hides which I have given to Ælmær, my page; and the land at Norton, and the land at Mollington, and the silver-hilted sword which Ulfkytel owned, and the coat of mail which is with Morkere; and the horse which Thurbrand gave me; and the white horse which Leofwine gave me. And I give to Eadmund, my brother, the sword that king Offa owned, and the sword with the 'pytted' hilt[2], and one brand[3], and one silver-coated blast-horn, and the lands which I owned in East Anglia, and the land at Peakdale. And I will that there be supplied, from this property, every year one day's sustenance to the convent at Ely, on St Ætheldryth's mass-day; and I give

[1] Afterwards king Eadmund Ironside.

[2] cum lacunato capulo. *Manning, apud Lye.*

[3] A sword with a wavy blade resembling flame, whence its name: now merely a sword *poetice.* Compare Fr. Flamberge.

þ ær· on þone dæg· c. þearfena· ⁊ sy æfre seo ælmesse gelæst gearhwamlice· age land se þe age· þa hwile þe cristendom stande· ⁊ gif þa nellaþ þa ælmessan geforðian þe þa land habbað· gange seo ār into Sc̃e Æðeldryðe. ⁊ ic geann Eadwige minon breðer anes seolfer hiltes swurdes. ⁊ ic geann Ælfsige bisceope þære gyldenan rōde þe is mid Eadrice Wynflæde suna· ⁊ ænne blacne stedan. ⁊ ic geann Ælmære þæs landes æt Hamelandene þe he ǽr ahte. ⁊ ic bidde minne fæder· for Godes ælmihtiges lufan· ⁊ for minon· ꝥ he þæs geunne þe ic him geunnen hæbbe. ⁊ ic geann Godwine Wulfnoðes suna þæs landes æt Cumtune· þe his fæder ær ahte. ⁊ ic gean Ælfswyðe minre fostermeder· for hire miclon geearnungon· þæs landes æt Westune þe ic gebohte æt minon fæder mid þridde healf hund mancusan goldes be gewihte. ⁊ ic geann Ælfwine minon mæssepreoste þæs landes æt Heorulfestune· ⁊ þæs malswurdes ðe Wiðer ahte· ⁊ mines horses mid minon gerædon. ⁊ ic geann Ælmære minon discðene þara ehta hida æt Cateringatune· ⁊ anes fagan stedan· ⁊ þæs

thereto a hundred pence, and on that day let be fed there c. poor; and let that alms ever be supplied yearly, whoever may own the lands, as long as Christianity may stand; and if they who have the lands will not afford the alms, let the property go to St Ætheldryth's. And I give to Eadwig, my brother, one silver-hilted sword. And I give to bishop Ælfsige the golden cross which is with Eadric, son of Wynflæd; and one black steed. And I give to Ælmær the land at Hambleden, which he before possessed. And I pray my father, for love of Almighty God, and for mine, that he grant that which I have given him (Ælmær). And I give to Godwine, Wulfnoth's son, the land at Compton, which his father before owned. And I give to Ælfswyth, my foster-mother, for her great deserts, the land at Weston, which I bought of my father for two hundred and fifty mancuses of gold by weight. And I give to Ælfwine, my mass-priest, the land at Harleston, and the cross-hilted sword that Wither owned; and my horse with my trappings. And I give to Ælmær, my sewer, the sceardan swurdes. ⁊ mines targan. ⁊ ic geann Siferðe þæs landes æt Hocganclife. ⁊ anes swurdes. ⁊ anes horses. ⁊ mines boc scyldes[1]. ⁊ ic geann Æðelwearde Stameran ⁊ Lyfingce þæs landes æt Tywinham. ⁊ ic geann Leofstane. Leofwines breðer Cwattes. þære landare þe ic of his breðer nam. ⁊ ic geann Leommære æt Biggrafan þæs landes þe ic him ǽr of nam. ⁊ ic geann Godwine Dreflan þara þreora hida æt Lutegaresheale. ⁊ ic geann Eadrice Wynflæde suna þæs swurdes þe seo hand is on gemearcod. ⁊ ic geann Æðelwine minon cnihte þæs swurdes þe he me ær sealde. ⁊ ic geann Ælfnoðe minon swurdhwitan þæs sceardan malswurdes. ⁊ minon heahdeor hunton þæs stodes þe is æt Colingahrycge. ⁊ gehealde man of minon golde Ælfric æt Bertune ⁊ Godwine Drefelan æt swa miclon swa Eadmund min broðor wat ꝥ ic heom mid rihte to gyldanne áh. Nu þancige ic minon fæder mid ealre eadmodnesse. on Godes ælmihtiges naman. þære andsware þe he me sende on Frigedæg æfter middes-

eight hides at Catherington, and one pied stallion, and the 'sceard'-sword, and my target. And I give to Siferth the land at Hockcliff, and one sword, and one horse, and my beechen shield. And I give to Æthelward Stamera and Lyfing the land at Tewin. And I give to Leofstân, Leofwine Cwatt's brother, the landed property which I took from his brother. And I give to Leofmær at Bygrave the land which I before took from him. And I give to Godwine Drefla the three hides at Ludgershall. And I give to Eadric, Wynflæd's son, the sword on which the hand is marked. And I give to Æthelwine, my page, the sword which he before gave me. And I give to Ælfnoth, my sword-furbisher, the 'sceard'-cross-hilted sword; and to my tall-deer huntsman the stud which is at Collingridge. And of my gold let there be retained, for Ælfric at Barton and Godwine Drefla, so much as my brother Eadmund knows that I have to pay them. I now thank my father, with all humility, in the name of

[1] So Cod. Winton. Manning (App. ad Lye) reads boh-scyld, from boh, *humerus*, i. e. *a shield borne on the shoulder*, scutum humerale.

sumeres mæssedæge· be Ælfgare Ælffan suna· ꝥ wæs ꝥ he me cydde mines fæder worde· ꝥ ic moste· be Godes leafe ⁊ be his· geunnan minre āre ⁊ minra æhta swa me mæst ræd þuhte· ægðer ge for Gode ge for worulde. ⁊ þysse andsware is to gewitnesse Eadmund min broðor· ⁊ Ælfsige bisceop. ⁊ Byrhtmær abb̄. ⁊ Ælmær Ælfrices sunu. Nu bidde ic ealle þa witan þe minne cwyde gehyron rædan· ægðer ge gehadode ge læwede· ꝥ hi beon on fultume ꝥ min cwyde standan mote· swa mines fæder leaf on minon cwyde stent. Nu cyðe ic ꝥ ealle þa ðingc þe ic to Gode· into Godes cyrican· ⁊ Godes þeowan geunnen hæbbe· sy gedon for mines leofan fæder sawle Æðelredes cyncges. ⁊ for minre· ⁊ for Ælfðryðe minre ealdemodor· þe me afedde· ⁊ for ealra þe me to þyson godan gefylstan. ⁊ se ðe ðysne cwyde· þurh ænig þingc awende· habbe him wið God ælmihtigne gemæne· ⁊ wið Sc̄a Marian· ⁊ wið Sc̄e Peter· ⁊ wið ealle þa þe Godes naman heriað.

Almighty God, for the answer which he sent me on the Friday after Midsummer's mass-day, by Ælfgar, Ælfa's son: that was, that he announced to me my father's words, that I might, with God's leave, and with his, give my property and my possessions as might to me seem most advisable, both before God and before the world. And to this answer there are for witness Eadmund my brother, and bishop Ælfsige, and abbot Byrhtmær, and Ælmær, Ælfric's son. I now pray all those 'witan' who may hear my testament read, both ordained and lay, that they give support that my testament may stand, as my father's leave stands on the testament. I now declare that all the things which I have given for God to God's church, and to God's servants, are done for the soul of my dear father, king Æthelred, and for mine, and for Ælfthryth, my grandmother's, who reared me, and for all theirs' who have aided me in this good [work]. And may he who shall in any way avert this testament, have to account with God Almighty, and with St Mary, and with St Peter, and with all those who praise the name of God.

WULFGYTH. M.XLVI.

✠ Her swutelað on ðyssum gewrite hu Wulfgyð gean hire þinga æfter hire forðsiðe· þe hire se ælmihtig God geuðe on līfe to brucanne. Ðæt is þonne ærest· minum hlaforde his rihte heriot. ⁊ ic gean þæs landes æt Stistede· be Godes gewitnesse ⁊ mīnra freonda· into Cristes cyrican· ðam munecum to fostre· on þam gerad· ꝥ Ælfcytel ⁊ Kytel mine bearn brucen þæs londes hyra dæg· ⁊ syððan gange ꝥ lond into Cristes cyrican· butan ælcre arentale· for mīne sawle· ⁊ for Ælfwines mines hlafordes· ⁊ for ealra mīnra bearna. ⁊ beon healf ða men freo æfter hira dæge. ⁊ ic gean into ðare cyrican æt Stistede· to þam ðe ic on līfe geuðe· Eldemes landes· ⁊ þærto Hyekenes· ꝥ ðær syn ealles fiftig æcera [on wude ⁊] on feld æfter mīnum forðsiðe. ⁊ ic gean to Wolk[ytele] ⁊ Kytele mīnum sunum þæs londes æt Wælsingaham· ⁊ æt Karltūne· ⁊ æt Herlingaham. ⁊ ic gean mīnum twam dohtrum· Gōde ⁊ Bōte· Seaxlingaham ⁊ Sumerledetūne. ⁊ into ðære cyrican æt Sumerledetūne sixtyne æceras

✠ Here is made known, by this writing, how Wulfgyth gives her things after her decease, which the Almighty God has granted her in life to enjoy. That then is first: to my lord his rightful heriot. And I give the land at Stistead, with the witness of God and my friends, to Christchurch, for the subsistence of the monks, on the condition that Ælfkytel and Kytel, my children, enjoy the land for their day, and afterwards the land go to Christchurch, without any 'arental', for my soul, and for Ælfwine's, my lord's, and all my children's. And let half the men be free after their day. And I give to the church at Stistead, besides what I have given in life, Eldemes land, and Hyekene's thereto, so that, after my decease, there may be altogether, in wood and field, fifty acres. And I give to Wolk[ytel] and Kytel, my sons, the land at Walsingham, and at Carlton, and at Harling. And I give to my two daughters, Gode and Bote, Sexlingham and Somerleyton. And to the church at Somerleyton, sixteen acres londes. ⁊ ænne æcer mæd. ⁊ ic gean Ælgyðe mīnre dehter þæs landes æt Certæcere ⁊ æt Essetesforde. ⁊ ðæs wuda ðe ic legde ðærto. ⁊ ic gean Godwine eorle ⁊ Haralde eorle Friðtūnes. ⁊ ic gean into Cristes cyrican. to Cristes weofede. ānre lytlere goldenre rōde ⁊ ānes sethrægles. ⁊ ic gean Sc̄e Eadmunde twegea gebonedra horna. ⁊ ic gean Sc̄e Æðelðryðe ānes wullenan kyrtles. ⁊ ic gean Sc̄e Osyðe healf pundes feos [⁊ ðe geue mine bearnes][1]. ⁊ ic gean Sc̄e Augustine ānes sethrægles. And seðe mīnne cwyde bereāfige þe ic nu becweden hæbbe on Godes gewitnesse. bereafod he wurðe ðisse eorðlicre myrgðe. ⁊ ascyrige hine se ælmihtiga Drihten. ðe ealle gesceafta gesceōp ⁊ geworhte. fram ealra haligra gemænysse on dōmes dæg. ⁊ sy he betaht Satane ðam deofle ⁊ eallum his awergedum geferum into helle grunde. ⁊ þær acwylmie mid Godes wiðsacum bute geswice. ⁊ mīne ærfenuman næfre ne aswence. Ðisses is to gewitnesse Eadweard cyning ⁊ manige oðra.

of land, and one acre of mead. And I give to Ælgyth, my daughter, the land at Chartacre and at Essetsford, and the wood which I added thereto. And I give to earl Godwine and earl Harold Fritton. And I give to Christchurch, for Christ's altar, one little golden rood, and one seat-cover. And I give to St Eadmund two polished horns. And I give to St Æthelthryth one woollen kirtle. And I give to St Osyth a half pound of money, [and let my children give that]. And I give to St Augustine one seat-cover. And whosoever shall bereave my bequest, which I have now bequeathed, in the witness of God, be he bereft of this earthly joy, and may the Almighty Lord, who hath created and wrought all creatures, sever him from the community of all his saints on doomsday; and be he delivered to Satan the devil and all his accursed companions, in the ground of hell, and there suffer torment with God's deniers without cessation, and never molest my heirs. Of this are witness, king Eadward and many others.

[1] Evidently an interpolation of a later period.

LEOFLÆD. M.XXIII.-M.L.

✠ Tibi domino delectissimo atque venerabili dominæ meæ reginæ omnibus modis gratias refero, quod circa me ancillam vestram benigne agere voluistis, et mihi de substantiis meis, ex quo vir meus ablatus est a me, pro libitu disponere indulsistis. Nunc igitur ostendo, in hoc libello, quod villam de Belesham Deo et Sancto Petro, et sanctæ virgini Æðeldredæ, cum omnibus ad eam pertinentibus post diem meum concedo, pro anima viri mei et liberis meis, seu vivis vel defunctis. Deinde duabus filiabus meis annuo Stevecheworde dum vivant tenere, Ælfwenne et Ælfswide, et ultra dies suos in locum sanctum Ely libere dimittant. Aliæ vero filiæ, scilicet Leosware, vicum illud de Weddreringesete, sub hac conditione permitto, ut caste se conservet, vel virum legitime accipiat, ne ipsa et progenies nostra lupanaris contagii notetur infamia. Hæc et alia ego, ancilla tua, tam æcclesiis quam domesticis, domine rex, tuo favore, post diem meum, esse dispono, et rata in ævum consistent, nemo ea præter te, quod absit, subtrahat vel minuat. Et quicunque aliud ex eis evellere tentaverit, maledictionem habeat Domini nostri Jhesu Christi, et cum Juda proditore auditionem malam audiat, "Ite maledicti in ignem æternum qui paratus est diabolo et angelis ejus." Hæc scripta tripliciter consignantur: unum est apud Ely, aliud in thesaurum regis, tertium Leofleda habet [1].

[1] "Quæ cum mortua fuit, corpus illius ad nos delatum in cimiterio fratrum sepelitur. Qua sepulta mox filia ejus præfata Ælfeswida, cum possessione de Stevecheworde, æcclesiæ se tradens viri consortium aspernatur, illic jugiter professa est permanere; cui tradita est Coveneia, locus monasterio vicinus, ubi aurifrixoriæ et texturis secretius cum puellulis vacabat, quæ de proprio sumptu albam casulam suis manibus ipsa talis ingenii peritissima fecit. Et soror ejus Leosware nobilissimo viro Leofwino sublimiter dotata, terram de Wedreringesete æcclesiæ postmodum adjecit, et plura," etc. *Hist. Eliens.* ap. Gale, i. pp. 496, 508.

ÆLFRIC MODERCOP. M.XXXVII.

TEMPORIBUS SANCTI EDWARDI, REGIS ANGLIÆ, FUIT VIR UNUS NOBILITATE INSIGNIS DICTUS ÆLFRICUS MODERCOPE, QUI, IPSO SANCTO REGE PER CARTAM SUAM TESTIMONIUM PERHIBENTE, DEDIT SANCTO EADMUNDO LODNE CUM THURWINEHOLM, CUJUS HÆC EST CARTA SIVE TESTAMENTUM.

✠ Ðis is se quide þe Alfric biquað ēr he ofer sē ferde. Ðat is erst Lodne into Seynt Eadmunde· be wude and by felde and be fenne· so ful and so forð so ic it formest ahte. And ic an þat lond at Birðe into Seynt Æðeldriðe· so ful and so forð so ic it bigeten hauede· eyðer on wude oðer on felde. And into Holm to Sainte Benedicte Berton· al so ful and so forð so ic it ahte. And ic an into Rameseye six marc silures· and ðat schal Godric mine broðer lesten. And ic an Ðurwineholm into Lodne· and Fuglholm into Berhe. And þa schep delen men on to· half into Lodne and half into Beorhe. And ic biqueðe to min heregete ane marc goldes· and þat schal Godric mine broðer lesten. And Alfric biscop I biqueðe mine teld and min bedreaf þat ic best hauede ut on mi fare mid me. And be Alfric biscop· and Tofi Prude· and Ðrunni þese

✠ This is the bequest that Ælfric bequeathed ere he journeyed over sea. That is first, Loddon to St Eadmund's, by wood, and by field, and by fen, as full and as free as I first possessed it. And I give the land at Birth to St Ætheldrith's, as full and as free as I acquired it, both in wood and in field. And to Holme, for St Benedict, Barton, all as full and as free as I possessed it. And I give to Ramsey six marks of silver, and that shall my brother Godric pay. And I give Thurwineholm to Loddon, and Fuglholm to Berh. And let the sheep be divided into two, half to Loddon, half to Berh. And I bequeath, for my heriot, one mark of gold, and that shall Godric my brother pay. And to bishop Ælfric I bequeath my tent, and my bed-hangings, the best I had out with me on my journey. And be bishop Ælfric, and Tofi Prude, and Thrunni, guarquides mundes hureþinge þat it no man awende. and gif it wa wille awenden. God almiðten awende is ansene fram him on domes day.

dians of this testament; at least, that no man avert it: and if any one will avert it, may God Almighty avert his countenance from him on doomsday.

BISHOP ÆLFRIC[1]. M.XXXVII.

✠ Her swytelað on þissum gewrite hu Ælfric ƀ. wille his are beteōn þe he under Gode geernode. ⁊ under Cnute kyncge his leofne laforde. ⁊ siþþan hæfð rihtlice gehealdan under Haralde cyncge. ꝥ is þonne ærest. ꝥ ic gean ꝥ land et Wilrincgawerþa into Sc̄e Eadmunde. for mira saule ⁊ for minas lafordas. swa ful ⁊ swa forð swa he it me to handa let. ⁊ ic gean ꝥ land et Hunstanestune be Æstanbroke. ⁊ mid þan lande et Holme. into Sc̄e Eadmunde. ⁊ ic wille ꝥ þa munecas on Byrig sellan syxtig punde for þan lande et Ticeswelle ⁊ et Doccyncge. ⁊ ꝥ þerto geherað. ⁊ ic gean Leofstane dæcane ꝥ land et Grimastune. swa ful and swa forð swa ic hit ahte. ⁊ ic gean mine cynelaforde Haralde II. marc gol. ⁊ ic gean

✠ Here is made known, in this writing, how bishop Ælfric desires to dispose of his property, which he has acquired under king Cnut, his dear lord, and has afterwards lawfully holden under king Harold. That then is first, that I give the land at Worlingworth to St Eadmund's, for my soul, and for my lord's, as full and as free as he bestowed it on me. And I give the land at Hunstanton by Eastbrook, and with the land at Holme, to St Eadmund's. And I will that the monks in Bury give sixty pounds for the land at Titchwell and at Docking, and what thereto belongs. And I give to Leofstân, the dean, the land at Grimstone, as full and as free as I possessed it. And I give to my royal lord Harold II. marks of gold. And I give to

[1] Of Elmham.

mire hlefdigen an marc gol. ⁊ gelæste man Ægelrice IIII. pund mire fatfylre. ⁊ sela man mina cnihtas þa mina stiwardas witan xxxx. punda. ⁊ fif pund into Elig· and fif pund into Holm· ⁊ fif pund Wulfwarde muneke minne mæge· ⁊ fif pund Ælffæhe min sæmestres. ⁊ ic wille ꝥ man sella ꝥ land et Walsingaham swa man derast mage· ⁊ gelesta man ꝥ feoh swa ic gewissod hæbbe. ⁊ ic wille ꝥ man selle ꝥ land et Fersafeld swa man derast mæge· ⁊ recna man iungere Brun ān marc gol· ⁊ mid þan laue scytte man mina borgas. ⁊ ic gean Ælfwine minan preoste et Walsingaham xxx. akera et Eggemæra· ⁊ Uui prouast habba þone ofaræcan. ⁊ ic gean Ædwine muneke þa mylne et Geeysæte þe Ringware ahte. ⁊ ic gean Ælfwig preoste ꝥ land et Rygedune þe ic bohte to Leofwenne. ⁊ ic gean ꝥ myln þe Wulnoð ahte into Sc̄e Eadmunde. ⁊ ic gean Sibriht ꝥ land þe ic gebohte on Mulantune. ⁊ ic gean ꝥ fen þe Þurlac me sealde into Ælmham· þa preostas to foddan. ⁊ ic gean into Hoxne· þa preostas· an þusend werð fen. ⁊ ic gean ꝥ fen þe Ælfric me

my lady I. mark of gold. And let IV. pounds be paid to Ægelric my cupbearer. And let xxxx. pounds be given to my pages whom my stewards know of. And five pounds to Ely, and five pounds to Holme; and five pounds to Wulfward the monk, my kinsman; and five pounds to Ælffæh my sempstress. And I will that the land at Walsingham be sold as dearly as possible, and let the money be paid as I have indicated. And I will that the land at Freshfield be sold as dearly as possible; and pay out to Junker Brun one mark of gold, and the residue disburse to my creditors. And I give to Ælfwine my priest at Walsingham xxx. acres at Egmere; and let Uvi the provost have the surplus. And I give to Eadwine the monk the mill at Guist that Ringwar possessed. And I give to Ælfwig the priest the land at Roydon, which I bought of Leofwen. And I give the mill which Wulnoth possessed to St Eadmund's. And I give to Sibriht the land which I bought at Moulton. And I give the fen which Thurlac sold me to Elmham, for the sustenance of the priests.

sealde into Holme. ⁊ ic gean þon hage binnon Norðwic for mire saule· ⁊ for ealra þe hit me geuðon· into Sc̄e Eadmunde. ⁊ ic gean þan hage into Sc̄e Petre binnon Lunden. ⁊ ic gean iungre Brun ꝥ healfe þusend fen.

And I give to the priests at Hoxne a thousand worth of fen. And I give the fen which Ælfric sold me to Holme. And I give the messuage within Norwich, for my soul, and for all theirs' who gave it me, to St Eadmund's. And I give the messuage within London to St Peter's. And I give to Junker Brun the half thousand fen.

LEOFGIFU. M.XLV.

LEOFGIUA INCLITA MATRONA, COGNATA ÆLFRICI FILII WITHGARI, DEDIT SANCTO EADMUNDO, TEMPORE ÆLFWARDI PRÆSULIS, HENTLESHAM ET GRISTLINGTHORP, SUBSCRIPTÆ CARTÆ TESTIMONIO.

✠ Leofgiue gret hire leuedi Godes gretinge. And ic kiðe þe mine quide· þat ic Crist an ⁊ his halegan mine louerdes soule to alisednesse and mine· into þe holy stowe þer ic self resten wille· þat is at Seynt Eadmundesbyri. Đat is þat lond at Hintlesham and þat lond at Gristlyngðorp· buten þat lond þat Ailsi hauede· þat he at his lauerde ernede and at me· and ilk þridde aker on þan wude at Hintlesham habbe Ailsi· and ingong and utgong· be felde and be fenne. And ic wille þat Ailric prest and Ailfric prest· and Ailri the diacon habben þat minstre at

✠ Leofgifu greets her lady with God's greeting. And I make known to thee my testament, what I give to Christ and his saints, for the redemption of my lord's soul and mine, to the holy place where I myself desire to rest, that is at St Edmundsbury. That is, the land at Hintlesham and the land at Gristlingthorp, except the land that Ailsi had, which he obtained from his lord and from me; and let Ailsi have the same third field in the wood at Hintlesham, and ingress and egress, by field and by fen. And I will that Ailric the priest,

Colne so here lofard it hem uðe. And ic wille ðat Ailfric prest beo on þat ilke loh þe Aignoð was. And be se mund ofer þan minstre ðe is ofer alle oðere. And ic an þan kinge to marc goldes· fon min eruenumen to· and gealæste þat gold· and mine lauede þat lond at Belhcham· buten þat lond þat Godric mine stiward haueð· þat habbe he· and Alfward biscop þat lond at Benetleye· buten half hide þe Osemund hauede· þat ic an Alfwy min stiward· and þat he on sit. And Alfnod min stiward þat lond þat Berric hauede under hande· and Alfgar mine mei þat lond at Borham· and Alfric mine mey Withgares sone þat lond at Bromford· and Stigand þat lond at Willauesham· ⁊ Æilric mine broðeres sone þat lond at Stonham and at Waldingfeld and at Lichtletic· and Alfled mine douhter þat lond at Hagele· and Godwine mine aðum and mine meygan þa þre hide at Werle· and Lefkyld þa to hide on fast his owen. And Æylmer habbe þat lond at Stonham þe ic hym er to hande let to reflande. And ic an Godric mine reue at Waldingfeld þa þritti acre ðe

and Ailfric the priest, and Ailri the deacon, have the monastery at Colne, as their lord gave it to them. And I will that Ailfric the priest be in the same place that Aignoth was. And be the guardianship over the monastery that which is over all the others. And I give to the king two marks of gold: let my heirs succeed to, and pay that gold: and to my lord the land at Belcham, except the land that Godric my steward has: that let him have; and bishop Alfward the land at Bentley, except the half hide that Osmund had, which I give to Ælfwy my steward, with that on which he resides. And to Alfnoth my steward the land that Berric had in hand; and to Alfgar my kinsman the land at Boreham; and to Alfric my kinsman, Wihtgar's son, the land at Bromford; and to Stigand the land at Willafesham; and to Ailric, my brother's son, the land at Stoneham, and at Waldingfield, and at Lichtletic; and to Alfled, my daughter, the land at Hagley; and to Godwine, my son-in-law and my kinsman, the three hides at Warley; and to Lefkyld the two hides near to his own.

ic hym er to hande let. And Ailric min hird prest· and Ailric mine cnihtes þat lond at Lalleford ðe me best heren willen. And Ailric prest habbe ān hide at Forendale. And ic wille þat alle mine men ben fre on hirede and on tūne· for me and for þo ðe me bigeten. And ic bidde mine leuedien· for Godes louen· þat þu [ne] ðolie ðat ani man mine quide awende· and se ðe hit awende God almiðin awende his ansene from him on domes day· buten ic it self do. God þe healde. Nu sinden þise write þre· on is mid þise kinges halidome· and oðer at Seynt Eadmunde· and þridde mid Leofgiue seluen.

And let Æylmer have the land at Stoneham, which I before let to him as reeveland. And I give to Godric, my reeve at Waldingfield, the thirty acres which I had before let to him. And to Ailric, my household priest, and to Ailric, my page, the land at Lalford, whichever shall best obey me. And let Ailric the priest have a hide at Forendale. And I will that all my men be free both in my household and vill, for me and for those who begot me. And I pray my lady, for love of God, that thou wilt not suffer that any man avert my testament; and who shall avert it, may God Almighty avert his countenance from him on doomsday; unless I do it myself. God preserve thee! Now of these writings there are three; one is with this king's relics, and the second at St Eadmund's, and the third with Leofgifu herself.

THURSTÂN. M.XLV.

[✠ O]n ure Drichtines name· ic Þurstan Wine sune kithe alle manne ihu ic an þe þing þe me God haueð lent so longe so his wille beth. Þat is þat ic an þat lond at Wimbisc into Cristes kirke for mine soule· and for Lef-

✠ In the name of our Lord: I Thurstân, son of Wine, make known to all men how I give the things which God hath lent me so long as it shall be his will. That is, that I give the land at Wimbish to Christchurch, wares. and for Egelgithes. after mine day and after Egelgithes. þo men fre. And leste man of Cristes kirke xii. pund be tale into Seynt Augustine. And ic an þat lond at Herlawe into Sc̃e Eadmunde buten þe halue hide þe Alfwine hauede at Gildenebrigge. and buten þat tuft þe Alfgor on sit. and þat hoo þerto. and alle þe men fre. And ic an þat lond at Sculham at þe Northhalle into Seynt Eadmunde. after unker bothre day. and þo men fre. And ic an þat lond at Wetheringsete into Ely. buten þat lond þat Aylri haueð. habbe he þat fre his day and his wiues. and after here bothere day into þe tunkirke. ⁊ þo men fre. And ic an þat lond at Cnapwelle into Ely. buten þat lond þat Ordeh haueð. ⁊ Aylric munek haueð. and þo men fre. And ic an þat lond at Westoñ Agilswiðe. buten þat lond þat Sewine haueð to Earninge. þat schal into tunkirke. and after hire day into Ely. ⁊ þo men fre. And ic an þat lond at Sculham at þe Middel halle half into Sc̃e Benedicte to Rameseye and half into Sc̃e Benedicte into Holm. so it þer to lith. after unker

for my soul, and for Leofwaru's, and for Egelgith's; after my day, and after Egelgith's; the men to be free. And let there be paid from Christchurch xii. pounds by tale to St Augustine's. And I give the land at Harlow to St Eadmund's, except the half hide which Alfwine had at Gildenbridge, and except the toft on which Alfgar resides, and the 'hoo' thereto; and all the men to be free. And I give the land at Sculham, at the North hall, to St Eadmund's, after the day of us both: and the men free. And I give the land at Wetheringsete to Ely, except the land that Aylri has: let him have it free for his day and his wife's; and after the day of them both, [let it go] to the 'tûn'-church; and the men be free. And I give the land at Knapwell to Ely, except the land that Ordeh has, and Aylric the monk has: and be the men free. And I give the land at Weston to Agilswid, except the land that Sewine has at Eorning: that shall go to the 'tûn'-church, and after her day to Ely: and the men be free. And I give the land at Sculham, at the Middle hall, half to S^t^ Be-bother day· and the men fre. And ic an mine kinelouerd for mine hergete to marc goldes· and to hors and sadelfate· and helm· and brinie· and suerd· and to scheldes· and to speren. And ic wille þat men selle þat lond at Bidicheseye and nime of þat lond to marc goldes to þe kynges heregete· and half marc goldes þe erl Harold· and half marc goldes Stigand bisscop· ⁊ an marc goldes mine felage· and an marc goldes Hisberne Þorþes brother· ⁊ an marc goldes sendi Arfast bisscop· and þat þe þerouer goð delen le . . . ermene men for his soule on his felawes witnesse· buten þat uttreste milne into Sc̃e Æthelburg at Berkynge. And [ic] wille þat min and Ulfketels felageschipe stonde to þat forwarde þe wit speken habben· þat is þat lond at Burg̃. And Ulfketel hauið leyd þerwith four marc goldes· so wether so leng libbe· buten half hide at Westle· and an hide at Dullingham þat ic an Wiking mine knihte. And ic an mine wife Ailgiðe al þe þing þe ic haue on Norfolke· so ic it her hire gaf to mund and

nedict's at Ramsey, and half to St Benedict's at Holme, as it thereto lies, after the day of us· both: and the men free. And I give to my royal lord, for my heriot, two marks of gold, and two horses and saddle-vessels[1], and a helm, and a coat of mail, and a sword, and two shields, and two spears. And I will that the land be sold at Bidichesaye; and let be taken from that land two marks of gold for the king's heriot, and a half mark of gold to earl Harold, and a half mark of gold to bishop Stigand; and one mark of gold to my fellow; and one mark of gold to Hisbern, Thorth's brother; and let one mark of gold be sent to bishop Arfast, and divide that which remains over * * * distribute to poor men for his soul, in his fellow's witness, excepting the furthermost mill to St Æthelburg at Barking. And I will that my and Ulfketel's fellowship stand according to the agreement that we have spoken; that is the land at Burg. And Ulfketel has laid thereto four marks of gold, whichsoever live the longer, except half a hide at Westley, and one

[1] Bottles hung from the saddle-bow?

to maldage· and þat lond at Pentelawe and at Æfredune· buten þat lond at Bromlege· þat schal into þe tunkirke ouer unker bother day. And ic an Agilgið þat lond at Henham· buten an half hide· þat schal into þe kirke. And ic an Alfwi prest· and Þurstan mine hirdprest· ⁊ Ordeh mine hirdprest· þat hi habben þat lond at Kydington after unker bother day. And ic an Meruyn and his wife and here bern þat lond at Dunmawe· buten an alf hide þat schal into þe kirke· and an tuft. ⁊ ic an mine cnihtes þat wude at Aungre· buten þat derhage ⁊ þat stod þe ic þer habbe. Þis is to witnesse innon Norfolk̄· Harold erl· and Stigand bisscop· and Osgote Clape· and Godwine· ⁊ Wlgeat· ⁊ Eadwine· and Osbern· and Ulf· and Gouti· and innon Suffolk̄· Lefstan decanus· and al se hird on Seynt Eadmundesbiri· ⁊ Eadric· and Alfric· and Ulfketel· ⁊ Lemmer· and in Grauntebreg̃schire· Leswi abbot· ⁊ al se hird bynnen Ely· and Ælfwine abbot· ⁊ al se hird into Rameseye· and Ælfwine· and Ulfketel kild· and Osgot Sveyn· and Ordger· and oþer Ordger·

hide at Dullingham, which I give to Wiking my page. And I give to my wife Ailgith all the things which I have in Norfolk, as I it ere gave her as 'mund' and on our wedding-day, and the land at Pentlow and at Æfredun, except the land at Bromley, which shall go to the 'tûn'-church, after the day of us both. And I give to Agilgith the land at Henham, except half a hide, which shall go to the church. And I give to Alfwi the priest, and to Thurstân my household priest, and to Ordeh my household priest, the possession of the land at Kydington after the day of us both. And I give to Merwyn and his wife and their children the land at Dunmow, except a half hide that shall go to the church, and a toft. And I give to my pages the wood at Ongar, except the deer-park and the stud which I have there. Of this are witness within Norfolk: Harold earl, and Stigand bishop, and Osgod Clapa, and Godwine, and Wulfgeat, and Eadwine, and Osbern, and Ulf, and Gouti; and in Suffolk: Leofstân dean, and all the convent at St Eadmundsbury, and Eadric, and innen Essex̃. Alfger þe erles sune. and Lefkild. ⁊ Osulf File. and Wlwine. and Sendi. and Leuerich discþeng. Se þe þis quide awenden wille buten ic self it be. God him fordo nu and on domesday. Amen.

and Alfric, and Ulfketel, and Lemmer; and in Cambridgeshire: Leswi abbot, and all the convent in Ely, and Ælfwine abbot, and all the convent in Ramsey, and Ælfwine, and Ulfketel child, and Osgot Sweyn, and Ordger, and the other Ordger; and in Essex: Alfger the earl's son, and Lefkild, and Osulf File, and Wulwine, and Sendi, and Leuerich sewer. Who shall avert this testament, unless it be myself, may God fordo him now and on doomsday. Amen.

Þise write sinden þre. on schal into Seynt Eadmunde. and on into Ely. and on schal ben innon min owen hird. And þat lond at Henham Þurstan and Ægelgið and Askil unnen Ægelswide after here aldre day. and after hire day go þat lond into Sc̃e Aetheldrith for hire owen soule. and for Þurstanes. and for Agelgið. and for Lefware. and for Askilles. boten þo tueye hidan þe Aylmer Parl haueð. and buten þat on hide þe Wlmare hauede. ⁊ an girde þe Lustwine hauede. And ic an Þurgot mine cnihte half hide þe Ælstan on sit at Aungre. ⁊ Meruin half hide. and þane litle hege with

Of this writing there are three: one shall go to St Eadmund's, and one to Ely, and one to my own family. And the land at Henham, Thurstân and Ægelgith and Askil give to Ægelswith, after her parents' day; and after her day, let the land go to St Ætheldrith's, for her own soul, and for Thurstân's, and for Ægelgith's, and for Lefwaru's, and for Askil's, except the two hides that Aylmer Parl has, and except the one hide that Wulmær had, and one rod that Lustwine had. And I give to Thurgot my page half a hide on which Ælstân resides at Ongar; and to Merwyn half a hide, and the

Meredene· and Sueyn half hide· and þat ouer beth ofgon he it on unker gemede· gif wit aleten willen.

little enclosure by Mereden; and to Sweyn half a hide, and what shall be over, let him hold it on at our pleasure whether we will relinquish it.

KING EADWARD THE CONFESSOR. M.XLV.

LICENCE TO TOLE TO BEQUEATH HER LAND AND PROPERTY.

✠ Edward kyng gret Heremann bisceop· ⁊ Harold eorl· ⁊ ealle mīne þegenas on Dorsætan freondlice. And ic cyðe eow ꝥ hit is mīn fulla unna ꝥ Tole mīn man Urces lāfe ꝥ heo becweðe hire land ⁊ ehta into Sancte Petre æt Abbodesbyrig swa hire leofest sy· be mīnan fullan geleafan· swa full ⁊ swa forð swa þa forewirda ǽr gewrhte wæran· ꝥ hit sceolde æfter heora begra dæge· hire ⁊ Urces hire hlāfordes· for heora sawle gān into ðam haligan mynstre. Nu wille ic ꝥ heora cwide stande swa swa hit geforewird wes on gōdre manna gewitnesse· þe þærwið wæran. ⁊ ic wille ꝥ swilc freols beo into ðam mynstre swilce is into elcan oðre ðær þe best is on eallan þingan. ⁊ ic me sylf wille beon geheald ⁊ mund þerofer· ⁊ ofer þa āre þe þar into hirð. ⁊ ic nelle

✠ I king Eadward greet bishop Heremann and earl Harold, and all my thanes in Dorsetshire, amicably. And I make known to you that it is my full permission, that Tole, my vassal, Urk's relict, may bequeath her land and property to St Peter's at Abbotsbury, as may to her be most agreeable, with my full leave, as fully and as freely as the agreements were before made: that it should, after the day of them both, hers, and Urk her lord's, for the souls of them both, go to that holy monastery. I now will that their bequest stand, as it was agreed with the witness of good men who were thereby. And I will that there be such freedom in that monastery as is in every other where it is best in all things. And I myself will be guardian and protector thereover, and over nanan menn geþafian ðe þar geũtige ænig ðæra þinga þæs ðe hig ðiderinn gedõn habbað.

the property which thereto belongs. And I will not permit any man that he there alienate any of the things which they have given thereto.

THURSTÂN. M.XLIX.

✠ Her cyð on þysan gewrite ꝥ Þurstãn gean þæs landes æt Wimbisc into Xp̃es cyrcean for his saule · ⁊ for Leofware · ⁊ for Æðelgyðe · þam hirede to fostre · æfter Þurstãnes dæge · ⁊ æfter Æðelgyðe · buton twam hidan. ⁊ gelæste se hired æt Xp̃es cyrcean for Þurstãnes saule ⁊ for Æþelgyðe þam hirede into Sc̃e Augustine · twelf pund be getale[1]. Þis syndon þa gewitnysse þæs cwydes · Eadwerd kyncg · ⁊ Ælfgyfu seo hlæfdige · ⁊ Eadsige arcebiscop · ⁊ Ælfric arceƀ. ⁊ Godwine eorl · ⁊ Leofric eorl · ⁊ Ælfgar þes eorlles sune · ⁊ Ælfweard ƀ. on Lundene · ⁊ Ælfwine ƀ. on Winceastre · ⁊ Stigand p̃. ⁊ Eadwold p̃. ⁊ Leofcild scirgerefa · ⁊ Osulf Fila · ⁊

✠ Here is made known, in this writing, that Thurstân gives the land at Wimbish to Christchurch, for his soul, and for Leofwaru's, and for Æthelgyth's, for the subsistence of the convent, after Thurstân's day, and after Æthelgyth's; except two hides. And let the convent at Christchurch pay, for Thurstân's soul and for Æthelgyth's, to the convent at St Augustine's, twelve pounds by tale[1]. These are the witnesses of this bequest: king Eadward, and Ælfgyfu the lady, and archbishop Eadsige, and archbishop Ælfric, and earl Godwine, and earl Leofric, and Ælfgar the earl's son, and Ælfward bishop of London, and Ælfwine bishop of Winchester, and Stigand

[1] oððe twa hida. ⁊ ælcon geare án pund to fulre sutelunge. þa hwile ðe we libban. ⁊ gelæste se hired æt Xp̃es cyrcean swa hwæder swa he wille.—*MS. Cant. add.*

or two hides; and every year one pound, in full acknowledgment, as long as we live; and let the convent at Christchurch pay whichsoever it will.

Ufic. ⁊ Ælfwine Wulfredes sunu. ⁊ Ælfric Wihtgares sunu. ⁊ ealle þa þegenas on Eastsexan. ⁊ beon heora menn frige æfter heora beira dæge. ⁊ na stinge nān mann æfter heora dæge on ꝥ land buton se hyred æt Xp̄es cyrcean. ⁊ yrfan hi swa hi wyrðe witan. ⁊ þissera gewrita sindan þreo. ān is æt Xp̄es cyrcean. oðer æt Sc̄e Augustine. þridde mid heom sylfan.

priest, and Eadwold pr̃., and Leofcild shire-reeve, and Osulf Fila, and Ufic, and Ælfwine Wulfred's son, and Ælfric Wihtgar's son, and all the thanes in Essex. And be their men free after the day of them both. And let no man exercise any authority over that land, after their day, except the convent at Christchurch; and let those inherit whom they know worthy. And of these writings there are three: one is at Christchurch, the second at St Augustine's; the third with themselves.

Dorso. Ðurstān dedit Winchest. eccle. X. I. cōvēto. Ãglice. Anno M°XLIX.

THURKETEL HEYNG. M.L.

✠ Her kyðet on þis write ihu ic Ðurketel an min ahte after min day. Ðæt is erst. ꝥ ic an ꝥ lond at Castre ⁊ at Ðorpe. mid medwe ⁊ mid merisce. ⁊ ingong ⁊ utgong. mine soule to alisednesse. God ⁊ Sancte Benedicte ⁊ Seynt Eadmunde to Biry ⁊ to Holme. ⁊ mine wiues del euere unbesaken to gyfen ⁊ to habben þere hire leuest be. ⁊ mine lafard richte heregete. And Alfwen mine douter habbe ꝥ lond at Ormisby. to þan forwarde ꝥ heo it ne may

✠ Here is made known, in this writing, how I Thurketel give my possessions after my day. That is first, that I give the land at Caistor and at Thorp, with meadow and with marsh, and ingress and egress, for the redemption of my soul, to God, and St Benedict, and to St Eadmund, at Bury and at Holme; and my wife's portion for ever uncontested, to give and to have where to her may be most desirable; and to my lord his rightful heriot. And let Alfforwirken. And after hire day go ꝥ lond into Holme· for mine soule ⁊ for hire· buten ꝥ lond ꝥ Omund ahte· ꝥ habbe Ketel mine nefe. And ꝥ lond at Scrouteby habben mine nefe Kild Swegnes sunen ⁊ Alemundes. And an pund habbe se abbot on Holm· anoðer se abbot on Byri· ⁊ mine men fre þo it ihernen wellen. And wo so þis quides bereuen wylle bereue hym God heueriche· buten he it her bete. Đise write sinden þre· an is on Holme· ⁊ oðer on Byri· þridde mid Đurketel seluen.

wen my daughter have the land at Ormsby, on the condition that she may not deteriorate it. And after her day, let that land go to Holme, for my soul and for hers, except the land that Omund possessed, that let Ketel my nephew have. And let my nephews, the sons of Kild Swegen and Alemund, have the land at Scroutby. And let the abbot of Holme have a pound; another the abbot of Bury; and let my men be free, those who shall deserve it. And whosoever will bereave this bequest, may God bereave him of the heavenly kingdom, unless he previously make amends for it. Of this writing there are three: one is at Holme, and the second at Bury; the third with Thurkytel himself.

THORED.

Ic Þored geann ꝥ land æt Horslege þam hirede æt Cristes cyrcean· for mine sawle· swa full ⁊ swa forð swa ic sylf hit ahte.

I Thored give the land at Horsley to the convent at Christchurch, for my soul, as full and as free as I myself possessed it.

THURKYTEL. M.L.

[H]er switeleþ ihu Þurketel an his ahte after his day.

Here is made known how Thurkytel gives his posþat is erst· for his soule· Palegraue into Seynt Eadmund· and Witingham half· and half þe bisscop. And alle mine men fre· and ilk habbe his toft· and his metecu· ⁊ his metecorn. And ic an at Reydoneberh þat midleste forlong fre into ðe kirke· and Scortland· and þe prestes toft· al into þe kirke fre. And ic an Lefwen mīn wif Simplingham· al þat ceaplond ⁊ þat oþer þat ic mid hire nam· and half Reydon· mid mete and mid erue[1]· to þat forwarde þat we spreken habben· ⁊ mīne men fre. And ic an Wingefeld mine broþeres sunes Ulfketel and Þurfketel. And ic an Lefquene fiftene acres at Palegraue and an toft. And Wlwine habbe þat lond þe he mines hafde· ⁊ Alfwold habbe mid ton þe he her hauede· xvi. acres mid tofte mid alle. And Osebern habbe þat lond be siden Þrandestoñ þat ic þer hauede. And ic an Lefric mine neue· and Godwine mine mey· and Wlwine ⁊ his brother xx. acres at Reydone· and þe mor þe ic ⁊ þo munekes soken ymbe min del· fremannen to note· so hi er deden· er daye

sessions after his day. That is first, for his soul, Palgrave to St Eadmund's, and half of Whittingham, and half to the bishop. And be all my men free, and let each have his toft, and his meat-cow, and his bread-corn. And I give at Reydon hill the midmost furlong free to the church; and Scortland, and the priest's toft, all to the church free. And I give to Lefwen, my wife, Simplingham, all the chap-land, and the other which I took with her, and half of Reydon, with meat and with cattle, according to our spoken agreement: and be my men free. And I give Wingfield to my brother's sons, Ulfketel and Thurfketel. And I give to Leofquen fifteen acres at Palgrave and one toft. And let Wulwine have the land that he had of mine, and let Alfwold have, with the vill which he had before, xvi. acres with toft altogether. And let Osbern have the land beside Thrandiston that I had there. And I give to Leofric my nephew, and to Godwine my kinsman, and to Wulwine and his brother, xx. acres at Reydon, and the moor, about

[1] For erue (erfe) we should probably read mannum, as in numerous other instances: as it now stands, the text seems devoid of sense.

⁊ after daye. Seþe þis awende wende him God fro heuene riche into helle witerbrogen· bute he hit þe deppere bete er his ending day. Ðise write sinden þre· on is at Seynt Eadmundesbiri· oþer haueð þe bisscop· þridde haueð Þurketel himself.

my part of which the monks and I contended, for the use of freemen, as they before did, in former times and aftertimes. Whoever shall avert this, may God turn him from the kingdom of heaven into the penal terrors of hell, unless he the more deeply compensate ere his final day. Of these writings there are three: one is at St Eadmundsbury, the second the bishop has; the third Thurkytel himself has.

KETEL ALDER. M.L.

✠ Her is on þis write Keteles quide. Ðat is þat ic an Stistede after mine tyme· for mine fader soule ⁊ for Sefledan· into Cristes kirke. And ic wille þat mine men ben alle fre· ⁊ Mann myne refe þat he sitte on þe fre lond þat ic him to honde habbe leten· his time euere fre· and after his time folege þat lond þen oþere. And ic an into þere kyrke þat lond þat Withrich hauede under hande· and Lewine· and Siric· and Goding· so so Gearagod to Leueriches hyge. And þat no man him ne forwerne þan utgang. And ic wille þat alle þo men þe ic an fre þat hi habben alle þinge þe hi under

✠ Here, in this writing, is the bequest of Ketel. That is, that I give Stistead, after my time, for my father's soul and for Seflæd's, to Christchurch. And I will that all my men be free, and that Mann my reeve reside on the free land which I leased over to him, for his time ever free; and after his time let that land follow the other. And I give to that church the land that Withric had in hand, and Lewine, and Siric, and Goding, so also Gearagod at Leofricshyge. And let no man refuse him the egress. And I will that all the men that I make free have all the things which they have in hand, honde habben buten þat lond. And ic an þat lond at Herlinge Stigand archebiscop mine louerd so it stant· buton þo men ben alle fre· and ten acres ic an into þe kirke· and gif ic ongein ne cume· þan an ic him to min heregete an helm and a brenie· and hors and gereade· and suerd· and spere. And ic wille· after þe forewarde· þat ic and Eadwine and Wlfric after mine time fon to alkere þinge ðe min ower is þer on tune[1]· buten so mikel so ic an into þe kirke· þat is þat eringlond þat Alfwold mine man haued under hande· and he sitte on þat oðer his time· and siðen al þat lond þat him to honde begeð folege mid ðe oðere into þe kirke. Gif Eadwyne min em wille helden se felageshipe mid me ⁊ min em Wlfric ymbe þat lond at Meþeltune· gif wit him ouerbiden· fon we to þat lond at Đorpe· into þat forewarde þat [ouer] ure boðere time go þat lond at Meðelton for ure heldren soule ⁊ ure awene soule into Seinte Benedicte at Holm· and þat lond at Đorpe into Seinte Edmundesbiri. And þat is min and mine sustres Boten þat foreward· gif ic

except the land. And I give the land at Harling to archbishop Stigand, my lord, as it stands, except that the men be all free, and ten acres which I give to the church; and if I come not again, then I give him, for my heriot, a helm, and a coat of mail, and a horse and trappings, and a sword and a spear. And I will, according to the compact, that I, and Eadwine and Wulfric after my time, succeed to everything that is anywhere mine in the 'tûn', save so much as I give to the church; that is the arable land that Alfwold my man has in hand: and that he reside on the other for his time; and afterwards that all the land that he has in hand follow with the other to the church. If Eadwine my uncle will hold the fellowship with me and Wulfric my uncle about the land at Metheltûn; if we two survive him, we succeed to the land at Thorp, with the understanding that, after the time of us both, the land at Metheltûn go, for the souls of our parents and for our own souls, to St Benedict's at Holme; and the land at Thorp to St Eadmunds-

[1] time, *both MSS.*

mine day do her his þat ic[1] fon to þat lond at Keteringham. and an marc goldes. oþer þe wrð. And gif ic hire ouerbide þanne schal ic habben þat lond at Somerledeton. And þat ilke forewarde ic and Gode mine soster habbet speken. gif he me ouerbide. gripe he to þat lond at Walsingham. buten ten acres þo schulen into þere kirke. And gif ic libbe leng þanne hio. þanne schal ic habben þat lond at Prestone. And ic an Godric mine broðer þat lond at Hemfordham[2] so it me on hande stand. and Keckeshale[3]. and he schal for þat lond at Strattune[4] gifen Alwy mine cnihte to pund. And ic and Algif min stepdouter wit habben wrouth þe forwarde ymbe þat lond at Anhus.[5] þat so weðer unker so lengere libbe habbe þat lond so mikel so wit ðer habben. and gif unc ban fordsið sceet on Romeweye. þanne go þat lond. for me and for Sefled. and for Algiue into Seint Eadmundesbiri. bute þo men ben alle fre. And ic an Harold erl. after mine time. þe halue lond at Moran.

bury. And that is my and my sister Bote's compact: if I end my day ere hers, that she succeed to the land at Keteringham, and one mark of gold, or the worth. And if I survive her, then I am to have the land at Somerleyton. And the same compact I and Gode, my sister, have spoken: if she survive me, let her take the land at Walsingham, except ten acres, which are to go to the church. And if I live longer than she, then I am to have the land at Preston. And I give to Godric, my brother, the land at Hemfordham[2], as it stands in my hand, and Buxhall: and for the land at Stratton he shall give to Alwy, my page, two pounds. And I and Algif, my stepdaughter, have made the agreement concerning the land at Onehouse, that whichsoever of us two live the longer, have of that land so much as we two have there; and if death befall us both on the way to Rome, then go that land for me, and for Sefled, and for Ælfgifu, to St Eadmundsbury, except that the men be all free. And I

[1] read he (heo). N.B. The masc. pronouns he, his, are here applied to the woman.
[2] Homfordham, MS. 14847.
[3] Boccheshale, *ib.*
[4] Stantone, *ib.*
[5] Onhus, *ib.*

so ful and so forð so ic it richt-like· on Godes witnesse and mani manne· mid mine wife bigat· and ic it siðen nawer ne forswat ne forspilde. And ic bidde þe· þurh þene Dricht-in se ðe and alle schefte schop· gif ic ongen ne cume· þat þu it nefre ne let weldon mine unwinan after me þe mid unrichte sitteð ðeron ⁊ nyttað it· me euere to un-ðanke. And ic an þe lond at Fretinge after þat ilke for-ward þat þu þe self and Stig-and archebiscop mine louerd wrouhten. And ic an Alfric mine prest and mine cuðen þat lond at Rissewrðe. And gif ani man si so disi þat wille mine quide bereuen· God him fordo on domesday· and alle his halegen.

give to earl Harold after my time half the land at Moran, as full and as free as I it rightfully, with God's witness and many men's, obtained it with my wife; and I afterwards have nowhere impaired or wasted it. And I pray thee, by the Lord who created thee and all creatures, that if I come not again, thou wilt never let my adversaries gain possession of it, who unrightfully reside thereon, and enjoy it, ever against my will. And I give the land at Fritton, according to the same agreement which thou thyself and archbishop Stigand, my lord, made. And I give to Ælfric, my priest and my kinsman, the land at Rushworth. And if any man be so foolish that he will bereave my testament, may God and all his saints fordo him on doomsday.

WULF.

In nomine Domini nostri Jhesu Christi. Ego Wulf inprimis concedo, pro anima mea, et Deo et Sancto Albano terram que vocatur Easttun, cum omnibus ad se pertinentibus, sicuti eam habui a rege, cum consensu illius, videlicet, Eadwardi regis; et illam terram similiter et Oxawicam sancte æcclesie Albani martyris, ubi et ego jacere volo; et unum de melioribus meis vestimentis que ego habeo, et unum calicem, et I. missalem, et I. dorsale, et palleam tunicam meliorem, que fuit Godgyue; alteram vero ad monasterium Ramesige; et IIII. marcas argenti ad ecclesiam Sancti Petri Rome; et IIII^or ad missas cantandas pro anima mea; et IIII. ad principales ecclesias hujus terræ; et sodalibus meis IIII. marcas auri, et omnes terras meas quas ego dimitto, preter illas duas quas Deo et Sancto Albano concessi. Et concedo Dagfino marcam auri, et Æfino II. marcas argenti, et I. equum; et Æþelrico ministro II. marcas; et Ædwardo I. equum; et singulis hominibus meis qui terras non habent, singulos equos. Et si adhuc de auro vel argento aliquid superest, ille plus habeat qui plus pro anima mea facere voluerit. Et XXX. de mancipiis meis libertatem pro anima mea habeant.

EADNOTH AND WIFE. M.XLIX.-M.LIV.

Notum sit universis hec legentibus, quod ego Ædnothus et uxor mea dedimus et concessimus Deo et Sancto Benedicto Ramesiæ terram nostram de Acleia in perpetuam elemosinam, pro nostris et patrum matrumque nostrarum et filiorum nostrorum animabus. Talem autem conventionem fecimus cum Ælfwino abbate et conventu Ramesie de eadem donatione. Nos quidem in vita nostra eandem terram nomine ecclesie tenebimus, sed neuter nostrum poterit ulla ratione eam alibi dare vel distrahere, vel ingenium querere per quod a prefate ecclesie dominio alienetur; sed post mortem utriusque, meam scilicet et mee uxoris, tota simul quieta et ab omni calumpnia libera in manum abbatis et fratrum transibit. Cum autem in dominio eam habuerint, duas libras singulis annis Ætherico monacho, filio nostro, inde ad vestitum procurabunt, quatinus idem Æthericus, hujus respectu beneficii, humilis et devotus Deo sit, abbati quoque et fratribus suis tractabilis. Qui si forte habitum suum et monasterium relinquens reverti voluerit, nichil omnino inde ulterius percipiat. Concessimus autem Lefwino homini nostro virgatam terre, in qua mansum suum habet, in vita sua quietam; post decessum vero ipsius, in possessionem ecclesie simul cum principali parte redibit; dimidiam vero partem hominum qui in memorata terra sub servitute degunt, libertate donavimus. Rogamus ergo et obsecramus, per Dei terribile nomen, ut nullus omnino hanc terram donet vel vendat vel aliquo modo ab eadem ecclesia alienet. Quod si quis fecerit, sit ille maledictus et alienatus ab omni beatitudine presentis vite et future, sitque ejus commoratio cum demonibus in inferno, ubi ignis eorum non extinguitur, et vermis eorum non morietur.

ÆGELRIC BIGGA. M.L.-M.LIV.

Hic notatur quod Ægelricus Bigga concedit Sancto Augustino post obitum suum, concessu domini sui Ædwardi regis, terras Bodesham et Wilrintun, eo pacto quod Wade ejus miles sedeat dies suos in Bodesham, et Lifwine Feireage sedeat dies suos in Wilrinton; et post obitum amborum terræ remaneant Sancto Augustino, et abbas procuret terras ad opus monasterii, sicut amorem habere Dei velit, et Sancti Petri, et Sancti Augustini. Et Dei odium habeat quisquis hanc donationem infregerit, nisi cicius emendaverit erga Dominum et sanctos ibi quiescentes.

Huic donationi sunt testes: Eadzinus archiepiscopus, et conventus Christi ecclesie, et Robertus episcopus Londoñ, et Godwinus episcopus Sancti Martini, etc.

QUEEN ÆLFGIFU EMMA. ABOUT M.LIII.

Her swytelað on þisum gewritæ þæt Ælfgifu seo hlefdige bæcweð v. hida æt Heilincigæ into Ealdan mynstræ[1]. and heo bæcwæð Wulfweardæ Hwitan v. hida of	Here is made known, in this writing, that Ælfgifu the lady has bequeathed v. hides at Hayling island to the Old monastery[1]; and she has bequeathed to Wulfweard

[1] At Winchester.

þam ilcan landæ his dæg· and æftær his dæge ga þa v. hida into Ealdan mynstræ. Þus seo hlæfdige hit bæcwed Wulfweardæ. Þa wes Wulfweard gyrnendæ þæt hæ mostæ ofgan his deg þa v. hida þæ wæron into mynstre bæcweðene· and sæ bisceop Stigandæ and sæ hiræd on Ealdan mynstræ him þæs gætiþodon wið swylcon gersumen swylce hi þa sehtæ wæron. Nū wæron þus heora forewæarð· þæt Wulfweard hebbæ þa v. hida his dæg· and æftær his dæge ga þa v. hida into Ealdan mynstræ· and þa oþræ v. hida forð mið þæ seo hlæfdige him bæcwæð· mid mæte ⁊ mid mannum· ⁊ mid eallum þingum swa hīt þonnæ stænt butan ælcon geantalæ.

Ðises is to witnæssæ Stigandæ bisceop· and Harold eorl· and sæ hired on Ealdan mynstræ· and Ælfwine abbod· and sæ hired on Niwan mynstræ· and Leofing stæallære· and Raulf stæallære· and Æscar steallære· and Eadsige scirgeræfa· and Wulfric æt Wernæforda· and Ælfwine· and Ælfweard· and Cupping· and eallæ scirþegnas on Hamtunscíræ.

White v. hides of the same land for his day; and after his day let the v. hides go to the Old monastery. The lady thus bequeathed it to Wulfweard. Wulfweard was at the time desirous of possessing for his day the v. hides that had been bequeathed to the monastery; and the bishop Stigand and the brotherhood of the Old monastery allowed it him for such consideration as they agreed on. Now their agreements were thus: that Wulfheard should have the v. hides for his day, and after his day the v. hides should go to the Old monastery, and the other v. hides along with them which the lady had bequeathed to him, with meat and with men, and with all things as they stand, without any gainsaying.

Of this are witness Stigand bishop, and Harold earl, and the convent at the Old monastery, and Ælfwine abbot, and the convent at the New monastery, and Leofing constable, and Rauf constable, and Æscar constable, and Eadsige shire-reeve, and Wulfric at Warnford, and Ælfwine, and Ælfweard, and Cupping, and all the shire-thanes in Hampshire.

Þissæ gewrita syndon III.· an is on Ealdan mynstræ· and þæt oþær is on Niwan mynstre· and þæt þridde heafð Wulfwearð.

Of this writing there are III.: one is at the Old monastery, and the second at the New monastery, and the third Wulfweard has.

ORDNOTH AND WIFE.

✠ Her is geswutelod on þisum gewrite hū Ordnoð ⁊ his wīf geūðan ðara x. hida æt Cendefer into þære ealdan cyrican to Wintanceastre ofer heora begra deg· ⁊ þa bōc þyderinnan sealdan to swutelunge· on þa gerād ꝥ seo bōc heam sy geara· gyf hy hyre hwer beðurfan to ænire rihtinge. ⁊ gange seo bōc æft into ðære stowe. ⁊ dæle man swylcne dæl heora æhta swylce hy gecwedan æfter heora dege. ⁊ gange seo ofereaca into þære stowe mid þam lande. On ða gereðnesse is ꝥ land geseld to þam mynstre· ꝥ man unc gefecce æt uncrum ændedege mid þes mynstres crafte· ⁊ unc swylce legerstowe forescewian swylc unc for Gode þearflice sy· ⁊ for worulde gerysenlic. Ðis is seo gewitnes ðe Ordnoð wile habban Godæs ⁊ his hiredes on Ealdan mynstre· ꝥ is ꝥ he ⁊ is wīf cwædan on heora

✠ Here is made known, in this writing, how Ordnoth and his wife have given the x. hides at Candever to the old church at Winchester, after the day of them both; and the charter have therein given as testimonial, on the condition, that the charter be ready for them, if they at any time stand in need of it for any rectification. And let the charter go afterwards to the convent. And let such part of their possessions be divided, after their day, as they have said, and the surplus go to the convent with the land. On this condition is the land given to the monastery: that they shall fetch us at our last day with the means of the monastery, and provide us such a resting-place as may be needful to us before God, and decent before the world. This is the witness that Ordnoth will have of God and his con-gewitnesse. ꝥ is æhta gangan on his freonda hand ofer his deg. se del ðe he cweðe. ⁊ se oðer dæl into ðære stowe ðær hi restað.

vent at the Old monastery, that is, that he and his wife have declared, with their witness, that his possessions pass into his friends' hands, after his day [i. e.] the part which he has said; and the other part to the place where they shall rest.

EADWINE DE CADENDUNE.

In nomine Domini nostri Jhesu Christi. Hic demonstratur quomodo Ædwinus de Cadendune suam hereditatem divisit. Hoc est, ego Eadwinus inprimis do terram que vocatur Watford, pro anima mea, Deo et Sancto Albano; et filio meo Leofuuino, Sunnandune, et Cadandune, et Stræstlea, et Hætlea, et Pirian, et Puttanho, et Beranlea. Et post obitum filii mei Leofuuini habeat Sanctus Albanus Beranlea et possideat in perpetuum. Et volo ut de pecoribus meis melioribus eligantur xx. boves et xx. vaccas ad sanctum locum ubi ego jacere cupio, id est, apud Sanctum Albanum.

EADWINE. M.LX.

✠ On min Drihtines name. Ic Eadwine kiðe ihu þat ic an ðe þinge ðe me God almichtin haue lent on þise liue. Þat is þat ic an þat land at Eskeresðorp into Seint Eadmund. buten ten acres ic giue þer into ðere kirke. and Lefric habbe ðe þre acres ðe he onsit. and ic an ðat lond at

✠ In the name of my Lord. I Eadwine make known how I give the things that God Almighty has given me in this life. That is, that I give the land at Eskeresthorp to St Eadmund, except ten acres which I give to the church there; and let Lefric have the three acres on which he re-

Litle Meddeltone into Sancte Benedicte[1]· ⁊ ten acres into ðe kirke· and ic an ðat lond at Beorh into Sancte Eðeldride bi suðen Kinges strete· buten ðat norðere hage at Appelsco and half ðe turfgret[2] ligge into Apetune· and ðerto weye to rode brod· and ten akres into Beorhkirke be suðen strete· and ten acres into Apetune kirke bi norðen strete· and four acres into Huluestou kirke· and four acres into Blitleford kirke· and x. acres into Sparham kirke. And alle mine men fre eywer after mine tyme.

Ðis is ðat frescet ðe Eadwine haued Crist unnen ⁊ Seynte Marie ⁊ alle Cristes halegen· his sowle to alisednesse ⁊ his sinne to forgiuenesse.

And ðis is ðe forward ðe Wlfric and Eadwine ða tueye breðere wrouhten hem bituen ymbe ða to lond at Ðorp and at Middelton. Þat is se ðe here so lenger libbe habbe boðe ðe lond· and after here boðere day go ðat lond at Middilton into Sancte Benedicte for here boðere soule. And ðat lond at Ðorpe after here boðere day fange Ketel

sides; and I give the land at Little Middleton to St Benedict[1], and ten acres to the church; and I give the land at Berg, south of King Street, to St Ætheldryth, except the north 'haga' at Applesco, and half the turfpit adjacent to Apton, and thereto a way two roods broad; and ten acres to Berg church, south of the street; and ten acres to Apton church, north of the street; and four acres to Hulveston church; and four acres to Blitleford church; and x. acres to Sparham church. And let all my men be everywhere free after my time.

This is the free gift which Eadwine has given to Christ and St Mary, and all Christ's saints, for the redemption of his soul and the forgiveness of his sins.

And this is the agreement that Wulfric and Eadwine, the two brothers, have wrought between them respecting the two lands at Thorp and at Middleton. That is, that whichsoever of them live the longer, have both the lands; and after the day of them both, the land at Middleton go to St Benedict, for the souls of them both. And to

[1] At Holme.

[2] turfgref ?

þerto· to swilke forwarde so ðer wrouht is· ðat is ðat Ketel leste alke iher to pund into Seynt Eadmunde· ðat is ðas londes gouel· and for here eyðeres soule ilke day ane messe. And after Keteles day go ðat lond into Seynt Eadmunde buton alken gentale· and at Meðeltone into ðere kirke ðe Đurwerd ahte· and ðat lond ðe Eadwine Ecferðes sune ahte fre into ðe kirke· and of ðat lond at Đorp VIII. acres into Æscewelle kirke· and of ðat lond at Wreningham VIII. acres into ðe elde kirke· and to acres into Fundenhale kirke and into Neolandes kirke.

Đise write sinden þre· on is binnen at Sancte Eadmunde· anoðer at Sancte Benedicte on Holm· ⁊ te þridde haued Eadwine himself.

the land at Thorp, after the day of them both, let Ketel succeed, under such agreement as there is made: that is, that every year Ketel pay two pounds to St Eadmund, which is the rent of the land, and, for the soul of each of them, every day one mass. And after Ketel's day, let the land go to St Eadmund, without any gainsaying, and [that] at Middleton to the church which Thurwerd possessed; and the land which Eadwine Ecgferth's son possessed, free to the church; and of the land at Thorp VIII. acres free to Ashwell church; and of the land at Wreningham, VIII. acres to the old church, and two acres to Fundenhall church and to Neoland church.

Of these writings there are three: one is in at St Eadmund's, the second at St Benedict's in Holme; and the third Eadwine himself has.

THURKIL AND ÆTHELGITH. M.LX.

[Th]urkil and Æþelgit unnen Wigorham into Seynt Eadmunde· so ful ⁊ so forth so wit it owen· after unker bother day· and þo men half

Thurkil and Æthelgith give Wigram to St Eadmund, as full and as free as we two possess it, after the day of us: and let half the men be fre. þeowe ⁊ lisingas. Se þe þis benime. God him benime heuene riche.

free, serfs and 'lisings'[1]. Whoso shall deprive them of this, may God deprive him of heaven's kingdom.

SIFLÆD. M.LX.

✠ Her switeleð ihu Sifled an hire aihte ouer hire day. Ðat is erst. into Seynte Eadmunde Marðingford for hire leue soule. al buten tuenti acres and tueye wainegong wudes. ⁊ þere wude norð ouer. And min kirke be fre. and Wlmer prest singe þerat. and his bearntem so long so he þen to þen hode. ⁊ fre leswe into þere kirke. and mine men fre. And be Seynt Eadmund mund þer ouer þene freschot. Se ðe þise cuide wille awenden be he amansid from God almichtin. and fram alle hise halegen. and fram Sancte Eadmunde.

✠ Here is made manifest how Siflæd gives her property after her day. That is first: to St Eadmund's, Mardingford, for her dear soul, all save twenty acres, and two waingangs of wood, and the wood north over. And be my church free; and let Wulmær the priest and his children sing thereat so long as he ministers to the cowl; and be there free pasture to the church, and be my men free. And be St Eadmund protector there over the 'freschot'. Whosoever will set aside this bequest, be he excommunicated from God Almighty and from all his saints, and from St Eadmund.

SIFLÆD. M.LX.

✠ Her switeleð on ðis write ihu Sifled uðe hire aihte

✠ Here is shown, in this writing, how Siflæd gave her

[1] Freed, or partially freed serfs?

ðo sche ouer se ferde. Ðat is erst into ðe tūnkirke on Mardingford v. acres and ane toft· and II. acres medwe· and to waynegong to wude. And ic [an] mine landseðlen here toftes to owen aihte· ⁊ alle mine men fre. And ic an eiðer mine broðer ane wayngong to wude. And ic an into Norðwich to Cristes kirke IIII. retheren· and to into Seynte Marian· and on into mine duzine[1]. And ic an into Seynt Eadmunde al þat þere to lafe gesceotte· þat beð on Mardingforda hus and hom· and wude and felde· and on medwe and on yrue. And gif ic hom cume· þanne wille ic sitten on þat lond mine day· and after mine day stonde þat cuide. And wo so þis awende God awende his ansene from him on domes day· buten he hit here bete.

property when she went over sea. That is first, to the village-church at Mardingford v. fields and one toft, and II. fields of meadow, and two waingangs at the wood. And I give my land-tenants their tofts for their own property: and be all my men free. And I give to both my brothers one waingang at the wood. And I give to Christchurch at Norwich IV. oxen; and two to S Mary's, and one to my 'duzine'[1]. And I give to S[t] Eadmund's all that there may prove of residue, that is at Mardingford, house and home, and wood and field, both in meadow and in cattle. And if I come home, then will I reside on the land for my day; and after my day, let the bequest stand. And whoso shall avert this, may God avert his countenance from him on doomsday, unless he make amends here.

WULFGEAT AND WIFE. ABOUT M.LX.

✠ Her swyteleþ on þise write þe forward þe Wlfgeat and his wif wrouhten wið þan abbot on Seynt Eadmundes-

✠ Here is made known, in this writing, the agreement which Wulfgeat and his wife made with the abbot of St Ead-

[1] fool, from dysig?

biri. and alle þe hirede. þat is þat he unnen ðat lond at Gyselingham to ðe forwarde ðat ðat ilke lond go into Sancte Eadmunde after Ælfwines day and his wiues. And ðat lond at Fakenham. so ful and so forð so Wlfgeat hit oh. go it into Seynt Eadmunde after here boðere day. buten alken gentale.

Ðise write sinden þre. on hauið Wlfgeat himself. oðer is in Seynt Eadmundesbiri. þridde hauið Stigand bisscop.

mundsbury and all the convent. That is, that they give the land at Gislingham on the agreement that the same land go to St Eadmund's after the day of Ælfwine and his wife. And let the land at Fakenham, as full and as free as Wulfgeat possessed it, go to St Eadmund's after the day of them both, without any gainsaying.

Of this writing there are three: one Wulfgeat himself has, the second is at St Eadmundsbury, the third bishop Stigand has.

ULF AND WIFE. ABOUT M.LXVI.

✠ Ðis is seo feorewearde þe Ulf and Madselm his gebedda worhtan wið [God] ⁊ wið Sc̃e Peter. þa hı̃g to Ierusalem ferdon. Þat is þat land æt Carlatune into Burh æfter heora dæge heora saule to alysednesse. ⁊ þat land æt Bytham into Sc̃e Guthlace[1]. ⁊ þat land æt Sempingaham into Sc̃e Benedicte to Ramesege. ⁊ þat land æt Lofintune ⁊ æt Heordewican Ealdrede b̄.. to fullon ceape. ⁊ þat land æt Scillintune. ⁊ æt

✠ This is the agreement that Ulf and Madselm his consort made with God and St Peter, when they went to Jerusalem. That is, [they give] the land at Carlton to Peterborough after their day, for the redemption of their souls; and the land at Bytham to St Guthlac's[1]; and the land at Sempringham to St Benedict's at Ramsey; and the land at Lofington and at Hardwick to bishop Ealdred, at full price; and the land at

[1] At Crowland.

Houcbig· ⁊ æt Mortune· þæron stent þam bisceope eahta marca goldes. ⁊ gif hĩg ham cuman· gylde þam ƀ. his gold· ⁊ gif heora naðer ne cumð· do se ƀ. for heora saule swa mycel swa þat land is betere þene þæt gold sy. ⁊ gif þam ƀ. getid buton eal teala· ga þe aƀƀ. Brand to þam ilcan foreweardan. ⁊ þæt land æt Mannethorp ic habbe geunnan þam abbot Brande· ⁊ þæt land æt Willabyg ic habbe geunnan Siferðe minen mæge· ⁊ þæt land æt Stoce heo hafað geunnan Lyfgyfan hyre magan· ⁊ þæt land æt Stroðistune heo hafað geunnan Ingemunde· ⁊ he hyre [an] þa Westhealle ongean æt Wintringatune. ⁊ ꝥ land æt Ofertune syllæ man ⁊ do for heora begra saule. ⁊ twa land ic habbe geunnen minre modar· ꝥ is Kitlebig ⁊ Cotum· ⁊ heo hæfð me geunnen Mæssingaham ⁊ Kytlebi. ⁊ gif ic ham ne· cume· habbe Ingemund ꝥ land æt Coringatune· ⁊ ꝥ land æt Cleaxbyg ic habbe geunnen Healþene minan breþer· ⁊ ꝥ land æt Urmesbyg into Sc̃e Marian stowe. ⁊ eal ꝥ ic þer ahte· ⁊ Lindbeorhge habban mine cnihtas· gif ic ham ne cume· ⁊ ꝥ land æt Lohtune ꝥ heo hafað þerinne into Þornege.

Shillington, and at Hoby, and at Morton, whereon are due to the bishop eight marks of gold. And if they come home, let the bishop be paid his gold; and if neither of them come, let the bishop do for their souls as much as the land is better than the gold is. And if it betide the bishop other than all good, let the abbot Brand enter on the same agreement. And I have given the land at Manthorp to the abbot Brand; and the land at Willoughby I have given to Siferth my kinsman; and the land at Stoke she has given to Lyfgyfu her kinswoman; and the land at Strothiston she has given to Ingemund; and he gives to her in return the Westhall at Winterton. And let the land at Overton be sold, and be applied for the souls of them both. And two lands I have given to my mother, viz. at Kettleby and Cotum; and she has given me Messingham and Kytleby. And if I come not home, let Ingemund have the land at Carrington; and the land at Claxby I have given to Healdene my brother; and the land at Ormsby and all that I there possessed, to St Mary's convent. And let my pages have the land at Linbeorh if I come not home; and let the land that she has at Loughton be given to Thorney.

ÆLFHELM.

✠ Her is seo swutelung hu Ælfhelm his âre ⁊ his æhta gefadod hæfð. for Gode ⁊ for worulde. Ðæt is þonne ǽrest his hlaforde ân hund mancosa goldes. ⁊ twa swurd. ⁊ feower scyldas. ⁊ feower speru. ⁊ feower hors. twa geraædode twa ungerædode. And he gean for his sawle þæs landes æt Wrættincge into Sc̃e Æðelðryðe. buton þam twam hydon ðe Æðelric hæfð. ⁊ ic gean þæs landes æt Brycandune into Sc̃e Petre to Westmenstre. buton ic wylle ꝥ man mæste minum wīfe twa hund swīna. ðænne þær mæsten sy. þider hire leofest sy. ⁊ ic gean Ælfgare minum suna þæs landes æt Hwipstede ⁊ þæs æt Wealtune his dæg. ⁊ æfter his dæge ga hit for uncra begra sawle þider him leofest sy. And ic cyðe hwæt ic minum wīfe to morgengife sealde. ꝥ is Beadewan. ⁊ Burgestede. ⁊ Strætford. ⁊ ða þreo hyda æt Heanhealan. ⁊ ic

✠ Here is the declaration how Ælfhelm has disposed of his property and his possessions, before God and before the world. That then is first, to his lord a hundred mancuses of gold, and two swords, and four shields, and four spears, and four horses, two caparisoned and two not caparisoned. And he gives for his soul the land at Wratting to St Æthelthryth's, except the two hides that Æthelric has. And I give the land at Brycandon to St Peter's at Westminster, except I will that there be masted for my wife two hundred swine, when there is mast there, where to her may be most desirable. And I give to Ælfgar, my son, the land at Whepstead and that at Walton, for his day; and after his day, let it go, for the souls of us both, whither to him it be most desirable. And I make known what I gave my wife for morning-gift: that is, gef hire· þa wit ǽrest togædere comon· ða twa hyda æt Wilburgeham· ⁊ æt Hrægenan· ⁊ ꝥ ðærto lið. ⁊ ic gean hire Carletunes· ⁊ ic gean hire ðæs heafodbotles æt Gyrstlingaþorpe· ⁊ ealra þæra æhta ðe þæron standað· mid mete ⁊ mid mannum· buton ic gean Godrice ⁊ minre dehter healfes þæs landes be wuda ⁊ be felda· buton ðam þe ic minum preoste gean. And ic gean minum wīfe ⁊ minre dehter healfes þæs landes æt Cunningtune to gedale· buton þam feower hydon ðe ic Æðelrice ⁊ Ælfwolde gean· ⁊ þa healfan hyde þe ic gean Osmære mīnum cnihte. And ic gean Ælfmære ⁊ his breðer Ælfstane þara twegra landa to gedale æt Hættanlea ⁊ æt Pottune· buton þam ðe ic Osgare gean. ⁊ ic gean Godere þæs ðe ic æt Wimunde gebohte. ⁊ ic gean Leofsige Lytlanbyrig æfter minum dæge· on ꝥ gerǽd ðe ꝥ stande þe wit beforan þam ealdormen lucan. ⁊ ic gean him ⁊ his wife þæs landes æt Stoctune wið ān hund mancosa goldes· ⁊ ic wylle ꝥ man selle minum hláforde ꝥ gold to minum heregeatum. ⁊ ic gean minum þrym broðrum

Baddow, and Burstead, and Stratford, and the three hides at Heanhall: and I gave to her, when we first came together, the two hides at Wilbraham, and at Rayne, and what is thereto adjacent. And I give her Carlton, and I give her the head dwelling at Gyrstlingthorp, and all the properties which stand thereon, with meat and with men; except that I give to Godric and my daughter half the land in wood and in field, except that which I give my priest. And I give to my wife and my daughter half the land at Cunnington in severalty, except the four hides which I give to Æthelric and Ælfwold, and the half hide which I give to Osmær my page. And I give to Ælfmær and his brother Ælfstân the two lands in severalty at Hatley and at Potton, except that which I give to Osgar. And I give to Godere that which I bought of Wimund. And I give to Leofsige Littlebury after my day, on the condition that that stand which we concluded before the alderman. And I give to him and his wife the land at Stockton, in consideration of a hundred mancuses of gold:

to gedale þæs landes æt Trostingtune· buton þam ðe ic gean Ælfwolde· ðæs ðe Æðelric hæfde. ⁊ ic gean Ælfhelme ðære hyde æt Icelingtune ⁊ þæs æt Mawurðe. ⁊ ic gean Wulfmære þæs ðe ic æt Biornham hæfde. ⁊ ic gean minre scæðe for minre sawle into Hramesege· healfe ðam abbode ⁊ healfe þam hirede. ⁊ ic gean minum wife healfes þæs stodes æt Trostingtune· ⁊ minum geferan healfes þe mid me ridað. ⁊ fo min wīf æfre to healfum þe on wealde is· ⁊ min dohter to healfum. ⁊ ic wille ꝥ min wīf fo æfre to healfum on ælcum tune· fo to lande se þe fo· swa hio[2] to forgifen wæs. Nu bidde ic þe leof hlaford ꝥ min cwide standan mote· ⁊ ꝥ ðu ne geþafige ꝥ hine man mid wuo wende. God is min gewita ic wæs þinum fæder swa gehyrsum swa ic fyrmest mihte· ⁊ fullice hold on mode ⁊ on mægene· ⁊ þe æfre on fullum hyldum hold ⁊ on fulre lufe· þæs me is God gewita. Se man se ðe minne cwide wende· buton þu hit sy leof· ⁊ ic hæbbe geleafan ꝥ þu nelle· God afyrre hine of his

and I will that that gold be given to my lord for my heriots. And I give to my three brothers in severalty the land at Troston, except that I give to Ælfwold that which Æthelric had. And I give to Ælfhelm the hide at Icleton, and the [land] at Maworth. And I give to Wulfmær that which I had at Barnham. And I give my 'scæð'[1], for my soul, to Ramsey, half to the abbot and half to the convent. And I give my wife half the stud at Troston, and half to my companions who ride with me. And let my wife succeed to half of what is in the forest, and my daughter to half. And I will that my wife always succeed to half in every vill, let whoever may succeed to the land, which to them was given. Now I pray thee, dear lord, that my bequest may stand, and that thou wilt not permit it to be wrongfully changed: God is my witness that I was ever so obedient to thy father as I best might, and wholly faithful in mind and deed; and to thee ever in full affection faithful, and in full love: of

[1] scægð, O. Nor. sceið, liburna; *a light swift vessel, introduced by the Northmen.*

[2] him?

rice. buton he ðe hraðor ongen wende. ⁊ God ⁊ ealle his halgan gehealde ælcne þara ðe þærto gefyrðrige ꝥ he standan mote. Gif hwa æfre ænig þing of þisum cwide awende oððe ætbrede. sy him Godes ār ⁊ his ece edlean æfre ætbroden. ⁊ he næfre ne wurðe on his myltse gemet. ac he sy amansumod of þam gemanan ealra gecorenra Cristes heapa. ge nu ge on ecnysse. buton he ðe hrædlicor ꝥ forlæte ⁊ on riht eac eft gewende.

this God is my witness. The man who shall change this my bequest (except it be thee, beloved, and I have faith that thou wilt not), may God exclude him from his kingdom, unless he the more quickly turn again. And may God and all his saints preserve each of those who are helpful that it may stand. If ever any one avert or withdraw anything from this bequest, be from him God's mercy and his eternal reward for ever withdrawn, and he be never found in his mercy; but be he excommunicated from the community of all the chosen companies of Christ, unless he the more quickly that forsake, and again turn to right.

BISHOP AILMER. M.XCVII.

[✠ O]n ure Drichtines name. Ic Ailmer biscop kithe alle manne ihwat ic habbe unnen into Sc̃e Eadmunde. þat is þat lond at Hindringham. and þat lond at Langham. and þat lond at Hildoluestone. ⁊ þat lond at Suanetone. and alle þe þinge þat ic þerto bigeten habbe. and þerto eken half hundred marc silueres. And ihu so ic wende mine cuiðe. ic wille þat þis stonde euere

✠ In the name of our Lord. I Æilmer bishop make known to all men what I have given to St Eadmund's: that is, the land at Hindringham, and the land at Langham, and the land at Hildolfston, and the land at Swanton, and all the things which I have acquired thereto; and thereto, besides, half a hundred marks of silver. And however I may alter my bequest, I will that this stand unawent· mine soule to lisidnesse. And se þe þise quide wenden wille· wende God his ansene him from on domisday.

ever unaltered, for the redemption of my soul. And whoever shall avert this bequest, may God avert his face from him on doomsday.

PRIVILEGIUM FRITHERICI.

Ego Fretherieus, licet inutilis Dei et Sanctæ Mariæ servus, sic res meas disposui sicut subscripta testantur. He sunt res quæ pertinent ad æcclesiam Sancte Helenæ. In Wica capella ipsius villæ; Capella de Wihtlega; Capella de Wiceneford; Capella de Chechingwica; Capella de Holt, cum dimidia virga terræ, quæ reddit v. solidos per annum: et in Lauuernæ dimidia hida terræ, quæ reddit x. solidos, et libera est a geldis. Et omnes decimæ, tam de dominica curte episcopi, quam de omni terra hominum ibi terram tenentium; et similiter de Mertlega, sed presbiter habet inde tertiam partem decimæ, et virgam terræ ad victum suum, ad servitium æcclesiæ. In Northuuica pertinent ad predictam æcclesiam omnes capellæ de feudo episcopi: Warmeduna, Hindelepe, Hudintuna, Circhul, Witintun, Cleinesse, et omnes decimæ, tam de dominica curte, quam de terra liberorum hominum et villanorum de episcopo tenentium. In Burgo autem ad ipsam æcclesiam pertinent novem mansuræ circa æcclesiam, quas partim extractas recongregavi, partim pretio et labore adquisivi, quæ si de incendio reparate fuerint possunt per annum reddere XL. solidos, et aliquid plus. Hec predicta æcclesia est de dominio Sanctæ Mariæ, et de victu monachorum. Hanc ipsi fratres, post obitum episcopi Wlstani, commiserunt mihi ad serviendum inde majori æcclesie, et ad faciendum proficuum eorum in vita mea. Post autem sine contradictione reciperent sua, et ideo unoquoque anno quicquid lucrari poteram de decimis, conferebam eis ad restaurationem æcclesiæ suæ. Hoc totum, scilicet æcclesiam, decimas, et terras, et laborem meum, reddo et clamo quietum Deo et Sanctæ Mariæ, pro remedio animæ meæ, ex parte mea et meorum. Terram autem ubi domum meam edificavi, et laborem meum in voluntate eorum dimitto, quia ortus eorum fuit, et petitione domni episcopi Samsonis eam mihi concesserunt in vita mea; et volo ut nichil per me perdant. Æcclesiam[1] etiam Sanctæ Mariæ de Lundonia reddo eis, quia illorum fuit et est. Dimidiam hidam de Lenc, quam Godricus de me libere tenet, reddo eis, et servitium ejus, quia juste ad eos pertinet. Et ipsi fratres concesserunt michi plenariam societatem in omnibus beneficiis æcclesiæ, ut fiat pro me in vita et post mortem sicut pro monacho.

[1] *In margine.* Primo tenuit eam Godwinus Brochesunche quidam vinitor; post eum Christianus Estissman, similiter vinitor; post eum filius ejus similiter vinitor; post eum Wilelmus filius Fulcredi; modo tenet eam filius ejus. Ipsa terra sita est juxta ecclesiam Sancti Jacobi*, fere ad IIII[or] pedes distans ab ea, ab aquilonari parte.

* Apparently St James's Garlick Hill, or Garlick Hithe.

PART III.

GUILDS.

III. GUILDS.

ORKY'S GUILD AT ABBOTSBURY.

DE FRATERNITATE, VULGO GYLDA, APUD ABBOTESBURIAM, PER ORCIUM INSTITUTA.

✠ Her cyð on þisum gewrite ꝥ Orcy[1] hæfð gegyfen þæ gegyldhealle ⁊ þone stede æt Abbodesbyrig Gode to lofe ⁊ Sc̄e Petre· ⁊ þam gyldscipe to āgenne· on dæge ⁊ æfter dæge· him ⁊ his gebeddan to langsumum gemynde. Se ðe þis awendan wyle hæbbe him wið Gode gemæne on þæm micclan dome.

Ðonne syndon ðis þa forword þe Orecy ⁊ þa gegyldan æt Abbodesbyrig gecoren habbað Gode to lofe· ⁊ Sc̄e Petre to wurðmynte· ⁊ heora sawlum to þearfe:·

Ðæt is ǣrost· ðrym nihton ǣr Petres mæssan· æt ælcon gegyldan ǣnne peningc· oððe ān peningcwurð weaxes· loc hwæðer māre neod sy into þam mynstre· ⁊ on

✠ Here is made known, in this writing, that Orky has given the Guildhall and the stead at Abbotsbury to the praise of God and St Peter, and for the guildship to possess now and henceforth, of him and his consort in long remembrance. Whoso shall avert this, let him account with God at the great doom.

Now these are the covenants which Orky and the guild-brothers at Abbotsbury have chosen, to the praise of God, and honour of St Peter, and for their soul's need.

That is first: Three nights before St Peter's mass, from every guild-brother one penny, or one pennyworth of wax, whichever be most needed in the monastery; and on the

[1] See pp. 414, 426, 576, where he is called Urk.

mæsse æfen æt twam gegyldum ǽnne brádne hláf well besewen[1] ⁊ well gesyfled. to urum gemænum ælmyssan. ⁊ fif wucan ǽr Petres mæssedæge sceote ælc gegylda ǽnne gyldsester fulne clænes hwætes. ⁊ ꝥ beo gelæst binnan twam dagum. be þæs inganges wite. ꝥ syndon þry sestras hwætes. ⁊ se wudu beo gelæst binnan ðrym dagum æfter ðam corngesceote. æt ælcon riht gegyldan áne byrðene wudes. ⁊ twa æt ðam ungyldan. oððe gylde ǽnne gyldsester cornes. And se ðe bryðene underfehð. ⁊ ꝥ gecweme ne deð. beo he his inganges scyldig. ⁊ þær ne beo nán gyfu. ⁊ se gylda þe oðerne misgret innan gylde on eornostne hige. gebete he ꝥ be his ingange wið ealre geferrædene. ⁊ syððan wið þone man þe he mysgrette. swa swa he hit findan mæge. ⁊ gif he nele to bote gebugan. þolige he þære geferrædene. ⁊ ælcere oðre gyldrædene. And se ðe má manna inlæde ðonne he sceole buton ðæs stiwerdes leafe ⁊ ðæra feormera. gylde his ingang:. And gyf ænigum on urum ge-

mass-eve, from every two guild-brothers, one broad loaf, well besprinkled, and well 'gesyfled', for our common alms; and five weeks before Peter's mass-day, let each guild-brother contribute one guild-sester full of clean wheat, and let that be rendered within two days, on pain of forfeiting the entrance, that is three sesters of wheat. And let the wood be rendered within three days after the corn-contribution, from every regular guild-brother one burthen of wood, and two from the non-regular, or let him pay one guild-sester of corn. And whoso undertakes a charge, and does it not satisfactorily, let him be liable in his entrance-fee, and let there be no remission. And let the guild-brother who insults another within the guild, with serious intent, make atonement to all the society, to the amount of his entrance, and afterwards to the man whom he insulted, as he may settle it; and if he will not submit to compensation, let him forfeit the fellowship, and every other guildship. And let him who introduces more

[1] besawen? I assume that the loaves contained or were sprinkled over with seeds, as dill, caraway, &c.

ferrædene his forðsið getide· sceote ælc gegylda ǽnne peningc æt þam lice for þære sawle· oððe gylde be þry gegyldum. ⁊ gyf ure ænig geuntrumod sy binnan syxtigu[m milan· þon]ne findon we fiftyne men ꝥ hine gefeccon· ⁊ gyf he forðfaren sy xxx.· ⁊ þa hine gebringon to þære stowe þe he to gyrnde on his life. ⁊ gyf he on neawyste forðfaren sy· warnige man þone stiwerd to hwylcere stowe ꝥ lic sceole· ⁊ se stiwerd warnige syððan ða gegyldan· swa fela swa he mæge mæst to geridan oððe to gesendan· ꝥ hi þærto cumon· ⁊ ꝥ lic wurðlice bestandan· ⁊ to mynstre ferian· ⁊ for þære sawle georne gebiddan. ꝥ byð rihtlice gecweden gyldrædene ꝥ we þus dōn· ⁊ hit geristð ꝥ well· ægðer ge for Gode ge for worolde· forðan ðe we nyton hwylc ure hraðost forðfærð. þonne gelyfe we· þurh Godes fultume· ꝥ us fremige eallon þas forword gecweden on ǽr· gif we hit rihtlice healdað.

Uton biddan God æl-

men than he ought, without leave of the steward and the purveyors, pay his entrance. And if death befall any one in our society, let each guild-brother contribute one penny at the corpse for the soul, or pay according to three guild-brothers. And if any one of us be sick within sixty miles, then we shall find fifteen men who will fetch him; and if he be dead, xxx.; and they shall bring him to the place which he desired in his life. And if he die in the vicinity, let the steward have warning to what place the corpse is to go, and let the steward then warn the guild-brothers, as many as ever he can ride to or send to, that they come thereto, and worthily attend the corpse, and convey it to the monastery, and earnestly pray for the soul. That will rightly be called a guildship, which we thus do, and it will beseem it well, both before God and before the world; for we know not which of us shall soonest depart hence. Now we believe, through God's support, that this aforesaid agreement will benefit us all, if we rightly hold it.

Let us fervently pray to

mihtigne georne mid inwerdre heortan· ꝥ he us miltsige· ⁊ eac swa his halgan apostol Sc̃e Petre· ꝥ he us geþingige ⁊ urne weg geryme to ecere reste· forðan ðe we for his lufon þis gegyld gegaderodon. He hæfð þone anweald on heofenum· ꝥ he mot lætan into heofenon þone þe he wyle· ⁊ forwirnan þam þe he nele· swa swa Crist sylf cwæð to him on his godspelle· Petrus ic betæce þe heofenan rı̃ces cæge· ⁊ swa hwæt swa þu wylt habban gebunden ofer eorðan ꝥ byð gebunden on heofenum· ⁊ swa hwæt swa ðu wylt habban unbunden ofer eorðan ꝥ byð unbunden on heofenum. Uton habban hyht ⁊ hopan to him ꝥ he us bewite ã her on worulde· ⁊ æfter forðsiðe ure sawla gehelpe· he us gebringe on ecere reste. Amen.

God Almighty, with inward heart, that he have mercy on us; and also to his holy apostle St Peter, that he intercede for us and make clear our way to everlasting rest; because for love of him we have gathered this guild. He has the power in heaven that he may let into heaven whom he will, and refuse whom he will not; as Christ himself said to him in his gospel: "Peter, I deliver to thee the key of heaven's kingdom; and whatsoever thou wilt have bound on earth, that shall be bound in heaven, and whatsoever thou wilt have unbound on earth, that shall be unbound in heaven. Let us have trust and hope in him, that he will ever have care of us here in the world, and after our departure hence, be a help to our souls: may he bring us to everlasting rest. Amen.

GUILD AT WOODBURY.

On Cristes naman· ⁊ Sc̃s Petrus apostolus· an gildscipe is gegaderod on Wudeburg lande· ⁊ se b̃. Osbern ⁊

In the name of Christ and St Peter the apostle, a guildship is gathered at Woodbury land; and the bishop Osbern þa canonicas innan Sc̃s Petrus minstre on Excestre habað underfangen þone ilcan geferscipe on broðorrædenne gemænelice forð mid oðrum gebroðrum. Nu doð hig æt ælcum heorðe to gecnawnisse þam canonicon anne penig to Eastron ælce geare· ⁊ ealswa æt ælcum forðfarenum gildan æt ælcum heorðe ænne penig to sawul sceote· se hit bonda se hit wif· þe on þam gildscipe sindon. ⁊ þat sawul gesceot sceulon þa canonicas habban· ⁊ swilce þenisce don for hig swilce hig agon to done. ⁊ þis sindon heora nama þe beoð on þam gildscipe. Brihtwi· Wilnoð· Ealdwine· Leofric· Brihtmær· Alfric· Eadmær· Edwine· Algar· Edwi· Wlword· Alword· Edwine· Godwi· Osgod· Aðeleoue· Brihtmær· Godric.

and the canons within St Peter's monastery at Exeter have adopted the same society in fellowship along with the other brethren. They will now, as an acknowledgment, pay to the canons yearly, for every hearth, one penny at Easter; and also for every departed guild-brother, for every hearth, one penny as soul-shot, be it a man be it a woman who belongs to the guildship. And the canons are to have the soul-shot, and perform such service for them as they ought to perform. And these are the names of those who are in the guildship.

On Wudeburge lande is eac an oðer gildscipe gegaderod Criste ⁊ Sc̃e Petre· ⁊ hig doð to Martinus mæssan of ælcum heorðe anne penig into Sc̃s Petrus minstre þam canonicon· and ælc sawul gesceot ealswa· æt ælcum heorðe anne penig. And þis sind þæra manna nama· Kytel· Ðeoderic· et rel.

In Woodbury land there is also another guildship gathered to Christ and St Peter; and they pay at Martinmas, from every hearth, one penny to St Peter's monastery, for the canons, and also every soul-shot, for every hearth one penny. And these are the names of the men: Kytel, Theodric, etc.

Of Cliftunes gildscipe· Isaac p̃.· Almær· Godwine· et rel.

From Clifton guildship, Isaac priest, Ælmær, Godric, etc.

Of Colatunes gildscipe· Orðric p̃.· Almer· Ailwine· et rel.

From Culliton guildship, Ordric pr., Almer, Ailwine, etc.

Of Alwines gildscipe on Wudebirig· Alstan· Leawine· Ailwine· et rel.

Of Bridafordes gildscipe· Edwine· Wlfric· Sæwine· et rel.

Of Cliftwike· Waltere p̃.· Eadmær· Leowine· et rel.

Of þam gildscipe on Lege· Ailwi p̃.· Tyrri p̃.· Wiłłm.· et rel.

Of Hnutwille· Godric· Alwine· Edwine· etc.

Of Colatune· Alwine Treddasunu· Godric· Ailric. et rel.

Of Sidemuða· Algar· Ailric· Wlwine· et rel.

Of Halsford· Ilberd p̃.· Edwine· Alwine· et rel.

Of Hwitastane· Edzi· Godric· Edwine· et rel.

Of Examuða· Godgið· Esgar· Edrid· et rel.

From Alwine's guildship at Woodbury, Alstan, Leawine, Ailwine, etc.

From Bideford guildship, Edwine, Wulfric, Sæwine, etc.

From Cliftwick, Walter pr̃., Eadmær, Leowine, etc.

From the guildship at Lege, Ailwi pr̃., Tyrri pr̃., William, etc.

From Nutwell, Godric, Alwine, Edwine, etc.

From Culliton, Alwine Tredda's son, Godric, Ailric, etc.

From Sidmouth, Algar, Wulwine, etc.

From Halsford, Ilberd pr̃., Edwine, Alwine, etc.

From Whitston, Edzi, Godric, Edwine, etc.

From Exmouth, Godgith, Esgar, Edrid, etc.

THANES' GUILD AT CAMBRIDGE.

Her is on þis gewrite siu geswitelung þære gerædnisse þe þius geferræden geræd hæfþ on þegna gilde on Grantabrycge. ꝥ is þonne ærest· ꝥ ælc oþrum āþ on haligdome sealde soþre heldrædenne for Gode ⁊ for worulde· ⁊ eal geferræden þæm ā fylste þe rihtost hæfde. Gif hwilc ge-

Here, in this writing, is the declaration of the agreement which this society has resolved in the Thanes' Guild at Cambridge. That then is first, that each should give oath on the holy relics to the others, before God and before the world, of true fidelity; and all the society should ever gilda forþfære gebrynge hine eal se gildscipe þær he to wilnie. ⁊ se þe þærto ne cume gylde syster huniges. ⁊ se gyldscipe hyrfe be healfre feorme þone forðferedan[1]. ⁊ ælc sceote twegen pænegas to þære ælmessan. ⁊ man þærof gebrynge ꝥ gerise æt Sc̃e Æþeldryþe. ⁊ gif þonne hwylcum gyldan þearf si his geferena fultumes. ⁊ hit gecӯd wyrþe þæs gildan nihstan gerefan[2]. butun se gilda sylf neah si. and se gerefa[3] hit forgymeleasi gegylde an pund. Gif se hlaford hit forgymeleasie gylde ān pūnd. butun he on hlafordes neode beo. oþþe legerbære. And gyf hwa gyldan ofstlea. ne si nan oþer butun eahta pund to bote. gif se stlaga þonne þa bote oferhogie. wrece eal gildscipe þone gildan. ⁊ eall beran[4]. Gif hit þonne ān dō. beran ealle gelice. ⁊ gif ænig gilda hwilcne man ofstlea ⁊ he neadwraca si. ⁊ his bismer bete. ⁊ se ofstlagana twelfhende sy. fylste ælc gegylda he[alf] mearc to fylste. Gyf se ofstlagena ceorl si. twegen oran. gif he Wylisc si. anne

support him who had most right. If any guild-brother die, let all the guildship bring him to where he desired; and let him who should not come thereto pay a sester of honey; and let the guildship * * * the deceased * * * * and let each contribute two pence to the alms, and thereof bring what is fitting to St Ætheldryth. And if any guild-brother be in need of his fellows' aid, and it be made known to the reeve (fellow) nearest to the guild-brother, and—unless the guild-brother himself be nigh—the reeve (fellow) neglect it, let him pay one pound. If the lord neglect it, let him pay one pound, unless he be on his lord's need, or confined to his bed. And if any one slay a guild-brother, let there be nothing for compensation but eight pounds; but if the slayer scorns the compensation, let all the guildship avenge the guild-brother, and all bear[4]. But if a guild-brother do it, let all bear alike. And if any guild-brother slay any man, and he be an avenger by com-

[1] ⁊ se gyldscipe . . . . forðferedan. This passage I do not understand: Mr. Kemble (Sax. in Engl. i. p. 513) renders it: "and let the gildship inherit of the dead half a farm."

[2] geferan? [3] gefera? [4] i. e. the fæhð, *feud*.

oran. Gif se gilda þonne hwæne mid dysie ⁊ myd dole stlea· bere sylf ꝥ he worhte. ⁊ gif gegilda his gegildan þurh his agen dysi ofstlea· bere sylf wiþ magas ꝥ he bræc· ⁊ his gegilde eft mid eahta pundum gebycge· oþþe he þolie â geferes ⁊ freondscipes. ⁊ gif gegilda myd þæm ete oððe drince þe his gegildan stlog· butun hit beforan cyninge· oððe leod bisceope· oððe ealdormen beo· gilde an pund· butun he ætsacan mæge mid his twam gesetlun ꝥ he hine nyste. Gif hwilc gegilda oþerne misgrete· gylde anne syster huniges· ⁊ gif hwa oþerne misgrete· gylde anne syster huniges[1] butun he hine mid his twam gesetlun geladie. Gif cniht wæpn brede· gilde se hlaford ân pund· ⁊ hæbbe se hlaford æt ꝥ he mæge· ⁊ him eal gildscipe gefylste ꝥ he his feoh of hæbbe. ⁊ gif cniht oþerne gewundie· wrece hit hlaford· ⁊ eal gyldscipe on· ⁊ sece þæt he sece· ꝥ he feorh næbbe. ⁊ gif cniht binnan stig sitte· gylde anne syster huniges· ⁊ gif hwa fotsetlan hæbbe do ꝥ ylce· ⁊ gif hwilc gegilda ut of lande forðfere· oððe beo gesycled· gefeccan hine his

pulsion, and compensate for his violence, and the slain be a twelve-hynde man, let each guild-brother contribute a half-mark for his aid; if the slain be a ceorl, two oras; if he be Welsh, one ora. But if the guild-brother slay any one through wantonness and with guile, let himself bear what he has wrought. And if a guild-brother slay his guild-brother through his own folly, let himself suffer on the part of the kindred for that which he has violated; and buy back his guildship with eight pounds, or for ever forfeit our society and friendship. And if a guild-brother eat or drink with him who slew his guild-brother, unless it be before the king, or the bishop of the diocese, or the aldorman, let him pay one pound, unless, with his two bench-comrades, he can deny that he knew him. If any guild-brother insult another, let him pay a sester of honey, unless he can clear himself with his two-bench-comrades. If a follower draw a weapon, let the lord pay one pound, and let the lord get what he can, and let all the guildship aid him in recovering his money. And

[1] This seems a repetition of the preceding passage.

gegildan. ⁊ hine gebringan d[ead]ne oððe cucene þær he to wilnie. be þæm ylcan wyte þe hit gecweden is. gif he æt ham forðferð ⁊ gegilda ꝥ lic ne gesecð. [⁊ se g]egilda þe [ne ge]sece his m[orgen spæce. gi]lde h[is syster huniges.]

if a follower wound another, let the lord avenge it, and all the guildship together; so that seek he whatever he may seek, he have not life. And if a follower sit within the 'stig', let him pay a sester of honey; and if any one have a 'fotsetla', let him do the same. And if any guild-brother die out of the land, or be taken sick, let his guild-brethren fetch him, and convey him, dead or alive, to where he may desire, under the same penalty that has been said, if he die at home, and the guild-brother attend not the corpse. And let the guild-brother who attends not his morning discourse, pay his sester of honey.

GUILD AT EXETER.

✠ Þeos gesamnung is gesamnod on Exanceastre. for Godes lufun ⁊ for usse saule þearfe. ægþer ge be usses lifes gesundfulnesse. ge eac be þæm æfteran dægum þe we to Godes dome for us sylfe beon willaþ. Þonne habbaþ we gecweden þæt ure mytting sie þriwa on XII. monðum. ane to Sc̃e Michaeles mæssan. oþre siðe to Sc̃e Marian mæssan ofer midne winter. þriddan siþe on eall hælegra mæsse dæg ofer Eastron. ⁊ hæbbe ælc gegilda II. sesteras mealtes. ⁊ ælc cniht anne. ⁊

✠ This association is associated at Exeter, for love of God, and for our souls' need, both as to our life's prosperity, and also to the latter days, which we desire for ourselves to be at God's doom. Now we have declared that our meeting be thrice in the twelve months, once at St Michael's mass, the second time at St Mary's mass, after Midwinter, the third time on Allhallows mass-day, after Easter. And let each guild-brother have two sesters of malt, and every follower one, sceat huniges· and se mæsse-preost a singe twa mæssan· oþre for þa lyfigendan frynd· oþere for þa forðgefarenan· æt ælcere mittinge· ⁊ ælc gemænes hades broður twegen salteras sealma· oðerne for þa lifgendan frynd· oþerne for þa forðgefarenan. ⁊ æt forðsiðe ælc monn VI. mæssan oððe VI. salteras sealma· ⁊ æt suþfore[1] ælc mon V. pening̃· ⁊ æt husbryne ælc mon anne peñ. ⁊ gif hwylc man þone andagan forgemeleasige· æt forman cyrre III. messan· æt oþerum cyrre V.· æt þriddan cyrre ne scire his nan man butun hit sie for mettrumnesse· oððe for hlafordes neode. ⁊ gif hwylc monn þone andagan oferhebbe æt his gescote· bete be twifealdun. ⁊ gief hwylc monn of þis geferscipe oþerne misgrete· gebete mid XXX. pening̃. Þonne biddaþ we for Godes lufun ꝥ ælc mann þæs gemittinge mid rihte healde· swa we hit mid rihte gerædod habbaþ. God us to þæm gefultumige.

and a 'sceat' of honey; and, at each meeting, let the mass-priest always sing two masses, one for living friends, one for those departed; and every brother of common condition two psalters of psalms, one for living friends, one for those departed. And after a death, each man VI. masses, or VI. psalters of psalms; and at a death, each man V. pence. And at a house-burning, each man a penny. And if any man neglect the day of meeting, for the first time III. masses, for the second time V., for the third time, let him have no excuse, unless it be for sickness or for his lord's need. And if any man neglect the appointed day for his contribution, let him make twofold compensation. And if any man of this society insult another, let him make compensation with XXX. pence. Now we pray, for love of God, that every man hold this meeting with integrity, as we with integrity have ordered it. May God support us thereto.

[1] forþfore? perhaps *funeral.*

ASSOCIATION OF BISHOP WULFSTÂN AND THE ABBOTS OF EVESHAM, CHERTSEY, BATH, PERSHORE, WINCHCOMBE, AND GLOUCESTER, AND THE DEAN OF WORCESTER.

On Drihtnes naman Hælendes Cristes· is ꝥ Wulstan ƀ. on Drihtnes naman· hæfð gerædd wið his leofan gebroðra· þe him getreowe synd· for Gode ⁊ for worulde. Ðæt is þonne ærest· Ægelwig abƀ. on Eofesham· ⁊ Wulfwold abƀ. on Ceortesige· ⁊ Ælfsige abƀ. on Baðan ⁊ þa gebroðra· ⁊ Eadmund abƀ. on Perscoran· ⁊ Rawulf abƀ. on Wincelcumbe· ⁊ Særle abƀ. on Gleweceastre· ⁊ Ælfstan decanus on Wigraceastre. Ðæt is· ꝥ we willað georne gehyrsume beon Gode· ⁊ S͞ca Marian· ⁊ S͞ce Benedicte· ⁊ us sylfe gerihtlæcan swa neah swa we nyhst[1] magon þam rihte· ⁊ beon swa swa hit awriten is· quasi cor unum et anima una. ⁊ we willað urum woruld hlaforde Willelme cinincge ⁊ Mahthilde þære hlæfdian holde beon· for Gode ⁊ for worulde :· ⁊ habbe we us gerædd betweonan to ure saule þearfe· ⁊ to ealra þara gebroðra þe us underþeodde synd· þe munuchades synd· ꝥ is ꝥ we willað beon

In the name of the Lord Jesus Christ, it is that bishop Wulstân, in the name of the Lord, has advised with his beloved brethren who are true to him before God and before the world. That then is first: Ægelwig abbot of Evesham, and Wulfwold abbot of Chertsey, and Ælfsige abbot of Bath, and the brothers, and Eadmund abbot of Pershore, and Ralph abbot of Winchcombe, and Særle abbot of Gloucester, and Ælfstân dean of Worcester. That is, that we will be earnestly obedient to God, and St Mary, and St Benedict, and direct ourselves as near as we nearest may to the right, and be, as it is written, quasi cor unum et anima una. And we will be faithful to our temporal lord king William, and to Matilda the lady, before God and before the world. And we have deliberated among ourselves for the need of our souls and of all the brothers' who are subjected to us, who are of monastic order: that

[1] MS. nyht.

on annesse· swylce ealle þas VII. mynstras syn an mynster· ⁊ beon swa hit her beforan awriten is· quasi cor unum, et anima una. Ðæt is ꝥ we ælcere wucan singan II. mæssan on ælcum mynstre· synderlice for eallum gebroðrum· monandæge ⁊ frigedæge. ⁊ wite se broður þe capitula mæsse wuca bið· ꝥ þas mæssan geforðige for þa gebroðra þe libbende synd· ⁊ for ælcan forðfarenan breðer· ælc þæra þinga fore don swylce hig ealle ætgædere on anum mynstre wæron:· ⁊ nu is þara abboda cwydrædene ꝥ hig willað beon Gode gehyrsume ⁊ heora bisceope· to heora gemænelicum þearfe· ꝥ is ꝥ heora ælc sceal don an c. mæssan of his agenra handa gebycge· ⁊ an c. þearfendra manna gebaðige· ⁊ þa fedan· ⁊ ealle þa gescygean· ⁊ ælc singe himsylf VII. mæssan· and him foredon xxx. nihta his mete beforan him· ⁊ ænne pænig on uppan þam mete:· God us gefultumige ꝥ we hit þus motan gelæstan· ⁊ mid suman gode geeacnian. Sic fiat.

Ðis synd þara gebroðra naman on Eofesham· ꝥ is ærest·

is, that we will be in unity, as if all the seven monasteries were one monastery; and be, as it is here before written, quasi cor unum et anima una. That is that we every week sing two masses in each monastery severally for all the brothers, on Monday and Friday. And be it known to the brother who is capitula mæsse wuca, that he perform these masses for the brothers who are living; and, for every departed brother, do each of those things as if they all were together in one monastery. And now it is the agreement of the abbots, that they will be obedient to God and to their bishop, for their common need: that is, that each of them shall perform and, for his own account, buy a hundred masses; and bathe a hundred needy men, and feed them, and shoe them. And each sing himself seven masses, and for thirty days set his meat before him, and a penny upon the meat. May God support us that we may perform this, and with some good augment it. Sic fiat.

These are the names of the brethren at Evesham: that is first,

Ægelwig abƀ. ⁊ Godric abƀ. ⁊ Ægelwine decanes· ⁊ Ordmær· ⁊ Godefrið· ⁊ Þeodred· Regnold ⁊ Eadric· ⁊ Ælfwine ⁊ Eadwig· Colling ⁊ Leofwine· Ælfric· ⁊ Wulfwine Sired ⁊ Bruning· Ælmær ⁊ Ælfwine· ⁊ Ægelric ⁊ Ægelwyrd· Dunning ⁊ Sægeat· Uhtred ⁊ Eadweard· Eadmund· Ulf· Brihtric· Wulfsige· Sexa· Ælfwine· Wlmær· Ægelwig.

Ðis syndon þara broðra naman on Ceortesige· ꝥ is ærest·	These are the names of the brothers at Chertsey: that is first:

Wulfwold abƀ. ⁊ Ælfward· ⁊ Sælaf· Oter ⁊ Godwine· Æþestan ⁊ Eadgar· Eadmær ⁊ Godwine· Ælfwine ⁊ Benedict· Siwine ⁊ Alfwold· Brihtnoð ⁊ Ælfric· Godric ⁊ Ælfric· Oswold ⁊ Ælfric· ⁊ Wulfward· ⁊ Wulfric·

Ðis syndon þara gebroðra naman on Baðan· ꝥ is ærest·	These are the names of the brothers at Bath: that is first:

Ælfsige abƀ. ⁊ Ælfric· Leofwig ⁊ Hieðewulf· Ælfwig ⁊ Ægelmær· Eadwig ⁊ Godwine· Ægelwine ⁊ Oswold· Ælmær ⁊ Þeodred· Eadric· Ægelmær· Sæwulf· Þured· Ægelric· ⁊ Hærlewine· ⁊ Godric munuc on Mældmesbyrig· ealswa ure an· ⁊ ealswa Wulfwerd Pīces broðor on Tantūne.

PART IV.

MANUMISSIONS.

ACQUITTANCES.

IV. MANUMISSIONS.

Geatfleda geaf freols· for Godes lufa ⁊ for heora sawla þearfe· ꝥ is Ecceard smið· ⁊ Ælstan ⁊ his wīf· ⁊ eall heora ofsprinc· boren ⁊ unboren· ⁊ Arcil· ⁊ Cole· ⁊ Ecferð Aldhunes dohter· ⁊ ealle þa men þe heo nam heora heafod for hyra mete on þam yflum dagum. Swa hwa swa þis awende ⁊ hyre sawla þises bereafie· bereafige hine God ælmihtig þises lifes ⁊ heofona rices· ⁊ sy he awyrged dead ⁊ cwic āā on ecnysse. ⁊ eac heo hafað gefreod þa men þe heo þigede æt Cwæspatrike· ꝥ is Ælfwald· ⁊ Colbrand· Ælsie· ⁊ Gamal his sune· Eðred· Tredewude· ⁊ Uhtred his stepsun[e]· Aculf· ⁊ Þurkyl· ⁊ Ælsige. Hwa þe heom þises bereafie· God ælmihtig sie heom wrað ⁊ Sc̄e Cuðberht.

Geatflæd has given freedom, for love of God, and for her soul's need, to Ecceard smith, and Ælstan and his wife, and all their offspring, born and unborn, and to Arkil, and Cole, and Ecferð Aldhun's daughter, and all the men whose persons[1] she took for their food in the evil days. Whoso shall alter this and bereave her soul thereof, may God Almighty bereave him of this life and of the kingdom of heaven; and be he accursed, dead and quick, ever to eternity. And she has also freed the men whom she solicited from Cwæspatric, that is: Ælfwald and Colbrand, Ælsie and Gamal his son, Eðred, Tredewude and Uhtred his stepson, Aculf, and Thurkyl, and Ælsige. Who shall bereave them of this, may God Almighty and St Cuthbert be wroth to them.

[1] Literally *heads*, as of cattle.

Æþelstan cyng gefreode Eadelm forraþe þæs ðe he ærest cyng wæs· ðæs wæs on gewitnesse Ælfheah mæssepreost· ⁊ se hired· ⁊ Ælfric se gerefa· and Wulfnoð Hwita· and Eanstan prafost· ⁊ Byrnstan mæssepreost. Se þe ðæt onwende hæbbe he Godes unmiltse ⁊ æalles þæs haligdomes þe ic on Angelcyn begeat mid Godes miltse. And ic an þan bearnan þæs ilcan þæs ic þan fæder an.

King Æthelstân freed Eadelm immediately after he was king. Of this were witness Ælfheah mass-priest and the convent, and Ælfric reeve, and Wulfnoth White, and Eanstân provost, and Byrnstân mass-priest. Who shall set this aside, may he have God's disfavour and all the relics' which I, with God's mercy, obtained in the English nation. And I grant to the children of the same what I have granted to the father.

Her kið on þissere bec ꝥ Aluric se canonica of Execestre alisde Reinold at Herberde ⁊ at his cilden ⁊ at geal hira ofspringe· mid II. scill. ⁊ Aluric hine clipað freon and saccles ā tūne ⁊ of tūne· for Godes luue. ⁊ ðis is seo gewitnisse: Iohan Alurices sune· ⁊ Nicole· ⁊ Ailric· ⁊ Randolf· Alword cild· Osbern Clopeles suñ· Ricard a Paules stret· ⁊ Ricard Theod. . . . .

Here is made known, in this book, that Aluric the canon of Exeter has redeemed Reinold from Herberd, and from his children, and from all their offspring, for two shillings. And Aluric declares him free and sackless, in town and out of town, for love of God. And these are the witnesses: John Aluric's son, and Nicol, and Ailric, and Randolf, Alword Child, Osbern Clopel's son, Ricard in Paul's street, and Ricard Theod . . . .

Eadwi cing het gefreon Abunet Ælfnoð cyrceweard an Exanceastre fryo ⁊ færewyrþe on Aþelwoldes ealdermannes gewitnesse· ⁊ Daniel bisc̃· ⁊ Byrhtrices profastes· ⁊ on Wulfrices cyrceweardes· ⁊ Eadwi cing het hit bryga[1] Bryhtric her binnon Cristes bec.

King Eadwig has pronounced Abunet Ælfnoth the sacristan at Exeter free and with liberty of going; in witness of Athelwold aldorman, and Daniel bishop, and Byrhtric provost, and Wulfric sacristan. And king Eadwig has commanded Brihtric to bring (insert) it here in Christ's book.

ON THE ALTAR OF ST. PETROC'S, BODMIN.

Hæc sunt nomina illorum hominum, Hûna et soror illius Dolo, quos liberavit Byrhtflæd, pro redemptione animæ suæ, super altare Sancti Petroci, coram istis testibus: Leofric prespiter[2], Budda prespiter, Morhayþo prespiter, Deui prespiter, Hresmen diaconus, Custentin laicus, Wurlowen laycus, ut libertatem habeant cum semine suo sine fine; et maledictus sit qui fregerit hanc libertatem.

Rumun liberavit Haluiu super altare Sancti Petroci, coram istis testibus: clerici Sancti Petroci.

Budic, Glowmæð quos liberavit Uulfsie episcopus super altare Sancti Petroci.

Hoc est nomen qui liberavit Duihon super altare Sancti Petroci: Leofstan, coram istis testibus: Byrhsie presbiter, Morhaðo diaconus, Britail, Iohann.

✠ Hæc sunt nomina illarum feminarum quas liberavit Wulsige: Cemoyre, Rum, Addalburg, et Ogurcen, coram istis testibus viden[tibus:] Osian pres̃, Cantgethen diaconus, Leucum clericus.

[1] bryngan?

[2] From the orthography observed in some of these proper names, as p for b, as prespiter for presbyter, c for g, as Codgivo for Godgifo, it appears that the Cornubian pronunciation, 900 years ago, resembled that of the present Welsh.

Wulfsige episcopus liberavit Ina Prost cum filiis ejus, pro anima Eadgar rex, et pro anima sua, coram istis testibus: Byrhsige presbiter, Electus presbiter, Abel presbiter, Morhaðo diaconus, Canreðeo diaconus, Riol diaconus.

Hec sunt nomina illorum hominum quos liberabit Ælfsie super altare Sancti Petroci, pro redemtione anime sue: Onwen, Ewsannec, Iesu, coram istis testibus: Byrhtsie presbyter, Mermen presbyter, Agustinus lector, Morhaiþo diaconus, Riol diaconus.

Hoc est nomen illius femine Gluiucen quem liberavit Ordulf, pro anima Ælfsie, super altare Sancti Petroci, coram istis testibus: Morhaðo diacono, Tithert clerico.

Þes ys þæs manes nama ðe Byrhsie gefreade et Petrocys stowe: Byhstan Hate Bluntan sunu, on Æþelhide gewitnyse hys agen wif, ⁊ on Byrhisi ys mæsepreostas, ⁊ on Riol, ⁊ Myrmen, ⁊ Wunsie, Morhæþþo, ⁊ Cynsie preost.

This is the name of the man whom Byrhtsige freed at Petroc's altar: Byhstân Hate son of Blunta, in witness of Æthelhid, his own wife, and of Byrhis his mass-priest, and of Riol, and Myrmen, and Wunsige, and Morhætho, and Kynsige preost.

Hec sunt nomina mulierum, Medhuil, Adlgun, quas liberavit Eadmunt rex, super altare Sancti Petroci, palam istis testibus: Cangueden diaconus, Ryt clericus, Anaoc, Tithert.

Hæc sunt nomina hominum quas liberavit Eadmund rex, pro anima sua, *super altare Sancti Petroci: Tancwoystel, Weneried, coram istis testibus: Wulfsie presbyter, Adoyre Milian clericus; atque in eadem die mandavit hanc feminam Arganteilin eisdem testibus.

Hæc sunt nomina hominum quas liberaverunt clerici Petroci: Sulleisoc, Ourduyþal, pro anima Eadgari regis, super altare Sancti Petroci, in festivitate Sancti Micaelis, coram istis testibus: Byrhsie presbiter, Osian presbiter, Austius lector, Riol diaconus.

Hoc est nomen mulieris Meonre quam liberavit Ullfrit, pro anima sua, super altare Sancti Petroci, coram istis testibus: Mermen presbiter, Morhaiðo diaconus, Guaiðrit clericus.

✠ Hec sunt nomina mulierum quas liberavit Wulfsie .episcopus et clerici Sancti Petroci: Proscen, Wuencen, Onncum, Illcum, super altare Sancti Petroci, coram istis testibus: Byrhsie presbiter, Riol diaconus, Morhaðo diaconus, Wuaðrit clericus.

✠ Hoc est nomen illius mulieris Wenceneðel quam liberavit Ordgar dux, pro anima sua, super altare Petroci Sancti, coram istis testibus: Wulfsige episcopus, Leumarh presbiter, Grifiuð presbiter, Morhaiðo diaconus.

✠ Hoc est nomen illius hominis Iliuþ, cum semine suo, quem liberavit Æþelræd rex, super altare Sancti [Petroci], coram istis testibus: Æþelwerd dux testis, Osolf prepositus testis, Mermen prespiter, Riol prespiter, Ret clericus, Lecem clericus, Bleþros clericus.

✠ Hoc est nomen istius hominis Madfuþ quem liberavit Iofa, pro redemtione animæ suæ, super altare Sancti Petroci, coram istis testibus videntibus: Tittherd presbiter, Aþalberþ presbiter, Budda presbiter, Brytthael presbiter, Cenmyn presbiter: hii sunt laici: Teþion filius Wasso, et Ungost Cilifri. Et quicumque fregerit hanc libertatem, anathema sit; et quicumque custodierit, benedictus sit.

Hec sunt nomina illarum feminarum quas liberavit Ermen, pro anima matris illius: Guenguiu et Elisaued, super altare Sancti Petroci, coram istis testibus videntibus: Osian presbiter, Leucum clericus, Ret clericus.

✠ Hoc est nomen istius hominis Teriþian, cum semine suo, quem liberavit Ordulf filius Brun, super altare Sancti Petroci, pro redemtione anime sue, ut libertatem habeat ab eo et a semine suo perpetualiter, coram istis idoneis testibus: Leofric presbiter, Prudens presbiter, Adalberd presbiter, Tittherd presbiter, Budda presbiter, Boia diaconus, Morayþo diaconus. Quicumque fregerit hanc libertatem, anathema sit; et quisquis custodierit, benedictus sit.

✠ Hoc est nomen illius mulieris Ælfgyþ quam liberavit Æþælflæd, pro anima sua et pro anima domini sui Æþælwerd dux, super cimbalum Sancti Petroci, in villa que nominatur Lyscerruyt, coram istis testibus videntibus: Æþæstan presbiter, Wine presbiter, Dunstan pƀ, Goda minister, Ælfwerd

Scirlocc, Æþælwine Muff, Ealdred frater ejus, Eadsige scriptor: et hii sunt testes ex clericis Sancti Petroci: Prudens presbiter, Boia diaconus, Wulfsige diaconus, Bryhsige clericus, ut libertatem . . . . Et postea venit Æþælwærd dux ad monasterium Sancti Petroci, et liberavit eam, pro anima sua, super altare Sancti Petroci, coram istis testibus videntibus: Buruhwold bisceop, Germanus abbas, Tittherd presbiter, Wulfsige diaconus, Wurgent filius Samuel, Ylcærþon præpositus, Teþion consul, ... filius Mór. Et ipse adfirmavit, ut quicumque custodierit hanc libertatem, benedictus sit; et quicumque fregerit, anathema sit a Domino Deo celi, et ab angelis ejus.

. . . .

Hoc est nomen illius hominis quem liberavit Cenmenoc, pro anima sua, super altare Sancti Petroci, Benedic, coram istis testibus videntibus: Osian presbiter, Morhaitho diaconus.

Hoc est nomen illius [mulieris] Anaguistl quem Eadgar rex liberavit, pro anima sua, super altare Sancti Petroci, coram istis testibus videntibus: Wulfsige presbiter, et Grifiuð presbiter, et Conredeu diaconus, et Byrehtsige cleric[us et] Elie laicus.

Wuenumon ⁊ hire team, Moruiw hire swuster [⁊] hire team· and Wurgustel ⁊ his team· wuarun gefreod her on tune· for Eadryde cyningc ⁊ for Æðelge[ard] biscop· an þas hirydes gewitnesse ðe her on tune syndun.

Wuenumon and her progeny, Morvith her sister, and her progeny, and Wurgustel and his progeny, were freed here in town, for king Eadred and for bishop Æthelgeard, in witness of the convent which is here in town.

Hoc est nomen illius hominis quem liberavit Perem, pro anima sua, Gurient, super altare Sancti Petroci, coram istis testibus: Adelces presbiter, Morhaedo diaconus, Guaedret clericus. Vale. Vive in Xp̄o.

✠ Wunstan, Bleðros, Hincomhal, Benedic, Wurcant, Otcer, Onnwuen, Argantmoet, Telent.

✠ Marh gefreode Leðelt ⁊ ealle hire team· for Eadwig

✠ Marh has freed Lethelt and all her progeny, for only

cyningc on his ægen reliquias· ⁊ he hie het lædan hider to mynstere· ⁊ her gefreogian on Petrocys reliquias· on þæs hirydes gewitnesse.

Her kyð on þissere bec ꝥ Æilsig bohte anne wifmann Ongyneþel hatte· ⁊ hire sunu Gyðiccael· æt Þurcilde· mid healfe punde· æt þære cirican dura on Bodmine· ⁊ sealde Æilsige portgereua ⁊ Maccosse hundredesmann IIII. pengas to tolle. Þa ferde Æilsig to· þe þa menn bohte· ⁊ nam hig ⁊ freode uppan Petrocys weofede æfre sacles· on gewittnesse þissa godera manna· ꝥ wæs Isaac messepreost· ⁊ Bleðcuf messepreost· ⁊ Wunning messepreost· ⁊ Wulfger messepreost· ⁊ Grifiuð messepreost· ⁊ Noe messepreost· ⁊ Wurþicið messepreost· ⁊ Æilsig diacon· ⁊ Maccos· ⁊ Teðion Modredis sunu· ⁊ Kynilm· ⁊ Beorlaf· ⁊ Dirling· ⁊ Gratcant· ⁊ Talan. ⁊ gif hwa þas freot abrece· hebbe him wið Criste gemene. Amen.

king Eadwig, on his own relics, and he ordered her to be led hither to the monastery, and here be freed on the relics of Petroc, in witness of the convent.

Here is made known, in this book, that Æilsige bought a woman called Ongynethel and her son Gythiccæl from Thurkild, for half a pound, at the church-door in Bodmin, and paid to Æilsige the portreeve and Maccos the hundredsman IV. pence as toll. Then went Æilsige, who had bought the persons, and took and freed them upon St Petroc's altar, ever sackless; in witness of these good men, viz. Isaac mass-priest, and Blethcuf mass-priest, and Wunning mass-priest, and Wulfger mass-priest, and Grifiuth mass-priest, and Noe mass-priest, and Wurthicith mass-priest, and Æilsige deacon, and Maccos, and Tethion son of Modred, and Kynelm, and Beorlaf, and Dirling, and Gratcant, and Talan. And if any one violate this manumission, let him have to account with Christ. Amen.

Hoc est nomen illius mulieris, Codgivo, quæ liberata fuit pro anima Maccosi centurionis, super altare Sancti Petroci, in vigilia Adventus Domini, istis testibus videntibus: Boia decanus, Godricus p̃r., Sewinus p̃r., Eli diaconus, Wulgarus diaconus, Godricus diaconus, Elwine diaconus, Edricus clericus, Elwinus, Elwerdus, Sicteicus, Waso, Wulwerdus, et alii quamplurimi de bonis hominibus. Si quis tam temerarius sit qui hanc libertatem fregerit, anathema sit a Deo et ab angelis ejus. Amen, fiat.

✠ Hæc sunt nomina illorum quos liberavit . . . . pro anima Etgar rex, super altare Sancti Petroci: Guene, Cen, Arganbri, et juniorum[1] dedit unum pro anima Etgar rex, id est nomen, Brethoc, coram istis testibus: Grifiud, Loumarch presbiter, Gaudreit clericus.

Her kyð on þissere bec ꝥ Ælfric Ælfwines sunu wolde þeowian Putraele him to nydþeowetlinge· þa com Putrael to Boia ⁊ bed his forespece to Ælfrice his breðere. þa sette Boia þas spece wið Ælfrice· ꝥ wes ꝥ Putrael sealde Ælfrice VIII. oxa æt þere cirican dura æt Bodmine· ⁊ gef Boia sixtig penga for þere forspæce· ⁊ dide hine sylfne ⁊ his ofspreng æfre freols ⁊ saccles· fram þam dæge· wið Ælfrice· ⁊ wið Boia· ⁊ wið ealle Ælfwines cyld ⁊ heora ofspreng· on þissere gewittnisse: Isaac messepreost· ⁊ Wunning p̃r.· ⁊ Sewulf p̃r.· ⁊ Godric diacon· ⁊ Cufure prauost· ⁊ Wincuf· ⁊ Wulfwerd· ⁊ Gestin þes bisceopes stiwerd· ⁊ Artaca· ⁊ Kinilm· ⁊ Godric Map· ⁊ Wulfger· ⁊ ma godra manna.

Here is made known, in this book, that Ælfric Ælfwine's son would enslave Putræl to him as a compulsory serf: then came Putræl to Boia, and prayed his mediation with Ælfric his brother. Then Boia made this agreement with Ælfric: that was, that Putræl should give to Ælfric VIII. oxen at the church door at Bodmin; and should give Boia sixty pence for the mediation; and should make himself and his offspring ever free and sackless from that day towards Ælfric and towards Boia, and towards all Ælfwine's children and their offspring: in witness of this: Isaac mass-priest, and Wunning presbyter, and Sewulf presbyter, and Godric deacon, and Cufure provost, and Wincuf, and Wulfwerd, and Gestin the bishop's steward, and Artaca, and Kinelm, and Godric Map, and Wulfger, and more good men.

[1] Very doubtful in MS.

✠ Hæc sunt nomina illorum hominum quos liberavit Ælfsie, pro anima Eadgari regis, et pro anima sua, super altare Sancti Petroci: Guenttinet, Cenhuiðel, David, Anau prost, coram istis testibus: Byrhtsie presbyter, Riol diac̄., Anaoc clericus, Tidherd clericus, Benjamen clericus.

✠ Hoc est nomen illius mulieris quam liberavit Gratcant: Ourdylyc cum filio suo Wurci, super altare Sancti Petroci, coram istis testibus: Hedyn presbiter, Lowenan diaconus, Leucum clericos, Bleþros clericos, Boia discipulus, Cenmyn clericos, Benjammen clericos.

Hoc est nomen illius mulieris, id est Madguistyl, cum progenie sua, id est, Bleidiud, Ylcerðon, Byrchtylym, quos liberaverunt clerici Sancti Petroci, super altare illius Petroci, pro remedio Eadryd rex, et pro animabus illorum, coram istis testibus: Comuyre presbiter, Grifiud presbiter, Oysian presbiter, Loumarch diaconus, Wudryt clericus, Loucum clericus, Tithert clericus.

Hær cyð on þyson bēc ꝥ Ælwold gefreode Hwātū· for hys sawle· a[t] Petrocys stow· a degye ⁊ æfter degye. An[d] Ælger ys gewytnisse· ⁊ Gotric· ⁊ Walloð· ⁊ Gryfyið· ⁊ Bleyðcuf· ⁊ Salaman. ⁊ hebbe he Godes curs ⁊ Sc̄s Petrocus· ⁊ æalle Welkynes sanctas þe ꝥ brece ðæ ydon ys. Amen.

Here is made known, in this book, that Ælwold has freed Hwatu, for his soul, at Petroc's altar, for his day and after his day. And Ælger is witness, and Godric, and Walloth, and Gryfyith, and Bleythcuf, and Salaman. And have he God's curse, and St Petroc's, and all the Welsh kin's saints, who violate this which is done. Amen.

Custentin liberavit Proscen, pro anima sua, super altare Sancti Petroci, coram istis testibus: Mermen presbiter, Riol diaconus, Cantgueithen diaconus, Tithert clericus, et aliis multis.

✠ Wulfsie episcopus liberavit Aedoc filiam Catgustel, pro anima sua et Eadgari regis, super altare Sancti Petroci: Cyngelt, et Magnus, et Sulmeaþ et Justus, et Rumun, et Wengor, et Luncen, et Fuandrec, et Wendeern, et Wurðylic, et Cengor, et Inisian, et Brenci, et Onwean, et Rinduran, et

Lywci. Hæc sunt nomina illorum hominum illarumque [feminarum] quos liberavit Wulfsige episcopus, super altare Sancti Petroci, pro anima sua et pro anima Eadgæri regis.

✠ Hæc sunt nomina illarum feminarum quas liberavit Ermen, pro anima matris illius: id est Guenguiu et Elisaued, coram istis testibus: Freoc p̃r., et Osian p̃r., et Leucum monachus.

✠ Hoc est nomen illius hominis quem liberavit Osferd, pro anima Eatgari regis: Gurheter, super altare Sancti Petroci, coram istis testibus: Comoere episcopus, Agustinus lector, Byrhsie sacerdos.

✠ Hoc est nomen [illius hominis] quem liberavit Eusebi, pro anima sua: Ceenguled, super altare Sancti Petroci, coram istis testibus: Grifiud, Leumarh, Riol.

✠ Hec sunt nomina illorum hominum quos liberavit Anaoc, pro anima sua: Otcer, Rannoeu, Muelpatrec, Josep, super altare Sancti Petroci, coram istis testibus videntibus: Cemoere episcopus, Osian sacerdos, Leucum clericus, Guaedret clericus.

✠ Hæc sunt nomina illorum hominum: Agustin, Ælchon, Sulcæn, Loi, Milcėnoc, Guenneret, Gurcencor, Riol, Anauclat, Æulcen, Gurcant, Cest, Æniucl, Oncenetll, Lucco, Iudhent.

✠ Þes sint þa menn þe Wulfsige byscop freode· for Eadgar cinig ⁊ for hyne sy[lfne]· æt Petrocys wefode· Leuhelec· Welet . . . nwalt· Beli· Iosep· Dengel· Proswite· Tancwuestel· an þas gewitnese· Byrhsige mæsseprost· Mermen masseprost· Mar· Catuutic· Wenwiu· Puer· Meðwuistel· Iosep.

✠ These are the men whom bishop Wulfsige freed, for king Eadgar and for himself, at Petroc's altar: Leuhelec, Welet . . . nwalt, Beli, Joseph, Dengel, Proswite, Tancwuestel, in the witness of Byrhtsige mass-priest, Mermen mass-priest, Mar, Catuuti, Wenwiu, Puer, Methwuistel, Joseph.

✠ Þys syndun þara manna naman ðe Wulfsige byscop gefreodet æt Petrocys wefode· for Eadgar ⁊ for hyne silfne·

✠ These are the names of the men whom bishop Wulfsige freed at Petroc's altar, for Eadgar and for himself:

⁊ Byrhsi ys gewitnese masseprost. ⁊ Mermen masseprost. ⁊ Morhi. ✠ Diuset ⁊ ealle here team.

and Byrhsi mass-priest is witness, and Mermen mass-priest, and Morhi, ✠ Diuset and all her progeny.

Ðys sindun þara manna naman ðe Wunsie gefreode at Petrocys stowe [for] Eadgar cinig. on ealle ðæs hiredys gewitnesse. Conmonoc. Iarnwallon. ⁊ Wenwærþlon. ⁊ Mæiloc.

✠ These are the names of the men whom Wunsie freed at Petroc's altar, for king Eadgar, in witness of all the convent: Commonoc, Iarnwallon, and Wenwærthlon, and Mæiloc.

✠ Hæc sunt nomina filiorum: Wurcon Aeðan, Junerð, Wurfoðu, Guruaret, quorum filii et nepotes posteritasque omnis defenderunt se per juramentum, Eadgari regis permisu, quoniam accussatione malorum dicebantur patres eorum fuisse coloni regi[s] : Comoere episcopo teste, Ælfsie præside teste, Dofagan teste, March teste, Ælfnoð teste, Byrhtsie prespiter teste, Mittuið prespiter teste, Abel prespiter teste.

Hoc est nomen illius viri quem liberavit Byrhtgyuo : Salenn, pro anima sua, super altare Sancti Petroci, coram istis testibus: Leof.... presbiter, Osian presbiter, Morcant.

Her kyð on þissere bec ꝥ Gesfræg Feala sune gebohte Gidið Edwiges docter æt Alpsta on Wunforda. ⁊ at Noæle Pincenne. to x. scill. freoh ⁊ sacles. ut of Wunforda. ⁊ Gyldeberd portgerefa nam ꝥ toll far þas kinges hand. ⁊ ðys ys seo gewitnisse. Gedmær on Cuike. ⁊ Sæger p̃. on Hefatriwe. ⁊ Randolf de Hãge. ⁊ Roggere on Pỹnnoc. ⁊ Morin at Gestgete. Riceard Alpstanes sune. ⁊ Wlfword

Here is made known, in this book, that Geoffrey son of Feala has bought Gidith Edwig's daughter of Alpsta at Winford, and of Noæle Pincenne, for x. shillings, free and sackless out of Winford; and Gyldeberd portreeve took the toll on the king's account. And these are the witnesses: Gedmer at Quick, and Sægar priest at Heavitree, and Randolf de Hage, and Roger at Pinnock, and Morin at Westgate, and hys broðer. Godwine Leowines sune ⁊ Goda his broðer. ⁊ Geda. ⁊ Sægær. Riceard Kykebeauw. ⁊ Edmær Norðmansun. ⁊ se þe þiss ũndõ. hæbbe he Godes curs. ⁊ Sc̃a Maria. ⁊ Sc̃s Petres. ⁊ ealle Xp̃es halgena ã butan ende. Amen.

Richard Alfstân's son, and Wulfword his brother, Godwine Leowine's son and Goda his brother, and Geda, and Sægar, Richard Kykebeaw, and Edmær Northman's son. And who shall this undo, have he God's curse, and St Mary's, and St Peter's, and all Christ's saints, ever without end. Amen.

Her kyð on þissere bẽc ꝥ Waltere Wulwordes sune ureode Aþeluue inna Sc̃es Petres minstre ouer his fæder lĩc. his feder saule to alisednisse ⁊ his. on Vuuenes gewitnisse. ⁊ mestre Odo. ⁊ mestre Leowines. ⁊ Godwines p̃. ⁊ Edwakeres. ⁊ his sune. ⁊ ag ealra þara hadeda ⁊ leweda þe þarig gewere. ⁊ se þiss undo habbe he Godes curs ⁊ þere hlefdia Sc̃e Marie. ⁊ Sc̃es Petres. ⁊ gealle Cristes halga. a butan ende. Amen.

Here is made known, in this book, that Walter Wulfword's son has freed Atheluve within St Peter's minster, over his father's corpse, for the redemption of his father's soul and his own: in witness of Wuene, and master Odo, and master Leowine, and Godwine priest, and Edwaker and his son, and also of all the ordained and lay who were therein. And who shall this undo, have he God's curse, and the lady St Mary's, and all Christ's saints', ever without end. Amen.

Her kið on þissere bec ꝥ Sewine Pinca bohte hine silfne to x. sciłł. at Willelme. on Edmæres gewitnisse pr̃.. ⁊ on Edwines. ⁊ on Tailiferes. ⁊ on Rodƀ.. ⁊ on ealles þas hundredes on Cuicu. ⁊ Alfric Hals nam ꝥ toll. ⁊ habbe he Godes curs þe hit æfre undo. Amen.

Here is made known, in this book, that Sewine Pinca has bought himself for x. shillings of William, in witness of Edmær priest, and Edwine, and Taillefer, and Robert, and all the hundred of Quick. And Alfric Hals took the toll. And have he God's curse who shall ever undo it. Amen.

Her kyð on þissere bec ꝥ Teolling gebohte Ælword Stamera ⁊ Edwine his broðor æt Coluwine to vii. mancson to cepe ⁊ to tolle· ⁊ Ælword portgerefa nam ꝥ toll. ⁊ herto is gewitnesse· Uiðel æt Culumtune· ⁊ Sæwulf· ⁊ Uitula· ⁊ Eadmund p̃.· ⁊ Snelling Tullinges sunu· ⁊ Leowine Leowerdes broðor· ⁊ Ælfgar Hellebula. ⁊ hæbbe he Godes curs þe þis æfre undo ã on ecnisse. Amen.

Here is made known, in this book, that Teolling has bought Ælword Stammerer and Edwine his brother from Coluwine, for vii. mancuses, as price and toll; and Ælfword portreeve took the toll. And hereto are witness: Vithel at Collumpton; and Sæwulf, and Vitula, and Eadmund priest, and Snelling Tulling's son, and Leowine Leowerd's brother, and Ælfgar Hellebula. And have he God's curse, who shall ever this undo, to all eternity. Amen.

Her kyþ on þissere bẽc ꝥ Huberd on Clist cræfede anne wifman þe Edit hatte Liuegeres wif mid unrihte· for þam Liueger hig alisde ut at Gosfreige bisceope ealswa man sceolde freohne wifman· ⁊ ealswa hit hriht wæs on þam dagum ælcne freohne man· wiþ xxx. p̃. ⁊ Huberd wæs leosende þære wifmanne for his unriht cræfinge þã ⁊ æfre mõ· hĩg ⁊ eal hire ofspring. ⁊ þærto is gewittnes Willm̃ de Buhuz· ⁊ Ruold se cniht· ⁊ Osbern Fadera· ⁊ Unfreig de Tettaborna· ⁊ Alword portgereua· ⁊ Iohan se cniht· ⁊ Rau Folcard. ⁊ þeos spæc wæs innan Willmes bure de Buhuz on Excestre gespæce.

Here is made known, in this book, that Hubert at Clist demanded a woman named Edith, wife of Liveger, with injustice, because Liveger had redeemed her of bishop Geoffrey as a man should [make] a free woman, and as it was right in those days [to make] every free man, for xxx. pence. And Hubert lost the woman, for his unjust claim, then and evermore, her and all her offspring. And thereto are witness, William de Buhuz, and Ruold the knight, and Osbern Fadera, and Humphrey de Tettaborne, and Alword portreeve, and John the knight, and Ralph Folkard. And this cause was argued in the chamber of William de Buhuz at Exeter.

Her cyþ on þissere bēc ꝥ Gedmer Spernægles sune hefð alised Leofilde his maga ut of Toppesham lande mid IIII. ⁊ XX. penuge· at Ceolrice· Heordinges gereua Eadnoðes sune· ⁊ þærto is gewittnes· Ælwine preost· ⁊ Ailword Pudding· ⁊ Heording· ⁊ his broðras· ⁊ Wulword at Iacobes circan· ⁊ Huga se rǣda· ⁊ eall ꝥ hundred at Toppeshamme. ⁊ se þe þis undo· habbe Godes curs· ⁊ Sc̃a Maria· efre butan ende.

Here is made known, in this book, that Gedmær Spernægle's son has redeemed Leoflæd his kinswoman (sister) out of Topsham, for XXIV. pence, from Ceolric Heording's reeve, son of Eadnoth: and thereto are witness: Alwine priest, and Ailword Pudding, and Heording, and his brothers, and Wulword at James's church, and Hugh the Red, and all the hundred of Topsham. And who shall this undo, have he God's curse and St Mary's, ever without end. Amen.

Her cyð on þisse bec þa Osbern ƀ. halgode Sc̃a Maria portic· þa freode Folcard þær Agelwine his man ⁊ his ofspring· Criste to lofe ⁊ Sc̃a Maria· ⁊ his sawle alisednisse· ⁊ let him ceosa hlaford loc hwær hig wolde. ⁊ hæbbe he Godes curs ⁊ ealra halgena þe þis æfre undo. Amen.

Here is made known, in this book, that when bishop Osbern hallowed St Mary's porch, Folcard there freed Agelwine his man and his offspring, for the glory of Christ and St Mary, and for his soul's redemption, and let him choose a lord where he would. And have he God's curse who shall ever undo this. Amen.

Capitulum Beati Petri Exonie omnibus fidelibus ecclesiæ salutem in Christo.

Noverint omnes tam futuri quam præsentes quod Willelmus Debuz, consensu uxoris et Johannis filii ejus, pro eterna retributione, coram justitia Exonie, Edwine Spileman ab omni servitute absolvit, et absolutum, provida deliberatione, sub præsentia Willelmi episcopi et nobilium, tam clericorum quam laicorum, matri æcclesiæ præsentavit, ut præsens ingenuitas tantorum astipulatione roborata omni tempore maneat inconvulsa. Si quis hanc absolutionem infestare temptaverit, ipse et ipsius factores subjaceant anatemati. Hujus rei testes sunt: Odo arch̄. Esuoldus arch̄. &c.

Her cyð on þissere bec ꝥ Bruning Cola sunu gebohte Roting æt Colewyne ⁊ æt Leofa· freoh ⁊ sacleas ut of Sceftbeara· on Særla gewytnisse þæs portgereua· ⁊ on Huberdes· ⁊ on Ælwerdes· ⁊ on Ælgares Paiardes· ⁊ on Wyllelmes his suna· ⁊ on Godwynes Colwynes suna· ⁊ on Esbernes Ælwerdes suna. ⁊ hebbe he Godes curs þe þis æfre undo. Amen.

Here is made known, in this book, that Bruning Cola's son has bought Roting of Colewine and of Leofa, free and sackless out of Sceftbeara. In witness of Særla the portreeve, and Hubert, and Ælwerd, and Algar Paiard, and William his son, and Godwyne Colwyne's son, and Esbern Alwerd's son. And have he God's curse who shall this ever undo. Amen.

Her kyð on þissere bec ꝥ Leowine Lundenisca ⁊ Ialdgið his wif gebohton Ælfilde æt Touie to feower ⁊ sixtuge penegon· ⁊ Ælfric Hals nam ꝥ toll innan Touies bure for þæs kynges hand. ⁊ herto is gewitnesse Roðsalin p̃.· ⁊ Ailword diacon· ⁊ Alwine deacon· ⁊ Dunstan Peoning.

Here is made known, in this book, that Leofwine the Londoner and Ealdgith his wife have bought Ælfhilde of Tovi for sixty-four pence; and Ælfric Hals took the toll within Tovi's chamber, on the king's account. And hereto are witness: Rothsalin priest, and Ailword deacon, and Alwine deacon, and Dunstân Peoning.

Her cyð on þissere bec ꝥ Huscarl lisde hine silfne wið Ealuwb . . . mid XL. p̃. on Godwines gewitnesse p̃. ⁊ on Alwordis portirefa· ⁊ on Ealdrides his suna· ⁊ on Osb̄. ⁊ on Walteres his broðra· ⁊ on Sæmæris· ⁊ Godwine p̃.

Here is made known, in this book, that Huscarl has redeemed himself from Ealuwb . . . . for XL. pence, in witness of Godwine priest, and Alword portreeve, and Ealdred his son, and Osbern, and Walter his brother, and

⁊ Swegn. ⁊ Wulfet namon ꝥ toll for þas cinges hand. ⁊ for Særles þe þa was portigerefa. Godes curs he habbe þe hit æfre undo. Amen.

Sæmar's, and Godwine priest, and Swegen. And Wulfet took the toll on the king's account, and Særla's, who was then portreeve. Have he God's curse who shall this ever undo. Amen.

Her cyð on þissere bec ꝥ Leowine Feala sunu bohte hine silfne ⁊ his ofspring æt Wulfworde Alfrices sunu at Iacobes cyrca to healfe punde. on Willelmes gewitnesse preostes. ⁊ on Godwines pr̃. ⁊ on Arnoldes pr̃. ⁊ on Edwines pr̃. ⁊ on Bartholomeus Floheres suna. on Floheres. ⁊ on Algares Pagardes. ⁊ on Cona. ⁊ Algares Leoflæde suna. ⁊ Haim. ⁊ Oter Dirlinges sunu. Edwacer. Agelword Ofstanes sunu. Osber. Alwordes sunu. Alfsta on Wunforda. Edwi. Nobol. Ocing. Agelword Pudding diac. ⁊ on ealles þa[s hun]dredes on Excestre. to ceosende him hlaford ⁊ his ofspring swa hwær swa hig woldon. ⁊ Alword portgerefa ⁊ Alwine Dirlinges aþum fangon to þam tolle for þæs cynges hand. ⁊ habbe he Godes curs ⁊ ealra halgena þe þis æfre undo.

Here is made known, in this book, that Leofwine Feala's son has bought himself and his offspring of Wulfword Alfric's son, at James's church, for half a pound; in witness of William priest, and Godwine pr̃., and Arnold pr̃. and Edwine pr̃., and Bartholomew Flohere's son, and Flohere, and Algar Pagard, and Cona, and Algar Leoflæd's son, and Haim, and Oter Dirling's son, Edwaker, Agelword Alfstân's son, Osbern Alword's son, Alfstân at Winford, Edwi Nobol, Oking, Agelword Pudding deacon, and all the hundred of Exeter: to choose a lord for himself and his offspring wheresoever they would. Alword portreeve and Alwine, Dirling's son-in-law, took the toll on the king's account. And have he God's curse, and all the saints', who shall this ever undo.

Her cyð on þissere bec ꝥ Ediþ Leofrices docter Locces bohte hi silue ⁊ hire ofspring

Here is made known, in this book, that Edith daughter of Leofric Loc has bought at Hul . . . . to IIII. ⁊ xx. p̃. on Willelmes gewittnisse stiwerdes· ⁊ on Agilwerdes Wudinges· ⁊ on Edmeres preostes· ⁊ on Edwies Hreawa suñ· ⁊ on Huscarles· ⁊ on Algeres Þr . . cge Godwines preost̃.· ⁊ on Leowines Lundeniscea. ⁊ habbe he Godes curs ⁊ ealra halgena þe hit æfre undo.

Her kið on þissere bec ꝥ Regenere bohte Alfriðe at Regenolde þam muneke at Cuicu wið v. scill̃. freoh ⁊ sacles uppan Cuiclande to beonde on fridome· on Edmæres gewitnesse p̃.· ⁊ on Edwines þas gereua· ⁊ on Rodberdes· ⁊ on Agelrices at Stanlince· ⁊ on ealles þas hundredes on Cuicu. ⁊ Alfric Hals nam ꝥ toll. ⁊ habbe Godes curs þe hit æfre undo. Amen.

Her kið on þissere bēc ꝥ Liueger se bacestere on Excestre alysde an wifman Ediþ hatte· Godrices dohter Cocraca ut of Clist lande at Gosfreige bisceope· to xxx. p̃. æfre mā freoh ⁊ saccles· heo ⁊ eal hire ofspring. ⁊ Gesfreig bisceop wæs hlaferd ofer Clist land on þam dagum. ⁊ þærto is gewitnis Colswein· ⁊ Roger on Buin· ⁊ Hereberd on Clist· ⁊ Edric se cipa. ⁊

herself and her offspring of Hul . . . . for XXIV. pence; in witness of William steward, and Agelword Wuding, and Edmer priest, and Edwi Hreawa's son, and Huscarl, and Alger . . . . Godwine's priest, and Leofwine the Londoner. And have he God's curse who shall this ever undo.

Here is made known, in this book, that Regenhere has bought Alfrith of Regenold the monk at Quick, for v. shillings, free and sackless, on Quickland, to be in freedom. In witness of Edmær priest, and Edwine the reeve, and Robert, and Agelric at Stanlinch, and all the hundred of Quick. And Alfric Hals took the toll. And have he God's curse who shall ever undo it. Amen.

Here is made known, in this book, that Liveger the baker (baxter) in Exeter has redeemed a woman named Edith, daughter of Godric Cocraca (Cockneck) from Clist, from bishop Geoffrey, for XXX. pence, evermore free and sackless, her and all her offspring. And bishop Geoffrey was lord over Clist in those days. And thereto are witness, Colswein, and Roger se þe þis undo hæbbe he Godes wræðe a butan ende. Amen.

at Buin, and Herbert at Clist, and Edric the chapman. And who shall this undo, have he God's wrath ever without end. Amen.

Halwun Hoce on Execestre freode Hægelflæde hire wiman þi hy bocte· ⁊ tilde for hire sawuale. Crist· ⁊ Sc̃e Peter· ⁊ ealle Cristes halga· hi wurðe wrað þe hi hæfre geþywie. Amen.

Halwyn Hoce in Exeter has freed Hægelflæd, her woman, whom she bought and fostered for her soul. May Christ and St Peter, and all Christ's saints be wroth with those who shall ever reduce her to servitude. Amen.

Her kyð on þysse bec ꝥ Æilgyuu Gode alysde Hig and Dunna and heora ofspring æt Mangode to XIII. mancson· ⁊ Æignulf portgerefa and Godsuc Gupa namon ðæt toll· on Manlefes gewitnesse· and on Leowerdes Healta· and on Leowines his broðor· and on Ælfrices Maphappes· and on Sweignes scyldwirhta. and hæbbe he Godes curs þe þis æfre undo â on ecnysse. Amen.

Here is made known, in this book, that Ælfgifu Gode has redeemed Hig and Dunna and their offspring from Mangod for XIII. mancuses; and Æignulf portreeve, and Godsuc Gupa took the toll, in witness of Manlef, and of Leowerd Healta, and of Leofwine his brother, and of Ælfric Maphap, and of Sweign shieldwright. And have he God's curse who shall ever this undo to all eternity. Amen.

Her kyð on ðys bec ꝥ Edwy Beorneges sunu lysde hine and his wif and his cild· on Edwerdes dæge cynges· æt Hunewine Hega suna ut of Toppeshamm lande· a Kinstanes gewitnysse p̃p̃. and a Leofsuna gewitnisse a Wun-

Here is made known, in this book, that Edwy Beornege's son has redeemed himself and his wife and his child, in the day of king Edward, from Hunewine Hega's son, out of Topsham, in witness of Kinstân priest, and of Leof-forda. and on Ælfrices Hwita. and on Wicinges batswegenes. ⁊ on Sæwines Lufa sunu. and on Leofsies. and on Ælfsies.

Her kyð on þissere bec ꝥ Godwine Blaca bohte hine sylfne ⁊ his wyf ⁊ his ofspring æt Willelme Hosethe mid xv. sciłł. on Edmæres gewitnes. ⁊ on Ælwies. ⁊ on Duninges. ⁊ on Sæmæres. ⁊ on Ælmæres. ⁊ on ealles þæs hundredes on Cuiclande. ⁊ Ælfric Hasl nam þæt toll for þæs kynges hand. ⁊ hæbbe he Godes curse þe hit æfre undo. Amen.

Her kyð on þissere bec þæt Ediuuu Sæuugeles laf bohte Gladu æt Colewine wyð healfe punde. to cepe ⁊ to tolle. ⁊ Ælword porhtgerefa nam ꝥ toll. ⁊ þærto was gewitnisse Leowine Leowordes broðor. ⁊ Ælwi Blaca. ⁊ Ælwine se cyng. ⁊ Landbyriht. ⁊ Alca. ⁊ Sæwerd. ⁊ hæbbe he Godes curs þe þis æfre undo on ecnisse. Amen.

Her cyð on þisse bec ꝥ Brihtmær æt Holacumbe hæfð geboht hine ⁊ Ælfgifu his wif ⁊ hira cild. ⁊ hira ofspring æt Rocgere Derendig. to twam pundum. æfre to freolse.

sunu at Winford, and of Ælfric White, and of Wiking boatswain, and of Sæwine Lufa's son, and of Leofsie, and of Ælfsie.

Here is made known, in this book, that Godwine Black has bought himself and his wife and his offspring from William Hoseth, for xv. shillings, in witness of Edmær, and of Ælwie, and of Dunning, and of Sæmær, and of Ælmær, and of all the hundred of Quick. And Ælfric Hasl took the toll for the king's account. And have he God's curse who ever shall undo it. Amen.

Here is made known, in this book, that Ediwu Sæfugl's relict has bought Gladu from Colewine for half a pound, as price and toll; and Ælword portreeve took the toll. And thereto were witness: Leowine Leoword's brother, and Ælwi Black, and Ælwine the king, and Landbyriht, and Alca, and Sæwerd. And have he God's curse, to eternity, who shall ever undo this. Amen.

Here is made known, in this book, that Brihtmær at Holcombe has bought himself and Ælfgifu his wife and their offspring of Roger Derendig, for two pounds, in perpetual on Dudemannes gewitnisse preostes on Exancestre· ⁊ on Leofwines p̃r. on Hwitastane· ⁊ on Ælfgæres portgerefa· ⁊ Ælfwerdes portgerefa· þe ꝥ toll namon for þæs cynges hand· ⁊ Leofwærdes his broðor· ⁊ Edwines Leoflede suna· ⁊ Oteres Dyrlinges suna· ⁊ Ælfgæres Ælfrices suna· ⁊ Blakemanes· ⁊ Leofrices Sæwines suna· ⁊ Dunstanes Sewines suna· ⁊ Randolfes· ⁊ Albaldes· ⁊ Smewines on Holacumbe· ⁊ Ægilwærdes Ælfsies suna· ⁊ Ælfmær Cynges suna· ⁊ Ælfsiges mid þam berde· ⁊ Edwine Leofrices suna· ⁊ Edwine Edmæres suna· ⁊ Edric on Hrenahricge· ⁊ on ealles þæs hundredes gewitnisse on Holacumbe. ⁊ hæbbe he Cristes curs ⁊ Sc̃a Marian· ⁊ Sc̃s Petrus þe þis æfre undo· ⁊ on ealles þæs hundredes gewitnisse on Exancestre.

freedom. In witness of Dudman priest at Exeter, and Leofwine p̃r. at Whitston, and Ælfgar portreeve, and Ælfwerd portreeve, who took the toll on the king's account, and Leofræd his brother, and Edwine Leofled's son, and Oter Dyrling's son, and Ælfgar Ælfric's son, and Blakeman, and Leofric Sæwine's son, and Dunstân Sewine's son, and Randolf, and Albald, and Smewine at Holcombe, and Ægilward Ælfsie's son, and Ælfmær King's son, and Ælfsige with the beard, and Edwine Leofric's son, and Edwine Edmær's son, and Edric at Renridge; and in witness of all the hundred of Holcombe. And have he Christ's curse, and St Mary's, and St Peter's, who shall ever this undo: and in witness of all the hundred at Exeter.

AT ST. PETER'S ABBEY-CHURCH, BATH.

Her swutelað on þisse Cristes bec ꝥ Leofenoð Ægelnoðes sunu æt Korstune hæfð geboht hine ⁊ his ofspring ūt æt Ælfsige abb̄. ⁊ æt eallon hirede on Baðon· mid fif

Here is shown, in this Christ's book, that Leofenoth, Ægelnoth's son at Harston, has bought out himself and his offspring from Ælfsige abbot and from all the con-oran ⁊ mid xii. heafdon sceapa· on Hascilles gewitnesse portgerēfan ⁊ on ealre þære burhware on Baðon. Crist hine ablende þe þis æfre awende.

✠ Her swutelað on þisse Cristes bēc ꝥ Ægelsige æt Linncūme hæfð geboht Wilsige his sunu ut æt Ælfsige abƀ. on Baðon ⁊ æt eallon hirede· to ēcean freōte.

✠ Her swutelað on þisse Cristes bēc ꝥ Ægelsige Byttices sunu hæfð geboht Hildesige his sunu ūt æt Ælsige abƀ. on Baðon ⁊ æt eallon hirede· mid syxtigon penegon· to ēcean freōte.

✠ Her swutelað on þisse Cristes bēc ꝥ Godwig se bucca hæfð geboht Leofgife þa dægean æt Norðstoke ⁊ hyre ofspring· mid healfan punde· æt Ælsige abbod· to ecan freote· on ealles þæs hiredes gewitnesse on Baðon. Crist hine ablende ðe þis æfre awende.

✠ Her swutelað on þisse Cristes bec ꝥ Ælsige abƀ. hæfð gefreod Godwine Bace æt Stāntune· for hine ⁊ for ealne þone hired on Baðan· on Sæmannes gewitnesse· ⁊ Wulwiges æt Prisetune· ⁊ Ælfrices Cermes.

vent at Bath, for five oras and for xii. head of sheep, in the witness of Leafcild the portreeve and all the township of Bath. May Christ blind him who shall ever set this aside.

✠ Here is shown, in this Christ's book, that Ægelsige at Linton has bought out Wilsige his son from Ælfsige abbot of Bath and from all the convent, in perpetual freedom.

✠ Here is shown, in this Christ's book, that Ægelsige Byttig's son has bought out Hildesige his son from Ælfsige abbot of Bath and from all the convent, for sixty pence, in perpetual freedom.

✠ Here is shown, in this Christ's book, that Godwig the Buck has bought Leofgifu the dough-woman at Northstoke, and her offspring, for half a pound, of abbot Ælsige, in perpetual freedom, in witness of all the convent at Bath. May Christ blind him who shall ever set this aside.

✠ Here is shown, in this Christ's book, that abbot Ælsige has freed Godwine Bake at Stanton, for himself and all the convent at Bath, in witness of Seman, and Wulwig at Priston, and Ælfric Cerm.

Her swutelað on ðissere Cristes bec ꝥ Ælfwig se red hæfð geboht hine sylfne ūt æt Ælfsige abbod ⁊ eallon hirede mid anon punde. Þar is to gewitnes eall se hired on Baðan. Crist hine ablende þe þis gewrit awende.

Here is shown, in this Christ's book, that Ælfwig the Red has bought out himself from abbot Ælfsige and all the convent, for one pound. Thereto is witness all the convent at Bath. May Christ blind him who shall set this writing aside.

Her swutelað on þissere Cristes bec ꝥ Edric æt Fordan hæfð geboht Segyfu his dohtor æt Ælfsige abbod and æt þam hirede on Baðan to ēcum freote· ⁊ eall hire offspring.

Here is shown, in this Christ's book, that Eadric at Ford has bought Sægyfu his daughter from Ælfsige abbot and from the convent at Bath, in perpetual freedom, and all her offspring.

Her swutelað on þisse Cristes bēc ꝥ Ælfric Scot ⁊ Ægelric Scot synd gefreōd for Ælsiges abbodes sawle to ēcan freōte. Þis is gedōn on ealles hiredes gewitnesse.

Here is shown, in this Christ's book, that Ælfric Scot and Ægelric Scot are freed for the soul of abbot Ælfsige, in perpetual freedom. This is done in witness of all the convent.

Her swutelað on þisse Cristes bēc ꝥ Iohann hæfð geboht Gunnilde Þurkilles dohter æt Gode Leofenaðes lafe to healfan punde· on ealles hiredes gewitnysse. Crist hine ablende þe þis gewrit awende. ⁊ he hæfð hi betæht Criste ⁊ Sc̄e Petre for his moder sawle.

Here is shown, in this Christ's book, that John has bought Gunnhild Thurkill's daughter from Gode Leofnath's relict, for half a pound, in witness of all the convent. May Christ blind him who shall set this writing aside. And he has committed her to Christ and St Peter, for his mother's soul.

Her swutelaþ on þyssere Cristes bēc ꝥ Sǣwi Hagg æt Widecume hæfþ gedon ūt his twegen sunu ætt Ælfsige

Here is shown, in this Christ's book, that Sæwi Hagg at Widcomb has emancipated his two sons from abbot Ælf-abbude· on ealles hiredes gewitnesse.

Her swutelað on þissere Cristes bec ꝥ Ægylmær bohte Sæþryþe æt Sewolde abbude mid III. maxan· on ealles hiredes gewitnysse· ⁊ ofer his dæg ⁊ his wifes dæg beo se man freoh. Crist hine ablende þe þis gewrit awende.

Her swutelað on þissere Cristes bec ꝥ Wulwine Hareberd bohte æt Ælfsige abbude Ælfgyþe mid healfan punde· on ealles hiredes gewitnysse. ⁊ Crist hine ablende þe þis gewrit awende.

Her swutelað on þissere Cristes bec ꝥ Ægylsige bohte Wynric æt Ælfsige abbude mid anon yre goldes. Þysses ys to gewitnysse Ælfryd portgereua ⁊ eal se hired on Baþon. Crist hine ablende þe þis gewrit awende.

Her swutelað on þissere Cristes bec þæt Siwine Leofwies sunu æt Lincumbe hafaþ geboht Sȳdeflæde ut mid fif scyllingum ⁊ . . . . . penegan æt Iohanne þam biscope ⁊ æt eallon þam hirede on Baþon· to ecum freote· ⁊ herto is gewittnesse Godric Ladda·

sige, in witness of all the convent.

Here is shown, in this Christ's book, that Ægelmær has bought Sæthryth, from abbot Sæwold, for III. mancuses, in witness of all the convent: and after his day and his wife's day, be the woman free. May Christ blind him who shall set this writing aside.

Here is shown, in this Christ's book, that Wulfwine Hareberd has bought, from abbot Ælfsige, Ælfgyth, for half a pound, in witness of all the convent. May Christ blind him who shall set this writing aside.

Here is shown, in this Christ's book, that Ægelsige has bought Wynric from abbot Ælfsige, for one ora of gold. Of this are witness Ælfred portreeve and all the convent at Bath. May Christ blind him who shall set this writing aside.

Here is shown, in this Christ's book, that Siwine Leofwi's son at Lincomb has bought out Sideflæd, for five shillings and . . . . . pence, from John the bishop and from the convent at Bath, in perpetual freedom: and hereto are witness: Godric Ladda,

⁊ Sæwold. ⁊ his twegen sunan. Scirewold ⁊ Brihtwold.

Her swutelað on þisse Cristes bẽc ꝥ Lifgið æt Forda is gefreod ⁊ hire twa cild. for þone biscop Iohann ⁊ for ealne þone hired on Baðon. on Ælfredes gewitnesse Aspania.

✠ Her cyþ on þisse bec ꝥ H[un]flæd gebohte Wulfgyþe æt Ælfrice Æþestanes su[na] Æþelminges. on Winemines gewitnisse eald portgerefan. ⁊ on Godrices his suna. ⁊ on Ælfwines Mannan suna. ⁊ on Leofrices cildes æt Nymed. ⁊ on Ælfrices Ælfhelmes suna geongan. ⁊ Brun bydel nam ꝥ toll on Ælfstanes gewitnisse mæssepreostes. ⁊ on Leofrices Winemines suna. ⁊ on ma l[eweda ⁊ gehādodra.]

and Sæwold, and his two sons, Scirewold and Brihtwold.

Here is shown, in this Christ's book, that Lifgith at Ford is freed, and her two children, before the bishop John, and before all the convent at Bath; in witness of Ælfred, Aspania.

✠ Here is made known, in this book, that Hunflæd has bought Wulfgyth from Ælfric son of Æthestân, son of Æthelm, in witness of Winemine senior portreeve, and of Godric his son, and of Ælfwine son of Manna, and of Leofric child at Nymed, and of Ælfric, son of Ælfhelm the Young. And Brun the crier took the toll in witness of Ælfstân the mass-priest, and of Leofric son of Winemine, and more, lay and ordained.

✠ Her geswutelaþ on þisum gewrite þæt Ægelsi on Wuldham hæfð gelened be Siwordes dægge biscopes his dohter ⁊ hiore dohter ut of Totteles cynne. ⁊ hæfð oþra mænn þærinn gedon. be þære burhwara gewitnysse on Hrouecæstre. ⁊ be ealle þæs biscopes geferan.

✠ Here is made known, by this writing, that Ægelsi at Wouldam has, during the life of bishop Siward, lent his daughter and her daughter out of Tottel's family, and has put other serfs therein, with the witness of the township of Rochester, and all the friends of the bishop.

ACQUITTANCES.

Her kyð on þissere becc ꝥ Aðelicc Ricardes swuster scirreua cwæð Hrodolf Sewies sune an Alfintune saccles of elcre crauigge. Ðarto is iwitnis Ricard se portreua· ⁊ Willelm Lambr̃.· Dunnig· Eorlawine· Reiner· Aluric Spoe· Rotberd Puddig· Wiggere· Dalfin· Gotselin· Gorpittel· Leggefot· Iohan· Osbern Ceaca· Rotbern Sceanca· Brihtric· Ailword Algar s̃.· Ricard Trencard· Iordan se prb̃.· Ricard· ⁊ ealle ꝥ hundred of Alfint̃. Se þe þis undo· habbe he Godes curs· ⁊ Sc̃e Marie· ⁊ ealle Cristes halgena· ã butan ende. Amen.

Here is made known, in this book, that Æthelice, sister of Richard the sheriff, has pronounced Hrodlof Sewie's son at Alphington sackless of every demand. Thereto are witness: Richard the portreeve, William Lambert, Dunning, Eorlawine, Reiner, Alfric Spot, Robert Pudding, Wiggere, Dalfin, Gotselin, Gorpettil, Leggefot . . . . . Osbern Ceaca, Rotbern Sceanca, Brihtric, Ailword Algar's son, Richard Trenchard, Jordan the presbyter, Richard, and all the hundred of Alphington. Who this undoes, have he God's curse, and St Mary's, and all Christ's saints', ever without end. Amen.

Her kyð on þissere becc ꝥ Rotberd a Poldraham cwæð saccles Willelm his broðer sune of Poldrahamlande ⁊ of elcre craufigge. Ðarto is iwitnis Reinald preost· ⁊ Dunnig· ⁊ Dalfin· ⁊ Seuara· ⁊ Sewi· ⁊ Girard· ⁊ Willelm Marescald· ⁊ Ricard ã Cuic· ⁊ Wulfric Wig· ⁊ Rau Sculdur· ⁊ Ricard Gealdulesc· ⁊ Herberd· ⁊ Segar· ⁊ Alger Innabusc· ⁊ Alger se webba· ⁊ Willelm se webba· ⁊ Roger

Here is made known, in this book, that Robert at Powderham has pronounced sackless of every demand William, his brother's son, of Powderham. Thereto are witness: Reinald priest, and Dunning, and Dalfin, and Sevara, and Sewi, and Girard, and William Mareścal, and Richard at Quick, and Wulfric Wig, and Rau Sculdur, and Richard Gildulesc, and Herbard, and Segar, and se stiwerd· ⁊ Rotberd Wianard· ⁊ Ricard Osannass· ⁊ Semer Swetleðer· ⁊· Iohel Uppacote· ⁊ Ascetill· ⁊ Rotberd Edwies meg. Se ðe þiss eure undo· habbe he Godes curs· ⁊ Sc̃a Maria· ⁊ ealle Cristes gecorena· ã butan ende. Amen.

Alger Innabusc, and Alger the weaver, and William the weaver, Roger the steward, and Robert Wianard, and Richard Osannass, and Semer Swetlether, and Joel Uppacote, and Arcetill, and Robert Edwis' kinsman. Who shall ever this undo, have he God's curse, and St Mary's, and all Christ's chosen's. Amen.

Her kyð on þissere boc ꝥ Oter ⁊ his cild cwede saccles Aluric þane Reda ⁊ his ofspring. ⁊ þarto is iwitnis Alword p̃s.· ⁊ Alured p̃.· ⁊ Waltere se cañ.· ⁊ Theodbald· ⁊ Semer Cipspones sune· ⁊ Waltere se Flemig· ⁊ Geffrei Hoel· ⁊ Randolf se cordewañ· ⁊ Alwine Modi· ⁊ Alwi Kya· and Alger Oxawamb· ⁊ Ailwerd· ⁊ Iordan· ⁊ Martin· ⁊ Osbern Hauoc· ⁊ Willemot Quikeuot. ⁊ Ricard se Flemig nam feor pengas to tolle. Se þe þiss mare undo· habbe he Godes curs· ⁊ Sc̃a Maria· and ealle Cristes gecorena· ã butan ende. Amen.

Here is made known, in this book, that Oter and his child have pronounced sackless Alfric the Red and his offspring. And thereto are witness: Alword priest, and Alured priest, and Walter the canon, and Theobald, and Semer Cipspone's son, and Walter the Fleming, and Geoffrey Hoel, and Randolf the cordwainer, and Alwine Modi, and Alwi Kya, and Alger Oxawamb, and Ailward, and Jordan, and Martin, and Osbern Hawke, and Willemot Quickfoot. And Richard the Fleming took fourpence for toll. Who shall ever this undo, have he God's curse, and St Mary's, and all Christ's chosen's, ever without end. Amen.

Her kyð on þissere bẽcc ꝥ Willelm bisceop of Execestre cwæð Wulfric Pĩg freoh ⁊

Here is made known, in this book, that William bishop of Exeter has pronounced saccles of þa lande a Teigtune ā þane dæ̃g þe ma dide Osbern bisceop. ⁊ Leofric bisceop of þa gealla minstre inna ꝥ niwe. ⁊ hine freode for Godes luue. ⁊ Sc̃æ Mariæ. ⁊ ealle Cristes halgena. ⁊ for þara bisceopa saule. ⁊ for his saule to alisednesse. Ðarto is iwitniss. Algar se bisceop of Constance. ⁊ se prior of Plimtune. ⁊ se prior of Tantune. ⁊ se prior of Sc̃es Nichol. minster. ⁊ se prior of Sc̃es Andreas. ⁊ Leowine se canon. ⁊ Waltere p̃.. ⁊ Willelm p̃.. ⁊ Rodberd se Blund. ⁊ Aluric p̃.. ⁊ Osbern se kapeƚ.. Wiƚƚm d.. ⁊ Osbern. Wiƚƚm ⁊ Barthōl.. Odo. ⁊ Hugo Ou. Gaisfreges s'. ⁊ Hugo Oc. Wiƚƚm Edwis s'. Alger Liffƚ. s'. ⁊ Iordan his s'. Randolf ⁊ Rau Mahtille. Waltere Dan. Osbern Hauoc. Ascetil Butaport. Seuara Jalewas s'. Dunnig. Rau. Theodƀ.. Teodbald. Wiƚƚm Selewies s'. ⁊ fela oðra þe ma nemna ne meg. Se þe þis efre undo. habbe he Godes curs. ⁊ Sc̃a Maria. ⁊ ealle Cristes gecorena. ā butan ende. Amen.

Wulfric Pig free and sackless of the land at Teignton, on the day that bishop Osbern and bishop Leofric were taken from the old monastery into the new. And he freed him for love of God, and St Mary, and all Christ's saints, and for the souls of those bishops, and for the redemption of his soul. Thereto are witness: Algar bishop of Coutances, and the prior of Plymton, and the prior of Taunton, and the prior of S[t] Nicholas' monastery, and the prior of St Andrew's, and Leowine the canon, and Walter priest, and William priest, and Robert le Blund, and Alfric p̃r., and Osbern the chaplain, William, and Osbern, William and Bartholomew, Odo, and Hugo Ou, Gaufreg's son, and Hugo Oc, William Edwi's son, Alger Lifflæol's son, and Jordan his son; Randolf and Rau Mahtille, Walter Dan, Osbern Hawke, Asketil Butaport, Sewara Salewa's son, Dunning, Rau, Theodbert, Theodbald, William Selewie's son, and many others that cannot be named. Who shall ever this undo, have he God's curse, and St Mary's, and all Christ's chosen's, ever without end. Amen.

Her kyð on þissere bec ꝥ Willelm de la Brugere cwæð saccles Wulwærd ðane webba· inna tune and ut of tune· of elce crafigge. ⁊ þarto is iwitnis Rau Teodb. sune ⁊ Teodb. his sune· ⁊ Atsun se hwita· Hroðolf Alcas s'· Hemeri Cutakig· Philippe Pagenes s'· Ricard Alkas s'· Geffrei Hoel· Herbð ⁊ Gollein· Ailwerd faber ⁊ his br̄.· Rau de Salcei· Herlawine· Brihtmer· Nidic. Se þe þis mare undō habbe he Cristes curs· ⁊ Sc̄e Maria· ⁊ ealle Cristes halgena· ā butan ende. Amen.

Here is made known, in this book, that William de la Brugere has declared sackless Wulward the weaver, in town and out of town, of every craving. And thereto are witness: Rau son of Theodbert, and Theodbert his son, and Atsun the White, Rotholf son of Alcas, Hemery Cutakig, Philip son of Pagan, Richard son of Alkas, Geoffrey Hoel, Herbth and Gollein, Ailwerd faber and his brother, Rau de Salcei, Herlawine, Brihtmer, Nidic. Whoever undoes this, may he have the curse of Christ, and St Mary, and all Christ's saints, ever without end. Amen.

Her kið on þissere becc ꝥ Gesfrei Foliot cweð saccles Semer Aluredes mæg ⁊ eall his ofspring· ⁊ þarto ys iwitnes Ricard se portgereua· ⁊ Rau Theodb.· ⁊ Waltere de S' Odin· ⁊ Willelm Pafard· ⁊ Willelm Spalla· ⁊ Ailwerd Sadelhack· ⁊ Seuara· ⁊ Edmer Burwolles s'. Se ðe þis undo habbe he Godes curs· ⁊ Sc̄e Marie· ⁊ ealle Cristes halgena· ā butan ende. Amen.

Here is made known, in this book, that Geoffrey Foliot has declared sackless Semer Alfred's son and all his offspring; and thereto are witness Richard the portreeve, and Rau Theodbert, and Walter of St Odin, and William Pafard, and William Spalla, and Ailwerd Sadelhack, and Sewara, and Edmer Burwolle's son. Who this undoes, may he have the curse of God, and St Mary, and all Christ's saints, ever without end. Amen.

Her kyð on þissere bec ꝥ Wulward bohte Leouede æt

Here is made known, in this book, that Wulward

Hierdinge Eadnoðes sune wið v. scill. to cepe ⁊ to tolle. ⁊ ꝥ toll nam Garwise gerefa to Toppeshamme. on Smecwines gewitnesse preostes. ⁊ on Alwines p̃r.. ⁊ on Ailwordes æt Oteri. ⁊ on Dunninges Tailiferes. ⁊ on Ailwordes Luunges sunu. ⁊ on Dunnewines. ⁊ on Godwines æt Hinatune. ⁊ on Hierdinges. ⁊ on Brihtmares Alfgares sunu. ⁊ se þe þiss undo habbe he Godes curs ā butan ende. Amen.

bought Leovede of Hierding son of Eadnoth, for v. shillings, as price and toll; and Garwise the reeve at Topsham took the toll, in witness of Smecwine the priest, and of Ailwine the priest, and of Ailword at Ottery, and of Dunning Tailefer, and of Ailword son of Luunge, and of Dunnewine, and of Godwine at Honiton, and of Hierding, and of Brihtmar son of Alfgar. Who this undoes, may he have God's curse ever without end. Amen.

✠ Dudda wæs gebur into Hæðfelda. ⁊ he hæfde þreo dohtor. an hatte Deorwyn. oðer Deorswyð. þridde Golde. ⁊ Wullaf on Hæðfelda hæfð Deorwynne to wife. ⁊ Ælfstan æt Tæccingawyrðe hæfð Deorswyðe to wife. ⁊ Ealhstan Ælfstanes broðar hæfð Goldan to wife. Hwita hatte wæs beocere into Hæðfelda. ⁊ Tate hatte his dohtor wæs Wulfsiges modor scyttan. ⁊ Lulle hatte Wulfsiges sweostar Hehstan hæfð to wife on Wealadene. Wifus ⁊ Dunne ⁊ Seoloce syndan inbyrde to Hæðfelda. Duding hatte

✠ Dudda was a boor at Hatfield, and he had three daughters: one was named Deorwyn, the second Deorswyth, the third Golde. And Wullâf at Hatfield has Deorwyn to wife, and Ælfstân at Tatchingworth has Deorswyth to wife, and Ealhstân, Ælfstân's brother, has Golde to wife. Hwita was the name of the beemaster at Hatfield, and his daughter named Tate was the mother of Wulfsige the shooter; and Hehstân at Walden has to wife Wulfsige's sister named Lulle. Wifus and Dunne and Seoloce

Wifuse sunu sit on Wealadene. ⁊ Ceolmund hatte Dunnan sunu sit eac on Wealadene. ⁊ Æðeleah hatte Seolecan sunu sit eac on Wealadene. ⁊ Tate hatte Cenwaldes sweostor Mæg hæfð to wife on Weligun. ⁊ Ealdelm Hereðryðe sunu hæfð Tatan dohtor to wife. Wærlaf hatte Wærstanes fæder wæs riht æht to Hæðfelda. heold ða grægan swyn.

✠ Brada hatte wæs gebur to Hæðfelda. ⁊ Hwite hatte þæs Bradan wif wæs gebures dohtor to Hæþfelda. seo Hwite wæs Wærstanes ⁊ Wærðryðe ⁊ Wynburge þridde modor. ⁊ se Wærstan[1] sit æt Wadtune. hæfð Winnes sweostor to wife. ⁊ Wine hæfð Wærðryðe to wife. ⁊ Dunne sæt on Wadtune wæs inbyrde to Hæðfelda. ⁊ Deorwyn hatte hire dohtor hæfð Cynewald on Munddene to wife. ⁊ Deornað hatte hire broðar bið mid Cynewalde. ⁊ Dudde hatte Wifuse dohtor sit æt Wilmundeslea. Cynelm hatte Cenwaldes fæder wæs gebur into Hæðfelda. ⁊ Manna

are inborn at Hatfield. The son of Wifus, named Duding, resides at Walden, and Dunne's son, named Ceolmund, also resides at Walden, and Seoloce's son, named Ætheleah, resides also at Walden. And Mæg at Welwyn has Cênwald's sister named Tate to wife, and Ealdelm, Herethryth's son, has Tate's daughter to wife. Wærstân's father, named Wærlâf, was a lawful serf at Hatfield: he kept the grey swine.

✠ Brada by name was a boor at Hatfield, and Brada's wife, named Hwite, was the daughter of a boor at Hatfield; Hwite was Wærstân's and Wærthryth's and Wynburh's great-grandmother. And Wærstân resides at Watton; he has Wine's sister to wife; and Wine has Wærthryth to wife. And Dunne resided at Watton; she was inborn at Hatfield; and Cynewald at Munden has her daughter, named Deorwyn, to wife; and her brother, named Deornað, is with Cynewald. And the daughter of Wifus, named Dudde, resides at Wymondley. Cênwald's father, named Cynelm, was a

[1] MS. swærstan.

hatte Cenwaldes sunu sit æt Wadtune under Eadwolde.

✠ Buhe hatte wæs Dryhtlafes moddrige. wæs afaren ut of Hæðfelda into Eslingadene. ⁊ Æþelwyn ⁊ Eadugu ⁊ Æþelgyð heo wæran ðreo gesweostra. ⁊ Tilewine ⁊ Duda wæron ealle þære Buge bearn. ⁊ Ealhstan Tilewine sunu. ⁊ Wulfsige Eaduge sunu. ⁊ Ceolem Æþelgyðe sunu. ⁊ Ceolstan. ⁊ Manwine. Þis cyn com of Felda. Deorulf Cyneburhe sunu ⁊ his twa sweostar. ⁊ Cynric æt Clæfring heora eam. Þas men synd Tatan magas æt Hæðfelda ðæs gebures.

boor at Hatfield; and Cênwald's son, named Manna, resides at Watton under Eadwold.

✠ Dryhtlâf's maternal aunt, named Buhe, went from Hatfield to Essendine: and Æthelwyn and Eadugu and Æthelgyth were three sisters, and Tilewine and Duda; these were all children of Buge. And Ealhstân Tilewine's son, and Wulfsige Eadugu's son, and Ceolelm Æthelgyth's son, and Ceolstân, and Manwine. (This kin came from Hatfield): Deorwulf, Cyneburh's son, and his two sisters; and Cynric at Clavering was their uncle. These men are the kinsmen of Tata at Hatfield, the boor.

This document is printed to show the care with which the relationship and connexions of the labouring class on an estate are recorded, on account, apparently, of the rights of the lord.

A COMPENDIOUS GLOSSARY

OF A FEW WORDS OCCURRING IN THE VOLUME, WHICH SEEM TO REQUIRE ILLUSTRATION.

A.

Æcer (m.), *Lat. ager, a field*, a measure of land, perhaps nearly the same as our *acre*.

Æfres. *See* Eafor.

Amber (m. f.), a measure containing four bushels. *See* Ellis, Introd. to Domesday, i. p. 133. Or half a mitta, 460.

Anstíge (m.), 160, a narrow gently rising path.

Armilcaisium, 2, an ecclesiastical vestment, probably the same as *dalmatica*. Du Cange prefers the form armilausa, connecting it with ἀρμελαύσια, *a military vestment*. If this form of the word is admitted, it may be compounded of armil, *sleeve* (Ohg. armilo, manica), and laus, *less*; and therefore signify a sleeveless garment. See Mr. Hardwick's Glossary to Hist. Mon. S. Augustini. I must, however, confess that in questions connected with ecclesiastical costume and furniture, I am no competent judge.

A'ð (m.), 432, *oath*, conjoined with ordælas (áðas ⁊ ordælas) it signifies one of the services from certain lands due to Taunton.

B.

Berewíc (f.), 382, *villa frumentaria*, Lye. But does it not rather signify a granary or storehouse for barley or corn in general? It may be synonymous with beretún, a *barton*, and berærn. At the time of the great survey, it seems to signify a hamlet. See Ellis, Introd. i. p. 240.

Blódwíte (n.), 359, 369, 384, 394, the penalty of bloodshed, or, LL. Hen. I. xxxix. forisfactura sanguinis; the fine imposed for drawing blood by wound or blow; reckoned (Hen. I. lxxxi. 3) among the minora forisfacta.

Bócland (n.), land held by book (bóc) or charter, in contradistinction to folc- or public-land.

Bonan, 429, 564. From this verb we have only the form geboned, applied to cups, horns, candlesticks, &c. Of its meaning I can only surmise that it may signify *polished, burnished*, and be akin to the Danish bone, *to rub, polish*.

Botl (n.), a dwelling, building, from bytlian, *to build*; heáfod-botl, *the principal mansion*.

Bovata, or Oxgang, 85, a measure of land, was originally as much as an Ox-team could plough in a year. Eight bovates are usually said to have made a carucate; but the number of acres which made a bovate are variously stated in different records, from eight to twenty-four. Introd. to Domesday, i. p. 156.

Burhbrice (m.), 411, the violation of a man's castle (burh), or dwelling; also the mulct for such violation. It was one of the rights of the crown. In later times the dative or abl. byrig appears to have been used for the nomin. burh, whence our local termination -bury.

Byrigels (m.), a burial-place, sepulchral mound, *tumulus*.

C.

Cassatus, 113, a word of frequent occurrence in Latin documents, for a hide.

Ciricsceat (m.), 263, church-, or kirk-shot; primitiæ seminum: an ecclesiastical due payable at Martinmas. From a voluntary offering this at length became a compulsory payment. The earliest mention of it in the Anglo-Saxon Laws occurs in Leges Inæ, 4. It was calculated at the rate of one seám, or horseload of winnowed grain for every hide of land occupied by a free tenant. For further information see the Glossaries to Die Gesetze der Angelsachsen, von Dr. Reinhold Schmid, and to the Anc. Laws and Instit. of England; Lingard's A. S. Church, i. p. 190; Kemble's Saxons in England, ii. 559, &c.

Ciricsócn (f.), 369, *a sanctuary*.

Crundel (m.). Of this word it is easier to say what it does not signify than what it does. Kemble (Cod. Diplom. Glossary, vol. iii.) says: "it seems to denote a sort of watercourse, a meadow through which a stream flows." But if so, how are we to understand the denominations Crawan crundel on Wereðanhylle (ib. iii. 301), *Crow's crundel on Weretha's hill*; stán crundel (ib. iv. 66); se þryscyta crundel (ib. v. 374), *the triangular crundel*. We have also se crundel þe se igð onstent (ib. v. 193), which I do not understand; but for which I would read, se crundel þe þam igðe onstent, *the crundel which stands on the islet*; and many others quite incompatible with Mr. Kemble's definition. Prof. Leo says: A crundel, or crundwel, is *a spring or well, with its cistern, trough, or reservoir*[1], &c. My belief is that the word is not Anglo-Saxon, nor Germanic, but British, and signifies a *tumulus*, or barrow, and is akin to the Welsh carneddaw, *a cairn*, or *heap of stones*.

In the Codex Diplomaticus mention is made of above sixty crundels, surely all these could not be meadows with streams flowing through them[2].

[1] Treatise on the local nomenclature of the Anglo-Saxons, as exhibited in the Codex Dipl. Ævi Sax., translated from the German of Prof. H. Leo, with additional examples and explanatory notes. Lumley, 1852.

[2] *Berks.* Farnborough, Stone C. Leckhamstead, Buccan (Buck's) C. Stanmore C. Mæres C. Asbury C. Ginge, Lillanhlæwes, C. Wilford Triangular C. Rugged (ruw) C. Beenham Clean C. Bagworth C. Lindford C. Wootton C. Chieveley CC. *Dorsets.* Piddleton, Hlosstedes C. Corscombe,

In a paper on heathen interment read before the Archæological Institute (*sine anno*), Mr. Kemble says:

"I think, when we bear in mind how very numerous and widely spread over all England were the Stone-beds, Circles, Dolmens, and the like, that the very rare notice of them in these documents (the Charters) is strange and unintelligible." Are not these missing monuments the Crundels?

Cumfeorm (f.), 102, *entertainment of strangers.*

D.

Defer, a termination, as in Candever. It is, no doubt, as Kemble suggests, a Keltic word: compare Brit. Dyffrin, *a valley through which water runs, and* Dwvyr, *water.*

Den (Denu) (f.), *a valley, -dean.*

Denbæru (m.), 119, 122, pl. denbæra, a pasture for swine: from den (denu) a *valley, hollow,* and bæro, a *wood, grove*; particularly, it would seem, one affording mast, &c. for swine.

Díc (m. f.), *a dike, ditch.* There seems great probability in what Mr. Kemble says regarding this word. "It signifies both the hollow (ditch) made by removing the earth, and the bank (dike) made by throwing it out. In the former case the word was probably feminine, and in the latter, masculine. This distinction, he adds, if it be substantiated, will add another evidence to the theory of the natural distribution of gender."

E.

Eafor (gen. æfres?), 102, *a wild boar*; apparently, like 'cumfeorm,' with which it is joined, a burthen on the monastery.

Edesc, ersc, (m.), 65, vivarium, *a preserve* or *enclosure* for the keeping of animals. Comp. edor, *sepes, septum.*

F.

Fæstingmen, 64, 65, 67, 79, 92, 100, 144, royal officers going on the king's errand. From fæsting, *commendatio.*

Fihtwite (n.), 138, 384, 411, one of the fines incurred for homicide. See Laws of Ælfred, vii., Ine vi.

Fleót (m.?), a running stream or small river; generally used in com-

---

Focga's C. Tarrant, Stony C. Lisbrook C. Winterborne, Deep C. Mapperton C. Corf Castle C. Plush, Ellene C. Burnston C. Chiselbourn C. *Gloucest.* Winterbourn, Putta's C. *Hants.* Alton C. and a little C. Stoke Crow's (Crawan) C. Wida's C. Clere C. on the isle. Easton C. Easingbourn CC. Overton C. *Kent.* Newnham C. *Northampt.* Badby, Boweles C. *Somers.* Swinford, Lulles C. Ashton CC. Hampton Crundelæcer. *Wilts.* Wiley, Morth C. Downton Crow's (Crawan) C., 3 CC. Enford, Dolh C. Fitelan Slædes C. Chatford, Rinda C. Abb's (Abban) C. Odbourn C. Pereston, Wolu C. Swallowcliff C. Newnton, Chalk C. Ashdown C. Idmiston, Pis C. Ebbesborne Crow's (Crawan) C., 3 CC. *Worcest.* South Stoke, King's C. Wenbury, Se durna C., C. Pidwylle C. Halling C. *County doubtful.* Beorhtwaldingtun, Stone crundel. Cusanhricg C.

position with a word limiting its application to a particular stream, as Ealhfleót, Mercfleót, &c.; though the simple word occurs as a proper name, as the river Fleet, now Fleet-ditch.

Flymena fyrmð (f.), 394, 411, the unlawful harbouring of a fugitive, and the penalty thereto attached. One of the rights of the crown in Wessex.

Folcland (n.), the land of the folk or people, the property of the community.

Forfang (m.), 384, 411, the seizing and rescuing of stolen or strayed property or cattle from the hands of the thief, or of those having illegal possession of it; also the payment by the owner for the delivery of such chattels.

Forsteal, 384, 411, according to the laws of Hen. I. lxxx. 2, 4, is thus defined: "Assultus super aliquem in via regia factus," or an assault on the king's highway. One of the rights of the crown in Wessex.

Fosterland (n.), 227, 329, 368, land given or bequeathed for the sustenance of the recipients or legatees, usually a religious fraternity or sisterhood.

Friðsócn (f.), a sanctuary, asylum.

Fyhfæng (Feohfang) (m.), 411. The receiving of money or chattels as a bribe, or the penalty for that offence. LL. Cnut. sec. xv.

Fyrd (f.), the military levy, constituting, with brygc-bót, *the keeping of bridges in repair,* and burh-bót, *the keeping of fortresses in repair,* what was called the Trinoda Necessitas, to which all landed property, that of the church not excepted, had to contribute.

Fyrdsócn (f.) at p. 389, is evidently used as the simple word, fyrd. Ettmüller (from Somner on Gavelkind) renders it *immunitas belli,* which certainly is not its meaning here. I am not aware of the occurrence of the term elsewhere.

Fyrdwite (n.), 359, 384, 411, the fine for neglecting to pay the contribution to the fyrd: one of the rights of the crown.

G.

Gemǽre (n.), plur. gemæru, -o, *a boundary.*

Griðbryce (m.), 369, 384, 394, *a breach of the peace,* more usually perhaps the king's or church's peace; the general, or public peace being denominated frið, Ger. Friede.

H.

Hæc, Hac (f.), 395, *a hatch, a half door or gate.*

Haga (m.), 355. 1. an enclosure made by a hedge (hæg); 2. a dwelling in a town so enclosed.

Hám (m.), Goth. haims, Ger. -heim, *a home, village.*

Hámsócn (f.), 332, 333, 359, 369, 384, 411, *domus invasio,* a breach of the peace by forcible entry into a man's house. In LL. Hen. I. lxxx. § 11, it is thus defined: Hamsocna est, si quis alium in sua vel in alterius domo cum *haraido* assaliaverit, vel persequatur, ut portam vel domum sagittet vel lapidet, vel colpum ostensibilem undecunque faciat. Hamsocna est, vel Hamfare, si quis premeditate ad domum eat, ubi suum hostem esse scit, et ibi eum invadat, si die vel nocte hoc faciat: et qui aliquem in molinum vel ovile fugientem prosequitur, hamsocna judicatur. Si in curia vel domo, sedicione orta, bellum eciam subsequatur, et quivis alium fugientem in aliam domum infuget, si ibi duo tecta sint, hamsocna reputetur. It was a right of the crown in Wessex.

For Haraidum, see Glossary to Anc. LL. & Inst. and Reinh. Schmid's Glossary to Die Gesetze der Angelsachsen.

Hangwite, Hængewite (n.), 384, 411, the fine for having hanged a thief without judgment, or for letting him escape from custody. Hængewite, for which we should perhaps read Hengwite, from hengen, *a prison*, may possibly signify the power of imprisonment, or the penalty for letting a criminal escape from prison.

Heal, Healh (f.), originally perhaps a stone structure; later a mansion or hall.

Heorþpenig (m.), 432, Romfeoh, Denarium S. Petri, Denier Sein Piere, a due payable to the see of Rome on St. Peter's day.

Híd (f.), *hide*, a space of land of uncertain extent, varying, it would seem, from 96 to 120 acres. It has been assumed to have originally been a sufficiency of land for the support of one family, a vague definition, though sanctioned by Beda, who in his Hist. Eccl. evidently employs *familia* as an equivalent to híd, or rather hiwisc, from hiw, *familia*. The form hígid appears in a Charter of Berhtwulf of Mercia, aº 840 (Cod. Dipl. ii. p. 5). Founded on calculation, Mr. Kemble's opinion is, that the híd contained about 30 acres of our measurement, but that the Saxons had a large and a small acre as well as a large and small hundred. See 'Saxons in Engl.' i. p. 96 *sq*.

The equivalents to híd found in the Charters are, mansus, mansa, mansio, manens, cassatus, terra tributarii.

Hlæsting, Hleasting, Lestagium, 359, 411, according to Bromton, consuetudo exacta in nundinis et mercatis; an impost on the lading of vessels, perhaps identical with seámpending, *load money*. A later signification seems to be: "a custom exacted in markets and fairs, for licence to carry goods from place to place, in the form of a packet or last."—Riley's Glossary to Liber Custumarum.

Hláw, Hlæ'w (m.), a *low, rising, tumulus*, as in Hundeshlaw, *Hounslow*; Leódhláw, *Ludlow*; Winneshláw, *Winslow*. It also occurs as *a sepulchral mound*.

Hlinc, 145, 149, 160, *link*. Though occurring only as a second component or termination, it still is known in Scotland, where, in the plural, the "links" signify, 1. "the sandy flat ground on the sea-shore;" 2. sandy and barren ground, though at a distance from any body of water; 3. rich ground lying among the windings of a river. Connected probably with ling, a species of rush, or thin long grass (Jameson, Dict.); or Dan. lyng, *heath, heather*.

Ho, Hoas (m.), a point of land, promontory.

Hundred-penig (m.), 432, 433, a collection made for the support of his office by the sheriff or lord of the hundred. (Riley, Gloss. to Liber Custumarum.)

Hundred-socn (f.), p. 187. This I take to mean sócn not limited to his (the abbot of Glastonbury's) particular domain, but extending over the whole hundred.

Hústing (O. Nor. Hússþing), 329, 533, a court, or tribunal (þing) held in a house or building (hús), while others were held in the open air. It appears that this court had the regulation of weights and measures.

I.

Igð (m.), an islet.

Infangenþeof, 359, 369, 384, 411, the privilege enjoyed by a landholder of jurisdiction over thieves taken on his land; but whether limited to his own men or not, seems not quite certain.

Ing (m.), chiefly occurring as a termination, and signifying *a meadow*; Fries. eng, inge; O. Nor. engi, Dan. eng. It sometimes stands first in a compound, as Ingatestone (Ing atte stone), Inghám, and others.

L.

Lád, Ládu (f.), a path, way, by land or water; a running water.

Landfeoh (n.), 138. The same perhaps as Landgafol. Kemble (Sax. in Engl. ii. p. 329) thinks it may be a recognitory rent for land held under the burh or city.

Leáh, Léh, Leág (f.), a *lea*. The difference between feld, *field*, and leáh seems not to be accurately known.

M.

Mancus, the eighth of a pound.

Manens. *See* Híd.

Miskenning, 359, 384, 411, "variatio loquelæ in curia; est autem loquela idem quod causa, placitum, juris sui prosecutio judicialis. Ita variare loquelam dicitur, qui alium petit quam quod initio et in prima litis contestatione petierat, vel qui in prosecutione juris sui non sibi constat."—*Du Cange*. Persons guilty of this offence were subject to a fine, called also *Miskenninga* and *Meschenninga*.

Missurium, 2, apparently a salver or similar vessel used in the celebration of mass (missa).

Mitta (Church), 144. ?A common mitta is equal to 2 ambers, 460.

Mundbryce (m.), 332, 333, 359, 369, 384, 411, the violation of the "mund" or protection, which the king or a superior extended to those subject or subordinate to him, and of which the pecuniary value was fixed according to the rank of the grantor. Also the penalty attached to this offence. It was one of the rights of the crown.

Mynster (n.), *a monastery*, from the Lat. monasterium. It is now incorrectly used for a monastic or abbey church, as Westminster-abbey, York-minster.

O.

Ordel (n.), 432, trial by hot iron, hot or cold water, and the corsnæd (panis conjuratus, offa consecrata); for which see Glossary to Anc. LL. & Inst. and Gloss. to Die Gesetze der Angelsachsen von Dr. Reinh. Schmid.

P.

Parafrithus, *a horse, palfrey*, 67, 79. It was the king's right to claim the service of horses or palfreys, for the carriage of effects from one royal vill to another, or for the furtherance of his messengers or the public servants. (Sax. in Engl. ii. p. 61.)

S.

Sac and Sóc, 369, 394, 404, Sacu and Sócn, Saca et Soche. "Sac was the power and privilege of hearing and determining causes and disputes, levying of forfeitures and fines, executing laws, and administering justice within a certain precinct. (Introd. to Domesd. i. 273.)

Sóc or Sócn was strictly the right of investigating or seeking; or, as Spelman defines it, "Cognitio quam dominus habet in curia sua, de causis litibusque inter vassallos suos exorientibus." It was also the territory or precinct in which the Sacu and other privileges were exercised.

Sawlsceat, Sawlgesceat (n.), 524. Symbolum animæ, Pecunia sepulturæ, *Soul-scot* or *-shot*, an ecclesiastical due payable at the open grave, for the repose of the soul of the departed.

Scapton (aureum), p. 2?

Sceawing (f. ?), 359, 411, *scavage*, a toll or duty paid for the oversight of certain officials upon the *showage*, or opening out of imported; the same as the "Ostensio" paid by foreign merchants, in the 'Instituta Londoniæ of Ethelred' (Anc. Laws and Inst. p. 127). (Riley's Gloss. to Liber Albus, v. Scawage.)

Scipbryce, Scipwreck, 384; whatever is cast on shore or found floating from wrecks, *jetsam and flotsam*.

Scipfylleð, Scipsócn, Naucupletio, 214, a ship's *lading*.

Scrippa, p. 495?

Sester (m.), 105, 158, *sextarius*, a measure both of solids and liquids; xv. pund wætres gaþ to sestre, fifteen pounds of water go to the sester. (Lib. Med. 2. 67, cited by Wanley, Catal.)

Stáca, 230, a pin *stake*, used in the kind of witchcraft called invultuatio (stácung). See p. 230, *note*, and Brand's Popular Antiquities, iii. p. 10, 11. edit. 1855.

Sufl, Sufol (n.), a kind of prepared loaf, but with what ingredient seems to be quite unknown. Kemble (Sax. in Engl. ii. p. 510) says: "I think these súfls must be *subflata,* raised or leavened bread. In the east of England still a kind of cakes are called *sowls,* probably sufls." The resemblance is specious, but, I fear, quite accidental. In Latin the word is rendered by *obsonium,* or anything eaten with bread, and in the A. S. Gospels the words "Habetis vos opsonium?" are rendered, Hæbbe ge sufol? Joh. xxi. 5. Lye, *voce* Gesyfled, has, without citing his authority: gesyfled hláf, *panis lacticinio et ovorum luteo maceratus;* and this closely accords with the O. Nor. sufl, *sorbillum, lacticinia.* Hence I am inclined to believe that a gesyfled hláf, or súfl, is either a loaf so macerated, or steeped in milk. Perhaps the sopcuppa mentioned in the Wills was for this purpose. As in Denmark and, no doubt, the other Northern nations, they have Melkbröd, *Milk-bread,* as distinguished from Vandbröd, *Common, or water bread,* it is not improbable that our sufol, &c. will answer to the former of these. In O. N. a sufla is a woman who sells milk.

Sulung, a measure of land used in Kent, probably equivalent to a hide.

T, Þ or Ð.

Tacc, i. e. swínsceade, 263. By the Latin term is probably to be understood the shade of beeches and oaks affording mast for swine, and is here apparently to be taken for the mast itself, not merely the shadow. With regard to Tacc, I can only conjecture that it may be a corruption of þac, *a covering, shelter,* from þeccan, *to cover, thatch.* Ellis (Introd. i. p. 98), quoting Bp. Kennet, says: "In Scotland the tithe or tenth hog was paid for pannage. This custom obtained in England, and was here called *Tack.*" Dabit pannagium vocatum Tack, videlicet, pro decem porcis unum porcum meliorem, &c.—*Ex libro Baroniæ de Sherborne,* MS. Gloss. Par. Antiq.

Teám (m.), 405, *vouching to warranty.* A process by which a person in whose possession lost or stolen property was found, was compelled to show from whom he bought or had it; which latter was, in like manner, bound to declare how it came into his hands, and so on to a third holder, beyond whom, provided he could prove lawful possession, it might not proceed. The person from whom the accused party had the property, and who came forth as his warrantor, was called the 'getyma,' or 'geteáma,' and the process itself 'Team.'

Þeoffang, Þiefphang, 125, 384, *the capture of a thief;* or his wite, if he escape: a right of the crown.

Þryh (f.), 241, a coffin.

Tóft (m.), 56, 580. O. Nor. Tóft, *an enclosed field,* a *vacant space,* from tómr, *empty, void:* a frequent termination of local names in the Danish parts of England.

Tol, Toll (m.), 263, 369, 384, 394, 404. Thelonium, 263, 369, 394, 404. The right of levying toll in ports, rivers, and high roads. It was a right of the crown.

Tún (m.). This word originally signified (like the Ger. Zaun) a hedge, enclosure, both as a separate word and as a termination; but later, not the enclosure, but that which was enclosed, until it finally became a town in its present acceptation. It is remarkable that while in England local terminations in *ton* (tún) are so numerous, its German correspondent zaun never occurs in the same sense.

U, V.

Uðleaw (m.), 359, the penalty for harbouring or concealing an outlaw.

Utleap, Uðleap (m.), 411, the penalty for suffering a culprit to escape.

Virgata, a measure of land, according to some authorities the fourth, to others the eighth of a hide, but altogether of uncertain quantity.

W.

Wagenscilling (m.), 138, a custom or toll on the loading of (salt-) wagons.

Wainegong, 592?

Walhfæreld (n.), 114, a company of pilgrims.

Weardwite (n.), 411, the penalty for neglecting the guard (weard) of the garrisons.

Weg, Wæg, Wæge, Pensa (f.), 460, 467, 468, 471, 472, 474, 479, *a wey*, according to Dr. Lingard (A. S. Church, ii. 65), is 246 lb., but he cites no authority.

Wér (m.), Wérgild (n.), Capitis æstimatio. The price at which every man was valued, according to his degree, which, in the event of his being slain, was to be paid to his relatives or to guild-brethren, and which he was himself condemned to pay if proved guilty of certain offences specified in the laws.

Wergeldþeof, 411, a thief of a class of society possessing a 'wér,' or who has forfeited his wer.

Wóh ceápung (f.), 138, buying or selling contrary to the laws of the market.

INDEX OF PLACES.

[*Names in italics are conjectural, and founded only on analogy.*]

A.

G.

I.

L, Hl.

T, þ.

Y.

THE END.

CORRIGENDA.

Page 106, note, *after* charters *add* with one at p. 94, a° 844.
,, 114, line 25, *for* Wahlfæreld *read* Walhfæreld.
,, 120, ,, 15, *after* Hedgeford *add* by Sturmead.
,, 250, ,, 7, *for* þurst an *read* þurstan.
,, 383, ,, 29, *for* Bichamdia *read* Bichamdic.
,, 499, ,, 13, *after* hides *add* as a clothing aid.
,, 520, ,, 20, *for* Bærorhtnoðæ *read* Bæorhtnoðæ.

N.B. I avail myself of the opportunity to correct an error in my edition of the Anglo-Saxon Chronicle, viz.

Preface, page xiii, line 3 from the bottom, *for* son *read* brother.

PRINTED BY TAYLOR AND FRANCIS, RED LION COURT, FLEET STREET.